Fodor's 93
Ireland

Fodor's Travel Publications, Inc.
New York • Toronto • London • Sydney

ISBN 0–679–02304–6

Fodor's Ireland

Editor: Andrew Collins
Contributors: Georgina Campbell, Anita Guerrini, Alannah Hopkin, Caroline Liou, Pat Mackey, Hugh Oram, Marcy Pritchard, Nan Richardson, Andrew Sanger.
Creative Director: Fabrizio La Rocca
Cartographer: David Lindroth
Illustrator: Karl Tanner
Cover Photograph: Peter Guttman

Design: Vignelli Associates

Special Sales

Contents

Maps and Plans

Foreword

We wish to express our gratitude to the staff of the Irish Tourist Board for their assistance in preparation of this guide.

While every care has been taken to ensure the accuracy of the information in this guide, the passage of time will always bring change, and consequently, the publisher cannot accept responsibility for errors that may occur.

All prices and opening times quoted here are based on information available to us at press time. Hours and admission fees may change, however, and the prudent traveler will avoid inconvenience by calling ahead.

Fodor's wants to hear about your travel experiences, both pleasant and unpleasant. When a hotel or restaurant fails to live up to its billing, let us know and we will investigate the complaint and revise our entries where the facts warrant it.

Send your letters to the editors of Fodor's Travel Publications, 201 E. 50th Street, New York, NY 10022.

Highlights'93 and Fodor's Choice

Highlights '93

Dublin The look of Dublin City Center continues to improve, with more pedestrianized streets and a greater variety of shops. In the South City Center, **Grafton Street** looks resplendent with its new red-brick walkways for shoppers. The **Temple Bar** area on the south side of the Liffey has also undergone extensive pedestrianization giving Dublin a revitalized "left-bank" area. The North City Center is also changing; **O'Connell Street** now features recently planted trees, a fountain near the General Post Office, and a new James Joyce statue at the O'Connell Street corner of **North Earl Street,** which has also been pedestrianized.

The **National Gallery, Civic Museum,** and **Municipal Gallery** were all refurbished in 1991, during Dublin's term as the Cultural Capital of Europe. Several new museums also opened: Foremost is the **Irish Museum of Modern Art,** which is housed in the beautifully restored **Royal Hospital Kilmainham,** a fine late-17th-century building also open to the public. The **Dublin Writer's Museum** honors the city's rich literary past and the interiors of **Newman House** and **Number Twenty Nine,** two typical late-18th-century family homes, have been fully restored in period detail. **Bloomsday,** June 16, the day made famous by James Joyce's *Ulysses* has become a festive annual occasion. Even those who have never read Joyce dress up in Edwardian attire and parade (preferably by horse-drawn carriage) around the areas detailed in the book. In the evening Joyce's works are celebrated at a series of light-hearted theatrical events, many of them in pubs associated with the author.

Dublin Environs The **Millmount Museum** in Drogheda was recently refurbished and is now one of the best exhibition halls in the country, with numerous relics of Drogheda's commercial and industrial past.

After thirty years of excavation, the site of the 18 megalithic passage-tombs at **Knowth** (dating from 3000 BC) is now open to the public; though, so far, only one-third of the site has been reconstructed. Many visit Knowth in conjunction with the completed excavation at **Newgrange,** one of the greatest—and most puzzling—megalithic tombs in Europe.

The Lakelands **Shannonbridge Bog Tour,** which takes visitors on an old works train for 8 kilometers (5 mi) across a raised peat bog, is a modest excursion, but it's been one of Ireland's most talked about attractions since opening in 1992. The wildlife, flora, and history of the bog—a site of international scientific interest—is discussed by the driver as the train makes its slow journey. **Strokestown Park House** in County Roscommon is adding a museum in 1993, documenting the disastrous 1845 famine, and its extensive gardens are in the early stages of a major restoration.

Visitors familiar with the traditionally unpretentious accommodations available in this area will be pleasantly surprised by the opulence of the **Slieve Russell Country Club and Hotel** at Ballyconnell near Cavan; the 300-acre compound features a luxurious indoor leisure center with a 20-meter pool, 18-hole golf course, and 50 acres of lakes for anglers.

The Southeast B & I Line recently launched a new luxury ferry, the *Isle of Inisfree*, on the Pembroke-Rosslare sea route. It's the largest car ferry on the Irish Sea route with a capacity of 2,000 passengers and 411 cars. **Sealink British Ferries** already has a comparable ultra-modern ferry on the Fishguard-Rosslare route, thus greatly improving the standards of sea transport. Three new parkland golf courses opened recently in the area: the Jack Nicklaus-designed course at **Mount Juliet** in Kilkenny, and 18-hole parkland courses adjoining the **Waterford Castle Hotel** and the **Dundrum House Hotel**.

The Irish National Heritage Park at Ferrycarrig, near Wexford Town, continues to enhance its attractions. This 35-acre open-air theme park, which covers Irish history from 9000 BC to AD 1100, is now handling up to 1,500 visitors per day. It has hired costumed craft workers and students to bring a human dimension to its full-scale replicas of Irish life in the distant past.

The Southwest Cork City Center's pedestrianized **Paul Street** area with its paved piazza has revitalized the whole area between Patrick Street and the river. Paul Street, French Church Street, and Carey's Lane are fast becoming the best addresses in town for lively moderately priced restaurants, adventurous fashion boutiques, specialty book shops, and top-quality craft shops.

Sheen Falls Lodge, a luxury development on Kenmare Bay, is the newest upscale hotel in the region. It has a magnificent location beside a waterfall and is surrounded by 300 secluded acres of lawn, semitropical gardens, and forest. **Adare Manor,** an even grander recent arrival on the scene in County Limerick, is a vast, Gothic Victorian manor on a 1,000-acre estate. It recently added an 18-hole golf course to its sporting facilities, which already included fishing, horseback riding, and a fitness center. The hotel is an ideal touch-down point for transatlantic passengers arriving at Shannon, which is only 25 km (16 mi) away. (*See* Dining and Lodging in Chapter 7.)

Where tourism is concerned, **Kinsale,** with its quaint narrow streets and fine restaurants, is the boom town of the Southwest; although Dingle, in the far west (favorite hideaway of actress Julia Roberts, among others), is equally attractive and offers a good choice of restaurants during its April-to-October high season. The completed **Dingle Way**

walking trail loops from Tralee for 95 miles around the Dingle peninsula and back. And the **Kerry Way,** which starts in
Killarney, now extends for 130 miles around the Ring of
Kerry. The **Skellig Experience,** beside the road bridge to
Valentia Island, combines an interpretative center telling
of **Skellig Michael** (an ancient Christian monastery on a conical rock 8 miles off the coast), with a 1½ hour cruise around
the islands.

The **Queenstown Centre,** a £3 million heritage center re-
creating the emigrant experience opens in **Cobh** in March
1993, and is expected to revitalize that comparatively ne-
glected Victorian seaport.

The West The development of regional airports is now making the
West more accessible than ever. Travelers can save time by
flying direct from the United Kingdom to Carnmore Airport, Galway City, or Horan International Airport at
Knock in County Mayo. Flights are also scheduled to these
airports from Cork and Dublin, eliminating a three- or four-
hour drive. The new **Connemara Airport,** serving the Aran
Islands, has cut the journey time to the island to 5 minutes,
and has also led to a significant price reduction.

The Northwest A new round of restoration work at **Donegal Castle** was begun in 1992, and may continue into 1993. You'll be able to
admire the castle's refreshed exterior, but you won't be
allowed inside.

Donegal Irish Parian China at Ballyshannon has opened a
visitor center at which you can see how the traditional fine
china is crafted, inspect and buy the finished pieces, and
have a snack at the café.

The **Sligo Park Hotel** has completed an extensive enlarge-
ment and refurbishment. It's now just about the best hotel
in Sligo Town.

Northern Ireland **Belfast** is in the midst of revitalization and improvement.
The huge **Laganside** development (which will take 15 years
to complete) aims to totally reconstruct Belfast's currently
unsightly 1½-mile stretch of riverside. The plans show
smart new business, leisure, and housing developments.
There is already some attractive construction going up
around the St. Anne's Cathedral and in the Golden Mile
area. **Northern Ireland** city hotels have been hit during the
past year's bombing campaign, keeping some visitors
away. Yet all the bad news comes from Belfast and, to a
much lesser extent, Derry; rural areas remain as inviting
and peaceful as ever. Despite the setbacks, there are good
things happening, too. In 1993, the European chain **Novotel**
is opening its first hotel in Ireland at Belfast Airport.

Derry City, for years considered a worse trouble spot than
Belfast, seems to have entered a new era as well. The high-
rise apartment buildings of the unsavory Bogside quarter
have been replaced by modern housing; now a substantial

area, situated between Shipquay Street and the city walls, will become a new commercial quarter called **The Village.** An **Interpretation Centre** telling the city's dramatic story has opened beside the city walls and will be expanded this year to include an Armada Exhibition with a display of Spanish treasure found in the Foyle estuary. Barbed wire and army stations on the historic city walls are due to be taken down this year, and guided walks on the ramparts may resume. A scaling-down of the army's presence in the town should soon be possible.

Fodor's Choice

No two people will agree on what makes a perfect vacation, but it's fun and helpful to know what others think. We hope you'll have a chance to experience some of Fodor's Choices yourself while visiting Ireland. For detailed information about each entry, refer to the appropriate chapters (given in the left-hand margin) within this guidebook.

Sights to Remember

Dublin	Sunset over the River Liffey
	Deserted Georgian squares on a Sunday
	Phoenix Park
Dublin Environs	Glendalough Valley
	Greystones Harbour at dusk
	Japanese Gardens, near Kildare Town
The Lakelands	Birr Castle Demesne, Birr
The Southeast	Ballyhack Village from Passage East
	Lismore Castle Gardens
	Mitchelstown Cave, Burncourt, Cahir
The Southwest	The view of the Blasket Islands from Slea Head
	Dusk over Killarney's Lower Lake as seen from Aghadoe Heights
	The view of Fastnet Rock Lighthouse from Cape Clear Island
The West	The view of the Aran Islands from the Cliffs of Moher
	Clifden's twin spires nestling in the mountains above the sea
	Salmon Weir Bridge, Galway
The Northwest	Peat cutters in the bog country
	Whitewashed single-story cottages with tied-on thatched roofs
Northern Ireland	Devenish Island viewed from Lough Erne's shore
	The Giant's Causeway
	Red, white, and blue curbstones in Protestant neighborhoods

Buildings and Monuments

Dublin	Bank of Ireland, College Green

National Library—the Reading Room

Royal Hospital, Kilmainham

Trinity College

Dublin Environs Castletown House, Celbridge

Church of Ireland cathedral and round tower, Kildare Town

Newgrange, Co. Meath

Russborough House, Blessington

The Lakelands Emo Court, near Portarlington

Clonmacnoise Monastery, Co. Offaly

Monastic remains, Ardmore

The Southeast Brown's Dolmen, Carlow Town

Kilkenny Castle, Kilkenny Town

Reginald's Tower, Waterford City

Rock of Cashel, Cashel

The Southwest Bunratty Castle, Bunratty

Charles Fort, Kinsale

Gallarus Oratory, Dingle Peninsula

Blarney Castle, Blarney

The West Ashford Castle, Cong

Dún Aengus, Inishmore, Aran Islands

Kylemore Abbey, Connemara

The Northwest Creevykeel megalithic court-cairn, near Cliffony

Donegal Castle, Donegal Town

Glenveagh Castle, Co. Donegal

Northern Ireland Belfast's Victorian pubs

Carrickfergus Castle, Carrickfergus

Castle Coole, near Enniskillen

Museums and Works of Art

Dublin Museum of Modern Art, Kilmainham

Guinness Hop Store

Treasury, at the National Museum

Dublin Environs Millmount Museum, Drogheda

Ledwidge Cottage and Museum, Slane

The Southeast Irish National Heritage Park, Ferrycarrig

Reginald's Tower Museum, Waterford City

The Southwest	Bantry House, Bantry
	Crawford Gallery, Cork
	Hunt Collection, Plassey
	Craggaunowen Project, Co. Limerick
The West	Dysert O'Dea Castle, Archaeology Center, Corofin
	Thoor Ballylee, Gort
The Northwest	Glebe Gallery, Church Hill
	Sligo County Museum, Sligo Town
Northern Ireland	Ulster Museum, Belfast
	Ulster Folk Museum, near Belfast

Scenic Drives and Views

Dublin	East pier, Dun Laoghaire
	Hill of Howth
Dublin Environs	Around the shores of Poulaphouca Reservoir, Co. Wicklow
	Banks of Grand Canal, Co. Kildare
	Hill of Tara, Co. Meath
The Southeast	Vee Gap scenic route, Co. Tipperary
The Southwest	Connor Pass, Dingle Peninsula
	Scenic route from Allihies to Eyeries, Beara Peninsula
	Tunnel road: Glengarriff–Kenmare–Killarney
The West	Atlantic drive around Achill Island
	The Burren: Cliffs of Moher to Ballyvaughan via Doolin and Fanore (coast road), returning to Lisdoonvarna via Corkscrew Hill
	Sky Road, Clifden
The Northwest	Killybegs to Glencolumbkille, Donegal Bay
	Around Sheephaven Bay
	The road along Errigal Mountain's south side
Northern Ireland	The Glens of Antrim
	Around Lower Lough Erne

Hotels

Dublin	Killiney Castle, Co. Dublin (*Expensive*)
	Shelbourne (*Expensive*)
	Towers (*Expensive*)
	Lansdowne (*Moderate*)

Ariel House (*Inexpensive*)

Dublin Environs Rathsallagh House, Dunlavin (*Very Expensive*)

Moyglare Manor, Maynooth (*Expensive*)

Tinakilly House, Rathnew (*Expensive*)

Tulfarris House, Blessington (*Expensive*)

Ballymascanlon House, Dundalk (*Moderate*)

The Lakelands Greville Arms, Mullingar (*Moderate*)

The White Horse, Cootehill (*Inexpensive*)

The Southeast Cashel Palace Hotel, Cashel (*Very Expensive*)

Mount Juliet, Thomastown (*Very Expensive*)

Ferrycarrig Hotel, Wexford (*Expensive*)

Kelly's Strand Hotel, Rosslare (*Expensive*)

Newpark Hotel, Kilkenny Town (*Moderate*)

The Southwest Adare Manor, Adare (*Very Expensive*)

Park Hotel, Kenmare (*Very Expensive*)

Longueville House, Mallow (*Expensive*)

Cahernane Hotel, Killarney (*Expensive*)

Benner's, Dingle (*Moderate*)

The West Dromoland Castle, Newmarket-on-Fergus (*Very Expensive*)

Ballynahinch Castle, Recess (*Expensive*)

Cashel House Hotel, Cashel Bay (*Expensive*)

Gregan's Castle, Ballyvaughan (*Expensive*)

Rock Glen Manor House, Clifden (*Moderate*)

The Northwest Rathmullan House, Rathmullen (*Expensive*)

St. Ernan's House, Donegal Town (*Moderate*)

Northern Ireland Culloden House, Belfast (*Very Expensive*)

Wellington Park Hotel (*Expensive*)

Londonderry Arms, Carnlough (*Moderate*)

Bed-and-Breakfasts

Dublin Iona House (*Inexpensive*)

Kilronan House (*Inexpensive*)

Dublin Environs Lennoxbrook, Kells (*Moderate*)

Old Rectory Country House, Wicklow Town (*Moderate*)

The Lakelands Ballycormac House, Borrisokane (*Inexpensive*)

Riverside House, Cootehill (*Inexpensive*)

The Southeast	Butler House, Kilkenny (*Moderate*)
	Diamond Hill Country House, Waterford City (*Inexpensive*)
The Southwest	Bantry House, Bantry (*Moderate*)
	Kathleen's Country House, Killarney (*Moderate*)
	Scilly House, Kinsale (*Moderate*)
The West	Currarevagh House, Oughterard (*Moderate*)
	Ballinalacken Castle, Lisdoonvarna (*Inexpensive*)
	Dun Aengus, Clifden (*Inexpensive*)
The Northwest	Coopershill, Riverstown (*Expensive*)
	Markree Castle, Collooney (*Expensive*)
	Bruckless House, Bruckless (*Moderate*)
	Temple House, Ballymote (*Moderate*)
	Woodhill Guest House, Ardara (*Inexpensive*)
Northern Ireland	Ash-Rowan Guest House, Belfast (*Moderate*)
	Jamestown House, Ballinamallard (*Moderate*)
	Camera House, Belfast (*Inexpensive*)

Restaurants

Dublin	Restaurant Patrick Guilbaud (*Very Expensive*)
	The Wine Epergne (*Very Expensive*)
	The King Sitric (*Expensive*)
	Les Frères Jacques (*Expensive*)
Dublin Environs	Rathsallagh House, Dunlavin (*Very Expensive*)
	Tinakilly House, Rathnew (*Very Expensive*)
	Roundwood Inn, Roundwood (*Expensive*)
	Tree of Idleness, Bray (*Expensive*)
The Lakelands	Crookedwood House, near Mullingar (*Expensive*)
	Moorhill House, Tullamore (*Expensive*)
The Southeast	Chez Hans, Cashel (*Very Expensive*)
	Marfield House Hotel, Gorey (*Very Expensive*)
	Waterford Castle, Waterford (*Very Expensive*)
	Dwyers of Mary Street, Waterford (*Moderate*)
	Neptune Restaurant, Ballyhack (*Moderate*)
The Southwest	Arbutus Lodge, Cork (*Expensive*)
	Cliffords, Cork (*Expensive*)
	Shiro Japanese Dinner House, Durrus (*Expensive*)

	Beginish, Dingle (*Moderate*)
The West	Drimcong House, Moycullen (*Expensive*)
	Claire's, Ballyvaughan (*Moderate*)
	Noctan's, Galway (*Moderate*)
	The Orchid Room, Sheedy's Spa View, Lisdoonvarna (*Moderate*)
The Northwest	Cromleach Lodge, Castlebaldwin (*Moderate–Expensive*)
	Restaurant St. John's, Fahan (*Moderate–Expensive*)
Northern Ireland	Roscoff, Belfast (*Very Expensive*)
	MacDuffs, Coleraine (*Expensive*)
	Restaurant 44, Belfast (*Expensive*)

After Hours

Dublin	Irish music session at O'Donoghue's
	National Concert Hall
	A play at the Abbey, the Gate, or the Project Arts Centre
	Abbey Tavern, Howth
Dublin Environs	Singing sessions at Black Bull and Gwent Arms pubs, Drogheda
	A pint of Guinness at Moran's Pub, Mornington
	Summer concerts at Castletown House, Celbridge
The Southeast	Portholes Bar, Hotel Rosslare, Rosslare
	Seanachie Pub, Ballymacart
	T & H Doolans Bar, Waterford City
The Southwest	Gleneagles Hotel, Killarney
	Mangan's Brasserie, Cork
	O'Flaherty's Pub, Dingle
The West	Abbeyglen Castle Hotel, Clifden
	Murray's Piano Bar, Hotel Salthill, Galway
	West County Hotel, Ennis
The Northwest	Abbey Hotel, Donegal Town
	Hargadon's Pub and Sligo Park Hotel, Sligo Town
	Nancy's and Peter Oliver's pubs, Ardara
Northern Ireland	Grand Opera House, Belfast
	Irish music sessions at the Rotterdam, Maddens, and Pat's Bar, Belfast

Ireland

Europe

Reykjavik

ICELAND

NORWAY

Bergen

NORTHERN
IRELAND

SCOTLAND

Edinburgh

*North
Sea*

Skagerrat

Belfast

IRELAND

*Irish
Sea*

GREAT

DENMARK

Dublin

BRITAIN

WALES

Hamburg

ENGLAND

HOLLAND

Amsterdam

Cardiff

The Hague

GERM

London

Rotterdam

*ATLANTIC
OCEAN*

English Channel

Brussels

Bonn

BELGIUM

Paris

LUXEMBOURG

Frankfurt

FRANCE

Zürich

Munich

Bern

Salzburg

SWITZERLAND

Lyon

LIECHTENSTEIN

Li

Milan

Venice

PORTUGAL

Madrid

ANDORRA

Marseille

Nice

Monaco

Lisbon

Barcelona

Corsica

Florence

SPAIN

Seville

Granada

*Balearic
Islands*

Sardinia

Tyrrhenian

Gibraltar

Mediterranean Sea

MOROCCO

ALGERIA

0   400 miles

TUNISIA

0   600 km

World Time Zones

Numbers below vertical bands relate each zone to Greenwich Mean Time (0 hrs.).
Local times frequently differ from these general indications,
as indicated by light-face numbers on map.

Algiers, **29**
Anchorage, **3**
Athens, **41**
Auckland, **1**
Baghdad, **46**
Bangkok, **50**
Beijing, **54**

Berlin, **34**
Bogotá, **19**
Budapest, **37**
Buenos Aires, **24**
Caracas, **22**
Chicago, **9**
Copenhagen, **33**
Dallas, **10**

Delhi, **48**
Denver, **8**
Djakarta, **53**
Dublin, **26**
Edmonton, **7**
Hong Kong, **56**
Honolulu, **2**

Istanbul, **40**
Jerusalem, **42**
Johannesburg, **44**
Lima, **20**
Lisbon, **28**
London (Greenwich), **27**
Los Angeles, **6**
Madrid, **38**
Manila, **57**

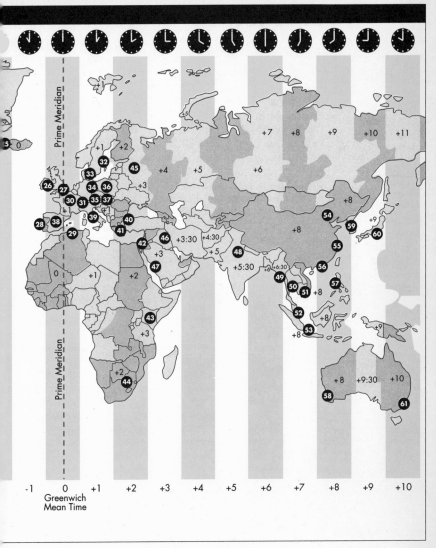

Introduction

By Nan Richardson

A frequent visitor to Ireland, Nan Richardson is the co-author of An Eye for an Eye: Northern Ireland. *Her articles and essays have appeared in* Art in America, Aperture, Granta, *and other publications.*

If you journey to Ireland by air, the descent is shrouded in gray, suddenly breaking through mists to that startling patchwork, "the forty shades of green," that leaves you breathless. But if you take the ferry (from say, Le Havre or Cherbourg to Cork or Rosslare; or from Liverpool or Holyhead to Dun Laoghaire or Belfast), you'll see the face of another Ireland, stained with the smell of peat from the braziers, the steaming pots of black tea, the tendrils of smoke from cigarettes passed silently around seated groups. You'll taste the sharp tang of golden whiskey, and hear the sounds of Gaelic-accented English that is the Irish brogue, as well as the noise of children: wheeling, crawling, climbing, laughing, bawling, like some untrammeled force.

While more prosperous countries of the EC vainly encourage barely a replacement birthrate, Ireland overflows with youth: 60% of its population is under the age of 25. But all this has its sober side, as Ireland's chief export is not linen and tweed, cut glass and wool, sheep and fat cattle, or music and literature. It is, as it has always been, her children, joining the great stream of the Irish in search of work and opportunity that the island cannot provide. History has willed it so, ever since the famines of the last century when the young and not-so-young fled or died, reducing a population from eight to three million in a generation's lifetime. Today whole rural counties are nearly depopulated, farms are abandoned, and houses are emptied—their occupants have disappeared to Dublin and beyond. History explains this, too, for Ireland has only been a Republic for barely 50 years, cut loose from the British Empire in 1923 and left with no cities, industry, or market for its products. Scrambling to make up for those centuries of exploitation has cost the Republic, which staggers under a third-world debt and cannot stem the dissolution of families and the tide of emigration to England, Australia, Canada, and the United States. The balladmakers sing emigre's songs, such as "A Long Way from Clare to Here," and it will be an equally long way to solvency for Ireland. For Ireland is two-faced, like the Janus-stones and sheel-na-gigs of its pre-Christian past; it's a complex place where the mystic lyricism of Yeats, the hard Rabelaisian passions of Joyce, and the spare, aloof dissection of Beckett grew not only from a rich and ancient culture but also from 20th-century upheavals.

A Friendly People

Simple customs tell a lot. Hospitality in Ireland is counted among the greatest of virtues, a legacy from Celtic times when anyone not offering the traveler food and drink was shamed; the country is justly legendary even now for the friendliness of its people. "You are welcome," people say in greeting the moment you cross the threshold of the poorest house, while total strangers will take you home for tea or supper and strike up conversations with ease and curiosity, entertaining you perhaps with an account of their second cousin's memorable fortnight in America (a fortnight's worth of stories if you have the time!).

Time, in fact, is one of the greatest luxuries of Ireland. On a fine day, along a lushly green country lane, you may pass a bicycle abandoned against a tree; looking for its owner, you'll find him reclining in the feathery hedgerows or on the long grass, contemplating fast-moving clouds like some philosopher-king. "Oh the dreaming, the dreaming, the heart-scalding bitter, maddening dreaming," cried the playwright George Bernard Shaw, but to knowing travelers in the stressed and industrialized world, this haven of dreamers is a pearl of great price, sought-after and kept secret. Not long ago, in a bar in Crossmaglen, a village in Armagh, a rugged farmer in oilskins and thornproof, chores over and done with (or just put on hold) turned an amused and quizzical eye as I fretted at the lateness of my appointment. "All that rushing about—and what for?" he reprimanded. "Give us a wee one there," he signaled the barman with a lift of his pipe, and pushed his glass to mine to toast the sentiment, "Life's for the living!" And, he concluded with another swallow, "Never put off for tomorrow a drink you can have today."

Much of the real beauty of Ireland is hidden on the back roads. If America is known for its car culture, Ireland is known for its cow culture, ever since the days of the "Tuigne na Cuailnge," or "The Cattle Raid of Cooley," the eighth-century epic that is the Iliad of Ireland, describing a marital dispute between the two leaders, King Ailill and Queen Maeve, over who had the finest herds in the land. Equal down to the last cow, Maeve had one item that Ailill lusted after: a giant brown bull; to win the wager, the king kidnapped the bull one night, kicking off a 50-year internecine war. Although Irish wealth today is not exactly measured in sirloin pound, the moo-cows seem to own the country lanes, staring haughtily and curiously at interloping motorists, lazily drooping timothy from their soft maws. In the end, with persuasion from harried livery equipped with frisky dogs and long-knobbed sticks, they'll share the road—but all in their time.

Somehow this may help explain why Ireland is what anthropologists call a "lived" culture, one that doesn't put much stock in the outward monuments of achievement; where the most potent history is oral, where storytelling is an art, and where people will travel miles for the "crack," the Irish synonym for a rousing good time. Ireland teaches you patience, reminds you of the rhythms of the natural world, and convinces you, reassuringly, of the essential well-being of man. French traveler LaTocnaye wrote in his journals in 1644, after a tour of the island, that "the Irish are very fond of strangers," and Oliver Goldsmith, later in the 18th century, observed, "The natives are peculiarly remarkable for their gaiety and the levity of their dispositions; English transplanted here lose their serious melancholy and become gay and thoughtless, more fond of pleasure and less addicted to reasoning."

The Price of a Pint

Hospitality finds its logical institution in the local pub, the center of social life in Ireland. Even a small town such as Dingle in County Kerry (population 1,000) boasts 52 watering holes, open day and night. Protocol dictates that you enter and greet everyone, taking a seat alone until invited (as you inevitably are) to join a table. Then the ancient custom of rounds begins, with the newcomer offering to buy the first set of drinks, and when the pints are barely half-full (half-empty from an Irish perspective), another imbiber stands the round, and so on, in turn. With a few companions, this makes it nearly obligatory to spend an afternoon in the pub. Similarly, if you're smoking, custom demands that you offer the pack to fellow socializers before you light up yourself. Women are often exempted from these rituals, if, indeed, they are allowed to join in at all, for in rural areas the sight of a woman drinking is still frowned upon, and if they do darken a publican's door they head for the "lounge," a slightly dressed-up version of the same establishment to drink glasses, never pints, even if they have a powerful thirst. Of course, "strangers," female or other, can be nonconformist with impunity.

These social and equitable customs help explain why 10% of Irish personal spending goes to alcohol like some unholy tithe and why these dark village pubs with their scratched wooden counters, dusty tiled floors, and the yeasty smell of Guinness have a feeling of sanctity and remove from wordly cares not unlike a church. It may also explain, incidentally, the historic Irish reputation for wit and bellicosity. The rumor of bellicosity, however, is ill-founded: "The only people in Europe who have never set out to conquer," my friend, a Dublin photographer claimed with pride, but wit flows untapped from unexpected sources. It might come from the use of a borrowed language, perhaps from the need of a subject people for subterfuge, but nuance and irony are the rules of conversation, and anything less would be considered flat-footed. Irish expertise in double-think and forked tongue makes for a universally acknowledged aptitude for legal affairs, a gift for words of imagination and persuasiveness that you can find in the crossroads *shebeen* (pub) much as in Dublin's Leinster House, where the Irish *Dail* (or legislature) sits.

The Grand Tour

You are never very far from anywhere in Ireland, but each of its 32 counties have their special character and history, and fierce loyalty from their sons and daughters. Dublin is the millennium-old capital, once a Celtic settlement by the ford of the River Liffey, later a Norse encampment for raiding Viking and Danish pirates, and finally the citadel-seat of the British colonizer's power for centuries. Today it is a graceful mix of fine Georgian buildings, a lively waterfront, wrought-iron canals and bridges, an army of booksellers, 800-odd pubs, and a rich cultural life. Ireland chooses to exempt artists from taxes, designating them national resources of sorts, and filmmakers, painters, and writers are part of the local scenery, along with the "rale Dubs," or "jackeens,"—the breezy natives born in the heart of the city between the Grand and Royal canals that divide North and South Dublin into two worlds. Although it can be a sophisticated city, with sushi bars, French restaurants and bold theater, it hasn't lost any of its simple pleasures, like waking to the tinkling of glass bottles with round silver caps, delivered to the stoop by a milkman dressed all in white; afternoon tea at Bewley's with scones slathered with Kerry Gold butter; soda farls heaped with clouds of whipped cream; waitresses in black dresses and starched aprons; or breakfast "the like of which you'll never see again," my landlady promised (though everywhere in Ireland seemed to be competing in this category). The silver pots of dark tea, the wheaten bread and toast in gleaming racks, the eggs, oatmeal, rashers (bacon), and sausages all done up with doilies, send you out into the permeating mists that the Irish ironically call "soft weather," fortified and content.

Nearby, the scenic Wicklow mountains and rich Boyne valley are home to the wealthier class. The ancestral homes of the dwindling members of the Anglo-Irish ascendancy dot the landscape throughout the country, and lords and baronets down on their luck have turned hoteliers and welcome guests to castle holidays with adaptable grace. Limerick County is famed as horse country. County Tipperary's rolling green flatlands and Galtee mountains are known for champion greyhounds and the stud farms that have turned out winners for generations. The Rock of Cashel, seat of the Kings of Munster for 700 years, (where St. Patrick said his first mass in Ireland) is here, along with Cahir Castle, one of the few places that managed to resist Cromwell's hordes, now restored to its former impressiveness.

The coast of County Wexford was the original beachhead of Ireland named by the Vikings after the consort of their one-eyed god Odin; it still bears the stamp of its fearless, sea-going settlers, in its steep pathways and fine seafood. Wexford is a quick trip to Kilkenny, the finest medieval city in Ireland and known for its artisans. Also nearby is Waterford City, where the crystal of the same name is produced, at the delta of three great rivers—the Nore, Barrow, and Suir. Waterford City has one of the oldest forts in Ireland, Reginald's Tower, built in 1013 and named for the Viking warrior who founded the city. But while the Southeast has its charm, for scenery, generally speaking, go to the counties in the West: from Cork and Kerry to Clare and Galway, from Sligo up to Donegal.

County Donegal, in the far northwest, is among the wildest, most ruggedly beautiful places in the world, with its long rocky coastline, white beaches, turbulent surf, and impressive mountains and plateaus, full of legendary lore of giants and witches, fairies, and pishogues. Irish is widely spoken here, and the music is famous; traditional groups, such as Clannad and De Dannaan, named after the prehistoric followers of the goddess Dana, are local heroes, and when Enya, daughter of local musicians, hit the top of the charts in Europe and the United States with her Irish-New Age instrumentals, the roof flew off Leo's pub in Gweedore, where spontaneous sessions for the music-loving community are regular happenings.

Galway City is a port and university town, bustling and businesslike, and the departure point for the Aran Islands, celebrated by playwright J.M. Synge in *Riders to the Sea* and Robert Flaherty in his classic documentary film *Man of Aran*. Just to the west of Galway City lies Connemara, loved by painters, who flock there in summer, by writers (from Yeats to Gogarty to Joyce), and by all seekers of silence and beauty. It, too, is a *Gaeltacht* (Irish-speaking) area, celebrated for its simplicity of lifestyle and genuinely warm natives. Connemara is also known for its ponies, descendants of the Andalusian horses that swam to shore from the Spanish fleet and bred with the local Celtic stock (direct descendants of the original Ice Age horse of 20,000 BC).

At the southwestern end of the Republic is County Kerry, full of soft accents and magic places. For centuries, summer travelers here have been thrilled by the surfeit of natural beauty as they've gazed at the black rocks and green waves glistening at Slea Head on the Dingle Peninsula or at the Blasket Islands, where St. Brendan the Navigator was said to have set sail in a wooden *curragh* (boat) to discover the Americas in the 7th century. Sea birds reel and wild donkeys graze among the fuschia hedges awash in crimson velvet flowers, and the fields explode with deep yellow gorse, may-blossom, and honeysuckle against a dark blue sky. County Kerry's special events and attractions include Killorgin's annual three-day Puck Fair in mid-summer (when a large billy goat is crowned king and garlanded with flowers, a residue of an old pre-Christian fertility rite) and Killarney, with its lakes, park lands, and jumping-off places for a drive around the Ring of Kerry.

Nearby Cork, (from the Gaelic "corcaigh," meaning marshes) has always been called "The Rebel County," and a quick tour of all the monuments will tell you why. Michael Collins, the general who won independence for Ireland was assassinated here, and Terence McSweeney, a former mayor of Cork, died on hunger strike here, to name a few. A Venice-like port city of canals and bridges, and a bustling mercantile center, Cork was once home to writers Sean O'Faolain and Frank O'Connor, and is today a city of sport. Its team is always in the championship finals of hurling, that fast and furious ancient game that makes soccer look like kick-the-can, and the city is one of the few places where they still play the traditional, two-thousand-year-old game of bowls that the Irish giant Cuchulain used to excel at. If your taste runs to less athletic entertainment, visit the exquisitely restored village of Kinsale, or the attractive historical and arts centers of West Cork, helped along by an influx of discriminating French and German settlers in this part of Ireland for the last 20 years.

Taking the main road from Dublin to Belfast is a reminder—as you pass bristling watchtowers, sandbagged forts and warpainted soldiers in camouflage who check your papers—that, as another song goes, "one of Ireland's four green fields are still in stranger's hands." While Munster, Leinster, and Connaught are in the south, six of the nine counties of Ulster remained part of Britain in 1921. Today Northern Ireland is definitely worth a trip, and the reward for a little courage is great: here you have the beauty of the Antrim Coast from Carncastle to Bushmills; the Giant's Causeway; the rich farmlands and lakelands of Fermanagh; and the austere beauty of the Mourne Mountains. People are as friendly and helpful here as they are in the Republic, and, probably because of their history, perhaps a little sharper and wittier. Northern Ireland is also fascinating for any follower of history and politics for you get an unforgettable glimpse of the winds of time changing, a scene not unlike the last days of the Raj, as Britain's first colony erodes to be her last.

Digging Up the Past

That sense of otherness which few destinations on this scale, or this accessible, can provide, cannot only be attributed to its evergreen climate and leisurely pace of life but also to the palimpsest of history and legend dug deep under Ireland's rich grassy surface. Its tumultuous past is in evidence everywhere, from the Neolithic tombs and defenses of Newgrange in County Meath and Dun Aengus on Inishmore Island, 5,000 years older than the pyramids of Giza, to the numerous other antiquities and archeological sites, registered and unregistered—standing stones and court graves, mottes and dolmens, raths and cairns, holy wells and mass stones, round towers and Celtic crosses.

The legacy of the first-known Scandinavian settlers in Ireland and the later influx of Bronze Age Celts from Central Europe was an agrarian society based on a democratic kingship, a justice system known as the Brehon laws, and an artisan caste proficient in gold and precious metals. Christianity followed in the 4th century, and while European culture flickered and died in the Dark Ages, priests nurtured knowledge in beehive huts and stone monasteries. About 800 AD Viking longboats scourged the island's coasts, leaving the mark of bright red hair behind on their Irish descendents. Brian Boru, last of the High Kings to sit at Tara, won the Battle of Clontarf against Danish armies in 1014, only to have his successors lose Ireland in 1169 to the Norman Strongbow, opening the door to 800 years of rebellion.

By 1609, the last of the Irish chieftains sailed for exile, making way for the "Plantation" of 200,000 Scottish Lowlanders on native Irish lands. Britain's Oliver Cromwell, "the Avenger," reinforced those Protestant claims, beheading thousands of men, women, and children in his devastating marches. In their wake came the "Penal Code," forbidding the Irish Catholics to practice their religion, exercise law, or own land, vote, and hold office. The crushing blow was the famine that struck after 1845, reducing the once-populous island from eight to three million inhabitants, through death or emigration, creating the first wave of the Irish diaspora and setting the stage for the ultimate uprising, on Easter morning, 1916, when Irish Nationalists proclaimed a republic. England's vengeance on the patriots galvanized the country to the bitter war of independence that ended in the partitioning of Ireland into twenty-six counties in the South and six in the North, a political struggle that continues today. Like many facets of history in Irish life, this conflict is subtle, often below the surface and invisible to the casual observer.

Ireland Today

Present-day Ireland encourages creativity that goes beyond history and tradition. In the music field, internationally known talents have emerged, such as the rock bands U2, the Hothouse Flowers, the Pogues, and In Tua Nua; top-of-the charts singers Sinead O'Connor, Van Morrison, Christy Moore, and Chris de Burgh; and folk musicians Sean Keane, Maggie Barrie, Liam Og O'Flynn, Paddy Reilly, Billy Bragg, and Mary Black. Theater is bursting with talent that often takes the centuries-old route across the water to London, with actors such as Richard Branagh, Brenda Fricker, Stella McCusker, Gabriel Byrne, and Daniel Day-Lewis, not to mention playwrights Brian Friel, Hugh Leonard, John Boyd, Graham Reid, Anne Devlin, John B. Keane, and the late Stewart Parker.

Contemporary filmmakers Pat O'Connor, Jim Sheridan, and Joe Comerford often draw from a rich source of narrative writing provided by novelists Neil Jordan, William Trevor, James Plunkett, Bernard McLaverty, Thomas Kinsella, Edna O'Brien, Benedict Kiely, and John McGahern. Irish poetry is alive and well in the hands of Seamus Heaney, Derek Mahon, Paul Muldoon, Seamus Deane, Tom Paulin, and Medh McGuckian.

While literature is certainly Ireland's single greatest contribution to the arts, with the shadow of giants like Jonathan Swift, Oscar Wilde, Patrick Kavanagh, Brendan Behan, Bernard Shaw, and others still casting a shadow, the country shows hidden strengths in other creative fields. In the visual arts, the legacy of Irish Impressionists Jack Yeats and Paul Henry, gave way to painters such as Tom Carr, David Crone, Felim Egan, Jack Pakeham, James Coleman, and Louis de Brocquy, whose subject matter is metaphor, "the secret logic of ambivalence." Meanwhile, a younger generation of artists, including Rita Duffy, Micky Donnelly, Fergus and Diarmuid Delargy, sculptor Ailish O'Connell, and others confront issues of social and political contradiction in their work. In its capacity for regeneration, irrepressible vitality, mordant wit, eerie spirituality, and culturally ingrained generosity, Ireland often seems to move backwards in time to the Tir-na-Og—the mythical land of the ever-young, an alternative world of fairies, pishogues, and hidden supernatural forces that remains alive in the Irish imagination.

1 Essential Information

Before You Go

Government Tourist Offices

Irish Republic Contact the Irish Tourist Board for information on all aspects of travel to and around Ireland.

In the U.S.: 757 Third Ave., New York, NY 10017, tel. 212/418–0800.

In Canada: 160 Bloor St., Suite 934, Toronto, Ont. M4W 1B9, tel. 416/929–2777.

In the U.K.: 150 New Bond St., London W1Y 0AQ, tel. 071/493–3201.

Northern Ireland The Northern Ireland Tourist Board (NITB) has its own overseas offices, which are the primary source of information for tourists planning to visit the province. Where there is no NITB office, however, the British Tourist Authority can usually supply information.

Addresses of the NITB are:

In the U.S.: 40 W. 57th St., 3rd Floor, New York, NY 10019, tel. 212/686–6250. **In the U.K.:** Ulster Office, 11 Berkeley St., London W1X 6BU, tel. 071/493–0601; 38 High St., Sutton Coldfield, B72 1UP, tel. 021/354–1431.

British Tourist Authority offices overseas are:

In the U.S.: 2580 Cumberland Pkwy., Suite 470, Atlanta, GA 30339, tel. 404/432–9635; 875 N. Michigan Ave., Chicago, IL 60611, tel. 312/787–0490; 2305 Cedar Springs Rd., Suite 210, Dallas, TX 75201, tel. 214/720–4040; World Trade Center, Suite 450, 350 Figueroa St., Los Angeles, CA 90071, tel. 213/628–3525. **In Canada:** 111 Avenue Rd., Suite 450, Toronto, Ont. M5R 3J8, tel. 416/925–6326.

Tour Groups

Care to ride round the Ring of Kerry, kiss the Blarney Stone, or pick up some Irish crystal? Then you might want to consider a package tour of Ireland's most famous highlights. Creative itineraries abound, hitting the traditional tourist spots as well as off-the-beaten-path places you might not be able to get to on your own. They also tend to save you money on airfare and hotels. If group travel is not your thing, look into independent packages (*see* Package Deals for Independent Travelers, *below*).

When considering a tour, be sure to find out (1) exactly which expenses are included, particularly tips, taxes, side trips, meals, and entertainment; (2) the ratings of all hotels on the itinerary and the facilities they offer; (3) the additional cost of single, rather than double, accommodations if you are traveling alone; and (4) the number of travelers in your group. Note whether the tour operator reserves the right to change hotels, routes, or even prices after you've booked, and check out the operator's policy regarding cancellations, complaints, and trip-interruption insurance. Many tour operators request that packages be booked through a travel agent; there is generally no additional charge for doing so.

Listed below is a sampling of operators and packages to give you an idea of what is available. For additional information, contact your travel agent, the Irish Tourist Board, or the Northern Ireland Tourist Board.

General-Interest Tours
Irish Republic

Maupintour (Box 807, Lawrence, KS 66044, tel. 913/843–1211 or 800/255–4266) sweeps through many of the Emerald Isle's highlights on its 15-day "Best of Ireland" tour. For shorter stays, **American Express Vacations** (300 Pinnacle Way, Norcross, GA 30093, tel. 800/241–1700 or, in GA, 800/421–5785) offers nine- and 12-day packages. **Trafalgar Tours** (21 E. 26th St., New York, NY 10010, tel. 212/689–8977 or 800/854–0103) has an eight-day package. **Globus-Gateway** (95–25 Queens Blvd., Rego Park, NY 11374, tel. 718/268–7000 or 800/221–0090) touts a seven-day introduction to Ireland, as well as a 13-day in-depth tour. **Cosmos,** the budget-minded affiliate of Globus-Gateway, does a 12-day "Jig Through Ireland." From May to October, **Brian Moore International Tours** (116 Main St., Medway, MA 02053, tel. 508/533–6683 or 800/982–2299) runs 10- and 14-day tours. One-week packages are offered year-round. **CIE Tours International** (108 Ridgedale Ave., Morristown, NJ 07960, tel. 201/292–3438 or 800/CIE–TOUR) brings you an eight-day "Irish Welcome," along with six other tours ranging from four to 13 days in length. **TWA Getaway Vacations** (tel. 800/GET-AWAY) hits Ireland's most popular sights in either eight or 12 days. **Delta Air Lines** (tel. 800/221–6666) offers a 17-day jaunt that covers both Great Britain and Ireland, and a 12-day "Grand Tour of Ireland." **Olson-Travelworld** (Box 10066, Manhattan Beach, CA 90226, tel. 310/546–8400, 800/421–2255, or in CA, 800/421–5785) offers a two-week "Irish Rhapsody" tour or a 20-day excursion to Ireland and Britain. At the upper end of the price spectrum, **Abercrombie & Kent** (1420 Kensington Rd., Oak Brook, IL 60521–2106, tel. 800/323–7308 or 708/954–2944) puts you in country houses and castle hotels on its deluxe 11-day "Magical Ireland" tour.

In the United Kingdom, contact **CIE Tours International** (185 London Rd., Croydon, CRO 2RJ, tel. 081/667–0011). They offer several coach tours as well as a variety of motoring, self-catering, and activity holidays.

Northern Ireland

The following companies run escorted tours combining Ireland and Northern Ireland, spending significant time in the North. **CIE Tours International** (*see above*) spends 12 days exploring the four Irish counties. Two overnight stops in the North are included. **Brendan Tours** (15137 Califa St., Van Nuys, CA 91411, tel. 818/785–9696 or 800/421–8446) runs the 13-day "Sights and Sounds of Ireland" tour. **Celtic International Tours** (161 Central Ave., Albany, NY 12206, tel. 518/463–5511 or 800/833–4373) offers the "Sojourn," a six-night trip with stops in the North, and **Brian Moore International Tours** (*see above*) provides the 10-day "Irish Landscape" tour, which includes a visit to the North.

Special-Interest Tours
Irish Republic

Cultural: Lynott Tours (Empire State Bldg., 350 5th Ave., Suite 2619, New York, NY 10118, tel. 212/760–0101 or 800/221–2474) customizes tours for groups of 10 or more. Possible themes include literature, history, and architecture. The leading specialist in cultural tours is **Abercrombie & Kent** (*see* General-Interest Tours, *above*). Itineraries can include social visits with the owners of Ireland's leading stately homes. U.K. visitors should contact **Elegant Ireland** (15 Harcourt St., Dublin 2, tel. 01/751665). This company offers a customized itinerary with overnight stops at a variety of Irish country homes for dinner, bed, and breakfast. **A Touch of Ireland** (92 Haddington Rd., Dublin 4, tel. 01/680888) organizes personalized itineraries and special interest tours for golfers, art connoisseurs, and those interested in crafts or large country homes. Driver guides and guides by the day are also available, and offered are an excellent range of unusual self-catering accommodations, from a four-bedroom Victorian gamekeeper's lodge on its own lake in County Sligo for £200 per week to a 700-year-old castle on Lough Corrib that sleeps 12 for £1,500 a week. An enthusiastic team at **The Hidden Ireland** (Kensington Hall, Grove Park, Dublin 6, tel. 01/686463) will arrange for you to stay in selected Irish country homes as paying guests. Hunting, shooting, fishing, and golf can be included in the itinerary. Houses range from small shooting lodges to great ancestral homes. Flights, itineraries, and self-driven or chauffeur-driven cars can be provided for groups of two to eight people. Alternatively, select your own destinations from the illustrated brochure.

Bicycling: Irish Cycling Safaris (7 Dartry Park, Dublin 6, tel. 01/978440) organizes week-long tours for groups of up to 20 cyclists in Connemara, Kerry, and the Southeast. Pace is tailored to group demand and averages 48 km/30 mi per day. Prices include bike rental, a guide, a tour van, and bed and breakfast accommodations.

Day Hiking: British Coastal Trails (150 Carob Way, Coronado, CA 92118, tel. 619/437–1211) features an excellent 11-day hiking tour of Southwest Ireland, held in May, July, and September. The itinerary covers some of the Republic's most scenic areas, including County Clare's lunar landscape in the Burren section; a ferry ride across the Shannon Estuary to County Kerry; the Ring of Kerry, including Valentia Island, Hog's Head, and the Dingle Bay coastline; and Killarney's lakes and national park. Walks are frequently away from the tourist track, along footpaths dating back to medieval Ireland, with views of such sights as Galway Bay, the Blasket Islands, and the Cliffs of Moher. The cost of the tour includes accommodations with private bath, an Irish breakfast and dinner daily, and a full-time guide.

Irish Wilderness Experience (50 Woodlawn Park, Killarney, Co. Kerry, tel. 064/32992), a Kerry-based company, aims to introduce people to the best that the West coast can offer the walker and naturalist. Tours are guided by experienced local experts who are highly knowledgeable about the region's ecology, natural history, archaeology, and folklore. The cost of the tours includes accommodations in hotels and guest houses, breakfast and dinner, and pickup from Killarney.

Golf: Value Holidays (10224 N. Port Washington Rd., Mequon, WI 53092, tel. 414/241–6373 or 800/558–6850) organizes golf vacations for two or more people at courses such as Ballybunion, Tralee, the Royal Dublin, and Portmarnock. Transportation, accommodations, greens fees, caddies, and optional matches are provided. Tours for nongolfers and evening entertainment can also be arranged. **Aer Lingus** (122 E. 42nd St., New York, NY 10168, tel. 212/557–1110 or 800/223–6537) organizes golf tours, as well as special shopping tours.

In the United Kingdom, **Atlantic Golf** (54A Richmond Rd., Twickenham, Middlesex TW1 3BE, tel. 081/891–6451) is a leading specialist in golfing holidays. Ballybunion, Lahinch, and Portmarnock are just three of the famous golf links served by the company. Four days, with unlimited golf, for four people traveling by air starts at £235. Other golf tours are run by **Aer Lingus Holidays** (223 Regent St., London W1R 0AJ, tel. 081/569–4001) and **Eurogolf** (3b London Rd., St. Albans, Herts, ALI ILA, tel. 0727/42256).

All Sports: Lismore Tours (106 E. 31st St., New York, NY 10016, tel. 212/685–0100 or 800/547–6673) organizes all aspects of an equestrian holiday, whether you aim to be a spectator at the Budweiser Irish Derby and the Dublin Horse Show or spend long hours in the saddle, either hunting or trail riding. Lismore also arranges golf, hunting, shooting, and fishing vacations, either in Ireland or in Ireland and Scotland.

In the United Kingdom, **B & I Line Holidays** (1st Floor, Port of Liverpool Bldg., Pier head, Liverpool L3 1BZ, tel. 051/236–8325) offers a wide range of packages, all with travel to Ireland on the company's ferries. Short vacations, motoring tours, farmhouse holidays, horseback-riding excursions, golf vacations, fishing holidays, riverboat cruises, bus tours, cottages, and city getaways are all available.

Avid anglers should contact **Cliff Smart Angling Holidays** (29 Bridle Rd., Burton Latimer, Northants NN15 5PQ, tel. 0536/725453), **Angler's World Holidays** (45 Knifesmithgate, Chesterfield S40 1QR, tel. 0246/221717), or **Kings Angling Holidays** (27 Minster Way, Hornchurch, Essex RM11 3TH, tel. 04024/53043). For golfing, fishing, farmhouse, and self-catering holidays, as well as bus tours, contact **PAB Travel** (Central Hall, 3 Ryder St., Birmingham B47 NH, tel. 021/2331252).

Northern Ireland **Sunquest Vacations Ltd.** (130 Merton St., Toronto, Ont. M4S 1A4, tel. 416/485–1700 or 800/268–8899) offers a seven-day tour giving access to 10 leading Northern Ireland courses.

Horseback Riding: A residential riding vacation with instruction at all levels (if required) in dressage, show jumping, and cross-country is offered at **Ashbrooke Riding School** (Brookeborough, Co. Fermanagh, tel. 0365/53242). Accommodation is available on Viscount Brookeborough's estate, either as a paying guest of the family or in self-catering units.

Irish/American Heritage: CIE Tours International (*see* General-Interest Tours, above) offers custom-designed group tours of Northern Ireland in virtually any area of special interest, including family lineage. Heritage holidays for groups or individuals are also arranged by the **Irish Genealogical Association** (162A Kingsway, Dunmurry, Belfast BT17 9 AD, tel. 0232/629595).

Walking: Ulster is encircled by a long-distance footpath called the **Ulster Way**, which is 790 km (491 mi) long. Accompanied walking holidays lasting a weekend or longer can be arranged through David Munnis (Secretary), **Ulster Rambling Federation,** 5 Rowan Rd., Ballymoney, Co. Antrim, tel. 02656/63360.

Package Deals for Independent Travelers

Irish Republic **CIE Tours International** (*see* General-Interest Tours, *above*) offers a three-night-minimum Dublin hotel package, which includes Irish breakfast daily, airport transfers, sightseeing tours, theater tickets, a four-day bus-and-rail pass, and a discount on rental-car rates. **British Airways** (tel. 800/AIRWAYS) gives you three nights in London and three in Dublin with the option to extend your stay in both cities. **Delta Air Lines** (*see* General-Interest Tours, *above*), **CIE Tours** (*see* General-Interest Tours, *above*), and **British Airways** all offer self-drive packages, which include accommodations at hotels or Irish town-and-country homes, a rental car, and full Irish breakfast daily. Some include round-trip airfare. **Brian Moore International Tours** (*see* General-Interest Tours, *above*) also has self-drive packages, plus weekend shopping sprees, and Dublin weekends from November to April. If you don't feel comfortable driving on the left side of the road, **Abercrombie & Kent** (*see* General-Interest Tours, *above*) will provide you with a private car and driver/guide. Follow A&K's suggested 14-day itinerary or design your own.

In the United Kingdom, **Aer Lingus Holidays** (*see* Special-Interest Tours, *above*) offers a variety of weekends in Ireland, both in Dublin and elsewhere in the country, along with motoring or golf holidays, coach tours, stays in castles and manors, and cruises on the Shannon. **CIE Tours International** (*see* General-Interest Tours, *above*) is another leading specialist. **Ryans Holidays** (200 Earls Court Rd., London SW5 9QX, tel. 071/244–6355) offers minibreaks in the west of Ireland, including three nights in Killarney, Westport, Galway, Limerick, or Sligo.

Northern Ireland **Celtic International Tours** (*see* General-Interest Tours, *above*) has self-drive packages of at least three nights, with farmhouse or hotel accommodations, unlimited mileage in a rental car, and Irish breakfast. **CIE Tours International** (*see* General-Interest Tours, *above*) also offers go-as-you-please self-drive packages, which include round-trip airfare; accommodations at farmhouses, town and country homes, or first-class hotels; unlimited rental car mileage; and full Irish breakfast daily.

In the United Kingdom, **Rainbow Holidays** (Ryedale Bldg., Picadilly, York YOI 1PN, tel. 0904/643355) offers short breaks to scenic spots in Northern Ireland, including air and hotel packages. **B&I Line Holidays** (*see* Special-Interest Tours, *above*) arranges a variety of touring packages and special-interest holidays in Northern Ireland and/or the Irish Republic, with car ferry and bed-and-breakfast included. Self-catering holidays in cottages and holiday homes are also available.

When to Go

The summer remains the most popular time to visit Ireland, and for good reason. The weather is pleasant, the days are long (daylight lasts until about 10 PM in late June), and the countryside is green and beautiful. But there will be crowds in popular holiday spots, and prices for accommodations are at their peak. As British and Irish school vacations overlap, covering the time from late June to mid-September, families, backpacking students, and other vacationers descend on popular coastal resorts in the South, the West, and the East. Unless you are determined to enjoy the short (July and August) swimming season, you would be well advised to take your vacation in Ireland outside these months.

Fall and spring are good times to travel, though the weather can be unpredictable. When hotels, restaurants, and accommodations are seasonal, they usually close from early or mid-November until mid-March or Easter. During this *off-season*, prices are considerably lower than at the summer peak, but your selection of hotels and restaurants is limited, and many minor attractions also close. St. Patrick's Week in March gives a focal point to a spring visit, but some American visitors may find the saint's-day celebrations a little less enthusiastic than the ones back home. Dublin, however, welcomes its American visitors on March 17 with a parade and then the Lord Mayor's Ball to round off the evening. If you're planning an Easter visit, don't forget that most theaters still close from Thursday to Sunday of Holy Week (the week preceding Easter), and all bars and restaurants, except those serving hotel residents, close on Good Friday.

If you want to feel like the only tourist in town, try a winter visit. Many hotels arrange special Christmas packages with entertainment and outdoor activities. Mid-November to mid-February is either too cold or too wet for all but the keenest golfers; however, horse races and hunting trips abound. There are cheerful open fires in almost all hotels and bars, and with extra time on their hands, people tend to take an added interest in visitors.

Climate What follows are average daily maximum and minimum temperatures for some major cities in Ireland.

Dublin

Jan.	47F	8C	**May**	59F	15C	**Sept.**	63F	17C
	34	1		43	6		49	9
Feb.	47F	8C	**June**	65F	18C	**Oct.**	58F	14C
	36	2		49	9		43	6
Mar.	50F	10C	**July**	68F	20C	**Nov.**	50F	10C
	38	3		52	11		40	4
Apr.	56F	13C	**Aug.**	67F	20C	**Dec.**	47F	8C
	40	4		52	11		38	3

Cork

Jan.	49F	9C	**May**	61F	16C	**Sept.**	65F	18C
	36	2		45	7		50	10
Feb.	49F	9C	**June**	67F	19C	**Oct.**	58F	14C
	38	3		50	10		45	7
Mar.	52F	11C	**July**	68F	20C	**Nov.**	52F	11C
	40	4		54	12		40	4
Apr.	56F	13C	**Aug.**	68F	20C	**Dec.**	49F	9C
	41	5		54	12		38	3

Belfast

Jan.	43F	6C	**May**	59F	15C	**Sept.**	61F	16C
	36	2		43	6		49	9
Feb.	45F	7C	**June**	65F	18C	**Oct.**	56F	13C
	36	2		49	9		45	7
Mar.	49F	9C	**July**	65F	18C	**Nov.**	49F	9C
	38	3		52	11		40	4
Apr.	54F	12C	**Aug.**	65F	18C	**Dec.**	45F	7C
	50	4		52	11		38	3

Current weather information for foreign and domestic cities may be obtained by calling The **Weather Channel Connection** at 900/WEATHER from a touch tone phone. In addition to the weather report, The Weather Channel Connection offers the local time and helpful travel tips as well as hurricane, foliage, and ski reports. The call costs 95¢ per minute.

Festivals and Seasonal Events

Irish Republic At least six major **horse races** are held at centers such as
January Thurles (Co. Tipperary), Naas (Co. Kildare), Leopardstown (Co. Dublin), and Gowran Park (Co. Kilkenny). The **Point-to-Point** season opens; these are small but exciting steeplechases, held in a different spot every Sunday until mid-May. The **Irish Crafts Fair** is held at the Royal Dublin Society.

February At the beginning of the month Dublin Airport hosts an **International Arts Festival,** which includes *artists at work* in the terminal building. The **Dublin Film Festival** starts at the end of the month, providing 10 days of the best in world cinema, plus lectures and seminars on all aspects of filmmaking. In Naas, County Kildare, the **Punchestown Bloodstock Sales** are held; this is one of the most important racehorse auctions in Ireland. There's an **international rugby match** between England and Ireland at Lansdowne Road, Dublin, in the middle of the month.

March **St. Patrick's Day,** March 17, is the focus of the month, with a parade in Dublin featuring guest bands from the United States and a festival of traditional Irish music, the Dublin **Feis Ceoil.** An **International Set Dancing Weekend** takes place in Galway. At the end of the month the **International Folk Dance Festival** gets underway at Cobh in County Cork. Motoring enthusiasts take part in the **Circuit of Ireland** rally.

April Easter provides one of the biggest events of the racing calendar, the two-day **Irish Grand National** race at Fairyhouse, County Meath, about 19 km (12 mi) from Dublin. The leadership of the Gaelic Football League is decided in the capital at Croke Park. The **Pan Celtic Week** in Killarney is an international celebration of Celtic music, dance, and song. The **West of Ireland Golf Championships** take place at Rosses Point in County Sligo.

May This month sees the opening of Ireland's agricultural showcase, the **Royal Dublin Society Spring Show,** at Ballsbridge. If you're interested in your ancestors, track down one of the seminars on Irish Origins held in Dublin, Kilkenny, and Tipperary. Festivals include the **Fleadh Nua** (traditional music, song, and dance) at Ennis, County Clare; the **International Choral and Folk Dance Festival** in Cork City; a **Maytime Festival** at Dundalk; a **Mussel Festival** at Bantry; and a **Walking Festival** in Kenmare.

June The **County Wicklow Gardens Festival** includes flower festivals, musical evenings, and garden tours. One of the richest and most exciting horse races in the world, the **Budweiser Irish Derby,** is run 48 km (30 mi) from Dublin at the Curragh, headquarters of Irish racing. The **Festival of Music in Great Irish Houses**—a delightful series of classical music concerts—is held in different stately homes around the Dublin area. **Bloomsday,** June 16, is celebrated in Dublin with readings and dramatizations of James Joyce's *Ulysses*, preceded by fancy-dress breakfasts and pilgrimages around the city.

July   There is an **International Coarse Angling** competition at Belturbet, County Cavan, and Athlone has a **freshwater angling festival** on the Shannon. The **Shannon Boat Rally** concludes with the sailing of an armada of small craft up the Shannon from Athlone to Carrick-on-Shannon. On the last Sunday in July many thousands of pilgrims, some in bare feet, climb the rocky slopes of Croagh Patrick (765 m/2,510 ft) in County Mayo to honor St. Patrick. The **Killarney Horse Racing Festival** attracts large crowds mid-month. The **Kerrygold Dublin Horse Show,** held in the third week of July, draws the best of Irish bloodstock and a highly fashionable crowd.

August   **The Summer Show of Flowers** is held in conjunction with the Horse Show. For golf enthusiasts, the month begins with the **Amateur Open at Lahinch** in County Clare and ends with the **Carroll's International** at the Royal Dublin. **Puck Fair** is a robust and entertaining occasion held at mid-month at Killorglin, County Kerry. At the end of the month in the same county, the *Rose of Tralee* is selected from among women of Irish descent from around the world; the competition coincides with the **Tralee Races.** The **Connemara Pony Show** at Clifden, County Galway, attracts a cosmopolitan crowd. **Kilkenny Arts Week** at the end of the month is renowned for interesting classical-music events.

September   In Galway, the oyster season opens with appropriate celebrations. The **Hurling and Gaelic Football finals** are played with great excitement at Croke Park in Dublin. The **Matchmaking Festival** in Lisdoonvarna, County Clare, is the traditional place for bachelor farmers to seek a wife; the revival of this informal tradition has become popular with American husband-seekers. The **Cork Film Festival,** the **Sligo Arts Week,** and the **Waterford International Festival of Light Opera** all start at the end of September and run into October, as does the **Dublin Theater Festival.**

October   The **Ballinasloe October Fair** in County Galway is one of the biggest and oldest horse and cattle fairs in Europe. Cork swings on the last weekend of October when the town and its environs are taken over by the **Guinness International Jazz Festival.** The **Dublin City Marathon** on the last Monday of the month attracts thousands of runners and engenders a carnival spirit.

November   The **Wexford Opera Festival** assembles international singers, directors, and conductors, all of whom present unfamiliar operatic gems in a tiny restored Georgian theater, the Theater Royal. The hunting season starts in November, continuing through April. The Irish Rugby Football season gets under way with hotly contested games between the four provinces: Connacht, Leinster, Munster, and Ulster (in Northern Ireland).

December   On **St. Stephen's Day,** December 26, the traditional *Wren Boys* in blackface and fancy dress still demand money and sing in the street, but these days most of the proceeds go to charity. If you miss them on the 26th, you can catch them at the **Wren Boy Festival** in Bunratty Folk Park on the 30th and 31st.

Northern Ireland   The **Ulster Harp National** is an exciting steeplechase held at
February   Downpatrick Race Course.

March The **Belfast Musical Festival** sponsors speech, drama, and music competitions for young people (Balmoral, Belfast). **St. Patrick's Day celebrations** include parades and pilgrimages at sites historically associated with the saint (Downpatrick, Newry, and Cultra). The **Horse Plowing and Heavy Horse Show** is an old-time plowing competition held for over 100 years at Fair Head, Ballycastle.

April The **Circuit of Ireland International Motor Rally,** with a 1,040-kilometer (650-mile) course, serves as a qualifying round for the **European Rally Championship. Belfast Civic Festival and Lord Mayor's Show** lasts 21 days and includes concerts, competitions, and exhibitions, starting on the second Saturday in May with floats and bands in the streets of Belfast.

May The **Belfast Marathon** is held. Anglers compete in the **P&O European Ferries Classic Fishing Festival** (Fermanagh Lakeland). The **Ballyclare Horse Fair** has horse-dealing in the old style on the village street. The **Royal Ulster Agricultural Society Show** includes international show-jumping and sheep-shearing competitions, parades, bands, and fashion shows (since 1855 at Balmoral, Belfast).

June At the **Belfast Midsummer Jazz and Blues Festival,** international jazz and blues players join local talent (Culloden Hotel, Belfast). The **Black Bush Amateur Golf Tournament** is played over four days using four courses (close to the Giant's Causeway, County Antrim). At the **Fiddle Stone Festival,** fiddlers from all over Ireland converge on the pretty village of Belleek.

July The **City of Belfast International Rose Trials** has over 100,000 roses in a riverside park (Dixon Park, Belfast). The **Northern Ireland Open Amateur Golf Championship** is held on the famous Royal Portrush links (County Antrim). **Battle of Boyne** festivities celebrate this 17th-century battle, in which the Protestant William of Orange defeated the Catholic James II (Belfast and other large towns). **Ulster Steam Traction Engine Rally** has vintage cars and field sports at Shane's Castle, Antrim.

August On the **Feast of the Assumption** on the 15th of the month, Hibernians in green sashes march to the music of Gaelic pipers (various Ulster cities). **Oul' Lammas Fair,** on the last weekend of the month, is a big social occasion, with trading in sheep and ponies, and about 100 stalls selling everything from antiques to ropes and ladders (Ballycastle).

September The **Belfast Folk Festival** provides a weekend of Irish folk talent in the center of Belfast. **Opera Northern Ireland** starts its autumn season at the end of the month in the Grand Opera House in Belfast.

October The **Ulster Antiques and Fine Art Fair** takes place at the Culloden Hotel in Belfast on the first weekend of the month.

November The **Belfast Festival** at Queen's University is a major arts festival featuring drama, ballet, cinema, and every kind of music from classical to jazz and folk.

December The **New Year Viennese Ball** is held, with music by Johann Strauss from the Ulster Orchestra (Belfast City Hall).

What to Pack

Clothing In Ireland you can experience all four seasons in one day, so pack accordingly. Even in July and August, the hottest months of the year, a heavy sweater and a good waterproof coat or umbrella are essential. (You may be tempted to buy an Irish hand-knit sweater or two while you're there, so don't pack more than one!) You should bring at least two pairs of walking shoes: It can and does rain at any time of the year, and rain showers can soak a pair of sneakers in minutes. In the coldest months, December and January, the average maximum temperature is around 7°C (45°F), while in the hottest months, July and August, it's about 19°C (66°F).

The Irish are generally informal about clothes. In the more expensive hotels and restaurants most people dress formally for dinner, but very few places operate a strict dress policy. Younger travelers should note that old or tattered blue jeans are forbidden in certain bars and discos.

Miscellaneous An extra pair of glasses, contact lenses, or prescription sunglasses is always a good idea; it is important to pack any prescription medicines you use regularly, as well as any allergy medication you may need.

Electrical Appliances The standard current in Ireland and Northern Ireland is 220 volts (50 cycles) AC. Most hotels have 220/110v sockets. Some shavers and hair driers have a built-in transformer, which can be set for 220v or 110v. If you will need a plug adapter or travel transformer, buy it before leaving home.

Carry-on Luggage Airlines generally allow each passenger one piece of carry-on luggage on international flights from the United States. The bag cannot exceed 45 inches (length + width + height) and must fit under the seat or in the overhead luggage compartment.

Checked Luggage Passengers are generally allowed to check two pieces of luggage, neither of which can exceed 62 inches (length + width + height) or weigh more than 70 pounds. Baggage allowances vary slightly among airlines, so check with the carrier or your travel agent before departure.

Taking Money Abroad

Before going, you may want to chart the U.S. dollar for a couple of weeks against the currency of the country you're visiting. This can be risky, but the savings may warrant the trouble. If the dollar is weakening, consider buying traveler's checks in foreign currency and paying in advance for such costly items as hotel rooms and train or plane tickets. If the dollar is improving, buy traveler's checks in U.S. currency, and use a credit card to pay for costly items after you've arrived at your destination. (Overseas credit charges often don't appear on your bill for two or three months, and you pay the exchange rate of the day the vendor posted the charge). Always carry some cash with you however, in smaller towns and rural areas, as well as in some of the smaller restaurants and shops. Regardless of how the dollar is faring abroad, it's wise to change a small amount of money into the currency of the country you're visiting (or the one you'll visit first) to avoid long lines at airport currency-exchange booths. Most U.S. banks will convert dollars into Irish pounds (Irish Republic) and pounds sterling (Northern Ireland). If your local bank can't provide this service, you can exchange money through **Thomas Cook Currency Services.** To find the office nearest you, contact Thomas Cook, 29 Broadway, New York, NY 10006, tel. 212/363–6207.

The most recognized traveler's checks are American Express, Barclays, Thomas Cook, and those issued through major commercial banks such as Citibank and Bank of America. American Express now issues "Travelers Cheques for Two"—a system that allows both you and your traveling companion to sign and use the same checks. Some banks will issue the checks free to established customers, but most charge a 1% commission fee. Buy part of the traveler's checks in small denominations to cash toward the end of your trip. This will save you from having to cash a large check and ending up with more foreign money than you need. Remember to take the addresses of offices where you can get refunds for lost or stolen traveler's checks.

Getting Money from Home

Cash Machines **Withdrawals** It's easy to use **automated-teller machines (ATMs)** to withdraw money from your checking account with a bank card. Just get the names of affiliated cash machine networks before your departure. (For locations for two of the larger networks, **Cirrus** and **Plus,** call 800/4–CIRRUS or 800/THE–PLUS.) Note that you may be charged a fee for withdrawals away from your home turf. Of course, you need to get a personal identification number (PIN) if you don't have one already.

Cash Advances You can also use ATMs to get cash advances on your credit card, providing you have a PIN number for your card. As with cash advances from tellers, you pay interest from the day of posting, and some banks tack on an additional service charge.

For both withdrawals and cash advances, there are usually limits on the amount you can access within given time periods. Know before you go.

Bank Transfers Just have your bank send money to another bank overseas. It's easiest to transfer money between like branches; otherwise, the process takes a couple days longer and costs more.

American Express Cardholder Services The company's **Express Cash** system links your U.S. checking account to your Amex card. Overseas you can withdraw up to $1,000 in a 21-day period (more if your card is Gold of Platinum). For each transaction there's a 2% fee (minimum $2, maximum $6). Call 800/227–4669 for information.

Cardholders can also cash personal or counter checks at any American Express office for up to $1,000, of which $500 may be claimed in cash and the balance in traveler's checks carrying a 1% commission.

Wiring Money To send or receive up to $10,000, you can use an **American Express MoneyGram,** and you don't have to have an American Express card. The sender goes to an American Express MoneyGram agent, specifies an amount, pays up to $1,000 with a credit card (anything over that in cash), and telephones the receiver with the reference number he is given. The receiver goes to the nearest MoneyGram agent, presents identification and the reference number, and picks up cash. Fees are 5% to

10%, depending on the amount and method of payment (AE, D, MC, V are accepted). For agent locations, call 800/543–4080.

If there are no American Express offices nearby, you can use **Western Union** (tel. 800/325–6000). A friend at home can bring cash or a check to the nearest Western Union office or pay over the phone with a credit card. Delivery usually takes two business days, and fees are roughly 5% to 10%.

Irish Currency

The unit of currency in the Irish Republic is the pound or punt, pronounced *poont*. It is divided into 100 pence (abbreviated 100p). **In this guide, the £ sign refers to the Irish pound; the British pound is referred to as the pound sterling and is written UK£.**

Irish notes come in denominations of £100, £50, £20, £10, and £5. Coins are available as £1, 50p, 20p, 10p, 5p, 2p, and 1p. £1 coins are not exchangable outside the Republic of Ireland. Dollars and British pounds are accepted only in large hotels and shops geared to tourists. Elsewhere you will be expected to use Irish currency.

At the time of writing (June 1992), the punt stood at around US$1.76, Canadian $2.10, and UK£.93; however, these rates will inevitably change both before and during 1993, making it advisable to keep a sharp eye on the exchange rate during your trip.

The unit of currency in Northern Ireland is the pound sterling, divided into 100 pence. Notes come in denominations of UK£50, UK£20, UK£10, and UK£5, and coins of UK£1, 50p, 20p, 10p, 5p, and 1p. At the time of writing (June 1992), the pound sterling stood at around US$1.80, Canadian $2.05, and IR1.07p.

What It Will Cost

The strength of the punt in comparison with the pound sterling is making some headway in reducing Ireland's high cost of living. Dublin, far more expensive than the rest of the country, is reputed to be one of Europe's most expensive cities for the business traveler. The independent traveler who is prepared to make a few not necessarily unpleasant concessions does not have to spend a fortune. A modest hotel in Dublin costs about £80 a night for two; this figure can be reduced to under £60 by staying in a registered guest house, and reduced to under £30 by staying in a suburban bed-and-breakfast (*see* Lodging, *below*). As far as food goes, lunch, consisting of a good *one-dish* plate of bar food at a pub, costs around £4.50; a sandwich at the same pub, about £1.40. Dinner in Dublin is more expensive; a fancy restaurant, though not an absolutely top spot, charges about £20 per person, excluding drinks and tip. On the other hand, theater and entertainment in most places are inexpensive—about £10 for a good seat, and double that for a big-name pop-music concert. For the price of a few drinks and (in Dublin and Killarney) a small entrance fee of about £1.50, you can spend a fun and memorable evening at a *seisún* (pronounced *say-shoon*) in a music pub. Entrance to most public galleries is free, but stately homes and similar attractions normally charge about £2 per person.

Just about everything is more expensive in Dublin, so add at least 10% to these sample prices, which apply in the rest of the country: cup of coffee, 60p; pint of beer, £1.85; soda, 85p; ham sandwich, £1.40; and 1-mile taxi ride, £3.

Northern Ireland is generally inexpensive compared with both the rest of the United Kingdom and the Republic of Ireland. By comparison, the lower level of taxation in Northern Ireland makes dutiable goods such as gasoline, alcoholic drinks, and tobacco cheaper. The cost of accommodations and restaurant meals is also less expensive.

Passports and Visas

U.S. Residents U.S. citizens need a passport to enter both Ireland and Northern Ireland. First-time applicants should apply at least five weeks before their departure to one of the 13 U.S. Passport Agency offices. Also, local county courthouses, many state and probate courts, and some post offices accept passport applications. Necessary documents include (1) a completed passport application (Form DSP-11); (2) proof of citizenship (certified birth certificate, issued by the Hall of Records of your state of birth, or naturalization papers); (3) proof of identity (valid driver's license, or state, military, or student ID card with your photograph and signature); (4) two recent, identical, two-inch-square photographs (black-and-white or color), with a white or off-white background; (5) $65 application fee for a 10-year passport (those under 18 pay $40 for a five-year passport). Check, cash (exact change), or money order are accepted. Passports are sent in 10 to 15 business days.

You may renew in person or by mail. Send a complete Form DSP-82; two recent, identical passport photographs; a passport less than 12 years old from the issue date; and a check or money order for $35.

A visa is not required for tourists staying in Ireland for up to 90 days, or in the North for up to 180 days. Tourists may be asked to show onward/return tickets. For further information, contact the **Embassy of Ireland** (2234 Massachusetts Ave., NW, Washington, DC 20008, tel. 202/462–3939), the **Embassy of Great Britain** (3100 Massachusetts Ave., NW, Washington, DC 20008, tel. 202/462–1340), or the nearest Consulate General.

Canadians Canadians need a passport to enter both Ireland and Northern Ireland. Send your completed application (available at any post office or passport office) to the **Bureau of Passports** (Suite 215, West Tower, Guy Favreau Complex, 200 René Lévesque Blvd. W., Montreal, Quebec H2Z 1X4). Include $25, two photographs, a guarantor, and proof of Canadian citizenship. Or apply in person at the regional passport offices in Edmonton, Halifax, Montreal, Calgary, St. John's (Newfoundland), Victoria, Toronto, Vancouver, or Winnipeg. Passports are valid for five years.

A visa is not required for tourists entering the Irish Republic or Northern Ireland. But you should contact your nearest Consulate General for information regarding stays exceeding 90 days.

Britons Neither a passport nor a visa is required for British citizens entering Ireland.

Customs and Duties

On Arrival   Two categories of duty-free allowance exist for travelers enter-
Irish Republic   ing the Irish Republic: one for goods obtained outside the European Community, on a ship or aircraft, or in a duty-free store
within the EC; and the other for goods bought in the EC, with
duty and tax paid.

In the first category, you may import duty-free: (1) 200 cigarettes or 100 cigarillos or 50 cigars or 250 grams of smoking tobacco; (2) 2 liters of wine, and either 1 liter of alcoholic drink
over 22% volume or 2 liters of alcoholic drink under 22% volume
(sparkling or fortified wine included); (3) 50 grams of perfume
and ¼ liter of toilet water; and (4) other goods to a value of
IR£34 per person (IR£17 per person for travelers under 15
years of age); you may import 12 liters of beer as part of this
allowance.

Duty paid allowances will be increased substantially beginning
January 1, 1993. Tentatively, under the new regime travelers
will be entitled to purchase (1) 800 cigarettes, (2) 10 liters of
spirits, (3) 45 liters of wine, and (4) 55 liters of beer. The allowances apply only to goods bought in shops in EC countries, including Britain and Northern Ireland, which already have the
duty paid.

Goods that cannot be freely imported include firearms, ammunition, explosives, drugs (e.g., narcotics, amphetamines), in-
decent or obscene books and pictures, oral smokeless tobacco
products, meat and meat products, poultry and poultry products, plants and plant products (including shrubs, vegetables,
fruit, bulbs, and seeds), domestic cats and dogs from outside
the United Kingdom, and live animals from outside Northern
Ireland.

Northern Ireland   Two levels of duty-free allowance exist for people entering
Northern Ireland: one for goods bought outside the European
Community (EC) *or* for goods bought in a duty-free shop in an
EC country; the other for goods bought in an EC country but
not in a duty-free shop.

In the first category you may import duty-free: (1) 200 cigarettes or 100 cigarillos or 50 cigars or 250 grams of tobacco (if
you live outside Europe these allowances are doubled); (2) 1 liter of alcoholic drink over 22% volume, or 2 liters of alcoholic
drink under 22% volume (fortified or sparkling wine, or 2 liters
of table wine); (3) 2 more liters of still table wine; (4) 60 millili-
ters of perfume and ¼ liter of toilet water; and (5) other goods
to the value of UK£32.

Duty paid allowances will be increased substantially beginning
January 1, 1993. Tentatively, under the new regime travelers
will be entitled to purchase (1) 800 cigarettes, (2) 10 liters of
spirits, (3) 45 liters of wine, and (4) 55 liters of beer. The allowances apply only to goods bought in shops in EC countries, including Britain and Northern Ireland, which already have the
duty paid.

Note that, though it is not classified as an alcoholic drink by EC
countries for customs purposes and is thus part of the "other
goods" allowance, you may not import more than 50 liters of
beer. No animals or pets of any kind can be brought into Northern Ireland without a six-month quarantine. Other items that

may not be imported include fresh meats, plants and vegetables, controlled drugs, and firearms and ammunition.

On Departure If you are bringing any foreign-made equipment from home, such as cameras, it's wise to either carry the original receipt with you or register it with U.S. Customs before you leave (Form 4457). Otherwise, you may end up paying duty on your return.

U.S. Residents You may bring home duty-free up to $400 worth of foreign goods, provided you have been out of the country for at least 48 hours and you haven't made an international trip in 30 days. Each member of the family is entitled to the same exemption, regardless of age, and exemptions may be pooled. For the next $1,000 worth of goods, a flat 10% rate is assessed; above $1,400, duties vary with the merchandise. Travelers 21 or older are entitled to bring in up to 1 liter of alcohol, 100 cigars (non-Cuban), and 200 cigarettes. Only one bottle of perfume trademarked in the United States may be imported. Antiques or works of art more than 100 years old are duty-free. Exceed these limits and you'll be taxed at the port of entry and additionally in your home state. Gifts valued at less than $50 may be mailed duty-free to friends or relatives stateside, with a limit of one package per day per addressee. Tobacco, liquor, and perfumes over $5 are prohibited.

Canadians Exemptions range from $20 to $300, depending on the length of trip. For the $300 exemption, you must have been out of the country for one week. In any given year, you are only allowed one $300 exemption. You may bring in duty-free up to 50 cigars, 200 cigarettes, 2.2 pounds of tobacco, and 40 ounces of liquor, provided these items are declared in writing to customs on arrival and accompany the traveler in carry-on or checked-through baggage. Personal gifts should be labeled "Unsolicited gift—value less than $40." Get a copy of the Canadian Customs brochure "I Declare" for further details. Copies can be obtained at local customs offices.

Britons You can expect tight security coming into Great Britain from both the Irish Republic and Northern Ireland. Customs regulations are the same for Great Britain and Northern Ireland. For details, *see* On Arrival for Northern Ireland, *above*. Further information can be obtained by contacting **HM Customs and Excise** (Dorset House, Stamford St., London SE1 9PS, tel. 071/620–1313).

Traveling with Film

If your camera is new, shoot and develop a few rolls of film before leaving home. Pack some lens tissue and an extra battery for your built-in light meter. Invest about $10 in a skylight filter: It will protect the lens and reduce haze.

Film doesn't like hot weather, so if you're driving in summer, don't store film in the glove compartment or on the shelf under the rear window. Put it behind the front seat on the floor, on the side opposite the exhaust pipe.

On a plane trip, never pack unprocessed film in check-in luggage; if your bags get X-rayed, you can say good-bye to your pictures. Always carry undeveloped film with you through security and ask to have it inspected by hand. (It helps to keep your film in a plastic bag, ready for quick inspection.)

medical plans cover emergency transportation, and some home-owner policies cover the theft of luggage.

Health and Accident

Several companies offer supplemental coverage for travelers:

Carefree Travel Insurance (Box 310, 120 Mineola Blvd., Mineola, NY 11501, tel. 516/294–0220 or 800/323–3149) provides coverage for emergency medical evacuation and accidental death and dismemberment. Medical phone advice is available 24 hours.

International SOS Assistance (Box 11568, Philadelphia, PA 19116, tel. 215/244–1500 or 800/523–8930), a medical assistance company, provides emergency evacuation services, worldwide medical referrals, and optional medical insurance.

Travel Assistance International (1133 15th St., NW, Suite 400, Washington, DC 20005, tel. 202/331–1609 or 800/821–2828) provides emergency evacuation services, 24-hour medical referrals, and medical insurance.

Travel Guard International, underwritten by Transamerica Occidental Life Companies (1145 Clark St., Stevens Point, WI 54481, tel. 715/345–0505 or 800/782–5151), offers reimbursement for medical expenses—with no deductibles or daily limits—and for emergency evacuation services.

Wallach and Company, Inc. (Box 480, Middleburg, VA 22117, tel. 703/687–3166 or 800/237–6615) offers comprehensive medical coverage, including emergency evacuation services worldwide.

Lost Luggage

On international flights, airlines are responsible for lost or damaged property at rates of up to $9.07 per pound ($20 per kilo) for checked baggage, and up to $400 per passenger for unchecked baggage. If you're carrying valuables, either take them with you on the plane or purchase additional insurance for lost luggage. Some airlines will issue extra luggage insurance when you check in, but many do not. Insurance for lost, damaged, or stolen luggage is available through travel agents or directly through various insurance companies. Luggage-loss coverage is usually part of a comprehensive package that includes personal accident, trip cancellation, and sometimes default and bankruptcy insurance. Two companies that issue luggage insurance are **Tele-Trip** (Box 31685, 3201 Farnam St., Omaha, NE 68131, tel. 800/228–9792), a subsidiary of Mutual of Omaha, and **The Traveler** (Ticket and Travel Dept., 1 Tower Sq., Hartford, CT 06183, tel. 203/277–0111 or 800/243–3174). Tele-Trip operates sales booths at airports, and it also issues insurance through travel agents. Tele-Trip will insure checked luggage for up to 180 days; rates vary according to the length of the trip. The Travelers Insurance Corporation will insure checked or hand luggage for $500–$2,000 valuation per person, also for a maximum of 180 days. The rate for one–five days for $500 valuation is $10; for 180 days, $85. Other companies with comprehensive policies include **Access America, Inc.,** a subsidiary of Blue Cross–Blue Shield (Box 11188, Richmond, VA 23230, tel. 800/334–7525 or 800/284–8300); **Near Services** (450 Prairie Ave., Suite 101, Calumet City, IL 60409, tel. 708/868–6700 or 800/654–6700); **Travel Guard International;** and **Carefree Travel Insurance** (*see* Health and Accident Insurance, *above*).

Before you go, itemize the contents of each bag in case you need to file an insurance claim. Be certain to put your home or business address on each piece of luggage, including carry-on bags.

The old airport scanning machines, still in use in some countries, use heavy doses of radiation that can make a family portrait look like an early morning fog. The newer models used in
all U.S. airports are safe for anything from five to 500 scans,
depending on the speed of your film. The effects are cumula-
tive; you can put the same roll of film through several scans
without worry. After five scans, though, you're asking for
trouble.

If your film gets fogged and you want an explanation, send it to
the **National Association of Photographic Manufacturers** (550
Mamaroneck Ave., Harrison, NY 10528). It will try to deter-
mine what went wrong. The service is free.

Language

Irish (also known as Gaelic), a Celtic language related to Scottish Gaelic, Breton, and Welsh, is the official national language.
Though English is technically the second language of the country, it is in fact the everyday language of the majority of the
population. Nowadays all Irish speakers are fluent in English.

Irish-speaking communities are found mainly in sparsely populated rural areas along the western seaboard, on some but not
all offshore islands, and in small pockets in West Cork and
County Waterford. Irish-speaking areas are known as Gaeltacht. While most road signs in Ireland are given in both English and Irish, within Gaeltacht areas the signs are often in
Irish only. A good touring map will give both Irish and English
names to places within the Gaeltacht. The most important
Irish words a visitor needs to recognize are *Fir* and *Mná*, used
frequently outside public toilets: *Fir* is Men and *Mná* is Women.

Staying Healthy

No special shots are required before visiting Ireland or Northern Ireland. If you may require purchasing prescription drugs,
have your doctor write a prescription using the drug's generic
name; brand names can vary widely.

**The International Association for Medical Assistance to Travel-
ers** (IAMAT) offers a list of approved, English-speaking doctors whose training meets British and U.S. standards. **In the
United States** contact: 417 Center St., Lewiston, NY 14092, tel.
716/754–4883. **In Canada:** 40 Regal Rd., Guelph, Ontario N1K
1B5. **In Europe:** 57 Voirets, 1212 Grand-lancy, Geneva, Switzerland. Membership is free.

In Washington, the **Department of State Citizens Emergency
Center** (tel. 202/647–5225) provides information about health
conditions in other nations; what U.S. citizens can do in the
event of an emergency overseas; whether any notices, cautions,
or warnings exist in the area to which you're traveling; and how
to obtain passports and visas.

Insurance

**In the
United States** Traveler insurance coverage is in four areas: health and accident, lost luggage, flight, and trip cancellation. Review your
existing health and home-owner policies to see if they already
cover health expenses incurred while traveling—some major

If your luggage is lost or stolen and later recovered, the airline will deliver the luggage to you free of charge.

Trip-Cancellation and Flight Insurance Consider buying it if your promotional or discounted ticket does not allow changes or cancellations. It's usually included in combination travel insurance packages available from most tour operators, travel agents, and insurance agents.

Flight insurance, which covers passengers in the case of death or dismemberment, is often included in the price of a ticket when paid for with major credit cards.

In the United Kingdom Always take out adequate insurance to guard against health problems, motoring mishaps, theft, flight cancellation, and loss of luggage. Most major tour operators offer holiday insurance, and details are given in brochures. But for free general advice on all aspects of holiday insurance, contact the **Association of British Insurers** (51 Gresham St., London EC2V 7HQ, tel. 071/600–3333). A proven leader in the holiday insurance field is **Europ Assistance** (252 High St., Croyden, Surrey CR0 1NF, tel. 081/680–1234).

Car Rentals

The best deals are on fly/drive packages or pre-booked rentals. Renting a car on impulse for a few days is the most expensive way.

All the major car rental companies have offices in Ireland, as do a number of Irish firms. All you need to rent a car is a valid driver's license; however, some companies will only rent to drivers between 23 and 70 years of age—Hertz and Avis are exceptions. Rental rates include only third-party insurance; a collision damage waiver, which protects against liability in the event of an accident, costs about another IR£50 per week.

Cars range from subcompacts to full-size sedans and chauffeured limousines. Unless automatic transmission is specified in advance, stick-shift cars are supplied. Rates vary according to car type and time of year: Do not expect to pay less than £25 a day, excluding the collision damage waiver. Most companies offer unlimited mileage and deliver the car with a full tank. When you return it the tank is refilled, and you pay the difference. The best place to pick up your car is at a major airport. Principal operators in each region are listed in the regional chapters; the following list gives the head offices of the major companies, all of which deliver nationwide. A full list of approved car rental operators, including their U.S. contact numbers, is available from the Irish Tourist Board.

Avis Rent-a-Car Ltd., 1 Hanover St., East, Dublin 2, tel. 01/776971; **Budget/Flynn Bros. Rent-a-Car,** Ballygar, Co. Galway, tel. 0903/4668; **Dan Dooley/Kenning Rent-a-Car,** Knocklong, Co. Limerick, tel. 062/53103; **Hertz Rent-a-Car,** Hertz House, 19/20 Hogan Place, Lower Grand Canal St., Dublin 2, tel. 01/767476; **Johnson & Perrott Ltd.,** Emmet Place, Cork, tel. 021/273295; **Murrays Europcar Rent-a-Car,** Baggot St. Bridge, Dublin 4, tel. 01/681777.

If you are renting a car in the Irish Republic and intend to visit Northern Ireland, make this clear when you get your car. Similarly, if renting in Northern Ireland and crossing the border, make sure that the rental insurance applies.

In Northern Ireland, as in the Republic, a stick-shift car is supplied unless automatic transmission has been specified. Picking up a car from the airport branches of the main firms can almost double the bill, so compare the airport rate with the city rate before deciding. Keep in mind that a surcharge is applied for dropping the car off in the Republic; it's cheaper to do a round-trip and leave it off where you picked it up.

Rail Passes

The **EurailPass,** valid for unlimited first-class train travel through 17 countries, including the Republic of Ireland but not Northern Ireland, is an excellent value if you plan on traveling throughout Ireland and on the Continent. The ticket is available for periods of 15 days ($430), 21 days ($550), one month ($680), two months ($920), and three months ($1,150). Prices are reduced for two or more people traveling together, so that a 15-day rail pass, for example, costs $340; between April 1 and September 30, you need a minimum of three in your group to get this discount. For those under 26 years old on the first day of travel, there is the **Eurail Youthpass,** for one or two months' unlimited second-class train travel at $470 and $640, respectively. For travelers who like to spread out their train journeys, there is the **Eurail Flexipass.** With the 15-day pass ($280), travelers get five days of unlimited first-class train travel, but they can spread that travel out over 15 days. A 21-day pass ($450) gives you nine days of travel; a one-month flexipass ($610) gives you 14 days of train travel.

The EurailPass does not cover Great Britain, and it is available only if you live outside Europe or North Africa. The pass must be bought from an authorized agent before you leave for Europe. Apply through your travel agent or through **Rail Europe** (226–230 Westchester Ave., White Plains, NY 10604, tel. 914/682–5172 or 800/345–1990).

The **Rambler Ticket,** for use on Ireland's railroads, bus system, or both, covers all the state-run and federal railways and bus lines throughout the Republic of Ireland. It does not apply to the North or to transportation within the cities. An eight-day bus or rail ticket is $96; a 15-day ticket is $114. The combination eight-day ticket for use on buses *and* trains during a 15-day period is $125; a 15-day ticket good for 30 days costs $184. For children under 16, the rates are $48 for an eight-day bus or rail ticket and $57.50 for an eight-day combination ticket.

The **Emerald Isle Card,** recently introduced by **CIE Tours International,** gives you unlimited bus and train travel anywhere in Ireland and Northern Ireland, valid within the cities as well. A 15-day pass gives you eight days of travel over a 15-day period; it costs $168, $84 for children. A 30-day pass for 15 days of travel over a 30-day period costs $288, $144 for children.

For more information on Rambler or Emerald Isle tickets, or to book in advance, contact CIE Tours International (108 Ridgedale Ave., Morristown, NJ 07960, tel. 201/292–3438 or 800/CIE-TOUR).

In Northern Ireland, **Rail Runabout** tickets, entitling you to seven days' unlimited travel on scheduled rail services April–October, are available from main Northern Ireland Railway stations. They cost UK£25 for adults, UK£12.50 for children under 16 and senior citizens. Inter rail tickets are also valid in Northern Ireland; tickets for eight days of unlimited travel cost £55 for adults, £27.50 for children under 16 and senior citizens; tickets for 15 days cost £80 for adults, £40 for children and senior citizens.

Student and Youth Travel

The **International Student Identity Card** (ISIC) entitles full-time students to rail passes, special fares on local transportation, student charter flights, and discounts at museums, theaters, sports events, and many other attractions. If purchased in the United States, the $14 cost of the ISIC card also includes $3,000 in emergency medical coverage, $100 a day for up to 60 days of hospital coverage, as well as a collect phone number to call in case of emergency. Apply to the **Council on International Educational Exchange** (CIEE, 205 E. 42nd St., New York, NY 10017, tel. 212/661–1414). In Canada, the ISIC is available for CN$13 from **Travel Cuts** (187 College St., Toronto, Ont. M5T 1P7, tel. 416/979–2406).

Travelers under age 26 can apply for a **Youth International Educational Exchange Card** (YIEE) issued by the **Federation of International Youth Travel Organizations** (81 Islands Brugge, DK-2300 Copenhagen S, Denmark). It provides similar services and benefits as the ISIC card. The YIEE card is available in the United States from CIEE (address above) and in Canada from the **Canadian Hostelling Association** (1600 James Naismith Dr., Suite 608, Gloucester, Ont. K1B 5N4, tel. 613/748–5638).

An **International Youth Hostel Federation** (IYHF) membership card is the key to inexpensive dormitory-style accommodations at thousands of youth hostels around the world. Hostels aren't only for young travelers on a budget, though; many have family accommodations. Hostels provide separate sleeping quarters for men and women at rates of $7–$20 a night, per person, and are situated in a variety of facilities, including converted farmhouses, villas, restored castles, and even lighthouses, as well as in specially constructed modern buildings. There are more than 5,000 hostel locations in 70 countries around the world. IYHF memberships, which are valid for one year from the time of purchase, are available in the United States through **American Youth Hostels** (Box 37613, Washington, DC 20013, tel. 202/783–6161), in Canada through the **Canadian Hostelling Association** (CHA, 1600 James Naismith Dr., Suite 608, Gloucester, Ontario K1B 5N4, tel. 613/748–5638), and in the United Kingdom through the **Youth Hostel Association of England and Wales** (Trevelyan House, 8 St. Stephen's Hill, St. Albans, Herts AL1 2DY, tel. 0727/55215). The cost for a first-year membership is $25 for adults 18–54. A renewal is $20. For youths (17 and under) the rate is $10, and for senior citizens (55 and older) the rate is $15. Family membership for $35 is available for two adults traveling with up to two children. Every national hostel association arranges special reductions for members visiting their country, such as discounted rail fare or free bus travel, so be sure to ask for a list of discounts when you buy your membership.

Council Travel, a CIEE subsidiary, is the foremost U.S. student travel agency, specializing in low-cost charters and serving as the exclusive U.S. agent for many student airfare bargains and student tours. CIEE's 72-page *Student Travel catalog* and "Council Charter" brochures are available free from any Council Travel office in the United States (enclose $1 postage if ordering by mail). In addition to the CIEE headquarters (205 E. 42nd St.) and branch office (35 W. 8th St.) in New York City, there are Council Travel offices in Tempe, AZ; Berkeley, La Jolla, Long Beach, Los Angeles, San Diego, San Francisco, and Sherman Oaks, CA; Boulder, CO; New Haven, CT; Washington, DC; Atlanta, GA; Chicago and Evanston, IL; New Orleans, LA; Amherst, Boston, and Cambridge, MA; Ann Arbor, MI; Minneapolis, MN; Durham, NC; Columbus, OH; Portland, OR; Providence, RI; Austin and Dallas, TX; Seattle, WA; and Milwaukee, WI.

Students who would like to work abroad should contact CIEE's **Work Abroad Department** (205 E. 42nd St., New York, NY 10017, tel. 212/661–1414, ext. 1130). The council arranges various types of paid and voluntary work experiences overseas for periods of up to six months. CIEE also sponsors study programs in Europe, Latin America, Asia, and Australia, and it publishes many books of interest to the student traveler. These include *Work, Study, Travel Abroad: The Whole World Handbook* ($12.95, plus $1.50 book-rate postage or $3 first-class postage); and *Volunteer! The Comprehensive Guide to Voluntary Service in the U.S. and Abroad* ($8, plus $1.50 book-rate postage or $3 first-class postage).

The Information Center at the **Institute of International Education** (809 UN Plaza, New York, NY 10017, tel. 212/984–5413) has reference books, foreign-university catalogues, study-abroad brochures, and other materials, which may be consulted by students and nonstudents alike, free of charge. The center is open Monday–Friday 10–4; it's closed on holidays.

Traveling with Children

Publications *Family Travel Times* is a newsletter published 10 times a year by **Travel With Your Children** (45 W. 18th St., 7th Floor Tower, New York, NY 10011, tel. 212/206–0688). A one-year subscription costs $35 and includes access to back issues and twice-weekly opportunities to call in for specific advice.

Great Vacations with Your Kids, by Dorothy Jordan and Marjorie Cohen, helps you plan your trip with children, from toddlers to teens ($12.95, E.P. Dutton, 375 Hudson St., New York, NY 10014, tel. 212/366–2000).

"Kids and Teens in Flight," a useful brochure about children flying alone, is available from the U.S. Department of Transportation. To order a free copy, call 202/366–2220.

Innocents Abroad: Traveling with Kids in Europe, by Valerie Wolf Deutsch and Laura Sutherland, is a new guide to child- and teen-friendly activities, food, and transportation in Britain and on the Continent, with individual sections on each country ($15.95 paperback, New American Library, Penguin USA, 375 Hudson St., New York, NY 10014, tel. 212/366–2000).

Home Exchange Exchanging homes is a surprisingly low-cost way to enjoy a vacation abroad, especially a long one. The largest home-exchange service, **Intervac U.S.** (Box 590504, San Francisco, CA 94159, tel. 415/435–3497), publishes three directories a year.

Membership, which costs $45, entitles you to one listing and all three directories. Photos of your property cost an additional $11; listing a second home costs $10. A good choice for domestic home exchange, **Vacation Exchange Club** (Box 820, Haleiwa, HI 96712, tel. 800/638–3841) publishes four directories a year as well as updated listings. Annual membership, which includes your listing in one book, a newsletter, and copies of all publications, is $50. **Loan-a-Home** (2 Park La., Apt. 6E, Mount Vernon, NY 10552, tel. 914/664–7640) is popular with academics on sabbatical and businesspeople on temporary assignment. There's no annual membership fee or charge for listing your home; however, one directory and a supplement cost $35. Loan-a-Home publishes two directories (in December and June) and two supplements (in March and September) each year. The set of four books costs $45 per year.

Getting There   On international flights, children under 2 not occupying a seat pay 10% of adult fare. Various discounts apply to children age 2–12, so check with your airline when booking. Reserve a seat behind the bulkhead of the plane. There's usually more leg room and enough space to fit a bassinet, which the airlines will supply. At the same time, ask about special children's meals or snacks; most airlines offer them. See TWYCH's "Airline Guide," published in the February 1990 and February 1992 issues of *Family Travel Times,* for more information about the children's services offered by 46 airlines.

Regulations governing infant travel on airplanes are in the process of changing. Until they do, however, if you want to be sure your infant is secure, you must bring your own infant car seat and buy a separate ticket. Check with the airline in advance to be sure your seat meets the required standard. For the booklet **"Child/Infant Safety Seats Acceptable for Use in Aircraft,"** write to the Federal Aviation Administration (APA-200, 800 Independence Ave. SW, Washington DC 20591, tel. 202/267–3479).

Hints for Disabled Travelers

The following organizations in the United States provide advice and services:

The **Information Center for Individuals with Disabilities** (Ft. Point Pl., 1st floor, 27–43 Wormwood St., Boston, MA 02210, tel. 617/727–5540) offers useful problem-solving assistance, including lists of travel agents who specialize in tours for the disabled.

Moss Rehabilitation Hospital Travel Information Service (1200 West Tabor Rd., Philadelphia, PA 19141–3099, tel. 215/456–9603; TDD 215/456–9602) provides information for a small fee on tourist sights, transportation, and accommodations in destinations around the world.

Travel Industry and Disabled Exchange (5435 Donna Ave., Tarzana, CA 91356, tel. 818/368–5648), for a $15 annual fee, provides a quarterly newsletter and a directory of travel agencies and tours to Europe, Canada, Great Britain, New Zealand, and Australia, all specializing in travel for the disabled.

Mobility International USA (Box 3551, Eugene, OR 97403, tel. 503/343–1284) is an internationally affiliated organization with 500 members. For a $20 annual fee, it coordinates exchange programs for disabled people around the world and offers information on accommodations and organized study programs. The organization also publishes *A World of Options for the 90s,* a guide to international exchange and travel for people with disabilities (available for $16 including postage, from the address above).

The **Society for the Advancement of Travel for the Handicapped** (SATH, 347 5th Ave., Suite 610, New York, NY 10016, tel. 212/447–7284) provides access information and lists of tour operators specializing in travel for the disabled. Annual membership costs $45 or $25 for students and seniors. Send $2 and a stamped, self-addressed envelope for information on a specific destination.

Publications   *The Itinerary* (Box 2012, Bayonne, NJ 07002, tel. 201/858–3400) is a bimonthly travel magazine for the disabled. Call for a subscription ($10 for one year, $20 for two); it's not available in bookstores.

Twin Peaks Press (Box 129, Vancouver, WA 98666, tel. 206/694–2462 or 800/637–2256 for orders only) specializes in books for the disabled.

Travel for the Disabled offers helpful hints as well as a comprehensive list of guidebooks and facilities geared to the disabled. *The Directory of Travel Agencies for the Disabled* lists more than 350 agencies throughout the world. *Wheelchair Vagabound* and *The Directory of Accessible Van Rentals* provide information for the worldwide RV/camping traveler. Twin Peaks also offers a "Traveling Nurse's Network," which provides registered nurses to accompany and assist disabled travelers.

Hints for Older Travelers

The **American Association of Retired Persons** (AARP, 601 E St., NW, Washington, DC 20049, tel. 202/434–2277) has two programs for independent travelers: (1) the **Purchase Privilege Program,** which comes with membership and offers discounts on hotels, airfare, car rentals, RV rentals, and sightseeing; and (2) the **AARP Motoring Plan,** provided by Amoco, which furnishes emergency aid (road service) and trip-routing information for an annual fee of $39.95 per person or couple. (Both programs include the member and member's spouse, or the member and another person who shares the household.) The AARP also arranges group tours, including apartment living in Europe and Australia, through **AARP Travel Experience from American Express** (400 Pinnacle Way, Suite 450, Norcross, GA 30071, tel. 800/927–0111). AARP members must be 50 or older; annual dues are $8 per person or per couple.

When using an AARP or other discount identification card, ask for reduced hotel rates at the time you make your reservation, not when you check out. At participating restaurants, show your card to the maître d' before you're seated because discounts may be limited to certain set menus, days, or hours. When renting a car, be sure to ask about special promotional rates, which may offer greater savings than the available discount.

Elderhostel (75 Federal St., 3rd Fl., Boston, MA 02110–1941, tel. 617/426–7788) is an innovative educational program for people 60 and older. Participants live in dorms on some 1,200 campuses around the world. Mornings are devoted to lectures and seminars; afternoons, to sightseeing and field trips. Fees for two- to three-week international trips, including room, board, tuition, and round-trip transportation, range from $1,800 to $4,500.

Mature Outlook (6001 N. Clark St., Chicago, IL 60660, tel. 800/ 336–6330), a subsidiary of Sears Roebuck & Co., is a travel club for people over 50, with hotel and motel discounts and a bimonthly newsletter. Annual membership is $9.95; there are 800,000 members currently. Instant membership is available at participating Holiday Inns.

The **National Council of Senior Citizens** (1331 F St., NW, Washington, DC 20004, tel. 202/347–8800) is a nonprofit advocacy group with about 5,000 local clubs across the country. Annual membership is $12 per person or per couple. Members receive a monthly newspaper with travel information and an ID card for reduced-rate hotels and car rentals.

Saga International Holidays (120 Boylston St., Boston, MA 02116, tel. 800/343–0273), an affiliate of Elderhostel, specializes in group travel for people over 60. A selection of variously priced tours allows you to choose the package that meets your needs.

Publications   *The International Health Guide for Senior Citizen Travelers,* by W. Robert Lange, MD, is available for $4.95 plus $1.50 for shipping, from **Pilot Books** (103 Cooper St., Babylon, NY 11702, tel. 515/422–2225).

Further Reading

History   For two intriguing studies that connect Irish culture and history, consult Constantine FitzGibbon's *The Irish in Ireland* and Sean O'Faolain's *The Irish: A Character Study,* which traces the history of Ireland from Celtic times. J.C. Beckett's *The Making of Modern Ireland,* a concise introduction to Irish history, covers the years between 1603 and 1923. *Modern Ireland,* a provocative new study by R.F. Foster, spans the years between 1600 and 1972. For an acclaimed history of Irish nationalism, refer to Robert Kee's *The Green Flag.*

Special-Interest   Readers can choose from several volumes on a specific region. Peter Somerville-Large's *Dublin* is packed with anecdotes relating to the famed Irish city. *Georgian Dublin,* by Desmond Guinness, the founder of the Irish Georgian Society, explores the city's architecture, with photographs and plans of Dublin's most admirable buildings. The most up-to-date work on the Aran Islands is Tim Robinson's award-winning *The Stones of Aran: Pilgrimage.* Though a little outdated, *The Aran Islands,* by J.M. Synge, is also worth reading. Tomas Ó Crohán's *The Islandman* provides a good background on Dingle and the Blasket Islands.

Autobiography   Several autobiographical accounts by both Irish natives and foreign visitors offer unique perspectives on Ireland. Deborah Tall's *The Island of the White Cow* chronicles five years spent with an Irish professor on an island off the coast of Connemara. In *An Only Child* and *My Father's Son,* Frank O'Connor, a well-known fiction writer, recounts his years as an Irish revolutionary and later as an intellectual in Dublin during the 1920s.

Niall Williams and Christine Breen, an American-Irish couple who started anew by moving to the County Clare countryside, recount their experiences in *O Come Ye Back to Ireland* and *When Summer's in the Meadow*. In *Round Ireland in Low Gear*, Eric Newby, a British travel writer, writes of his bicycle journey with his wife around the Emerald Isle. Christy Brown's *My Left Foot*, recently made into an award-winning film, is the autobiographical account of an artist crippled with cerebral palsy.

Fiction Ireland has a long, impressive history of great novelists and story writers. For a literary history exploring the influence of Ireland's changing landscape on its writers, look at *A Writer's Ireland*, by William Trevor. Samuel Beckett, the well-known playwright, fills his story collection *More Pricks than Kicks* with Dublin characters; if you enjoy literary gamesmanship, you may also want to try Beckett's trilogy—*Molloy*, *Malone Dies*, and *The Unnamable*. James Joyce, certainly one of the most acclaimed writers of the 20th century, is world renowned for *Ulysses*, a classic, linguistically innovative work, which follows a group of Dublin characters through the course of a single day; shorter introductions to Joyce's writing include *A Portrait of the Artist as a Young Man* and *Dubliners*, a story collection.

Maeve Blinchy's *Light a Penny Candle* traces the friendship of two women, one of whom escapes to Ireland during World War II. If you're drawn to tales of unrequited love, turn to Elizabeth Bowen's stories and her novel, *The Last September*, set in Ireland during the Irish Civil War. Coming-of-age novels include *Under the Eye of the Clock*, a somewhat autobiographical work by Christopher Nolan, which takes as its subject a handicapped youth discovering the pleasures of language; and *Fools of Fortune*, by William Trevor, which treats the loss of an ideal childhood, brought about by a changing political climate.

Thomas Flanagan's *The Year of the French* is a historical novel about the people of County Mayo, who revolted in 1798 with the help of French revolutionaries. *A Nest of Simple Folk*, by Sean O'Faolain, follows three generations of an Irish family between 1854 and 1916. Leon Uris's *Trinity* covers the years 1840–1916, as seen through the eyes of British, Irish Catholic, and Ulster Protestant families. Jennifer Johnston, admired for her verbal economy, sets her best novels (including *The Captains and the Kings*, *The Gates*, and *How Many Miles to Babylon*) in the declining world of the Anglo-Irish "big house" in the early 20th century. In *No Country for Young Men*, Julia O'Faolain writes of two Irish families struggling to overcome the effects of the Irish Civil War. Bernard MacLaverty's two novels *Cal* and *Lamb* deal with modern-day Irish political and social barriers that can stand in the way of love.

If you prefer reading a more magical rather than a realistic novel, take a look at James Stephens's *A Crock of Gold*, a charming and wise fairy tale written for adults, or Flann O'Brien's *At Swim-Two-Birds*, a surrealistic tale full of Irish folklore.

Edna O'Brien writes often about romantic relationships in a trilogy of short novels titled *The Country Girls* and a collection of stories called *A Fanatic Heart*. Wayward characters, such as loners, prostitutes, and immigrants, abound in Desmond Hogan's volume of stories, *A Link with the River*. Other superbly crafted story collections, full of acute observations of Ireland's social and political landscape, include Benedict Kiely's *The State of Ireland*, Mary Lavin's *Collected Stories*, Frank O'Connor's *Collected Stories*, and William Trevor's *Stories*.

Theater Ireland claims a range of fine playwrights as well. Samuel Beckett, who moved from Ireland to Paris and began writing in French, is the author of the comic modernist masterpiece *Waiting for Godot*, among many other plays. *The Importance of Being Earnest* is perhaps the most acclaimed work of Oscar Wilde, a major proponent of "art for art's sake" and a dramatist, poet, and wit of the late 19th century. Among the many plays of George Bernard Shaw, who grew up in Dublin, are *Arms and the Man, Major Barbara, Pygmalion*, and *Saint Joan*.

The history of Irish theater includes a good number of controversial plays, such as J.M. Synge's *The Playboy of the Western World*, which was considered morally outrageous at the time of its opening in 1907, and is still appreciated today for its poetic language. Sean O'Casey wrote passionately about social injustice and working-class characters around the time of the Irish Civil War in such plays as *The Plough and the Stars* and *Juno and the Paycock*. *The Quare Fellow*, by Brendan Behan, challenged accepted mores in the 1950s and at the time could only be produced in London. Behan is also well known for his play *The Hostage* and for *Borstal Boy*, his memoirs. Two playwrights who have been recognized more recently internationally are Hugh Leonard (*Da* and *A Life*) and Brian Friel (*Philadelphia, Here I Come!, The Faith Healer*, and *Dancing at Lughnasa*), whose work often illuminates Irish small-town life.

Poetry No list of Irish literature would be complete without mention of the country's poets. The most celebrated of these is William Butler Yeats, whose poems often describe the Irish landscape, including the Sligo and Coole countryside. A favorite poet among the Irish people themselves is Patrick Kavanagh, whose distinguished career was devoted to writing exceptionally about ordinary lives. Thomas Kinsella's *Poems 1956–1973* and Seamus Heaney's *Selected Poems* are both highly recommended. Kinsella is also the editor of *The New Oxford Book of Irish Verse* and a translator of Irish (Gaelic) poetry. Heaney is considered one of the most compelling Irish poets since Yeats; Northern Ireland serves as the setting for many of his recent poems.

Periodical *Ireland of the Welcomes* (U.S. and Canada: Box 2745, Boulder, CO 80322; Europe and elsewhere: Box 84, Limerick, Ireland), a magazine published six times a year by the Irish Tourist Board, features articles on aspects of Irish culture and travel, including driving tours.

Arriving and Departing

Visitors have a choice of three types of flights: nonstop—no changes, no stops; direct—no changes, but one or more stops; and connecting—two or more planes, one or more stops.

From North America by Plane

Irish Republic The main post of arrival for transatlantic flights is **Shannon**
Airports and **Airport** (tel. 061/61444) on the west coast, 25½ km (16 mi) west
Airlines of Limerick City. Shannon is a small airport, with only one
modest terminal building. If you have some time to pass there,
visit the duty-free shop, the first of its kind to open. It's
stocked with last-minute buys such as sides of smoked salmon,
handmade chocolates, whole farmhouse cheeses, and sweaters
and tweed caps. Shannon is the place where Irish coffee—black
coffee and sugar, bolstered with a shot of Irish whiskey and
topped with whipped cream—was invented; sipping a cup at
the airport is another good way to pass the time. All transatlantic flights touch down at Shannon, even if their destination is
Dublin. The Shannon–Dublin flight takes 30–40 minutes.

Dublin Airport (tel. 01/379900) is 9.5 km (6 mi) north of the city
center. Most of the flights it handles come from Europe, the
United Kingdom, or inside of Ireland. It has just one terminal
building, but the well-stocked duty-free shop boasts an unusual
concession: Books can be sold prior to their official launch, so
you can pick up the latest work by your favorite author even before it's been reviewed in the papers.

Only three airlines have regularly scheduled flights from the
United States: **Aer Lingus** (tel. 212/557–1110 or 800/223–6537),
Aeroflot (tel. 202/429–4922 or 800/535–9877), and **Delta** (tel.
800/722–9230 or 800/241–4141). **Aer Lingus** flies from New
York, Chicago, or Boston to Shannon and Dublin. **Aeroflot** flies
from Washington, D.C. **Delta** flies from Atlanta to Shannon or
Dublin. A number of charter flights operate from the United
States and Canada between May and September. No direct
commercial flights are scheduled from Canada.

Flying Time The shortest scheduled transatlantic flight to Shannon leaves
from Boston (Aer Lingus); it takes five hours and 35 minutes. If
you're flying on to Dublin, there is a 45-minute stopover at
Shannon and then a 40-minute onward flight. New York to
Shannon takes about 6½ hours; Chicago to Shannon, 7½ hours;
and Atlanta to Shannon, seven hours.

Northern Ireland No scheduled transatlantic flights are available to Belfast, al-
Airports though some charter flights can be found in the summer. For
details, check with your travel agent. Otherwise, pick up a connecting flight to Belfast in Shannon, Dublin, London, or Manchester. Two airports serve Belfast: **Belfast International
Airport at Aldergrove** (tel. 0232/229271), 24 km (15 mi) from the
city, handles all international traffic; **Belfast Harbour Airport**
(tel. 0232/57754), 6½ km (4 mi) from the city, handles local and
U.K. flights only. In addition, **Eglinton,** Derry's airport, receives flights from Manchester and Glasgow in the United
Kingdom (Loganair).

Enjoying If you're lucky enough to be able to sleep on a plane, it makes
the Flight sense to fly at night. Many experienced travelers, however,
prefer to take an afternoon flight to Ireland and arrive in the
evening, just in time for a good night's sleep. The air on a plane
is dry, so it helps to drink a lot of nonalcoholic beverages while
flying; drinking alcohol contributes to jet lag, as does eating
heavy meals on board. Feet swell at high altitudes, so it's a good
idea to remove your shoes at the beginning of your flight. Sleep-
ers usually prefer window seats to curl up against; those who

like to move around in the cabin should ask for aisle seats. Bulkhead seats (located in the front row of each cabin) have more legroom, but seat trays are attached rather awkwardly to the arms of the seat rather than to the back of the seat ahead. Generally, bulkhead seats are reserved for the disabled, the elderly, or parents traveling with babies.

Discount Flights The major airlines offer a range of tickets that can increase or decrease the price of any given seat by more than 300%, depending on the day of purchase. As a rule, the further in advance you buy the ticket, the less expensive it is but the greater the penalty (up to 100%) for canceling. Check with airlines for details.

The best buy is not necessarily an APEX (advance purchase) ticket on one of the major airlines. These tickets carry certain restrictions: They must be bought in advance (usually 21 days); they restrict your travel, usually with a minimum stay of seven days and a maximum of 90; and they also penalize you for changes—voluntary or not—in your travel plans. But if you can work around these drawbacks (and most travelers can), they are among the best-value fares available.

Charter flights offer the lowest fares but often depart only on certain days, and they are seldom on time. You may be able to arrive at one city and return from another; however, you may lose all or most of your money if you cancel your trip. Don't sign up for a charter flight unless you've checked with a travel agency about the reputation of the packager. It's particularly important to know the packager's policy concerning refunds in the event of a canceled flight; some agents recommend that travelers purchase trip-cancellation insurance if they plan to book charter flights. One of the most popular charter operators to Europe is **Council Charter** (205 E. 42nd St., New York, NY 10017, tel. 212/661–0311 or 800/800–8222), a division of the **Council on International Educational Exchange** (CIEE). Other companies advertise in Sunday travel sections of newspapers.

Somewhat more expensive—but up to 50% below the cost of APEX fares—are tickets purchased through consolidators, companies that buy blocks of tickets on scheduled airlines and sell them at wholesale prices. Tickets are subject to availability, so passengers must generally have flexible travel schedules. Here again, you may lose all or most of your money if you change your plans, but at least you will be on a regularly scheduled flight with less risk of cancellation than on a charter. As an added precaution, you may want to purchase trip-cancellation insurance. Once you've made your reservation, call the airline to confirm it. Among the best-known consolidators are **UniTravel** (Box 12485, St. Louis, MO 63132, tel. 314/569–2501 or 800/325–2222) and **Access International** (101 W. 31st St., Suite 1104, New York, NY 10001, tel. 212/465–0707 or 800/825–3633). Others advertise in the Sunday travel sections of newspapers.

A third option is to join a travel club that offers special discounts to its members. Among such organizations are **Discount Travel International** (114 Forrest Ave., Narberth, PA 19072, tel. 215/668–7184 or 800/334–9294), **Moment's Notice** (425 Madison Ave., New York, NY 10017, tel. 212/486–0500), **Travelers Advantage** (CUC Travel Service, 49 Music Sq. W., Nashville, TN 37203, tel. 800/548–1116), and **Worldwide Discount Travel**

Club (1674 Meridian Ave., Miami Beach, FL 33139, tel. 305/534–2082). These cut-rate tickets should be compared with APEX tickets on the major airlines.

Smoking As of late February 1990, smoking was banned on all routes within the 48 contiguous states; within the states of Hawaii and Alaska; to and from the U.S. Virgin Islands and Puerto Rico; and on flights of less than six hours to and from Hawaii and Alaska. The rule applies to both domestic and foreign carriers.

On a flight where smoking is permitted, you can request a non-smoking seat during check-in or when you book your ticket. If the airline tells you there are no seats available in the nonsmoking section on the day of the flight, insist on one: Department of Transportation regulations require carriers to find seats for all nonsmokers, provided they meet check-in time restrictions. These regulations apply to all international flights on U.S. carriers; however, the Department of Transportation does not have jurisdiction over foreign carriers traveling out of or into the United States.

From North America by Ship

The days are long gone when almost all transatlantic liners made Cobh in County Cork their first or last European port of call. The only regular visitor these days is Cunard's superliner, the *Queen Elizabeth 2*. For the last several years, she has called at Cobh in mid-July and mid-September en route to New York (a four-day trip). Confirmation of her 1993 schedule will be available early 1993 from **Cunard** (555 5th Ave., New York, NY 10017, tel. 212/661–7777 or 800/5–CUNARD). Inclusive tours that coincide with the sailings are offered by **O'Connor Fairways Tours** (800 2nd Ave., New York, NY 10017, tel. 212/661–0550 or 800/288–7609). Rates for the four-day crossing start at around $1,785 per person, including one-way economy-class airfare.

From Britain by Plane

Irish Republic Airports and Airlines The major carriers are **Aer Lingus** and **Ryanair.** There are 12 flights every day to Dublin from Heathrow, operated by Aer Lingus. Aer Lingus also operates frequent daily flights to Dublin from Gatwick. In addition, flights to Dublin leave from Birmingham, Bristol, East Midlands, Liverpool, Manchester, Leeds/Bradford, Newcastle, Edinburgh, and Glasgow. There are at least two flights daily from Heathrow to Shannon, and three flights daily to Cork. There are also flights to Cork from Birmingham, Manchester, and Plymouth, and to Dublin, Cork, Knock, Shannon, and Waterford from Luton or Stansted (near London). Flying time to most Irish airports is around one hour.

The wide range of fares reflects the number of flights available—and the competition: Most fares offer good value. The season you travel, the length of time you stay in Ireland (with all cheaper fares you have to spend at least one Saturday night in the country), and the amount of time between your trip and the purchase of your ticket (generally, the further in advance you make your reservations, the cheaper the flight will be) dictate the cost of the flight. It's always worth shopping around before making your reservation. A range of business-class fares is also available. There are no first-class fares to Ireland.

For reservations and information in Britain: **Aer Lingus** (tel. 081/569–5555); **British Midland Airways** (tel. 071/589–5599); **Brymon Airways** (tel. 0345/090000); **Loganair** (tel. 041/889–3181); **Manx Airlines** (tel. 0624/824313); **Ryanair** (tel. 071/435–7101); **SAS** (tel. 071/734–4020).

Northern Ireland *Airports and Airlines*

Frequent flights are scheduled throughout the day to Belfast from Heathrow, Gatwick, and 17 other U.K. airports. Flights take about 1¼ hours from London. British Airways's and British Midland Airways's shuttle services from London are walk-on, no-reservation flights, and the airlines claim that no passenger is turned away; another plane would be employed if necessary. **Belfast International Airport at Aldergrove** is Northern Ireland's principal air arrival point. **Belfast Harbour Airport** receives flights from U.K. provincial airports and from Luton. **Eglinton Airport,** a few miles from Derry City, receives flights from Manchester and Glasgow. Call 0504/261911, 0504/44100, or 0504/43813 for a taxi into town.

British Airways and **British Midland Airways** (*see* above) operate most flights into Belfast, but cheaper flights may be available from **Brittania** (tel. 0582/405737) or **Loganair** (*see* above).

From Britain by Ferry, Car, and Bus

By Ferry *Irish Republic*

Getting to Ireland by train/ferry is simple, though slow. There are two principal routes: to Dublin from Holyhead on the Isle of Anglesea, and to Rosslare from Fishguard or Pembroke in Wales. Two companies sail the Dublin route: **B&I** (tel. 071/734–4681) and **Sealink** (tel. 0223/647047), whose ferries go to Dun Laoghaire, a few miles south of Dublin. Buses into Dublin from the docks meet all the ferries. Total journey time from London is around 11 hours.

B&I operates the Pembroke–Rosslare route; Sealink operates the Fishguard–Rosslare route. To connect with the Fishguard sailings, take one of the many direct trains from London (Paddington). Sailing time is 4½ hours. A connecting train at Rosslare will get you to Waterford by about 8:30 PM, to Cork by about midnight. For the Pembroke sailings, you have to change at Swansea. Sailing time is again 4½ hours.

Swansea Cork Ferries (tel. 0792/456116) operate a service between Swansea and Cork from April to October. The crossing takes 12 hours, but easy access by road to both ports make this longer sea route a good choice for motorists heading for the Southwest.

The cost of your trip can vary substantially. It's worth spending time with a travel agent and comparing prices carefully; flying is sometimes cheaper. Fares to Dublin are cheapest, starting at around UK£50 off-season round-trip and rising to UK£80 round-trip in summer. Book well in advance at peak periods. Students and others under 26 should take advantage of the cheap fares offered by **Eurotrain** and **Transalpino.**

For reservations and information, contact: **B&I; Eurotrain** (tel. 071/730–3402); **Sealink;** and **Transalpino** (tel. 071/834–9656).

Northern Ireland Car ferries run to the port of Larne from the Scottish port of Stranraer. Trains leave London (Euston) for Stranraer Harbour several times a day. **Sealink Ferries** (tel. 0776/22620) crosses the water to Larne, where you pick up a train to Belfast. The whole trip is around 13 hours. There is also a nine-hour crossing from Liverpool to Belfast, operated by **Belfast Ferries** (tel. 0519/226234). Trains leave London (Euston) for Liverpool throughout the day.

If you're traveling from Dublin, you can take the Belfast–Dublin Express, which goes nonstop between the two cities in two hours. Six trains run daily in both directions (only three on Sundays).

By Car
Irish Republic

All ferries on *both* principal routes to Ireland—Holyhead–Dublin and Fishguard/Pembroke–Rosslare—take cars. Fishguard and Pembroke are relatively easy to reach by road. The car trip to Holyhead, on the other hand, is sometimes difficult: Delays on the A55 North Wales coastal road are not unusual.

For reservations and information, *see* From Britain by Ferry, above.

Northern Ireland

Car ferries to Belfast leave from Liverpool; those to Larne, from the Scottish ports of Stranraer and Cairnryan. For more information, *see* From Britain by Ferry, above.

Many roads from the Republic into Northern Ireland have been closed, but a score of legitimate crossing points, as well as another score of "unapproved" routes, exist. There's an army checkpoint, with relatively few formalities, at all approved frontier posts. The fast N1/A1 connects Belfast to Dublin (161 km/100 mi); there are sometimes border delays on this road.

By Bus
Irish Republic

Numerous bus services run between Britain and Ireland. Those traveling with young children should beware the long hours and possible delays. All bus services use either the Holyhead–Dublin or Fishguard/Pembroke–Rosslare ferry routes.

Services are operated by **National Express–Supabus** (tel. 071/730–0202), a consortium of British bus companies, and **Slattery's** (tel. 071/482–1604), an Irish bus operator. Supabus has services from all major British cities to more than 90 Irish destinations. Slattery's has services from London, Manchester, Liverpool, and North Wales to Dublin, Tralee, Listowel, Ennis, and Galway.

Northern Ireland

Buses to Belfast run from London and from Birmingham, making the Stranraer–Larne crossing. For reservations and information, contact **National Express** (tel. 071/730–0202).

Staying in the Irish Republic

Getting Around

By Plane

Ireland is not a large country, so air travel does not play a big role in internal travel; however, an increase primarily in internal business travel has led to the development of provincial airports, some of which now have regular daily flights from the United Kingdom. They can also be very useful to vacationers. See relevant regional chapters for details on airports at Kerry, Sligo Town, Galway, Knock, Waterford, and Derry City (for Donegal). Several flights daily are scheduled between Shannon, Dublin, and Cork, with a flying time of 30–40 minutes between each city. There is also a regular air service to all three of the Aran Islands from Connemara Airport. Operated by Aer Arann, the flights take 6 minutes, weather permitting (*see* Chapter 8).

By Car A car is the ideal way to explore Ireland, a country of small back roads and predominantly rural attractions. Roads are generally good, although four-lane two-way roads are the exception rather than the rule. Most National Primary Routes (designated by the letter "N") have two lanes with generous shoulders on which to pass. In general, traffic is light, especially off the National routes, but it's wise to slow down on the smaller, often twisty roads. The general speed limit in Ireland is 88 kph (55 mph) on the open road and either 48 kph (30 mph) or 64 kph (40 mph) in urban areas. Beware of high speeds on the back roads; you may find a herd of cattle or a donkey and a cart around the next corner.

Road signs are generally in both English and Irish (Gaelic). The Republic is currently undergoing a slow changeover from miles to kilometers. There simply is not enough money in the road budget to change all the signs at once: you'll understand why when you see how many signs can be attached to a single post in rural Ireland. As a general rule, distances on the new *green* signposts (which cover most of the National Primary Routes) are in kilometers. Most white signposts are older, and they give the distance in miles. (The *new* white signposts, however, give the distance in kilometers!)

Because of the coexistence of both old and new signs, the route number is not always referred to on the signpost, particularly when traveling on a National Secondary Road (also N-numbered routes) or a Regional road (R-numbered routes). In these cases, the name of the next town on your itinerary is more important to know than the route number: Neither small local signposts nor local people refer to roads by these relatively new official numbers.

The Irish, like the British, drive on the left-hand side of the road. Safety belts must be worn by the driver and front passenger, and children under 12 must travel in the back. It is also compulsory for motorcyclists and their passengers to wear helmets.

Traffic signs are the same as in the rest of Europe, and roadway markings are standard. Note especially that a continuous white line down the center of the road prohibits passing. Barred markings on the road and flashing yellow beacons indicate a crossing, where pedestrians have the right of way. At a junction of two roads of equal importance, the driver to the right has the right of way.

Despite the relatively light traffic, parking in towns can be a problem. Signs with the letter *P* indicate that parking is permitted, but a stroke through the *P* warns you to stay away or you'll be liable for a fine of £15 to £40. In Dublin and Cork, parking lots are your best bet, but check the rate first in Dublin; they can vary wildly.

Drunk-driving laws are strict. Like the United Kingdom, Ireland has a Breathalyzer test, which the police can administer anytime. If you refuse to take it, the odds are you'll be prosecuted anyway. As ever, the best advice is not to drink if you're going to be driving.

By Train   Ireland's train services are operated by the state-owned **Irish Rail (Iarnrod Éireann)**, the rail division of **CIE (Coras Iompair Éireann)**. They are generally reliable, reasonably priced, and comfortable. All the principal towns are easily reached from Dublin, though services between provincial cities are roundabout. If you want to go to Cork City from Wexford, for example, you have to go via Limerick Junction. It is often quicker, though perhaps less comfortable, to take a bus.

Most mainline trains have two classes: standard and superstandard. A round-trip ticket is usually cheapest to buy. For information on long-term passes, *see* Rail Passes, *above*.

By Bus   The long-distance services are operated by Irish Bus **(Bus Éireann)**, a subdivision of CIE. Bus Éireann also provides local services in Cork, Galway, Limerick, and Waterford. Expressway bus services, with the most up-to-date buses, cover the major routes throughout the country.

Buses are a cheap and flexible way of exploring the countryside. Bear in mind that outside the peak season, services are limited, and some routes (e.g., Killarney–Dingle) disappear altogether. There is often only one service a day on the Express routes—and one a week to some of the more remote villages! To ensure that your proposed bus journey is feasible, buy a copy of Bus Éireann's timetable—45p from any bus terminal.

Many of the destination indicators on bus routes are in Irish, so make sure you get on the right bus. For example, a bus to Wicklow marked "Baile Átha Cliath" would in fact be going to Dublin, as that is the Irish name for the capital. Asking someone to translate is often the best way to avoid a mishap.

By Ferry   Ferries provide two very useful shortcuts. If you're traveling from County Kerry to County Clare and the West of Ireland, you can take the ferry from Tarbert (in County Kerry), leaving every hour on the half hour. Going the other way, ferries leave from Killimer (in County Clare) every hour on the hour. The boat takes 30 minutes to cross the Shannon Estuary. It costs £5 per car, £1 for foot passengers.

A 10-minute car ferry crosses the River Suir between Ballyhack in County Wexford and Passage East in County Waterford. It not only saves you a boring drive through New Ross on the N25 but also introduces you to two pretty fishing villages, Ballyhack and Arthurstown. It operates continuously during daylight hours and costs £3 per car, 70p for foot passengers.

Many, but not all, of Ireland's offshore islands can be reached by ferry. There are regular services to the Aran Islands from Galway City, Rossaveale in County Galway, and Doolin in County Clare. Ferries also sail to Inishbofin off the Galway coast and Arranmore off the Donegal coast, and to Bere, Sherkin, and Cape Clear islands off the coast of County Cork. The islands are all small enough to explore on foot, so the ferries are for foot passengers and bicycles only. Other islands— the Blaskets and the Skelligs in Kerry, Rathlin, and Tory off the Donegal coast—can be reached by private arrangements with local boatmen (*see* relevant regional chapters). Full details on ferries to the islands are available in *Islands of Ireland* (£1.50) from the Irish Tourist Board.

Telephones

Public pay phones are located in all towns and villages. They can be found in street booths and in bars and shops, some of which display a sign saying "You can phone from here." There are currently at least three different models of pay phones in operation; read the instructions or ask for assistance. A local call costs 20p for three minutes; long-distance calls within Ireland are around 60p for three minutes. The whole country is covered by a direct dialing (STD) system. If you have trouble getting through, dial 10 for operator assistance; however, if the operator has to connect your call it will cost at least one-third more than direct dial. Do not make calls from your hotel room unless it's absolutely necessary. Practically all hotels add 200% to 300% to the cost of a call.

International calls can be made from only the most up-to-date pay phones. Most towns and villages have this facility in the post office; in Cork City and Dublin, the general post offices are located on Oliver Plunkett Street and O'Connell Street, respectively.

Calls can be dialed directly to over 75 countries worldwide, with access to 120 more via the operator. International dialing codes can be found in all telephone directories. The international prefix from Ireland is 16. Calls to the United States cost about £4.50 for three minutes, less after 10 PM and on Saturdays, Sundays, and bank holidays. Calls to Canada cost the same.

AT&T and **MCI** both have direct calling systems in Ireland. AT&T's **USADirect,** which charges $1.63 the first minute and $1.04 for each additional minute, allows you to call collect or charge calls from abroad to your AT&T calling card. Either way, you pay AT&T rates. For information, tel. 412/553–7458, ext. 314 (collect from outside the U.S.), or 800/874–4400. MCI charges nearly identical rates and works the same way as AT&T. For information tel. 800/950–5555, or from Ireland 800/551001.

For calls to Great Britain, dial 03 before the exchange code, followed by the local number. Calls to Britain cost about £2.10 for three minutes, about one-third less after 6 PM and on Saturdays, Sundays, and public holidays.

For operator assistance, dial 10. To call the international operator in the Dublin area, dial 114; in all other areas, dial 10. The international operator covers collect calls, person-to-person calls, and calls to ships.

For international telegrams, dial 196; for audio conference calls, dial 114. To find out the time, dial 1191; the weather forecast is 1199. For directory inquiries within Ireland and Northern Ireland, dial 1190.

Mail

Postal Rates Airmail rates to the United States and Canada are 52p for letters, 38p for postcards. Mail to all European countries goes by air automatically, so airmail stickers or envelopes are not required. Rates are 32p for letters, 28p for postcards. These rates may change before or during 1993, so be sure to check them.

Receiving Mail Mail can be held for collection at any post office free of charge for up to three months. It should be addressed to the recipient "c/o Poste Restante." In Dublin, use the General Post Office (O'Connell St., Dublin 1, tel. 01/728888).

Tipping

In some hotels and restaurants a service charge of around 12%—rising to 15% in some plush spots—is added to the bill. If in doubt, ask whether service is included. In places where it is included, tipping is not necessary unless you have received particularly good service. But if there is no service charge, add a minimum of 10% to the total.

Tip taxi drivers about 10% of the fare displayed by the meter. Hackney cabs, who make the trip for a prearranged sum, do not expect tips. There are few porters and plenty of baggage trolleys at airports, so tipping is usually not an issue; if you use a porter, 50p is the minimum. Tip hotel porters about 50p per large suitcase. Hairdressers normally expect about £1. You don't tip in pubs, but for waiter service in a bar or hotel lounge or a Dublin lounge bar, leave about 20p.

Opening and Closing Times

Most shops are open from 9 to 5:30 or 6, Monday–Saturday. Once a week—normally Wednesday, Thursday, or Saturday—they shut at 1 for the afternoon. These times do *not* apply to Dublin, and they can vary from region to region, so it's best to check locally. Larger shopping malls usually stay open late once a week—generally until 9 PM—on Thursday or Friday.

Banks are open from 10 to 12:30 and 1:30 to 3, Monday–Friday. They remain open until 5 one afternoon per week; again, the day of week varies locally.

Pubs are open Monday–Saturday from 10:30 AM to 11:30 PM May–September, closing at 11 the rest of the year. The famous Holy Hour, which required city pubs to close from 2:30 to 3:30, was abolished in 1988, and afternoon opening is now at the discretion of the owner or manager; few bother to close. On Sundays, the pubs are open from 12:30 to 2 and from 4 to 11. All pubs are closed on Christmas Day and Good Friday, but hotel bars are open for residents.

Shopping

Few visitors leave Ireland without purchasing at least a tweed hat or a hand-knitted Aran jersey, and if not one of these, then a linen tablecloth or a piece of Waterford crystal. All four items are reasonably priced investments that, given a little care, will last a lifetime.

Irish crafts have come a long way over the last 20 years. The range of Irish-made goods available in the shops is no longer limited to the ethnic and the traditional: high-fashion garments and household goods combining traditional materials with the very best modern designs have added a new dimension to the market.

The best selection of shops and the most sophisticated goods are found in Dublin—especially if high fashion and antiques are among your tastes. Cork City offers less choice but quite a few surprises, and Galway features crafts galleries and off-beat boutiques.

A logical shopping scheme would entail tweeds in County Donegal, Aran sweaters in County Galway, Waterford crystal in Waterford, and so on, but the dedicated shopper soon realizes that most crafts shops sell a mix of goods drawn from all over the country. If you're after something a little different, keep an eye open for signs indicating "craft workshops": There are at least 16 of them around the country. In each of these workshops, you'll find independent craftspeople with different skills selling directly from their studios. Craft workshops have helped increase the variety and quality of Irish souvenirs.

U.S. and Canadian visitors have a great advantage in shopping; they get a refund of the **value added tax**—called VAT— which currently accounts for a hefty 21% of the purchase price of many goods and 16% of those that fall outside the *luxury* category. Apart from clothing, most items of interest to visitors, right down to ordinary toilet soap are rated at 21%. Most crafts outlets and department stores operate a system called Cashback, which enables U.S. and Canadian visitors to collect VAT rebates in the currency of their choice at Dublin or Shannon Airport on departure. Otherwise, refunds can be claimed from individual stores after returning home. Forms for the refunds must be picked up at the time of purchase, and the form must be stamped by customs before leaving Ireland. Most major stores deduct VAT at the time of sale if goods are to be shipped overseas; however, there is a shipping charge.

Antiques   Top-quality antiques shops are concentrated in Dublin's Grafton Street area, but it's still possible to pick up modestly priced pieces of 18th- and 19th-century silver, 19th-century pewter, and antique period furniture elsewhere in the country. Try Cork City, Castlecomer, Kilkenny, Galway City, and Limerick.

Crystal   Irish lead crystal is justifiably world famous. The best known of all, Waterford Glass, is on sale all over Ireland in department stores and crafts shops. The demand is so great that substantial export orders can take weeks or even months to fill. Check out the lesser known crystals—Cork, Dublin, Tyrone, and Galway crystal—and the less formal uncut glass from Jerpoint and Stoneyford.

Drinkables   Irish whiskey has an altogether different taste from Scotch whisky, and a different spelling, too. Well-known brands include Powers, Paddy, Jameson, and Bushmills. There are also two excellent Irish liqueurs: Irish Mist, which contains whiskey and honey, and Bailey's Irish Cream, a concoction of whiskey and cream, sometimes drunk on ice as an aperitif.

Edibles   Smoked salmon can vary greatly in taste and quality. Make sure it's wild salmon, not farmed, and if the label tells you what sort of wood it was smoked over, opt for oak chips. Nowadays smoked salmon is sold in plastic packages, sliced or unsliced. A cheaper but also delicious alternative is smoked trout. Whole farmhouse cheeses like St. Killian's—a Camembert-like pasteurized cheese—are becoming popular gifts. More exotic and more expensive are the handmade farmhouse cheeses, each from an individual herd of cows. Milleens, Durrus, and Gubbeen are all excellent, though strong when ripe. A milder alternative is the Gouda-like Coolea cheese, found in most duty-free shops.

Jewelry Dublin and Cork City are the best spots for antique jewelry, but do not despair if the prices there are beyond your resources. Beautiful modern reproductions of such Celtic treasures as the Tara brooch are on sale for a fraction of the antique price. Other good buys include Claddagh friendship rings, in silver or gold, and beautiful pieces made by modern silversmiths using polished Connemara marble.

Knitwear Aran sweaters were developed by the women of the Aran Isles to provide a working garment that was warm, comfortable, and weatherproof. The religious symbols and folk motifs woven into distinctive patterns once enabled local people to identify one another's families and localities. Even today, no two Arans are alike: If you want to buy a handknit, take your time and wait till you find one that really takes your fancy. After all, it should last the rest of your life. Cheaper and less durable Arans are described as "hand-loomed," which is just another way of saying "machine-made," so be sure you are getting what you want. There is a wealth of other types of sweaters: classic blue fisherman's rib sweaters, homespun hand-dyed handknits, picture sweaters, and sophisticated mohair garments.

Linen A pure linen blouse, like an Aran sweater, can last forever. Designs are classic, so they will not date. Linen handkerchiefs for men make useful gifts. Damask tablecloths and crochet-linen place mats make ideal wedding gifts.

Rugs, Shawls, and Blankets All crafts shops sell fleece floor rugs made of goat- or sheepskin. Handwoven shawls made from unspun, undyed wool are even more luxurious than mohair, though not as easy to find. Lightweight woolen blankets in traditional plaids are always popular gifts.

Tableware The Arklow pottery in County Wicklow is famous for its fine china, sold at all major department stores. Belleek, on the border with Northern Ireland, produces delicate bone china, which is widely collected. Tableware by Ireland's many ceramic artists, with striking modern designs, can be a real bargain, especially if four or six place settings are ordered at once.

Tweeds The best selection of traditional tweeds is still found in the specialist tweed shops of Counties Galway and Donegal. Weavers can also be found at work in Kerry, Dublin, County Wicklow, and elsewhere in Connemara. Tweeds vary a good deal in type, from rugged-looking garments to clothes with jewellike colors that have been popularized by Avoca Handweavers and worn by some of Ireland's most fashionable citizens.

Sports and Outdoor Activities

Participant Sports
Bicycling The combination of numerous side roads and very light traffic makes Ireland an attractive destination for cyclists. The less energetic can concentrate their itinerary on the relatively flat central area of the country; those who brave the mountains of the West and Southwest will be rewarded by magnificent scenery and a wonderfully varied coastline.

Boardsailing and Dinghy Sailing	Boardsailing has caught on in the last 10 years. There are numerous locations suitable for the sport: inland lakes, river estuaries, and sheltered harbors. Dinghies can be hired at most of Ireland's sailing schools, which will also teach you how to sail them in five-day courses. Bring your own wet suit, if possible; you'll need it, even in July and August.

Cruising   Fully equipped boats are rented by the week on the Shannon and the Grand Canal. It's a simple and relaxing holiday, allowing you to explore lesser-known, but beautiful, corners of Ireland. Boats can accommodate up to eight people and have showers, toilet, and well-equipped galleys. Prices start at about £190 per week.

Fishing   Ireland is well known as a game-angling resort: wild Atlantic salmon, wild brown trout, and sea trout abound in the rivers, lakes, and estuaries, and offshore is the deep-sea challenge. Coarse fishing (for all fish that are not trout or salmon) is also available. The salmon season is normally from January 1 to September 30, but dates vary from one district to another. The best period for sea trout is June to late September.

Permits are necessary on privately owned waters or club waters: The latter will cost £5–£15 a day for salmon, £2–£10 for trout. There is no closed season for coarse angling. Besides the permit for the use of a certain stretch of water, those who wish to fish for salmon and sea trout by rod and line must also have a state national license. This costs £25 annually, or £10 for 21 days. It is available in some tackle shops or from the **Central Fisheries Board** (Balngowan House, Mobhi Boreen, Glasnevin, Dublin 9, tel. 01/379206). No license is required for brown trout, rainbow trout, or coarse fish, including pike. Sea angling is available on rocks and piers around the coast. A day of offshore fishing from an open launch costs about £18 per head.

Golf   There are nearly 200 golf courses in Ireland, from world-famous championship courses to scenic nine-hole courses. Choose between the challenging links of the Atlantic coast, the more subtle layouts on the eastern seaboard, and the mature parklands of the inland courses. Killarney's two courses are unmatched for scenery; Arnold Palmer says **Portmarnock** (near Dublin) is among the world's best. He himself designed the new course at **Tralee,** and there's a second 18-hole course at **Ballybunion** designed by Robert Trent Jones. The historic **Royal Dublin** on the shores of Dublin Bay is another course not to be missed.

Greens fees average about £15 but can be as much as £55 at the most prestigious places. Only **Waterville** and **Ashford** have electric carts. Very few places rent out clubs.

Hiking   The Irish Tourist Board provides free information sheets on long-distance paths, set up throughout the country over the last few years with the consent of local landowners. Routes are indicated by trail markers and signposts. Most are between 30 and 60 km (18 and 37 mi), with the exception of the **Wicklow Way,** the first to be opened and still one of the best, which is 137 km (85 mi) long. Alternatively, you can plan your own walks with the help of a good touring map: Ireland is an excellent walking country, with its mild climate and virtually traffic-free byroads.

Horseback Riding Several riding stables offer all-inclusive holidays combining long days in the saddle with home-cooked food and bed-and-breakfast accommodations. Most stables charge about £8 for an hour's ride, a little more if tuition is included.

Hunting If you're staying in hunting country, your hotel will arrange an introduction to the local hunt. The season runs from November to March, and the meet makes a fine spectacle, with the pink-coated hunt officials and their large, heavy-footed hounds milling around outside the village pub before the start. Special hunting packages can be pre-booked (*see* Special-Interest Tours, *above*) for real enthusiasts; they make exceptionally memorable holidays.

Jogging Early risers are amazed to find that no one in rural Ireland drives much before 8 AM, turning the place into a jogger's paradise. Phoenix Park is the place to go in Dublin; most hotels are a 10- or 15-minute jog from the park. The many long sandy beaches around the country are popular with runners, but you may find yourself sharing space with a string of racehorses: Beaches are favorite spots for practice gallops.

Sailing There are several companies around the coast offering bare-boat charters to experienced skippers, but cruises must be booked well in advance. The coastline is endlessly varied and remarkably uncrowded compared with, say, the southern coast of England. Formalities are minimal, harbor dues are low, and facilities are extremely simple.

Tennis Tennis has gained in popularity over the last few years, but it's not really suited to the rainy Irish climate. More than 100 hotels and guest houses have hard or grass courts—usually just one or two—and the cities and larger towns have public courts. Fees are low, but finding equipment to rent can be difficult.

Spectator Sports
Gaelic Games Gaelic football and hurling are played in most parts of the Republic. Gaelic football is an extremely fast and rough form of football (closer to rugby than American football), which involves two teams of 15 who kick and run around a field with a round, soccer-like ball. The rules of this game are complicated, but the skill and speed of the players make it exciting and impressive to watch, even if you don't quite understand what is going on. Hurling, considered by many to be the fastest field game in the world, also involves two teams of 15 who use a three-foot wood stick with a broad base aggressively to catch and hurl a leather-covered ball toward goalposts; the game can result in several injuries. Gaelic games are organized by the Irish Gaelic Athletic Association (GAA) and can be observed free of charge at local GAA fields and sports centers around the Republic. Inter-provincial games and All-Ireland finals are played throughout July and August at the GAA stadiums in Cork and Dublin. Croke Park in Dublin is the setting for the end of the annual All-Ireland finals. Tickets for these matches can be hard to obtain, but the events are also televised.

Horse Racing There is a horse race somewhere in Ireland almost every day of the year. The flat season runs from March to November; steeplechases are held throughout the year. Several courses—about 28 of them altogether—are within easy reach of Dublin. Irish classics are run at the Curragh in County Kildare, and the **Irish Grand National** is at Fairyhouse in County Meath. Some of the best meetings are held in the summer at smaller courses: Killarney in mid-July, Galway in late July–early August,

Tramore in mid-August, Tralee in late August, and Listowel at
the end of September.

Beaches

Ireland has over 3,200 km (2,000 mi) of coastline, with an abundance of beaches—or strands, as they are called locally. Some
are small rocky coves with shingle where you can enjoy utter
privacy; others, like Tramore, County Waterford; Courtown,
County Wexford; Salthill, near Galway; and Bundoran in County Donegal are long sandy beaches fronting bustling resort
towns. The Irish like their beaches kept simple, so you will not
find much in the way of facilities outside the resort towns. At
most, there might be a public toilet, or an isolated hotel or bar,
but don't count on it. If bathing is unsafe there will probably be
a notice to that effect, or a red flag. You should not assume that
bathing is safe in the absence of any warnings: Ask locally to
make sure. Few people swim outside the months of July and
August, but beaches remain popular with walkers and runners
throughout the year.

Dining

The quality and variety of Ireland's restaurants has improved
greatly in the past 15 years. The soggy vegetables and over-
cooked meat that once characterized Irish hotel and restaurant
food are becoming increasingly obsolete. A new generation of
imaginative chefs has begun to capitalize on what are some of
the best raw materials in the world for gourmet cooking.

Lavish hospitality has always been a characteristic of Irish society, and the generous portions offered in Irish hotels and restaurants prove the point. Breakfast starts with fruit juice,
followed by cereal or porridge, and then a *fry* consisting of bacon, sausage, egg, and tomato, with local variations such as potato cakes or black pudding. This is accompanied by toast or
soda bread (whole-meal bread made with bicarbonate of soda
and buttermilk instead of yeast), orange marmalade, and a pot
of tea or coffee.

Many people find that this is enough to keep them going until
teatime or early dinner. Others tide themselves over with a
one-dish pub lunch—an open smoked-salmon sandwich or a
bowl of Irish stew (mutton, potatoes, onions, carrots, and parsley, simmered together).

Most towns have at least one restaurant of some sort. In less
commercial areas such as the midland counties, the best bet is
usually the local hotel. Irish pubs have taken over the role filled
elsewhere by cafés and coffee shops. Most pubs serve tea, coffee, and sandwiches, and many offer simple bar food at lunchtime. Requests for tea, coffee, and food (and the presence of
small children) are generally not welcome in the evenings,
when the main business becomes the provision of alcoholic
drinks.

Many Irish people eat their main meal at midday, so most restaurants are open at lunchtime—from 12:30 to 2:30. Dinner
service begins at around 6, but 7:30 to 8:30 is the most popular
time to eat. The many small Irish restaurants make reservations advisable on weekends and during the peak season. As
you will see from the listings, in all but the fanciest top spots,

informal dress is acceptable—casual but neat. This does not include beachwear, shorts, skimpy or tattered T-shirts, or torn or cutoff jeans.

Ireland is renowned for its dairy products, its meat, and its seafood. The dominant school of cooking, best described as Irish with a French accent, combines classic French and traditional Irish cooking, and includes some nouvelle cuisine influence as well. Irish cream and butter are blended with wine and herbs to produce light sauces that complement rather than dominate the excellent meat and fish. Steak, which appears on nearly all menus, is always a reliable option. A juicy, charbroiled sirloin needs no embellishment—but if you want it rare, be sure to ask. Lamb and pork are both of high quality. Lamb is at its best from March to September, which is also the best time for seafood—lobster, crab, prawns, fresh salmon, trout, mussels, scallops, sea urchin, sole, brill, monkfish, turbot, skate, and, except in summer, oysters. The coast is never more than an hour and a half away, so you can expect all seafood to be freshly caught and high in quality.

Winter travelers can look forward to sampling the game. Kerry venison is a famous specialty beginning in October; the pheasant season starts on November 1 and lasts for about three months. Quail, woodcock, wild duck, rabbit, and hare all appear frequently on the menus of the better restaurants—either roasted or in pâtés and pies.

Several exceptionally good Irish cheeses have been developed recently, notably Cashel Blue, St. Killian, Coolea, Milleens, and Durrus. Many of the various fruits and vegetables are still imported, but outside Dublin the best places limit themselves to the locally grown seasonal crop. The more old-fashioned restaurants offer at least two kinds of potatoes, sometimes more: chipped (french fried), boiled, sautéed, mashed, and *dauphinois* (sliced in a gratin dish), to name a few. But usually the Irish like their potatoes plainly boiled in their jackets, piled high on a serving dish and bursting open. Peel one on your side plate, smother it with butter, and you'll understand why.

Nowadays most restaurants have a license to serve alcoholic drinks. There are two kinds of licenses: a wine license allows a restaurant to serve wine and wine-based drinks such as sherry and vermouth; however, it cannot serve spirits or beer of any sort—canned, bottled, or draft. Restaurants with a full license can serve the full range of liquors and beers.

To help visitors on a budget, more than 360 restaurants participate in a *tourist menu* scheme. Up to three three-course menus are available at set prices—£6, £8.25, and £12. The Irish Tourist Board's *Dining in Ireland* (£2) gives full details on participating restaurants. Some places limit this menu to lunchtime and early evening.

Lodging

Accommodations in Ireland range from deluxe renovated castles and stately homes to thatched cottages and farmhouses. Room standards are rising all the time, especially in the middle and lower price ranges. Pressure on hotel space reaches a peak from June to September, but it's always a good idea to reserve in advance. Many Irish hotels can be booked directly from the

United States. Ask your travel agent for details. The **Irish Tourist Board's Central Reservations Service** in Dublin (14 Upper O'Connell St., Dublin 1, tel. 01/747733) makes reservations in hotels and other accommodations; local tourist offices do the same.

The Irish Tourist Board (ITB) has an official grading system and publishes a list of "approved accommodations," which includes hotels, guest houses, bed-and-breakfasts, farmhouses, hostels, and camping parks. For each accommodation, the list gives a maximum charge that no hotel may exceed without special authorization. Prices must be displayed in every room, so if the hotel oversteps its limit, do not hesitate to complain to the hotel manager and/or the ITB.

Ideally, visitors should sample a range of accommodations. The very expensive country-house hotels and renovated castles offer a unique combination of luxury and history. Less impressive, but equally charming, are any number of provincial inns and country hotels with simple but adequate facilities. Many visitors, seeking to meet a wide cross section of Irish people, prefer a different B&B every night. Others enjoy the simplicity of self-catering for a week or two in a thatched cottage.

Guest Houses
Some guest houses, particularly in Dublin, are hard to distinguish from hotels, and they're cheaper as well; however, less is expected in terms of public rooms, bars, restaurants, and front-desk service, so, in general, guest houses are not for the business traveler. Most are owner-run, and with good standards of cleanliness and hospitality, they're often ideal for vacationers. They must have at least five bedrooms, but in Dublin and major cities they're often much bigger; many offer bathrooms in the suites, and TV and direct-dial phones in the bedrooms. The larger guest houses are sometimes built above an existing bar or restaurant. Others are part of a large family home. The cost at these places may or may not include an optional evening meal.

Bed-and-Breakfasts
This is a well-established and well-regulated form of accommodation in Ireland. B&Bs are classified by the Irish Tourist Board as either town homes, country homes, or farmhouses. Many now have at least one bedroom with a bathroom, but don't expect this as a matter of course. B&Bs often charge an extra 50p–£1 for a bath or shower. If this is taken in the family bathroom, you should ask first whether you can use the facility. Many travelers do not bother booking a B&B in advance. They are so plentiful in rural areas that it's often more fun to leave the decision open, allowing yourself a choice of final destinations for the night.

Farm Vacations
Many Irish farms offer holidays with part board or full board on a weekly basis. These are listed in the ITB's illustrated publication *Farm Holidays in Ireland* (£1.50). You will notice at once from the booklet that very few Irish farmhouses are picturesque: they are more likely to be modern bungalows or undistinguished two-story houses than creeper-clad Georgian mansions—though exceptions do exist. Room and part board—breakfast and an evening meal—costs from £150–£200 per week.

Cottages
In more than 30 locations there are clusters of holiday cottages for rent. Although built in the traditional style, they have central heating and all the other conveniences of modern life. A

three-bedroom cottage equipped for six adults is around £240 per week in mid-season. It is essential to reserve in advance. The ITB's publication *Self-Catering* lists individual properties and clusters of traditional cottages available by the week. For information on booking, contact the ITB.

Camping This is the cheapest way of seeing the country, and facilities for campers and caravaners are improving steadily. An abundance of coastal campsites compensates for the shortage of inland ones. All are listed in *Guest Accommodation* (£4), available from the ITB. Rates start at about £4 per tent, £5 per caravan overnight.

Youth Hostels **An Oíge** (The Irish Youth Hostels Association, 39 Mountjoy Sq., Dublin 1, tel. 01/363111) has a chain of 40 youth hostels ranging from a castle in Kilkenny to cottages at Killary Harbour on the edge of the Atlantic. You must have an International Youth Hostel card to stay in an Irish youth hostel, and it is advisable to book in advance if you're traveling in summer. Charges for adults are £4.50 per night in city hostels, around £3.80 in rural hostels. All have a curfew and are closed between 10 AM and 5 PM.

Another 93 hostels are linked together in the **Association of Independent Hostels.** These budget accommodations range from small cottages to rambling old mansions, each with an informal, friendly atmosphere. Some hostels have private rooms and all offer self-catering kitchens and hot showers. There is no late-night curfew at independent hostels, and no daytime closing rules either. Many have a small shop and offer evening meals of wholesome (often vegetarian) home-cooked food. For a copy of a leaflet listing Independent Hostels and their facilities and locations, write to **Patrick O'Donnell, Dooey Hostel** (Glencolumcille, County Donegal, tel. 073/30130).

Credit Cards

The following credit card abbreviations have been used: AE, American Express; D, Discover; DC, Diners Club; MC, MasterCard (known as Access in the Republic); V, Visa. It's a good idea to call ahead to check current credit card policies.

Staying in Northern Ireland

Getting Around

By Car The road network in Northern Ireland is excellent and, outside Belfast, uncrowded. Road signs and traffic regulations conform to the British system. The speed limit is 48 kph (30 mph) in towns, 96 kph (60 mph) on country roads, and 112 kph (70 mph) on two-lane roads and motorways.

There are plenty of parking lots in the towns (usually free except in Belfast), and visitors are advised to use them. Control zones in town centers, where parking is prohibited, are indicated by yellow signs: CONTROL ZONE. NO UNATTENDED PARKING. An unattended car in a control zone is treated as a security risk.

If you are crossing into the Republic, be sure to use an approved road. Crossing the border on the clearly marked unapproved roads is strictly prohibited. Approved roads connect the following towns on either side of the border (the Northern Ireland town is first; the Republic town, second):

Newry–Greenore, Newry–Dundalk (via Killeen).

Armagh–Dundalk (via Newtown Hamilton).

Crossmaglen–Carrikmacross.

Armagh–Castleblayney, Armagh–Monaghan.

Roslea–Monaghan.

Enniskillen–Clones, Derrylin–Belturbet, Enniskillen–Swanlinbar.

Enniskillen–Manorhamilton, Enniskillen–Ballyshannon (via Belleek).

Kesh–Pettigo.

Castlederg–Castlefin, Strabane–Lifford.

Derry–St. Johnston.

Derry–Bridgend, Derry–Muff, Derry–Newton Hamilton.

Posts are normally staffed from 8 AM to 8 PM, and some are staffed until midnight. On both sides of the border, formalities are quick and friendly; a lengthier stop is more likely at a checkpoint a mile or so from either side of the border. North of the frontier you may be stopped by either the army or the police. Have your passport or driver's license handy.

By Train The state-owned **Northern Ireland Railways** has three main rail routes, all operating out of Belfast's **Central Station** (tel. 0232/ 230310). These are north to Londonderry, via Ballymena and Coleraine; east to Bangor along the shores of Belfast Lough; and south to Dublin and the Irish Republic.

Other than on the Dublin line, all trains are one class only, with reasonably priced fares similar to those in the Republic. The Belfast–Dublin nonstop express takes about two hours.

For information on long-term passes, *see* Rail Passes in Before You Go, *above*.

By Bus All services are operated by the state-owned **Ulsterbus** company. Services are generally good, with particularly useful links to those towns not served by train. In addition, there is a **Freedom of Northern Ireland** ticket costing UK£25 for seven days' unlimited travel. A one-day ticket costs UK£15. Ulsterbus also operates a wide range of bus tours. (For details, *see* Essential Information, *Chapter 10*.)

Telephones

Northern Ireland is part of the United Kingdom telephone system. A local call costs 10p.

If you are dialing Northern Ireland from the Republic, codes are different than they would be otherwise. For example, the code for Belfast is 0232 from anywhere within the United Kingdom including Northern Ireland, or indeed from anywhere in the world, but from the Republic of Ireland it's 084. This is explained in detail in phone directories on both sides of the border. In the Republic, you can find the appropriate code for a Northern Ireland number either in the phone directory or by dialing 10. For all operator services in Northern Ireland, dial 100.

Mail

Postal Rates Airmail rates to the United States and Canada are 39p for letters and 33p for postcards (not over 10 grams). To the rest of the United Kingdom and the Irish Republic, rates are 24p for first-class letters and 18p for second class. These rates may well increase before or during 1993.

Tipping

Northern Ireland follows Great Britain, rather than the rest of Europe, in keeping tipping to a minimum. In restaurants, check the bill to see if service is included. If it isn't, tip about 10% if you're satisfied with the service you've received. Taxi drivers don't normally expect tips, but again, tip about 10% of the fare if you think it's appropriate.

Opening and Closing Times

Shops in Belfast are open 9 to 5:30, Monday–Friday, with a late closing on Thursday, usually at 9 PM. Elsewhere, shops close for the afternoon once a week, usually Wednesday or Thursday, but it's best to check locally. In addition, most smaller shops close for an hour or so at lunch.

Bank hours are 9:30 to 12:30 and 1:30 to 3, Monday–Friday. All banks are closed on Saturdays.

Post offices are open 9 to 5:30, Monday–Friday, and 9 to 1 on Saturday. Some close for an hour at lunch.

Pubs in Northern Ireland are open from 11:30 AM to 11 PM Monday–Saturday, and 12:30 PM to 2 PM and 7 PM to 10 PM on Sundays. Sunday opening is at the owner or manager's discretion.

Shopping

The range of Irish-made goods is roughly similar to that available in the Republic (*see* Staying in the Irish Republic, *above*). Most Irish linen is made in Northern Ireland; other items of interest include delicate Belleek porcelain, Carrickmacross lace, musical instruments (such as harps and bagpipes), Tyrone crystal, and silver jewelry and ornaments using polished Mourne granite. Keep an eye out also for traditionally woven tweeds and wall hangings—as well as items of clothing—designed by handweavers. Bushmills whiskey is made in County Antrim.

Sports and Outdoor Activities

Fishing With a long coastline (750 km, 466 mi), part of it on the Atlantic and the other on the Irish Sea, Northern Ireland offers plenty of choices for shore angling and offshore excursions. Rivers and lakes, including large *loughs* such as Strangford, Neagh, and Erne, add to the variety.

To game fish in Northern Ireland, you need a rod license. The **Foyle Fisheries Commission** (FFC, 8 Victoria Rd., Londonderry BT47 2AB, tel. 0504/42100) distributes licenses for game fishing in the Foyle area, and the **Fisheries Conservancy Board** (FCB, 1 Mahon Rd., Portadown, Craigavon, Co. Armagh BT62 3EE, tel. 0762/334666) handles all other regions. A license costs between UK£5 and UK£10 for 15 days. You must also obtain a permit from the owner of the waters in which you plan to fish. Most of the waters are owned by the **Department of Agriculture** (Fisheries Division, Stormont, Belfast BT4 3PW, tel. 0232/63939), which charges about UK£10 for a 15-day permit, UK£3.50 for a daily one. If you plan to fish outside the jurisdiction of the Department of Agriculture, you must obtain a permit from one of the local clubs. For more information, and for Department of Agriculture permits and FFC and FCB rod licenses, contact the Northern Ireland Tourist Bureau.

Some of the same regulations apply to coarse fishing (for all fish that are not trout or salmon). A rod license is required by the FCB, though the cost is much less than that of the game-fishing license; the FFC requires no license for coarse fishing. In addition, you need a permit from the owner of the waters in which you plan to fish.

Golf   Northern Ireland has 60 golf courses in a territory the size of Connecticut. These include some of the most challenging and scenic golf courses in the world. In Newcastle, the **Royal County Down Golf Club,** which features two 18-hole courses, is considered one of the finest courses in the world. Visitors are welcome. In general, greens fees are modest (about UK£9 per day), and reductions are made for groups. There are plenty of caddies, but motorized carts are not available.

Hiking   For serious hikers there is the challenge of the 790-km (491-mi) **Ulster Way,** a footpath that travels through spectacular coastal scenery.

Horseback Riding and Pony Trekking   These are popular sports throughout the area, particularly in the forest parks and the Glens of Antrim. Several Northern Ireland hunting clubs welcome visitors and will provide a mount if you have an introduction to the master of the hunt. This can be arranged through the Northern Ireland Tourist Board.

Sailing   Two of the best places for offshore sailing are Strangford Lough and Ballyholme Bay, Bangor. Lough Erne is a popular inland sailing spot; you can rent a craft at Kesh in County Fermanagh for sailing there.

Dining

Visitors can choose from a number of pleasant restaurants in Northern Ireland, mainly in the middle and lower price range. *Where to Eat* (UK£1.95), published by the Northern Ireland Tourist Board, contains a comprehensive list of places. Prices are notably lower than in the Republic, but the style and presentation of the food are similar.

Lodging

Hotels and other accommodations in Northern Ireland are similar to those in the Republic of Ireland. The Northern Ireland

Tourist Board publishes a complete list—called *Where to Stay* (UK£2.95)—of hotels, guest houses, farmhouses, bed-and-breakfasts, self-catering accommodations, youth hostels, and camping and trailer parks; prices and full information are included. There is more of a choice in the middle and lower price ranges than at the top.

Information on the nine hostels in Ulster is provided by **The Youth Hostel Association of Northern Ireland** (56 Bradbury Pl., Belfast, tel. 0232/324733). All hostels should be booked in advance for July and August.

Credit Cards

The following credit card abbreviations have been used: AE, American Express; D, Discover; DC, Diners Club; MC, MasterCard (known as Access in Northern Ireland); V, Visa. It's a good idea to call ahead to check current credit card policies.

Great Itineraries

Introduction to Scenic Ireland (One Week)

Although Ireland is not a large country, a week allows only enough time for a quick overview. A car is essential for this itinerary.

Day 1: Arrive in Shannon. Have a look at Bunratty Castle and Folk Park before heading south for Killarney. Take a break in Rathkeale for a tour of Castle Matrix.

Day 2: In Killarney, take a full-day organized tour through the Gap of Dunloe and on the Killarney lakes by jaunting car (pony and trap) and boat.

Day 3: Choose between the lush sub-tropical vegetation of the Ring of Kerry or the rugged mountains of the Dingle Peninsula. Both options involve a full-day trip, either by car or organized excursion from Killarney.

Day 4: Head for Galway City by crossing the Shannon estuary on the ferry from Tarbert to Killimer. Follow the coast road through Kilkee, Ennistymon, and Ballyvaughan past the spectacular Cliffs of Moher and into the extraordinary limestone landscape of The Burren.

Day 5: After a walk around Galway City, drive through the famous blue and purple Connemara landscape to Castlebar; then continue on to Sligo and "Yeats Country."

Day 6: Set off early for Dublin. After a lunch in one of Dublin's famous pubs, spend the afternoon on a walking and shopping tour of the City Center.

Day 7: Take the time to see the famous *Book of Kells* in Trinity College's Old Library (closed Sunday) before heading for the airport.

An Extended Tour of Scenic Ireland (Two Weeks)

The scenic contrasts within Ireland are remarkable. The classical splendor of the great buildings in and around Dublin, the rural simplicity of the West Coast, the lush vegetation of the

Southwest, the ruggedness of Counties Sligo and Donegal, and the neatness of the Antrim Coast are all just a few hours' drive from one another. Listen for the astonishing variety of accents that you'll hear along the way—conclusive proof that there is no such thing as a "typical" Irish accent.

Day 1: Walk around Dublin City Center, taking time to see the *Book of Kells* at Trinity College and the State Apartments at Dublin Castle.

Day 2: Visit Boyne Valley by car or by organized tour, stopping at the Hill of Tara, Slane Castle, and the megalithic tombs at Newgrange, Knowth, and Dowth.

Day 3: Take a trip to County Wicklow, either by car or organized tour, taking in such sights as Powerscourt Estate, Glendalough, Mount Usher Gardens, and Russborough House at Blessington.

Day 4: Drive to Cork City via Kildare Town (stopping there perhaps to look at the National Stud or the Japanese Gardens) and the Rock of Cashel.

Day 5: Walk around Cork City and visit Kinsale, stopping there overnight to sample one of the latter's many fine restaurants.

Day 6: Proceed to Killarney with a short detour to Blarney if you wish to kiss the famous stone. Spend the afternoon riding around the Muckross Estate in a jaunting car.

Day 7: Either take a tour through the Gap of Dunloe by jaunting car and on the lakes by boat, or drive around the Ring of Kerry, one of Europe's premier scenic routes.

Day 8: Head north from Killarney, traveling up the West Coast toward Galway City. Cross the Shannon estuary by ferry from Tarbert to Killimer and follow the coast road through Kilkee, Ennistymon, and Ballyvaughan past the Cliffs of Moher to the extraordinary limestone landscape of The Burren.

Day 9: If the weather is fine, head for Rossaveale and take a day trip to the middle Aran Island, Inishman—or fly there from Oranmore Airport. If the weather is unsuitable for visiting the Aran Islands, take a driving tour through the famous Connemara landscape, following the coast road to Clifden and returning to Galway City on the inland Maam Cross road.

Day 10: Head for Westport; for an unforgettable view of Clew Bay and its many islands, climb the mountain of Croagh Patrick. If the weather is unsuitable, take a drive to Achill Island, which is connected to the mainland by a highway.

Day 11: Drive through "Yeats Country" in County Sligo to Donegal Town, turning left at Donegal Town to visit Donegal tweed country–Ardara, Gweedore, and Dunfanaghy.

Day 12: Head through Letterkenny toward Derry City. Before crossing the border to Northern Ireland, stop at the Grianan of Aileach, a huge stone fort dating from 1700 BC. Drive through Derry City to the Causeway Coast, stopping overnight in Portrush or Bushmills.

Day 13: Spend the morning climbing over the Giant's Causeway and then drive through the Glens of Antrim to Belfast.

Day 14: Leave Belfast, and return over the border to the Republic, through Newry and Bundalk to Dublin.

Ireland by Rail (One Week)

All too many travelers who use Shannon as their gateway to Europe miss the opportunity of taking a quick look around Ireland before continuing their journey. This tour starts in Shannon and ends in Dublin, where you can either proceed by plane to mainland Europe or take a ferry to the United Kingdom. While not as flexible as travel by rental car, rail travel in Ireland is a less expensive alternative (especially on a rail pass). Your range of destinations can be extended by taking local buses and organized excursions.

Day 1: The bus from Shannon Airport to Limerick passes Bunratty Castle and Folk Park (both worth a look). Take a walk around old Limerick City and visit St. John's Castle and the city walls.

Day 2: Proceed by train to Killarney. After lunch, take either a half-day excursion to the Gap of Dunloe or (in bad weather) an organized orientation tour.

Day 3: Take an organized tour to either the Ring of Kerry or the Dingle Peninsula.

Day 4: Travel to Cork City by train. Explore the city on foot either before or after an organized excursion to Blarney Castle or a ride on the regular bus to the lovely port of Kinsale.

Day 5: Take the train to Kilkenny City and spend the day exploring this historic place.

Day 6: Get an early train to Dublin and allow a full day to explore the City Center on foot. Spend an evening at one of the traditional music pubs.

Day 7: Head for the airport or the ferry in the Dublin vicinity.

Great Irish Houses and Castles (8–12 Days)

Although it is physically possible to accomplish this tour in 8 days, we suggest you allow 3 or 4 more days, if possible, to relieve the somewhat hectic pace. The itinerary is best undertaken between June and September, when the maximum number of houses are open to the public. Outside these months, you may often find that it is possible to view a house by phoning a day or so in advance and making an appointment, even if the house is officially closed. This tour will appeal to those with an interest in history, architecture, or interior decoration. You might wish to stay at one of the grand and often historic country house hotels along the way.

Day 1: The Dublin Castle State Apartments and the Royal Hospital, Kilmainham, are the two must-sees in Dublin. A walk along the inner city stretch of the River Liffey provides excellent views of two of architect James Gandon's Georgian masterpieces, the Custom House and the Four Courts. South of the river, Georgian domestic town architecture at its best can be seen at Merrion Square and on the continuation of its east side, Fitzwilliam Street.

Day 2: Head north of Dublin to visit Slane Castle, Newbridge House, and Malahide Castle.

Day 3: Castletown House in Celbridge, County Kildare, is one of Ireland's most magnificent Georgian structures; it serves as the headquarters of the Irish Georgian Society, which works hard to preserve Ireland's Georgian heritage. Russborough House near Blessington, County Wicklow, has a good European art collection.

Day 4: Take the main road to Cork City, turning off at New Inn just beyond Monasterevin to visit Emo Court. You will pass the Rock of Cashel en route to Cahir, with a castle in the town center that is worth visiting.

Day 5: Riverstown House and Dunkathel House are both situated near the village of Glanmire, just outside the city on the Dublin road.

Day 6: A short detour from the main Killarney road will lead you to Blarney Castle and Blarney House. Muckross House in Killarney, a mid-Victorian manor house, is one of the least interesting on the tour, but it should be seen for its attractive location.

Day 7: From Killarney, head north to the Shannon estuary, on whose shore you will find Glin Castle, the ancestral home of the FitzGeralds. Take the Rathkeale road to Limerick in order to visit Castle Matrix; also stop at Cratloe Woods, on the other side of Limerick City, the only remaining 17th-century "longhouse" still inhabited. Stay overnight in or near Limerick City or Ennis.

Day 8: If you have enough time, visit Knappogue Castle and Bunratty Castle in the morning before heading for the airport.

2 Portraits of Ireland

Bogland

for T. P. Flanagan

By Seamus Heaney

Born in County Derry, Seamus Heaney is one of Ireland's most respected living poets. A new edition of his Selected Poems *appeared in 1990.*

We have no prairies
To slice a big sun at evening—
Everywhere the eye concedes to
Encroaching horizon,

Is wooed into the cyclops' eye
Of a tarn. Our unfenced country
Is bog that keeps crusting
Between the sights of the sun.

They've taken the skeleton
Of the Great Irish Elk
Out of the peat, set it up
An astounding crate full of air.

Butter sunk under
More than a hundred years
Was recovered salty and white.
The ground itself is kind, black butter

Melting and opening underfoot,
Missing its last definition
By millions of years.
They'll never dig coal here,

Only the waterlogged trunks
Of great firs, soft as pulp.
Our pioneers keep striking
Inwards and downwards,

Every layer they strip
Seems camped on before.
The bogholes might be Atlantic seepage.
The wet centre is bottomless.

Ireland at a Glance: A Chronology

ca. 6000 BC Mesolithic (middle Stone Age) hunter-gatherers migrate from Scotland to the northeastern Irish coast.

ca. 3500 BC Neolithic (new Stone Age) settlers (origins uncertain) bring agriculture, pottery, and weaving. They also build massive megaliths—stone monuments with counterparts in England (Stonehenge), Brittany (Carnac), and elsewhere in Europe.

ca. 700 BC Celtic tribes begin to arrive via Britain and France; they divide Ireland into "fifths" or provinces, including Ulster, Leinster, Connaught, Meath, and Munster.

ca. AD 100 Ireland becomes the center of Celtic culture and trade without being settled by the Romans.

432 Traditional date for the arrival of St. Patrick and Christianity; in fact, Irish conversion to Christianity began at least a century earlier.

ca. 500–800 Golden Age of Irish monasticism; as many as 3,000 study at Clonard (Meath). Irish missionaries carry the faith to barbarian Europe; art (exemplified by the *Book of Kells*, ca. 700) and Gaelic poetry flourish.

795 First Scandinavian Viking invasion; raids continue for the next 200 years. Viking towns founded include Dublin, Waterford, Wexford, Cork, and Limerick.

1014 Vikings decisively defeated at Clontarf by Irish troops under King Brian Boru of Munster. His murder cuts short hopes of a unified Ireland.

1066 Normans (French descendents of Viking invaders) conquer England and set their sights on Ireland as well.

1169 Dermot MacMurrough, exiled king of Munster, invites the Anglo-Norman adventurer Richard FitzGilbert de Clare ("Strongbow") to help him regain his throne, beginning a pattern of English opportunism and bad decisions by the Irish.

1172 Pope Alexander III confirms Henry II, king of England, as feudal lord of Ireland. Over the next two centuries, Anglo-Norman nobles establish estates, intermarry with the native population, and act in a manner similar to the neighboring Celtic chieftains. Actual control by the English crown is confined to a small area known as "the land of peace" or "the Pale" around Dublin.

1366 Statutes of Kilkenny attempt belatedly to enforce ethnic divisions by prohibiting the expression of Irish language and culture and intermarriage between the Irish and English, but Gaelic culture prevails, and the Pale continues to contract. Constant warfare among the great landowners keeps Ireland poor, divided, and isolated from the rest of Europe.

1477–1513 Garret Mor ("Gerald the Great") FitzGerald, eighth earl of Kildare, dominates Irish affairs as lord deputy (the representative of the English crown).

1494 Henry VII removes Kildare from office (he is soon reinstated), and initiates Statute of Drogheda (Poyning's Law), which is in force until 1782—Irish Parliament can only meet by consent of the king of England.

1534–40 Henry VIII's break with the Catholic Church leads to insurrection in Ireland, led by Garret Mor's grandson Lord Offaly ("Silken Thomas"). He is executed with five of his brothers.

1541 Parliament proclaims Henry VIII king of Ireland (his previous status was merely a feudal lord). Irish magnates reluctantly surrender their lands to him as their overlord. Hereafter, a constant English presence is required to keep the peace; no single Irish family replaces the FitzGeralds.

1558–1603 Reign of Queen Elizabeth I; her fear of Irish intrigue with Catholic enemies of England leads to expansion of English power, including the Munster "plantation" (colony) scheme and the division of Ireland into English-style counties.

1580–88 Edmund Spenser, an administrator for the Crown in Ireland, writes *The Faerie Queene*.

1591 Trinity College, Dublin, is founded.

1595–1603 Rebellion of Hugh O'Neill, earl of Tyrone (Ulster). Defeats England at Yellow Ford (1598), but assistance from Spain is inadequate; Tyrone surrenders at Mellifont six days after Queen Elizabeth's death.

1607 The Flight of the Earls, and the beginning of "the Troubles." The earl of Tyrone and his ally Tyrconnell flee to Rome; their lands in Ulster are confiscated and opened to Protestant settlers, mostly Scots.

1641 Charles I's policies provoke insurrection in Ulster and, soon after, Civil War in England.

1649 August: British leader Oliver Cromwell, having defeated Charles and witnessed his execution, invades Ireland, determined to crush Catholic opposition. Massacres at Drogheda and Wexford.

1652 Act of Settlement—lands of Cromwell's opponents are confiscated, and owners are forced across the Shannon to Connaught. Never fully carried out, this policy nonetheless establishes Protestant ascendancy.

1678 In the wake of the Popish Plot to assassinate King Charles II, Catholics are barred from British parliaments.

1683 Dublin Philosophical Society founded, modeled on the Royal Society of London.

1689 Having attempted, among other things, to repeal the Act of Settlement, King James II (a Catholic) is deposed and flees to Ireland. His daughter Mary and her husband William of Orange assume the throne.

1690 James is defeated by William III at the Battle of the Boyne.

1704 First laws of the Penal Code are enacted, restricting Catholic landowning; later laws prohibited voting, education, and military service among the Catholics.

1775 American War of Independence begins, precipitating Irish unrest. Henry Grattan (1746–1820), a Protestant barrister, enters the Irish Parliament.

1778 Land clauses of Penal Code are repealed.

1782 Grattan's Parliament—Grattan asserts independence of Irish Parliament from Britain. Britain agrees, but independence is easier to declare than to sustain.

1798 Inspired by the French Revolution and dissatisfied with the slow progress of Parliament, Wolfe Tone's United Irishmen rebel but are defeated.

1800 The Irish Parliament votes itself out of existence and agrees to Union with Britain, effective January 1, 1801.

1823 Daniel O'Connell (1775–1847), "the Liberator," founds the Catholic Association to campaign for Catholic Emancipation.

1828 O'Connell's election to Parliament (illegal, because he was a Catholic) leads to passage of Catholic Emancipation Act in 1829; later, he works for repeal of the Union.

1845–48 Failure of potato crop leads to famine; thousands die, others migrate.

1848 "Young Ireland," a radical party, leads an abortive rebellion.

1856 Birth of George Bernard Shaw, playwright (d. 1950).

1858 Fenian Brotherhood founded in New York by Irish immigrants with the aim of overthrowing British rule. A revolt in 1867 fails, but it compels Gladstone, the British prime minister, to disestablish the Anglican Church (1869) and reform landholding (1870) in Ireland. The government also increases its powers of repression.

1865 Birth of William Butler Yeats, the great Irish poet (d. 1939).

1871 Isaac Butts founds parliamentary Home Rule Party, soon dominated by Charles Stewart Parnell (1846–91, descendant of English Protestants), who tries to force the issue by obstructing parliamentary business.

1881 Gladstone's second Land Act opposed by Parnell, who leads a boycott (named for Captain Boycott, its first victim) of landlords.

1882 Phoenix Park murders—British officials murdered by Fenians. Prevention of Crime bill that follows suspends trial by jury and increases police powers. Acts of terrorism increase. Parnell disavows all connection with Fenians. Birth of James Joyce, novelist (d. 1941).

1886 Gladstone introduces his first Home Rule Bill, which is defeated. Ulster Protestants fear Catholic domination and revive Orange Order (named for William of Orange) to oppose Home Rule.

1890 Parnell is named co-respondent in the divorce case of Kitty O'Shea; his career is ruined.

1893 Second Home Rule Bill passes Commons but is defeated by Lords. Subsequent policy is to "kill Home Rule with kindness" with land reform, but cultural nationalism revives with founding of Gaelic League to promote Irish language. Yeats, John

Synge (1871–1909), and other writers find inspiration in Gaelic past.

1898 On the anniversary of Wolfe Tone's rebellion, Arthur Griffith (1872–1922) founds the Dublin newspaper the *United Irishman,* preaching *sinn fein* ("we ourselves")—secession from Britain; Sinn Fein party founded 1905. Socialist James Connolly (executed 1916) founds the *Workers' Republic.*

1904 Abbey Theatre opens in Dublin.

1912 Third Home Rule Bill passes Commons but is rejected by Lords. Under new rules, however, Lords' veto is null after two years. Meanwhile, Ulster Protestants plan defiance; the Ulster Volunteers recruit 100,000. Radical Republicans such as Connolly, Patrick Pearse, and others of the Irish Republican Brotherhood (IRB) preach insurrection and recruit their own volunteers.

1914 Outbreak of war postpones implementation of Home Rule until peace returns. Parliamentarians agree, but radicals plan revolt.

1916 Easter Uprising—IRB stages insurrection in Dublin and declares independence; the uprising fails, but the execution of 15 leaders by the British turns public opinion in favor of the insurgents. Yeats writes "a terrible beauty is born."

1919 January: Irish Parliamentarians meet as the *Dail Éireann* (Irish Assembly) and declare independence. September: Dail suppressed; Sinn Fein made illegal.

1920–21 War breaks out between Britain and Ireland: the "Black and Tans" versus the Irish Republican Army (IRA). Government of Ireland Act declares separate parliaments for north and south and continued ties to Britain. Elections follow, but the Sinn Fein majority in the south again declare themselves the Dail Éireann under Eamonn de Valera (1882–1975), rejecting British authority. December 1921: Anglo-Irish Treaty grants the south Dominion status as the Irish Free State, allowing the north to remain under Britain.

1922 De Valera and his Republican followers reject the treaty; civil war results. The Irish Free State adopts a constitution; William T. Cosgrave becomes president. In Paris, James Joyce's *Ulysses* is published.

1923 De Valera is arrested and the civil war ends, but Republican agitation and terrorism continues.

1932 De Valera, who had founded the *Fianna Fáil* party in 1926, is elected president.

1932–36 Tariff war with Britain.

1938 New constitution creates Republic of Eire with no ties to Britain.

1969 The annual Apprentice Boys' march in Londonderry, Northern Ireland, leads to rioting between Catholics and Protestants. British troops, called in to keep the peace, remain in Northern Ireland to this day.

1972 Republic of Eire admitted to European Economic Community. Troubles continue in the north—January 30, British troops shoot 13 unarmed demonstrators on "Bloody Sunday."

Stormont (the Northern Parliament) is suspended and direct rule from London is imposed. Acts of terrorism on both sides leads to draconian law enforcement by the British.

1986 Anglo-Irish Agreement signed, giving the Republic of Eire a stronger voice in northern affairs.

Irish Miles

By Frank
O'Connor

Born in County
Cork, Frank
O'Connor
(1903–66), a
pseudonym for
Michael
O'Donovan, was
a Republican
rebel and one of
Ireland's
best-loved fiction
writers. The
essay reprinted
here is taken
from the first
chapter of Irish
Miles, a chronicle
of a bicycle trip
around Ireland
taken by
O'Connor, his
wife, and a
friend.

Exploring the Boyne Valley in the early days of our married life, before we yet knew what we were looking for and when anything from a high cross to a keep could lure us off our road, Célimène and I came on the prehistoric necropolis of Newgrange. Prehistory or high crosses, all were the same to us. It was a showery day, and after cycling a mile and a half in the rain to find the caretaker so kindly provided by the Board of Works, we found he had already gone back to the tombs with a couple of military officers. We returned. The rain cleared off as quickly as it had begun, and the blue plains of Meath sparkled and steamed all round us, and there in the heart of them was the great tumulus, overgrown with grass and bushes, and surrounded by its circle of monoliths. The two officers were there, but the caretaker had gone off to find some candles—the Board of Works, as we learned later, hasn't yet heard of electric light and will probably drop dead when it does. Dwarfed by the tall stones with their mysterious patterns, the two young men, one plump and cheery, the other slim and good-looking, looked damned unhistoric. Somehow you could never imagine them turning into spirals and trumpets in the National Museum or being lectured on as a style or period. We nodded to one another and tried not to look too self-conscious, but all the same the atmosphere was rather like that of a doctor's waiting-room. The slim officer broke the silence in a rather startling way.

"I wonder would you consider it—what's the word?—if I said this was Egyptian?"

"It's been called a lot of things in its time," I replied, so taken aback that I broke into a Belfast accent which made the other officer hoot with delight. He obviously thought I was a great card.

"Up the Six Counties!" he said.

"No, but I mean it," the first officer went on eagerly—he was a different type entirely; clever and highly strung. "I understand that all these spirals and things are really sun symbols."

"I think you'd be quite safe in calling them anything," said I. "You couldn't very well be contradicted."

"Oh, yes," he said, by no means satisfied with the reply. "I read that in a book somewhere. I wish I could remember the name of it. It's the same thing as you find in the Pyramids."

We were interrupted by the caretaker bringing back the bits of sacred candle which looked as if they might be contemporary, and we solemnly lit them and crawled after him through the depths of the hillside, under the great half-human shoulders of crude stone, giving ourselves a crick in the neck while we tried to study the patterns on them. In the central chamber we were able to stand, and the officer flicked his torch rapidly up the walls to the roof. I knew I ought to feel moved, but while I tried to remember that this was the heart of Irish prehistory, I found myself watching the shadows which the candle-light threw on the young, warm, eager faces. The second officer didn't seem to be altogether sure of himself, and waited for me to make another joke just to reassure him that history didn't apply to him. Personally, at that moment I very much doubted if it did. I felt sure he would get out of it somehow. But his friend was absolutely determined on the point.

"It was the Milesians who built this, wasn't it?" he asked, looking about him.

"It's supposed to have been the Tuatha De Danann," said I. "Whoever the blazes the Tuatha De Danann were."

"That's right," he said quickly. "They were priestly johnnies, weren't they?"

"At any rate, the people who came after them adopted them as gods," said I.

"That's just the same thing that happened in Crete," he said. "Crete was a daughter-civilization of Egypt. It was started by a priestly caste, just like the Tuatha De Danann, and then the Dorians came and booted them out. The Dorians were soldiers. That's how civilization began. It's all in a book I read once, but I can't remember the name of it. Can you?"

"No," I said firmly, "I can't."

"But that's what happened here all right," he said with conviction. "The Milesians were a military caste; they came from the Mediterranean, and booted out the priestly johnnies and took over the show."

I was just on the point of suggesting that I didn't notice any shortage of priestly johnnies, but decided that, having once talked in a Belfast accent, the less I had to say about the clergy the better. The other officer mightn't understand that I was joking.

"That's how civilization began," the first officer continued eagerly, "with priests and soldiers. It all centres on the Mediterranean. The first time it happened was on the banks of the Nile. A lot of priestly johnnies learned to calculate the time of the Nile floods so that they could have three crops of wheat instead of one. It's all in that book I've been telling you about if only I could remember the name."

I was just as glad he couldn't. I shouldn't have been able to believe in its existence. History simply vanished before the pair of them with their eagerness and good looks. I had no doubt it must be subjective. We left them with real regret, and cycled on uphill through a wooded glen, and downhill again into a secluded valley. This was Mellifont, Honey Fountain, St. Malachy's first settlement in his attempt to Europeanize the Irish Church. A French master-builder had supervised its erection, but his monks and the Irish monks didn't agree on the principles of architecture, so after some time they returned to France. But he must, I believe, have been still in Ireland at the time of the consecration, and seen all the famous figures of the tragedy which led up to the Norman invasion. They were all there: O'Connor, the last Irish king; his ruffianly lieutenant, O'Rourke, with his middle-aged wife Darvorgilla, and her lover-to-be, Diarmuid MacMurrough, prince of Leinster, a ruffian even more abominable than her husband. A pretty gang of thieves they were, and Brother Robert of Citeaux must have had a rare time showing them the marvels of this new type of architecture. Up to this, they had seen nothing but the little churches of out-of-the-way monasteries which they were so fond of burning, but this great type of Cistercian architecture with its massive walls and vaulted roofs must have posed them some nice problems in arson. Not that we saw much of it. There was a ruined tower on the right, a tiny, ruined parish church on the side of the hill, an old mill where they sold picture postcards, and the octagon of a lavabo in beautiful European Romanesque. They were cutting the hay, and perhaps if we had come a day later we might have seen a bit more of the lay-out, but now there was nothing to assist us except a big blue notice-board, the contents of which I had to read to Célimène, who fondly believed that there ought to be something to guide us. It ran:

Abstract of a Letter of the Lord Abbot of Mount St. Joseph, Roscrea, dated June 10th, 1929, to Very Rev. Francis Canon—, P.P. Mellifont.

" 'Mellifont Abbey Items.

" '3,000,000 Masses celebrated, Community assembled in Choir 1,160,000 times to say Divine Praises, 4 Bishops, 2 of them Archbishops of Armagh, 25 Abbots and 3,000 Monks buried in Monastery. These Items—' "

" 'Items is good', " interrupted Célimène.

" 'These Items'," I continued firmly, " 'have been Drawn Up by a Young Monk who was asked to make a *Special* Study of your Questions.' "

"Is he in the Board of Works too?" asked Célimène.

"His father was a labouring man in regular employment," I added.

"Is that there?" she asked in surprise, screwing up her eyes to look at the board.

"No," I said. "I just made it up."

That sprightly pair of lads had cast a spell on the day. We went on to Monasterboice, skipping back a couple of centuries to the days of the Culdees. They were making the hay there, too. We looked for a while at the beautiful old crosses, and then had our lunch and fell fast asleep propped up against a grave. We might of course have dreamed of some old abbot or stone-cutter, in which case this chapter would have been much more exciting, but the fact is that we didn't dream at all. There was no history on us, and in the cool of the evening we cycled under awnings of blue shadow into the little village of Slane. It was dark on the steep road down to the river, with its great avenue of trees and Gothic gateway. By the bridge was a handsome old mill and mill-house, and the great span of the slow, sedgy Boyne. On the far bank a few country boys were playing pitch-and-toss by the light of an electric torch.

We went back and stood in the square. In the whole square there are only four houses; four three-story houses set back a little from the four corners, with flanking walls leading to pavilions in the shape of coach-houses, each facing on to a different road. There were two wrought-iron lanterns in each roadway. That was all; four houses, eight coach-houses, sixteen arches, eight lanterns; and even then the lanterns are now only stumps, the arches hidden with shrubbery. One house belongs to the police, another to the doctor, while the parish priest's house has had its roof raised, and its little Georgian panes replaced by stained glass.

But it is clear that the architect had another story in mind when he found the solution to the problem of his square. I feel sure it was a love story, and that from one of the small-paned Georgian windows he intended some woman to look out night after night on the eight lanterns which shut in her little world, and the carriages that rolled in and out of it with their officers, duellists and squireens from Trim and Drogheda. Was she married, and, if so, for whom did he intend the other two houses? Was it perhaps one of the four-sided comic intrigues that 18th-century dramatists delighted in? The sense of the past swooped down and enveloped us. Below on the riverbank it all began, ages and ages ago, with priestly johnnies and soldier johnnies, and all the trouble they started hasn't yet come to an end.

I feel sure the architect's tale had a happy ending, for though the Gothic gateway under the trees may have been in existence, it had not yet set the fashion for unhappy love, Shelley's poetry and Robert Emmet's speech from the dock. Wolfe Tone, rationalism and married love were still the rage, and I fancy the architect saw a carriage waiting one night on the road down to the river, a coach-house door opening quietly, and a young woman tripping out with lifted skirts. Then a few whispered words, and the carriage rattled over the bridge in the direction of Dublin.

So, at least I fancy, but it is all hard to read, and it is only when darkness falls, and the four old houses cease to whisper correct, serious, official things to one another about the decline in morals and the decay of children's teeth, compulsory Irish and the licensing of dogs, that the old wrought-iron lanterns seem to glow again, the four houses become a string quartet, and the tune they play a Boccherini minuet or a Mozart serenade, melancholy and gay.

The Stone Walls of Ireland

By Richard Conniff

Author Richard Conniff is a former managing director of Geo magazine.

The walls look as though they have been there forever: mottled with lichen and bearded with moss; woven together with vines, hedges, and trees; running, in more than one place, straight across a shallow stream bed, as if the wall were there before the water; emerging, in other places, from the low tide mark, as if the walls splashed ashore with the first settlers in Ireland, 8,000 years ago.

"All the people are dead now who was building walls," a man known locally as the Kaiser assured me one afternoon in County Kerry. It was the sort of remark you heard everywhere in Ireland: the walls were built "centuries ago, I suppose." Even "thousands and thousands of years ago." Or "in olden times." And what did he himself do for a living, I asked the Kaiser. Well, he built walls.

Long ago, of course? Not at all, he said. There was the one in Ballyferriter, built a year or two ago to "close up" around a man's house, and another outside the church. There was a fine new wall across from the pub in Ventry. There was the wall he was going to be building soon around Paudy O'Shea's new pub. And of course there was Sean Moran's wall on the Conor Pass Road in Dingle—I must've heard about it—a wall of such magnificence that people stopped their cars dead in the middle of the road to admire it: "You'd *have* to stop to look at it," he said, as if to explain away their poor driving habits. "You'd be blind if you didn't." He would show it to me himself, in fact.

The following Saturday, as arranged, we headed off around the tip of the Dingle Peninsula, stopping at a number of places not listed, including Sean Moran's wall—a structure of double thickness, six feet in height, around a field where sheep grazed. "The best wall around, I'd say, in Kerry," the Kaiser ventured, on his own craftsmanship. "There are no sheep going to be coming out of there soon. Or cattle."

As we drove, he talked about his craft. The common stone in the area was red sandstone, which breaks away in relatively flat tablets well suited to construction. "There's a bed for every one," the Kaiser explained. "You put it there and say, 'Get in it.'" It was sound material for a wall like, well, Sean Moran's. He'd set the stones there so snugly, he said, that "you couldn't pass a blade of grass across it with a pliers. Sean Moran'll be dead and rotting before it falls down. You'd travel a long time before you saw the likes of that again. You'd travel all Ireland, I suppose."

He lamented the tendency to use barbed wire and electric fencing, which give no shelter for the crops or the animals. Some farmers even bulldozed stone walls to make bigger fields. Sean Moran, of course, would need no wiring. One local man so admired the towering wall at Moran's place that he went out every day with his dog and gazed at it for a half-hour at a time, until one day the dog (gone mad with boredom) got away from him and was killed (doubtless by a driver who was looking at the wall instead of the road). "A lot of people came out to look at it when it was built. Thousands of people. All Dingle came." The wall achieved its rightful status as a conversation piece; it became that estimable thing in Irish country life—a "talking point." For its builder, anyway.

The Kaiser complained about a local farmer who wanted a wall built. "He told me, 'My cattle don't wear glasses looking at the wall. I don't want no fancy work.' The man had red trousers on and a white jacket and he only wanted a plain wall. 'Something thrown up. No fancy work.' And then he put in this big white stone that looks like the arse of a tank in there." Sean Moran's wall, by contrast, was a subtle masterpiece. "You don't see the likes of that in Connemara, do you? You'd travel the world. 'Tis a job forever and ever. And no cement."

Any comparison with Sean Moran's wall is of course invidious, but in that regard it was like a number of others we passed that day on the Dingle Peninsula: dry stone walls, built "forever and ever," of a sort that would make even a modern wall-builder think the craft was one practiced mostly long ago, in days gone by. At the end of the peninsula, for instance, the ancient fort of Dunbeg walls off a small promontory from attack by land. The final line of defense is a massive stone barrier stepped up on the inside with walkways for men fighting with their backs to the Atlantic. No one really knows who built it, or against what foe. Farther on toward Slea Head, the slopes are dotted with beehive huts, monastic dwellings huddled together within small stone circles built high to shut out the world. Around the forts and these anchoritic retreats, the land is of a sort to keep monks and other farmers thin. But it is also well walled, and the field walls, too, look as if they have been there forever. Some of them are sod and stone. The grass grows sideways on them, and they look like yard-high ridges—elongated fins—of lawn. Elsewhere the walls are densely packed piles of flat sandstone. They run up to the mountaintops, enclosing fields pitched at an angle of 30 degrees. The scenery, out to the Blasket Islands, is spectacular, but it's the slope that takes your breath away.

If these walls appear ancient, it may be with good reason. A few Irish walls are as modern as Sean Moran's, and many are of far more recent vintage than a passer-by would surmise. But archeologists have established that the building of walls in Ireland goes back to the Neolithic Age. They have found walls running *underneath* a prehistoric burial cairn in County Down. There, and all along the coast from Kerry to Antrim, farmers cutting turf have stumbled onto field walls—whole systems of walls, in some cases—hidden for millennia by the peat blanket. These subterranean walls run, in one case, from the waterline to a point 600 feet above sea level. At another site, the buried farm has much the shape of a modern one, with half-acre tillage plots, fields of 3 or 4 acres, and a long straight fence more than a mile long, apparently separating one family's holdings from another's. The blanket peat that hid these old fields began to build up around 1000 BC, as a result of early land clearing and deforestation. The walls beneath this blanket are thus probably 3,000 to 4,000 years old and are compounded of stone and sod, in the same manner as walls built on the present surface within the last century. In some places, the old walls emerge from the turf and continue on the surface as present-day boundaries. Like modern countrymen, prehistoric farmers doubtless cast a cool, appraising eye on one another's fields from across such walls.

But while the Irish landscape abounds in prehistoric and Early Christian antiquities, the walls generally do not date back that far, and the sense of continuity between modern walls and those of prehistoric farmers is an illusion. Most walls in Ireland went up no earlier than the agricultural revolution. The network of walls and hedges that we think of as timelessly defining the Irish countryside was, in fact, cast over the landscape like a web beginning in about 1750. Before that, much, if not most, of Ireland was, in effect, a great unfenced cow pasture. "Their fields lie open and unclosed," declared *Advertisements for Ireland* in 1623. Where proper fields existed, an anonymous writer added a few years later, they were "no better fenced than a midwife's toothless gums." In Donegal, in the middle of the 19th century, a landlord declared: "We suppose it would not be believed that in this district, until very lately, fences were altogether unknown."

Indeed, the Irish seem to have had something close to a split personality on the subject of walls. Scattered across the landscape by their pastoral, cattle-herding way of life, with nothing like the security of a town or village nearby, early Irish farmers commonly walled themselves in. The strongest farmers put up their houses within raths or ringforts, a form associated with Celtic settlers of the first millennium AD Thirty thousand of these raths survive around Ireland, visible, in the words of a Kerry farmer, as "old roundish rings of mouldy stone and sods." These grassy corrugations in the earth are all that remain even of Tara, once the seat of power over much of Ireland.

The raths are so well preserved partly because grazing was always more important in Ireland than the plow, but also

because farmers regarded the raths as "fairy forts" and
would not touch them. In Ulster in 1958, for example, a
Land Commission work crew was building a fence in the
course of rearranging land holdings in a congested district.
"But an ancient rath lay in the path of the fence," a local
newspaper reported. "The workmen refused to dig holes in
the rath. They said they would die soon if they lifted a sod.
A Land Commission supervisor suggested that two of the
oldest men in the locality might have no fear of death. Two
men, one of 97, the other 95, were asked and indignantly refused. They said that life was 'as sweet as the fairy music
they often heard from the rath.'" Such caution has given
the Irish landscape the quality of a palimpsest, with the
earthworks of earlier civilizations still visible in the modern
fields. But that is changing. Unfearing bulldozers now frequently level raths, and at Tara the raths sometimes serve
as a sort of makeshift dirt bike course. Carrot-haired boys
on fat-wheeled bicycles rise and disappear over the humpy
landscape as if pedaling over waves.

The raths were once a place for a farmer to drive his livestock, to protect his wealth from hit-and-run cattle raiders.
What field walls existed seem mostly to have been huddled
around these refuges and around monastic sites. They
formed the tillage plots of the "infield." But beyond them,
in the "outfield," Irish farmers seem to have felt something
like an abhorrence for walls. The occasional crop planted in
a portion of the outfield would necessarily be enclosed, to
keep the animals from trampling it. But the enclosure
would be wicker, with stakes driven into the ground and
rods woven around them. When the crop came in, the fence
came down. The rods served as fuel in winter, and the outfield survived as open range. . . .

As English landlords and settlers took over [in Ire-
land] during the 17th century, widespread fencing
of the land began almost immediately. Their methods had obvious and impressive advantages. In County
Meath, for example, 5,000 acres of "waste sheep walk" were
drained, limed, and fenced off into arable fields of ten acres
each, for settlement by French and English Protestants.

These fences were elaborate affairs. An 18th-century visitor described them as typically consisting of an earthen em-
bankment between drainage ditches 6 feet wide and 5 feet
deep. The bank was usually planted with hedges and with
trees for lumber. (In Ireland, for unknown reasons, the
word "ditch" came to apply to the raised bank, rather than
to the trenches from which it was formed. The word is now
used to denote almost any form of raised boundary, including an unmortared—but not a mortared—stone wall; a
mortared stone wall is known as a "wall." By the same logic,
the word "moat" or "mote" refers in Ireland not to a water-
filled trench around a castle, but to the raised and fortified
platform enclosed by the trench; it derives from the Nor-

man French word for "mound." The traveler in Ireland must therefore be prepared to hear about people climbing ditches and walking, like Christ, on moats. These are merely lexical differences, not miracles.)

The single most important benefit of enclosing the countryside was that it made the livestock farming for which Ireland was best suited more systematic and productive. Confining the movement of cattle within an enclosed field meant that the grass would be grazed more thoroughly and the manure concentrated in a field that could subsequently be planted with crops. With cattle no longer wandering freely over the open outfield, more land came under cultivation. Crop rotation was possible, along with the use of hay and roots as winter fodder.

Unfortunately for the Irish, the countryside that was being fenced in had been their common grazing ground. Not only were their ancient ways being supplanted by new and foreign methods; they were themselves being forced out, especially in the fertile lowlands. They responded, in places, by hacking down the landlords' hedges to burn for winter fuel. Later, in the 18th century, secret societies like the Ribbonmen vented their anger at a variety of grievances by mutilating the landlords' livestock. In Munster, the Whiteboys burned the alien settlers' crops and leveled walls across former common grazing ground. By then, however, the walls had already wrought a singular, irreversible change in Irish life: they had made the herder obsolete. . . .

But if enclosure ended one way of life, it also began another, drawing out the latent Irish mania for walls. . . . The walls entered not just every field, but every life and every aspect of life. They became drying racks, clotheslines, coat hooks, scratching posts, hiding places for poteen, and dumps for weapons. They served as shelter for outdoor classrooms—the so-called hedge schools—when formal education of Catholics was for a time outlawed. The walls were a place for lovers to hide, and also for eavesdroppers. They were instruments of spite and weapons for assault, but they were also children's playthings. (Outside Mullingar, for instance, children running small stones across the resonant coping stones have worn a long groove in a "musical wall"; the groove is generations old, but it is also still fresh.) They were a source of entertainment and of "divilment," which was and is a national sport.

As boundaries, the walls became manifestations of the Irish fondness for small fiefdoms and the gleeful cultivation of petty divisions, but they were at times also instruments of self-destructive generosity by enabling the land to be further and further subdivided. For peasant and landlord alike, the walls were a way of showing wealth, power, craftsmanship. As such, like Sean Moran's wall, they were talking points. They were also objects of delight entirely on their own. If the walls closed off the Irish from certain wilder, more naturalistic feelings, still they had a beauty of their own, to which the Irish were hardly blind. (*Tarry Flynn*, Patrick Kavanagh's novel of country life in County Monaghan, is, for example, shot through with walls and hedges. One moment the excitable protagonist is counting the stones in a wall as an exercise in self-control; the next he is suffused with lyrical feelings: "The snails climbing up the stones of the fences and the rushes and thistles in the meadow beyond seemed to be putting a quilt of peace around his heart.")

Finally, of course, the walls had something to do with the business of farming. They were a place to put stones when the fields were being picked clean. They were a way to mark field boundaries. And they were barriers to keep cattle in the pasturage and donkeys out of the cabbages. Indeed, building good walls quickly became synonymous with sound farming in Ireland. It was something that got into the blood. The story is told of County Galway farmers who had complained all their lives about the miserable land, where stones grew like mushrooms and walls divided farms less into fields than into cubicles. In time, the Land Commission relocated them to the rich, wide fields of County Meath. They complained then, of course, that they hadn't enough stones to build a decent fence. There is a saying, still repeated in parts of Ireland: "You can tell a farmer by his ditches."

3 Dublin

By Hugh Oram

Updated by
Alannah Hopkin

Dublin: of all the capital cities in Europe, it is the most intimate in scale and easiest to explore. Although one of its names in Irish (Gaelic), *Dubhlinn*, means "dark pool," most visitors to the city find it a friendly, lighthearted place. Its setting is definitely an added attraction: It is looped around the edge of Dublin Bay, and to the immediate south of the city rise the Wicklow Mountains, 620 meters (2,000 feet) high. From many neighborhoods of the city's southern suburbs, these mountains appear to block off the ends of the streets. From north to south, Dublin stretches 16 km (10 mi), and from its center, immediately adjacent to the port area and the River Liffey, the city spreads westwards for an additional 10 km (6 mi); in total, it covers 28,000 acres.

As recently as 1600, Dublin was little more than a large village, with a population of 15,000. Much of its huge growth in population has occurred during this century; the capital has become the center for government offices and many new service industries. As a result, many people from other parts of Ireland have settled in here. Greater Dublin, with its 1 million residents, now claims nearly one-third of the population of the whole Irish Republic. Yet the city hardly ever seems too crowded, except for a few jam-packed pedestrian-only streets.

The population of Dublin is remarkably heterogeneous, reflecting the many invasions and settlements of the city over the years. From 1880 onwards, Jewish people fled the pogroms of eastern Europe and came to live in Ireland, and until the 1950s, the capital had a substantial Jewish population. (Much of the younger Jewish population has left the city to live in Israel and other countries.) Over the past decade, a large number of Middle Easterners and many American, Dutch, German, and Japanese immigrants have settled here.

Dublin first became a crossroads in Ireland some 1,500 years ago. Four of the main thoroughfares that traversed the country led to the site of present-day Dublin. Today, the area where the city's first inhabitants, members of the Gaelic order, built their dwellings is known as the Liberties; sections of the first town walls, dating back nearly 1,000 years, can still be seen off Thomas Street.

In 837, Norsemen from Scandinavia carried out the first outside attack on Dublin, arriving in a fleet of 60 long ships. Four years later, the Vikings built their first port here and used it for raiding large tracts of the countryside. Despite the resistance of the Irish against Viking rule, the Norsemen made Dublin one of the principal centers of their empire, from Russia in the east to Ireland in the west and Iceland in the north. The power of the Scandinavians was finally broken by the Irish at the Battle of Clontarf in 1014, which took place north of Dublin. Native rule, however, was short-lived; the Anglo-Normans landed in County Wexford, in southeast Ireland, in 1169; a mere two years later, King Henry II of England finally subdued some of the Irish chieftains and granted Dublin its first charter.

Through the Middle Ages, the city developed as a trading center, though fraught with political difficulties; the last remaining relic of medieval trade in Ireland can be seen nearly opposite the Christ Church Cathedral, in Tailor's Hall. In 1651, English soldier Oliver Cromwell occupied and ransacked

Dublin. Not until the 18th century did Dublin reach a period of glory, when a golden age of enlightened patronage by wealthy members of the nobility turned the city into one of Europe's most prepossessing. Still, until the early 19th century, social and economic power rested exclusively in Protestant hands.

New streets and squares, such as Merrion and Fitzwilliam squares, were constructed with a classical dignity and elegance. Handel, the German-born English composer, wrote much of his great oratorio, the *Messiah*, in Dublin, where it was first performed in 1742. Many other crafts, such as bookbinding and silver making, flourished to cater to the needs of the often titled and usually wealthy members of society. Ireland was granted a certain measure of political autonomy by the British, and in the new government buildings (now the Bank of Ireland) in College Green, opposite Trinity College, the independent parliament met for the first time in 1783.

However, this period of glory was short-lived; in 1800, the Act of Union brought Ireland and Britain together in a common United Kingdom, and the seat of political power and patronage moved from Dublin to London. Dublin quickly lost its cultural and social sparkle, as many members of the nobility moved to London. The 19th century proved to be a time of political turmoil and agitation, although Daniel O'Connell, a lord mayor of Dublin, won early success with the introduction of Catholic emancipation in 1829.

During the late 1840s, Dublin escaped the worst effects of the famine, caused by potato disease, that blighted much of southern and western Ireland. New industries, such as mineral-water manufacturing, were established, and with an emerging Victorian middle class introducing an element of genteel snobbery to the city, Dublin began its rapid outward expansion. Until the mid-19th century, Dublin extended little beyond St. Stephen's Green, but with the sudden demand for additional housing by the newly wealthy, many new suburbs were established, such as Ballsbridge, Rathgar, and Rathmines on the south side, and Clontarf and Drumcondra on the north side.

At the same time, Dublin's cultural activity blossomed, particularly in literature. Two main literary movements grew up side by side. In 1893, Douglas Hyde, later the first president of Ireland, founded the Gaelic League (Conradh na Gaelige) with the aim of restoring the Irish language. At the same time, W. B. Yeats played a pivotal role in the Irish literary renaissance; with the foundation of the Abbey Theatre in 1904 and the coming to prominence of other playwrights like Sean O'Casey and J. M. Synge, Irish literature thrived. The cultural ferment of Dublin in the first decade of this century inevitably had its political apotheosis in the uprising of 1916, which lasted a week, damaging many buildings in the central O'Connell Street area of the city. In 1919, the war aimed at winning independence from Britain began in County Tipperary and lasted for three years. Dublin was comparatively unscathed during this period, but during the Civil War, which followed the setting up of the Irish Free State in December 1921, more harm came to a number of the city's historic buildings, such as the Four Courts and the Custom House, which both burned down. The capital had to be rebuilt during the 1920s. After the Civil War was over,

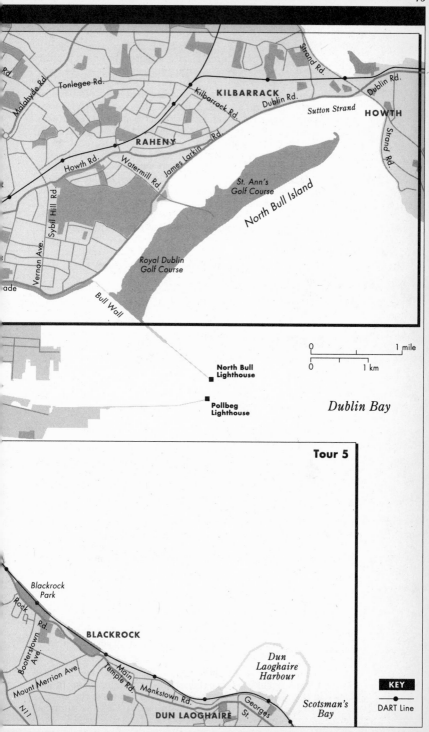

Rd.

Malahyde Rd.

Tonlegee Rd.

Strand Rd.

Kilbarrack Rd.

KILBARRACK

Dublin Rd.

Dublin Rd.

HOWTH

Sutton Strand

RAHENY

James Larkin Rd.

Howth Rd.

Watermill Rd.

Strand Rd.

St. Ann's
Golf Course

Sybil Hill Rd.

North Bull Island

Vernon Ave.

ade

Royal Dublin
Golf Course

Bull Wall

0   1 mile

0   1 km

■ North Bull
Lighthouse

■ Pollbeg
Lighthouse

Dublin Bay

Tour 5

Blackrock
Park

Rodk
Rd.

BLACKROCK

Booterstown Ave.

Mount Merrion Ave.

Main Temple Rd.

Monkstown Rd.

N11

Georges St.

*Dun
Laoghaire
Harbour*

*Scotsman's
Bay*

DUN LAOGHAIRE

KEY
—●— DART Line

Dublin entered a new era of political and cultural conservatism, which continued until the late 1950s.

In the 1960s, an era of economic optimism pervaded the city, with many new internationally oriented businesses established. Much of this enthusiasm waned again during the recessionary years of the 1970s, but then in the 1980s the city became a world center for rock music, with artists such as Bob Geldof, Chris de Burgh, and U2. With the 1990s, a new spirit of economic enterprise is underway with a recently opened international financial services center, next to the two-centuries-old Custom House, drawing many leading business clients to the city. And the pedestrianization and refurbishment of the narrow lanes and alleys of Temple Bar with cobblestone and old-style lighting has brightened up this already lively inner-city area. 1992 was the year of *The Commitments*, the film that showed off modern, working-class Dublin to the world and provoked euphoric levels of patriotism. The mood created by the film will be tough to match in 1993, but Dublin's pride and energy will no doubt carry on.

Essential Information

Arriving and Departing

Airport and Airlines — Dublin Airport (tel. 01/379900), 9½ km (6 mi) north of the city center, serves international and domestic airlines. Only two airlines have regularly scheduled flights from the United States to Dublin: **Aer Lingus** (tel. 212/557–1100 or 800/223–6537 in the U.S; 01/370011 in Dublin) flies from New York, Chicago, or Boston to Dublin, and started handling flights from Los Angeles in 1991; **Delta** (tel. 800/722–9320 or 800/241–4141 in the U.S.; 01/794744 in Dublin) flies from Atlanta to Dublin.

Flying to Ireland from Britain has never been easier, with 7 airlines serving destinations in Ireland from 19 British airports. The major carriers are Aer Lingus, British Airways, and Ryanair. There are 12 flights daily from London's Heathrow Airport to Dublin, operated by Aer Lingus. Aer Lingus operates frequent daily flights from London's Gatwick Airport to Dublin. Ryanair has several flights daily from London's Luton and Stansted airports to Dublin. In addition, flights to Dublin leave from Birmingham, Bristol, East Midlands, Liverpool, Luton, Manchester, Leeds/Bradford, Newcastle, Edinburgh, and Glasgow. Aer Lingus operates flights from Dublin to Waterford, Cork, Kerry, Shannon, Galway, Knock in County Mayo, Sligo, and Derry.

For reservations and information in Dublin, contact: **Aer Lingus** (tel. 01/370011) or **Ryanair** (tel. 01/774422).

Major European carriers such as Air France, Lufthansa, Sabena, and KLM run direct services to Dublin from most European capital cities and major regional airports, especially those in Germany.

When you arrive at Dublin Airport, currency can be exchanged at the Bank of Ireland in the arrivals hall or at the bank branch in the main check-in area. Just before you leave the arrivals hall, the **Tourist Information Centre** (tel. 01/376387) will answer any questions relating to Dublin.

Between Airport and City Center
By Bus The **Dublin Bus** (tel. 01/734222) starts outside the arrivals gateway; pay the driver inside the coach. The single fare is £2.50. Service runs all day, from 7:30 AM to 11 PM, at intervals of about 30 minutes, as far as **Busaras** (tel. 01/302222), the main provincial bus station in the city center. Journey time from the airport to the city center is normally 30 minutes, but it may be longer in heavy traffic.

By Taxi A taxi is a quicker alternative than the bus to get from the airport to Dublin center. A line of taxis waits by the arrivals gateway; the fare for the 30-minute journey to any of the main city-center hotels is about £10. It's advisable to ask about the fare before leaving the airport.

Getting Around

Traveling around Dublin by public transport is comparatively easy, although a car is useful for getting around the outlying suburbs. The city center, with its maze of one-way streets and parking restrictions, is best negotiated on foot.

By Train An electric railway system, the **DART** (Dublin Area Rapid Transport; tel. 01/366222) connects Dublin with Howth to the north and Bray to the south on a fast, efficient line. There are 25 stations on the route, which is the best means of getting to seaside destinations such as Howth, Blackrock, Dun Laoghaire, Dalkey, Killiney, and Bray. The service starts at 6:30 AM and runs until 11:30 PM; at peak periods, 8–9:30 AM and 5–7 PM, trains arrive every five minutes. At other times of the day, the intervals between trains are 15 to 25 minutes.

Tickets can be bought at stations, but it is also possible to buy weekly (£10) or monthly (£40) rail tickets, as well as weekly (£14) or monthly (£55) "rail-and-bus" tickets, from the **Irish Rail Travel Centre** (35 Lower Abbey St., tel. 01/366222). Individual fares begin at 55p and range up to £2.70. There are heavy penalties for traveling the DART without a ticket.

Diesel train services run from Connolly Station (Amiens St.) to more distant locations like Malahide, Skerries, and Drogheda to the north of Dublin, and Wicklow and Arklow on the south side.

By Bus Dublin offers an extensive network of buses, but due to heavy traffic, bus service is not always reliable. Fares begin at 55p and have to be paid to the driver on entry to the bus, another cause of delays. Some bus services run on cross-city routes, but most buses start in the city center. Buses to the north of the city begin in the Lower Abbey Street/Parnell Street area, while those to the west begin in Middle Abbey Street and in the Aston Quay area. Routes to the southern suburbs begin at Eden Quay and in the College Street area. A number of services are links to DART stations, and another regular bus route connects the two main provincial railway stations, Connolly and Heuston. For Dublin Bus information, call 01/734222.

By Taxi The taxi service in Dublin is comparatively inexpensive, with a pick-up charge of £2 and a further charge of about £1.50 a mile thereafter. Many taxi stands, where a cab may be found at most times of the day and night, are located throughout the city center and suburbs, and are listed in the Dublin telephone directory. Alternatively, you may phone a taxi company and ask for a cab to meet you at your hotel, but this may cost up to £4 extra.

Although the taxi fleet in Dublin is large, the cabs are non-standard and some cars are neither spacious nor in pristine condition. Local taxi companies include **VIP Taxis** (tel. 01/783333), **Metro** (tel. 01/683333), and **Mercs and Perks** (tel. 01/842–1341).

By Hired Car Two companies will supply a car with a driver for an individual guided tour of the city, which will cost between £50 and £100 a day, depending on the size of car: **Co-op Taxis** (tel. 01/777777) and **Tailors' Tours** (tel. 042/76393).

By Rental Car Renting a car in Dublin is extremely expensive, with high rates and a 10% local tax. Gasoline is also expensive by U.S. standards, at around 60p a liter. Peak-period car-rental rates begin at around £200 a week for the smallest models, like a Ford Fiesta. Dublin has many car rental companies, and it pays to shop around and to avoid "cowboy" outfits. Some reliable car rental firms in the Dublin vicinity are: **Avis** (Jury's Hotel, tel. 01/683394; 51 Grafton St., tel. 01/778877; Hanover St., tel. 01/774010; Dublin Airport, tel. 01/372369), **Hertz** (O'Connell St., tel. 01/788862; Leeson St. Bridge, tel. 01/602255; 19 Hogan Place, tel. 01/765921; Dublin Airport, tel. 01/842–9333), and **Murray's Rent-a-Car** (Baggot St. Bridge, tel. 01/681777; Dublin Airport, tel. 01/378179).

Important Addresses and Numbers

Tourist Information The main Dublin **Tourist Information Office** (14 Upper O'Connell St., tel. 01/747733) is open weekdays 9–5:30 and Saturday 9–1. Because the office is located in one of the busiest areas of town, you are advised to go there as early as possible. The head office of the **Irish Tourist Board** (Baggot St. Bridge, tel. 01/765871) is open weekdays 9–6. Tourist Information Offices are also located at Dublin Airport (arrivals level, tel. 01/376387), which is open daily 8–8, and at St. Michael's Wharf (Dun Laoghaire, tel. 01/280–6984), which is open daily 7 AM–8 PM.

Emergencies For **gardai** (police), **ambulance**, or **fire**, dial 999.

Medical Check the main newspapers to see which public hospitals offer emergency services on any given day. For minor ailments, hotels have access to their own doctors and also to private hospitals, such as the Blackrock Clinic, south of Dublin.

Dentists The **Dublin Dental Hospital** (20 Lincoln Pl., tel. 01/679–4311) has emergency facilities and lists of dentists offering emergency care.

Embassies Embassies are open weekdays 9–5, but are closed for lunch 1–2.

U.S. Embassy (42 Elgin Rd., tel. 01/688777).
Canadian Embassy (65 St. Stephen's Green, tel. 01/781988).
British Embassy (31 Merrion Rd., tel. 01/269–5211).
Australian Embassy (Fitzwilton House, Wilton Terr., tel. 01/761517).

Travel Agencies **American Express** (116 Grafton St., tel. 01/772874).
Thomas Cook (118 Grafton St., tel. 01/771721).

Lost and Found **Dublin Bus:** Contact its headquarters (59 Upper O'Connell St., tel. 01/734222).
Railways, including the DART: Contact **Iarnrod Éireann/Irish Rail** (Travel Centre, 35 Lower Abbey St., tel. 01/366222).

Opening and Closing Times

Dublin is gradually becoming a 24-hour city, even though the bus and DART train services close down for the night at 11:30 PM. Many taxis run all night, so there is no problem getting around. Many of the clubs on the Leeson Street Strip stay open until 4 AM or later. Even Sunday, once a day of sabbatical rest in Dublin, is lively in Continental style. Many smaller city-center shops and boutiques are open on Sundays; department stores are occasionally open on Sundays.

Banks are open weekdays 10–12:30 and 1:30–3. On Thursdays, they remain open until 5. Banks may have lunchtime opening shortly. Most branches now have automatic cash dispensers.

Post offices are open weekdays 9–1 and 2–5:30. On Saturdays, they are open 9–12:30. Main post offices are open Saturday afternoons, too. The General Post Office (GPO) on O'Connell Street, which has foreign exchange and general delivery facilities, is open Monday–Saturday 8–8. On Sunday, it is open 10:30–6:30.

Museums are normally open Tuesday–Saturday and also Sunday afternoon. Monday is the usual closing day.

The city's main **stores** are open Monday–Saturday 9–5:30 or 9–6. Department stores are closed on Sunday. Smaller specialty stores open on Sunday as well, usually 10–6.

Crime

Crime, often drug related, is a problem in Dublin, so visitors should watch over their wallets, handbags, and other personal possessions. Great care should be taken when parking a car not to leave any valuables inside, even under a raincoat on the back seat or in the trunk. Certain areas demand caution: The city center is where pedestrians and motorists should be especially careful. Another danger area for parking cars is in the vicinity of the Guinness Brewery Hop Store and Irish Whiskey Corner (*see* Tour 3: Dublin West, *below*). Side streets off O'Connell Street can also be dangerous, especially at night.

Guided Tours

Orientation Tours   **Bus Éireann** (tel. 01/366111) provides a four-hour city sightseeing tour that covers the main sights in the city center, including St. Patrick's Cathedral, Trinity College, the Royal Hospital, and Phoenix Park. The company also features day tours to country destinations out of the main bus station, Busaras, in Dublin.

Dublin Bus (tel. 01/734222) offers a three-hour city-center tour, taking in sights similar to the Bus Éireann tour (*see above*). During the summer, this tour runs daily, using open-topped buses weather permitting. The company also conducts a north-city coastal tour, going to Howth, and a south-city tour, traveling as far as Enniskerry.

Gray Line Tours (tel. 01/619666) runs city-center tours that cover the same sights as the Bus Éireann and Dublin Bus itineraries (*see above*).

Special-Interest Tours *DART Train Tours*	Guided tours of Dublin using the DART system are organized by **Views Unlimited** (8 Prince of Terrace, Bray, tel. 01/286–0164 or 01/286–2861).
Horse-Drawn Carriage Tours	Horse-drawn carriage tours are available around Dublin and in Phoenix Park. For tours of the park, contact the **Office of Public Works** (tel. 01/613111). For other tours through the city, contact **Paddy Sarsfield** (tel. 01/755995).
Pubs	Evening tours of the literary pubs of Dublin are offered by **Colm Quilligan** (tel. 01/540228).
Walking Tours	**Tour Guides Ireland** (Glendenning House, Wicklow St., tel. 01/679–4291) conducts walking tours of the city, including Georgian Dublin. **Eamonn MacThomais** offers entertaining walking tours of the Liberties and Literary and Georgian Dublin; tours begin at 2 PM on weekends at the statue of Molly Malone's barrow, Grafton Street. Tourist Information Offices also provide leaflets describing walking tours that follow signposted itineraries.

Exploring

Highlights for First-time Visitors

Book of Kells at Trinity College (*see* Tour 1)
Chester Beatty Library (*see* Tour 5)
Guinness Brewery Hop Store (*see* Tour 3)
Howth Peninsula (*see* Tour 6)
Hugh Lane Municipal Art Gallery (*see* Tour 2)
Merrion Square (*see* Tour 1)
National Gallery of Ireland (*see* Tour 1)
Phoenix Park (*see* Tour 3)
Royal Hospital, Kilmainham (*see* Tour 3)
St. Stephen's Green (*see* Tour 1)

Tour 1: South City Center

Numbers in the margin correspond to points of interest on the Tours 1 and 2: Dublin City Center map.

A good place to start your tour of Dublin is the city-center area south of the River Liffey; it contains a majority of the city's historic buildings and monuments. Let's begin south of O'Connell Bridge and Westmoreland Street at College Green, once a Viking meeting place and burial ground. East of College Green

❶ stands **Trinity College,** the sole college of Dublin University, Ireland's oldest, dating back to 1592, when it was founded by England's Queen Elizabeth I on the site of the confiscated Priory of All Hallows. For centuries, Trinity was the preserve of the Protestant church, and it is only within the past 30 years that final prohibitions barring Catholics from studying there have been lifted. Among the distinguished alumni of the college are Jonathan Swift, Thomas Moore, Sheridan LeFanu, George Berkeley, Oscar Wilde, J. M. Synge, Bram Stoker, and Samuel Beckett. Trinity served as a stand-in for an English university in the popular 1983 movie *Educating Rita*.

Trinity's grounds cover 40 acres, and most of its buildings were constructed in the 18th and early 19th centuries. The extensive West Front, with a classical portico in the Corinthian style, faces onto College Green; now grimy with age, it was built between 1755 and 1759, possibly the work of Theodore Jacobsen, architect of London's Foundling Hospital. Statues of orator Edmund Burke and dramatist Oliver Goldsmith are positioned close to the front gate. Parliament Square, the cobbled quadrangle that is the visitor's first introduction to the grounds, also dates back to the 18th century. On the right of the square, you'll find the Theatre, or Examination Hall, which features an impressive organ retrieved from an 18th-century Spanish ship and a gilded oak chandelier from the old House of Commons; concerts are sometimes held here. The Chapel, which stands on the left of the quadrangle, has stucco ceilings and fine woodwork. Both the Theatre and the Chapel were designed by Scotsman William Chambers in the late-18th century. The looming Campanile, or bell tower, erected in 1853, dominates the center of the square. *College information, tel. 01/772941. Grounds open daily 8AM–10PM.*

At the right-hand corner of the second quadrangle, called Library Square, the **Old Library** houses Ireland's most valuable collection of ancient volumes and priceless manuscripts; the most famous of these is the Book of Kells, a splendidly illuminated version of the Gospels, designed by unknown monks, perhaps in Kells, County Meath, in the 9th century. The 680-page book was rebound in four volumes in 1953, and two of these are usually displayed at a time, with pages turned periodically, in the library's two-story Long Room. This room, which is 13 meters (41 feet) wide by 65 meters (210 feet) long, has a high-pitched barrel-vaulted ceiling and contains approximately 200,000 of the 3 million volumes in Trinity's collection. Since the 1801 Copyright Act, the college has received a copy of every book published in Britain and Ireland, and a great number of these publications must be stored in other parts of the campus and beyond. The carved Royal Arms of Queen Elizabeth I, above the library exit, is the only surviving relic of the original college buildings. *Admission: £2.50 adults, £2 children 12–18, senior citizens, and students, free to children under 12. Open weekdays 9:30–4:45, Sat. 9:30–12:45.*

At the east end of the Old Library stands the **New Berkeley Library,** built in 1967. Behind the Old Library, you'll find the concrete Arts and Social Sciences Buildings, with an entrance on Nassau Street; this complex houses the **Douglas Hyde Gallery of Modern Art,** which concentrates on contemporary art exhibitions and has its own bookshop. *Tel. 01/772941, ext. 1116. Admission free. Open Mon.–Thurs. 11–6, Fri. 11–7, Sat. 11–4:45.*

In the Thomas Davis Theatre in the Arts Building, Trinity recently introduced the **Dublin Experience,** an elaborate audiovisual presentation devoted to the history of the city over the past 1,000 years. *Tel. 01/772941. Admission: £2.75 adults (£5 with Old Library), £2.25 students and senior citizens (£4 with Old Library), £1.50 children under 18. The show runs every hour on the hour. Open May–Oct., daily 10–5.*

Directly opposite the front entrance of Trinity College in College Green stands one of Dublin's most striking buildings, now serving as a branch of the **Bank of Ireland.** This grand structure, with a facade incorporating Corinthian pillars into its Ionic porticos, was first designed by Sir Edward Lovett Pearce to house the Irish Parliament, which resided here for 17 years;

Tours 1 and 2: Dublin City Center

when the Parliament was abolished in 1803 under the Act of Union, the building was bought by the Bank of Ireland. Today the main banking hall is set in the old Court of Requests where citizens' petitions were heard. The former House of Lords, which may be viewed by small groups upon request, features a coffered ceiling, an exquisite 18th-century Waterford glass chandelier, and two large tapestries depicting the Battle of Boyne and the Siege of Derry. *College Green, tel. 01/776801. Admission free. Open weekdays 10–12:30 and 1:30–3; Thurs. until 5.*

From the Bank of Ireland, turn left onto College Green, which becomes Dame Street; continue for less than 1 km (½ mi) to **3** Cork Hill and **City Hall,** the seat of the Dublin Corporation, the elected body that governs the city. This edifice, with its great domed entrance hall, was built as the Royal Exchange in 1769 and contains many notable historical artifacts, including 102 royal charters and the mace and sword of the city. *Tel. 01/679–6111. Admission free. Open weekdays 9–5.*

4 Behind City Hall (west) is **Dublin Castle,** the seat of British administration in Ireland from the 13th century to 1922. It is now heavily restored and is used mostly for government and conference purposes. In the Lower Castle Yard, the Record Tower, built by King John between 1208 and 1220, and the earliest of several towers on the site, is the largest remaining relic of the original Norman buildings. Guided tours are offered around the principal State Apartments (on the southern side of the Upper Castle Yard), which are furnished with rich Donegal carpets and illuminated by Waterford glass chandeliers; today these elaborate rooms are used largely for ceremonial occasions. The largest and most impressive of these chambers, St. Patrick's Hall, with its gilt pillars and painted ceiling, is used for the inauguration of Irish presidents. The Round Drawing Room, in Bermingham Tower, dates from 1411 and was rebuilt in 1777; a number of Irish leaders have been imprisoned in the tower, from the 16th century to the early 20th century. The blue oval Wedgwood Room contains Chippendale chairs and a marble fireplace.

Also on the castle grounds is the **Church of the Holy Trinity** (formerly called Chapel Royal), designed in the early 19th century by Francis Johnston, who also designed the original General Post Office building on O'Connell Street. Carved oak panels and stained glass depicting viceroys' coats of arms grace the interior. *Castle St., tel. 01/777129. Admission to State Apartments: £1 adults, 50p children, including guided tour. Open weekdays 10–12:15 and 2–5; Sat., Sun., and public holidays 2–5. Call ahead, because apartments are sometimes closed for state occasions.*

From the main entrance of the castle, turn right onto Cork Hill and Dame Street until you reach South Great George's Street on your right. The covered markets here (open Mon.–Sat. 9–6), a Victorian legacy, have changed little despite their restoration; you'll find many lines of food, fashion, and trinkets for sale.

Time Out   Take a look at the **Long Hall Pub** (51 S. Great George's St., tel. 01/751590), one of Dublin's most ornate traditional taverns, full of lamps, woodwork, mirrors, and chandeliers, all at least 100 years old. The pub serves sandwiches, beers, and whiskeys.

5 South Great George's Street eventually turns into Aungier Street. The inside of the **Carmelite Church** on Whitefriar Street, off Aungier Street, contains an unusual bequest from an early 19th-century pope, Gregory XVI, who gave the prior of the church, in recognition of the latter's work, the remains of St. Valentine, the patron saint of lovers, who was martyred in Rome about AD 269. *Tel. 01/758821. Admission free. Open daily 8–8.*

6 Return to the market area on South Great George's Street; behind the shops on the right, approached by a pedestrian walkway, is the **Dublin Civic Museum.** In the 18th century, the building housed the City Assembly Hall, precursor of City Hall. The museum's small, esoteric collection includes Stone Age flints, Viking coins, old maps and prints of the city, and the sculptured head of British admiral Horatio Nelson, which used to top Nelson's Pillar, beside the General Post Office on O'Connell Street (*see* below); the column was toppled by an explosion in 1966 on the 50th anniversary of the Easter Rising. Often the museum runs exhibitions relating to the city. *South William St., tel. 01/679–4260. Admission free. Open Tues.–Sat. 10–6, Sun. 11–2.*

From the museum, walk east, passing Clarendon Street and the Catholic **St. Theresa's Church;** continue along Johnson's Court, beside the church, onto Grafton Street.

7 Part of Dublin's most famous chain of coffee houses, dating back to 1840, **Bewley's Café** on Grafton Street with its dark wood and marble tables is renowned for its stained-glass windows by Harry Clarke (1889–1931), Ireland's most distinguished early 20th-century artist in this medium. The café, which serves reasonably priced tea, coffee, meals, and desserts, is a fine place in which to observe Dubliners of all ages and occupations. On the first floor, a small museum deals with Bewley's history. (Other branches of Bewley's are located at South Great George's and Westmoreland streets.) *Tel. 01/776761. Open weekdays 10–6.*

8 Cross Grafton Street and walk east along South Anne Street to **St. Ann's Church** (Church of Ireland) on Dawson Street. Its plain neo-Romanesque granite exterior, designed in 1868, belies its rich, 18th-century Georgian interior, with polished wood balconies and ornate plasterwork. *Dawson St., tel. 01/762186. Admission free. Open weekdays 10–3 and Sun. for services. Closed Sat.*

9 Steps away from the church is the **Royal Irish Academy,** which houses old scientific texts, a large collection of ancient Irish manuscripts, including the 11th–12th century Book of the Dun Cow and 18th-century poet Thomas Moore's library. *19 Dawson St., tel. 01/762570. Admission free. Open weekdays 9:30–5:30.*

10 From Dawson Street, walk along Molesworth Street, where you'll pass the **Freemasons Hall** (tel. 01/761337), a large 18th-century building with a pillared portico. At the end of the street, turn left onto Kildare Street. At 2 Kildare Street, the full records of the **Genealogical Office** can help people who are searching for Irish ancestors. *Tel. 01/618811. Open weekdays 9:30–5:30.*

⑪ At the same address, you'll find the **Heraldic Museum,** founded in 1911 and once located in Dublin Castle. It now displays a collection of family coats of arms. *2 Kildare St., tel. 01/614877. Open weekdays 10–12:30 and 2–4:30.*

⑫ West of the museum stands the **National Library.** Its main Reading Room opened in 1890 to contain the collections of the Royal Dublin Society. Beneath its dramatic domed ceiling, countless authors have researched and written their books over the years. The library accommodates an important collection of first editions and works by Irish writers, including ones by Swift, Goldsmith, Yeats, Shaw, Joyce, and Beckett. Virtually every book ever published in Ireland is kept here, as well as an unequaled selection of old maps and an extensive collection of Irish newspapers and magazines. *Kildare St., tel. 01/618811. Admission free. Open Mon. 10–9; Tues. and Wed. 2–9; Thurs. and Fri. 10–5; Sat. 10–1.*

⑬ Next to the library you'll find the impressive **Leinster House** (Kildare St., tel. 01/789911), constructed in 1745 as a lavish town house for the duke of Leinster and now the seat of the Dáil Éireann (House of Representatives) and the Seanad Éireann (Senate), which constitute the National Parliament. The public is admitted to the Dáil visitors' gallery only with an introduction from a member of the House; local Tourist Information Offices can make arrangements.

⑭ The **National Museum** is located west of Leinster House. Extensively renovated in recent years, the museum features several rooms devoted to artifacts from prehistoric Ireland, including carved stones, weapons, and jewelry. The Treasury collection, including some of the museum's most renowned pieces, is open permanently. Among the priceless relics on display are the 8th-century Ardagh Chalice, a two-handle silver cup with gold filigree ornamentation; the bronze-coated iron St. Patrick's Bell, the oldest surviving example (5th–8th centuries) of Irish metalwork; the 8th-century Tara Brooch, an intricately decorated piece made of white bronze, amber, and glass; and the 12th-century bejeweled oak Cross of Cong, covered with silver and bronze panels. Another room is devoted to the 1916 Easter Rising and the War of Independence (1919–1921); displays include uniforms, weapons, banners, and a piece of the flag that flew over the General Post Office during Easter Week, 1916. Other exhibits showcase Irish glass, lace, and instruments, including pipes, harpsichords, and 17th- and 18th-century harps.

In contrast to the convoluted late-Victorian architecture of the main museum building with its balustrades and fancy ironwork, the design of the **National Museum Annexe** (located around the corner on Merrion Row, just past the Shelbourne Hotel) is purely functional; it houses temporary shows of Irish antiquities. *National Museum, Kildare St., tel. 01/618811; Annexe, 7–9 Merrion Row, tel. 01/601117. Admission free, except for certain exhibitions. Open Tues.–Sat. 10–5, Sun. 2–5.*

Across from the National Museum, at 30 Kildare Street, a plaque records that Bram Stoker, creator of the 19th-century classic horror story *Dracula,* once lived here, quite peacefully.

Time Out Right opposite the main museum entrance, **Cunningham's** (35A Kildare St., tel. 01/762952), a cozy tearoom and snack bar, serves all kinds of tantalizing sandwiches and salads.

⑮ At the south end of Kildare Street lies **St. Stephen's Green,** a verdant city-center square, with extensive lakeside paths. It was an open common until 1663, but the houses and buildings that now stand on its four sides were not constructed until the late 18th century. (Unfortunately, several of these old structures have been modernized without charm.) Lord Ardiluan, a member of the Guinness brewery family, paid for the space to be laid out as a public park in 1880. The green features flower gardens, formal lawns, a Victorian bandstand, and an ornamental lake that is home to many waterfowl. Among the park's many statues are a memorial to Yeats by Henry Moore, and the Three Fates, a dramatic group of bronze female figures watching over Man's destiny by a fountain.

To see inside one of the fine Georgian houses on the green, head for the **Newman House** on the south side. It was in these two houses that the Catholic University of Ireland was established in 1850, with Cardinal John Henry Newman as its first rector. James Joyce describes turn-of-the-century life at this university in *A Portrait of the Artist as a Young Man.* Recently, University College, which no longer uses these houses, restored them to their original 18th-century splendor. No. 85, the smaller of the two, has exuberant baroque plasterwork inside, while the style of No. 86 is quite different, containing rococo plasterwork, floral swags, and musical instruments. Built in 1765, they are furnished and decorated in period style. *85–86 St. Stephen's Green, tel. 01/757255. Admission: £1 adults, 75p children, students, and senior citizens. Open June–Sept., Tues.–Fri. 10–4:30, Sat. 2–4:30, Sun. 11–2.*

On the north side of the green—referred to in the 18th century as the Beaux Walk—you'll find the imposing Victorian-era **⑯** redbrick **Shelbourne Hotel** (27 St. Stephen's Green, tel. 01/766471), where in a first-floor suite the Irish Free State's constitution was drafted in 1921. A center for Dublin's high society, the Shelbourne is a friendly place despite its grandeur, and nonguests can stop here comfortably for a drink or meal (*see* Lodging, below).

Next to the Shelbourne Hotel is the **Huguenot Cemetery,** the last such burial ground in Dublin, which was used in the late 17th century by French Protestants who had fled persecution in their native land. The gates to the cemetery are rarely open, but you can observe its grounds from the street.

Across the road from the Huguenot Cemetery, in Ely Place, is the Royal Hibernian Academy's exhibition hall, known as the **⑰** **RHA Gallagher Gallery.** This old institution is now housed in one of Dublin's newest spaces, a large, well-lit building; it holds adventurous exhibitions of the best in contemporary art, both from Ireland and abroad. *Ely Pl., off St. Stephen's Green, tel. 01/612558. Admission free. Open Mon.–Wed. and Fri.–Sat. 10–5, Thurs. 10–9, Sun. 2–5.*

From the corner of Merrion Row and Lower Baggot Street, **⑱** turn left onto Upper Merrion Street, where the **Natural History Museum** houses a collection of mounted mammals and birds, with examples of extinct species, including skeletons of prehis-

toric giant deer. *Merrion Sq. W, tel. 01/618811. Admission
free. Open Tues.–Sat. 10–5, Sun. 2–5.*

⑲ The **National Gallery of Ireland,** on Merrion Square West, owes
its existence to William Dargan (1799–1867), who was responsible for building much of Ireland's railway network in the 19th
century (he is honored by a statue on the front lawn). The building was designed by Francis Fowke, who was also responsible
for London's Victoria and Albert Museum. Rated as one of the
best smaller public museums in Europe, the National Gallery
contains more than 2,000 paintings, with a large number representing the Irish School, including the work of Jack B. Yeats,
the brother of W. B. Yeats and considered by many to be one of
Ireland's finest painters. The collection also includes work by
French Impressionists, a small selection of Dutch masters (including some fine Rembrandts), and exceptional paintings from
the 17th-century French, Italian, and Spanish schools.
*Merrion Sq. W, tel. 01/615133. Admission free. Open Mon.–
Wed. and Fri.–Sat. 10–6, Thurs. 10–9, Sun. 2–5.*

⑳ Across from the gallery, you'll come to **Merrion Square,** created
in the late 18th century after the construction of the surrounding homes. This oasis of lawns and flower beds takes you away
from the roar of city traffic. During the famine years of 1845–
1847, soup kitchens were established here to feed starving refugees. The square has formerly been the home of several distinguished Dubliners, including Oscar Wilde's parents, Sir
William and "Speranza" Wilde (No. 1), Irish national leader
Daniel O'Connell (No. 58), and authors W. B. Yeats (Nos. 52
and 82) and Sheridan LeFanu (No. 70). Visitors can walk past
the houses and read the plaques on the house facades, which
identify the former inhabitants. Until 50 years ago, the square
was a fashionable residential area, but today most of the houses
are used for commercial purposes.

At the southeast corner of Merrion Square is another carefully
refurbished and fully furnished 18th-century home, less grand
㉑ than Newman House. **Number Twenty Nine,** as it's known, depicts the elegant lifestyle of the Dublin middle-class between
1790 and 1820, when the house was owned by a wine merchant's
widow. The National Museum of Ireland has re-created the period's style with authentic furniture, paintings, carpets, curtains, painting, wallpapers, and even bell-pulls. The house is
refurbished from basement to attic showing everything from
the kitchen, nursery, and servant's quarters to the formal living areas. *29 Lower Fitzwilliam St., tel. 01/765831. Admission:
free. Open Tues.–Sat. 10–5, Sun. 2–5.*

Tour 2: North City Center

The northern part of the city center beyond the River Liffey—a
mixture of densely thronged shopping streets and run-down
sections of once genteel homes—is less attractive today than
the south city center. But during the 18th century, most of the
upper echelons of Dublin society lived in the Georgian houses
around Mountjoy Square and shopped along Capel Street,
which was lined with pricey shops that sold fine furniture and
silver. However, with the construction of Merrion Square on
the south side (completed in 1764) and the nearby Fitzwilliam
Square (completed in 1825), the city's fashionable social center
switched decisively and permanently from north to south of the

River Liffey. Although some of the illustrious inhabitants in the north city center clung to their houses, this area gradually became more run down over time.

㉒ Off Upper Gardiner Street, **Mountjoy Square,** built in the mid-18th century, once had four sides of elegant terraced houses, but today only the northern side remains intact. Irishman Brian Boru, who led his soldiers to victory against the Vikings in the Battle of Clontarf in 1014, was said to have pitched camp before the confrontation on the site of Mountjoy Square. Playwright Sean O'Casey once lived here at No. 35 and used the square as a setting for *The Shadow of a Gunman.*

㉓ A block and a half north of the square stands the Jesuit **St. Francis Xavier,** one of the city's finest churches in the classical style, begun in 1829, the year of Catholic Emancipation, and completed three years later; the building is designed in the shape of a Latin cross, with a distinctive Ionic portico and an unusual coffered ceiling. The striking faux–green marble high altarpiece, decorated with lapis lazuli, came from Italy. The church appears in James Joyce's story "Grace." *Upper Gardiner St., tel. 01/363411. Admission free. Open daily 8–6.*

A walk west from Mountjoy Square along Gardiner Place and Great Denmark Street leads you to Parnell Square and the **㉔ Hugh Lane Municipal Art Gallery,** built originally as a town house for the earl of Charlemont in 1762 and named after an art benefactor who drowned on the *Lusitania,* which was sunk off the County Cork coast in 1915. The small museum features an impressive collection of paintings and sculpture by 19th- and early 20th-century French and Irish artists and strikingly displayed stained-glass work by Harry Clarke and Evie Hone. *Parnell Sq., tel. 01/741903. Admission free. Open Tues.–Sat. 9:30–6, Sun. 11–5.*

㉕ The **Garden of Remembrance,** which faces the gallery, was opened in 1966 to commemorate all those who died fighting for Irish freedom. The garden has a large plaza at its entrance; steps lead down to the fountain area, which has a sculpture by contemporary Irish artist Oisin Kelly based on the mythological Children of Lir, who were turned into swans. Most of the **㉖** remainder of Parnell Square is occupied by the **Rotunda Maternity Hospital** (Parnell St., tel. 01/730700), founded in 1745 as the first of its kind in Ireland or Britain. The hospital, with a three-story tower and copper cupola, was designed on a grand scale by architect Richard Cassels (1690–1751). Its exquisite chapel features elaborate plasterwork, appropriately honoring motherhood, executed by Bartholomew Cramillion in 1757–1758.

㉗ Parnell Square is also the site of the **Gate** (Cavendish Row, tel. 01/744045), one of Dublin's main theaters. For five decades, from the 1930s to the 1970s, Mícheál MacLiammóir and Hilton Edwards staged many startling and memorable productions here by Irish playwrights and introduced Dublin audiences to foreign writers. Orson Welles and James Mason both performed here early in their careers. Today the Gate continues to mount exciting plays, particularly by young Irish dramatists.

㉘ The **Dublin Writers Museum** opened in 1991 to celebrate Ireland's literary achievements past and present. Besides exhibits relating to Irish writers, the museum has a writers' center where authors can meet informally. *8–11 Parnell Sq., tel. 01/*

722077. Admission: £1 adults, 50p children. Open Mon.–Sat. 10–5, Sun. and bank holidays 2–6.

Parnell Square leads to the top (north) end of **O'Connell Street,** Dublin's most famous thoroughfare. Previously known as Sackville Street, its name was changed in 1924, two years after the setting up of the Irish Free State. After the devastation of the 1916 Easter Rising, the street had to be almost entirely reconstructed, a job that took until the end of the 1920s. The main attraction of the street, Nelson's Pillar, a Doric column towering over the city center and a marvelous vantage point, was blown up by an unknown group in 1966, the year that the 50th anniversary of the Easter Rising was celebrated.

At the corner of Henry and O'Connell streets, you'll see the **29** massive **General Post Office** (known as the **GPO**), with the original facade and Ionic portico designed by the neoclassical architect Francis Johnston in the early 1800s. The building was destroyed during the Easter Rising and was then rebuilt in its original style; it reopened in 1929. Inside the main concourse of the building, the bronze sculpture depicts the dying Cuchulainn, a leader of the Red Branch Knights in Celtic mythology. *O'Connell St., tel. 01/728888. Open Mon.–Sat. 8–8, Sun. 10:30–6:30.*

From the GPO, cross O'Connell Street and walk down Cathe-**30** dral Street to Marlborough Street and the Catholic **Pro-Cathedral,** built between 1815 and 1825. Although the severely classical church design is on a suitably epic scale, the building was never granted full cathedral status. The church's facade with its six-pillared portico is based on the Temple of Theseus in Athens; the interior is modeled after the Grecian-Doric style of St. Philippe du Roule of Paris. The Pro-Cathedral has been used over the years for important state funerals. A Palestrina choir, in which the great Irish tenor John McCormack began his career, sings in Latin here every Sunday at 11. *Marlborough St., tel. 01/745441. Admission free. Open daily 8–6.*

Time Out **Café Kylemore** (1 Upper O'Connell St., at North Earl St., tel. 01/722138) offers a plain menu, but its neo-Viennese decor is charming, with many unusual prints on the walls. **Conway's** (Parnell St., near Upper O'Connell St., tel. 01/732687), the second-oldest pub in Dublin, was founded in 1745; little has changed in it since Victorian times. Among its antique furnishings is a real gem: a 130-year-old eight-day grandfather clock.

Tour 3: Dublin West

Numbers in the margin correspond to points of interest on the Tour 3: Dublin West map.

If you follow the River Liffey upstream from the north city center, keeping to the north bank, the streets along the quays lead **31** you to the classical edifice of the **Four Courts,** the seat of the Irish Law Courts. Built between 1786 and 1802, this massive structure was designed by architect James Gandon, who was also responsible for another Dublin landmark, the **Custom House,** downstream on the same side of the River Liffey. In 1922, during the Irish Civil War, the Four Courts was almost totally destroyed by shelling, and the adjoining Public Records Office was gutted, many of its priceless legal documents de-

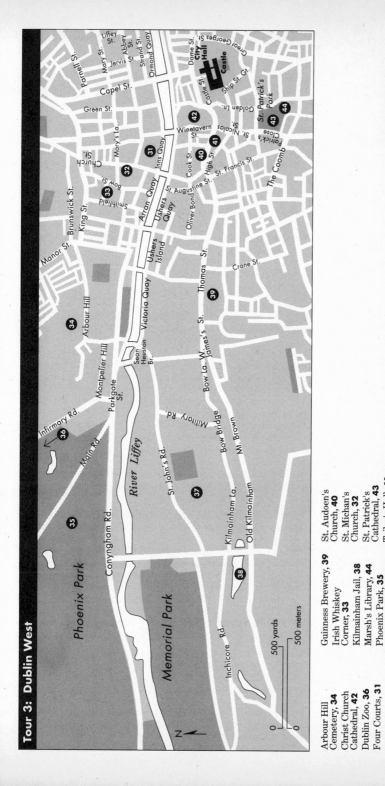

Tour 3: Dublin West

0 — 500 yards
0 — 500 meters

N

Arbour Hill
Cemetery, **34**
Christ Church
Cathedral, **42**
Dublin Zoo, **36**
Four Courts, **31**

Guinness Brewery, **39**
Irish Whiskey
Corner, **33**
Kilmainham Jail, **38**
Marsh's Library, **44**
Phoenix Park, **35**
Royal Hospital, **37**

St. Audoen's
Church, **40**
St. Michan's
Church, **32**
St. Patrick's
Cathedral, **43**
Tailor's Hall, **41**

stroyed, including innumerable family records; restoration to the building's original style took 10 years. Today the stately Corinthian portico and the circular central hall are worth viewing. The upper rotunda of the Four Courts' distinctive lantern dome provides a good view of the city. *Inns Quay, tel. 01/ 725555. Admission free. Open weekdays 10–4.*

32 Around the corner from the Four Courts on Church Street is the Anglican **St. Michan's Church,** dating from 1685 and on the site of an 11th-century Danish church. The church, which is architecturally undistinguished except for its 37-meter (120-foot) bell tower, features an 18th-century organ, supposedly played by Handel, and the Stool of Repentance, the only one still in existence in the city; parishioners who were termed "open and notoriously naughty livers" used it to do public penance. St. Michan's main claim to notoriety, however, is down in the vaults, where the totally dry atmosphere has preserved a number of corpses in a remarkable state of mummification. They lie in open caskets, and strong-hearted visitors can shake hands with a former religious crusader or nun. Most of the preserved bodies are thought to have been Dublin tradespeople. *Church St., tel. 01/724154. Admission free. Open weekdays 10–12:45 and 2–4:45, Sat. 10–1.*

33 From St. Michan's, turn left from Church Street onto May Lane and continue through to the **Irish Whiskey Corner.** Jameson's Whiskey Distillery was built here in 1791. After local distilleries merged in 1966 to form Irish Distillers, part of the old Jameson's complex was converted into the new group's head office and one of the bonded warehouses was turned into a whiskey museum. Visitors can watch a short audiovisual history of the industry, which actually had its origins 1,500 years ago in Middle Eastern perfume making. Mementos of whiskey making on display include antique posters and a large scale model of an old distillery; you can also view a reconstruction of a former warehouse, where the colorful nicknames of former barrel makers are recorded. In the Ball o' Malt bar, you're invited to taste the different blends of Irish whiskey and compare them against bourbon and scotch. *Bow St., tel. 01/725566. Guided tour: £2. Tours weekdays 3:30 PM.*

34 From the whiskey museum, turn right on Bow Street and make a left onto King Street North; proceed to Blackhall Place and then make a left onto Arbour Hill, the location of **Arbour Hill Cemetery,** where the leaders of the 1916 Easter Rising are buried. A total of 14 Irishmen were executed by the British; these included Patrick Pearse, who led the rebellion, and James Connolly, a labor leader wounded in the battle. The burial ground is a simple but formal area, with the names of the dead leaders carved in stone beside an inscription of the proclamation they issued during the uprising. *Arbour Hill. Admission free. Open Mon.–Sat. 9–4:30, Sun. 9:30–12.*

Walk south toward the quays and then west along Parkgate Street, a distance of 1 km (½ mi).

Time Out **Ryans Pub** (Parkgate St., tel. 01/776097) is one of Dublin's last genuine late-Victorian-era pubs; it has changed little since its last (1896) remodeling. Its dark-mahogany bar counters and old-fashioned lamps and *snugs* (small drinking alcoves) create a restful setting.

At the end of Parkgate Street, opposite the bus depot, entrance
35 gates lead to the 1,752 attractive acres of **Phoenix Park,**
Europe's largest public park, with lakes, woods, gardens, and
expansive playing fields. The main road that bisects the park
for 4 km (2½ mi) was laid out by Lord Chesterfield, a lord lieutenant of Ireland, in the 1750s; old-fashioned gas lamps that
line both sides of the road were recently renovated. By the entrance to the park is the People's Garden, a charming and colorful flower garden.

Among the park monuments worth noting are the Phoenix Column, erected by Lord Chesterfield in 1747, and the 60-meter
(198-foot) obelisk, built in 1817 to commemorate the Duke of
Wellington, the Irish general who defeated Napoleon for the
British. A much more recent edifice marks the visit to Ireland
by Pope John Paul II in 1979, when he addressed more than a
million people here. Both the president of Ireland and the U.S.
ambassador have official residences in the park, but neither
building is open to the public. The Garda Siochana (police) has
its headquarters here; a small museum contains many relics of
Irish police history, including old uniforms. *Park: tel. 01/
771156, ext. 2250. Admission free. Open weekdays 9–5, but
phone in advance to confirm.*

36 **Dublin Zoo** may be found on the northern fringes of Phoenix
Park; founded in 1830, it is the third-oldest public zoo in the
world. Many animals from tropical climes are housed in barless
enclosures, while Arctic species swim the lakes, complementing the deer that roam free in the adjoining park. The zoo is one
of the few places in the world where lions will breed in captivi-
ty. The children's corner features goats, guinea pigs, and
lambs. *Tel. 01/771425. Admission: £4 adults, £1.75 children.
Open daily 9:30–sunset.*

Return to the main park entrance and walk east on Parkgate
Street to the Sean Heuston Bridge; cross the River Liffey to
the Heuston Railway Station, continue past the station's main
entrance, cross St. John's Road, and walk on Military Road to
37 the **Royal Hospital** on Kilmainham Lane. Built in the late 17th
century to house military pensioners, it is a replica of Les
Invalides in Paris. After the founding of the Irish Free State in
1922, the building fell into disrepair, but over the last 15 years,
a huge restoration program has returned the whole edifice to
its former glory. The structure consists of four galleries around
a courtyard with a grand dining hall and a chapel with a stucco
ceiling and fine wood carvings. Today the Royal Hospital offers
a series of musical events and houses the **Irish Museum of Modern Art,** a survey of 20th-century Irish and international art
that includes the prestigious Gordon Lambert collection of
Irish contemporary art and the Sidney Nolan collection, featuring recent works by the Irish-Australian artist. The international collection includes work by Picasso and Miro and op
art; among the Irish artists featured are Richard Deacon, Richard Gorman, Dorothy Cross, Sean Scully, Matt Mullican, and
James Colman. *Kilmainham La., tel. 01/718666. Royal Hospital: admission free, but individual shows may have separate
charges. Open Tues.–Sat. 2–5, Sun. noon–5. Guided tours every 30 min on Sun. Museum of Modern Art: Admission to permanent collection free; small charge for special exhibitions.
Open Tues.–Sun. 11–6.*

Immediately beyond the front gates of the Royal Hospital grounds lies **Kilmainham Jail,** a grim, forbidding structure where leaders of the 1916 Easter Rising, including Patrick Pearse and James Connolly, were held before being executed in the prison yard. In the 19th century, other inmates here were the revolutionary Robert Emmet and Charles Stewart Parnell, a leading politician. You can visit the cells, a chilling sight, while the guided tour and a 30-minute audiovisual presentation relate a graphic account of Ireland's political history over the past 200 years from a nationalist viewpoint. *Inchicore Rd., tel. 01/535984. Admission: £1.50. Open June–Sept., daily 11–6; Oct.–May, Wed. and Sun. 2–6.*

From the jail, turn right (east) onto Old Kilmainham, which turns into Mount Brown, James's Street, and then Thomas Street (a 1½-km/1-mi walk). Here you'll reach the vast **Guinness Brewery** complex, the largest brewery in Europe, where a 19th-century **Hop Store** has been skillfully converted into a museum and exhibition space for art shows. An elaborate audiovisual presentation details Guinness's history since the brewery was established on this spot in 1759. The show ends with the curtain rising on the kind of old-fashioned pub, with mahogany decor, mirrors, and snugs, that has become hard to find in modern Dublin. *Guinness Hop Store, Crane St., tel. 01/536700. Admission: £1. Open weekdays 10–3; show every 20 min.*

Return to Thomas Street and continue east for 1 km (½ mi) in the direction of the south city center. Thomas Street becomes Cornmarket and then High Street, where you'll find the Catholic **St. Audoen's Church,** with an elegant classical interior, completed in 1847, and a striking Corinthian pillared portico, added at the end of the 19th century. The church provides a well-produced audiovisual presentation, which tells the story of ancient Ireland before the arrival of the Vikings 1,200 years ago. St. Patrick and the Celtic gods figure prominently in the show. *High St., tel. 01/679–1855. Admission: £1.50. Open daily 10–4:30.*

An alley below the church takes you to the 13th-century archway of the only remaining stretch of Dublin's medieval city wall. South of the church across the road stands **Tailor's Hall,** built in 1706–07; the only surviving guildhall or crafts workers' center in Dublin, the structure is now the headquarters of An Taisce, the Irish National Trust, committed to restoring ancient buildings. Visitors can request to see the exquisite 18th-century interior, especially the main hall with its lofty ceiling, tall Queen Anne windows, and a carved balcony for musicians. The basement bar has an authentic early 18th-century stone fireplace. *Back La., tel. 01/544794. Admission free. Open weekdays 9–5.*

If you return to High Street and walk east, the street quickly becomes Christ Church Place, where you'll reach **Christ Church Cathedral,** one of two Protestant cathedrals in Dublin, built on the site of a Viking wooden church founded in 1038; this church was replaced by a new stone church in 1173, constructed by the Norman invader Strongbow, who is said to be buried here. The cathedral was largely reconstructed from 1871 to 1878 in early Gothic style. Remains from the 12th-century building include the north wall of the nave, the west bay of the choir, and the transepts, featuring fine stonework with pointed arches and supporting columns. *Christ Church Pl., tel. 01/ 778099. Admission free. Open May–Sept., Mon.–Sat. 10–5, Sun. between church services; Oct.–Apr., Tues.–Fri. 10–12:45 and 2:15–4:30, Sun. between services.*

Next walk west from Christ Church Place to Nicholas Street, which turns south into the nearby incline of Patrick Street; this **㊸** leads you to **St. Patrick's,** the national cathedral of the Church of Ireland. Sir Benjamin Guinness, of the brewing family, paid for its renovation in the 1860s. The original building, dedicated in 1192, was an unsuccessful attempt to assert supremacy over Christ Church Cathedral. In the present-day St. Patrick's, a memorial to Jonathan Swift, the author of *Gulliver's Travels,* is located in the south aisle; Swift was dean of the cathedral between 1713 and 1745. Other interesting tributes include the 17th-century Boyle Monument with its numerous painted figures of family members and the monument to Turlough O'Carolan, the last of the Irish bards and one of the country's finest harp players. To the immediate north side of the cathedral is a small park, with statues of many of Dublin's literary figures. *Patrick St., tel. 01/754817. Admission: 80p adults, 30p students. Open Mar.–Oct., weekdays 9–6; Mar.–Apr., Sat. 9–4; May–Oct., Sat. 9–5; Easter–Oct., Sun. 10–11:15 and 12:45–3. Nov.–Feb., weekdays 9:30–12:30 and 1:30–6, Sat. 9–4, Sun. 12:45–3.*

㊹ Near the cathedral entrance is **Marsh's Library,** the oldest public library in Ireland, founded and endowed in 1701 by Narcissus Marsh, the Archbishop of Dublin. Housed in a modest two-story brick Georgian building approached through a small garden, the library stores a priceless collection of 200 manuscripts and 25,000 16th- to 18th-century books; many of these rare volumes are locked inside cages, as are any readers who wish to look at them. In recent years, the library has been restored with great attention to its original architectural details, especially in the book stacks. *St. Patrick's Close, off Patrick St., tel. 01/543511. Admission free. Open May–Sept., weekdays 9–6, Sat. 9–4, Sun. 10–11 and 2:15–3; Oct.–Apr., weekdays 9–12:30 and 1:30–6, Sat. 9–12:30 and 1:30–4, Sun. 10–11 and 2:15–3.*

Tour 4: James Joyce's Dublin

Numbers in the margin correspond to points of interest on the Tour 4: James Joyce's Dublin map.

James Joyce (1882–1941), one of Ireland's greatest 20th-century writers, set his major achievements (*Dubliners, A Portrait of the Artist as a Young Man, Ulysses,* and *Finnegans Wake*) in Dublin; he never wrote about another place. He was, however, unsentimental about his native city, and at one time referred to it as the Center of Paralysis. Joyce spent the first 22 years of his life in Dublin and the last 36 in self-imposed exile, in several locations including Trieste, Paris, and Zurich. Yet he knew and remembered Dublin in such incredible detail that he used to claim that if the city were destroyed, it could be rebuilt in its entirety from his written works, particularly *Ulysses.*

㊺ Begin your tour of Joyce's Dublin in the very heart of the city, on **Prince's Street,** next to the General Post Office. The office of the old and popular *Freeman's Journal* newspaper (published 1763–1924) was located here, but the building was destroyed

Tour 4: James Joyce's Dublin

Bailey Restaurant, **51**

Bella Cohen's
Brothel, **49**

Belvedere College, **47**

Davy Byrne's Pub, **52**

Eccles Street, **46**

James Joyce Cultural
Centre, **48**

Molesworth Street, **53**

National Library, **54**

New Ormond
Hotel, **50**

Prince's Street, **45**

Sweny's
Pharmacy, **55**

during the 1916 Easter Rising. The central character of *Ulysses*, Leopold Bloom, a newspaper advertisement canvasser, worked at the *Freeman's Journal* office. Next, travel northward up O'Connell Street and Parnell Square, into Dorset

46 Street, before turning right, then left into **Eccles Street.** No. 7 no longer exists, but the site is revered by Joycean scholars, since this was the fictional home of Bloom. Cross Dorset Street and walk down Temple Street into Great Denmark Street,

47 where you'll find **Belvedere College** (tel. 01/774795), a well-preserved 18th-century mansion where Joyce studied between 1893 and 1898. You can visit the interior during term time (September–June, excluding holidays). The entrance lobby, the classrooms, the rich Venetian plasterwork, and the staircase with bronze Apollo medallions are worth a look.

48 The **James Joyce Cultural Centre,** off Great Denmark Street at 35 North Great George's Street (tel. 01/731984), is a center for Joycean studies and events related to the author. Though not open to the general public, visitors may phone to hear of lectures and other events organized by the center. The restored 18th-century Georgian town house, once the dancing academy of Professor Dennis J. Maginni, has a library and archives. (Call the Tourist Information Office, tel. 01/747733, for further details.) Turn left at the foot of North Great George's Street and continue through to Parnell Street before turning right into the much redeveloped Lower Gardiner Street. Retrace your steps in the direction of the Custom House, with its green cupola dominating the foot of the street. Take the second turn

49 left, into Railway Street; No. 82 was the site of **Bella Cohen's Brothel,** a key location in Bloom's travels around Dublin on June 16, 1904. This immediate area contained many such houses of ill repute in the early years of this century. From here, return to the city center and travel westward along the

50 quays, toward the Guinness Brewery. The **New Ormond Hotel** (Upper Ormond Quay, tel. 01/721811), an afternoon rendezvous spot for Leopold Bloom, has been restored in recent years, and plaques in the Siren Suite Ballroom and Malachy's Bar note their connections with Joyce's writings. On Bloomsday, June 16 of each year, special Joyce-related events are organized at the hotel.

Return once more to the city center, eastward along the quays to O'Connell Bridge; walk south on Westmoreland and Grafton

51 streets to the **Bailey Restaurant** (tel. 01/773055) on Duke Street, which will be on your left off Grafton. Inside the restaurant, the actual door from No. 7 Eccles Street is carefully pre-

52 served (*see above*). Right across the road from Bailey's is **Davy Byrne's Pub** (tel. 01/711298), another historic Dublin hostelry frequented by Joyce; here Bloom, on his peregrinations, has a glass of burgundy and a Gorgonzola cheese sandwich. Then he leaves the pub and walks to Dawson Street, where he helps a

53 blind man cross the road. He then walks along **Molesworth Street** (which leads eastward) from Dawson Street; next he en-

54 ters the **National Library** (tel. 01/618811; *see* Tour 1: South City Center, *above*), on Kildare Street at the far end of Molesworth Street, where he has a near meeting with Blazes Boylan, his wife's lover. In the library, Bloom looks for a copy of an advertisement.

Walk north on Kildare Street toward the grounds of Trinity College, and head east on Leinster Street. On Lincoln Place, at

55 the back of Trinity College, **Sweny's Pharmacy,** which appears in *Ulysses*, remains close to its original Joycean splendor. No other establishment mentioned by James Joyce in his literary works, whether shop or pub, has changed so little since early this century. Sweny's still has its black and white exterior and atmospheric interior, with its potions and phials. The shop is at the west end of Westland Row, at the other end of which is the Pearse railway station, a stop on the DART electric line.

Four other destinations related to Joyce and his writings are located outside of Dublin's city center:

Brighton Square. From Kildare Street, you can take a 5-km (3-mi) journey by the 15A or 15B bus, or by taxi, to the southern suburb of Rathgar, a genteel neighborhood even today. James Joyce was born at 41 Brighton Square, on February 2, 1882. Joyce spent the first two years of his life here; during the next 20 years, he lived at more than 20 addresses in the city.

James Joyce Martello Tower (Sandycove, tel. 01/280–9265). Sandycove Station on DART (*see* Tour 5: Dublin Southside, *below*).

One Martello Terrace (Bray, Co. Wicklow, tel. 01/286–8407). Bray Station on DART (*see* County Wicklow in Chapter 4, Dublin Environs).

Sandymount Strand (Sandymount). Sandymount Station on DART (*see* Tour 5: Dublin Southside, *below*).

Tour 5: Dublin Southside

Numbers in the margin correspond to points of interest on the Tour 5: Dublin Southside map.

South of City Center Take the 47A bus from Hawkins Street in the city center to the suburb of Rathfarnham, where you may explore the 50-acre **St. 56 Edna's Park,** which features a charming small-scale lake and nature trails. St. Edna's 18th-century house has been turned into a museum commemorating Patrick Pearse, leader of Dublin's 1916 Easter Rising. In the early years of this century, the house was a progressive boys' school, which Pearse and his brother Willie founded. The museum preserves Pearse family memorabilia, documents, and photographs. *Grange Rd., Rathfarnham, tel. 01/934208. Admission to park free. Open daily 10–sunset. Admission to museum free. Open May–June, daily 10–12:30 and 2–6; Sept.–Apr., the museum closes sometime between 3:30 and 5:30, depending on the month. Call ahead.*

Leaving the park, turn on to Grange Road and walk up the hill for about 1 km (½ m), turning left at the T junction and continu-**57** ing for a farther ½ km (¼ mi), as far as **Marlay Park,** an extensive parkland with woodlands and nature walks; it is also the start of Wicklow Way, a well-defined walking route that crosses the Wicklow Mountains for 48 km (30 mi), through some of the most rugged landscapes in Ireland. Marlay Park has a cobbled courtyard, which is home to brightly plumaged peacocks. Surrounding this courtyard are crafts workshops, where visitors are welcome to watch the craftspeople in the process of bookbinding and making jewelry and furniture. *Grange Rd., Rathfarnham, tel. 01/942834. Admission free. Open weekdays 9:30–5.*

Tour 5: Dublin Southside

Dublin Bay

SANDY-MOUNT

Scotsman's Bay

James Joyce Martello Tower

Dun Laoghaire Harbour

Georges St.

DUN LAOGHAIRE

64

63

62

Monkstown Rd.

61

Main

Temple Rd.

BLACKROCK

59

Rock Rd.

60

Booterstown Ave.

Mount Merrion Ave.

N11

Merrion Rd.

Nutley In.

Ailesbury Rd.

58

Stillorgan Rd.

MOUNT MERRION

DONNY-BROOK

Sandford

Milltown Rd.

Dundrum Rd.

Drumartin Rd.

Kilmacud Rd.

Main Sandyford Rd.

Adelaide Rd.

Ranelagh Rd.

RATHMINES

RATHGAR

Churchtown Rd.

CHURCHTOWN

DUNDRUM

Rd.

57

S. Circular Rd.

Grand Canal

Harold's Cross Rd.

Rathmines Rd.

Nutgrove Ave.

RATH-FARNHAM

56

Crumlin Rd.

Clonard Rd.

Terenure Rd.

TERENURE

Rathfarnham Rd.

Ballyboden Rd.

DRIMNAGH

N17

Dunmagh Rd.

Kildare Rd.

Cromwell Rd.

CRUMLIN

Kimmage Rd.

Templeville Rd.

Templeogue Rd.

TEMPLEOGUE

N81

KEY

DART Railway

Stations

N

0   1 mile

0   1 km

Blackrock, **61**
Booterstown, **60**
Chester Beatty Library, **58**
Dalkey, **64**

Dun Laoghaire, **63**
Marlay Park, **57**
Monkstown, **62**
Sandymount Strand, **59**
St. Edna's Park, **56**

Ballsbridge To reach the prestigious suburb of Ballsbridge, take the DART local train to Sydney Parade; the No. 7 or 8 bus from Eden Quay; or the No. 45 bus from Burgh Quay in the city center. From the DART station, walk west on Ailesbury Road to **58** Shrewsbury Road, where you'll reach the **Chester Beatty Library,** which houses one of the most significant collections of Islamic and Far Eastern art in the Western world. Sir Alfred Chester Beatty (1875–1968), a Canadian mining millionaire, donated the collection to Ireland. Among the library's exhibits are clay tablets from Babylon dating from 2700 BC, Japanese color wood-block prints, Chinese jade books, and Turkish and Persian paintings. *20 Shrewsbury Rd., Ballsbridge, tel. 01/ 269–2386. Admission free. Open Tues.–Fri. 10–5, Sat. 2–5. Conducted tours, Wed. and Sat. 2:30.*

Next return east from the museum, walk the length of Ailesbury Road, cross the DART railway line, and continue on **59** Sydney Parade Avenue until you reach **Sandymount Strand.** This beach stretches for 5 km (3 mi) from Ringsend to Booterstown. It was cherished by James Joyce and his beloved from Galway, Nora Barnacle, and figures as one of the settings in *Ulysses.* When the tide recedes, the beach extends for 1½ km (1 mi) from the foreshore, but the tide sweeps in again very quickly. A small park lies between the main Strand Road and the beach. You can take a bracing walk along the 1½-km (1-mi) breakwater at Ringsend, approached by passing the electricity-generating station. Poolbeg Lighthouse stands at the end of this seawall walk. About ½ km (¼ mi) inland from Sandymount Strand is the village of the same name, built round a large green that is lined with small shops. Some of the stores sell antiques, and you can also stop for a drink at one of the plain but cozy pubs. From the green, the No. 2 or 3 bus will take you back to the city center, or you can return by the DART train.

Outer Southern The outer southern suburbs of Dublin offer a choice of attrac-
Suburbs tions with historical and literary associations, enough for several day trips. These destinations can be reached most easily by the DART local train or by car, taking the R118 from the corner of Lower Merrion Street and Merrion Square. Near **60** **Booterstown,** along the R118 on the way south to Blackrock, lies the largest wildlife preserve in the Dublin area. Many fairly rare migratory species of birds, such as curlews, herons, and kingfishers, come to nest here; information boards along the road describe these birds for visitors. Also on this main road you'll pass Glena, the house where Athlone-born John McCormack, the world-famous tenor, died in 1945.

61 Continue on 3 km (2 mi) to **Blackrock,** a bedroom community with a popular shopping center, fine sea views, and swimming. Idrone Terrace, above the DART railway station, provides a view across the bay to Howth Peninsula. The old-fashioned lamps on the terrace were recently renovated.

62 **Monkstown,** 3 km (2 mi) south beyond Blackrock on Temple and Monkstown roads (the R119) to Dun Laoghaire, boasts two architectural curiosities. The first is a strange-looking **Anglican Parish Church** in the main square, built in 1833. Its architect, John Semple, was inspired by two entirely different styles, the Gothic and the Moorish, which blend into an unlikely composite of towers and turrets. The church is only open during Sunday services. About 1 km (½ mi) south of town you'll find the well-preserved ruins of **Monkstown Castle,** a 15th-century edifice with a keep, a gatehouse, and a long wall section, all surrounded by greenery.

63 Once a Protestant stronghold of the old ruling elite, **Dun Laoghaire,** a further 2½ km (1½ mi) beyond Monkstown along Monkstown Crescent (the R119), was once called Kingstown, after the British monarch, King George IV, disembarked for a fleeting visit in 1821. The town reverted to its original Irish name 99 years later. In some of the neo-Georgian squares and terraces behind George's Street, the main thoroughfare, a little of the community's former elitist elegance can still be felt.

Dun Laoghaire has long been known for its great harbor, enclosed by two piers, each 2½ km (1½ mi) long. The harbor was constructed between 1817 and 1859, using granite quarried from nearby Dalkey Hill; the west pier has a rougher surface and is less favored for walking than the east pier, which features a bandstand where musicians play during summer. The workaday business here includes passenger-ship and freight services sailings to Holyhead in north Wales, 3½ hours away. Dun Laoghaire, however, is also a yachting center with the members-only Royal Irish, National, and Royal St. George yacht clubs, all founded in the 19th century, lining the harbor area.

The first railway in Ireland was built from Westland Row (now Pearse Station) in Dublin to Dun Laoghaire, opening in 1834. Much of the original station's entrance and booking hall has been converted into the fine but expensive **Restaurant na Mara** (Railway Station, Harbour Rd., tel. 01/280–6767), a fish restaurant owned and run by the Irish Rail company.

The former Mariners' Church, west of the harbor and across from the Royal Marine Hotel and the People's Park, now houses the **National Maritime Museum.** The former nave of the church makes a strangely ideal setting for such exhibits as the French longboat captured at Bantry, County Cork, in 1796, as part of an aborted French invasion. A particularly memorable exhibit is the old optic from the Baily Lighthouse on Howth Head, across Dublin Bay; the herringbone patterns of glass reflected light across the bay until 20 years ago. *Haigh Terr., Dun Laoghaire, tel. 01/280–0969. Admission: £1. Open May–Sept., Tues.–Sun. 2:30–5:30; Oct.–Apr., weekends 2:30–5:30.*

From the harbor area, **Marine Parade** leads alongside Scotsmans Bay for 1¼ km (¾ mi), as far as the **Forty Foot Bathing Pool,** once a male-only preserve but now sometimes used by brave women.

A few steps away stands the **James Joyce Martello Tower,** originally built in 1804 as one of a series along Ireland's east coast, when Napoleon's invasion seemed imminent. Its first civilian tenant in 1904 was Oliver St. John Gogarty, a medical student who was known for his poetry and ready wit; Joyce spent time with Gogarty at the tower, and described it in the first chapter of *Ulysses,* using his friend as a model for the character of Buck Mulligan. The tower now houses a Joyce Museum, founded in 1962 thanks to Sylvia Beach, the first publisher of *Ulysses,* in Paris. The exhibition hall contains first editions of most of Joyce's works. Joycean memorabilia include his waistcoat, embroidered by his grandmother, and a tie that he gave to Samuel Beckett. The gunpowder magazine stores the Joyce Tower Library, including a death mask made of Joyce on January 13,

1941. *Tel. 01/280–8571 or 01/280–9265. Admission: £1.50. Open Apr.–Oct., Mon.–Sat. 10–1 and 2–5, Sun. 2:30–6; rest of year, by appointment.*

Time Out **Marine Parade** has a choice of fine restaurants serving international cuisine, such as **Les Relais des Mouettes** (tel. 01/280–9873) for classical French cuisine and **Pier 3** (tel. 01/284–2234), a converted house with simply prepared but substantial dishes, such as mignon of pork and grilled minute steak in mustard sauce.

From the James Joyce Tower at Sandycove, walk the short distance to the main Sandycove Road and continue for 1 km (½ mi) **64** to the next seaside village, **Dalkey.** Along Castle Street, its main thoroughfare, you'll observe substantial stone remains, resembling small turreted castles, of two 15th- and 16th-century fortified houses. From the center of the village, walk up the coastal Coliemore Road as far as Coliemore Harbour, where small boats during the summer make the 15-minute crossing to **Dalkey Island,** which is uninhabited except for a herd of goats. The island, which is covered in long grass, has its own Martello tower. Return to the mainland and continue up the hill to Vico Road, where you'll have astounding bay views (similar to those near Italy's Bay of Naples) as far as Bray in County Wicklow. Return to Dalkey Village by Sorrento Road.

Tour 6: Dublin Northside

Numbers in the margin correspond to points of interest on the Tour 6: Dublin Northside map.

Glasnevin Dublin's northern suburbs remain predominantly working class and largely residential but they do offer a few places worth an extra trip. To reach the suburb of **Glasnevin,** drive from the north city center by Lower Dorset Street, as far as the bridge over the Royal Canal. Turn left, go up Whitworth Road, by the side of the canal, for 1 km (½ mi); at its end, turn right onto Prospect Road and then left onto the Finglas Road, the N2. You may also take the No. 40 or 40A bus from Parnell Street, next to Parnell Square, in the north city center.

65 **Glasnevin Cemetery,** on the right-hand side of Finglas Road, is the best-known burial ground in Dublin; it contains the graves of many distinguished Irish leaders, including Eamon De Valera, a founding father of modern Ireland and a former Irish *taoiseach* (prime minister) and president. Other notables interred here include late-19th-century poet Gerard Manley Hopkins and Sir Roger Casement, an Irish rebel hanged for treason by the British in 1916. The cemetery is freely accessible all day.

66 From the eastern side of the cemetery, enter the **National Botanic Gardens,** which date back to 1795 and feature more than 20,000 different varieties of plants, a rose garden, and a vegetable garden. The main attraction is the curvilinear range of greenhouses, more than 124 meters (400 feet) long, designed and built by a Dublin ironmaster, Richard Turner, between 1843 and 1869. The Palm House, with its striking double dome, was built in 1884 and houses orchids, palms, and tropical ferns. In recent times, these buildings have become run-down, but an extensive restoration program is under way. Visitors here can

Tour 6: Dublin Northside

Casino, **67**
Glasnevin Cemetery, **65**
Howth, **70**
Malahide Castle, **71**
National Botanic Gardens, **66**
Newbridge House, **72**
North Bull Island, **68**
St. Anne's Park, **69**

KEY

DART Railway Stations

stroll along the River Tolka. *Glasnevin Rd., tel. 01/374388. Admission free. Open summer, Mon.–Sat. 9–6, Sun. 11–6; winter, Mon.–Sat. 10–4:30, Sun. 11–4:30.*

Marino Casino To reach the Casino in the suburb of Marino by car, take the Malahide Road from Dublin's north city center for 4 km (2½ mi). You can also take a No. 20A or 24 bus to the Casino from Eden Quay in the north city center.

㊐ The **Casino** is one of Dublin's most exquisite, yet also most underrated, architectural landmarks; a former summerhouse that has never had anything to do with gambling, it rests on part of what was once Lord Charlemont's estate. The main grand mansion was demolished in 1921, but the delightful small-scale Palladian-style casino, built between 1762 and 1771 from a plan by William Chambers, was luckily saved. Although it remained in a decayed state for years, it has now been fully restored, complete with ornate fireplaces and authentic period furnishings in the 16 rooms. Outside, four stone lions grace the terrace, while on the roof, gracious urns hide the chimneys. *Malahide Rd., Marino, tel. 01/331618. Admission: £1. Open June–Sept., daily 10–6:30.*

North Bull Island To reach North Bull Island from Dublin's north city center by car, take the Clontarf Road for 4 km (2½ mi) to the causeway that leads out to Bull Wall, a walkway that stretches for 1½ km (1 mi) seawards, as far as the North Bull Lighthouse. Bull Wall

㊈ also extends on the southern end of **North Bull Island,** a 5-km-(3-mi-) long island created in the last century by the action of the tides. With its vast beach and dunes, it serves as a nature conservancy area and an interpretive center that details bird life on the island, including mallards, moorhens, and sandpipers. Telescopes and binoculars are available to rent, and guided tours can be arranged daily. *Center, tel. 01/338341. Open daily 9–6.*

The most northerly causeway from the island, halfway along the inland side, leads to the main James Larkin Road, which at

㊉ this point fronts **St. Anne's Park.** The green area features extensive rose gardens, with many prize species, and woodland walks. The park is freely accessible all day.

Howth From Dublin, you can easily get to Howth by the DART train, which takes about 30 minutes, or by the No. 31B bus from Lower Abbey Street in the city center. By car, take the Howth Road from the north city center for 16 km (10 mi) to Howth.

㊐ **Howth,** a fishing village set at the foot of a long peninsula, was an island inhabited as long ago as 3250 BC. Its name is derived from the Norse *hoved*, meaning head. The village served as the point for the sea crossing to Holyhead in north Wales between 1813 and 1833, but it was then superseded by the newly built harbor at Kingstown (now Dun Laoghaire), on the other side of Dublin Bay. Today, Howth Harbour is home to an extensive fishing fleet, and it also features a new marina. Both arms of the harbor pier form extensive walks. **Ireland's Eye,** an island with a prominent craglike profile, is separated from the harbor by a channel nearly 1½ km (1 mi) wide. In calm weather, local boatmen make the crossing to the island, where visitors will find an old stone church on the site of a 6th-century monastery and also a Martello tower dating back nearly two centuries.

At the King Sitric Restaurant on the East Pier (*see* Dining, *below*), a 2½-km (1½-mi) cliff walk begins, leading to the white **Baily Lighthouse,** which was built in 1814. At times, the cliff path is narrow, with sheer drops to the sea, but the views out over the Irish Sea are very rewarding. The lighthouse, approached by a footpath on a narrow spit of land, may be visited by obtaining written permission in advance from the Commissioners for Irish Lights (Lower Pembroke St., Dublin 2, tel. 01/682511). From the car park above the lighthouse, you'll have access to perhaps the best views in the Dublin area, over the entire bay as far south as Dun Laoghaire, Bray, and the north Wicklow coast. Much of Dublin can also be seen.

North of the lighthouse at Howth Summit, you can take a local bus to complete the circuit of the peninsula. The 5½-km (3½-mi) journey takes about 10 minutes. Just before the DART station at Howth, disembark for the **Transport Museum.** The star of the collection here is the open-topped Hill of Howth tram. Until 1959, a tram service ran from the railway station in Howth, over the summit and back down to the station. Volunteers have spent several years restoring the tram, which stands alongside other unusual vehicles, such as old horse-drawn bakery vans. *Tel. 01/480831. Admission: £1. Open weekends and public holidays 2–5.*

Next door to the museum lie the **Howth Castle Gardens,** at the rear of the Deerpark Hotel. The rambling castle, which dates back to 1464 and has been much altered in the intervening centuries, is not open to the public. However, visitors can revel in the beautiful gardens. A formal garden with high beech hedges was laid out in the early 18th century, and the rhododendron garden boasts many rare varieties, which can be seen in full flower during April, May, and June. The grounds also feature the ruins of a tall, square 16th-century castle and a Neolithic dolmen (a prehistoric free-standing structure made from boulders). *Tel. 01/322624. Admission free. Open daily 8–sunset.*

Malahide To reach Malahide by car from Dublin, drive from the north city center on the R107 for 14½ km (9 mi). You can also get to Malahide by taking a train from Connolly Station, Dublin, which runs every hour and takes about 20 minutes. A bus to Malahide also leaves from Talbot Street, near Connolly Station; while service is more frequent (every 15 minutes), the ride takes about an hour.

71 Southwest of **Malahide** village stands **Malahide Castle,** which was occupied by the Anglo-Irish and aristocratic Talbot family from 1185 until 1976, when it was sold to the Dublin County Council. The great expanse of parkland around the castle includes a botanical garden with more than 5,000 species and varieties of plants, all clearly labeled. The castle itself is a combination of styles and periods; the earliest section, the three-story tower house, dates from the 12th century. The medieval Great Hall is the only one in Ireland that is preserved in its original form, while the National Portrait Gallery features many fine portraits of the Talbot family and 18th- and 19th-century Irish notables. Other rooms are well-furnished with authentic 18th-century pieces. *Malahide, Co. Dublin, tel. 01/845-2655. Admission: £2.35 adults, £1.15 children. Open weekdays 10–5, weekends 2–5.*

If you're driving, continue from Malahide through Swords on
the coastal road (the R106) for 8 km (5 mi), turning off the N1
road as signposted to **Newbridge House** in Donabate. (You can
also travel from Malahide to Donabate by train, which takes
about 10 minutes. From the Donabate train station, the walk to
the Newbridge House grounds takes 15 minutes.) This 18th-
century mansion, now publicly owned, features its original furnishings, and its drawing room is considered to be one of the
best examples of Georgian domestic design in Ireland. The
kitchens of the house are furnished with their original utensils,
while in the courtyard, visitors find crafts workshops and some
examples of old-style transportation, such as coaches. Beyond
the walled garden are innumerable acres of parkland and an
animal farm. *Donabate, Co. Dublin, tel. 01/843–6534. Admission: £2.10 adults, £1 children. Open Apr.–Oct., weekdays
10–5, Sun. and bank holidays 2–6; Nov.–Mar., Sun. and bank
holidays 2–5.*

Dublin for Free

Bank of Ireland (College Green, tel. 01/776801) (*see* Tour 1:
South City Center, *above*).
Dunsink Observatory, north of Phoenix Park, is one of the oldest in the world, dating back to 1783. A small museum section
features astronomical instruments. As the location is isolated,
visitors are recommended to either drive there or take a taxi.
*Castleknock, Dublin, tel. 01/387911. Open Mar.–Aug., 1st and
3rd Sat. of the month, 8–10 PM.*
Guinness Hop Store (Crane St., off Thomas St., tel. 01/536700).
Visitors to the Hop Store can enjoy a complimentary half-pint
of Guinness stout, brewed in Dublin since 1759, at the ground-
floor bar (*see* Tour 3: Dublin West, above).
Four Courts (Inns Quay) (*see* Tour 3: Dublin West, *above*).
The **Irish Stock Exchange,** though now computerized, has a delightfully old-fashioned air compared with that of Wall Street.
Visitors can take a seat in the tiny spectators' gallery. *28
Anglesea St., opposite Blooms Hotel, tel. 01/778808. Gallery
open to the public weekdays 9:30–10:30 and 2–2:45.*
Lunchtime concerts are presented free during the summer by
brass bands and other musical ensembles in the bandstand in
the heart of St. Stephen's Green (*see* Tour 1: South City Center,
above) and in other parks around the city, such as Herbert Park
in Ballsbridge.
Marlay Park Craft Courtyard (Grange Rd., Rathfarnham, tel.
01/942834) (*see* Tour 5: Dublin Southside, *above*).
Rathborne's Candle Factory (East Wall Rd., tel. 01/743515 or
01/749222), Ireland's oldest candle making firm, dates back to
1488. You can make an appointment to watch the candle making
process.
Tower Design Centre (Pearse St., tel. 01/775655) (*see* Shopping,
below).

What to See and Do with Children

Dublin Zoo (Phoenix Park, tel. 01/771425) (*see* Tour 3: Dublin
West, *above*).
Fry Model Railway is a museum on the grounds of Malahide
Castle, 16 km (10 mi) north of the city, offering a unique collec-
tion of models of Irish trains from their introduction in 1834 un-
til the present day. They are displayed on an authentic layout

built by a master craftsman, Tom Tighe, and feature city landmarks such as the River Liffey and the Hill of Howth. An hourly train runs from Dublin's Connolly Station to Malahide. *Tel. 01/452337. Admission: £2.25 adults, £1.15 children. Open weekdays 10–5, Sat. 11–6, Sun. 2–6.*

Lambert Puppet Theatre (Clifton La., Monkstown, Co. Dublin, tel. 01/280–0974) stages regular puppet shows and also has a puppetry museum. Visitors can take the DART train from the city center to the Monkstown and Seapoint stations.

Marlay Park (Grange Rd., Rathfarnham, tel. 01/942834), on the southern fringes of the city, provides a free ride for children every Saturday 3–6 PM, on the model steam railway. The No. 47B bus from Hawkins Street in the city center stops outside the park (*see* Tour 5: Dublin Southside, *above*).

Museum of Childhood, located in a large 19th-century house, has a fascinating collection of dolls and toys. *20 Palmerstown Park, Rathmines, tel. 01/973223. Admission: £1 adults, 75p children under 12. Open July–Aug., Wed. and Sun. 2–5:30; rest of year, Sun. 2–5:30. Closed Oct.*

The **National Wax Museum** is Ireland's only such museum, accommodating more than 100 wax replicas. A favorite with many children is the Chamber of Horrors. *Granby Row, tel. 01/726340. Admission: £2.50 adults, £1.50 children. Open Mon.–Sat. 10–5:30, Sun. noon–5:30.*

Newbridge House (Donabate, Co. Dublin, tel. 01/843–6534) features Tara's Palace, a doll's house that was made to raise funds for children's charities. The palace has 25 rooms, all fully furnished in miniature. The exterior of the doll's house is based on the facades of three great Irish houses—Carton, Castletown, and Leinster (*see* Tour 6: Dublin Northside, *above*).

Shopping

Dublin's central shopping area, from O'Connell to Grafton streets, is the best place in Ireland for concentrated general and specialty shopping, at prices competitive with most other European countries. The big department stores stock the internationally renowned fashion lines and accessories, while alongside them stand small, owner-managed boutiques that make shopping in the city a personalized and pleasurable event. Prices can be higher in the smaller shops, but the department stores are less likely to stock specifically Irish crafts lines.

Shopping in central Dublin can mean pushing through crowds, especially in the afternoons and on weekends. Most large shops and department stores are open Monday–Saturday 9–6. While department stores are closed on Sundays, most smaller specialty shops stay open Sunday 10–6. Shops with later closing hours are noted below.

Shopping Districts

O'Connell Street The main thoroughfare of the city offers perhaps too many fast-food outlets, but it also has some worthwhile stores. One of Dublin's largest department stores, Clery's, faces the General Post Office (GPO), and on the same side of the street as the post office is Eason's, another big department store.

Henry Street Running westward from O'Connell Street, this street features Arnotts department store and a host of smaller specialty stores

Dublin Shopping

KEY

AE American Express Office

Arnotts, Grafton St., **9**
Arnotts, Henry St., **2**
Best of Irish, **11**
Blarney Woollen Mills, **20**
Brown Thomas, **13**
Claddagh Records, **7**
Clery's, **4**
Dublin Woollen Company, **6**
Eason's, **3**
Fred Hanna's, **19**

Gael Linn, **24**
Greene's, **23**
HMV, **14**
Hodges Figgis, **17**
Kevin & Howlin, **18**
The Kilkenny Shop, **22**
Marks & Spencer, Grafton St., **15**

Marks & Spencer, **1**
Powerscourt Townhouse Centre, **8**
Royal Hibernian Way, **16**
St. Stephen's Green Centre, **12**
Switzers, **10**
Tierneys, **12**
Tower Design Centre, **25**
Waterstone's, **21**
The Winding Stair, **5**

selling records, footwear, and fashion. Henry Street's continuation, Mary Street, has a branch of Marks & Spencer.

Grafton Street Dublin's main shopping street is now closed to vehicles for most of the day. Two substantial department stores face each other here, while the rest of the street is taken up by smaller shops, many of them branches of international chains, such as Benetton, Next, and Principles. Smaller streets off Grafton Street, especially Duke Street, South Anne Street, and Chatham Street, have interesting crafts and fashion shops.

Francis Street The new hub of Dublin's antiques trade, this street and surrounding areas such as the Coombe offer a concentration of shops where you can browse at will. The largest shop in the district is Cooke's (79 Francis St., tel. 01/542057), a veritable emporium of antiques of all ages and conditions. The smaller shops are more specialized. With a whole network of dealers, if what you want cannot be found, you will be quickly passed along the line to someone who carries what you seek. This area in the Liberties, the oldest part of the city, has largely replaced the quays upstream from O'Connell Bridge as the chief source of antiques.

Specialty Shopping Centers

Blackrock (Blackrock, Co. Dublin) is technically outside of Dublin's city center, but it deserves special mention as one of the most customer-friendly shopping centers around. It's built on two levels, looking onto an inner courtyard, with the giant Superquinn Center, cafés, and restaurants. Blackrock can be reached conveniently on the DART train line.

Powerscourt (S. William St.), a fashionable town house built in 1771, housed a wholesale textile company for many years until it was updated nearly 15 years ago. The interior courtyard has been thoroughly refurbished and roofed over; on the dais at ground-floor level, live piano music is often heard. Two floors of galleries have a maze of small crafts shops interspersed with coffee shops and restaurants.

Royal Hibernian Way (between S. Anne and Duke Sts., off Dawson St., tel. 01/679–5915), a small development, stands on the former site of the two-centuries-old Royal Hibernian Hotel, a coaching inn that was demolished in 1983. The stylish shops are small in scale and include a branch of Leonidas, the Belgian chocolate firm.

St. Stephen's Green Centre (NW corner of St. Stephen's Green), Dublin's largest and most ambitious shopping center, resembles a giant greenhouse, with ironwork in the Victorian style. On three floors overlooked by a vast clock, the 100 mostly small shops sell a variety of crafts, fashions, and household goods.

Tower Design Centre (Pearse St., tel. 01/775655) is the most imaginative of Dublin's crafts centers, fashioned from an 1862 sugar-refinery tower. Taken over in 1978 by Ireland's Industrial Development Authority, the tower now houses more than 35 separate crafts firms. On the ground floor, visitors can stop at workshops devoted to heraldry, stained glass, and Irish pewter; the sixth floor features hand-painted silks, handknits, and silver jewelry.

Department Stores

Arnotts has two stores; its main one on Henry Street (tel. 01/ 721111) has three levels. On the top floor, the exhibition hall often has unusual art shows with a Dublin theme. The other store on Grafton Street (tel. 01/721111) concentrates exclusively on fashion.

Brown Thomas (Grafton St., tel. 01/679–5666) is Dublin's most elegantly decorated department store, with many international fashion labels on sale.

Clery's (O'Connell St., tel. 01/786000) has four floors of merchandise; the ground floor has a *bureau de change*.

Eason's (O'Connell St., tel. 01/733811) is a multipurpose store with four floors. The basement, with its rows of souvenirs, and the ground floor, with an especially large book section, are particularly worth browsing in.

Marks & Spencer has its main store on Mary Street (tel. 01/ 728833) with a larger range of fashions and foods than its three-story shop on Grafton Street (tel. 01/679–7855).

Switzers (Grafton St., tel. 01/776821) remains a middle-of-the-road department store; the ground floor carries a good selection of Royal Doulton porcelain, Wedgwood china, and Waterford crystal.

Specialty Shops

An increasing number of Irish-made crafts and souvenir lines reflect an increasing demand by visitors for specifically Irish goods. Some newer specialty shops sell nothing else.

Books   Books are ideal presents from Ireland. With nearly 1,000 titles now published a year in Ireland, the breadth and choice of material is quite impressive. The range of texts is particularly wide in relation to Irish history and travel and the production quality of such titles compares very favorably with such books published outside Ireland.

Fred Hanna's (27 Nassau St., tel. 01/771255) sells old and new books, with a good choice of travel and Irish books.

Greene's (Clare St., tel. 01/762544) carries an extensive range of secondhand volumes.

Hodges Figgis (54 Dawson St., tel. 01/774754) stocks 1½ million books on three floors.

Waterstone's (7 Dawson St., tel. 01/679–1260), a large branch of a British chain, has two floors featuring a fine selection of Irish books.

The Winding Stair (40 Lower Ormond Quay, tel. 01/733292) sells second-hand books and a café that overlooks the River Liffey.

CDs, Records,   An increasing amount of Irish-recorded material, covering tra-
Tapes   ditional folk music, country and western, rock, and even a smattering of classical music, is now available on records, compact discs, and tapes. **HMV** (65 Grafton St., tel. 01/679–5334; and 18 Henry St., tel. 01/732899) is one of the larger record shops in town. **Claddagh Records** (2 Cecilia St., tel. 01/679–3664) and **Gael Linn** (26 Merrion Sq., tel. 01/767283) specialize in traditional Irish music and Irish-language recordings.

China, Crystal,   Ireland is synonymous with Waterford crystal, which is avail-
Ceramics   able in a wide range of products, including relatively inexpensive items such as ashtrays or sets of glasses. But other lines

are now gaining recognition, such as Cavan, Galway, and Tipperary crystal. At **Dublin Crystal** (Carysfort Ave., Blackrock, Co. Dublin, tel. 01/288–7932), visitors can watch the crystal being cut. The best city-center retail outlets are **Blarney Woollen Mills** (tel. 01/710068) and **The Kilkenny Shop** (tel. 01/777066), both on Nassau Street, and **Best of Irish** (Westbury Hotel, Harry St., tel. 01/679–1233). The above outlets are also good for Irish-made ceramics, such as Belleek, Galway, and Donegal Parian. **Tierneys** (St. Stephen's Green Centre, tel. 01/782873) carries a good selection of crystal and china.

Irish Tweeds Suits and other garments, such as skirts for women and jackets for men, come ready-made in this durable and popular cloth. It can also be bought by the length for making your own clothes. The tweed on sale in Dublin comes from two main sources, Donegal and Connemara; labels inside the garments guarantee their authenticity. The following are the largest retailers of Irish tweeds in the city: **Dublin Woollen Company** (Metal Bridge Corner, tel. 01/775014); **Kevin & Howlin** (31 Nassau St., tel. 01/770257); **Blarney Woollen Mills** (College Park House, Nassau St., tel. 01/710068); and **The Kilkenny Shop** (Nassau St., tel. 01/777066).

Outdoor Markets

Dublin has a number of open-air markets, selling mostly men's and women's fashions. **Moore Street** is open from Mondays to Saturdays, 9–6; stalls lining both sides of the street sell fruits and vegetables. The traditional Dublin repartee here is renowned in the city. Other open markets are only open at the weekends. A variety of bric-a-brac is sold at the **Liberty Market** on Meath Street, open on Fridays and Saturdays, 10–6, and Sundays, 12–5:30. The indoor **Christchurch Market,** opposite St. Audeon's Church, is open Saturdays and Sundays, 10–5; come here for antiques and bric-a-brac.

Hotel Shops

Several of the leading hotels have shops. The **Berkeley Court** (Lansdowne Rd., Ballsbridge, tel. 01/601711) features a crafts shop and boutique that is open all year, adjoined by a branch of Weir's, the Grafton Street jewelers. The Irish gift shop and boutique in the adjacent **Jury's** (Northumberland Rd., tel. 01/605000) stocks a wide selection of Irish tweeds and crystalware. The **Burlington** (Upper Leeson St., tel. 01/605222) has a small crafts shop with pottery and jewelry.

Sports, Fitness, and Beaches

Participant Sports

Bicycling Dublin streets have no special lanes for bicycles, but the flat countryside to the north and the west of Dublin and the mountains to the south are ideal territories for cycling. Bicycles can be rented for around £25 a week, with an equivalent amount charged for deposit. Nearly 20 firms in the Dublin region rent bicycles; Tourist Information Offices have a full list. Some of the best firms include **Joe Daly** (Lower Main St., Dundrum, tel. 01/298–1485), **McDonald's** (38 Wexford St., tel. 01/752586), and **Ryan's** (115 Upper Dorset St., tel. 01/305090).

Bowling Bowling continues to be a popular sport in Dublin; two kinds are played locally. The sedate, outdoor variety is played at a dozen outdoor areas; among the most attractive of these are **Herbert Park** (Ballsbridge, tel. 01/269–5637) and **Moran Park** (Dun Laoghaire, tel. 01/280–1179). The city has three indoor bowling centers: **Crumlin Super Bowl** (Crumlin Rd., tel. 01/559659), **Dundrum Bowl** (Dundrum, tel. 01/298–0209), and **Stillorgan Bowl** (Stillorgan, tel. 01/288–1656).

Fitness Centers Two major fitness centers in the Dublin vicinity are **Fitzwilliam** (Appian Way, tel. 01/603988), a privately owned club offering a swimming pool, 10 tennis courts, six squash courts, a gym, and a sauna; and **RiverView Sports Club** (Beech Hill, Clonskeagh, tel. 01/830322), with a full gymnasium and sauna facilities. Both clubs offer temporary memberships.

Golf The Dublin region is an idyllic place for golfers, with a total of 26 18-hole courses and around 15 nine-hole courses, with several more in the development stage. Major 18-hole courses include **Deer Park** (Howth, tel. 01/322624), with appealing views of the water; **Elm Park** (Donnybrook, tel. 01/693438), in a south city suburb location, but with a rural ambience; **Foxrock** (Torquay Rd., tel. 01/289–3992), in an exclusive residential area; **Newlands** (Clondalkin, tel. 012/592903), an inland course west of Dublin; **Portmarnock** (Portmarnock, tel. 01/324674), one of Ireland's premier courses, situated above a beach northeast of Dublin city center and host to several international tournaments; **St. Margaret's** (St. Margaret's, Co. Dublin, tel. 01/361897), a championship parkland course 10 minutes north of the airport, is one of the area's newest courses; **Sutton** (Sutton, tel. 01/323013), a seaside course north of Dublin; and **Woodbrook** (Bray, tel. 01/282–4799), south of Dublin city center, with stunning mountain views and sea breezes.

Horseback Riding About 20 riding stables in the greater Dublin area have horses for hire by the hour or the day, for novices and experienced riders. A few of these stables also operate as equestrian centers with full tuition facilities. Some major stables in the vicinity include **Ashton Equestrian Center** (Castleknock, tel. 01/383236), **Castleknock Riding Center** (Castleknock, tel. 01/201104), and **Riding and Driving Club** (Willow Rd., Dundrum, tel. 01/298–6112).

Jogging Joggers can enjoy running in Dublin's 40 parks and open squares and along the footpaths of the city's main roads after 6 PM, when traffic has become less heavy. The south city center around Merrion Square is ideal for the sport, but only after business hours and during weekends.

Squash Dublin has about 10 privately owned squash centers; **Squash Ireland** (tel. 01/280–1515) runs four main centers in various city locations.

Swimming Dublin has 12 public pools, but only two can be recommended to visitors, at **Townsend Street** (off Tara St., tel. 01/770503) and **Williams Park** (Rathmines, tel. 01/961275). **Fitzwilliam** (Appian Way, tel. 01/603988), a private fitness club, features a fine pool, and offers temporary memberships. Privately owned pools open to the public for a small fee are located at **Dundrum**

Family Recreation Center (Meadowbrook, Dundrum, tel. 01/298–0183), **Fitzpatrick's Killiney Castle Hotel** (Killiney, tel. 01/285–1533), **Jury's Hotel** (Ballsbridge, tel. 01/605000), **St. Vincent's** (Navan Rd., tel. 01/384906), and **Terenure College** (Templeogue Rd., tel. 01/908822). For hardier spirits, there is year-round sea swimming at the **Forty Foot Bathing Pool** in Sandycove, County Dublin. Traditionally open only to men, it now admits women.

Tennis   Tennis is one of Dublin's most popular participant sports, and some public parks have excellent tennis facilities that are open to visitors. Among these are **Bushy Park** (Terenure, tel. 01/900320), **Herbert Park** (Ballsbridge, tel. 01/684364), and **St. Anne's Park** (Dollymount, tel. 01/313697); these parks each have six courts. Several private tennis clubs are open to visitors, such as **Donnybrook** (Brookvale Rd., tel. 01/269–2838), with six courts; **Fitzwilliam** (Appian Way, tel. 01/603988), with eight outdoor and two indoor courts; and **Kilternan Tennis Centre** (Kilternan Golf and Country Club Hotel, Kilternan, tel. 01/295–3729), with four outdoor and four indoor courts. For more information, contact the **Irish Lawn Tennis Association** (22 Upper Fitzwilliam St., tel. 01/610117).

Spectator Sports

Football   Although football, played in Ireland with a soccerlike ball, is the country's latest big-time sport, following some impressive international wins, facilities for watching it are not so ideal. **Dalymount Park,** north of the city center, is the main center for international matches.

Gaelic Games   The traditional Gaelic games of Ireland, including football and hurling, still attract a large following with intensely exciting big national matches, full of roaring crowds as they cheer on their county teams; games are held at **Croke Park,** the main stadium, located just north of the city center. For details of matches, contact the **Gaelic Athletic Association** (Croke Park, tel. 01/363222).

Horse Racing   Horse racing is one of the great sporting loves of the Irish; nothing attracts the crowds like a race meeting. The sport is closely followed, with keen interest in betting, but the social side of attending racing is also important to Dubliners. The main course in Dublin is **Leopardstown** (tel. 01/289–3607), an ultramodern course on the south side. In the greater Dublin region, other courses include **Fairyhouse** (Co. Meath, tel. 01/256167) and **Curragh** (tel. 045/41205), west of Dublin, a setting for classic races on the vast Curragh plain.

Rugby   International rugby matches are staged at the vast **Lansdowne Road Stadium,** normally during the winter and spring. Local matches are played every weekend, also during the winter and spring. For details, contact the **Irish Rugby Football Union** (62 Lansdowne Rd., tel. 01/684601).

Beaches

The immediate Dublin area has two main beaches. On the north side of the city lies **Bull Island,** created over the years by the action of the tides and offering an almost 3-km- (2-mi-) long stretch of fine sand. The No. 30 bus from Lower Abbey Street stops by the walkway to the beach. The main beach for swimming on the south side of the city is situated at **Killiney**, 13 km (8 mi) south of the city center; this shingly beach stretches for 3 km (2 mi). The DART train station is right by the beach. Much nearer the city center, **Sandymount Strand** is a long expanse of fine sand where the tide goes out nearly 3 km (2 mi), but it is not suitable for swimming or bathing because the tide races in so fast. The strand also can be reached easily by the DART train.

Dining

By Georgina Campbell

A resident of Howth in County Dublin, Georgina Campbell is the food writer for Dublin's The Sunday Press *and the author of* Classic Irish Recipes *and the soon to be published* Meals For All Seasons.

Until recently, most Irish people thought of going out for a meal as a treat reserved for special occasions, such as birthdays and anniversaries, and the most likely dining choice was usually the local hotel restaurant. During the last two decades, however, Ireland has experienced a gastronomic revolution. A new interest in dining out has paved the way for smaller, more individualized restaurants to do well, often in the well-tried French tradition of family ownership, with a chef-patron overseeing every detail. Many of these chefs have studied abroad and been influenced by recent trends; a disproportionately high number of recommended restaurants can be described as French. Nevertheless, although nouvelle cuisine will undoubtedly have a long-term effect on presentation, regional food is making a comeback, which is a positive trend. Traditional Irish dishes used to be thought too ordinary for restaurant menus, but talented young chefs are now keen to revive them, and, indeed, to demonstrate the goodness of Irish ingredients in any way possible. The Green movement is also on Ireland's side, with the potential of unpolluted Irish produce at last being properly valued.

Not many restaurants in Dublin have yet had the courage to specialize entirely in traditional Irish food, but two establishments reviewed below that concentrate on Irish cuisine— Oísins and Gallagher's Boxty House—are excellent in their own fashion. Meanwhile, even what is probably the smartest Dublin restaurant, Restaurant Patrick Guilbaud, at least makes a gesture (albeit more Gallic than Gaelic) toward regional specialties.

The hotels, conscious of having lost their dining business to smaller restaurants, are fighting back, creating fine gourmet restaurants, such as the Aisling at the Shelbourne, the Kish at Jury's, the Berkeley Room at the Berkeley Court, the Russell Room at the Westbury, and now the Alexandra at the new Conrad/Hilton. Yet despite the improved standards at these places, they still tend to lack atmosphere and generally aren't worth the price compared to the independent restaurants. Getting good value for your money is, in fact, a big problem when dining in Ireland. In a comparable British city, lively ethnic restaurants provide above-average meals at reasonable prices, but the ones that exist in Dublin tend to be at the top end of the market. Still, good and less expensive restaurants are starting to fill in the gaps.

Situated as it is beside the sea and with easy access to fresh fish from all around the coast, Dublin offers several places to eat where seafood is the specialty. These restaurants feature not only the traditional cockles and mussels (although these dishes are reappearing on menus) but also wild salmon and oysters from the clear Atlantic waters off the west coast; deep-sea fish trawled off the Donegal coast and the Irish Sea; and lobsters, crabs, and more unusual creatures, such as sea urchins, from rocky coastal waters. Pork, bacon, lamb, and beef still provide the backbone for such traditional dishes as Dublin coddle, Irish stew, and corned beef with cabbage, but game, such as venison and quail, has also increased in popularity. The biggest culinary success story of the last decade has to be the growth of the farmhouse cheese industry: Whenever you see Irish farmhouse cheese on the menu, make a point of trying it; you'll now find dozens of cheeses from which to choose.

Dining hours in Dublin are much the same as elsewhere in Europe, with the main rush at lunchtime from 1 to 2 and at dinner from 8 to 9. VAT (value added tax) will automatically be added to your bill—a 10% tax on food, a 25% tax on drinks. Check to see, however, if service has been included before paying. If so, it can be paid with a credit card and there is no need to leave a tip. If not, it is more considerate to the staff to pay the main bill by card but leave the tip (10%–15%) in cash.

Highly recommended restaurants are indicated by a star ★.

Category	Cost*
Very Expensive	over £20
Expensive	£15–£20
Moderate	£10–£15
Inexpensive	under £10

per person, without tax (10%), service, or drinks

City Center

Very Expensive

Celtic Mews. Turn off busy Baggot Street under an archway and, immediately on your right, you'll find this long-established oasis of calm in a Georgian mews. Over the years, the chefs have successfully blended classical French and Irish cooking styles. Despite the elegance of the setting—a deep wine-colored background sets off a collection of fine antiques, as black-tied waiters provide full silver service at polished or white-clothed tables—the atmosphere is cozy and informal. The cuisine tends toward richness; if you enjoy a bit of showmanship, try the Celtic filet mignon, cooked at the table and served with a mushroom-and-tomato sauce with whiskey and cream. Simpler tastes will be satisfied with an upscale version of traditional Irish stew, made with center loin lamb chops. If you seek privacy, ask for one of the banquette-style tables. *109A Lower Baggot St., tel. 01/760796. Reservations advised. Dress: casual but neat. AE, DC, MC, V. Dinner only. Closed Sun., bank holidays, Easter weekend, Christmas.*

L'Ecrivain. Set in a basement in the heart of Georgian Dublin, this traditional French restaurant is within pleasant walking distance of St. Stephen's Green. Derry Clarke, the owner-chef, has steadily built up its reputation as one of the city's best and most enduring eating places and he and the younger members of his staff have won numerous prizes at international culinary competitions. It's a small and cozy restaurant (seating only 34), but the menu and wine list are both generous and wide-ranging. The table d'hôte menus, especially at dinner, provide

Dublin Dining

excellent variety and value—quality seasonal ingredients are cooked with care and imagination. Try one of the unusual first course salads followed, perhaps, by game when in season. Dessert is a specialty; save room for it. *112 Lower Baggot St., tel. 01/611919. Reservations advised (required on weekends). Jacket required; jacket and tie suggested. AE, DC, MC, V. Closed Sat. lunch, Sun.*

Number 10. This elegant new restaurant in the basement of the lovely Longfield's Hotel comprises two Georgian townhouses that have been converted into a small hotel and decorated with period furnishings. Imagination has been used to create a bower-like antechamber in what was once a coal bunker. The main dining room is decorated in warm neutral colors and glows in the light of an open fire. Tables are set with white linen cloths and napkins and fine modern crystal. Although the place is a popular lunch spot for the local business community, the atmosphere is best at dinner, especially when there is a violinist—on Saturdays all year and on additional evenings in summer. The cuisine combines French-influenced post-nouvelle cooking with the increasingly popular traditional Irish style. A warm salad of lardons of bacon and croutons makes a good appetizer, to be followed, perhaps, by chicken in a creamy smoked salmon sauce or Barbary duck with brandy and green peppercorn sauce. The delicious desserts include simple choices like a puff pastry cream slice with fresh strawberries, and more sophisticated offerings, such as a vanilla and cassis bavarois with a fresh fruit coulis. *Fitzwilliam St. Lower, tel. 01/761060. Reservations advised; weekend reservations required. Dress: casual but neat; jacket and tie suggested weekends. AE, DC, MC, V. Closed Sat.–Sun. lunch.*

★ **Restaurant Patrick Guilbaud.** Discreet to the point of austerity, the modern and quiet ambience features pink and gray decor and large hanging plants. The formality of the service attracts the local business community, as does the air of professional calm combined with absolute reliability; corner tables are often in demand for meetings. Officially, the cuisine is "classic and nouvelle French," yet in keeping with the current revival of interest in regional food, a selection of homemade black pudding, sweetbreads, and *crúbeens* (pigs' trotters) served with a pepper and red wine sauce, appears on the menu alongside more predictable dishes, such as casserole of Dublin Bay prawns and lobster served with aromatic butter. *46 James Pl., Lower Baggot St., tel. 01/764192 or 01/601799. Reservations advised. Jacket and tie suggested. AE, DC, MC, V. Closed Sun., Mon., bank holidays.*

Expensive **Chapter One.** This new restaurant beneath the Dublin Writers Museum has vaults, arches, old stone walls, and a warm, soothing decorative scheme in sophisticated shades and discreet patterns. Effectively lit busts and paintings of famous writers echo the theme of the museum above. Although large, the restaurant consists of a network of small rooms linked by arches, creating an intimate atmosphere, even at quiet times. Short but imaginative set menus might start with warm salad of calves liver, flavored with strips of bacon and served on a bed of tossed salad, or delicate quenelles of fish poached in white wine with cream dill and fresh tomato sauces. As an entrée, sample slices of pork fillet served on delicious little potato cakes, stuffed chicken breast with whiskey sauce, or pan-fried lamb cutlets with vegetables in a rosemary sauce; the food is well cooked, the ingredients fresh. Desserts are attractive and tempting, but don't overlook the farmhouse cheese selection. *18/19 Parnell Square, tel. 01/732266 or 01/732281. Reservations accepted; weekend reservations advised. Dress: jacket and tie suggested. AE, DC, MC, V. Closed Sat. lunch (and Sun. lunch low season), Sun.–Thurs. dinner, holidays.*

The Commons Restaurant. On the south side of St. Stephen's Green, this airy restaurant has French doors that open onto a pleasant paved courtyard used for al fresco lunches. The elegantly modern cream and deep blue decor is enhanced by thick Oriental rugs. Competently prepared food is served from an international menu with classical French and Middle-Eastern influences. Start off, perhaps, with avocado in a yogurt-lime dressing, or sweetbreads with port and leaf spinach. Main courses lean toward fish, and game in season, but other favorites include lamb cutlets roasted in garlic and thyme, or beef medallions grilled to your liking with shallot sauce. *85/86 St. Stephen's Green, tel. 01/780530 or 01/780539. Reservations required for dinner, advised for lunch. Dress: casual but neat. AE, DC, MC, V. Lunch weekdays; dinner Mon.–Sat. Closed Sun., bank holidays.*

★ **Les Frères Jacques.** Housed in a late-Victorian corner house next door to the Olympia Theatre, this restaurant offers something special, exemplified by the Gallic charm of *le patron* and the nostalgic prints of Paris and Deauville on the green-papered walls. The French waiters, dressed in white Irish linen and black bow ties, are all very proper, yet the atmosphere is far from stiff; romantic souls will enjoy the piano player who performs in the evening. Expect traditional French cooking, with the emphasis on the changing seasons. You'll find a good choice of game in season. Fish lovers can dive into such delights as fresh turbot stuffed with mushroom duxelles, served with basil sauce; also recommended is the *magret de canard*—roast breast of duck, served with a ginger and grapefruit sauce. Chocolate marquise, well laced with rum and served with two sauces, provides a suitably dramatic ending. *74 Dame St., tel. 01/679–4555. Reservations advised. Dress: casual but neat. AE, DC, MC, V. Lunch weekdays; dinner Mon.–Sat. Closed Sun., holidays.*

The Grey Door. This establishment, which is located just off Fitzwilliam Square and only a five-minute walk from St. Stephen's Green, is right in the heart of Georgian Dublin and takes its style from the elegance of the restored terraced building it occupies. The menu offers a unique combination of classical Scandinavian and Russian cuisine—the owners call it "the food of the Tsars." The restaurant, which is richly furnished with antiques and gleaming cut glass, is suitably sumptuous. Although the building is large (there is a less expensive, informal restaurant, Blushes Bistro, in the basement and a beautiful private dining room upstairs), the ground-floor restaurant is small and intimate, with tables in the front half of the room grouped around a magnificent Georgian fireplace, complete with open fire. Specialties include gravlax (dill-cured salmon) served with a light mustard sauce and dill potatoes, and beef Novgorod, a center-cut fillet, pan fried and served on sauerkraut, fried barley, vegetables, garlic butter, and sour cream. The extensive wine list begins with a flourish—an 1892 Château Margaux, Premier Grand Cru, at £550—but the house wines are more accessible at £9.50; a good selection is available in the £10–£15 range. *23 Upper Pembroke St., tel. 01/763286 or*

01/766011. Reservations advised. Dress: casual but neat. AE, DC, MC, V. Closed Sun., holidays.

★ **Oĭsins Irish Restaurant.** A restaurant that demonstrates the goodness of traditional Irish cuisine at its best is a rare treat, not to be missed. Although true to their origins, all the old favorites at Oĭsins have actually been improved by a lightness of touch that is utterly modern. Up-to-date sauces add interest to otherwise familiar dishes; garnishes provide color and a variety of texture pleasing to the modern palate. Situated on the first floor of a Victorian terrace, with a little bar below, this small, intimate, and relaxing place features modern Irish art on the walls, pottery on the polished tables, and a piano player performing the old airs in the corner. Dinner consists of a six-course menu, starting with a house specialty—tasty little sausage slices flambéed in *poĭtin* (a spirit made from potatoes). The next course includes appetizer-size portions of dishes, such as Dublin coddle (the traditional Saturday-night dish, for after the pub—bacon, sausages, onion, carrot, and potatoes, all boiled together) and, perhaps, a chowder made with cockles and mussels. Among the main-courses are Irish stew and other specialties such as baked ham and spiced beef. If you want a truly Irish dessert, go for the carrageen moss pudding, a cold sweet based on a seaweed and served with Bailey's Irish Cream. *31 Upper Camden St., tel. 01/753433 or 01/783635. Reservations advised. Dress: casual but neat. Dinner only. No credit cards. Closed Sun.–Mon., Christmas week, Easter week.*

The Pavilion Restaurant. This restaurant is situated uniquely in the middle of Dublin Zoo in Phoenix Park on the first floor of a Victorian building (Haughton House), about a 10-minute drive from the city center. The place recently changed hands and is now under French management. The smart decor includes a parquet floor, a cool, understated color scheme, heavy linen napery, white china, and sparkling glasses. The French menu leans toward *cuisine moderne*—warm salads, chicken breast with wild mushroom sauce, beef and pepper sauce with fettuccine. If you go for dinner, when the zoo is closed, ask ahead for directions. *Dublin Zoo, Phoenix Park, tel. 01/775283. Reservations advised. Jacket suggested. AE, DC, MC, V. Dinner Fri.–Sat. only. Closed Sat. lunch, Dec. 25–26, Jan. 1.*

Moderate **Ayumi-Ya Japanese Steakhouse.** This more casual, city-center branch of the well-established Ayumi-Ya in Blackrock opened in 1992 and has been an immediate success. Situated in a basement in a busy business area and convenient to St. Stephen's Green, it is easily seen from the street, and the basement is bright and cheerful. The simple but well-cooked dishes are prepared and served by an extremely helpful staff. Specialties include *kushi-yaki* (food cooked on skewers), *teriyaki* (food marinated then grilled over charcoal), and *teppan-yaki steaks* (cooked on a hot iron plate). Try *ebifari* (big prawns, deep fried in breadcrumbs), a very light and crisp starter served with a *wakame* (seaweed) green salad and bean curd. Next comes fragrant miso soup, based on traditional seaweed stock and soybean paste. Typical main courses include beef and salmon teriyaki, both presented sizzling on board-mounted iron dishes, the chunks of marinated, grilled meat served with a lightly cooked mixture of vegetables—onion, sweet peppers, and others—complemented by a light soy-based sauce. Fresh fruit is offered in place of dessert. *Basement, 132 Lower Baggot*

St., tel. 01/6620233 or 01/6620223. Reservations accepted. Dress: casual but neat. MC, V. Closed Sat. lunch, Sun.

Caesar's. The friendly, efficient staff and good food make for a warm atmosphere at this unpretentious Italian restaurant, with its rows of white-clothed tables. This is a good place for a late meal after visiting the Olympia Theatre across the road. Fresh pasta is made on the premises daily; fresh fish (especially prawns) and veal are other specialties. Favorite dishes include veal parmigiana or prawns with garlic and wine, served, perhaps, with spaghetti *alla carbonara* as a side dish. Across the road, you'll find a sister restaurant, Nico's (53 Dame St., tel. 01/773062), which is run on the same lines but also serves lunch. *18 Dame St., tel. 01/679-7049. Reservations advised. Dress: casual but neat. AE, DC, MC, V. Dinner only. Closed Sun., holidays.*

The Imperial Chinese Restaurant. In a city belatedly developing a wide choice of ethnic restaurants, this has long been (and remains) the preferred choice for the local Chinese community. Occupying two floors on a busy street very close to the fashionable Grafton Street shopping area, this recently refurbished eatery presents a restful and elegant facade, with deep blue carpets, warm pink walls, a fountain, and an arch, which breaks up the main ground-floor seating area and allows a more intimate dining experience. Although, like other Chinese restaurants, the Imperial offers a number of interesting set menus, the specialty of the house is *dim sum* (little heart), myriad small portions of steamed and deep-fried meats and vegetables. *12A Wicklow St., tel. 01/772580. Reservations accepted; weekend reservations advised. Dress: casual but neat. AE, MC, V. Closed 2 days at Christmas.*

Le Caprice. Situated right in the city center, this Italian restaurant features white linen–covered tables and lots of bric-a-brac and busy decorations. The place also has a reputation for a real party atmosphere later in the evening if the pianist is in the right mood, or if musicians from the nearby National Concert Hall happen to be among the guests and an impromptu session gets going. The menu includes several old favorites, traditional Continental dishes such as prawn cocktail, deep-fried scampi, roast duckling à l'orange, and so on. Go, instead, for the Italian dishes, such as tortellini *alla panna* (cooked in broth, drained, and heated in cream) or *melanzane parmigiana* (a sort of pie made of eggplant, interspersed with layers of mozzarella cheese and tomato sauce) and finish up with *cassata*, the classic Sicilian ice cream with candied fruit. *12 St. Andrew's St., tel. 01/679-4050 or 01/770033. Reservations accepted. Dress: casual but neat. AE, DC, MC, V. Dinner only. Closed New Year's Day, Good Friday, Easter Sunday, Dec. 24-26.*

★ **Eastern Tandoori.** This popular Indian restaurant makes no concessions to European tastes; although it's on the ground floor of a modern office block in the very center of town, the decor is traditional Indian, with beautiful brasses, wall plaques, and lanterns (all imported from India). The staff wears traditional waistcoats and shirts, and Indian music plays in the background. The menu includes an extensive vegetarian choice, but no European alternatives for the faint-hearted. The cuisine tends to be aromatic rather than burning hot; chicken is a specialty—try, for instance, tandoori makhan chicken (spring chicken marinated in yogurt, herbs, and spices, first cooked over charcoal, then in butter with tomatoes and cream, and served topped with nuts). Or sample the hotter pasanda (lean pieces of chicken, lamb, or beef, cooked in an almond sauce with fresh cream, highly spiced, and also served with nuts). *34 South William St., tel. 01/710428 or 01/710506. Reservations advised. Dress: casual but neat. AE, DC, MC, V.*

Pigalle. Housed in a very old building at the archway leading to Ha'penny Bridge, this charming restaurant built up a strong local following within six months of opening in 1988; it's located in an interesting area of antique shops, galleries, unusual boutiques, and restaurants (now dubbed Dublin's Left Bank). The place features pleasantly old-fashioned decor, a relaxed atmosphere, and good food. Moroccan by birth, the owner-chef trained in the south of France. The menu is unashamedly French. It changes daily, but typical dishes include *le gâteau aux asperges fraîches* (fresh asparagus tart), *filet de truite saumonée à l'oseille et au muscadet* (fillet of sea trout with sorrel and muscadet), or *magret de canard au calvados et aux pommes* (duck breast with calvados and apples). Try to get the window table overlooking bustling Crown Alley. *14 Temple Bar, tel. 01/719262 or 01/679–6602. Reservations advised; weekend reservations required. Dress: informal. MC, V. Lunch weekdays; dinner Mon.–Sat. Closed Sun., 1 wk at Christmastime.*

Elephant & Castle. American visitors may be familiar with its Irish cousin of the same name in New York. Traditional American food in a similar tradition is served in this lively and cheerful restaurant. Bare tables and generally sparse decor contribute to a clatter that heightens the overall noise level. When the service is up to scratch, the turnover tends to be quick, and the slightly Bohemian "Left Bank" location tends to attract a young crowd. The food is varied and colorful, and portions are generous. The huge bowls of mixed leaf salad are a positive adventure, and the cosmopolitan contributions ranging from spicy nachos to ginger-laced stir-fries demonstrate the menu's eclectic and highly flavored nature. Seasoning is perhaps a bit strong for sophisticated palates, and main courses tend to be filling—but this suits the typically voracious clientele: Nobody ever leaves hungry. *18 Temple Bar, tel. 01/679–3121. Reservations accepted. Dress: casual but neat. AE, DC, MC, V.*

Inexpensive **The Bad Ass Café.** This lively restaurant in the Left Bank area between the Central Bank and Ha'penny Bridge is set in a converted warehouse and retains a distinctly barnlike atmosphere, with primary colors used inside and out. Bulbs and floor alike are bare, but there's plenty to watch—notably the old-fashioned cash shuttles whizzing around the ceiling. Although the food (pizzas, burgers, etc.) is unexceptional, the Bad Ass can be great fun and is popular with all age groups. Children will enjoy the special Kidz Bizz menu and the ongoing coloring competition. *9–11 Crown Alley, tel. 01/712596. Reservations only for groups of 8 or more. Dress: casual. AE, MC, V. Open daily 9 AM–"late." Closed Jan. 1, Good Friday, Dec. 25–26.*

Bewley's. This famous chain of coffeehouses is dear to the nation's hearts; recent threat of closure provoked an unprecedented emotional response, even from respected national figures. Although no longer under family ownership, Bewley's now seems safe, and a massive restoration program is well under way. Completed branches have now returned to their original style, with dark mahogany trim, stained-glass windows, bentwood chairs, and the much-loved waitresses in black dresses with white aprons and headbands. Specialties include the traditional Irish breakfast (eggs, bacon, sausage, black-and-white pudding, tomatoes, and mushrooms) and a wide range of home-baked breads, cakes, and pastries, which can be washed down with Bewley's own teas or coffees—the shops have 11 blends of tea and 15 of coffee from which to choose. *Westmoreland St., Grafton St., South Great George's St., and suburban branches, tel. 01/776761 (head office). No reservations. Dress: casual. AE, DC, MC, V. Open daily 8–7. Closed Dec. 25–26.*

Burdock's. In the heart of Viking Dublin, next door to the Lord Edward Pub, Dublin's most famous take-out fish-and-chipper is determinedly old-fashioned: Vegetable oil is scorned in favor of real beef drippings; it's also the only chipper in town that still fries over a coal fire. Joining the inevitable queue is part of the fun. As your meal should be consumed as quickly as possible, the traditional place to sit and eat is on the steps of St. Patrick's Cathedral. *Werburgh St., tel. 01/540306. No credit cards. Dinner only. Closed Tues. and Sun.*

Cornucopia Wholefoods. Vegetarian restaurants often provide the best value for the money, and this spot is no exception. Access is through the Cornucopia unrefined food shop (which offers plenty of distractions on the way), and the restaurant features lots of well-cared-for plants, as well as recycled paper and handmade pottery for sale. The seating consists of bar stools at high, glass-topped, narrow tables; locals often slip advertisements under the glass, which makes for some interesting reading. The menu includes red lentil soup, avocado quiche, vegetarian spring roll, and vegetarian curry, all of them regular favorites. *19 Wicklow St., tel. 01/777583. No reservations. Dress: casual. No credit cards. Open weekdays 8 AM–9 PM, Sat. 8–6. Closed Sun.*

Fat Freddy's Pizza Warehouse. Fat Freddy and his cat occupy the ground floor of this white-walled, timber-floored 18th-century warehouse in the lively Temple Bar area; various bands and artists add to the atmosphere (and noise level) in the practice rooms upstairs. Although this is mainly a student hangout, no upper age limit exists here—anyone who appreciates a good pizza (not to mention Grandma's homemade apple pie) is welcome. Customers have a reasonable choice apart from pizzas, including baked potatoes with various fillings, quiches, lasagna, and chili con carne, as well as half a dozen wines. *20 Temple La., Dame St., tel. 01/679–6769. Weekend reservations advised. Dress: casual but neat. MC, V.*

Gallagher's Boxty House. Located in a late-Victorian building behind the Central Bank, right in the heart of the thriving Temple Bar area, this highly original restaurant features a lovely country ambience, with lots of dark-green decor complementing the antique pine furniture and trim, the stone floors, and the handmade pottery; everything is Irish made. The main dish, Boxty, is a traditional Irish potato bread or cake that has been cleverly adapted by the Gallaghers to make a potato pancake that is thin enough to wrap around all kinds of fillings, such as bacon and cabbage, chicken with leeks, and smoked fish. Other recommended dishes include bacon and cabbage with parsley sauce and champ (potato mashed with scallions, milk, and butter), followed by brown bread and Bailey's ice cream or the superb bread and butter pudding. Expect to share a table. *20 Temple Bar, tel. 01/772762. No reservations. Dress: casual. V. Closed Christmas and Good Friday.*

Independent Pizza Company. This small operation just off Grafton Street claims their crusts are lighter and crisper than those of their rivals, but in fact it's probably the "fresh ingredients only" policy practiced here that makes regulars swear the pizzas are the best in town. The modern and spacious city-center place opened only recently (the original store is north of the river, in Drumcondra); it features black and gray decor, lots of plants everywhere, and a lemon tree in the back. *8 South Anne St., tel. 01/679–5266. No reservations. Dress: casual. No credit cards. Closed 4 days around Christmas and Good Friday.*

The Kilkenny Kitchen. Uniquely situated in a modern shop specializing in the best of Irish craftsmanship and overlooking Trinity College, this tweed-carpeted self-service restaurant decorated with natural wood showcases wholesome home cooking in the traditional style. The menu includes a house quiche (combining Irish bacon, herbs, and fresh vegetables), a good traditional Irish stew, casseroles, and an imaginative selection of salads. The choice of Irish farmhouse cheeses and the home-baked scones, bread, and cakes are all tempting. Lunchtime is busy; expect to share a table. *6 Nassau St., tel. 01/777066. No reservations. Dress: casual. AE, MC, V. Open Mon.–Sat. 9–5. Closed Sun., public holidays.*

Mitchells Cellars. Situated comfortingly in the vaulted basement of a wine shop, this place hasn't really changed since the early '70s: It still has the same bustling lunchtime crowd, the quarry-tiled floor, whitewashed walls, red and white lamp-shades hanging over pine tables, waitresses neatly dressed in navy and white—and much the same menu. Country French-influenced home cooking dominates on the menu, which includes soups and pâtés, quiche lorraine and salads, beef braised in Guinness, and chocolate and brandy meringue. The restaurant's perennial popularity may be attributed to its attachment to the revered wine merchants upstairs (there's usually something interesting on the wine list at the right price) and to its location just off St. Stephen's Green. Get here early, or expect a line. *21 Kildare St., tel. 01/680367. No reservations. Dress: casual but neat. AE, DC, MC, V. Lunch only. Closed Sun.; Sat. in June, July, and Aug.; bank holidays; Dec. 24–28.*

Paddy Kavanagh's. Tucked away in a lane behind the Bord Failté (Tourist Board) head office, Paddy Kavanagh's isn't a place you're likely to come across by chance, but it's very popular with local office workers. This informal, friendly place in an old building has been transformed into an atmosphere well-suited to the restaurant's reputation for good home cooking—the decor features country tones of dark green and terra-cotta and plenty of natural wood. The main dishes tend to be fairly traditional and homey; fish pie is a typical specialty. Tasty vegetarian alternatives and an unusually wide range of salads are also on the menu. This weekday place opens early, with breakfast from 8 AM; it closes following afternoon tea. *6 Pembroke Row, tel. 01/765056. Limited reservations accepted for lunch. Dress: casual but neat. No credit cards. Open Mon.–Thurs. 8–5, Fri. 8–4. Closed weekends, Christmas week.*

Pasta Fresca. Situated on one of Dublin's most interesting thoroughfares, just off Grafton Street, this stylish little Italian restaurant and delicatessen squeezes a surprising number of people into a small area; it's comfortable, however, once you're settled, and the high ceiling does create a sense of space. Antipasto *misto* (assorted sliced Italian meats) makes a good appetizer—or go for a single meat like prosciutto (Italian cured ham), or *carpaccio della casa* (wafer-thin slices of beef fillet, with fresh Parmesan, olive oil, lemon juice, and black pepper). The main courses consist mainly of Pasta Fresca's own very good versions of well-known dishes such as spaghetti *alla bolognese*, cannelloni, and lasagna *al forno*. The pasta is freshly made each day. You'll find lines at lunchtime. *3–4 Chatham St., tel. 01/679–2402 or 01/679–8965. Reservations accepted; weekend reservations advised. Dress: casual but neat. No credit cards. Open daily 8 AM–11 PM. Closed public holidays.*

Il Primo. Nothing has been wasted on the decor at this spartan little upstairs Italian restaurant situated just a few hundred yards from St. Stephen's Green. Bare boards and tables, simple (but comfortable) old-fashioned wooden-armed office chairs, stainless steel cutlery, and paper napkins all indicate economy—the (rather good) pictures are even for sale. Lovely large, modern crystal wine glasses, however, give a hint of the good things to come: The generosity here is evident on your plate. Sound, middle of the road Irish-Italian cuisine changes seasonally. Typical offerings include a starter of warm spinach salad—wilted in a balsamic vinegar dressing and shallots, then served with Parma ham and new potatoes—followed by a creamy delicious risotto—with chunky chicken breasts, a scattering of chicken livers, and some wild mushrooms. Pizzas are sizzling, aromatic, and inexpensive, and there's a choice of salads. Desserts include homemade ice cream, and the Italian cheeses are superb. *16 Montague St. (off Harcourt St.), tel. 01/ 783373. Reservations advised. Dress: casual but neat. DC, MC, V. Closed Sun., Mon. dinner, holidays.*

The Periwinkle Seafood Bar. This informal daytime restaurant is located in what was once the stable area of Lord Powerscourt's town house (now imaginatively converted into Dublin's most attractive shopping center); it features the original low arched ceiling and even the cauldron that was once used to prepare the horses' bran mash. The modern quarry-tiled floor, pine tables, and chunky pottery complement the old building's architecture; the kitchen is open, with a gray marble counter the only barrier. Expect home cooking with a leaning toward Cordon Bleu: The emphasis is on freshness, quality, and simplicity. Sample the seafood chowder, served with homemade brown bread, or the toasted crab claws in garlic butter, cheese, and breadcrumbs. *Unit 18, Powerscourt Townhouse Centre, South William St., tel. 01/679–4203. No reservations. Dress: casual. No credit cards. Open 10:30–5. Closed Sun., Christmas, Easter, bank holidays.*

Suburbs and County Dublin

Very Expensive **La Vie en Rose.** The Taillebauds have moved their well-known city-center restaurant to a famous spot in Sandycove and, although the surroundings here are grander and the sea view desirable, the French proprietor-chef has not changed his classic French style; a nouvelle flair still influences the presentation. You might try a *flan de poivrons doux aux trois sauces* (a flan consisting of green, red, and yellow sweet peppers, served with three sauces), and follow this with a *tresse de poissons, sauce verte* (plait of salmon and brill served with a slightly creamed spinach sauce). The desserts are especially good: Don't miss the liqueur-laced ices topped with crunchy nuts and served in delicate brandysnap baskets. From the wine list, house selections are the best value. *Marine Parade, Sandycove, tel. 01/*

280–9873. Reservations advised; weekend reservations required. Jacket required; jacket and tie suggested. AE, MC, V. Closed Sat. lunch, Sun., holidays.

★ **Le Coq Hardi.** This successful restaurant, close to the city center and most of the major hotels, is consistently popular with the business community. Rosewood furniture, gilt-framed pictures and mirrors, Irish linen, Newbridge silver, and Rosenthal china create a reassuring, clublike atmosphere. The house style is classical French, with some concessions to *cuisine moderne* in the choice and presentation of vegetables. Specialties include "smokies," an appetizer made with Scottish smoked haddock, marbled with tomato, double cream, and Irish cheese and baked "en cocotte" (in an ovenware dish), and *coq* Hardi, which is chicken filled with potatoes, mushrooms, and special herbs, wrapped in bacon, oven-baked, and finished with Irish whiskey. The outstanding wine list concentrates on the great wines of Bordeaux, Burgundy, Loire, and Champagne; bear in mind, however, that there are very few selections under £15. *35 Pembroke Rd., Ballsbridge, tel. 01/268–9070 or 01/268–4130. Reservations required. Jacket required; tie advised. AE, DC, MC, V. Lunch weekdays; dinner Mon.–Sat. Closed Sun. and bank holidays.*

The Wine Epergne. This delightful restaurant, a 10-minute drive from the city center, has a strong local following. Once a Victorian shop (and still connected to Findlater's Wine Merchants next door), it now features polished floors, Turkish carpets, Victorian furniture, and old cutlery that is charmingly mismatched. The feeling of being in a private home is emphasized by the family portraits on the walls. The new owner-chef, Kevin Thornton, has made a great impact on the Dublin dining scene with his post-nouvelle style based on a seasonal approach. Using only the best of natural/organic products, he changes the menu once or twice a week according to the markets, and varies vegetables to complement each dish. A typical meal might start with a terrine of rabbit and capon set in a saffron jelly, followed by fillet of rouget with a fresh shrimp mousse and a citrus and lemon grass sauce. For dessert, don't miss the house special, a memorable *tarte au citron*. (Lunch costs about £12.) *147 Upper Rathmines Rd., tel. 01/962348. Reservations advised. Jacket suggested. MC, V. Dinner Tues.–Sat. Closed Tues. and Sat. lunch, Sun.–Mon., Christmas.*

Expensive– **Ernie's Restaurant.** This long-established single-story restau-
Very Expensive rant in Donnybrook, only a few minutes by taxi from the city center, is built around a large tree and fountain that are particularly pretty when lit up at night. Almost as famous for the late Ernie Evans' personal collection of original paintings—which cover virtually all the available wallspace—as for the food, the dining room offers a welcoming atmosphere, with distinctive blue Irish linen tablecloths and sparkling crystal on the tables. The restaurant is still owned by the Evans family. The cuisine is basically classic French, with concessions to traditional Irish—dishes like moules à la marinière (mussels cooked with chopped shallot, bouquet garni, and white wine) or fillets of sole Bonne Femme (fillets baked with chopped mushrooms, parsley and white wine) are typical. A seasonal vegetarian platter, willingly made to order, is a nice touch in an establishment where high-quality ingredients, attention to detail, and consistency are still the hallmarks. *Mulberry Gardens, Donny-*

brook, tel. 01/269–3300 or 01/269–3260. Reservations required.
Jacket and tie suggested. AE, DC, MC, V. Closed Sat. lunch,
Sun., Mon., 10 days at Christmas.

Il Ristorante. Roberto and Celine Pons have moved their well-
known Kinsale restaurant up to south Dublin, where it's already a major hit. Situated over the popular Club Bar in
Dalkey, only the most discreet signs (a small brass plate and
neat menu) give away the presence of the quiet but stylish restaurant upstairs. It's small and intimate—only about 20 tables—with paintings decorating the walls, a muted color
scheme, and lots of plants and fresh flowers. Fans of the previous restaurant will recognize the new-wave Italian cooking
style in this new venture, although Roberto's strikingly original touches always have the power to surprise. Look for combi-
nations like fillet steak with pesto or sea trout baked in sea salt.
Or try the calves' liver Venetian-style—thin strips of pink liver
served on a bed of caramelized onions. The wickedly rich desserts include *tiramisu,* an irresistible pudding of cream, coffee, and brandy. *108 Coliemore Rd., Dalkey, tel. 01/284–0800.
Reservations advised. Dress: casual but neat. AE, DC, MC, V.
Dinner daily, except Mon. Closed Christmas week.*

Expensive
Abbey Tavern. Situated in the fishing port of Howth, 14 km (9
mi) north of the city center, this Old World tavern is only a five-
minute walk from the DART station. The ancient building's
original stone walls, flagged floors, and old gaslights are more
effective than anything a decorator might conceive; blazing turf
fires add to the historic atmosphere. The upstairs restaurant
specializes in fish dishes, with the traditional Irish and Continental cuisine. Sole Abbey—fillet of sole stuffed with prawns,
mushrooms, and herbs—is a house specialty, and fresh Dublin
Bay prawns can be cooked to order. Traditional Irish music is
offered in a different part of the building. *Abbey St., Howth,
tel. 01/390282. Reservations advised; weekend reservations required. Jacket suggested. AE, DC, MC, V. Dinner only: Apr.–
Sept., daily; Oct.–Mar., closed Sun. eves.*

Ayumi-Ya Japanese Restaurant. This is Dublin's first Japanese
restaurant, located in a small shopping complex 8 km (5 mi)
from the city center. Customers have a choice of seating at regular tables; on the floor, Japanese-style; or at *teppan-yaki*
(iron-grill) tables (offered by reservation). Japanese decorations and porcelain are used throughout and the waiting staff
wear kimonos or Japanese-style shirts. The Japanese proprietor-chef is a qualified dietician and has won numerous
awards for her cuisine. Choices include *sushi* and *sashimi* (a selection of ultrafresh, thinly cut raw fish), *tempura* (a deep-fried
selection of prawns, vegetables, and fish), beef teriyaki, and
teppan-yaki, which the chef cooks right at the tables; Ayumi-
Ya is the only restaurant in Ireland offering this iron-grill style
of cooking. *Newpark Centre, Newtownpark Ave., Blackrock,
tel. 01/283–1767. Reservations advised; weekend reservations
required. Dress: casual but neat. AE, DC, MC, V. Closed Dec.
25–26, Jan. 1–2.*

Beaufield Mews. A 10-minute taxi ride from the city center,
this 18th-century coach house with stables still has its original
cobbled courtyard and is even said to be haunted by a friendly
monk. Inside it's all black beams, old furniture, and bric-a-
brac, including stable artifacts. The most desirable tables overlook the courtyard or the garden, or are, less predictably, "under the nun" (the nun in question is a 17th-century portrait).

The traditional food makes use of the best of seasonal ingredients; you'll find old favorites like roast duckling à l'orange but also fresh wild salmon steaks simply grilled or poached and served with hollandaise sauce. The menu also includes game in season—venison and pheasant are specialties—and homemade ice cream. *Woodlands Ave., Stillorgan, tel. 01/288–6945. Reservations required. Dress: casual but neat. AE, DC, V. Dinner only (other meals by arrangement). Closed Sun., Mon., bank holidays.*

Bon Appetit. Owner-chef Patsey McGuirk brought a loyal following from his previous city-center restaurant of the same name when he moved, in 1989, to this substantial Georgian terraced building in Malahide, only a 10-minute drive from Dublin Airport and a half hour from the city center. The striking floral decor in warm shades of pink creates a cozy traditional atmosphere, an impression heightened by the staff of black-jacketed waiters. Patsey's wife, Catherine, manages the front of the house. The traditional Continental menu includes such entrées as escargots and mushrooms in garlic and cream sauce, and a generous choice of desserts. Especially recommended are sole McGuirk, boned sole stuffed with prawns and turbot and baked with white wine and cream, and duckling Montmorency served with black cherries and a cherry brandy and orange sauce. *9 James's Terr., Malahide, tel. 01/450314. Reservations advised. Jacket and tie advised. AE, DC, MC, V. Lunch weekdays; dinner Mon.–Sat. Closed Sundays, bank holidays, Christmas week.*

Broph's. Near the American Embassy and over a (very exclusive) nightclub, Broph's restaurant is upstairs in a Georgian terraced building. It's interestingly furnished in warm colors—Afghan rugs on the terra-cotta walls, lamps, and wall lights all create a relaxing atmosphere. The chef-owner takes pride in making imaginative use of the best Irish ingredients in his own style. For instance, he may take some wild sea trout, make it into *quennelles* (dumplings), and serve them in a delicate sauce with saffron and chives; another evening, he may fan out a panfried duck breast, give it a game glaze, and add baby corn for color. Desserts tend to be classical, but often with a twist—crème brûlée, for example, comes with a pretty net of caramelized sugar spun over it. *16 Merrion Rd., Ballsbridge, tel. 01/602236 or 01/605288. Reservations advised; weekend reservations required. Dress: casual but neat. AE, DC, MC, V. Lunch weekdays, dinner Mon.–Sat. Closed Sun., bank holidays.*

Digby's Restaurant and Wine Bar. Situated in a terraced Georgian house on the seafront in Dun Laoghaire, this is a well-established favorite with locals. The smart upstairs restaurant is often used for special occasions; the rustic stone-flagged wine bar on the ground floor, for inexpensive, casual meals. In the restaurant, recently redone in pinks and grays with art deco mirrors, owner-chef Paul Cathcart practices "cuisine du marché" to emphasize the seasonal nature of his approach to fresh products—using a lot of game in winter and seafood in summer, for instance. For starters, you might try aubergine cake (sliced panfried eggplant layered with tomato and basil and baked with grated sheep's cheese) and follow with steamed medallions of monkfish with wild mushrooms. If you still have room, you can order chocolate pecan truffle pie. *5 Windsor Terr., Dun Laoghaire, tel. 01/280–9147. Reservations advised. Dress: casual but neat. AE, DC, MC, V. Dinner Wed.–Mon.;*

lunch Sun. only. Closed Tues., Dec. 25–26, Good Friday, bank holidays.

★ **The King Sitric.** This well-known seafood restaurant is a main attraction in the fishing port of Howth, north of the city center; it's situated in a Georgian house on the harbor front, with the yacht marina and port on one side, and with sea views from the upstairs bar/reception area. The restaurant consists of a series of rooms on the ground floor, furnished traditionally with antiques and white linen; try to get a table in the middle, near the kitchen. The menu makes little concession to non–fish eaters, although there's usually some alternative, such as chicken Kiev or some game, when in season. But who could resist fish that is so utterly fresh? Lobster, caught just yards away in Balscadden Bay, is the big treat; it's best at its simplest, in butter sauce. Crab is equally fresh and scrumptious here, dressed with mayonnaise or mornay sauce. *Calmar frites* (deep-fried squid) is a special starter served with fresh tomato or tartar sauce. For dessert, don't miss the house specialty, meringue Sitric (hollow meringues, filled with homemade vanilla ice cream, covered with dark chocolate sauce, and scattered with flaked almonds). *East Pier, Howth, Co. Dublin, tel. 01/325235 or 01/326729. Reservations advised; weekend reservations required. Jacket advised; jacket and tie suggested. AE, DC, MC, V. Dinner only. Private dining by arrangement. Closed Sun., bank holidays, and at Christmas and Easter, 10 days each.*

★ **Roche's Bistro.** About a 15-minute drive out of Dublin and handy to the airport, Roche's is part of an old terraced house in the main street of a pretty coastal town. Orla Roche is a Francophile, and it shows—the particular brand of relaxed Gallic charm and good country French cooking found here is rare in Ireland. The small and cozy place, with white walls covered with French prints and antique copper utensils, has cheerful blue-and-white-check tablecloths and an open coal fire in winter. The cooking is done in full view of clients, in a minuscule kitchen behind the bar. Seafood figures strongly on the wide-ranging menu. You might start with a mousseline of scallops (scallops pureed with egg white, Noilly Prat, cream, and grated orange zest, cooked in a mold and served with orange *beurre blanc*) and follow with breast of duck with cassis. *12 New St., Malahide, tel. 01/452777. Reservations accepted; weekend reservations advised. Dress: casual but neat. AE, DC, MC, V. Lunch Mon.–Sat., dinner Thurs.–Sat.*

Trudi's. Situated in a late-19th-century building on Dun Laoghaire's main street, this informal bistro has become something of an institution, with a devoted local clientele. The restaurant has two floors, with a small wine bar on the ground floor and an intimate upper balcony area. The menu reflects seasonal changes, with food prepared to allow the natural flavor of ingredients to predominate. Typical entrées include braised lambs' tongues with mustard sauce and poached salmon with watercress sauce, in the summer. Game is served in season. *107 Lower George's St., Dun Laoghaire, tel. 01/280–5318. Reservations advised, especially on weekends. Dress: casual but neat. AE, DC, MC, V. Dinner only. Closed Sun.–Mon., Dec. 25–26, Good Friday.*

Moderate   China-Sichuan Restaurant. This restaurant has the distinction of being state-owned by the Szechuan Province of the People's Republic of China; the ingredients (and the chefs) are supplied directly by China. The establishment is situated in an ordinary

terraced building about a 15-minute drive from the city center.
The focal point here is a giant ceramic water-lily fountain. Traditional scarlet lanterns and velvet-covered booths set in private areas help create an intimate ambience. Recommended
specialties include duck skin stuffed with seafood, and whole
steamed sole. Desserts are unexceptional. *4 Lower Kilmacud
Rd., Stillorgan, tel. 01/288–4817 or 01/288–9560. Reservations
required. Jacket and tie required. AE, MC, V. Closed Good
Friday and 3 days at Christmas.*

De Selby's. Named after a character in James Joyce's writings,
this family restaurant is very close to the shopping center in the
middle of Dun Laoghaire town. Situated in a Victorian terraced building, the restaurant is in one large room, but the
space has been divided to create a more intimate atmosphere.
A strikingly fresh blue-and-yellow color scheme complements
the varnished wooden tables and chairs; the many paintings on
display by young local artists are for sale. Good, reasonably
priced food of this type is rare in the Dublin area: De Selby's
specializes in fresh seasonal food with the emphasis on fish and
steak, including delicious homemade burgers. The warm salad
of chicken livers and mixed leaves makes a delicious starter,
and the pasta entrées are also recommended. Seafood pasta
and rack of lamb are house favorites. *17–18 Patrick St., Dun
Laoghaire, tel. 01/284–1761 or 01/284–1762. No reservations.
Dress: casual. AE, DC, MC, V. Dinner daily; lunch Sat.–Sun.
only. Open every day except Dec. 24, 25, 26 and Good Friday.*

The Old Schoolhouse. Although it's a half-hour drive from the
city center, this attractively converted Victorian schoolhouse
is only a five-minute drive from the airport. The stone-walled
garden makes a delightful setting for alfresco dining in summer; guests can relax in the reception/lounge area of the recently added conservatory. Inside, you'll find an informal
atmosphere, with old pine furniture and local pottery complementing the original wood floors and paneled walls. Traditional
Irish home cooking is served, with the emphasis on fresh fish
and steaks. Recommended dishes include the lemon sole
stuffed with crab, or Irish potato cakes with crispy bacon. A
vegetarian option is always available, such as mushrooms in
garlic butter, followed by spinach roulade and salad. A garden
room downstairs allows private dining for 14. *Coolbanagher,
Swords, tel. 01/402846. Reservations advised. Dress: casual
but neat. AE, DC, MC, V. Closed Sat.–Sun. lunch, Sun. dinner.*

The Orchid Szechuan Restaurant. Just outside the city center,
in the basement of an early Victorian terraced house, this pretty Chinese restaurant, with its unusual cool, monochromatic
black color scheme, is one of the friendliest dining spots in
town. The chef, from Hong Kong's Riverside Restaurant, has a
talent for turning an ordinary meal into a banquet with specialties like hot-and-sour soup, king prawns with hot garlic sauce,
and crispy deep-fried shredded fillet of beef with spicy sauce.
*120 Pembroke Rd., Ballsbridge, tel. 01/600629. Reservations
accepted; weekend reservations advised. Jacket and tie suggested. AE, DC, MC, V. Closed Dec. 24–26.*

Lodging

Dublin's city center and the immediate southside of the city offer a number of first-class hotels. Rates for these hotels are reasonable by international standards, although suites, usually a bedroom and a sitting room, are increasingly popular but very expensive, at around £500 a night plus 15% service charge. Service charges range from 15% in expensive hotels to zero in moderate and inexpensive ones. Be sure to inquire at time of booking. Some city-center hotels are located in drab parts of town, such as Upper O'Connell Street. For travelers with their own cars, it is worth considering a location out of the city center, such as Dalkey and Killiney, where the surroundings are more pleasant.

The city also has a good choice of less expensive accommodations, with many moderately priced and inexpensive hotels offering basic but agreeable rooms. Bed-and-breakfast establishments, long the mainstay of the economy end of the market, have upgraded their facilities and now provide rooms with their own bathrooms or showers, as well as multichannel color televisions and direct-dial telephones, for around £20 a night per person.

A new development in Dublin is the renting of apartments and houses to visitors; the travelers usually cook their own meals. Most of these apartments and houses provide maid service that is responsible for daily cleaning. These apartments and houses are well decorated and furnished, offering travelers total freedom to come and go as they please.

Bord Failté (Irish Tourist Board) publishes a complete *self-catering* guide; these recommended properties can be booked through any Tourist Information Office (*see* Important Addresses and Numbers in Essential Information, above).

Category	Cost*
Very Expensive	over £100
Expensive	£75–£100
Moderate	£50–£75
Inexpensive	under £50

*All prices are per person for a standard double room, including 10% local sales tax (VAT) but excluding service charge.

Highly recommended hotels are indicated by a star ★.

City Center

Very Expensive **Shelbourne.** This grand old Dublin hotel may have an imposing
★ redbrick front with white trim, but you'll find it far from unfriendly. Its guest book contains names ranging from the Dalai Lama to Laurel and Hardy to Richard Burton to Peter O'Toole. (In the 19th century, writer William Makepeace Thackeray stayed here for six shillings and eight pence a day.) The blazing open fire in its bustling lobby, flanked by two huge rose brocade sofas, is proof that the hotel has not lost its past grandeur. The Shelbourne first opened in 1824, in modest houses facing St. Stephen's Green; over the years, the buildings were ex-

132

Dublin Lodging

panded considerably, but also became run-down until, between 1986 and 1988, £7 million was lavished on a tip-top refurbishment. No two bedrooms are the same size or shape, but all have fine, carefully selected furniture and luxurious drapes, with splendid antiques in the older rooms. Rooms at the front of the hotel face lovely St. Stephen's Green, and in the distance are the Dublin mountains; it's the only side of the hotel with good views. Although the back rooms face a service yard, you'll find them far quieter. The impressive suites have separate sitting rooms and dressing areas; the largest, with a mini-network of interconnecting rooms, is named in honor of the late Princess Grace of Monaco, who visited in the 1960s and 1970s. On the ground floor, the Horse Shoe Bar is a small, popular rendezvous spot; tea in the adjoining lounge, with its deep, comfortable armchairs and views of the green, is a real Dublin tradition. The distinguished Aisling Restaurant serves a varied, expensive menu with excellent seafood appetizers and such entrées as crab, duck, grilled salmon, and veal. *St. Stephen's Green, Dublin 2, tel. 01/766471, fax 01/616006. 143 rooms, 22 suites. Facilities: 2 restaurants, bar, lounge, gift shop/ newsagent, parking. AE, DC, MC, V.*

Expensive **Berkeley Court.** This quietly elegant hotel with efficient service which opened more than a decade ago, in the verdant residential district of Ballsbridge, attracts both local and foreign celebrities. Although the glass-and-concrete exterior is designed in a modern blocklike style, the vast, recently renovated lobby is attractive, with plush carpeting, roomy sofas, white tiles, and antique planters. The large bedrooms are decorated in light pastel shades, with antiques or reproductions of period furniture; bathrooms feature marble tiling. The Berkeley Room restaurant offers improved table d'hôte and à la carte menus; the more informal Conservatory restaurant, with hanging plants and large windows, serves grilled food and snacks. The hotel is a 10-minute cab ride from the city center. *Lansdowne Rd., Dublin 4, tel. 01/601711. 207 rooms, including 20 suites. Facilities: 2 restaurants, 2 shops, hairdresser, barbershop, Jacuzzis in suites, indoor pool, tennis. AE, DC, MC, V.*

Conrad. Rising seven stories, Dublin's latest expensive hotel opened in 1989 and is well placed opposite the National Concert Hall and within a two-minute walk of St. Stephen's Green. Gleaming light marble graces the large, formal lobby. Bedrooms are furnished with sand-colored decor and natural wood furniture, offer uninspiring views of the adjacent tower blocks, and are rather cramped. The air-conditioning/heating systems can also be quite noisy. The suites, however, are spacious enough, with stylish, dark furniture in the sitting area. On the first floor, guests have a choice of two restaurants: The airy Plurabelle serves informal lunches and evening meals, and the more enclosed Alexandra room, with heavy wood paneling and drapes, has formal menus emphasizing elaborately prepared fish, fowl, and meat dishes. In the basement, the Alfie Byrne Bar, named in honor of Dublin's lord mayor for most of the 1930s, has a black bar counter in the center of the room that some may find a bit gloomy. Overall, the hotel has a sophisticated ambience; while the service is efficient, it lacks the spontaneous Irish warmth of smaller establishments. *Earlsfort Terr., Dublin 2, tel. 01/765555. 179 rooms, 9 suites. Facilities: 2 restaurants. AE, DC, MC.*

Gresham. This mid-19th-century hotel has been substantially refurbished within the past five years, but it is located in a drab part of town. In the past, the hotel attracted many celebrities, such as Richard Burton and Elizabeth Taylor, but more recent VIPs have gravitated to newer and more expensive accommodations. Bedrooms are reached via long windowless corridors. The somewhat antiquated bathrooms lend character to the bland modern-repro style of the newly decorated rooms, which are nevertheless clean and comfortable. The Gresham's restaurant is still a pleasant place to stop for lunch and dinner, with an emphasis on meat and fish dishes. Although you're right near the historic GPO, you'll also have to watch out in the area for pickpockets. *Upper O'Connell St., Dublin 1, tel. 01/746881. 200 rooms. Facilities: restaurant, bar, nightclub/disco. AE, DC, MC, V.*

Westbury. This hotel has an excellent location, right off the fashionable shopping mecca of Grafton Street in the city center. The spacious main lobby is furnished with attractive antiques and comfortable armchairs where guests sit to take afternoon tea. Despite these efforts, the Westbury offers little period atmosphere. Bedrooms are rather utilitarian, with pastel color schemes; suites, which combine European decor with tasteful Japanese screens and prints, are much more inviting. The flowery Russell Room serves formal lunches and dinners, and the downstairs Sandbank, a seafood restaurant and bar, features decor imitating a Joycean-period establishment. The food and service can be disappointing. *Grafton St., Dublin 2, tel. 01/679–1122. 206 twin/double rooms, 8 suites. Facilities: 2 restaurants; shops in Westbury Mall beside hotel entrance. AE, DC, MC, V.*

Moderate **Burlington.** Opened in 1969, the first and largest of Dublin's modern hotels has an impersonal glass-and-concrete facade, but the staff here is quite friendly and attentive. The hotel attracts a number of tour groups. Public rooms are well decorated, especially the large bar, with mahogany counters and hanging plants that enhance the conservatory-style setting. The generous-size bedrooms have large picture windows. For such a big hotel, the Burlington is surprisingly lacking in sports and health facilities, and the pool was removed to make way for the bar extension. *Upper Leeson St., Dublin 4, tel. 01/605222. 477 rooms. Facilities: 2 restaurants, nightclub, gift shop/newsagent, Irish cabaret in summer. AE, DC, MC, V.*

Jury's and **the Towers.** These two hotels offer striking contrasts in decor and design. Jury's is a seven-story, concrete-and-glass blocklike building; it adjoins the Towers, which is the same height with a light finish to its facade. Jury's, the older hotel, dating back 30 years, offers large, plainly decorated bedrooms with light walls and brown drapes; furnishings are functional but uninspired, especially for an expensive hotel. The Towers' bedrooms are a third larger than those of Jury's, with subtle, sand-colored decor, complemented by natural built-in wood furniture. Both the large beds and the armchairs are blissfully comfortable. Rooms also have plenty of storage space. Suites are even grander, with their own sitting rooms and kitchenettes. Entry to the Towers is restricted to guests, who can enjoy their own lounge and well-stocked reading room. All shop and restaurant facilities are located in Jury's. The Kish serves only fish and features an elaborate bar; the Embassy Room has a green garden-theme decor; and the Coffee Dock, serving light fare, is open 23 hours a day (closed 4 AM–5 AM). The Dubliner's Bar, in a setting reminiscent of a farmhouse kitchen, has a collection of memorabilia, old photographs, and newspaper clippings, as well as a century-old printing press. Although both hotels are popular with businesspeople and vacationers, you'll probably be happier at the Towers, if you can afford the extra cost. *Ballsbridge, Dublin 4, tel. 01/605000. Jury's, 300 rooms, 8 suites; the Towers, 100 rooms, 4 suites with kitchenettes. Facilities: 2 restaurants, coffee shop, bar, pool, shop/boutique, Irish cabaret in summer. AE, DC, MC, V.*

★ **Lansdowne.** In the leafy suburb of Ballsbridge, convenient to the city center, this small establishment offers a very friendly ambience. The cozy, modest rooms are painted in pastel shades, and they have all the basics. The basement bar is a popular hangout for local businesspeople and fans of the international rugby matches held at nearby Lansdowne Road; photos of sports personalities hang on the walls. Next to the bar is the Bonne Bouchée Restaurant, which serves lunch and dinner, specializing in seafood and grilled steaks. *27 Pembroke Rd., Dublin 4, tel. 01/684079 or 01/682522. 28 rooms. Facilities: bar, restaurant, TV. AE, DC, MC, V.*

★ **Mont Clare Hotel.** Rarely has a Dublin hotel undergone such a complete personality change; this establishment used to be a rather drab place offering modest accommodations and undistinguished dining facilities. A new wing, however, opened in 1990, and all the bedrooms in the original part of the hotel were refurbished to match the standards of the new section. Bedrooms feature deep-pile carpeting and vibrant colors, such as deep-red walls and white ceilings. All rooms provide a computerized minibar, individual heat/air-conditioning controls, trouser presses, tea- and coffee-making facilities, and an in-house film channel. The immaculate bathrooms have marble floors and tile walls. Corridors seem a bit cramped, and guests may not find the low ceilings in the older rooms to their liking. The new Goldsmith's Restaurant specializes in Irish fish and beef, while the Merrion Lounge serves Irish bar food, such as sandwiches and stews. The location of the hotel could not be better, just behind Trinity College and near St. Stephen's Green, Grafton Street, and museums. *Merrion Sq., Dublin 2, tel. 01/616799 or 01/619555. 80 rooms. Facilities: restaurant, bar, parking. AE, DC, MC, V.*

Stephen's Hall. This is a new venture on the Dublin hotel scene: All accommodations are suites consisting of a sitting room, kitchen, bathroom, and one or two bedrooms. This arrangement is proving popular with both business travelers and tourists. The hotel is in a tastefully modernized Georgian townhouse just off St. Stephen's Green. Rooms are comfortably equipped with quality modern furniture, and are far more spacious than the average hotel room. *14–17 Lower Leeson St., Dublin 2, tel. 01/610585. 37 suites. Facilities: restaurant, bar, basement bar, parking. AE, DC, MC, V.*

Inexpensive **Ariel House.** This redbrick Victorian guest house, dating from
★ 1850, stands conveniently near bus routes and the DART line, a five-minute ride to the center of Dublin; it is also just down the road from the Berkeley Court and Jury's (*see above*). Michael O'Brien, the amiable owner, returned to Ireland from San Francisco and London, and he turned his home into this immaculate lodging with a new extension in the back. The lobby, lounge, and restaurant are graced with Victoriana and lace

curtains in the Irish style; the lounge features comfortable leather chairs, a white marble fireplace, lovely oil portraits, a Waterford crystal chandelier, and an exquisite Japanese doll. In the afternoon, Victorian tea is served. The bedrooms are plain with light walls and contemporary furniture, though some rooms in the main house have high ceilings. Number 27, which faces a neat garden, is especially charming, with Victorian-style furniture and a Jacuzzi. A well-prepared breakfast is served in the cozy dining room with a special glass-roofed area and fine wood furnishings. This is a good economical alternative to the more expensive hotels. *52 Lansdowne Rd., Dublin 4, tel. 01/685512. 27 rooms. Facilities: wine license, light refreshments, TV and phones in rooms. MC, V.*

Dublin International Youth Hostel. Housed in a converted convent, it offers dormitory accommodations (up to 25 people per room) and also family-size rooms that can take up to four people. This is a spartan, low-cost alternative to hotels; nonmembers of the international youth hosteling organization can stay for a small extra charge. The hostel is located north of Parnell Square, near the Mater Hospital. *51 Mountjoy St., Dublin 1, tel. 01/301766. 500 beds. Facilities: restaurant. No credit cards.*

Iona House. This northside family-run guest house was converted from a large Victorian redbrick home. The genial Shoulderdice family make sure travelers have a comfortable visit at a reasonable price. All the modestly furnished rooms have showers and TVs. *5 Iona Pk., Dublin 9, tel. 01/306217. 11 rooms. MC, V.*

Isaac Tourist Hostel. This cheap alternative for young people has bunk beds in a dormitory situation. Bathrooms are also shared. You can't get any cheaper (around £5 a night), but if you're prepared to pay around £12 a night, you can get a private room. The hostel is close to the Busaras bus station and the city center. *2 Frenchman's La., Dublin 1, tel. 01/363877. 21 private rooms, 16 dormitory rooms. No credit cards.*

★ **Kilronan House.** This guest house, only a five-minute walk from St. Stephen's Green, remains a longtime favorite with vacationers, perhaps because of the friendly welcome they receive from the Murray family, who have run the place for 30 years. The large, late-19th-century terraced house, with a white facade, was well-converted, and the owners can be commended for updating decor and furnishings each year. Bedrooms are pleasantly furnished, with plush carpeting and pastel-colored walls. Another welcome plus for visitors, and rather rare in Dublin hotels, let alone guest houses, is the orthopedic beds, which guarantee a restful night's sleep. *70 Adelaide Rd., Dublin 2, tel. 01/755266. 12 rooms. Facilities: TV, radio, direct-dial phone in room, tea-making equipment. AE, DC, MC, V.*

Leeson Court. Two 18th-century terraced houses have been combined to form this recently opened hotel, which stands close to St. Stephen's Green and is just around the corner from the new Conrad (*see* above). The first sight to greet arrivals are two enormous bookcases in the lobby, filled with an enticing selection of old volumes. The tiny breakfast room is a real pleasure, with blue table linen, walls, and curtains, and a view of the garden. The small bedrooms are all cheerfully decorated in matching colors, with thick carpeting and stained-wood furnishings. The tiled bathrooms are surprisingly spacious. Although the windows in the front are double-glazed against traffic noise, some sounds do filter in, especially around 9 AM and 6 PM. The wood-paneled Darby O'Gill bar looks like a very old-fashioned country pub; during the late evening, there is real Irish music to set a lively mood. The conservatory at the back of the hotel faces a pleasant patio and beer garden. A nightclub is located in the basement, but it is fully sound-insulated from the rest of the building. *26–27 Lower Leeson St., Dublin 2, tel. 01/ 763380. 20 rooms. Facilities: bar, nightclub, restaurant. AE, DC, MC, V.*

Montrose House. Located on a secluded road near Herbert Park in Ballsbridge, this small 19th-century redbrick B&B features lovely gardens that rival the floral splendor of the nearby park. Mrs. Ryan's welcome will be warm, but the clean, no-frills rooms have no individual bath or shower facilities. Breakfast is the only meal served. *16 Pembroke Pk., Ballsbridge, Dublin 4, tel. 01/684286. 4 rooms. No credit cards.*

Mount Herbert. This rather sprawling guest house, derived from combining a number of large Victorian-era houses, overlooks fine rear gardens in the residential Ballsbridge district, right near the main rugby stadium and a 10-minute bus ride from Dublin center. The simple rooms are painted in light shades with little furniture besides the beds, but all of them have bathrooms and TVs. Guests can relax in the lounge, and a large restaurant, overlooking the back garden, serves three meals a day, with unpretentious dinners of steaks and stews. The place is a great favorite with budget-minded visitors from all over the world who seek comfortable accommodations. *7 Herbert Rd., Dublin 4, tel. 01/684321. 144 rooms. Facilities: restaurant, shop. AE, DC, MC, V.*

Suburbs and County Dublin

Expensive **Killiney Castle.** A 13-km (8-mi) drive from the Dublin city cen-
★ ter, this hotel is more agreeably situated than any lodging in the capital, for its lofty location allows guests sweeping views over south Dublin and parts of Dublin Bay. The original part of the hotel is a 19th-century stone castle, with a substantial modern addition where you'll find the bedrooms. Although some of these rooms are narrow, many are furnished with antiques and four-poster beds; they also feature large bathrooms and plenty of storage space. Ask for a room at the front of the building; the nighttime view over the lights of Dublin is spectacular. Restaurants include Jesters, in the basement disco, which has a mediocre grill menu, and Truffles, on the ground floor, which serves more formal breakfasts, lunches, and dinners. The health center is equipped with treadmills, bicycles, a sauna, squash and tennis courts, and a 25-meter (82-foot) indoor heated pool, and the hotel is convenient to golfing, horseback riding, and fishing. At the side of the hotel stands Killiney Hill, a viewpoint in a public park; the seaside village of Dalkey and Killiney Beach are both within comfortable walking distance. *Killiney, Co. Dublin, tel. 01/284–0700. 88 rooms. Facilities: 2 restaurants, indoor pool, tennis, squash, parking. AE, DC, MC, V.*

Moderate **Dalkey Island.** To get to this converted 19th-century two-story mansion on the edge of the sea, you take a pleasant drive out to Dalkey, a seaside village 13 km (8 mi) south of the city center; the village is also easily accessible by DART train. In the lobby, you'll find a photograph that shows the house 70 years ago. Although the pale pastel rooms are a bit cramped, they all look out to the Dalkey Island, and their balconies are useful in the summer. You'll find the service here friendly and informal. The relaxing bar and restaurant are popular with local residents. *Coliemore Harbour, Dalkey, Co. Dublin, tel. 01/285–0377. 20 rooms. Facilities: restaurant. AE, DC, MC, V.*

Forte Crest. The only hotel at Dublin Airport, this low-rise redbrick structure with a plain exterior has roomy but characterless sleeping accommodations. The lively bar features music during the weekends, while the usually crowded dual-level Garden Room restaurant serves mostly fish and meat entrées, as well as a good selection of vegetarian dishes. Some of the public rooms display interesting photographs from the early days of Irish aviation. *Dublin Airport, Dublin 1, tel. 01/ 379211. 195 rooms. Facilities: bar, restaurant, gift shop/ newsagent. AE, DC, MC, V.*

Kilternan Golf Hotel. This grand, rambling hotel, originally a 19th-century mansion, is set splendidly overlooking the rugged, wooded mountains around Enniskerry. The 16-km (10-mi) journey from Dublin center can be tedious when the traffic is slow moving, especially from 5 to 6 PM on weekdays, but the hotel's location is more than ample reward. Each of the spacious bedrooms has a double and a single bed, as well as a balcony and private bath. Ask for a room that overlooks the golf course and Scalp Mountain. The extensive sports facilities include an artificial ski slope, a golf course, a tennis court, and a full gym with exercise bicycles and a sauna. *Kilternan, Dublin 18, tel. 01/295– 5559. 53 rooms. Facilities: restaurant, sports gym, tennis, 18-hole golf course, indoor pool, gym, sauna, TV. AE, DC, MC, V.*

Montrose. This well-designed hotel, located near the Irish TV and radio studios (RTE) and across the road from University College's Belfield campus, features large, relaxing bedrooms that were recently repainted. It is only a 15-minute cab ride from the city center. *Stillorgan Rd., Dublin 4, tel. 01/269– 3311. 190 rooms. Facilities: bar, restaurant, gift shop/ newsagent, hairdresser. AE, DC, MC, V.*

Royal Marine. This 19th-century seaside hotel has been totally overhauled in recent years, and its public areas, bar, and restaurant have been completely modernized. The comfortable, capacious bedrooms have also been refurbished with contemporary decor; the eight suites with four-poster beds and separate sitting rooms preserve the lofty ceilings of the original building. Ask for a room at the front of the hotel, facing a gorgeous view of Dun Laoghaire harbor. *Dun Laoghaire, Co. Dublin, tel. 01/280–1911. 104 rooms. Facilities: restaurant. AE, DC, MC, V.*

Skylon. This modern five-story hotel, designed as a square box, with a concrete-and-glass facade, is located on the main road into the Dublin city center from the airport. The generous-size rooms have been plainly decorated in cool pastel shades; they have little furniture other than double beds and a couple of easy chairs. The ground-floor area has been substantially renovated, with a large bar and a restaurant. The cooking is adequate but uninspired, with dishes such as grilled steak, poached cod, and omelets. *Upper Drumcondra Rd., Dublin 9, tel. 01/379121. 92 rooms. Facilities: bar, restaurant, gift shop/ newsagent. AE, DC, MC, V.*

Tara Tower. A seven-story minitower in the Doyle chain, this unpretentious, informal hotel is not far from the Booterstown bird sanctuary. Its best rooms face Dublin Bay, stretching to the Howth peninsula. On the ground floor, you'll find a large

bar and a restaurant attractively refurbished with rustic woodwork. The menu includes grilled fish, steaks, and omelets, but
the food quality varies. The hotel service, though, is very per-
sonable. *Merrion Rd., Dublin 4, tel. 01/269–4666. 84 rooms.
Facilities: bar, restaurant, gift shop/newsagent. AE, DC, MC,
V.*

The Arts and Nightlife

Compared with most large cities, nightlife in Dublin may seem
distinctly unglamorous, though it begins around 10 PM and runs
until 4 AM. The plethora of pubs, some 900 in the city, is one
source of entertainment, and many in the city center offer musical
performances, often folk or jazz. For a good listing of cultural and
evening events, consult *The Irish Times*, which has a daily guide
to what's happening in Dublin and in the rest of the country, as
well as complete film and theater schedules; *The Evening Her-
ald* and *Evening Press*, with useful listings of theaters, cine-
mas, and pubs offering live entertainment; and *In Dublin*, a
fortnightly guide to all film, theater, and musical events
around the city.

The Arts

Classical Music The main theater for classical-music performance is the **National Concert Hall** (Earlsfort Terr., tel. 01/711888), which stages
orchestral concerts and smaller recitals throughout the year.
The **Royal Hospital Kilmainham** (Military Rd., tel. 01/718666)
also presents frequent classical concerts.

Films Dublin has two dozen cinema screens in the city center, but
only a few in the suburbs, which show a selection of current releases made in Ireland and abroad. Two theaters popular with
movie buffs are the **Lighthouse** (Middle Abbey St., tel. 01/679–
2644) and the **Screen** (College St., tel. 01/714988). **The Irish
Film Institute** (6 Eustace St., tel. 01/679–5744) has ambitious
plans for a new Irish film center, including two theaters.

Theater For theatrical productions, the main venues are the **Abbey**
(Lower Abbey St., tel. 01/744505), which stages mainstream
traditional plays, mostly Irish, and its sister theater at the
same address, the **Peacock,** which offers more experimental
drama. The Abbey originally opened in 1904 and became an important center for the Irish cultural renaissance. Poet W. B.
Yeats and Lady Gregory, an aristocratic writer and patron of
the arts, were prominent in the early Abbey, encouraging
young playwrights such as J. M. Synge. The original theater
burned down in 1951, but it reopened with a modern design in
1966.

The **Gate** (Cavendish Row, Parnell Sq., tel. 01/744045; *see* Tour
2: North City Center, above) stages a range of contemporary
plays, while the **Gaiety** (South King St., tel. 01/771717) and the
Olympia (Dame St., tel. 01/778962) both provide family-style
entertainment. The **Project Art Centre** (39 E. Essex St., tel. 01/
712321), the **Andrew's Lane Theatre** (9–11 Andrew's La., tel.
01/679–5720), and the **Tivoli** (Francis St., tel. 01/535998) present experimental productions.

Nightlife

Irish Cabarets/ Dance Clubs	**Leeson Street,** off St. Stephen's Green, is a main nightclub area from 10 PM to 4 AM. Clubs on this street include **Fanny Hill's, Suesey Street,** and **Von B's.** Dress at these places is informal, but jeans and sneakers are not welcome. Drink prices can be exorbitant, up to £20 for a mediocre bottle of wine, and these clubs are not licensed to sell beer or liquor. **Abbey Tavern** (Howth, Co. Dublin, tel. 01/390307) offers a rip-roaring cabaret with rousing Irish traditional songs. **Braemor Rooms** (Churchtown, tel. 01/298–8644) presents Irish and international stars in cabaret, with backing groups. **Burlington Hotel** (Upper Leeson St., tel. 01/605222) features a well-performed Irish cabaret, with dancing, music, and song. **Jury's Hotel** (Ballsbridge, tel. 01/605000) stages a cabaret show similar to that at the Burlington Hotel. **Pink Elephant** (S. Frederick St., tel. 01/775876), a noted night spot with a young crowd, has a full bar and books the latest rock stars.
Irish Music and Dancing	**Comhaltas Ceoltóiri Éireann** (35 Belgrave Sq., Monkstown, tel. 01/280–0295) offers boisterous summer evenings of genuine Irish music and dancing.
Pubs	**Bad Bob's Backstage Bar** (34 E. Essex St., tel. 01/775482) is a very popular pub with the young; the late-night crowd enjoys its live rock music. **Bartley Dunnes** (32 Lower Stephen St., tel. 01/533137), with its near-dark interior, attracts black-leather-and-chain-clad young people; its atmosphere is unusual because of its clientele, but it can be fun. **Brazen Head** (Bridge St., tel. 01/779549), Dublin's oldest pub, dates back to 1688; with its stone walls and open fires, it has changed little over the years. The place is renowned for traditional-music performances, as well as for lively sing-along sessions on Sunday evenings. **Dockers** (5 Sir John Rogerson's Quay, tel. 01/771692) is a trendy riverside establishment, just round the corner from Windmill Lane Studios, where U2 and other noted bands record. Bono of U2 is a frequent visitor here. You'll find sing-alongs here by the piano. **Doheny & Nesbitt** (5 Lower Baggot St., tel. 01/762945), a traditional spot with dark wooden decor and smoke-darkened ceilings, has hardly changed over the years. **Horse Shoe Bar** (Shelbourne Hotel, St. Stephen's Green, tel. 01/766471) has comparatively little space for drinkers around the semicircular bar; it's a popular meeting place for Dublin's smart social set, including politicians. **McDaid's** (3 Harry St., tel. 01/679–4395) attracted boisterous Brendan Behan and other leading writers in the 1950s; its wild literary reputation still lingers, although the bar has been discreetly modernized, and the atmosphere is altogether quieter. **Mother Redcap's Tavern** (Back La., tel. 01/538306) is an authentic re-creation of a 17th-century Dublin tavern, with stone walls from an old flour mill, beams, and plenty of old prints of the city, as well as trendy Victorian posters. **Neary's** (1 Chatham St., tel. 01/777371), with an exotic Victorian-style interior, was once the haunt of music-hall artists, as well as of a certain literary set. Today, actors and actresses from the adjacent Gaiety Theatre enliven the scene. **O'Donoghue's** (15 Merrion Row, tel. 01/762807), a cheerful,

smoky hangout, offers impromptu musical performances that often spill out onto the street.

Ryan's Pub (28 Parkgate St., tel. 01/776097) is one of Dublin's last genuine late-Victorian-era pubs, and has changed little since its last (1896) remodeling. Its dark mahogany counters, old-fashioned lamps, and snugs create a marvelously restful setting.

Slattery's (129 Capel St., tel. 01/727971) has an undistinguished decor, but it remains one of the city's best traditional-music showcases, with performances held almost every night.

Stag's Head (1 Dame Ct., tel. 01/6793701) dates back to 1770 and was rebuilt in 1895; it has a smoky atmosphere and an unusual counter, fashioned from Connemara red marble.

Toner's (139 Lower Baggot St., tel. 01/763090), though billed as a Victorian bar, actually goes back 200 years, with an original flagstone floor to prove its antiquity, as well as wooden drawers running up to the ceiling, a relic of the days when bars doubled as grocery shops.

4 Dublin Environs

County Wicklow, the Boyne Valley, and County Kildare

By Hugh Oram

Only an hour or two from Dublin, you can find yourself deep in the countryside, with landscape ranging from County Wicklow's magnificent rugged mountain scenery to County Kildare and County Meath's flat pastoral lands rich in historical remains. Newgrange in County Meath is perhaps Ireland's most important prehistoric site. Astride the River Boyne in County Louth is Drogheda, a fascinating town settled by the Vikings in the early 10th century. The Dublin environs also have an impressive eastern coastline stretching from Counties Wicklow to Louth, punctuated by delightful harbor towns and fishing villages. The coast is virtually unspoiled for its entire length.

Essential Information

Important Addresses and Numbers

Tourist Information
To answer questions on travel in the Dublin environs and for help in making lodging reservations, contact one of the following Tourist Information Offices: **Dublin City Center** (Upper O'Connell St., tel. 01/747733), **Dublin Airport** (tel. 01/379900), **Dun Laoghaire** (tel. 01/280–6984), **Dundalk** (tel. 042/335484), or **Mullingar** (tel. 044/48650).

Mullingar is the head office of tourism covering the counties of Wicklow, Louth, Meath, and Kildare. During the summer, temporary Tourist Information Offices are open throughout the environs, in towns such as Arklow, Bray, and Wicklow Town, in County Wicklow; Drogheda, in County Louth; Trim, in County Meath; and Athy, Kildare, Naas, and Newbridge, in County Kildare.

Emergencies
For **police, fire,** or **ambulance,** dial 999.

Getting Around

By Car
The easiest and best way to tour Dublin's environs is by car, because public transportation to the more outlying areas is infrequent. Dublin Airport offers a choice of a dozen car rental companies, and all the main national and international firms have branches in Dublin's city center. Some reliable car rental firms in the Dublin vicinity include **Avis** (Jury's Hotel, tel. 01/683394; 51 Grafton St., tel. 01/778877; Hanover St., tel. 01/774010; Dublin Airport, tel. 01/372369), **Hertz** (O'Connell St., tel. 01/788862; Leeson St. Bridge, tel. 01/602255; Dublin Airport, tel. 01/842–9333), and **Murray's Rent-a-Car** (Baggot St. Bridge, tel. 01/681777; Dublin Airport, tel. 01/378179).

By Bus
Bus services link Dublin with main and smaller towns in the environs. All bus services for the region depart from Busaras, the central bus station, at Store Street. For bus inquiries, contact **Bus Éireann** (tel. 01/366111).

By Train
Train services run the length of the east coast, from Dundalk to Arklow, with many intervening stops, including Dublin, where the main stations are Connolly Station (Amiens St.) and Pearse Station (Westland Row). From Heuston Station, trains run westward to Newbridge, The Curragh, and Kildare Town. Contact **Iarnród Éireann (Irish Rail,** tel. 01/366222).

Guided Tours

Bus Éireann (tel. 01/366111; information available Mon.–Sat. 9–7, Sun. 10–7) runs guided bus tours to many of the historic and scenic locations throughout the Dublin environs on a daily basis during the summer. Most tours depart from Busaras Station, Dublin, but some leave from regional destinations, such as Dun Laoghaire.

Gray Line (tel. 01/619666), a privately owned touring company, also runs many guided bus tours throughout the Dublin environs between May and September.

Exploring the Dublin Environs

Numbers in the margin correspond to points of interest on the Dublin Environs map.

County Wicklow

East Wicklow   Begin your tour of the eastern part of County Wicklow, often called the Garden of Ireland, in its main town and administrative center, **Wicklow Town,** 51 km (32 mi) south of Dublin on the N11, about one hour's driving time. Frequent train services to Wicklow Town run about every two hours from Connolly and Pearse Stations in Dublin. Buses leave from Dublin about every two hours. Train and bus times are both about 1¼ hours.

The English name of Wicklow derives from the Danish words *Wyking alo* (Viking meadow). The town's Main Street is attractive, divided into two levels and framed by trees. On this street at the entrance of the town are the extensive ruins of a 13th-century Franciscan friary, which was closed down under the 16th-century dissolution of the monasteries in the area. Inquire at the nearby priest's house (Main St., tel. 0404/67196) to view the ruins. Also on Main Street is a statue in honor of the town's most famous resident, Captain Robert Halpin (1836–1894). Wicklow has long had a strong seafaring tradition, but Halpin's career culminated in his commanding the *Great Eastern*, the pioneer mid-19th-century ironclad steamship that laid the first transatlantic cable. A grateful British government awarded Halpin a substantial pension, and he used the money to build Tinakilly House, 3 km (2 mi) on the Dublin side of the town, which is now a hotel and restaurant (*see* Dining and Lodging, *below*).

The most appealing area of Wicklow Town lies around the harbor. Harbour Road leads down to the pier; several alleyways connect this road to Main Street. A bridge across the River Vartry leads to a second, smaller pier, which is situated at the northern end of the harbor. From this end, follow the shingle beach, which stretches for 5 km (3 mi); behind the beach is the broad Lough, a lagoon noted for its wildfowl. Immediately to the south of the harbor, perched on a promontory that is a good viewing point for much of the Wicklow coastline, is the ruin of the **Black Castle.** This structure was built in 1176 by Maurice Fitzgerald, an Anglo-Norman lord who arrived with the English invasion of Ireland in 1169. The freely accessible ruins ex-

Dublin Environs

NORTHERN IRELAND

Castleblayney

Coothill

MONAGHAN

CAVAN

Bailieborough

Virginia

Lough Ramor

Crossakiel

R195 R154

28

Kells

Delvin

Kinnegad

Edenderry

Prosperous

Robertstown **32**

R409

Hill of **35**
Allen

Newbridge

36 **34**

Monasterevin

Kildare **The Curragh**

KILDARE

Dunlavin

Ardscull

Stradbally

37

Athy

38

39

Moone High
Cross

Castledermot **40**

Carlow

Castlecomer

Kilkenny

CARLOW N80

Omeath **15**

Carlingford Lough

Kilkeel

Greenore

14

13 **Carlingford**

R173 **Cooley**
Peninsula Drive

Dundalk **12**

R178

Inniskeen **16**

Carrickmacross

Kingscourt

R164

17 **18** **Louth**

Rathnetty

R171

R161

Ardee R170 Dunleer

LOUTH

Collon R168 **20** **Monasterboice**

N52

Mellifont Abbey **21**

King William's Glen **22** **19**

24 N51

Slane **Drogheda**

23 **Newgrange**

N51

25

Navan

MEATH

Athboy

Trim **27**

Laracor

R158

Summerhill

R156

Kilcock

Enfield

N4

Leixlip

Lucan

Maynooth **30**

Celbridge

Straffan **31** **29**

Liffey

Naas **33**

R410

Blessington

Russborough **8**
House

9

Poulaphouca
Reservoir

R759

Roundwood

3

WICKLOW

R756

Glendalough **4**

WICKLOW
MOUNTAINS

Laragh

R755

Rathdrum

5

Aughrim

R747

Woodenbridge

6 **Avoca**

7 **Arklow**

Tullow

Tinahely

R725

Shillelagh

Carnew

Bunclody

R725

Gorey

WEXFORD

N11

Dundalk Bay

Clogher Head

Clogherhead

Baltray

Irish Sea

Duleek R108

Balbriggan

Skerries

Garristown

Rush

Swords

Malahide

DUBLIN

Howth

★ **Dublin**

Dún Laoghaire

Dalkey

N81

R115

Bray **11**

Enniskerry

10 **Powerscourt Gardens**
and Waterfall

Newtownmountkennedy

R765 **Mount Usher**
Gardens

2 Ashford

N11 Rathnew

1 Wicklow
Head

Wicklow R750
Town

Glenealy R752

Brittas Bay

Avondale Forest
Park and House

N

0   6 miles

0   9 km

KEY

—— Rail Lines

Monasterboice

tend over a large area; with some difficulty, you can climb down to the water's edge.

Between one bank of the River Vartry, which flows into the harbor, and the road to Dublin stands the 18th-century **St. Lavinius Church** (Church of Ireland). The building is worth a visit to investigate the Romanesque door from a medieval church, the pews, the 12th-century stonework, and the atmospheric graveyard. The church is topped off by a green onion-shaped cupola, made from copper, which was added as an afterthought in 1771. *Admission free. Open daily 10–6.*

The old town jail, just above Market Square, has been transformed into a **Heritage Center** which not only displays exhibits on aspects of County Wicklow's rich and stormy history but also acts as a genealogical center. *Tel. 0404/67324, ext. 126. Admission free. Open weekdays 9–5, but call in advance, as the center closes when hosting field trips.*

Time Out | **Pizza del Forno** (Main St., tel. 0404/67075) serves inexpensive pizzas and steaks, as well as vegetarian dishes. With its red-and-white-check tablecloths, low lighting, and pizza oven blazing away, it provides an agreeable stop for the whole family.

From Wicklow Town, travel 6½ km (4 mi) north along the R750 and N11 roads to **Ashford.** Just before the village of Ashford, ② turn directly off the main road into **Mount Usher Gardens.** At the entrance to the gardens, you'll find a cluster of crafts shops, including a pottery workshop, as well as a bookshop. You pass through the self-service restaurant to reach the gardens, which cover more than 20 acres on either side of the River Vartry. Edward Walpole, who owned a Dublin textile firm, took over the mill in 1868 and converted the site to gardens. Succeeding generations of the Walpole family maintained the grounds so that today the gardens, under new ownership, have more than 5,000 species, including eucalypti, azaleas, camellias, and rhododendrons. Visitors can wander along the garden paths, through woodland glades, and across bridges that span the river. *Tel. 0404/40116. Admission: £2 adults, £1.30 children. Open Mar. 17–Oct. 31, Mon.–Sat. 10:30–6, Sun. 11–6.*

From Ashford, drive north on the N11; after 11 km (7 mi), you'll reach the small town of **Newtownmountkennedy.**

Time Out | **Harvey's Bistro** (tel. 01/819203), on the Dublin end of Newtownmountkennedy, is a two-story cottage that has been converted into a restaurant; it specializes in tasty Irish home cooking, with dishes such as corned beef and cabbage.

Turn off by the Catholic St. Joseph's Church on Newtownmountkennedy's main street and take the R765 west for 9½ km (6 mi)—past the reservoirs that supply Dublin's drinking water—as far as Roundwood.

③ **Roundwood,** standing 279 meters (900 feet) above sea level, is the highest village in Ireland. It consists of little more than a broad main street, although the Sunday-afternoon market held in the village hall, where cakes, jams, and other homemade goods are sold, can be a lively affair. From the main street, by the Roundwood Inn (*see* Dining and Lodging, *below*), a minor road leads west for 8 km (5 mi) to two lakes, **Lough Dan** and

Lough Tay, lying deep between forested mountains like Norwegian fjords.

Leave Roundwood by driving south on the R755, the main road to **Glendalough,** for 9½ km (6 mi). (Glendalough can also be easily reached from Dublin by taking the St. Kevin's bus service, which departs daily at 11:30 AM from the front of the Royal College of Surgeons on St. Stephen's Green; cost: £7 round-trip.) This valley with two lakes, situated between forested mountains, is the setting of some of Ireland's most significant monastic ruins. The 6th-century missionary St. Kevin, a descendant of the royal house of Leinster, came to the valley to live as a hermit. According to one tale, St. Kevin was pursued here by a stunning redhead named Kathleen, whom he proceeded to throw from a cliff into one of the nearby lakes. Whether or not the story is true, St. Kevin did indeed found a monastery here. Despite the attacks of the Vikings in the 9th and 10th centuries, the religious settlement continued to develop, only waning when English forces overran it in 1398. Substantial ruins were left behind and can be viewed today. Most of the buildings among the ruins are open all day and are freely accessible. The best introduction to the glories of the valley and lakeside is the new **Visitor Center,** which has models of Glendalough and an audiovisual presentation that tells its whole history. *Tel. 0404/45325. Admission: £1 adults, 70p senior citizens, 40p children. Open Mar.–May and Sept.–Oct., daily 10–5; June–Aug., daily 10–7.*

The **Teampaill na Skellig** (Church of the Oratory), on the south shores of the Upper Lake in Glendalough, is probably the oldest building on the site, dating from St. Kevin's time. A little to the east of this oratory is **St. Kevin's Bed,** a tiny cave in the rockface, about 9¼ meters (30 feet) above the level of the lake, where St. Kevin lived his hermit's existence in the 6th century. It is not easily accessible; you approach the cave by boat, but climbing the cliff to the cave can be dangerous and is not recommended. At the southeast corner of the Upper Lake is **Reefert Church,** also dating from the 6th century, whose ruins consist of a nave and a chancel. The saint also lived in the adjoining ruined beehive hut with five crosses, which marked the original boundary of the monastery. At this point, you'll have a superb view up the valley.

The ruins by the edge of the Lower Lake are the most important part of the whole Glendalough site. The gateway, beside the Royal Hotel, is the only surviving entrance to an ancient monastic site anywhere in Ireland. Inside, you'll observe an extensive graveyard, with many elaborately decorated crosses. The perfectly preserved, six-story **Round Tower,** which was built around the 11th or 12th century, stands 31 meters (100 feet) high. The entrance to the first story stands 8 meters (25 feet) above ground level. The largest building here, and on the entire Glendalough site, is the 7th- to 9th-century **Cathedral,** which is substantially intact, with the nave, chancel, and ornamental oolite limestone window, which may have been imported from England. The nave is small for a large church, only 9 meters (30 feet) wide by 15½ meters (50 feet) long.

South of the cathedral is the 3½-meter- (11-foot-) high Celtic **St. Kevin's Cross.** Made of granite, it is the best-preserved such cross on the site. **St. Kevin's Church,** an early barrel-vaulted oratory with a high-pitched stone roof, is also worth a visit. Besides exploring all the ruins, you can also take extensive walks around the lakes; the scenery around the Upper Lake is particularly awesome.

South of
Wicklow Town
From Glendalough, drive for 1½ km (1 mi) to the crossroads of Laragh, then 5 miles on the R755 to Rathdrum. South of here, signposted off the R752 to Woodenbridge, is the entrance to **⑤ Avondale Forest Park,** the location of **Avondale House.**

Avondale House resonates Irish history, for this was the home once owned by Charles Stewart Parnell, the 19th-century nationalist leader, who fell in love with a married woman named Kitty O'Shea; when her husband instituted divorce proceedings in 1890, the revelation of Parnell's affair during court hearings ruined his political career. The house, built in 1779, was acquired by John Parnell, great-grandfather of Charles Stewart, in 1795; Charles was born here in 1846. The two-story dwelling was used by the political leader as a residence and for social occasions, until his premature death in 1891.

The whole house has been flawlessly restored, with the reception and dining rooms on the ground floor filled with Parnell memorabilia, including many political cartoons of his time, which portray his efforts to secure home rule for Ireland. The surrounding estate and forest park are equally impressive. The park, which extends 523 acres, mainly on the west bank of the Avondale River, was the first forest in Ireland to be taken over by the state, in 1904; in subsequent years, a forestry school has been active here. Visitors can take a 5½-km (3½-mi) walk along the river or stroll along a pine trail and an exotic tree trail. They may also observe the ruins of a teahouse and the stump of a 350-year-old beech tree, with all the rings marked in relation to historic events in Ireland and the world. *Tel. 0404/46111. Admission: £2 adults, £1 senior citizens and children. Car park fee: £2. Open May–Sept., daily 10–1 and 2–6; Oct.–Apr., weekends noon–6.*

⑥ Return to the main road, the R752, and continue south for a further 6½ km (4 mi) to **Avoca,** a small hamlet set amid heavily forested hills at the confluence of the Rivers Avonbeg and Avonmore. At this deeply peaceful setting, beneath a riverside tree, the great poet Thomas Moore (1779–1852) composed his 1807 poem "The Meeting of the Waters." You can take some pleasant forest walks here, and visit **Avoca Handweavers** (tel. 0402/5105), the oldest handweaving mill in Ireland, with colorful tweed fabrics for sale.

Three km (2 mi) south of Avoca is another attractive village, **Woodenbridge,** situated at a meeting of the Rivers Aughrim and **⑦** Avoca. Continue for 8 km (5 mi) on the R747 to **Arklow,** the only industrialized town in County Wicklow; it has a fertilizer factory. The town is also an important fishing and maritime town in the county; though much of its appearance is somewhat grim, you can take restful walks along the river bank and around the harbor area. At the **Arklow Pottery Factory** on the quays, you can take guided tours and look at its crafts shop. *Tel. 0402/ 32401. Open weekdays 9:30–1 and 2–4:45, weekends 10–4:45.*

Arklow has a small **Maritime Museum,** set in the public library building by the railway station; it traces the town's distinguished seafaring traditions. *Tel. 0402/32868. Admission: £1 adults, 50p children. Open June–Sept., weekdays 10–1 and 2–5.*

To the immediate north of Arklow, off the R150 coastal road, are sandy beaches and quiet coves. The largest beach on **Brittas Bay** is popular in the summer with those on holiday from Dublin.

From Arklow, drive on the R747 road, passing Aughrim, a lovely little town, after 14½ km (9 mi). From Aughrim, take the R747, passing another small village, Tinahely; continue 8 km (5 mi) south of Tinahely on the R749 road, as far as **Shillelagh,** an attractive one-street village lined with stone cottages. About 3 km (2 mi) to the east of Shillelagh is **Coolattin Wood,** one of the last original native woods left in Ireland, with impressively tall oak trees. The timber for the roof of Dublin's St. Patrick's Cathedral came from here.

West Wicklow

8 **Russborough House** is one of the highlights of the western part of County Wicklow; it is situated just off the N81, 3 km (2 mi) south of Blessington, which can also be reached from Dublin by bus. To reach Russborough House from Wicklow Town by car, drive in the direction of Ashford on the main N11 road (in the direction of Dublin); then take the minor road that leads to Glendalough. From here, take the R756 across the Wicklow Gap as far as the main N81 road. When you reach the N81, right in the direction of Dublin; this road will lead directly to Russborough. To reach Russborough House from Shillelagh, head west on the R725, then turn right (north) at Tullow onto the N81 and drive toward Blessington.

Faced in gray Wicklow granite, this outstanding Palladian structure, built between 1740 and 1750, was designed by the architect Richard Castle, the first earl of Milltown. From the main block of the house, two semicircular loggias reach out to embrace the wings.

The main rooms of the building are decorated in baroque-style plasterwood, executed by the Francini brothers, Italian craftsmen who were active in Dublin in the mid-18th century. The house belongs to Sir Alfred Beit, the nephew of a German entrepreneur, and the Beit art collection that is on display includes works by Gainsborough, Goya, Rubens, and Velázquez, as well as bronzes and porcelain. Russborough looks out over an impressive artificial lake to the mountains of Wicklow; the extensive woodland on the estate is open to visitors. *Tel. 045/ 652329. Admission: £2.50, upstairs £1. Open Oct. 31, Sun., and public holidays 2:30–5:30; June–Aug., daily 2:30–5:30.*

Leave the grounds of Russborough House, turn right onto the main N81 road, and travel north for 3 km (2 mi) to **Blessington,** with its very wide main street lined on both sides by tall trees. This small market town, founded in the second half of the 17th century, used to be a stop on the Dublin–Waterford mail-coach service in the mid-19th century, and until 1932 a quaint steam train ran from here to Dublin, along the side of the main road. **9** Near Blessington is the great **Poulaphouca Reservoir,** which provides water for Dublin. At the southern end of the reservoir lie two glens of outstanding natural beauty, Poulaphouca and Hollywood. Near the latter glen are fine views from the summit of Church Mountain. You can drive around the entire perimeter of the reservoir on minor roads.

From Blessington, drive north on the N81 for 8 km (5 mi), then turn right onto the R759 and continue through wild upland country for 25½ km (16 mi) to the Sally Gap, a bleak crossroads.

At this junction, turn left onto the R115 for a further 13 km (8 mi) to Glencree; from here drive another 25½ km (16 mi) east along minor roads to Enniskerry.

The village of **Enniskerry** is a pretty spot, built around a central square and surrounded by the wooded Wicklow Mountains. (Enniskerry can also be reached directly from Dublin by taking the No. 44 bus from the Dublin quays area.) The main reason to visit here, however, is the estate of the **Powerscourt Gardens and Waterfall.** The grounds were originally granted to Sir Richard Wingfield, the first viscount of Powerscourt, by King James I of England in 1609. Richard Castle, the architect of Russborough House (*see* above), designed the grand Powerscourt House in the Palladian style; it was constructed between 1731 and 1740. In 1974 the house burned down, but there are now plans to restore the house to its original splendor, complete with antique furnishings and paintings. However, the Powerscourt Gardens, which were laid out from 1745 to 1767 and redesigned from 1843 to 1875, survived beautifully and are considered among the finest in Europe. The gardens were originally planned by Daniel Robertson, who drew his inspiration from two sources: the Villa Butera in Sicily, and copious amounts of sherry.

The gardens feature sweeping terraces, antique sculptures, and a circular pond and fountain flanked by winged horses; you have a magnificent view of the Italianate patterned ramps, lawns, and pond across the Dargle Valley to Sugar Loaf Mountain, one of Ireland's most dramatic vistas. The grounds include many specimen trees, an avenue of monkey puzzles, a parterre of brightly colored summer flowers, and a Japanese garden. The kitchen gardens, with their modest rows of flowers, are a striking antidote to the classical formality of the main sections. The gardens also offer a restaurant, a crafts center, and a children's play area. *Tel. 01/867676. Admission: £2 adults, £1 children. Open Mar.–Oct., daily 9–5:30.*

The equally renowned Powerscourt Waterfall, with a great height of nearly 124 meters (400 feet), is situated 5 km (3 mi) south of the gardens; it is the highest falls in the British Isles. *Admission: £1 adults, 50p children. Open daily 10:30–7, or until dusk in winter.*

From Enniskerry, travel 8 km (5 mi) along the road that skirts the River Dargle toward **Bray,** an unspectacular seaside community that offers a good sea walk along a 1½-km- (1-mi-) long promenade. (Bray may also be reached easily by the DART train from Dublin.) At the top of Main Street, the Heritage Center in the town hall houses many artifacts from Bray's history, such as old photographs and household items. *Tel. 01/ 868205. Admission free. Open Wed., Sat., Sun. 2–6.*

Bray is perhaps more well known for **One Martello Terrace** (tel. 01/286–8407), immediately by the harbor, where James Joyce (1882–1941) lived between 1887 and 1891. The writer used this house as the setting for the Christmas dinner in *A Portrait of the Artist as a Young Man.* Today the house is privately owned, but if you catch the owners on a good day, you may persuade them to show you the dining room; they recommend calling on Thursdays 10 AM–1 PM. Although the residence has been renovated, the dining room portrayed in Joyce's novel still maintains the spirit of his time.

Immediately off the Bray–Greystones Road just south of Bray, the **Kilruddery Gardens,** dating from the 17th century, have fine beech hedges, Victorian statuary, and a parterre of lavender and roses. *Tel. 01/863405. Admission: £1. Open May, June, Sept., daily 1–5; groups by appointment Apr.–Sept.*

County Louth

Dundalk and the Cooley Peninsula ⑫ The first stop on our tour of County Louth, **Dundalk,** lies 83 km (52 mi) from Dublin on the N1, about a 1½-hour drive. Frequent train services run to Dundalk from Dublin's Connolly Station, departing at roughly 1½-hour intervals. The fastest express train is one hour. Buses to Dundalk leave Dublin about every 1½ hours; the trip takes about two hours.

The history of Dundalk, the main town of County Louth, dates back to the early Christian period, around the 7th century. The area near the town is closely connected with Cuchulainn, a renowned figure in Irish mythology. Today, it is a frontier town, only 9½ km (6 mi) from the Northern Ireland border, and few traces of its past remain. The remnants of two early religious foundations do survive, however; on Mill Street, the **bell tower** of a Franciscan monastery with Gothic windows dates from the 13th century, while the Church of Ireland's **St. Nicholas,** on Market Square, incorporates a 15th-century tower. The church was rebuilt in 1707 and has a large, early 19th-century transept. In the graveyard lies the tomb of Agnes Galt, sister of Robert Burns, the 18th-century Scottish poet. The church is open only during services.

In the town center stands the Catholic **St. Patrick's Cathedral,** built between 1835 and 1847 when the Gothic revival was at its height. It is modeled on the 15th-century King's College Chapel, at Cambridge in England, with its buttresses and mosaics lining the chancel and the side chapel walls. *Open daily 8–6.*

Other 19th-century buildings in Dundalk include the **Market House,** the **Town Hall,** and the **Courthouse,** which is the most impressive of these, built in the 1820s in a severe Greek-revival style, with Doric columns supporting the portico. The Courthouse stands north of St. Patrick's Cathedral.

On the seaward side of Dundalk, extensive salt marshes and mud flats lie on the edge of Dundalk Bay. This area is one of the largest bird sanctuaries in Ireland: Species such as Brent geese, curlews, and oystercatchers are regular visitors. Leave Dundalk by the N1 road, driving northward for 6½ km (4 mi) to Ballymascanlon. Behind the Ballymascanlon Hotel (*see* Dining and Lodging, below), you'll find the neolithic **Proleek Dolmen,** a huge mushroomlike stone structure that dates back to the third millennium BC. Its capstone weighs nearly 50 tons.

⑬ From Ballymascanlon, you can begin the **Cooley Peninsula Drive.** Continue for 9½ km (6 mi) along the R173 road to **Gyles Quay,** a small coastal village with a clean, safe beach. From the village, you'll have excellent views southward along the County Louth coast to Clogher Head. The R173 continues round the east of the peninsula to **Greenore,** a distance of 11 km (7 mi). The town was built in Victorian times as a ferry-boat terminal, and today it has become a port for container traffic.

⑭ Continue 5 km (3 mi) eastward from Greenore along the R176 to **Carlingford,** a small fishing town dating from medieval times.

King John's Castle, a massive 13th-century fortress, still dominates the entrance to Carlingford Lough. An unusual feature of
this structure is the west gateway, which is only wide enough
to admit one horseman. At present, out of the historic buildings
in the town, only the castle is freely accessible to the public.
Other remnants from the medieval days include a tower from
the town wall and one of its gates, which later became the town
hall. The 15th-century **Mint Tower House** with mullioned windows also survives. The final survivor from the Middle Ages is
Taaffe's Castle, a 16th-century fortified town house.

Carlingford also has some striking thatched cottages, but what
makes it particularly attractive is its natural setting; the mountains of the Cooley Peninsula rise up from behind the town, the
Carlingford Lough lies at its front, and the Mountains of the
Mourne rise only 5 km (3 mi) away across the lough.

From Carlingford, drive for 6½ km (4 mi) northwest along the
R173 to reach **Omeath,** the final town on the peninsula.

Omeath was until recently the last main *Gaeltacht* (Irish-
speaking) village in this vicinity. On the eastern side of the village, you'll find the open-air Calvary and Stations of the Cross
at the monastery of the Rosminian Fathers. Jaunting cars
(traps pulled by ponies) take visitors to the site from the
quayside, which has stalls selling all kinds of shellfish from the
nearby lough, including oysters and mussels. A ferry service
runs from the quay to Warrenpoint, across the lough in Northern Ireland.

A narrow road climbs the mountains behind Omeath; as you
climb higher, the views become ever more spectacular, stretching over the Mountains of Mourne in the north and as far south
as Skerries, 32 km (20 mi) north of Dublin. This narrow road
leads back to Dundalk.

At **Inniskeen,** 14½ km (9 mi) west on the R178 from Dundalk
and just over the county boundary in Monaghan, the area's
most famous poet is commemorated at the **Inniskeen Folk Museum,** in a converted church next to a round tower. Patrick
Kavanagh (1906–1969), born and raised here, became one of
Ireland's leading poets and was brought back to the village for
burial. *Tel. 042/78102. Donations appreciated. Open May–
Aug., Sun. 2–5; other times, call for an appointment.*

In **Rathnetty,** 4.8 km (3 mi.) southwest of Dundalk on the R171,
the landmark known as **Cuchulainn's Stone** is said to be the
place where the ancient hero threw away his swords. He is reputed to have bound himself to this stone, so that even in death,
he would face his enemies standing. Not until a bird perched on
his shoulder could his adversaries be sure that Cuchulainn was
really dead.

Continue for 1.6 km (1 mi) southwest on the R171 off of the
R178, to the small village of **Louth,** set on a hill affording commanding views of the surrounding countryside. St. Patrick,
Ireland's patron saint, was reputed to have built his first
church in this village in the 5th century. He made St. Mochta
the first bishop of Louth; still standing in the village is the ex-
cellently preserved **St. Mochta's House,** an oratory dating from
the 10th century, with a high-pitched stone roof. The house is
freely accessible, but visitors should watch out for cattle in the
surrounding field.

From Louth, continue on the R171 passing **Ardee,** a market town with a broad main street. Ardee features two 13th-century castles that are presently closed to the public. **St. Mary's Church of Ireland** on Main Street incorporates part of a 13th-century Carmelite church. Proceed south from Ardee to Drogheda, taking the N2, the R168, and the N51 for a total of 20 km (12½ mi).

Drogheda
⑲

Drogheda is one of the most enjoyable historic towns to visit on the east coast of Ireland. It was colonized in 911 by the Danish Vikings; two centuries later, the town was taken over by Hugh de Lacy, the Anglo-Norman lord of Trim, in the neighboring county of Meath. At first, two separate towns existed on the northern and southern banks of the River Boyne. By the 14th century, Drogheda was not only heavily walled and fortified but also unified, making it one of the four most important towns in Ireland. Today it is an industrial town, with cement-making one of its key industries, but its setting on the River Boyne dispels any grim industrial feeling. Even the new ring road, which runs along the southern bank of the river, has not done too much visual damage to the urban landscape.

Originally, Drogheda had 10 gates in its town walls, but only one survives today: **St. Laurence's Gate,** with two four-story drum towers, is one of the most perfect examples in Ireland of a medieval town gate. Nearby, on Chord Road, is the **Siena Convent,** with a delightfully peaceful little chapel, well worth a visit. *Admission free. Open daily 8–8.*

From the St. Laurence's Gate, walk down the steep incline to the dock area, 400 yards away. The northern bank of the river is lined with the imposing warehouses built in the 18th century; this modern port is one of the busiest on the east coast. Towering over the river is the great length of the railway viaduct. Built around 1850 as part of the railway line from Dublin to Belfast, it is still used and is a splendid example of Victorian engineering; because of its height above the river, the viaduct remains the most prominent landmark in the town.

The center of the town, around West Street, is the historic heart of Drogheda. The bank building on the corner of West and Shop streets, called the **Tholsel,** is an 18th-century square granite edifice with a cupola; it used to house the town hall. Further along West Street is **St. Peter's,** a Roman Catholic parish church, built in striking Gothic style. It features a rather macabre point of interest for visitors: The preserved head of St. Oliver Plunkett is on display. He was a primate of Ireland who was martyred at Tyburn in London, in 1681. At the far end of West Street, where it becomes Narrow West Street, turn left toward the river, where you'll reach a well-preserved 13th-century tower. Rising 31 meters (100 feet), it is the only remaining portion of an Augustinian foundation.

On the heights above West Street, approached by streets and laneways that climb upward, you'll reach Fair Street. The 19th-century gray stone **Courthouse** displays 17th-century municipal charters and a sword and mace presented to the town council by William III after the Battle of the Boyne in 1690. *Admission free. Open weekdays 9–5:30.*

At the eastern end of Fair Street, turn left into the grounds of **St. Peter's Church of Ireland,** built in a severe 18th-century style, with a tower and a steeple. The building is rarely open except for Sunday services, but it has an impressive interior, with wooden pews, memorial tablets, an organ loft, and statuary. However, if the church is closed, you'll still have access to the fine views over the town from the churchyard. From this vantage point, Drogheda, despite all its recent development, still looks very much like a medieval town, with its uneven lines of slate roofs and chimneys.

The most striking feature on the horizon, seen from here, is the great mound of Millmount, on the other side of the river. You can reach this landmark off the Dublin Road, immediately south of town. The tower on top of this mound was built comparatively recently—two centuries ago—but the mound is said to be the site of an 11th-century BC burial place. The gateway to the top of the mound is usually open during the day; if you go to the top, you'll have more extensive views across Drogheda.

The old British Army barracks forming a square at the foot of the tower have been renovated and contain crafts workshops, including a weaver's shop, and the recently refurbished **Millmount Museum.** The museum houses many relics of eight centuries of Drogheda's commercial and industrial past, including painted banners of the old trade guilds; a circular, leather-covered coracle (the traditional fishing boat on the River Boyne); and many instruments and utensils from domestic and factory use. Rather surprisingly, the museum does not have many mementos of the most infamous episode in Drogheda's history, when the English leader Oliver Cromwell sacked the town in 1649, killing 3,000 people. *Tel. 041/36391. Admission free. Open summer, daily 3–6; Nov.–Apr., Wed.– Sun. 3–6. Crafts shops open all year, Mon.–Sat. 9:30–6.*

North of Drogheda From Drogheda's center, take the minor road north that follows the northern bank of the River Boyne estuary for 11 km (7 mi) to **Baltray,** which still bears a close resemblance to an 18th-century Irish fishing village; from Baltray, continue north another 8 km (5 mi) to the fishing village of **Clogherhead.** Take a walk above the local harbor to the heights of Clogher Head for outstanding views north to the Mountains of the Mourne and south to Skerries.

From Clogherhead, take the R170 for 23 km (15 mi) to Dunleer, then turn south onto the N1 Dublin–Belfast road, returning in the Drogheda direction for 13 km (8 mi) to the small village of **20** **Monasterboice,** with its fine collection of high crosses. The 10th-century **Muireradach Cross,** which stands nearly 6 meters (20 feet) high, is considered to be the best-preserved example of a high cross anywhere in Ireland; it features elaborate panels depicting biblical scenes, including a centerpiece of the Last Judgment. From the adjacent Round Tower, 34 meters (110 feet) high, the extent of the former monastic settlement at Monasterboice can be ascertained. The key to the tower door is held at the nearby gate lodge.

From Monasterboice, return to Dunleer and drive 9½ km (6 mi) west, passing through the small village of **Collon,** laid out in the 18th century with just a single main street. Continue 8 km (5 mi) south of Collon on the R168 and then take the signposted **21** right turn down the minor road to **Mellifont Abbey,** founded in 1142 as the first Cistercian monastery in Ireland; only fragments of the original ground plan survive. Some arches of the Romanesque cloister still exist, and substantial portions of the abbey buildings can still be seen, including the two-story chapter house in the 12th-century English-Norman style. This structure was once a daily meeting place for the monks and now stores a collection of medieval glazed tiles. The lavabo is a curious structure, originally octagonal; it is now roofless, and only four walls are left. *Tel. 041/26459. Admission: free. Open May–mid-June, Tues.–Sat. 9:30–1 and 4–5:30; Sun. 2–5:30; mid-June–mid-Sept. daily 9:30–6:30.*

West of Drogheda **King William's Glen** lies 6½ km (4 mi) west of Drogheda, off the
㉒ N51, following the northern bank of the River Boyne. A portion of King William's Protestant army hid here before the Battle of the Boyne (1690), which they won, and the nearby site of the battle is marked; many of the Protestant-Catholic conflicts in present-day Northern Ireland can be traced to the immediate aftermath of this battle. Part of the battle site is also incorporated in the nearby **Townley Hall Estate,** which offers forest walks and a nature trail. Continue on a farther 13 km (8 mi) west, branching off the N51, onto the signposted minor road leading to the prehistoric sites at Dowth, Knowth, and Newgrange.

However, it's only part of an even larger prehistoric burial ground, which includes the sites of **Dowth,** a mile to the northeast, and **Knowth,** about two miles northwest. These sites have been under excavation since 1962, and while Dowth is still closed to the public, the partially excavated site at Knowth opened recently. It is far larger and more diversified than Newgrange, with a huge central mound and 17 smaller ones. About one-third of the site has been excavated, and there are seven passage tombs open to visitors. You can also watch archaeologists at work on the rest of the site. The earliest tombs and carved stones here date from the Stone age (3000 BC), although the site was in use up until the early 14th century. In the Early Christian era (4th–8th centuries AD) it was the seat of the High Kings of Ireland. *Tel. 041/24824. Admission: £1 adults, 70p senior citizens, 40p children and students.*

㉓ **Newgrange** is one of the most spectacular prehistoric tombs in Europe. It was built in the fourth millennium BC with some 250,000 tons of stones that were brought to the site by people with only a primitive knowledge of architectural technology. How they transported the thousands of stones to the site remains a mystery, but the grave may have been the world's earliest observatory. The mound above the tomb is more than 11 meters (36 feet) at the front; white quartz stones were used for the retaining wall. The tomb is so carefully constructed that on the day of the winter solstice, the rays of the rising sun hit a roof box above the entrance to the grave. Then the rays shine for about 20 minutes down the passageway that leads to the interior and illuminate the burial chamber. Visitors to the interior of this Bronze Age tomb may see the effect re-created artificially. The geometric designs on some stones at the center of the burial chamber continue to baffle experts. The entire history of the site is narrated in the adjoining interpretive center. *Tel. 041/24488. Admission: £1.50. Open mid-June–mid-Sept., daily 10–7; Apr.–mid-June and mid-Sept.–mid-Oct., Mon.–Sat. 10–5, Sun. 2–5. Rest of year, Tues.–Sat. 10–1 and 2–5, Sun. 2–5.*

Return to the N51 and continue westwards for 5 km (3 mi) to the
㉔ agreeable crossroads village of **Slane.** Here you can visit the

Slane Castle demesne (estate) and take a fine walk to a 16th-century building known as the **Hermitage,** constructed on the site where St. Erc, a local man who was converted to Christianity by St. Patrick led a hermit's existence. Another pleasant tree-lined walk takes you along the River Boyne. The castle itself is not generally open to the public, but it does have a nightclub and a restaurant.

The **Old Mill Transport Museum,** situated near the River Boyne, features about 20 antique cars, as well as old commercial vehicles, motorcycles, horse-drawn carts, and bicycles. You can also stop here for tea. *Tel. 041/51827. Admission: £1. Open May–Aug., daily noon–6; Sept.–Apr., Sun. 2–6.*

About 1½ km (1 mi) to the north of Slane is the 155-meter- (500-foot-) high **Slane Hill,** where St. Patrick proclaimed the arrival of Christianity in 433 by lighting the Paschal Fire. From the top of the hill, you'll have sweeping views of the Boyne valley; on a clear day, the panorama stretches from Trim to Drogheda, a vista extending for 40 km (25 mi).

Ledwidge Cottage and Museum is located about 1 km (½ mi) east of Slane, on the road to Drogheda. This humble stone, slate-roofed cottage formerly belonged to Francis Ledwidge (1887–1917), a farm laborer who wrote lyric poetry. Just as he was beginning to win acknowledgment for his work, he joined the British Army and was killed in action in World War I. His cottage has now been furnished as it was in his time, a tribute to his short life. *Tel. 041/24285. Admission: £1. Open Mon.– Wed. 10–1 and 2–6; Sat. 10–1 and 2–7; Sun. 2–6.*

Time Out   The **Conyngham Arms Hotel** (tel. 041/24155), at the crossroads in Slane, is an agreeable, family-run establishment with a self-service buffet during the day and set meals at dinner, including such entrées as chicken cooked in Irish-whiskey cream sauce and shrimp scampi.

County Meath

Navan and the Hill of Tara   Begin your tour of County Meath at **Navan,** which is 48 km (30 mi) from Dublin on the N3 or a short drive on the N51 from Slane. Allow one hour's driving time from Dublin. Navan is also ㉕ 27 km (17 mi) on the N51 from Drogheda, about a half-hour drive. No trains run from Dublin to Navan, but buses leave Dublin every 1½ hours; the journey takes about 1¼ hours.

Navan, in County Meath, is a busy market and mining town of considerable antiquity, with evidence of prehistoric settlements, but its real development did not begin until the 12th century, when Hugh de Lacy, Lord of Trim, had the place walled and fortified, making it a defensive stronghold of the English Pale in eastern Ireland. On the main thoroughfare, Trimgate Street, the Catholic **St. Mary's Church,** built in 1839, features an interesting late-18th-century wood carving of the Crucifixion, the work of a local artist, Edward Smyth, who at the time was the greatest sculptor Ireland had produced since the Middle Ages. On Fridays, the Fair Green, beside the church, is the site of a bustling outdoor market. *Church open daily 8–8.*

You'll have the best view of the town from the motte of Navan, an artificial hill that may have once been the tomb of a prehistoric queen, but was more likely an Ice Age gravel deposit; it was adapted for use by D'Angulo, a 12th-century baron. D'Angulo was responsible for the first fairs in Navan. He also built a defensive castle on the hill, and today from its summit, visitors have panoramic views of the area and the River Black. Navan also offers a tree-lined walk along the Ramparts, the towpath of the now disused Navan–Drogheda canal. With some difficulty, because of the undergrowth, you can walk along the canal for 13 km (8 mi), as far as Slane.

26 The **Hill of Tara** is situated 13 km (8 mi) south of Navan; follow the main N3 road in the direction of Dublin. The hill is signposted to the right; take the minor road for 1½ km (1 mi). The site was originally the location for an Iron Age Celtic hill fort, surrounded by multiple ring forts; some of these were ruined in the 19th century by religious zealots from England who thought that they would find the ark of the covenant here. The hill gained prominence when used as the residence of one of the high kings of Ireland until the 11th century; the site became an inspiration for many Irish legends. The last king to live here was Malachy II, who died in 1022. While the Hill of Tara was used as a royal residence, a great national assembly *(feis)* was held here every three years, when laws were passed and tribal disputes were settled. Tara's influence waned with the arrival of Christianity.

Today on the hill, you can only see a modern statue of St. Patrick and a pillar stone that may have been the coronation stone of the early kings. In the graveyard of the adjacent Anglican church, you'll find a pillar with the worn image of a pagan god and a Bronze Age standing stone. However, the main attraction of the Hill of Tara is its height: It stands more than 155 meters (500 feet) above sea level, and from its top on a clear day, you can see across the flat central plain of Ireland, with the mountains of east Galway rising nearly 160 km (100 mi) away.

Trim Return from the Hill of Tara to Navan; 16 km (10 mi) south of **27** Navan is **Trim**, which has some of the finest medieval ruins in Ireland. In 1359, the town was walled on the instructions of the English king and its fortifications strengthened; several parliaments were held here in the 15th century. Oliver Cromwell captured the town in 1649 and killed most of its inhabitants.

On the southern side of the town, **Trim Castle**, the largest Anglo-Norman fortress in Ireland, is by far the most imposing ruin in present-day Trim. In 1173, it was built by Hugh de Lacy on a site that slopes down to the placid waters of the River Boyne; it was soon destroyed and then rebuilt from 1190 to 1200. The ruins cover two acres and include an enormous keep with 21-meter- (70-foot-) high turrets, flanked by rectangular towers; the outer castle wall is almost 500 yards long, and five D-shaped towers survive. The castle remains are freely accessible at all times. Facing the river is another ruin, that of the Royal Mint, an indication of Trim's political importance in the Middle Ages.

The **Yellow Steeple** overlooks the town from a ridge opposite the castle. Dating from 1368, it is a remnant of the 13th-century Augustinian abbey of St. Mary's. Much of the tower was destroyed in 1649 to prevent its falling into Cromwell's hands, and today, only the striking, 38-meter- (125-foot-) high east wall remains. On Loman Street, the Church of Ireland cathedral, **St. Patrick's**, is of recent origin, dating back to the early 19th century, but the square tower belongs to an earlier structure built in 1449. The town hall on Castle Street has records of Trim dating back to 1659; these papers may be seen during business hours on weekdays. The nearby Education Centre (tel. 046/ 31158), also on Castle Street, has regular exhibitions of historical material.

Several places of interest lie on the outskirts of Trim. At **Newtown,** 1¼ km (¾ mi) east of Trim on the banks of the River Boyne, is the ruin of what was the largest cathedral in Ireland, built by Simon de Rochfort, the first Anglo-Norman bishop of Meath, in 1210. At **Laracor,** 3 km (2 mi) south of Trim on the R158, there is a wall left of the rectory where Jonathan Swift, the great 18th-century satirical writer, was rector from 1699 to 1714. Nearby are the walls of the cottage where Esther Johnson, the "Stella" who inspired much of Swift's writings, once lived. From Laracor, continue for 8 km (5 mi) southeast along the R158 to **Summerhill,** one of the most pleasant villages of south County Meath; it has a large square and a village green with a 15th-century cross. Adjacent to Summerhill is **Cnoc an Linsigh,** an attractive area of forest walks with picnic sites, ideal for a half day's meandering. Many of the lanes that crisscross this vicinity of County Meath provide delightful driving between high hedgerows and afford occasional views of the lush pastoral countryside.

Kells ㉘ From Navan take the N3 northwest for 16 km (10 mi) to **Kells,** where St. Columba founded a monastery in the 6th century. In the 9th century, a group of monks from Iona in Scotland took refuge at Kells after being expelled by the Danes. Early in that century, these monks wrote and illustrated the Book of Kells, the Latin version of the four Gospels and one of Ireland's greatest medieval treasures. During the mid-17th-century Cromwellian wars, it was removed to Trinity College, Dublin, for safekeeping and remains there to this day, where it is on view in the Old Library (*see* Tour 1: South City Center in Chapter 3). A facsimile copy is on display in the Church of Ireland **St. Columba's,** in Kells. In the church graveyard stand four elaborately carved high crosses, while the stump of a fifth is in the marketplace; during the 1798 uprising, it was used as a gallows. Near the church is **St. Columba's House,** a small two-story 7th-century building measuring about 24 feet square; it is nearly 40 feet high with a steeply pitched stone roof, similar in appearance to St. Kevin's Church at Glendalough in County Wicklow (*see* County Wicklow, above) and Cormac's Chapel at Cashel in County Tipperary (*see* Chapter 6). Also adjacent to the church is the nearly 31-meter (100-foot) high Round Tower, in almost perfect condition, dating from before 1076. Unusually, its top story has five windows, each pointing to an ancient entrance to the medieval town.

County Kildare

North Kildare ㉙ **Celbridge,** the first stop on our tour of County Kildare, is 24 km (15 mi) from Dublin; take the N4 road out of Dublin. Between Lucan and Leixlip, turn onto the R403 and continue on the last 6½ km (4 mi) to Celbridge. The drive from Dublin will take 30 minutes. No train service runs between Dublin and Celbridge.

The Dublin City No. 67 bus leaves Middle Abbey Street, Dublin, at intervals of about one hour; the journey to Celbridge takes about one hour.

Celbridge is a rather nondescript market town, with a straggling main thoroughfare, but at the eastern end of this street, the gateway leads into one of Ireland's architectural glories, **Castletown House.** This immaculate Palladian-style house, with colonnaded wings at each side of the main building, was built in 1722 for William Conolly, the speaker of the Irish House of Commons. The house was designed by Alessandro Galilei, an Italian architect who created interiors as pleasing as the neoclassical facade. The intricate plasterwork in the halls was executed by the Italian Francini brothers; at the back of the house, the long gallery, painted in the blue Pompeian style and decorated with Venetian chandeliers, is the most notable of all the public rooms, which also include an 18th-century print room and a red drawing room. Downstairs, you'll find the nursery and the Victorian kitchen. The gardens are designed in the formal 18th-century style, with clipped hedges and neat lawns. The entire property is in an excellent state of preservation; the Irish Georgian Society was responsible for the renovation of both the house and the gardens. *Tel. 01/628–8502. Admission: £2.50. Open Apr.–Oct., weekdays 10–5, Sat. 11–6, Sun. 2–6; Nov.–Mar., weekends and public holidays 2–5.*

③⓪ From Celbridge, take the R403 west and turn north on the R406 to **Maynooth.** This tiny university town houses St. Patrick's College, a center for the training of Catholic priests that also serves as a lay university, much expanded in recent years. The ruins of **Maynooth Castle** are at the entrance to the college; the oldest part of the castle is the keep, which probably dates from the 13th century; although the keep and the great hall are still in reasonable condition, much of the castle was destroyed in 1647. The key to the castle can be obtained from Castleview House, opposite. *Tel. 01/628–5222. Admission free. Open June–Sept., daily 3–6. At other times, by appointment.*

At the eastern end of Maynooth is **Carton House,** once the residence of the dukes of Leinster. The house was designed about 1740 in the classical style by Richard Castle, who also designed Russborough House, near Blessington. The grounds feature The Shell House, whose interior is decorated entirely with seashells. *Tel. 01/628–6250. Admission: £1.50 adults, 50p children. The house can be seen by appointment.*

③① From Maynooth, take the minor road due south for 13 km (8 mi), to the village of **Straffan,** attractively situated on the banks of the River Liffey. The butterfly farm in Straffan is the only one of its kind in Ireland, featuring a tropical house with exotic plants, butterflies, and moths. Mounted and framed butterflies are available for sale. *Tel. 01/627–1109. Admission: £1. Open May–Aug., daily 10–6.*

Straffan's **Steam Museum** at Lodge Park is a relatively new attraction covering the history of Irish steam engines. These handsome machines were often used agriculturally to help in such operations as churning butter and threshing corn. The steam engines stand in the courtyard of an 18th-century house; there is also a collection of model locomotives. If you want to be sure of arriving on a "live steam day," when one or more engines will be in operation, phone in advance to confirm. *Tel. 01/*

628–8412. Admission: live steam days—£4 adults, £2 children; otherwise £3 adults, £2 children. Open mid-June–mid-Sept., Thurs.–Sun. 11:30–1 and 1:30–4:30.

From Straffan, follow the R403 for 16 km (10 mi) westwards; in **(32)** Prosperous, take the signposted turn to **Robertstown,** 2½ km (1½ mi) southwest. Here you can take scenic walks along the canal and boat trips on the water during the summer. The renovated late-18th-century canal hotel at Robertstown is now used for candlelighted dinners and musical entertainment. Dinners are preceded by an hour-long trip up and down the canal on the boat *Eustace. Tel. 01/452655 or 045/60020. Canal trip and dinner cost about £21 per person. Canal trips and dinners are offered in May and Sept. on Sun. and public holidays; June, July, and Aug., they are offered daily.*

From Robertstown, drive eastwards for 5 km (3 mi) along the minor road, then turn right (heading southeast) onto the R409. Just past this junction is **Mondello Park,** where frequent motor **(33)** races are held; drive for a further 11 km (7 mi) into **Naas,** a busy market town that St. Patrick is said to have visited more than once. Today, however, Naas is best known for the **Punchestown Racecourse,** which is located 3 km (2 mi) from the town. The racecourse has a wonderful setting amid rolling plains, and 16 km (10 mi) away, the Wicklow Mountains form a spectacular backdrop. Although horse races are held regularly here, the most popular event is the April steeplechase festival.

Time Out **Lawlor's Restaurant** (tel. 045/97085) at Poplar Square in Naas has been catering for visitors to the racecourse since the last century with its tradition of hearty meals of fish and steaks. Light meals are served in the bar, and as a gesture to modern tastes, vegetarian dishes are also available.

The Curragh and About 8 km (5 mi) south of Naas, past the uneventful town of
Kildare Town **Newbridge,** the **Curragh** starts; this broad plain, bisected by
(34) the main N7 road, is Ireland's major racing center, where each year several international horse races awarding substantial prize money are held; these meetings attract the upper echelons of Irish society, who enjoy intermingling four loves: horse racing, betting, champagne, and the social whirl. The Curragh is also the location for a large camp used by the Irish Army, whose main barracks are situated here; one of its prize relics is the armored car once used by Michael Collins, a leading Irish political leader who was assassinated in 1922. It can be seen with permission from the commanding officer (tel. 045/41301).

If time permits, a detour worth taking lies 8 km (5 mi) north-**(35)** west of Newbridge: the **Hill of Allen,** which is an outstanding landmark in the vicinity, rising 209 meters (676 feet) high. Because it is one of the few high points on the surrounding plain, it offers wonderful views. The hill also has a special place in Irish mythology, since it was the site of one of three royal palaces in Leinster some 1,500 years ago; Fionn Mac Cumhaill, the hero of many Irish folk tales, also lived here.

From the Curragh, continue along the N7 for a further 5 km (3 **(36)** mi) to **Kildare,** one of the most enjoyable towns to visit in this part of the country. **St. Brigid's Cathedral** (Church of Ireland), with its stocky tower, is immediately off the market square in the center of town. St. Brigid founded a religious settlement here in the 5th century; the present cathedral is a restoration of a building that dates from the 13th century. By the mid-17th century, the cathedral was in decline; it was partially rebuilt about 1686, but restoration work wasn't completed until much later, between 1875 and 1896. The stained-glass west window of the cathedral depicts three of Ireland's greatest saints: Brigid, Patrick, and Columba. *Admission free. Open daily 10–6.*

Outside, in the graveyard of the cathedral, but immediately adjacent to the main door, is the 33-meter- (108-foot-) high Round Tower, the second highest in Ireland, possibly dating from the 12th century. Energetic visitors can climb the stairs to the top, for extraordinary views across much of the Midlands. *Tel. 045/ 41654. Admission: 60p adults, 30p children. Open May–Sept., daily 10–6; Oct.–Apr., Sun. 2–5.*

South of the town about 2½ km (1½ mi), clearly signposted to the left of the market square, are the **Japanese Gardens,** considered by many experts to be the finest in Europe. They were founded in the early years of this century by Lord Wavertree, a brewing millionaire, who also owned the National Stud (*see* below), immediately adjacent. A Japanese gardener, Tassa Eida, laid out the gardens between 1906 and 1910, and they have been kept in perfect condition ever since. The gardens symbolize the passage of humanity through life. With miniature lakes, little rivers spanned by bridges, and a profusion of Asian trees and flowers, the gardens form an absolute oasis. The section depicting eternity has been created in the Japanese Karesansui style, with emblematic features in sand and stone. Visitors can visit a small tearoom and also a garden center with a good selection of bonsai trees. *Tel. 045/21617. Admission: £1.50. Open Easter–Oct., weekdays 10:30–5, Sat. 10:30–5:30, Sun. 2–5:30.*

The **National Stud,** where breeding stallions are stabled, is a main center of Ireland's racing industry. On application, visitors can tour the Stud and its fine selection of Thoroughbred horses. You can also enjoy the **Irish Horse Museum,** a small, modern building where displays are devoted to the history of the horse in Ireland. Its most outstanding exhibit is the skeleton of Arkle, the Irish racehorse that won outstanding victories in races in Ireland and England during the late 1960s. The museum also contains medieval evidence of horses, such as bones from 13th-century Dublin, and also some early examples of equestrian equipment. *Admission and hours for the museum are the same as for the Japanese Gardens; the entrance fee to the Gardens covers the museum.*

Time Out The **Silken Thomas** (tel. 045/22232), a pub in the market square of Kildare Town, re-creates an Old World atmosphere with open fires, dark wood decor, and leaded lights.

South Kildare From Kildare Town, take the N7 for 11 km (7 mi) to Monasterevin on the banks of the Grand Canal; then take the R417 for 19 km (12 mi) south as far as Athy. For most of its distance, the road runs in close proximity to the River Barrow, one of Ireland's major waterways; from the road, you'll have fine views across the river to the low range of wooded hills on the County Laois side of the river. **Athy** is an industrial and market town on the River Barrow, which widens considerably here. Overlooking the river, by the bridge, is a 16th-century castle, now a private house, that was built by the earl of Kildare to defend this strategic crossing. On the other side of the bridge from the castle is a pleasant park and the Catholic church, built in a pentagonal shape between 1963 and 1965; its striking interior features Stations of the Cross by George Campbell, a noted Irish artist; statues; and a crucifix on the high altar by local artist Brid ni Rinn. *Admission free. Open daily 8–6.*

Northeast of Athy, 6½ km (4 mi) off the N78, is the **Motte of Ardscull,** a large hillock by the roadside; from the crossroads here, turn right onto the minor road that leads for 8 km (5 mi) eastward toward **Ballitore,** a former Quaker settlement in the 18th and 19th centuries. An old schoolhouse here has been converted into a small Quaker museum. Among the pupils at the school was Edmund Burke (1729–1797), the great orator and political philosopher. *Tel. 045/31109. Admission: £1. Open sporadically, usually Sun. afternoons.*

Ballitore also has the **Crookstown Heritage Centre,** an old mill that has been converted into a museum of the flour milling and baking industries. *Tel. 0507/23248. Admission: £1 adults, 50p children. Open Apr.–Sept., daily 9–7, or on request.*

From Ballitore go to the main N9 road and drive south for 3 km (2 mi), as far as Timolin, where you'll reach the **Irish Pewter Mill,** a splendid tribute to an old Irish craft. Jugs, plates, and other pewter items are sold. *Tel. 0507/24164. Open weekdays 9:30–5; adjoining crafts center is also open weekends.*

Continue for a farther 1½ km (1 mi) south on the N9, and at the Moone Post Office, take the signposted right turn, continuing for 3 km (2 mi) to the **Moone High Cross,** an ancient Celtic cross that stands 5½ meters (17½ feet) high, with 51 sculptured panels showing scriptural scenes. From the main road at Moone, continue southwards on the N9 for 3 km (2 mi), as far as **Castledermot.** On the left-hand side of the village, you'll find an almost perfectly preserved 10th-century round tower together with two high crosses, equally well conserved, on the grounds of the local church. From the church gate, you can walk back to the main road along the footpath that is totally enclosed by trees. On the right-hand side of the road in the village, the substantial ruins of a Franciscan friary, mostly dating from the 14th century, are freely accessible.

From Castledermot, you can return to Naas on the N9 (43 km/ 27 mi).

Dining and Lodging

By Georgina Campbell and Hugh Oram

Updated by Alannah Hopkin

Highly recommended restaurants and hotels are indicated by a star ★. For further information about dining and lodging, *see* Chapter 1, Essential Information, and Chapter 3, Dublin.

Dining

Category	Cost*
Very Expensive	over £25
Expensive	£17–£25

Moderate	£12–£17
Inexpensive	Under £12

*per person, without service or drinks

Lodging

Category	Cost*
Very Expensive	over £100
Expensive	£80–£100
Moderate	£60–£80
Inexpensive	under £60

* All prices are for a double-size room, except where stated, and include a 10% local sales tax (VAT) and a 12% service charge.

County Wicklow

Blessington
Dining and Lodging

Tulfarris House. A restored 18th-century Georgian house in the grand style, this hotel features a comfortable sitting room with a large window facing the gardens and a marble fireplace. The 21 charming bedrooms, including some suites, all have private baths; the more expensive rooms are not only larger, they also have striking views out across Poulaphouca Lake. The French restaurant in the main house specializes in more expensive cuisine, while the courtyard bistro serves plainer fare. Isolated on its own grounds, the property offers sports facilities, including its own lakeside nine-hole golf course, fishing, croquet, and peaceful walks through its own woods. *Blessington, Co. Wicklow, tel. 045/64574. 21 rooms with bath. Facilities: 2 restaurants, bar, golf course, fishing, croquet, leisure center with swimming pool, gymnasium. AE, DC, MC, V. Very Expensive.*

Bray
Dining
★

The Tree of Idleness. This Greek-Cypriot restaurant, located on the extreme southern stop on the DART line from Dublin, happens to be one of the best restaurants in the country. Located near the seafront on the ground floor of a Victorian house, this pleasant dining spot specializes in classic dishes and good hearty portions. Roast lamb stuffed with feta cheese and olives is highly recommended. The extensive wine list includes Greek and Cypriot house wines. *Bray, Co. Wicklow, tel. 01/286–3498. Reservations advised. Dress: casual but neat. DC, MC, V. Dinner only. Closed Mon., Christmas, last week of Aug. and first fortnight of Sept. Expensive.*

Dunlavin
Dining and Lodging
★

Rathsallagh House. Joe and Kay O'Flynn's delightful home is well signposted, 56 km (35 mi) southwest of Dublin on the edge of the Wicklow Hills not far from where the N756 meets the N81. Set in 500 acres of parkland in some of the most beautiful countryside in the east of Ireland, this large, comfortable farmhouse was converted from Queen Anne stables in 1798 when the original house burned down; it's now run as a Grade A country-house hotel. Double rooms are each decorated in different colors and have large bathtubs. The homey atmosphere is accentuated by the ample cupboard space and the good selection of books in each room. Kay's talents in the kitchen are legendary, and the equally famous relaxed atmosphere belies a high standard of professionalism. Although the dining room is small, tables are tastefully set with linen cloths and napkins, silver cutlery, enormous wine glasses, candles, and fresh flowers. French doors open onto the croquet lawn and, on cool evenings, guests have a welcoming fire blazing in the grate. In the kitchen, homegrown vegetables and fruit complement hearty roasts of local lamb or beef. Specialties include twice-baked cheese soufflé and warm salad of pigeon breast. Sports facilities include a small golf course, a tennis court, an indoor heated swimming pool, and a sauna. *Near Dunlavin, Co. Wicklow, tel. 045/53112. 12 rooms with bath. Facilities: bar, restaurant. DC, MC, V. Very Expensive.*

Glendalough
Dining and Lodging

Glendalough Hotel. This old-fashioned 19th-century hotel, which sits in the glen at Glendalough, was recently refurbished. Upstairs, the cozy bedrooms, all with private baths, are decorated in quiet pastel colors; four rooms are triples. Downstairs, the bar has been modernized and the main restaurant, a long room with grand windows, looks out onto the Glendalough monastery and wooded mountain scenery, with the sound of running water from the stream outside. The rather plain menu features fish and meat dishes, but helpings are hearty. The hotel is a favorite stopping point in the area for visitors from around the world. *Glendalough, Co. Wicklow, tel. 0404/45135. 16 rooms with bath. Facilities: bar, restaurant, tennis, fishing. AE, DC, MC, V. Moderate.*

Rathnew
Dining and Lodging
★

Tinakilly House. This impressive Victorian mansion, situated on seven acres, was built in the 1870s by Captain Robert Halpin, a Wicklow man who made his fortune at sea. The great lobby at the entrance to the house stores mementos of Captain Halpin and his nautical exploits, including paintings and ship models. The house has been lovingly restored by William and Bee Power; the whole home is filled with impeccable Victorian antiques, and woods used originally in its construction, such as mahogany and pitch pine, have been meticulously replaced. Bedrooms have private baths, and some offer four-poster beds, Jacuzzis, and fine views of the Wicklow landscape. First-floor rooms are larger than the second-floor attic rooms, which are snug yet comfortable. A new wing of 15 suites named after sea captains was opened in 1991. The seven acres of Victorian gardens feature giant California redwoods at each end of the tennis court. The Irish country-house cuisine, with French influences in the presentation, uses fresh produce from the vegetable garden on the grounds. Specialties include roast breast of Barbary duck with fruit sauce, Wicklow lamb, and quail. *Rathnew, Co. Wicklow, tel. 0404/69274. 14 rooms with bath. Facilities: restaurant, bar, tennis court, golf and horseback riding nearby. MC, V. Very Expensive.*

Hunter's Hotel. This old coaching inn, first opened in 1830, has a lovely rural setting on the banks of the River Vartry, only 1 km (½ mi) east of Rathnew Village. A delightful Old World atmosphere has been maintained in the period prints, beams, and antique furnishings; the inn is a favorite place with local hunters and many foreigners. The magnificent garden stretches down to the river. All bedrooms are cozily furnished with Victorian-style flower-print wallpaper. Only 10 rooms have private tiled bathrooms; communal bathrooms for the remaining rooms can be rather Spartan. Ask about Room 17 on the ground floor, with a private garden entrance. Original Georgian furnishings have been extended to the dining room, where window tables are much in demand. In the summer, afternoon tea with homemade scones and jams served in the garden is delightful. The restaurant serves traditional country-house cuisine using homegrown produce in such entrées as roast Wicklow lamb with herbs and mint sauce, and baked sea trout with herbs and parsley butter. *Rathnew, Co. Wicklow, tel. 0404/40106. 18 rooms, 10 with bath. Facilities: restaurant (Moderate–Expensive), bar. AE, DC, MC. Moderate.*

Roundwood
Dining
★

Roundwood Inn. South of Dublin on the Glendalough road, amid spectacular scenery, you come to the highest village in the Wicklow Hills and this 17th-century inn. Furnished in a traditional style, with wooden floors and diamond-shaped windows, this place is remarkable for having changed so little over the years. Although the inn is best-known for good, reasonably priced bar food—homemade broth, Irish stew, Galway oysters, or smoked Wicklow trout—eaten at sturdy tables beside an open fire, the more expensive restaurant offers a combination of Continental and Irish cuisines, reflecting the traditions of the German proprietor, Jurgen Schwalm, and his Irish wife, Aine. In the long dining room, the most coveted of the dark wooden tables are the ones in front of the big log fires. Local produce figures prominently on the menu, especially roasts like rack of Wicklow lamb, prime Irish beef, and local game in winter. Wiener schnitzel is a house special, and the featherlight fresh cream *gâteau* dessert is not to be missed. *Roundwood, Co. Wicklow, tel. 01/281–8107 or 01/281–8125. Reservations required. Dress: casual but neat. MC, V. Closed Sun. dinner and Mon. except on public holidays, Christmas Day, Good Friday. Expensive.*

Wicklow Town
Dining and Lodging
★

Old Rectory Country House. Once a 19th-century rectory, this splendid country house in the Greek-revival style stands on a hillside just off the main road from Dublin on the approach to Wicklow Town. Owners Paul and Linda Saunders have successfully transformed the interior with dark marble fireplaces, bright colors, original oil paintings, and antique and contemporary furniture, all blending together beautifully. The light, spacious rooms with private baths are decorated in white and pastel shades with Victorian antique furniture. 1992 sees the dining room move into the new conservatory, built in the same period style as the house. Linda's innovative country-house cooking is based on pure ingredients, especially seafood and organic vegetables, and she specializes in salads and desserts, often including, or garnished with, edible flowers and herbs. Specialties include fillet of black sole stuffed with salmon and spinach terrine, and roast sea trout with a fresh herb sauce. Don't miss the house dessert, "Swan Lake" meringues, piped in the shape of swans and cygnets. *Wicklow Town, Co. Wicklow, tel. 0404/67048. 5 rooms, all with bath. Facilities: restaurant. AE, MC, V. Closed Oct.–Easter. Moderate.*

Grand Hotel. On the main Dublin road just as you come into Wicklow Town, this solid redbrick Victorian edifice has been thoroughly refurbished in recent years. Downstairs the bar serves plain yet tasty meals all day until 9 PM, while the large restaurant offers more elaborate lunch and dinner menus, featuring fish and lamb specialties of the region. Upstairs, on two floors, the clean and simple rooms all have private baths. The hotel makes no pretense to luxury, but it offers a very friendly and comfortable ambience. *Wicklow Town, Co. Wicklow, tel. 0404/*

67337. 14 rooms with bath. Facilities: bar, restaurant, TV and direct-dial phones in rooms. AE, DC, MC, V. Inexpensive.

County Louth

Ardee
Dining

The Gables House and Restaurant. Situated just off the Dublin–Derry road (the N2), not far from the Dundalk junction, this restaurant was originally a 1940s house built on a school playground. The place features traditional decor, with antique mahogany furniture, deep-burgundy velvet curtains, and oil paintings by local artists. Mats on the polished tables, silver cutlery, linen napkins, lace coasters, and gleaming lead crystal glasses all contribute to the intimate atmosphere. Expect generous portions and a French-influenced cooking style; dishes include seafood from the Celtic Sea—poached wild salmon, turbot, hake, and prawns, finished in a sauce of carrots, celery, and chives (the colors of the Irish flag)—and a chocolate mousse with Frangelico liqueur and chopped hazelnuts layered with meringue. *Dundalk Rd., Ardee, Co. Louth, tel. 041/ 53789. Reservations advised. Dress: casual but neat. AE, DC, MC, V. Dinner only. Closed Sun.–Mon.; first fortnight of June and first fortnight of Nov. Moderate–Expensive.*

Collon
Dining

Forge Gallery Restaurant. This well-established restaurant is located in a converted forge north of Dublin on the N2, just north of Slane. The reception area displays paintings by local artists for sale. Warm tones of rose and plum work well with the antique furniture; the old fireplace contributes real warmth to the atmosphere. The cuisine is a mixture of French provincial with a strong hint of traditional Irish in winter, when old favorites like silversides or boiled mutton with caper sauce appear on the menu. Two popular specialties are salmon and crab in phyllo pastry, and the Rendezvous appetizer with prawns and scallops in a cream and garlic sauce. Be sure to try one of the seasonal homemade soups. *Collon, Co. Louth, tel. 041/26272. Reservations advised; weekend reservations required. Dress: casual but neat. MC, V. Closed Sun.–Mon.; 4 days at Christmas and all of Jan. Expensive.*

Drogheda
Dining and Lodging

Boyne Valley Hotel. A converted 19th-century mansion that once belonged to a brewing family in Drogheda, this hotel is situated on extensive parkland. The hotel is approached by a 1-km- (½-mi-) long drive. Bedrooms are adequately comfortable, with uninspired decor. The new wing of the hotel, completed in 1990, has double rooms, all with private baths and contemporary furnishings. Other additions to the hotel include an attractive, plant-filled conservatory bar looking out over the parkland and the basement, which has been converted into the Sennhof Restaurant. With its wooden beamed ceiling and many posters from Switzerland, it offers an authentic Swiss menu, which includes such delicacies as *Berner Platte*, a mixture of many kinds of meat, such as pork and lamb. The wine list carries Swiss wines, a real rarity for Ireland. *Dublin Rd., Drogheda, Co. Louth, tel. 041/37737. 38 rooms with bath. Facilities: bar, restaurants, pitch-and-putt golf course. AE, DC, MC, V. Moderate.*

Dundalk
Dining and Lodging

Ballymascanlon Hotel. This converted Victorian mansion standing on its own grounds, just north of Dundalk, has long had a fine reputation in the area for comfort and good cuisine. Bedrooms have private baths, and the hotel offers a sports complex with an indoor heated swimming pool, a gymnasium, and a sauna. Other sports facilities include two squash courts, two tennis courts, and a nine-hole golf course. The main restaurant, serving Irish and French cuisine, specializes in fresh seafood entrées, such as lobster in season; the menu also includes vegetarian platters. The hotel grounds also feature an unusual historical artifact, a prehistoric monument known as the Proleek Dolmen. *Dundalk, Co. Louth, tel. 042/71124. 36 rooms with bath. Facilities: 2 bars, restaurant, pool, table tennis, billiards, squash, tennis, golf, gym. AE, DC, MC, V. Moderate.*

County Meath

Kells
Dining and Lodging

Lennoxbrook. This fine country home, run by Paul and Pauline Mullan, dates back over 200 years; it is situated 5 km (3 mi) north of Kells on the N3 road from Dublin to Cavan. The Mullans are the fifth generation of the family to occupy the house, which is filled with antiques and family heirlooms. Upstairs, the five rooms, all doubles, are furnished in the old style, with finely patterned wallpaper and period furniture; they share two bathrooms. Dinner may include freshly caught fish or locally raised lamb. The house is convenient to the Newgrange monument. *Kells, Co. Meath, tel. 046/45902. 5 rooms. Facilities: restaurant. No credit cards. Inexpensive.*

Kilmessan
Dining and Lodging

Station House Hotel and Restaurant. For anyone who likes the atmosphere of old railways, or simply good food served in unusual surroundings, the Flynn family's establishment is recommended. You reach the place by traveling up the N3 from Dublin to Navan and turning off the main road at the sign for the Hill of Tara, 9½ km (6 mi) before Navan. Continue down the side road for 6½ km (4 mi), past the Hill of Tara to Kilmessan. The railway station was once the junction for a hub of lines linking Dublin with County Meath, but it was closed down in 1952. The Flynns did a restoration job but kept the main features of the station. Diners can have their aperitifs on what was the old platform, while the old ticket office forms the dining room. The emphasis here is on local produce, including meat, vegetables, and fish, despite the inland location. Bedrooms are pleasantly decorated in a floral style; only half the rooms have private baths. Outside, the grounds have been well landscaped, but remnants of the old train station may still be seen, such as the signal box, the turntable for engines, and the engine shed (part of it used for bedrooms). *Kilmessan, Co. Meath, tel. 046/25239. 10 rooms, 5 with bath. Facilities: bar, restaurant. AE, MC, V. Moderate.*

County Kildare

Castledermot
Dining
★

Doyle's Schoolhouse Country Inn. Situated on the main Waterford–Dublin road (the N9) in south County Kildare, bordering on Counties Wicklow and Carlow, this renovated 1930s schoolhouse is slightly off the main tourist trail, but it has a strong local following. Small, intimate, and furnished with a homey mixture of antiques and newer furniture, the cozy atmosphere is appropriate to owner-chef John Doyle's wholesome country-house cooking, with a strong seasonal bias; entrées might include pike baked with sorrel stuffing served with cream and mustard sauce in the summer, or roast venison and pheasant in the autumn and winter. Especially recommended are the country pâtés and rough terrines, usually based on pork with legs of pheasant or duck liver. *Castledermot, Co. Kildare, tel. 0503/ 44282. Reservations advised; reservations required Sun.– Mon. Dress: casual but neat. AE, DC, MC, V. Lunch Sun. only; Apr.–Oct., informal lunch daily; dinner Nov.–Mar., Tues.–Sat.; Apr.–Oct., nightly. Moderate–Expensive.*

Dining and Lodging **Kilkea Castle.** Built in the 12th century as a defensive Anglo-Norman castle, this was the home of the FitzGerald family for centuries. The castle is said to be haunted by apparitions and the sounds of battle, even in its new role as a luxury hotel. Eleven rooms are situated in the castle itself, while the rest are found around the adjacent courtyard. Although most rooms are rather plainly furnished, all have private baths; bedrooms in the castle tend to be more luxuriously furnished. The restaurant is now located in what was the great hall of the castle; in these grand surroundings, typical Irish dishes are served, such as sirloin steak and grilled salmon steak. The hotel features its own sports complex and river fishing. *Castledermot, near Athy, Co. Kildare, tel. 0503/45156. 46 rooms with bath. Facilities: 2 bars, restaurant, heated indoor swimming pool, gymnasium, sauna, 2 tennis courts, river fishing for trout, clay-pigeon shooting, bowls, archery; horseback riding nearby. AE, DC, MC, V. Expensive.*

Maynooth **Moyglare Manor.** Just a half-hour drive southwest of Dublin,
Dining and Lodging this imposing Georgian mansion, set on 16 pastoral acres dotted with cows and sheep, is renowned for its magnificent antique furnishings. The gracious drawing room has velvet chairs, oil paintings, and thickly draped windows. The grand bedrooms feature four-poster canopy beds, roomy wardrobes, marble fireplaces, and comfortable chintz armchairs. Some of the bathrooms alone are as large as a room in a modern home. A cocktail bar is decorated with portraits of residents of the house over the past 150 years. Despite the grandeur of the surroundings, the romantic dining room can be pleasantly intimate, with a large mahogany sideboard, silver dishes, and fine crystal. The traditional French menu includes *crêpes au gruyère* and baked plaice stuffed with shrimps. Desserts tend to be rich and sophisticated; white-chocolate mousse is a typical choice. *Maynooth, Co. Kildare, tel. 01/628–6351 or 01/628–6469. 17 rooms with bath. Facilities: restaurant, 2 bars, tennis court; horseback riding nearby. AE, DC, MC, V. Very Expensive.*

Naas **Curryhills House Hotel.** This Georgian farmhouse with modern
Dining and Lodging additions and elegantly landscaped surroundings stands on the flat plain of Kildare, 11 km (7 mi) northwest of Naas on the R403. The spacious bedrooms are unremarkably furnished but relaxing, and they all have either a bath or a shower. The basement restaurant serves local country-style specialties, such as turkey raised by the owners and served with mushrooms. The bar is a popular local meeting spot, and during weekends, traditional Irish music livens up the atmosphere. The hotel offers no sports facilities, but guests can participate in coarse angling, horseback riding, and golf nearby. *Prosperous, near Naas, Co. Kildare, tel. 045/68150. 10 rooms. Facilities: bar, restaurant. AE, DC, MC, V. Moderate.*

Newbridge **Hotel Keadeen.** This modern, single-story hotel is set beside
Dining and Lodging the main N7 Dublin–Limerick road. The unpretentious, well-maintained rooms feature contemporary furnishings with

matching floral wallpaper and bedcovers. You can have lunch in the lounge bar, or lunch and dinner in the main restaurant, which overlooks neatly manicured lawns and flower beds. *Newbridge, Co. Kildare, tel. 045/31666. 37 rooms with bath, including 1 suite, 3 studios. Facilities: 2 bars, restaurant, parking, TV. AE, DC, MC, V. Moderate.*

5 The Lakelands

By Pat Mackey

*A resident of
Waterford, Pat
Mackey is the
author of the
travel guides*
Sunny South East
by Hook and by
Crook *and*
Lakeland.

*Updated by
Alannah Hopkin*

Irish schoolchildren were once taught to think of their country as a saucer with mountains around the edge and a dip in the middle. The dip is the Midlands—or the Lakelands, as the Irish Tourist Board prefers to call it, and this often overlooked region comprises seven counties: Cavan, Laois (pronounced "leash"), Westmeath, Longford, Offaly, Roscommon, and Monaghan, in addition to North Tipperary.

Appropriately, a fair share of Ireland's 800 bodies of water speckle this lush countryside. Many of the lakes which were formed by glacial action some 10,000 years ago are quite small, especially in Cavan and Monaghan. Anglers who come to the area have learned to expect a lake to themselves, and many return year after year to practice the sport. The River Shannon, one of the longest rivers in Europe, bisects the Lakelands from north to south piercing a series of loughs (lakes): Lough Allen, Lough Ree, and Lough Derg. The Royal Canal and the Grand Canal cross the Lakelands from east to west, ending in the Shannon north and south of Lough Ree. Stretches of both canals are now being developed for recreational purposes.

Quiet and unspectacular, the Lakelands demand thorough and leisurely exploration—the rewards are many, but night owls and thrill-seekers should probably head elsewhere. The towns themselves—including Nenagh, Roscommon, Athlone, Boyle, Mullingar, Tullamore, Longford, and Cavan—are not especially interesting, but they appeal strongly to people hungry for a time when the pace of life was slower and every neighbor's face was familiar. Accommodations in the area are simple but offer good value. The Lakelands is an important cattle area, and the local cuisine reflects this. And since no place in Ireland is more than an hour and a half from the sea, you can also expect to find fresh ocean fish—not to mention salmon and trout from the many rivers and lakes. A town's main hotel is usually the social center, a good place from which to study local life. You might witness a wedding reception (generally a boisterous occasion for all age groups), a First Communion supper, a meeting of the local Lions Club, or a gathering of the neighborhood weight-watchers group. In the countryside around the small, friendly towns, you'll discover several well-maintained historic homes with carefully tended gardens; the impressive monastic remains at Clonmacnoise, Boyle, and Fore; excellent fishing and uncrowded parkland golf courses; and numerous lovely country walks along the water.

Essential Information

Arriving and Departing by Plane

Airports The principal international airport serving the Lakeland region is **Dublin Airport** (tel. 01/379900). **Connaught International Airport** (tel. 094/67222) in Knock, County Mayo, is much smaller, and **Sligo Regional Airport** (tel. 071/68280) has daily flights from Dublin on Aer Lingus. Car rental facilities are available at Dublin and Knock Airports. For more information on these airports, *see* Chapters 3 (Dublin) and 9 (The Northwest).

Arriving and Departing by Car, Train, and Bus

By Car Mullingar, the regional capital, and Boyle are on the main N4 route between Dublin and Sligo. It takes one hour to drive from Dublin to Mullingar (55 km/34 mi), and two hours from Mullingar to Sligo. To get from Mullingar to the southwest of the country, you can take the N52 to Nenagh where it meets the N7 and follow that into Limerick—a trip (150 km/94 mi) of about two hours. The R390 from Mullingar leads you west to Athlone, where it connects with the N6 to Galway. The drive (120 km/75 mi) takes about 2½ hours.

By Train A direct rail service links Mullingar to Dublin, with three trains every day making the 1½-hour journey. It costs £10 one-way and £18 round-trip. Contact **Irish Rail** (tel. 01/366222) for information.

By Bus **Bus Éireann** (tel. 01/366111) runs an express bus from Dublin to Mullingar in 1½ hours, with a round-trip fare of £10. Buses depart three times daily. A regular-speed bus, leaving twice daily, makes the trip in two hours.

Getting Around

By Car Most of the winding roads in the Lakelands are uncongested, although you may encounter an occasional animal or agricultural machine crossing the road. If you're driving in the north of Counties Cavan and Monaghan, be sure to avoid "unapproved" roads crossing the border into Northern Ireland. The approved routes into Northern Ireland connect the towns of Monaghan and Aughnacloy, Castlefinn and Castlederg, Swalinbar and Enniskillen, Clones and Newtownbutler, and Monaghan and Rosslea. Those driving a rented car should make sure it has been cleared for cross-border journeys. You can rent a car at **Hamill Car and Van Rentals** (Dublin Rd., Mullingar, Co. Westmeath, tel. 044/48682), **Hanlon Bros. Ltd.,** (Dublin Rd., Longford, Co. Longford, tel. 043/46421), or **O'Meara's Car Hire** (Baylough, Athlone, Co. Westmeath, tel. 0902/92325).

By Train Trains from Mullingar, departing twice daily every weekday and Sunday, stop at Longford (35 minutes), Carrick-on-Shannon (1 hour), Boyle (1¼ hours), and Sligo (2 hours).

By Bus The express buses leaving Dublin (*see* Arriving and Departing by Bus, *above*) make stops at Mullingar (1½ hours), Longford (2¼ hours), Carrick-on-Shannon (3 hours), Boyle (3¼ hours), and Sligo (4¼ hours). There is also a daily bus from Mullingar to Athlone, and an express service connecting Galway, Athlone, Longford, Cavan, Clones, Monaghan, and Sligo. Details of all bus services are available from Bus Éireann depots at the following locations: **Athlone Railway Station** (tel. 0902/72651), **Cavan Bus Office** (tel. 049/31353), **Longford Railway Station** (tel. 043/45208), **Monaghan Bus Office** (tel. 047/82377), **Sligo Railway Station** (tel. 071/60066), and **Bus Éireann** (Dublin, tel. 01/366111).

Important Addresses and Numbers

Tourist Information Offices Information is available from Tourist Information Offices in **Mullingar** (Dublin Rd., tel. 044/48650), **Athlone** (Church St., tel. 0902/94630), **Banagher** (Crank House, tel. 0902/51458), **Birr** (Emmet Sq., tel. 0509/20110), **Roscommon** (The Square, tel. 0903/26342), **Boyle** (Bridge St., tel. 079/62145), **Cavan** (Farnham St., tel. 049/31942), and **Monaghan** (Market House, tel. 047/81122).

Hospitals and Pharmacies For medical and ambulance service, contact Mullingar's **General Hospital** (tel. 044/40221). You can buy pharmaceutical supplies from **Fairgreen Pharmacy** (Quinnsworth Shopping Centre, Mullingar, tel. 044/48471).

Exploring the Lakelands

Numbers in the margin correspond to points of interest on the Lakelands map.

Highlights for First-time Visitors

Birr Castle Demesne (*see* Tour 1)
Bord na Mona Bog Rail Tour (*see* Tour 1)
Clonmacnoise (*see* Tour 1)
Emo Court, near Portarlington (*see* Tour 3)
Shannon Boat Trip from Athlone or Banagher (*see* Tour 1)

Tour 1: North Tipperary and the West Lakelands

❶ This tour starts in the southwest corner of the region, in **Nenagh,** a small town on the N7—the busy main road that crosses the country from Dublin to Limerick. Nenagh was originally a Norman settlement; it grew to a market town in the 19th century. All that remains of the original settlement is **Nenagh Castle Keep,** in the center of town; it is about 31 meters/ 100 feet high and 16 meters/53 feet across the base. Opposite the castle is the old county jail. Its gatehouse and governor's house now form the **Nenagh Heritage Centre,** which has permanent displays on "Lifestyles in North West Tipperary" and Gaelic sports (football and hurling), as well as temporary painting and photography exhibits. *Tel. 067/32633. Admission: £1 adults, 50p children. Open mid-May to Oct. 31, weekdays 10:30–5, weekends 2:30–5.*

❷ Continue east on the N7 for 32 km/20 mi to **Roscrea.** The main road cuts through a 7th-century monastery founded by St. Cronan; you'll pass the west facade of a 12th-century Romanesque church that now forms an entrance gate to a modern Catholic church. Above the structure's round-headed doorway is a hood-moulding enclosing the figure of a bishop, probably St. Cronan. Roscrea's main attraction is located in the very center of town: **Damer House** and the **Roscrea Heritage Centre.** Damer House, a superb example of an early 18th-century townhouse on the grand scale, was used as a barracks during most of the 19th century; it was rescued from decay by the Irish Georgian Society. It was built in 1725 within the curtain walls of a Norman castle. In those days, homes were often constructed beside or attached to the strongholds they replaced. Damer House has a plain, symmetrical facade, and there's a magnificent carved pine staircase inside. The house contains the collection of the Irish Country Furniture Society, supplemented by pieces from the National Museum—a treat for those interested in antiques. In the adjoining building, exhibits take up monastic settlements in the Midlands, the old Irish kitchen, and other local and national themes. *Tel. 0505/21850. Admission: £1.20*

The Lakelands

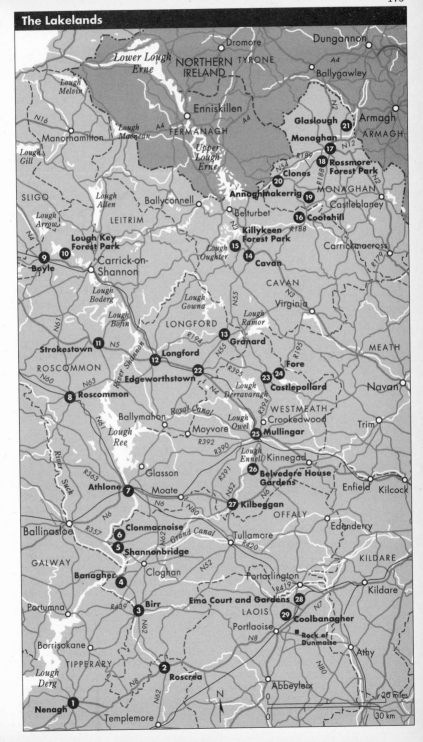

Dungannon

Dromore

Lower Lough Erne

NORTHERN IRELAND

TYRONE

Ballygawley

Lough Melvin

Enniskillen

FERMANAGH

Glaslough

Armagh

21

Monaghan

ARMAGH

17

Manorhamilton

Lough Maonean

Upper Lough Erne

R189

18 **Rossmore Forest Park**

Lough Gill

N16

Ballyconnell

N54

20 Clones

Belturbet

19 Annaghmakerrig

MONAGHAN

Castleblaney

SLIGO

Lough Allen

LEITRIM

16 Cootehill

Lough Arrow

N4

Lough Key Forest Park

Lough Oughter

15 Killykeen Forest Park

R188

Carrickmacross

9 Boyle

10

Carrick-on-Shannon

N3

14 Cavan

R179

Lough Boderg

CAVAN

N61

Lough Bofin

LONGFORD

Lough Gowna

Virginia

N3

MEATH

11 Strokestown

N5

River Shannon

R194

13 Granard

Lough Ramor

R195

ROSCOMMON

N60

N63

12 Longford

N55

R395

23 **24** Fore

Navan

8 Roscommon

22 Edgeworthstown

N4

Lough Derravaragh

23 Castlepollard

R394

N61

Ballymahon

Royal Canal

Lough Owel

WESTMEATH

Crookedwood

Trim

Lough Ree

Moyvore

25 Mullingar

R392

Lough Ennell

Kinnegad

River Suck

R363

Glasson

R391

26 **Belvedere House Gardens**

N6

Enfield

Kilcock

Athlone 7

Moate

N6

N52

N6

Ballinasloe

R357

N80

27 Kilbeggan

OFFALY

Edenderry

6 **Clonmacnoise**

Grand Canal

Tullamore

KILDARE

5 **Shannonbridge**

N62

R420

Kildare

GALWAY

Banagher 4

Cloghan

N52

Portarlington

Portumna

R439

3 Birr

R419

Emo Court and Gardens 28

N7

Kildare

Borrisokane

N62

LAOIS

29 Coolbanagher

TIPPERARY

Portlaoise

N8

Rock of Dunmaise

Athy

Lough Derg

2 Roscrea

Abbeyleix

N80

20 miles

1 **Nenagh**

Templemore

N

0   30 km

adults, 50p children. Open mid-May–Oct. 31, weekdays 10–5, weekends 2–5.

❸ Leave Roscrea on the N62 and head north for 19km (12 mi) to one of the most attractive towns in the region: **Birr,** a quiet, sleepy place with tree-lined malls and modest Georgian houses. All roads lead to the gates of **Birr Castle Demesne,** an imposing Gothic castle dating from the early 17th century that is still the home of the earls of Rosse; it is not open to the public. However, you can visit the surrounding 100 acres of gardens, the oldest of which was planted three centuries ago. The present earl and countess of Rosse continue the family tradition of making botanical expeditions for specimens of rare trees, plants, and shrubs from all over the world. The formal gardens contain the tallest box-hedges in the world (10 meters/32 feet). In spring, you'll see a wonderful display of flowering cherries, magnolias, crab apple blossom, and naturalized narcissi; in autumn, the maples, chestnuts, and weeping beeches blaze red and gold. The grounds are laid out around a lake and along the banks of two adjacent rivers; above one of these stands the castle. The grounds also contain the remains of a giant (72-inch) reflecting telescope built in 1845, which remained the largest in the world for the next 75 years. Allow at least two hours to see all the features here. *Tel. 0509/20056. Admission: £3 adults, £1.50 children. Open daily 9–1 and 2–5:30.*

❹ From Birr take the R439 9.5 km/6 mi northwest to **Banagher,** a village on the Shannon that is a popular base for water-sports fans. If you happen to be in Banagher on a Thursday or a Sunday, you can take a two-hour Shannon Cruise on the *River Queen,* an enclosed launch that seats 54 passengers and has a full bar on board. *Silver Line Cruisers Ltd., The Marina, Banagher, Co. Offaly, tel. 0902/51112. Cost: £3 adults, £2 children. Departures mid-May–mid-Sept., 3 PM Thurs.; 2:30 and 4:30 PM Sun., weather permitting.*

Time Out **Flynn's** (Main St., Banagher, tel. 0902/51566), a light and spacious Victorian-style bar in the village center, offers a lunch menu of generously filled sandwiches, salad platters, a roast meat of the day, chicken, fish, or burgers and chips. It's a popular spot with the boating crowd and can be busy on weekends.

Leave Banagher by the R456, turning off after about 2 km/1 mi, and follow signposts for Shannonbridge and Clonmacnoise. On either side of the road, you'll notice vast stretches of chocolate-brown boglands and isolated industrial plants for processing this area's natural resource. Bog is used in peat-fired electricity-generating stations, compressed into briquettes for domestic hearths, and made into moss peat and plant containers for gardeners. Ireland's liberal use of a resource that is scarce elsewhere in Europe provoked an indignant reaction from botanists and ecologists in the 1980s, which resulted in the setting aside of certain bog areas for conservation. Among these are the Clara Bog and Mongan's Bog in County Offaly, both relatively untouched, raised pieces of land with unique flora, and the Scragh Bog in County Westmeath. Because of the preservative qualities of peat, it is not unusual to come across bog timber 5,000 years old, or to dig up perfectly preserved domestic implements from more recent times—not to mention the occasional cache of treasure. Deer, badgers, and wild dogs inhabit the boglands, along with a rich bird and plant life. These areas are being preserved by Bord na Mona, the same government agency that makes commercial use of other boglands.

If you would like to have a close look at a bog, follow the signs in **⑤** **Shannonbridge** for the **Bord na Mona Bog Rail Tour,** which leaves from **Uisce Dubh,** 10 km/6 mi from Shannonbridge. A small green and yellow diesel locomotive pulls one coach across the bog at an average of 24 km/15 mi per hour while the driver provides commentary on a landscape unchanged for millennia. There are over 1,200 km/745 mi of narrow-gauge bog railway, and the section on the tour, known as the Clonmacnoise and South Offaly Railway, is the only part accessible to the public. *Uisce Dubh, near Shannonbridge, Co. Offaly, tel. 0905/74114. Admission: £2.50 adults, £1.50 children. Tours on the hour, Mon.–Sun. 10–6, Sun. 2–6, but Oct.–Apr. call ahead to confirm weekday schedule.*

⑥ **Clonmacnoise,** once one of Ireland's most important monastic settlements, is clearly signposted from Shannonbridge. The remaining buildings are situated on an esker, or natural gravel ridge, that overlooks a large marshy area beside the River Shannon. When the settlement was founded by St. Ciaran in 545, the Shannon was an important artery of communication, so that the site was not as remote as it appears now. Take time to survey the surrounding countryside from the higher parts of Clonmacnoise, and you'll get a good idea of the strategic advantages of its commanding riverside location.

In its heyday, Clonmacnoise was the burial place of the kings of Connaught and of Tara. It survived raids by feuding Irish tribes, Vikings, and Normans until 1552, when the English garrison from Athlone reduced it to ruin. Since then it has remained a prestigious burial place; among the ancient stones are many other graves of local people dating from the 17th to the mid-20th century, when a new graveyard was consecrated on adjoining land. The older surviving buildings include the shell of a small cathedral, two round towers, the remains of eight smaller churches, and several high crosses, the best preserved of these being the Cross of the Scriptures, also known as Flann's Cross. Some of the treasure and manuscripts originating from Clonmacnoise are now housed in the National Museum in Dublin. *Co. Offaly, tel. 0905/74195. Admission: £1 adults, 40p children. Open mid-June–Sept., daily 9–7; Oct.–May, daily 10–6.*

Turn left out of the car park at Clonmacnoise, and signposts will lead you to the village of Ballynahown where you'll turn **⑦** north onto the N62 Athlone road. **Athlone** originated as a crossing point of the Shannon, at first as a ford. It marks the boundary between the old provinces of Leinster (to the east) and Connacht (to the west). **Athlone Castle** was built beside the river in the 13th century. After their defeat at the Battle of the Boyne in 1691, the Irish retreated to Athlone and made the Shannon their first line of defense. The castle was extensively renovated in 1991, the 300th anniversary of this rout. It remains an interesting example of a Norman stronghold and houses a small museum of artifacts relating to Athlone's eventful past. *Town Bridge, Athlone, Co. Westmeath, tel. 0902/ 94360. Admission: £1 adults, 40p children. Open June–Sept., Mon.–Sat. 11–1 and 3–6.*

Athlone, the main shopping hub for the surrounding area, is an important road and rail junction, but it contains nothing of great interest to the visitor. Rather than explore its narrow, congested streets, take a ride on the *M. V. Avonree* riverboat up the Shannon to nearby Lough Ree. *The Strand, Athlone, tel. 0902/92513. Admission: £3.50 adults, £2.50 children. Sailings July–Sept. at 11, 2:30, and 4, except Wed. 4:30 only. 1½ hours duration; light refreshments on board.*

8 To explore the region west of the Shannon, take the N61 from Athlone for 32 km/20 mi to **Roscommon,** the capital of County Roscommon, where sheep and cattle raising is the main occupation. As you enter this pleasant little town on the southern slopes of a hill, you'll pass the remains of **Roscommon Abbey** on your right. The principal ruin is a church; at the base of the choir stand eight sculpted figures representing gallowglasses, or medieval Irish professional soldiers. The ruins are freely accessible. To the north of the town are the weathered remains of **Roscommon Castle,** a large Norman stronghold dating from the 13th century. After seeing it, wander around the town center, a quiet place with buildings designed mainly in late-Georgian and Victorian styles. Note the Bank of Ireland in the main square: This gracious Georgian building, once the courthouse, served as the Catholic Church until 1902.

9 Those with an interest in fishing and walking will want to continue north on the N61 for 43 km/26 mi to **Boyle,** a delightful, old-fashioned town situated on the Boyle River midway between Lough Gara and Lough Key. The ruins of **Boyle Abbey** (on the N4), dating from the late 12th and early 13th centuries, still convey an impression of the splendor of this richly endowed Cistercian foundation. The nave, choir, and transept of the cruciform church are in good condition. The ruins are freely accessible.

10 Boyle is a mecca for anglers and walkers who can choose between the challenges of the Curlew Mountains to the north of the town, or **Lough Key Forest Park** to the east, a popular base for campers and backpackers. The park consists of 340 hectares/840 acres on the shores of the lake, and contains a bog garden, a deer enclosure, and a cypress grove; boats can be hired on the lake. *Tel. 079/62214. Car park: £2. Freely accessible.*

11 The main tour leaves the N61 after about 12 km/8 mi at Tulsk, turning right (east) on to the N4 for **Strokestown Park House.** Like many villages near a "big house," **Strokestown** was designed to complement the house. The widest main street in Ireland—laid out to rival the Ringstrasse in Vienna—leads to a Gothic arch, the entrance to the house grounds. As you can see from its facade, this enormous house, seat of the Pakenham Mahon family from 1660 to 1979, has a complicated architectural history. The Palladian wings were added in the 18th century to the original 17th-century block, and the house was extended again in the early 19th century. The interior is full of curiosities, such as the gallery above the kitchen, which allowed the lady of the house to supervise domestic affairs from a safe distance. Menus were dropped from the balcony on Monday mornings with instructions to the cook for the week's meals. One wing houses lavish stables with vaulted ceilings and Tuscan pillars. There is also a distillery and a fully equipped nursery. The gardens are undergoing an ambitious restoration plan that will include the widest and longest herbaceous borders in Ireland. A museum documenting local events during the disastrous Famine (1845–1850) is due open in 1993. *Strokestown, Co. Roscommon, tel. 078/33013. Admission: £2 adults, £1 children. Open June 1–Sept. 15, Tues.–Sun. 12–5.*

From Strokestown, continue east on the N4 for 23 km/14 mi to Longford, the starting point of the next tour.

Tour 2: The Northern Lakelands

⑫ **Longford,** the county seat of County Longford, is a typical little market community on the main (N5) Dublin–Sligo road. Pick up the R194 Ballinalee–Granard road to visit **Carriglass Manor,** 5 km/3 mi outside town. The romantic Tudor-Gothic house was built in 1837 by Thomas Lefroy. His descendants still reside here, and they are proud that as a young man in England, Lefroy was romantically involved with the novelist Jane Austen. Just why they never married is a mystery, but it is believed that she based the character of Mr. Darcy in *Pride and Prejudice* on Mr. Lefroy. The house features some good plasterwork and many of its original mid-19th-century furnishings. A magnificent stableyard belonging to an earlier house on the site dates from 1790. Visitors also have access to a small costume museum. *Co. Longford, tel. 043/45165. Admission: stableyards and gardens 50p; house tour £1 adults, 50p children. Open Mon., Tues., Fri., Sat. 12–5, Sun. 2:30–6.*

⑬ Continue east from the manor on the R194 to **Granard.** This market town and fishing center stands on high ground near the Longford–Cavan border. The **Motte of Granard** at the southwest end of town was once the site of a fortified Norman castle. In 1932 a statue of St. Patrick was erected here to mark the 15th centenary of his arrival in Ireland. (At least a dozen statues of the patron saint, all virtually identical, were put up that year; see how many others you can spot on your travels.)

Leave Granard on the N55 and drive north for 30½ km/19 mi to **⑭** **Cavan.** Cavan is an undistinguished little town serving the local farming community, but it has two attractions that you might like to visit. **Cavan Crystal** is an up-and-coming rival to Waterford in the cut-lead-crystal line; the company offers guided factory tours and access to their factory shop. This is a good opportunity to watch skilled craftspeople at work if you can't make it to Waterford. *Cavan Town, tel. 049/31800. Guided tours: weekdays 10:30, 11:30, 2:30, 3:30.*

The **Cavan Folk Museum** holds what is called with pride "the Pig House Collection": costumes, kitchen and household goods, farmyard tools, machinery, and other bric-a-brac tracing the rural lifestyle from the 1700s to the present. At some quarters in the area, that way of life has changed so little that the "museum pieces" are still in use around the farm—which may be why the locals are so fond of this collection. *Cornafean, Cavan Town, tel. 049/37248. Admission: £1.50 adults, 50p children. Phone to confirm opening hours.*

Time Out **The Annalee Restaurant** (Hotel Kilmore, Dublin Rd., tel. 049/32288) is a bright two-tier room overlooking landscaped gardens. Fresh local produce is cooked in traditional Irish style, and vegetarian dishes are also available.

Traveling north from Cavan on the N3, you can follow signs to
(15) Killykeen Forest Park. Organized within the beautiful mazelike
network of lakes called **Lough Oughter,** this 600-acre park offers a series of planned and signposted walks and nature trails.
*Tel. 049/32541. Admission free. Parking £1.50. Open Feb.–
Dec., daily 9–5; closed Jan.*

Beyond Cavan you enter the heart of the northern Lakelands,
with lakes both large and small on either side of the road. County Cavan and County Monaghan each have at least 180 lakes.
The countryside is characterized by drumlins—small, steep
hills consisting of boulder clay left behind by the glacial retreat
10,000 years ago. The boulder clay also filled in many of the pre-
glacial river valleys, causing the rivers to change course and
create shallow lakes, which provide excellent fishing.

(16) The route then takes you northeast up the R188 to **Cootehill.**
Fans of the songwriter Percy French (1854–1920) will recall
the opening lines of his famous song "Come Back; Paddy Reilly,
to Ballyjamesduff," which instruct the traveler in search of
that little paradise to "turn to the left at the bridge of Finea,
and stop when halfway to Cootehill." In fact, as locals will delight in telling you, if you follow these instructions you will not
get to Ballyjamesduff at all—you'll get hopelessly lost.

Cootehill is one of the most underestimated small towns in Ireland. It has a lovely setting on a wooded hillside, and its wide
streets, with their intriguing old shops, are always busy without being congested. Most of its visitors are anglers from Europe, the United Kingdom, and the rest of Ireland. Walk up to
"the top of the town" (past the White Horse Hotel) and you will
see the entrance gates to **Bellamont Forest.** Only pedestrians
are allowed through the gates, which lead, after about a mile of
woodlands, to an exquisite hilltop Palladian villa, small but perfectly proportioned, and virtually unaltered since it was built
in 1728. It is now a private home but is occasionally opened to
the public. If you are interested, inquire locally or at the Tourist Information Office in Cavan (tel. 049/31942).

Leave Cootehill for Monaghan on the R188, and enjoy the lack
of traffic, which is typical of the undulating backroads in drum-
(17) lin country. **Monaghan** is an attractive county town built
around a central diamond. The old market house, dating from
1792, is now the **County Museum.** Its display tracing the history of Monaghan from earliest times to the present day is the
winner of a European Community Heritage Award. *Tel. 047/
82928. Admission free. Open Tues.–Sat. 11–1 and 2–5.*

Leave Monaghan on the R189 Newbliss road. Just outside the
(18) town you will pass **Rossmore Forest Park,** 280 hectares/691
acres of low hills and small lakes with pleasant forest walks and
signposted nature trails that are freely accessible. At Newbliss
you can follow an optional excursion (about 4.8 km/3 mi)
(19) signposted **Annaghmakerrig.** Here you will find a small forest
park with a lake, and above it Annaghmakerrig House, home of
the stage director Sir Tyrone Guthrie until his death in 1971.
He left it to the nation as a residential center for writers, artists, and musicians. It is not officially open to the public, but
anyone with a special interest in the arts or in its previous owner can ask to be shown around.

(20) Continue on the R183 from Newbliss to **Clones.** This is border
country—also known as bandit country—and aimless explor-

ing, especially on roads marked "Unapproved Road" (which lead to unmanned border crossings), is not recommended. In early Christian times, Clones was the site of a monastery founded by St. Tighearnach, who died here in AD 458. An Augustinian abbey replaced the monastery in the 12th century, and its remains can still be seen near the 23-meter/75-foot **Round Tower.** In the central diamond of the town stands a 10th-century Celtic high cross, with carved panels representing scriptural scenes. Nowadays Clones, a small agricultural market town, is known chiefly for lace making. A varied selection of lace is on display around the town and can be purchased at the **Clones Lace Centre.** *Co. Monaghan, tel. 047/51051. Admission free. Open Mon., Wed., Sat. 9:30–5.*

Return to Monaghan on the N54 (21 km/13 mi). If you have time for one more excursion in the area, leave Monaghan on the N12 11km/7 mi out of town and take the first left (R185) for **㉑ Glaslough,** which means "green lake." On the shores of its deep, beautiful waters is **Castle Leslie,** originally a medieval stronghold, which has been the seat of the Leslie family since 1664. The present castle was built in 1870 in a mix of Gothic and Italianate styles. The Leslie family, a mildly eccentric one known for its literary and artistic leanings, has many notable relations by marriage, including the duke of Wellington, who defeated Napoleon at Waterloo, and Sir Winston Churchill. Wellington's death mask is preserved at Castle Leslie, as is Churchill's baby dress, along with an impressive collection of Italian artworks. *Co. Monaghan, tel. 047/88109. Admission to house: £2, adults, £1 children. Open July 19–Aug. 19, daily 2–6; other times by appointment. Admission to gardens: £1 adults, 50p children. Open May–Oct., daily 10–5.*

Tour 3: The Eastern Lakelands

This tour takes Longford as its starting point, exploring the areas to the east and south. Those with literary interests may **㉒** wish to stop in **Edgeworthstown** (also known as Mostrim), 12 km/8 mi east of Longford on the N4. This town was the home of the novelist Maria Edgeworth (1769–1849), whose highly original satirical works, the best known of which is *Castle Rackrent*, were admired by such contemporaries as Sir Walter Scott and William Wordsworth, both of whom visited here. The family residence, Edgeworthstown House, at the eastern end of the village, is now a private nursing home and not open to the public. The Edgeworth family vault, where Maria and her father, Richard Lovell Edgeworth, an author and inventor, are interred, is located in the churchyard of St. John's Church.

㉓ From Edgeworthstown take the R395 for **Castlepollard,** a pretty village of multicolored houses laid out around a triangular green. One and a half km (1 mi) outside the village you'll find **Tullynally Castle and Gardens,** seat of the earls of Longford and the Irish home of the literary Pakenham family, whose members include the prison reformer and antipornography campaigner Frank Pakenham (the current earl of Longford); his wife Elizabeth and his daughter Antonia Fraser, both historical biographers; and his brother Thomas, a historian. The original 18th-century building was extended in the Gothic style in the 19th century, making it the largest castellated house in Ireland, with an elaborate facade of turrets and towers. In addition to a fine collection of portraits and furniture, the house contains many fascinating 19th-century domestic gadgets, as well as an immense kitchen. The grounds also include a landscaped park and formal gardens. *Co. Westmeath, tel. 044/61159. Admission to castle and gardens: £2 adults, £1 children; admission to gardens only: £1 adults, 50p children. Gardens open June–Sept., daily 10–5; castle rooms open July 16–Aug. 15, daily 2:30–6, and by appointment to groups.*

㉔ From Castlepollard take the R195 and follow signposts to **Fore,** where you will find the remains of **Fore Abbey.** The oldest structure here is St. Fechin's Church, dating from the 10th century, with a massive cross-inscribed lintel stone. Nearby are the remains of a 13th-century Benedictine abbey, whose imposing square towers and loophole windows resemble a castle rather than an abbey. The site is freely accessible.

Before leaving Fore, you might wish to visit the **Ben Breeze Open Farm,** just outside the village on the Kells road. The farm is basically a traditional dairy and pig farm, with 40 cows and 40 sows on 40 hectares/80 acres. There is also a large collection of fowl, including peacocks, quail, doves, and several varieties of hens and chicks; the most popular attraction is usually the baby pigs. *Fore, Co. Westmeath, tel. 044/66338. Admission £1. Open Mon.–Sat. 10–6. Closed Sun.*

㉕ Return to Castlepollard and take the R394 to **Mullingar,** a busy commercial and cattle-trading center situated on the Royal Canal midway between two large, attractive lakes, Lough Owel and Lough Ennel. This is an area of rich farmland, and the town is known as Ireland's beef capital; farmers all over Ireland describe a good young cow as "beef to the ankle, like a Mullingar heifer." The buildings in the town date mostly from the 19th century, with the exception of the large **Catholic Cathedral of Christ the King,** which was completed in 1939 in the Renaissance style. Finely carved stonework decorates the front of the cathedral, and the spacious interior has mosaics of St. Patrick and St. Anne by the Russian artist Boris Anrep. *Admission free. Open daily 9–5:30.*

The **Military and Historical Museum** is also worth a visit. On display here are weapons from the two World Wars, boats of oak from the 1st century AD, and uniforms and other articles of the old IRA. *Columb Barracks, tel. 044/48391. Admission free. Open to the public by appointment only.*

Time Out The **Bloomfield House Hotel** (Mullingar, Co. Westmeath, tel. 044/40894) is just outside Mullingar on the N52 Kilbeggan road on the shores of Lough Ennell. The castellated white building dates from 1837 and was previously a convent. A selection of salads and sandwiches is served in the bar, while the more formal Lakeview Restaurant offers classic French cuisine.

㉖ Leave Mullingar on the N52 heading south. You might like to stop 5 km/3 mi out of town to visit **Belvedere House Gardens,** remarkable for a beautiful setting on the northeast shore of Lough Ennel. Terraced gardens descend in three stages to the waters of the lake and provide a panoramic view of its islands. The estate also contains a walled garden with many varieties of trees, shrubs, and flowers, and parkland landscaped in the 18th-century style. *Mullingar, Co. Westmeath, tel. 044/40861. Open May–Sept., daily 12–7. Admission £1 adults, accompanied children free.*

27 **Kilbeggan,** 24 km/15 mi south of Mullingar on the N52, is known mainly for its distillery, which was established in 1757 to produce a traditional Irish malt whiskey. It closed down in 1954 and was re-opened in 1987 by Cooley Distillery. Cooley makes its whiskey in County Louth but brings it to Kilbeggan to be matured in casks. The Kilbeggan distillery has been restored as a museum of industrial archaeology illustrating the process of Irish pot whiskey distillation. The site also features a crafts center with a resident potter and a demonstration of coopering—the making of the oak barrels in which the whiskey matures. *Kilbeggan, Co. Westmeath, tel. 0506/32134. Admission: £1.50 adults, £1 children. Open Apr.–Oct., Mon.–Sat. 9–6, Sun 10–6; Nov.–Mar., Mon–Sat. 10–4:30, Sun 2–6. Guided tours every half-hour April–Oct.*

Continue on the N52 to **Tullamore,** the county seat of Offaly, on the Grand Canal. Turn left on the R420 and drive 27 km/17 mi until you reach **Portarlington,** a charming Old World town that until quite recently had a sizable bilingual (English/French) population of Huguenot origin. Next, proceed 8 km/5 mi south
28 of the town on the R419 to **Emo Court and Gardens.** The house was designed by James Gandon, architect of the Custom House and the Four Courts in Dublin, on a similarly grand scale. The domed rotunda, inspired by the Roman Pantheon, is one of the most impressive rooms in Ireland. This vast circular space is lit by a lantern in the coffered dome, which rests on gilded capitals and marble pilasters. The house has been magnificently restored by its present owner; it's a wonderful example of living on the grand scale. The grounds also include formal gardens with classical statuary and rare trees and shrubs. *Emo, Co. Laois, tel. 0502/26110. Admission to gardens: £2 adults, £1 children and senior citizens. Admission to house: £2.50. Gardens open daily 10:30–5:30; house open mid-Mar.–mid-Oct., Mon. 2–6 and by arrangement.*

If Emo Court has turned you into an admirer of the work of James Gandon, you will enjoy a visit to the exquisite **Church of**
29 **St. John the Evangelist** in **Coolbanagher,** 1½ km/1 mi south on the R419. Gandon's original 1795 plans are on view inside the building, which also has an elaborately carved 15th-century font. *Open daily 9–6.*

The R419 joins the main N8 Cork–Dublin road about 1⅝ km/1 mi south of Coolbanagher.

Sports and Fitness

Bicycling

One of the best ways to immerse yourself in the natural beauty of the Lakelands is to tour the region on a bicycle. Twisting roads, generally in good condition, lead from one magnificent view to another, and there are picnic places in the state-owned forests just off the main road. The Irish Tourist Board recommends two long tours: one of the Athlone-Mullingar-Roscommon area, and another of the Cavan-Monaghan-Mullingar region. But part of the pleasure of traveling on bicycle is breaking away from the prescribed routes and making discoveries on your own. Shops that rent cycles in the Lakelands region include the following: **M.R. Hardiman** (Irishtown, Athlone, Co.

Westmeath, tel. 0902/78669), **Brendan Sheerin** (Main St., Boyle, Co. Roscommon, tel. 079/62010), **E. Clerkin** (Main St., Monaghan, Co. Monaghan, tel. 047/81434), and **Leo Hunt** (Main St., Roscommon, Co. Roscommon, tel. 0903/26299).

Boating

There are 300 miles of navigable rivers and island-studded lakes in the region, and several companies rent out charter boats of varying sizes for vacations on the water. Most of these vessels hold from six to eight people, and all are operated by the parties who rent them: **Athlone Cruisers Ltd.** (The Jolly Mariner Marina, Athlone, Co. Westmeath, tel. 0902/72892), **Carrick Craft** (The Marina, Banagher, Co. Offaly, tel. 0902/51187), **Celtic Canal Cruisers Ltd.** (24th Lock, Tullamore, Co. Offaly, tel. 0506/21861), **S.G.S. Marine** (Glasson, Athlone, Co. Westmeath, tel. 0902/85163), and **Silverline Cruisers** (Banagher, Co. Offaly, tel. 0902/51112).

Fishing

For pike, you'll find the most fruitful areas around Cavan, Clones, Cootehill, Castleblaney, Kingscourt, Carrick-on-Shannon, Boyle, Belturbet, and Butlersbridge. Keep in mind, however, that certain laws have been passed to protect and conserve the dwindling population of Irish pike: You are forbidden to use live fish bait, to fish with more than two rods, to transfer live roach from one water to another, or to kill more than three pike in a day. For rudd fishing, the best places are the waters around Mullingar (Lough Patrick, Lough Analla, and the Royal Canal) and Monaghan (Lough na Glach, Lough Moynalty, Lough Corcrin); and tench fishers seem to favor Carrick-on-Shannon, Boyle, Strokestown, Lanesborough, Athlone, Carrickmacross, and Shercock.

The Lakelands region hosts several angling festivals, with prize money and fringe events such as sing-alongs, dart games, and card competitions. Castleblaney has a tournament in March; Carrickmacross and Ballinsasloe, in May; Athlone, in July and October; and Cootehill, in September. Contact the Irish Tourist Board for more details on these tournaments.

For information on necessary licenses and permits, *see* Sports and Outdoor Activities in Chapter 1.

Golf

The golfing clubs in the region offer fine courses and moderate greens fees and are generally uncrowded, especially on weekdays. All of the following places welcome visitors: **Athlone Golf Club** (Hoosens Bay, Athlone, Co. Westmeath, tel. 0902/92073 or 0902/92235), **Birr Golf Club** (The Glens, Birr, Co. Offaly, tel. 0509/20082), **County Cavan Golf Club** (Aranmore House, Cavan, tel. 049/31283), **Longford Golf Club** (Glack, Longford, Co. Longford, tel. 043/46310), **Mullingar Golf Club** (Belvedere, Mullingar, Co. Westmeath, tel. 044/48629), **Nenagh Golf Club** (Beechwood, Nenagh, Co. Tipperary, tel. 067/31476), **Portlaoise Golf Club** (The Heath, Portlaoise, Co. Laois, tel. 0502/26533), **Tullamore Golf Club** (Brookfield, Tullamore, Co. Offaly, tel. 0506/21439), and **Virginia Golf Club** (Virginia, Co. Cavan, tel. 049/47110).

Walking

Forest park trails (Killykeen, Lough Key, and Dun a Ri forest parks) and narrow country roads invite visitors to tour parts of the Lakelands on foot. One impressive walking trail to the east of Birr, called **the Slieve Bloom Way,** runs through the Slieve Bloom Mountains on a 50-km/31-mi circular route; its attractions include deep glens, rock formations, waterfalls, and views from mountain peaks.

Dining and Lodging

Dining

Category	Cost*
Very Expensive	over £20
Expensive	£17–£20
Moderate	£12–£17
Inexpensive	under £12

per person, excluding drinks and service

Lodging

Category	Cost*
Expensive	over £75
Moderate	£60–£75
Inexpensive	under £60

All prices are for a standard double room, including tax.

Highly recommended restaurants and hotels are indicated by a star ★.

Athlone

Dining and Lodging **Prince of Wales.** Although situated in the busy town center, this well-run modern hotel is only a few minutes' walk from the River Shannon. It welcomes a varied clientele: local patrons of the bar and coffee shop, business travelers, tour-bus groups, and independent travelers. The bright and modern bedrooms, with large bathrooms, are very well-maintained. The restaurant is a cheerful, rustic room with Tiffany lamps hanging from the roof beams and bright green plush chairs; it serves a set lunch menu and a better-than-average à la carte selection in the evening. The emphasis is on classic French dishes (such as black sole in lobster sauce or roast pheasant with cranberry sauce), and portions are generous. *Church St., Athlone, Co. Westmeath, tel. 0902/72626. 72 rooms with bath. Facilities: 2 restaurants, bar, gift shop, fishing. AE, DC, MC, V. Moderate.*

Ballyconnell

Dining and Lodging

Slieve Russell Hotel and Country Club. This magnificent hotel, 16 miles west of Cavan, makes a convenient break on the Dublin-Sligo journey. A fountain plays before the palatial floodlit neoclassical-style facade, and the spacious lobby gleams with polished marble. Most bedrooms have a Jacuzzi, super-king-size beds, floor-to-ceiling drapes, and chunky art deco-style furniture reminiscent of the great ocean liners. The sports and spa facilities are outstanding, but for many guests the excellent coarse and trout fishing—some of which is available within the hotel's 300-acre grounds—is the main attraction. The Conall Cearnach Restaurant is a formal spot with white napery and wrought-iron chandeliers. The extensive menu includes a variety of traditionally prepared seafood dishes, such as black sole on the bone or salmon hollandaise. The Brackley Buttery offers a more informal ambience. *Ballyconnell Co. Cavan, tel. 049/26444. 144 rooms with bath. Facilities: 2 restaurants, 2 bars, indoor pool, gym, sauna, solarium, steam bath. 2 squash courts, 4 tennis courts, fishing, 18-hole golf course. AE, DC, MC, V. Expensive.*

Birr

Dining

The Stables. People travel from miles around to dine in this small restaurant situated behind a Georgian townhouse opposite the castle gates. There's a tiny room, with a chaise longue and an open fire, where you can study the menu. The dining room—which was once the stables—is an open room with a high-beamed ceiling and plain whitewashed walls; the small tables have red napery and oak chairs. The *Cordon Bleu*–trained cook uses only fresh local produce. The menu features such old favorites as grilled sirloin steak *maître d'hotel* (with a spicy butter sauce), chicken Kiev, and stuffed paupiettes of pork with cider. *Oxmantown Mall, Birr, Co. Offaly, tel. 0509/ 20263. Reservations advised. AE, DC, MC, V. Open Wed.– Sat., dinner only. Moderate.*

Lodging

County Arms. Built in 1810, this small country house, just outside Birr on the Roscrea road (N62), was converted into a modest hotel in the late-1960s. Its last private owners were two elderly sisters, and the furnishings in the public rooms still recall an old-fashioned private home, with Victorian day couches, deeply cushioned armchairs, a grandfather clock, undistinguished paintings and brass bric-a-brac. The lovely walled garden to the left of the house has a small conservatory and gravel walks. The most attractive bedrooms, with tall Georgian windows, are found at the front of the house, but they overlook a dull suburban stretch of main road beyond the gardens. The more modestly proportioned back rooms have a better view of open countryside. All rooms have been refurbished recently in shades of dusty pink. *Roscrea Rd., Birr, Co. Offaly, tel. 0509/ 20791. 18 rooms with bath. Facilities: bar, restaurant, fishing, horseback riding. AE, DC, MC, V. Moderate.*

Dooley's. This old coaching inn occupying a corner of the main square is an excellent value. In the lobby, a turf fire glows under a carved mahogany chimney piece. The oak-beamed bar with private alcoves and ruched blinds is a popular local meeting place. The renovated bedrooms have modern bureaus and bedside tables, bright floral drapes and spreads, and large, fully tiled bathrooms. They are also scrupulously clean and offer a variety of quaint views of the pretty Georgian town. The rather overdecorated dining room serves a selection of Continental and Irish dishes, such as beef bourguignonne or roast lamb with mint sauce. *Emmet Sq., Birr, Co. Offaly, tel. 0509/20032. 18 rooms with bath. Facilities: restaurant, coffee shop, bar, fishing. AE, DC, MC, V. Inexpensive.*

Borrisokane

Dining and
Lodging
★

Ballycormac House. This country hideaway is situated 11 km/7 mi southwest of Birr and 7 km/3 mi from Lough Derg. Leave Birr on the N52 Borrisokane road and turn right for Aglish after about 11 km/7 mi. Signposts will direct you from there. Guests stay in a 300-year-old farmhouse whose owners now breed Irish hunting horses. Gardens surround the quaint cottage-style building, which is set amid 20 secluded acres. The cozy house features open fires and central heating and has been decorated with antiques and curios. Your hosts, the Paxman family, are known as much for their high standard of hospitality as for their equestrian pursuits. Dinner, prepared by a *Cordon Bleu* cook, is from organically grown produce and local meat and fish, and all breads, jams, and cakes are homemade. Each relaxing bedroom is pleasantly furnished in its own way. *Aglish, Borrisokane, Co. Tipperary, tel. 067/21129. Advance booking essential. 5 rooms with bath. Facilities: evening meal (residents only), horseback riding, fox hunting, rough shooting, TV in one room only. AE, DC, MC, V. Closed Christmas week. Inexpensive.*

Clones

Lodging

Hilton Park. Look for a large set of black gates with silver falcons 5 km/3 mi outside Clones on the R183 Ballyhaise road to find this large and stately early Georgian country house. It has three private lakes on its 500-acre grounds, which include 50 acres of gardens and parkland, a working sheep farm, and an organic market garden. Your friendly hosts, Johnny and Lucy Madden, run their magnificent house with stylish informality. All rooms are individually decorated with antiques and have lovely views; some have four-poster beds. Dinner, which consists of freshly prepared produce from their market garden and local meat and fish, is available for residents. *Clones, Co. Monaghan, tel. 047/56007. 5 rooms, 3 with bath. Advance booking essential. Facilities: trout and pike fishing, boating, lake swimming, croquet, golf, TV room (no TV or direct dial phones in rooms). AE, V. Closed Oct.–Mar. Expensive.*

Cootehill

Dining and
Lodging
★

The White Horse. This property typifies the better sort of market-town hotel, which serves as a focal point for the local community as well as providing a good grade of budget accommodation for the traveler. Some rooms in the rambling Victorian hotel building are on the small side; all of them are plainly decorated but well-maintained, with a variety of town views. The quieter ones are situated in the back. The restaurant, a softly lit mahogany-furnished room in the interior of the hotel, is known far and wide for its very generous portions of plainly cooked local meat and fish. *Main St., Cootehill, Co.*

Cavan, tel. 049/52124. 30 rooms, 24 with bath. Facilities: bar, restaurant, TV lounge. AE, MC, V. Inexpensive.

Lodging **Riverside House.** The unpretentious, genuine old-fashioned Irish hospitality at Joe and Una Smith's farm is appreciated by both serious anglers and nonsporting guests. (The lodging is signposted 1 km/.5 mi outside town off the R188 Cavan road). You'll stay in a substantial Victorian house situated on 100 acres overlooking the River Annalee, which are worked as a dairy farm (bring your boots if you want to explore). All rooms have peaceful views and are individually decorated with modest antiques and family hand-me-downs. There is a play area for children, who are especially welcome. *Cootehill, Co. Cavan, tel. 049/52150. 6 rooms, 2 with bath. Facilities: evening meal by arrangement (BYOB), TV room, fishing, boats for hire. No credit cards. Inexpensive.*

Crookedwood

Dining **Crookedwood House.** This large old country house, 13 km/8 mi
★ north of Mullingar on the R394 Castlepollard road, is something of a surprise in the area—well off the beaten track and yet producing the sort of food you would expect to find in a fashionable city restaurant. Orders are taken by the fire in a comfortable sitting room overlooking the lake, and served in the basement in three interconnecting rooms with whitewashed stone walls, an open fire, and a cozy dark-red color scheme. Starters may include warm salad with duck livers and pistachio nuts or mousseline of salmon with leek sauce; main courses on the changing menu might be a duet of scampi and salmon parcels in champagne sauce, medallions of pork steak in lemon butter sauce, or such vegetarian daily specials as rosti (potato pancake) with creamed mushrooms. The chef uses predominantly local produce and organically grown vegetables. *Near Mullingar, Co. Westmeath, tel. 044/72165. Reservations advised. AE, DC, MC, V. Open Tues.–Sat. 7:30–9:30 (last orders), Sun. 12:30–2. Closed 2 weeks in Oct. Expensive.*

Longford

Dining and **Longford Arms.** Conveniently situated in the town center, this
Lodging pleasantly refurbished Victorian hotel has spacious public rooms decorated in art nouveau style, with light woods, stained glass, and flounced drapes. Rooms are small, with plain modern furnishings, and most of them overlook an internal roof, but they are quiet and clean. The well-run restaurant serves generous portions of local meat (roast or grilled) and a choice of fish dishes such as salmon hollandaise. *Main St., Longford, Co. Longford, tel. 043/46296. 51 rooms with bath. Facilities: bar, restaurant. AE, DC, MC, V. Inexpensive.*

Mullingar

Dining and **Greville Arms.** As you check into this old coaching inn, look out
Lodging for the tall, bespectacled man in the glass case beside the recep-
★ tion desk, but do not be alarmed. He is a life-size wax effigy of James Joyce, who stayed here once in his youth and wrote about the visit in *Stephen Hero*. Deep carpets, dark paneled walls, and soft lighting give the public rooms an impression of luxury, while the spacious bedrooms are simpler in decor but

have good modern amenities. The inn's dining room overlooks a pleasant stretch of the Royal Canal, and its walls are covered with photos and drawings of Joyce. The menu, though not exactly adventurous, is better than average, relying heavily on grilled or roast beef, pork, and lamb. Dishes prepared with local fish are also offered. *Pearse St., Mullingar, Co. Westmeath, tel. 044/48563. 33 rooms with bath. Facilities: restaurant, coffee shop, 2 bars, nightclub, fishing, DC, MC, V. Moderate.*

Roscommon

Dining and Lodging   **Abbey Hotel.** This 18th-century castellated Gothic lodge on the edge of town takes its name from the ruined abbey behind it. It is surrounded by well-tended flower gardens, and a thriving rookery lies between the hotel and the abbey. A few original features, such as the marble mantelpiece in the bar, have been retained in the lodge, but most of the hotel has been redone in a mishmash of styles. The clean and spacious bedrooms on a new ground-floor extension have large bathrooms. The open-plan restaurant overlooks the gardens and has cane-seated bentwood chairs and Tiffany lamps under a cantilevered beamed roof. Baked stuffed duckling with citrus sauce and poached fillets of plaice bearnaise are typical main courses. *Co. Roscommon, tel. 0903/26240. 20 rooms with bath. Facilities: bar, restaurant, nightclub (weekends). AE, DC, MC, V. Hotel: Inexpensive. Restaurant: Moderate.*

Tullamore

Dining   **Bridge House.** This large, multipurpose establishment in the town center offers several options. At the front, the lounge bar has a self-service food area and carvery, with waitress service for drinks and cakes (open until 6 PM). Besides the roast of the day, you can try generous platters of cold meats, seafood, and salads. The central bar is surrounded by comfortable wicker chairs and tables. The nicest seating area overlooks the Grand Canal. The Charleville Room, in a separate area with soft lighting and a red color scheme, provides a set or à la carte menu from 12:30 to 2:30 and from 5:30 to 10. The menu combines French and traditional Irish cooking, with such dishes as beef Stroganoff or rack of lamb with rosemary served in large portions. Service here is prompt. *Bridge St., Tullamore, Co. Offaly, tel. 0506/21704. Reservations advised for Charleville Room. AE, MC, V. Inexpensive (self-service), Moderate (restaurant).*

Dining and Lodging ★   **Moorhill House.** Surrounded by pretty gardens, this modest detached Victorian house (about 1 km/.6 mi outside Tullamore on the N80) features large and comfortable rooms with wool carpets, floral drapes, and some antiques. Five new rooms in a separate wing on the ground floor have separate entrances and windows overlooking the garden. All the accommodations are maintained at a high standard. The expensive, award-winning restaurant in the converted stables is now a bright, whitewashed room looking onto a patio where barbecues are held in good weather. The four-course set menu includes such main courses as chicken in filo pastry, king scallops in saffron sauce, and fresh fish. *Clara Rd., Tullamore, Co. Offaly, tel. 0506/21395. 12 rooms with bath. Facilities: bar, restaurant, tennis, fishing, horseback riding. No TV in rooms. AE, DC, MC, V. Hotel: Moderate. Restaurant: Expensive.*

Virginia

Dining and Lodging **The Park Hotel, Deer Park Lodge.** This 18th-century hunting lodge on the shores of Lough Ramor is a fine place to take a few days' break from sightseeing. It has good sporting facilities and interesting walks nearby. While the exterior of the house has a certain charm, the decor inside is an uninspired mix of modern and reproduction-Victorian styles. The rooms are all different shapes and sizes; the four at the front have the best views of the lake. The expensive restaurant, in a pleasant Georgian room, serves classic French dishes—salmon, duck, and beef—featuring local produce. *Virginia, Co. Cavan, tel. 049/ 47235. 18 rooms with bath. Facilities: bar, restaurant, tennis, 9-hole golf course, fishing, sauna. AE, DC, MC, V. Closed Nov. 1–Mar. 1. Moderate.*

6 The Southeast

Kilkenny Town, Wexford Town, Waterford City, Tipperary Town

By Alannah Hopkin and Pat Mackey

The Southeast will surprise visitors who expect Irish scenery to be rugged and wild. The coastal counties of Wexford and Waterford are low-lying and relatively flat, with long sandy beaches and low cliffs; inland, counties Carlow, Kilkenny, and Tipperary consist of lush, undulating pastureland bisected by winding river valleys. This region has the mildest, sunniest, and also the driest weather in Ireland, with as little as 30 inches of rainfall per year—compared to an average of 80 inches on parts of the west coast.

The combination of sunshine and sandy beaches makes the Southeast's coast a popular vacation area with Irish families; but except for the resort of Tramore, it is relatively undeveloped. Its main attractions remain the natural beauty of its landscape and its small and charming fishing villages.

Both coastal and inland areas have a rich and interesting history. There is evidence of settlements from some 9,000 years ago in the Slaney Valley near Wexford. The Kings of Munster had their ceremonial center on the Rock of Cashel, which in the 7th century became an important monastic center and bishopric. There were other thriving early Christian monasteries at Kilkenny, Ardmore, and Lismore.

The quiet life of early Christian Ireland was disrupted from the 9th century onward by a series of Viking invasions. The Vikings liked what they found here—a pleasant climate; rich, easily cultivated land; and a series of safe, sheltered harbors—so they stayed and founded the towns of Wexford and Waterford. (Waterford's name comes from the Norse *Vadrefjord*, Wexford's from *Waesfjord.*) Less than two centuries later, the same cities were conquered by Anglo-Norman barons and turned into walled strongholds. The Anglo-Normans and the Irish chieftains soon started to intermarry, but the process of integration halted with the Statute of Kilkenny in 1366, for the English feared that if such intermingling continued they would lose whatever control over Ireland they had.

The next great crisis was Oliver Cromwell's Irish campaign of 1650, which in attempting to crush Catholic opposition to the English parliament brought widespread slaughter. The ruined or extensively rebuilt condition of most of the region's early churches is a result of Cromwell's desecrations. His outrages are still a vivid part of local folk memory, but not as vivid as the 1798 Rebellion, an ill-timed and unsuccessful bid for a united Ireland inspired by the French Revolution. The decisive "battle" took place at Vinegar Hill near Enniscorthy, where some 20,000 rebels, armed only with pikes, were cut down by British cannon fire. Songs commemorating these events of almost 200 years ago, such as "The Rising of the Moon" and "The Croppy Boy," are still sung in local bars.

Outside the months of July and August, the region is relatively free of traffic, making it ideal for leisurely exploration. Wexford, Waterford, and Kilkenny all have compact town centers best explored on foot, and they also make good touring bases. Wexford's narrow streets are built on one side of a wide estuary, and it has a delightful maritime atmosphere. The new National Heritage Park at nearby Ferrycarrig is well worth a visit, which will contribute enormously to an understanding of Irish history up to the 12th century. Waterford is less immediately attractive than Wexford, but it offers a richer selection of

Viking and Norman remains, some good Georgian buildings, and also the famous Waterford Glass Factory, open to visitors. Kilkenny, an important ecclesiastic and political center up to the 17th century, is now a lively market town whose streets still contain many remains from medieval times, most notably the beautiful St. Canice's Cathedral and a magnificent 12th-century castle.

Among the inland riverside towns, Carrick-on-Suir and Clonmel each have a special quiet charm, while the village of Lismore has a hauntingly beautiful castle set in wooded gardens. Anglers will scarcely believe the variety of fishing and scenery along the Rivers Barrow, Nore, Suir and especially in the Blackwater Valley area. County Tipperary is the location of the Rock of Cashel, ancient seat of the kings of Munster, which can be seen from miles around in all directions; this vast, cathedral-topped rock rising up above the plain is one of Ireland's most impressive sights.

Essential Information

Arriving and Departing by Plane

Airports and Airlines
Waterford Regional Airport (tel. 051/75580) is located on the Waterford–Ballymacaw road in Killowen. **RyanAir** (tel. 051/78272) schedules flights out of this small regional airport three times daily to Luton, England, and weekly to Liverpool, England. **Aer Lingus** (tel. 01/377777) provides daily scheduled flights to Cork, Dublin, and other regional airports.

Between the Airport and Center City
Waterford City is 9½ km (6 mi) from the airport. **Suirway Bus Service** (tel. 051/82209) provides transportation between the airport and town, with a station located opposite the Tourist Information Office on Merchant's Quay. A hackney cab from the airport into Waterford will cost approximately £10, and there are car-rental facilities at the airport.

Arriving and Departing by Car and Ferry

By Car
Waterford, the regional capital, is easily accessible from all parts of Ireland. From Dublin, take the N7 southwest, change to the N9 in Naas, and continue along this highway through Carlow and Thomastown until it terminates in Waterford. The N25 travels east–west through Waterford, connecting it with Cork in the west and Wexford in the east. And from Limerick and Tipperary, the N24 stretches southeast until it, too, ends in Waterford.

By Ferry
The region's primary ferry terminal is found just south of Wexford at Rosslare. **Sealink Ferries** (tel. 053/33115) sails directly between Rosslare Ferryport and Fishguard, Wales. Pembroke, Wales, can be reached on the **B+I Lines** (tel. 053/33311), and there are three sailings weekly to France's Le Havre and Cherbourg on **Irish Ferries** (tel. 053/33158).

Rental Cars
The major car rental companies have offices at Rosslare Ferryport, and in most large towns rental information can be found through the local tourism office. Typical car-rental prices start at about £40 per day with unlimited mileage, and they usually include insurance and all taxes. **Budget** has offices in both Rosslare Harbour (The Ferryport, tel. 053/33318) and

Waterford (41 The Quay, tel. 051/21670), as does **Hertz** (tel. 053/33238 in Rosslare Harbour; Cork Rd., tel. 051/72886, in Waterford).

Getting Around

By Train Waterford is linked by **Irish Rail** (tel. 01/366222 in Dublin; 051/73401 in Waterford) service to Dublin. Trains run from Plunkett Station in Waterford to Dublin four times daily, making stops at Kilkenny, Thomastown, and Carlow. The daily train between Waterford and Limerick makes stops at Tipperary and Clonmel. The train between Rosslare and Waterford runs twice daily.

By Bus **Bus Éireann** (tel. 01/366111 in Dublin, 051/73401 in Waterford) makes the Waterford–Dublin journey four times daily for about £6. There are three buses daily between Waterford and Limerick, and three between Waterford and Rosslare. The Cork–Waterford journey is made twice daily. In Waterford the terminal is Plunkett Station.

By Car For the most part, the main roads in the Southeast are of good quality and are free of congestion. Side roads are generally narrow and twisting, and drivers should keep an eye out for farm machinery or animals on country roads.

Important Addresses and Numbers

Tourist Information **Carlow Tourist Information Office** (Hadden Shopping Center, Tullow St., Carlow, tel. 0503/31554).

Cashel Tourist Information Office (Town Hall, Cashel, Co. Tipperary, tel. 062/61333).

New Ross Tourist Information Office (Harbour Centre, The Quay, New Ross, Co. Wexford, tel. 051/21857).

Tipperary Tourist Information Office (3 James St., Tipperary, tel. 062/51457).

Kilkenny Tourist Information Office (Rose Inn St., Kilkenny, tel. 056/21755).

Rosslare Tourist Information Office (Rosslare Ferry Terminal, Kilrane, Rosslare Harbour, Co. Wexford, tel. 053/33232).

Tramore Tourist Information Office (Railway Sq., Tramore, Co. Waterford, tel. 051/81572).

Waterford Tourist Information Office (41 Merchant's Quay, Waterford, tel. 051/75788).

Wexford Tourist Information Office (Crescent Quay, Co. Wexford, tel. 053/23111).

Emergency Numbers **Waterford Regional Hospital** (Ardkeen, Co. Waterford, tel. 051/73321).

Gardai (Police) Emergency (tel. 999).

Ambulance and Fire (tel. 999).

Guided Tours

Walking tours of historic Wexford, arranged by the **Old Wexford Society,** meet at the Talbot Hotel on Trinity Street (tel.

053/22566) and at White's Hotel on George's Street (tel. 053/22311) every evening during the summer.

Walking tours of Kilkenny are arranged by **Tynan Tours** and operate daily from the Kilkenny Tourist Information Office (Rose Inn St., tel. 056/21755).

Exploring the Southeast

Highlights for First-time Visitors

Irish National Heritage Park (*see* Tour 1)
Kilkenny Castle (*see* Tour 1)
Lismore Castle Gardens (*see* Tour 3)
Monastic Remains at Ardmore (*see* Tour 3)
Rock of Cashel (*see* Tour 3)
Waterford Glass Factory (*see* Tour 2)

Tour 1: Carlow, Kilkenny and Wexford Towns

Numbers in the margin correspond to points of interest on the Southeast map.

This tour covers a region rich in historical and maritime attractions. From Carlow's small county seat you travel through the rich farmlands of the Barrow valley to the city of Kilkenny, pausing to explore the historic city center on foot. From Thomastown, just outside Kilkenny, another cross-country drive follows the River Nore to New Ross, where it meets the River Barrow, and on to John F. Kennedy's ancestral home and the Arboretum planted in his memory. The tour ends in the old Viking port of Wexford.

❶ Begin at **Carlow Town** (83 km/52 mi south of Dublin on the N9), which was established by the Anglo-Normans in the 12th century. Its position on the border of the English Pale—the small area around Dublin that was dominated by the English from Elizabethan times on—made it an important strategic center and hence the scene of many battles and sieges.

Today Carlow is a modern market town on the banks of the River Barrow, with a population of about 11,700 employed in such industries as sugar beet refining, flour milling, and malting. One of its most prominent sights is the Roman Catholic **Cathedral of the Assumption.** Completed in 1883, the Gothic-style cathedral is notable for its stained-glass windows and the magnificent monument on the tomb of its builder, Bishop James Doyle (1786–1834), a champion of Catholic emancipation; the monument was carved by the acclaimed Irish sculptor John Hogan (1800–1858). *Tullow St., tel. 0503/31227. Open daily 10–8.*

The ruins of the 13th-century **Carlow Castle** can be found near the bridge on the grounds of Corcoran's Mineral Water Factory. This castle withstood a siege by Cromwell's troops in 1650, only to be destroyed accidentally in the early 19th century when a Dr. Philip Middleton attempted to renovate the castle for use as a mental asylum. While setting off explosives to reduce the thickness of the walls, he managed to demolish all but the west wall and its two flanking towers.

The Southeast

Nenagh

Rathdowney

LAOIS

Silvermines

Templemore

Templetuohy

Johnstown

Borrisoleigh

Urlingford

Freshford

Dur

Milestone

Thurles

Holycross 52

Cappamore

Cappawhite

Killenaule

Ballingarry

Caherconlish

Callan

Herbertstown

Rock of Cashel **Cashel**

51

TIPPERARY

Kno

Tipperary Town 50

Fethard

SLIEVENAMON MOUNTAIN

Windgap

Knocklong

Aher

Kilfinane

Ballylanders

Glen of Aherlow

Cahir 49

N24

53 **Clonmel**

R697

GALTEE MOUNTAINS

Mitchelstown Caves

54

LIMERICK

N8 Burncourt

Carrick-on-Suir

Portlav

Ballyporeen 48

Clogheen

Mitchelstown

Knockmealdown Mountains

Kilmacthomas

N25

Kildorrery

Mount Melleray Abbey

Shanballymore

Lemybrien

Fermoy

Ballyduff R666

Cappoquin

R675

44

R. Blackwater

47 **Lismore**

N72

WATERFORD

Bunmahon

Rathcormac

Conna

Tallow

45

Clonea

Watergrasshill

N8

Ballyknock

Dungarvan

Ring

CORK

Youghal

46

N25

Ardmore

Cork

Midleton

Cobh

Ballycotton

Castlecomer
Ballyragget
R78
Old Leighlin
Kilkenny Town
4 — 11
SEE DETAIL MAP
N10
nsmore
Cave
R430
N9
Carlow Town
Tullow
R726
WICKLOW
R725
Woodenbridge
Arklow
Kildavin
Shillelagh
Leighlinbridge
Muine Bheag
(Bagenalstown)
R705
CARLOW
Borris
Graiguenamanagh
R729
St. Mullins
R700
N9
Stoneyford
ocktophet
12
Thomastown
R. Nore
R. Barrow
KILKENNY
Mullinavat
N25
13
N25
Bunclody
Ferns
Gorey
Enniscorthy
15
R744
R741
R742
Clonroche
N79
WEXFORD
R. Slaney
N11
Blackwater
Oylgate
Wexford Town
16 — 25
SEE DETAIL MAP
St. George's
Channel
JOHN F.
KENNEDY PARK
14
Dunganstown
R733
26
Ferrycarrig
*Wexford
Harbour*
R. Suir
N24
Cheekpoint
28
Ballyhack
Duncannon
Passage
East
Waterford
Harbour
R684
R685
Waterford City
29 — 40
SEE DETAIL MAP
42
43
R675
Tramore
Annestown
41
**Dunmore
East**
Fethard-
on-Sea
*Forlorn
Pt.*
R736
Wellington
Bridge
Piercetown
Duncormick
Tomhaggard
Rosslare
*Rosslare
Harbour*
N25
R730
Lady's Island
27
Kilmore Quay
Saltee
Islands
*Hook
Peninsula*
**TO WALES,
FRANCE**

Celtic Sea

KEY
— Rail Lines
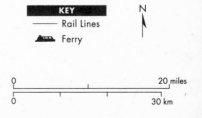 Ferry

N

0 _____ 20 miles
0 _____ 30 km

One last stop is the **County Museum** in the town hall, whose exhibits include a reconstructed blacksmith's forge and a pre-industrial kitchen. *Centaur St., tel. 0503/43299. Admission: 50p adults, 30p children. Open May–Sept., daily 11–5:30; Oct.– Apr., Sun. only 2:30–5:30.*

A brief 3¼ km (2 mi) detour on the road to Tullow (R725) east of Carlow Town will bring you to the famous **Browne's Hill Dolmen.** This stone monument dates from 2000 BC and, with a capstone weighing in at 100 tons, is considered the largest in Ireland. Nineteenth-century historians thought that dolmens were Druidic altars, while the peasantry believed them to be giants' graves. They are, in fact, megalithic tombs dating from the Stone Age (c.3000–2000 BC). The dolmen is accessible through a field gate along the road; there is no admission fee.

② Double back to Carlow Town and pick up highway N9 south for some 10 km (6¼ mi) into **Leighlinbridge,** where the first bridge over the River Barrow was built in 1320. On the east bank lie the ruins of **Black Castle.** Built in 1181, this fortress was one of the earliest Norman defenses in Ireland, and has been the scene of countless battles and sieges over the centuries. Just one ruined 400-year-old tower stands today.

③ Just 4¾ km (3 mi) west of Leighlinbridge, signposted to the right off the N9, is the tiny village of **Old Leighlin,** site of a monastery founded in the 7th century by St. Laserian. It was rebuilt in the 12th century as **St. Laserian's Cathedral** and enlarged in the 16th century. Worth noticing here are the Gothic doorway, some curiously carved 16th-century grave slabs, and St. Laserian's cross and holy well.

Return to the N9 and continue south, taking the N10 (right hand fork) in Whitehall after 8 km (5 mi), and continuing for another 16 km (10 mi) to Kilkenny Town.

④ The best example of a medieval community in Ireland, **Kilkenny Town** (pop. 10,000) is attractively situated on the River Nore, which forms the moat of its magnificently restored castle. The name Kilkenny comes from the Irish for "Canice's Church," which nowadays refers to the splendid 13th-century St. Canice's Cathedral, with its ancient stone tower and imposing Gothic interior.

Kilkenny holds a special place in the history of Anglo-Irish relations. The infamous 1366 Statute of Kilkenny was intended to strengthen English authority in Ireland by keeping the heirs of the Anglo-Norman invaders from becoming absorbed into the Irish way of life. Intermarriage became a crime punishable by death. Irish cattle were barred from grazing on English land. Anglo-Norman settlers could forfeit their estates for speaking Gaelic, for giving their children Irish names, or for dressing in Irish clothes. The native Irish were forced to live outside town walls in shantytowns. The intermingling of the Irish and the Anglo-Normans was well under way when the Statute went into effect; perhaps if this fusion had been allowed to continue, Anglo-Irish relations in this century might have been more harmonious.

By the early 17th century, the Irish Catholics had grown impatient with such repression; they tried to bring about reforms with the Confederation of Kilkenny, which governed Ireland for six years. Pope Innocent X sent money and arms. Cromwell responded in 1650 by overrunning the town and sacking the cathedral, which he used to stable his horses.

Numbers in the margin correspond to points of interest on the Kilkenny Town map.

⑤ St. Canice's Cathedral, on the corner of Dean Street and Parliament Street, is the best place to begin your walking tour. In spite of Cromwell's defacements, this is still one of the finest cathedrals in Ireland. The bulk of the 13th-century structure (restored in 1866) is in the early English style. Within the massive walls is an exuberant Gothic interior, given a somber grandeur by the extensive use of a locally quarried black marble. Many of the memorials and tombstone effigies represent distinguished descendants of the Normans, some depicted in full suits of armor. Look for a female effigy in the south aisle wearing the old Irish or Kinsale cloak; the 12th-century black marble font at the southwest end of the nave; and St. Ciaran's Chair in the north transept, also made of black marble, with 13th-century sculptures on the arms.

The Round Tower on the cathedral grounds is all that is left of the 6th-century monastic development around which the town developed. If you have the energy to climb the tower's 167 steps, you'll have a good vantage point at the top. Next door is **St. Canice's Library,** containing some 3,000 16th- and 17th-century volumes. *Dean St. Open daily 9–1 and 2–6.*

Across the street from the cathedral, you'll be able to see the **⑥** back of the **Black Abbey** on the next block south. This 13th-century friary, named after the black capes of the Dominican friars, has recently been restored as a Dominican church. A museum displaying a number of historical artifacts is located next door in the presbytery. From the Black Abbey, turn left and follow narrow Abbey Lane—one of the town's more medieval-looking streets—to Parliament Street. Turn right. Two blocks down on your right, across the street from the **⑦ ⑧ Courthouse,** is the late-16th-century **Rothe House,** the restored home of a wealthy Tudor merchant and now the headquarters of the Kilkenny Archaeological Society, which mounts a number of special exhibitions here each year. *Parliament St., tel. 056/22893. Admission: £1 adults, 50p children. Open Mon.–Sat. 10:30–5, Sun. 3–5.*

Time Out   For a meal in an unusual setting, take the left fork off Parliament Street onto St. Kieran Street and try **Kyteler's Inn** (tel. 056/21064); this restaurant is in the cellar of a building notorious as the place where Dame Alice Kyteler, an alleged witch, was accused of poisoning her four husbands. The restaurant retains its 14th-century stonework and exposed beams. Its menu features a respectable French-influenced à la carte dinner and a fixed-price lunch. However, the owners can't resist serving witch's broth—really just a homemade vegetable soup.

Continue along Parliament Street, which is called High Street at this point. You'll notice as you walk through the town the many old-fashioned, brightly painted shop and bar facades, each with an individual color scheme and handcrafted details. The Victorian tradition of painting store fronts has nearly died out in many towns, but since the 1980s Kilkenny has led the **⑨** field in its revival. You'll find the town hall, or **Tholsel,** which

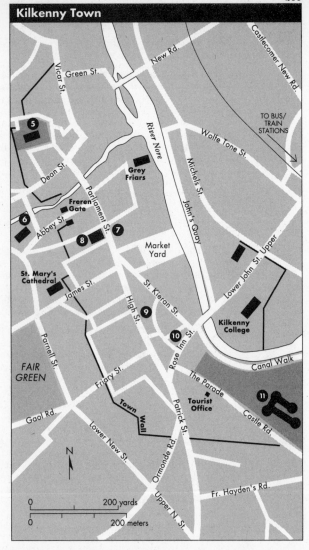

Kilkenny Town

was built in 1761 near the site of the medieval Market Cross, on the left.

Make a left off High Street onto Rose Inn Street to find the **Shee Alms House**, on the left side of the street. It was founded in 1582 by Sir Richard Shee as a hospital for the poor and served in that capacity until 1895. Today it houses the **Tourist Information Office** and CityScope, a sound-and-light show on 17th-century Kilkenny. *Rose Inn St., tel. 056/21755. Open Mon.–Sat. 9–5:15. CityScope admission: £1.*

High Street splits into Patrick Street and the Parade at Rose Inn Street, and you should veer left onto the Parade to reach **Kilkenny Castle**. Kilkenny was the seat of the dukes of

Ormonde, the powerful Butler family, for over 500 years. In 1967 they donated the present building, which dates from 1820, to the state. The gray stone building has two turreted wings and numerous chimneys poking over the battlements. It stands amid rolling lawns beside the River Nore in 20 hectares (49 acres) of landscaped parkland. Restoration work on the west wing is currently in progress; it should be completed by May 1993, but there are guided tours of the fully restored east wing. There is also an impressive portrait gallery, 46 meters (150 feet) long, and a modern-art gallery with frequently changing exhibitions. *The Parade, Kilkenny, tel. 056/21450. Admission: £1 adults, 40p children; grounds free. Open Tues.–Sat. 10–7, Sun. 2–5.*

About 11 km (7 mi) north of Kilkenny on the N78 (follow signposts for Castlecomer and Athy) is **Dunmore Cave,** a natural limestone cavern containing weird rock formations. The cave is mentioned in the ancient Book of Leinster as the dwelling place of Lord of the Mice, a giant cat killed by a female warrior named Aithbel. In the late 19th century, the bones of some 44 individuals, 25 of them children, were found here; they were probably seeking refuge from a Viking attack. Like many other Irish caves, Dunmore was considered the entrance to hell until well into the 17th century. Nowadays the cave is equipped with pathways, catwalks, and bridges to enable you to explore the eerie beauty of its formations in safety. *Dunmore, tel. 056/67726. Admission: £1 adults, 40p children. Open mid-Mar.–Sept. 30, daily 10–4:15; Oct. 1–mid-Mar., weekends 2–4:15.*

Numbers in the margin correspond to points of interest on the Southeast map.

⑫ Return to Kilkenny on the N78 and pick up the R700 for **Thomastown,** a pretty, stone-built village 14½ km (9 mi) to the south. Here the River Nore and its tributaries have been used to create **The Water Garden,** a small but charming haven which is at its best in early July, when the aquatic plants are in full bloom. *Ladywell, tel. 056/24478. Admission: £1 per car. Open May 1–Sept. 30, daily 10–6.*

Time Out **The Jerpoint Inn** (Market St., tel. 056/24234) may not be the most picturesque pub in Thomastown, but it does serve exceptional grub at lunchtime. The short menu includes lamb baked in cider and honey and chicken breast stuffed with ham and cheese. Portions are generous, and the service is friendly and efficient.

A short detour 2 km (1 mi) to the south from Thomastown on the N9 will bring you to **Jerpoint Abbey,** a ruined Cistercian monastery dating back to about 1180. Guide service is available in July and August only, but interesting sculptures and restored Romanesque cloisters decorated with human figures are accessible year-round. *Tel. 056/21755. Admission: 60p. Open daily 10–6.*

Return to Thomastown and rejoin the R700, heading south 24 km (15 mi) for New Ross. This is a very pretty stretch of road, skirting the River Nore and crossing it over a nine-arched stone bridge in the village of Inistioge.

⑬ **New Ross** is a busy inland port on the banks of the River Barrow. Even though it is one of the oldest towns in County Wexford, only the most dedicated history buffs will be tempted to stop and explore the steep narrow streets above its unattractive docks.

Time Out The major attraction in New Ross is a cruise up the River Barrow on the **Galley Cruising Restaurant** (tel. 051/21723). You can take in the peaceful farmlands along the river bank while sampling lunch, afternoon tea, or dinner. The emphasis is on fresh local produce and seafood.

The **John F. Kennedy Memorial Forest Park** is clearly signposted from New Ross on the R733, which follows the banks of the Barrow southwards. The cottage where the President's ⑭ great-grandfather was born may be found in **Dunganstown.** Kennedy relatives are still living in the house. About 2 km (1 mi) down the road at Slieve Coillte is the entrance to the park, which features over 600 acres of forest, nature trails, and gardens, as well as an ornamental lake. The grounds contain some 4,500 species of trees and shrubs and serve as a training center for botanists and foresters. The top of the park offers fine panoramic views. *Dunganstown, tel. 051/88171. Admission: £1. Open daily, May–Aug. 10–8; Sept. and Apr. 10–6; Oct.–Mar. 10–5.*

Return to New Ross and either pick up the N25 to go direct to Wexford (37 km/23 mi) or join the N79 to take in Enniscorthy en route to Wexford (56 km/35 mi).

⑮ **Enniscorthy,** a thriving market town with a rich history, is built on the steeply sloping banks of the River Slaney. Dominating the town is its castle, built by a Norman knight in 1199 and once owned by the English poet Edmund Spenser, who gave us *The Faerie Queene.* The site of fierce battles against Oliver Cromwell in the 17th century and during the Uprising of 1798, the square-towered keep of Enniscorthy Castle now houses the **County Wexford Museum.** The museum contains thousands of historical items, including a reconstructed dairy and displays of pottery and military memorabilia; you'll find the curator eager to provide commentary on the exhibits. *Castle Hill, tel. 054/35926. Admission: £1 adults, 30p children. Open weekdays 10–6, weekends 2–6.*

On the east side of town is the famous **Vinegar Hill,** where the most important battle in the Uprising of 1798 took place. Here some 20,000 rebels, armed only with pikes, made a last desperate stand against the continuous bombardment of the British Army's cannon fire.

St. Aidan's Cathedral stands on a commanding site overlooking the Slaney. This Gothic-revival building was built in the mid-19th century under the direction of Augustus Welby Pugin, the celebrated architect of London's Parliament building.

From Enniscorthy, take the N11 south for about 24 km (15 mi) ⑯ into the town of **Wexford,** an ancient place defined on maps by the Greek cartographer Ptolemy as long ago as the 2nd century AD. Its Irish name is Loch Garman, but the Vikings called it *Waesfjord*—the harbor of the mud flats—which became Wexford in English.

Numbers in the margin correspond to points of interest on the Wexford Town map.

The River Slaney empties into the sea at Wexford. The harbor has silted up since the days when the Viking longboats docked here; nowadays only a few small trawlers fish out of here. The town is situated on the south bank of the Slaney, with its main street running parallel to the quays on the riverfront. The opposite, or north, bank of the Slaney, a short walk across the new bridge, forms the **Wexford Wildfowl Reserve.** The mud flats, known locally as slobs, are home to various species of ducks, geese, and swans. Screened blinds and an observation tower are provided for visitors, and a collection of the various species who live on the slobs has been established at the reception center. *Tel. 053/23129. Freely accessible.*

The **Tourist Information Office** on the waterfront at Crescent Quay is a good place to start exploring Wexford's compact town center on foot. Here you can find out about guided walking tours organized by local historians.

In the center of Crescent Quay is a large bronze **Statue of Commodore John Barry,** the father of the American navy. Born in 1745 in nearby Ballysampson, he settled in Philadelphia by the age of 15 and became a brilliant naval fighter during the American Revolution.

Walk up Peter Street from the quay to Main Street. This narrow thoroughfare is the main shopping street of the town, with a pleasant mix of old-fashioned bakeries, butchers, and sweetshops, stylish boutiques, and friendly pubs. A browse around may delight visitors seeking provincial Irish charm. The town is at its best in late October, when the famous Wexford Opera Festival engenders a carnival atmosphere that affects all walks of life.

Turn left into Main Street South and make a right onto Bride Street. From here you can see, rising above the rooftops, the graceful spires of the **Church of the Immaculate Conception** on Rowe Street, and the **Church of the Assumption** on Bride Street. These elegant examples of 19th-century Gothic architecture are known as "the twin churches" because their exteriors are identical, their foundation stones were laid on the same day, and their spires both reach a height of 70 meters (230 feet).

From Bride Street travel through St. Peter's Square to School Street and the **Franciscan Church.** The ceiling of this church is worth noting for its fine, locally crafted stucco work. Continue along School Street, turn right onto Rowe Street, and head downhill, passing the Church of the Immaculate Conception, mentioned above. At Main Street North, turn left to reach the **Wexford Bull Ring,** once the scene of bullbaiting, a cruel medieval sport that was popular among the Norman nobility. This arena was also the site of another, far more tragic event in 1649, when Cromwell's soldiers massacred 300 panic-stricken townspeople who had gathered here to pray as the army stormed their town.

A few last addresses worth noting as you wander the town's narrow, winding streets include Oliver Cromwell's temporary residence at 29 Main Street South; the birthplace of Oscar Wilde's mother, Jane Elgee (who wrote as "Speranza"), in the old rectory on Main Street at the Bull Ring; the birthplace of William Cody, father of the famous American showman "Buffalo" Bill Cody, on King Street; and the 19th-century poet Thomas Moore's home at the Cornmarket.

Wexford Town

Wexford Harbor

Continue along Main Street North and turn left at Slaney Street to reach the remains of the old town walls. There were originally five fortified gateways in the walls, but only the largest one, the red sandstone **Westgate Tower,** remains standing. South of Westgate Tower, you'll come across the ruins of the 12th-century **Selskar Abbey,** where the first treaty between the Irish and the Normans was signed in 1169.

Numbers in the margin correspond with points of interest on the Southeast map.

It is not only visitors who find Irish history, with its Celtic background and its successive waves of invaders—Christians, Vikings, Normans—confusing at times, but also many of the Irish themselves. One of the most successful and enjoyable attractions to be opened in recent years is the **Irish National Heritage Park** at **Ferrycarrig,** 5 km (3 mi) from Wexford Town on the N25. This 35-acre open-air theme park beside the River Slaney should not be missed. In about an hour and a half, a guide takes you through 9,000 years of Irish history—from the first evidence of man on this island, at around 7000 BC, to the Norman settlements of the mid-12th century. Full-scale replicas of typical dwelling places illustrate the changes in beliefs and lifestyles. Highlights of the tour include a prehistoric homestead, a *crannóg* (lake dwelling), an early Christian *rath* (fortified farmstead), a Christian monastery, a horizontal water mill, a Viking longhouse, and a Norman castle. There are also examples of pre-Christian burial sites and a stone circle. Most of the exhibits are "inhabited" by students in appropriate dress who will answer questions. Naturalists will enjoy the unspoiled riverside site, which includes several nature trails. *Ferrycarrig, tel. 053/41733. Admission: £2 adults, £1 children. Open Apr. 1–Oct. 31, daily 10–7.*

Time Out Before heading back into town, stop for a pint and a plate of food at the **Oak Tavern** (Ferrycarrig, tel. 053/24922), a riverside bar about 2 km (1 mi) from the gates of the park on the Enniscorthy road. Log fires blaze in the lounge, while in good weather you can relax on the riverside terrace of this charming Old World inn.

Return to Wexford on the N25, and follow it for 5 km (3 mi) in the Rosslare direction until you reach the signpost for **Johnstown Castle Gardens** and **The Irish Agricultural Museum.** The castle itself, a massive Victorian Gothic building in gray stone, is now an agricultural college, but the attractive and well-maintained grounds, with ornamental lakes and over 200 different trees and shrubs, are open to the public. The main attraction is the museum, housed in the quadrangular stable yards. Extensive displays are devoted to rural transport, farming, and the activities of the farmyard and the farmhouse, with a special exhibit on dairying. The museum also contains an important collection of Irish country furniture. *Johnstown Castle, tel. 053/42888. Admission £1.25 adults, 50p children. Open Mon.–Sat. 9–12:30 and 1:30–5; Sun. 2–5.*

Tour 2: Coastal Drive from Wexford Town to Ardmore via Waterford City

This tour follows mainly minor roads along the prettiest parts of the coast in Counties Wexford and Waterford, pausing midway to explore Waterford City on foot. **Rosslare,** a seaside resort with a long sandy beach, lies 18 km (11 mi) southwest of Wexford off the N25 on the R470. The terminus for car ferries from Fishguard, Pembroke, Le Havre, and Cherbourg is on the N25 5 miles south of the village. Instead of taking in Rosslare, the route leaves the N25 at Piercetown, 8 km (5 mi) south of

27 Wexford following the right-hand fork, R739, to **Kilmore Quay.**

This seaside village of thatched and whitewashed cottages, noted for its fishing industry, offers a pleasant view from the harbor over a flat coast that stretches for miles eastward. The village is the point of departure for day trips offshore to the **Saltee Islands,** Ireland's largest bird sanctuary. (From mid-May to the end of July, look for boats at the village waterfront to take you to the islands.) In late spring and early summer, several million sea birds nest among the dunes and on the rocky scarp on the south of the islands. Even if you are not an ornithologist, it's worth making the trip at these times to observe the sheer numbers of gulls, kittiwakes, puffins, guillemots, cormorants, and petrels.

On leaving Kilmore Quay, make your way northwest on the R736, then head west through Duncormick and on to Wellington Bridge. Past the bridge, head toward Fethard-on-Sea on the R733, following signs for the **Ring of Hook** drive. This is a strange and atypical part of Ireland, where the land is exceptionally flat and the narrow roads are straight. Except during July and August, when the many sandy beaches attract vacationing families, the roads are virtually empty, and the tiny hamlets appear eerily deserted. But the area has its own special charm, a peace and quiet enhanced by small thatched cottages with tiny but carefully tended gardens.

The Ring of Hook leads to **Duncannon,** a small resort with a good sandy beach and a delightful nautical atmosphere, on the north side of Waterford harbor. Its history is marked by the visits of two kings; James II beat a hasty retreat out of Ireland through Duncannon port after his defeat at the Battle of the Boyne in 1690, and his successor, William III, also spent some days here before leaving for England.

From Duncannon, follow the signposts to Arthurstown and

28 **Ballyhack.** This attractive village on the upper reaches of Waterford Harbour, with its square castle keep and green hilly background, is much admired by painters and photographers. The castle was once owned by the Knights Templars of St. John of Jerusalem, who held the ferry rights by royal charter; traditionally they were required to keep a boat at Ballyhack to transport injured knights to the King's Leper Hospital at Waterford. Nowadays a small car ferry plies the same route in a five-minute crossing to Passage East.

Time Out   Seafood, renowned in this region, is the reason to drop in at Ballyhack's **Neptune Restaurant,** just below the castle. If you aren't looking for a full meal, try a plate of local oysters or a fresh salmon sandwich in the conservatory, which overlooks the harbor.

29 Cross the estuary by ferry to Passage East and follow the R683 into the center of **Waterford City.** Like Wexford, Waterford was founded by the Vikings in the 9th century, and occupied by the Normans in the late 12th century. The city was overrun by

Cromwellian forces in the 17th century and did not prosper again until the late 18th century. During this period, the city's famous glass-manufacturing industry was established. The best Waterford glass was produced from the late 1780s to the early 19th century. This early work, examples of which can be found in museums and public buildings all over the country, is characterized by a unique, slightly opaque cast that is absent from the modern product.

Numbers in the margin correspond to points of interest on the Waterford City map.

Initially, the slightly run-down commercial center doesn't look too promising. You'll need to park your car and proceed on foot to discover the heritage that the city has made admirable efforts over the past decade to preserve. Begin your tour at the corner of Greyfriar's Street and Custom House Parade down at the quays. (The **Tourist Information Office** is also down there at No. 41 Merchants Quay.) The city quays stretch for nearly a mile along the River Suir and were described in the 18th century as the best in Europe. Here you'll find the **Waterford Heritage Centre,** home to some of the 75,000 historical artifacts excavated from beneath the city in the mid-1980s. Parts of Viking houses are displayed alongside samples of leather work, bone carvings, pottery, and ornate jewelry. *Greyfriar's St., tel. 051/71227. Admission: 50p. Open Mon.–Sat. 10–5.*

Make a right on the Parade and head along the water to the massive pepperpot-shaped **Reginald's Tower,** built by the Vikings for the city's defense in 1003. The walls of this 25-meter-(80-foot-) high circular fortification are 3 meters (10 feet) thick; an interior stairway leads to the top. Reginald's Tower marks the apex of a triangle that contains the old walled city of Waterford. Since 1955 the tower has been used as a civic museum, but historically it served in turn as the residence for a succession of Anglo-Norman kings, including Henry II, John, and Richard II; a mint for silver coins; a prison; and an arsenal. It is said that Strongbow's marriage to Eva, the daughter of Dermot MacMurrough, took place here in the late 12th century, thus uniting the Norman invaders with the native Irish. *The Mall, tel. 051/73501. Admission 50p. Open Mon.–Sat. 10–5.*

Proceed south along the Mall to **City Hall,** one of Waterford's finer Georgian buildings, dating from 1783. On the way you'll pass some good examples of domestic Georgian architecture—tall, well-proportioned houses with typically Irish semicircular fanlights above the doors. As you enter the imposing yet simply designed City Hall, be sure to notice the arms of Waterford over the entrance. The building contains two lovely theaters, an old Waterford dinner service, and an enormous 1802 Waterford-glass chandelier, which hangs in the Council Chamber; a copy of the chandelier hangs in Independence Hall in Philadelphia. The Theatre Royal is the setting for the annual Festival of Light Music in October. A small collection of military memorabilia includes the uniform, sword, and battle flag of the Irish Brigade carried by Thomas Francis Meagher at the battle of Fredericksburg. Meagher (1823–1867), an Irish-American hero, was born nearby in the building on the quays that is now the **Granville Hotel.** Also on display is the old American Union flag with 34 stars. *The Mall, tel. 051/73501. Admission free. Open weekdays 9–1 and 2–5.*

Waterford City

River Suir

John's R.

Adelphi Quay

Rose Lane

William St.

PEOPLE'S PARK

Court House

Fire Station

Beau St.

Catherine St.

Parnell St.

The Mall

Bailey's New St.

Greyfriar's St.

Henrietta St.

Colbeck St.

City Wall

Garden

Spring

Michael St.

Olaf St.

Peter St.

New St.

The Quay

Custom House Parade

High St.

Broad St.

Castle St.

Browne's Lane

City Wall

Barronstrand St.

Patrick St.

Alexander St.

Health Centre

Meagher's Quay

Great George's St.

Green

Mayors Walk

Ballybricken

Tourist Office

Govt. Office

O'Connell St.

Granville Hotel

Arts Centre

Barker St.

Thomas St.

James St.

Merchants Quay

The Glen

Morgan St.

Lower Yellow Rd.

Bridge St.

Summer Hill

Military Rd.

30 · 31 · 32 · 33 · 34 · 35 · 36 · 37 · 38 · 39 · 40

200 yards
200 meters

Bishop's Palace, **33**

Blackfriars Abbey, **35**

Christ Church Cathedral, **38**

City Hall, **32**

French Church, **39**

Holy Trinity Cathedral, **37**

Reginald's Tower, **31**

St. Olaf's Church, **34**

Victorian Clock Tower, **36**

Waterford Glass Factory, **40**

Waterford Heritage Centre, **30**

Time Out The **Reginald** restaurant and pub (The Mall, tel. 051/55087) is worth a look for its unusual decor: A section of the city's 9th-century Viking wall has been incorporated into the restaurant's interior. This is a popular place with locals for lunch and snacks.

㉝ Alongside City Hall on the Mall is the **Bishop's Palace,** another building that is among the most imposing of the remaining Georgian town houses. Only the foyer is open and free to the public (weekdays, 9–5).

Turn right once you leave the Bishop's Palace and then make a right on to Colbeck Street. On your left you'll see one of the remaining portions of the old city wall; there are sections all around the town center. A left at the top of Colbeck Street and **㉞** then an immediate right will bring you to the site of **St. Olaf's Church**—built, as you might guess from the name, by the Vikings in the mid-11th century. All that remains of the old church is its original door, which has been incorporated into the wall of the existing building (a meeting hall).

Continue north up St. Olaf's Street and make a left into High **㉟** Street. On your right is the ruined tower of **Blackfriars Abbey,** a Dominican abbey founded in 1226 and returned to the crown in 1541 after the dissolution of the monasteries. It was used as a courthouse until Cromwellian forces destroyed it in the 17th century.

From the crossroads ahead looking down Barronstrand Street **㊱** toward the quays, you can see the **Victorian Clock Tower** on Merchant's Quay, built in 1864 with public donations. Although it has no great architectural merit, it serves as a reminder of the days when Waterford was a thriving, bustling port with almost full employment. Now, as elsewhere in Ireland, the unemployment figure for its 38,500 inhabitants is high.

㊲ **Holy Trinity Cathedral** (Roman Catholic), on Barronstrand Street between High Street and the clock tower, has a simple, classic facade, but its interior is richly (some would say garishly) decorated with high vaulted ceilings and ornate Corinthian pillars. More interesting than its architecture is the fact that it was built in the late 18th century, when the Catholic religion was barely tolerated, on land granted by the Protestant city fathers.

Retrace your steps back along High Street until it joins **㊳** Henrietta Street. A right turn here brings you to **Christ Church Cathedral** (Church of Ireland). Although its facade is in a more ornate Renaissance style than the classic Catholic Cathedral's, both buildings were designed by the same architect, a Waterford man named John Roberts. Christ Church Cathedral occupies the site of an 11th-century church, which was torn down in the 18th century and replaced with the current structure. Take note of the tomb of James Rice, an unusual *memento mori;* a high-relief effigy depicts him wrapped in his shroud in a state of decay, with all manner of frogs and bugs climbing out of his corpse.

Across Cathedral Square you can see the roofless ruins of the **㊴** **French Church,** a 13th-century Franciscan abbey, also known as Greyfriars, that was given to a group of Huguenot refugees (hence the "French") in 1695. A splendid east window remains amid the ruins. A short walk down Henrietta Street will bring you back to the quays, close to the starting point of the tour.

Time Out The **Olde Stand Victorian Pub and Restaurant** (Michael St., tel. 051/79488) serves lunch and snacks at reasonable prices. Old paintings, city maps, and a handcrafted wooden bar add touches of nostalgia.

40 Last, but certainly not least, is the almost mandatory trip to the **Waterford Glass Factory,** which lies about 2 km (1 mi) from the Tourist Information Office. Take the N25 Waterford–Cork road south from the quay, or ask at the tourist office about the regular bus service.

On guided tours of the glass factory, you observe the specialized crafts of blowing, cutting, and polishing glass. Busy barearmed workmen in leather aprons carry out their intricate tasks against a noisy background of glowing furnaces and ceaseless bustle. Children under 14 are not allowed on the tour, but they can watch videos of the process from the showroom. An extensive selection of crystal is on view (and for sale) in the showroom. Tours, which take 40 minutes, should be arranged in advance with the factory or through the tourist office. *Cork Rd., Kilbarry, tel. 051/73311. Admission free. Open weekdays 10:15–2:30.*

Numbers in the margin correspond to points of interest on the Southeast map.

41 Leave Waterford on the R683, picking up the R684 after about 5 km (3 mi). After another 8 km (5 mi) you'll reach **Dunmore East,** a fishing village of thatched cottages at the head of Waterford Harbour and the site of an attractive lighthouse. There are plenty of small beaches and cliff walks nearby, and you get a wonderful view of the estuary from the hill behind the village.

42 Double back on the R684 and take the R685 to the left, following signposts for **Tramore.** The 5-km- (3-mi-) long beach at Tramore is a popular escape for families from Waterford and other parts of the Southeast, as the many vacation homes and camper parks show. It is Ireland's biggest seaside resort and a dream-come-true for young children, but it is not to everybody's taste. One part of the seafront is taken over by a 50-acre amusement park, a miniature railway, and a boating lake, while the upper half of town is rather more quiet and reserved. Tramore's newest attraction, which opened in 1992, is **Celtworld,** a multi-media experience of the myths and legends of Celtic Ireland. Old hippies will find nostalgia in the Pre-Raphaelite–style graphics by flower-power artist Jim Fitzpatrick, and children of all ages will enjoy the Marvel comic–style approach to Celtic mythology. Anyone with a serious interest in the subject, or even minimal intellectual pretensions, should probably keep well away. *Tramore, Co. Waterford, tel. 051/86166. Admission: £3.95 adults, £3.25 students and senior citizens, £2.75 children under 16. Open daily March–May and Oct. 10–5; June–Sept. 10 AM– 1 PM. Call for hours Nov.–Feb.*

At the western end of the beach the sand gives way to rocky cliffs guarded by the **Metal Man,** a giant cast-iron figure. He stands on top of a great pillar, and it is said that if a young woman hops on one foot around the base of the pillar three times, she will be married within a year. This custom, which is still observed in a lighthearted way, can be traced back to a stone that stood on the spot centuries ago and was used in ancient Celtic fertility rites.

Time Out **The Esquire** (Cross Market St., tel. 051/81324) is a quiet retreat where the internationally trained owner-chef applies his skills to fresh local produce. Originally built in 1937 as a "Gentleman's Bar," the establishment retains an air of gentility. A full à la carte menu with such dishes as smoked salmon, Irish peppered steak with brandy, and vegetarian specials is served in the restaurant, while a simpler—and faster—bar-food menu is also available.

Eleven km (7 mi) west of Tramore on the R675, you join the coast again at **Annestown,** a smaller, quieter resort town with a good sandy beach; 8 km (5 mi) beyond this is the former copper-mining center of **Bunmahon,** now a fishing village popular with holiday makers. This area offers a pleasant coastal drive with good views—unusual rock formations in the cliffs interspersed with sand dunes. Both towns are home to various rare flowers and birds. You will find attractive and easily accessible beaches at Stradbally and Clonea.

Gradually the lowlands of Wexford and eastern Waterford, with their covering of soft grasses, give way to heath and moorland; the bog is created and maintained by the wetter climate of the hillier western Waterford countryside. You will see the mountains responsible for this change in climate rising up behind **Dungarvan,** a small town on Dungarvan Harbour and the administrative center for the part of the county outside Waterford City. It is a quiet town with good facilities for deep-sea fishing and sailboating, and is a popular base for climbers and hikers.

Time Out Dungarvan has several waterside bars with a relaxed, nautical atmosphere. One of the best is **The Moorings** (Davitt's Quay, tel. 058/41461) where you can feast on local seafood. **Merry's** (Lower Main St., tel. 058/41974), once a 17th-century wine merchant's establishment, is a reasonably priced restaurant with plenty of Old World atmosphere and decorated with unusual bygones.

Tour 3: The Blackwater Valley and County Tipperary

This tour takes you inland, through some of Ireland's lushest pasturelands, to some of its most romantic sites. The Blackwater Valley is famed for its beauty, its peacefulness, and its excellent fishing. Some of the finest racehorses in the world are raised in the fields of Tipperary, which is also the county in which you will find the magnificent monastic remains on the Rock of Cashel.

Leave Dungarvan on the N25 and head south, following signposts for Cork. The road climbs steeply past moorland interspersed with woodland. After about 16 km (10 mi), look out for a signpost to Ardmore on the left. **Ardmore** is a delightful little resort at the base of a tall cliff, far more restrained in tone than Tramore. Follow the signs to the top of the cliff to reach

Ardmore's monastic remains. The **Ardmore Tower** is 31 meters
(97 feet) high, and is in exceptionally good condition. Such
structures were built by the early Christian monks as watchtowers and belfries but came to be used as places of refuge for
the monks and their valuables during Viking raids. This is the
reason the doorway is 15 feet above ground level: Once inside,
the monks could pull the ladder into the tower with them. Some
70 round towers remain in Ireland, but none has such a spectacular setting as this one's clifftop location. The tower is freely
accessible.

Nearby is the ruined **Cathedral of St. Declan,** an ancient structure named after the founder of a monastic community; it has
some weathered but interesting biblical scenes carved on its
west front. The saint is said to be buried in **St. Declan's Oratory,** a small early Christian church that has been partially reconstructed in modern times.

Return to the N25 and turn left to cross over Youghal Bridge.
After the bridge turn right onto the R634, and follow this road
through Tallow to pick up the N72 into the lovely little town of
47 **Lismore** on the banks of the Blackwater, a river famous for its
trout and salmon. You will immediately be struck by a dramatic
view of the magnificent **Lismore Castle,** a vast turreted gray
stone building atop a wooded rock that overhangs the river.
There has been a castle here since the 12th century, but the
present structure, built by the sixth duke of Devonshire, dates
from the mid-19th century. The castle still remains in the same
family, and was for many years the Irish home of Fred Astaire's
sister, Adele, who married the duke of Devonshire. The upper
and lower gardens, open to the public, consist of woodland
walks, including an unusual yew walk said to be over 800 years
old, and an impressive display of magnolias, camellias, and
shrubs. *Tel. 058/54424. Admission: £1.50 adults, 50p children.
Open May–Sept., Sun.–Fri. 1:45–4:45.*

Today, with a population of only 920, Lismore is a sleepy village, popular with anglers and romantics. From the 7th to the
12th century, however, it was an important monastic center,
founded by St. Carthac (or Carthage), and one of the most renowned universities of its time. The only reminders of those
days are the village's two cathedrals, a Roman Catholic one
from the late-19th century, and the Church of Ireland St.
Carthage's, which dates from 1633 and incorporates fragments
of an earlier church. The latter cathedral also has some interesting tombs and effigies.

Leave Lismore, heading east on the N72 for 6½ km (4 mi), for
Cappoquin, a well-known coarse-angling center, and pick up
the R669 north into the **Knockmealdown Mountains.** Your route
is signposted as the **Vee Gap** road, the Vee Gap being its summit, from which you get superb views of the Tipperary plain,
the Galtee Mountains in the northwest, and a peak called
Slievenamon in the northeast. If the visibility is good, you
should be able to see the Rock of Cashel, ancient seat of the
kings of Munster, some 32 km (20 mi) away. Just before you enter the Vee Gap, look for a 6-foot-high mound of stones on the
left side of the road. It marks the grave of Colonel Grubb, a local landowner who liked the view so much that he arranged to
be buried here standing up so that he could look out on the
scene for all eternity.

As you travel on the R669, you might like to stop and visit the **Mount Melleray Abbey.** The monastery was founded in 1832 by the Cistercian Order in what was then a barren mountainside wilderness. Over the years the order has succeeded in transforming the site into more than 600 acres of fertile farmland. The monks maintain strict vows of silence, but visitors are permitted into most areas of the abbey. It is also possible to stay in the guest lodge by prior arrangement. *Tel. 058/54404. Admission free. Open daily 9–6.*

Continue north through Clogheen and pick up the R655 west to **(48) Ballyporeen,** a town best known as the ancestral home of Ronald Reagan. The town's special **Visitor Center** (tel. 052/67106) documents Reagan's 1984 visit. Despite the fame—and the tour buses—that the Reagan connection has brought the place, it remains a pleasant, friendly rural backwater with wide streets built to accommodate the cattle fairs that were held here until the 1960s. There is an undeniable charm to this quiet, low-lying village on an open plain midway between the mountains of western Waterford and southern Tipperary.

Mitchelstown Caves are clearly signposted from Ballyporeen to the right by the town church. Follow this road for 5 km (3 mi) to explore one of the finest subterranean limestone formations in Ireland, created by the motion of water against the rock over millions of years. Some of the caves are massive, extending for miles. Although only a part of the system is open to the public, it is still an impressive and uncommercialized sight. *Tel. 052/67246. Admission: £2 adults, 50p children. Open daily 10–6.*

Rejoin the N8 about 1½ km (1 mi) north of the caves and turn **(49)** right to reach **Cahir** (pronounced "care"). Cahir is a small market town on the River Suir, at the crossroads of the busy N24 and N8 roads. **Cahir Castle,** its main attraction, is a massive limestone structure dating from 1164 and built on rock in the middle of the river. There are regular guided tours and an audiovisual display in the lodge. *Tel. 052/41011. Admission £1 adults, 40p children. Open June–Sept., daily 10–7:30; Oct.–May, Tues.–Sat. 10–6; Sun. 2–6.*

Tipperary Town can be reached by following the N24 northwest from Cahir past the **Glen of Aherlow,** a lovely wooded stretch skirting the River Aherlow and its tributaries between the Galtee Mountains and the Slievenamuck Hills.

Time Out This beautiful woodland setting is the site of the **Glen Hotel** (Glen of Aherlow, tel. 062/56146), a country-style inn with an amiable and spacious interior. You'll find light snacks, salads, and an à la carte menu available here throughout the day.

(50) Tipperary Town, a dairy-farming center at the head of a fertile plain known as the Golden Vale, is a good starting point for climbing and walking in the hills around the Glen of Aherlow. Racehorses are County Tipperary's most famous export, and it has four racecourses—at Tipperary Town, Clonmel, Thurles, and Limerick Junction. Try to catch a meeting if you can: it makes an enjoyable and inexpensive day out.

(51) Take the N74 east from Tipperary Town to **Cashel.** A visit to the **Rock of Cashel** will appeal to almost anyone who cares about the past. The rock itself rises as a giant circular mound 60 meters (200 feet) above the surrounding plain; it is crowned by a tall cluster of gray monastic remains. Cashel means "stone fort" in Gaelic. Legend has it that the devil, flying over Ireland in a hurry, took a bite out of the Slieve Bloom Mountains to clear his path (the gap, known as the Devil's Bit, can be seen to the north of the rock) and spat it out here in the Golden Vale.

The town of Cashel has a lengthy history as a center of royal and religious power. It was the pre-Christian seat of the kings of Munster and was probably at one time a center of Druidic worship. Here, according to legend, St. Patrick baptized King Aengus, who became Ireland's first Christian ruler. It was also at Cashel that St. Patrick is said to have plucked a shamrock to explain the mystery of the Trinity, thus giving a new emblem to Christian Ireland.

The best approach to the Rock is along the **Bishop's Walk,** a 10-minute hike from the Cashel Palace Hotel on Main Street. As you enter the royal town, you'll see ahead a rough stone with an ancient cross; this is where, according to legend, St. Patrick baptized King Aengus. (Patrick was old then and drove his staff into the earth to support himself. After the ceremony, it was discovered that the staff had passed through the king's foot and the grass was soaked with blood. Aengus thought that this suffering was part of the Christian ceremony.) The stone at this site was also the Coronation Stone of the Munster kings; it dates from as early as the 4th century.

Actually, the stone that you see upon arrival is a replica; the real one is on display in the new museum across from the town entrance. Although the museum is an innovation that some find inappropriate and unnecessary, it does provide enthusiastic young guides, who will ensure that you do not miss the many interesting features of the buildings atop the Rock of Cashel.

The largest building on the summit is the shell of **St. Patrick's Cathedral,** while the best-preserved is **Cormac's Chapel.** The 13th-century cathedral was originally built in a flamboyant variation on Romanesque style, but was destroyed by fire in 1495; the restored building was desecrated during the 16th century. There is a series of sculptures in the north transept representing the Apostles and other saints and the Beasts of the Apocalypse. Look for the octagonal staircase turret that ascends beside the Central Tower to a series of defensive passages built into the thick walls. From the top of the Central Tower, you'll have a wonderful view of the surrounding plains and mountains. Another passage gives access to the Round Tower, a well-preserved building 30 meters (92 feet) high.

The entrance to Cormac's Chapel is behind the south transept of the Cathedral. Note the high corbeled roof, modeled on the traditional covering of early saints' cells (as at Glendalough and Dingle); the typically Romanesque twisted columns around the altar; and the unique carvings around the south entrance. The chapel was built in 1127 by Cormac Macarthy, king of Desmond and bishop of Cashel (combination bishop-kings were not unusual in the early Irish church). *Rock of Cashel, tel. 062/61437. Admission: £1. Open May–Sept., daily 9–7:30; Oct.–Apr., daily 9:30–4:30.*

Take some time to linger at the Rock of Cashel, sitting on the short grass admiring the view of the plains of Tipperary, and absorbing the atmosphere of its pagan and Christian pasts. At the base of the rock is the **Bru Boru Heritage Center,** where

Irish music, dancing, and culture are studied. Exhibits on aspects of Irish heritage change seasonally, and you can visit the craft shop, genealogy center, and restaurant. *Cashel, Co. Tipperary, tel. 062/61122. Admission to Heritage Center: free. Open year-round Mon.–Sat. 9–5, Sun. 2–5. Admission to evening song and storytelling (see Arts, below): £5 adults, £2 children. Tues.–Sun. 9 PM, mid-June–mid-Sept.*

When you leave, you might want to look around the town of Cashel, which has a few interesting shops selling modern crafts and some well-preserved examples of the Victorian Irish shop front, with four-part windows divided by timber pilasters. Look for a run of six such windows on Main Street. The **GPA Bolton Library,** on the grounds of the St. John the Baptist Church of Ireland Cathedral, has a fascinating collection of rare books and manuscripts on display. *John St., tel. 062/61944. Admission: £1 adults, 50p children. Open Mon.–Sat. 9:30–5:30, Sun. 2:30–5:30.*

You can also visit the **Cashel Folk Village,** which features a series of reconstructed 18th-century houses and shops as well as a range of antiques and tools from that period. *Main St., tel. 062/ 61333. Admission: 50p adults, 30p children. Open daily 9:30–8.*

Time Out The **Bishop's Buttery** (tel. 062/61411) in the Cashel Place Hotel on Main Street is an informal restaurant, adorned with elaborate Celtic-style hangings, in the cellar of a former bishop's palace. There are always such traditional Irish dishes on the menu as Irish stew (mutton, onion, carrots, and potatoes) and Colcannon (a creamy combination of leeks, potatoes, butter, and nutmeg).

If the Rock of Cashel has left you in a mood for more ecclesiastical remains, make a detour on the R660, traveling 14 km (9 mi) **52** to the north of Cashel, to **Holycross,** site of **Holycross Abbey,** a Cistercian abbey church named after a relic of the True Cross. The abbey, which incorporates late-12th- and early 15th-century architecture, has been carefully restored and has some well-preserved stone carvings and window traceries. It is attractively situated on the banks of the River Suir. *Holycross, near Thurles, tel. 0504/43241. Freely accessible.*

53 Return to Cashel and pick up the R688 southeast to **Clonmel** (24 km/15 mi), the county seat of Tipperary, which is set on the loveliest part of the River Suir, with wooded islands and riverside walks. With a population of about 12,500, it is one of Ireland's largest and most prosperous inland towns. There has been a settlement here since Viking days; in the 14th century the town was walled and fortified as a stronghold of the Butler family. The novelist Laurence Sterne (1713–1768), author of *Tristram Shandy,* was born here, and the English novelist Anthony Trollope (1815–1882) served for a time in the post office. O'Connell Street, the main thoroughfare, runs east-west and close to the river. At one end is the West Gate, built in 1831 on the site of the medieval one. Among other notable buildings are the Court House (designed by Sir Richard Morrison), and the Franciscan Friary and St. Mary's Church of Ireland, both of which incorporate remains of earlier churches and some interesting tombs and monuments.

Clonmel is well-known in sporting circles, being the base of the Tipperary foxhounds and a greyhound-racing center. It is also the headquarters of the Irish Coursing Club. At greyhound races, the dogs chase an electronic "hare" around a fenced-in miniature racecourse; at a coursing meet they chase and kill a real hare in an open field. The latter, although an ancient sport with its own rules, is not for the squeamish, and meets are frequently disrupted by animal lovers. You will often see sleek, slim greyhounds in the area being exercised on leashes along the road. Some of them are worth thousands of pounds.

Time Out **Mulcahy's of Clonmel** (47 Gladstone St., tel. 052/22825) is an award winning bar-restaurant. A selection of salads, snacks, and hot dishes is served all day in the Carvery Food Bar; from 6 PM an extensive à la carte menu is available in the Melleray Restaurant.

54 About 20 km (12 mi) east of Clonmel on the N24 is a smaller riverside town, **Carrick-on-Suir.** This town is something of an oddity, as it lies partly in County Tipperary and partly in County Waterford. The beautifully restored **Ormonde Castle** is the main attraction here. The most interesting part of the castle is a Tudor manor house, one of the best-preserved Tudor buildings in Ireland; it was built in 1584 beside an older castle keep overlooking the river. The town is one of several claiming to be the birthplace of Anne Boleyn, and the house is said to have been built in order to entertain her daughter, Queen Elizabeth I, who never visited here. It contains some good early stucco work and many arms and busts of the English Queen. *Tel. 051/ 40787. Admission: 80p adults, 30p children. Open mid-June– Sept., daily 9:30–5.*

From Clonmel the N24 continues east to Waterford and west to Limerick. The Cork–Dublin road can be picked up by following the N24 west to Cahir for 16 km (10 mi).

Shopping

Enniscorthy In Enniscorthy, stop by **Kiltrea Bridge Pottery** (Kiltrea Bridge, Caim, tel. 054/35107) and **Carley's Bridge Pottery** (Carley's Bridge, tel. 054/35312) for handcrafted pottery work.

Kilkenny Don't miss the **Kilkenny Design Centre** at Kilkenny Castle (tel. 056/22441) in the old stable yard opposite the castle. The establishment sells a range of goods that combine traditional crafts with modern design—ceramics, jewelry, sweaters, handwoven textiles, and so on. Also check out **The Sweater Shop** (High St., tel. 056/63405), and **P.T. Murphy** (85 High St., tel. 056/21127), which specializes in heraldic jewelry. **Richard Duggan and Sons Ltd, The Monster House** (High St., tel. 056/22016) is a small department store with a good selection of Irish crystal and other souvenirs. **Nicholas Mosse Pottery** (Bennettsbridge, tel. 056/ 27105) stocks an attractive array of handmade spongeware.

Tipperary The **Tipperary Crystal factory** (Ballynoran, Carrick-on-Suir, tel. 051/41188) is a facility similar to that at Waterford, and purchases made at this showroom can also be shipped overseas with ease.

Waterford Outside of Waterford City, definitely pay a visit to the world-famous **Waterford Glass Factory** (Cork Rd., Kilbarry, tel. 051/

73311). The showroom at the factory displays an extensive selection of both Waterford crystal and Wedgwood pottery, and overseas orders are handled promptly (*see* Tour 2, above). Numerous shopping arcades in Waterford provide ample opportunity for browsing. You'll notice an emphasis on tweeds, knitwear, and crystal in the arcades at Broad Street Centre and George's Court, as well as along The Quay and on Barronstrand and Broad streets. Try **Quay Antiques** (128 The Quay, tel. 051/77784), **Kelly's** department store (75 The Quay, tel. 051/73557), and **Joseph Knox** (3 Barronstrand St., tel. 051/75307) for crystal and china.

Wexford   County Wexford is a major center for pottery, leatherwork, weaving, silversmithing, and other crafts. In Wexford Town you'll want to visit the **Wool Shop** (39 S. Main St., tel. 053/22247) or **Casket Fabrics** (50 Patrick St., tel. 051/75304) for Aran sweaters, **John Hore's** (31 S. Main St., tel. 053/22200) for handmade Irish linen, and **Lowney Antiques, Ltd.** (61 S. Main St., tel. 053/23140) for your own small slice of Ireland's past.

Sports and Fitness

Participant Sports

Bicycling   Maps outlining suggested bicycling routes are available from most tourist board information offices throughout the Southeast. Bikes can be rented through **J.J. Wall** (88 Maudlin St., Kilkenny, tel. 056/21236), **Colum's Shop** (O'Connell St., Dungarvan, Co. Waterford, tel. 058/41278), or **The Bike Shop** (9 Selskar St., Wexford, tel. 053/22514).

Fishing   Although most of Ireland's angling is concentrated in the northern center of the country around the counties of Leitrim, Cavan, and Monaghan, there is good fishing in the Southeast around Carlow Town and in parts of County Waterford. Carlow Town and Graiguenamanagh, both on the River Barrow, are also the sites of a popular angling festival held every May. Contact the **Southern Regional Fisheries Board** (Anglesea St., Clonmel, Co. Tipperary, tel. 052/23971) for further information. For deep-sea fishing, contact Cormack Walsh at the **Sea Angling Service** (29 Abbots Close, Sea Park, Dungarvan, Co. Waterford, tel. 058/43514).

Golf   Some of Ireland's best parkland golf courses can be found in the Southeast. Among them are **Carlow Golf Club** (Deerpark, Co. Carlow, tel. 0503/31695), **Tramore Golf Club** (Tramore, Co. Waterford, tel. 051/86170), **Mount Juliet Golf Club** (Thomastown, Co. Kilkenny, tel 056/24725), **Kilkenny Golf Club** (Glendine, Co. Kilkenny, tel. 056/22125), **Waterford Castle Golf and Country Club** (The Island, Ballinakill, Co. Waterford, tel. 051/71633), **Rosslare Golf Club** (Rosslare Strand, Co. Wexford, tel. 053/32203), **Clonmel Golf Club** (Lyreanearle, Clonmel, Co. Tipperary, tel. 052/21138), **Dundrum House Golf Club** (Dundrum, near Cashel, Co. Tipperary, tel. 062/71116), and **Courtown Golf Club** (Kiltennel, Gorey, Co. Wexford, tel. 055/21533).

Hiking   A number of hiking trails crisscrossing the Irish countryside have been designed and maintained by the National Sports Council, and several of these fine trails are located in the Southeast. The **South Leinster Way** begins in the County Carlow town of Kildavin and makes its way southwest over Mt. Leinster and the River Barrow, terminating in Carrick-on-Suir. A second trail, the **Munster Way,** picks up where the first ends and leads through the Vee Gap in the Knockmealdown Mountains and on to Clogheen. Contact the tourist board for further information.

Horseback Riding   If you have any equestrian skills at all, you will probably want to ride some of the fine horses bred in this part of Ireland. The following places all offer riding by the hour or by the day; expect to pay about £12 for a two-hour trek, and about £32 for a full day, including packed lunch: **Carrigbeg Stables** (Carrigbeg, Bagenalstown, Co. Carlow, tel. 0503/21962), **Kilotteran Equitation Centre** (Kilotteran, near Waterford, tel. 051/84158), **Melody's Riding Stables** (Ballymacarberry, near Clonmel, Co. Waterford, tel. 052/36147), **Horetown Equestrian Centre** (Horetown House, Foulksmills, Co. Wexford, tel. 051/63706), **Grianan Riding School** (Comer Rd., Kilkenny, tel. 056/22872), **Mount Juliet Equestrian Centre** (Thomastown, Co. Kilkenny, tel. 056/24455), **Thomastown Equitation Centre** (Thomastown, Co. Kilkenny, tel. 056/24112), and **Warrington Riding School** (Warrington, Co. Kilkenny, tel. 056/22682).

Spectator Sports

The people of the Southeast are a sporting lot, and on any given day in this region you're likely to find the stands at the races or the hurling matches full to brimming.

Dog Racing   **Greyhound racing** is extremely popular here, and Irish dogs are considered to be among the best in the world. Races are held at night, and the main dog tracks in the Southeast are **Clonmel Greyhound Racetrack** (Davis Rd., Clonmel, Co. Tipperary, tel. 052/21118), **Enniscorthy Greyhound Racetrack** (Showgrounds, Enniscorthy, Co. Wexford, tel. 054/33172), **Kilkenny Greyhound Racetrack** (St. James Park, Co. Kilkenny, tel. 056/21214), **Thurles Greyhound Racetrack** (Town Park, Thurles, Co. Tipperary, tel. 0504/21013), and **Waterford Greyhound Racetrack** (Kilcohan Park, Co. Waterford, tel. 051/74531).

Gaelic Football and Hurling   Tickets to Gaelic football and hurling matches are available through the **Gaelic Athletic Association** (GAA, Croke Park, Dublin, tel. 01/363222) or at the entrance to the local stadium. In the Southeast, games are played on Sundays at the following county grounds: **Clonmel GAA Grounds** (Western Rd., Clonmel, Co. Tipperary, tel. 52/21806), **Carlow GAA Grounds** (Dr. Cullen Park, Co. Carlow, tel. 503/32414), **Kilkenny GAA Grounds** (Nowlan Park, Co. Kilkenny, tel. 056/22841), **Waterford GAA Grounds** (Walsh Park, Co. Waterford, tel. 056/77798), and **Wexford GAA Grounds** (Wexford Park, Clonard Rd., Co. Wexford, tel. 053/24620).

Horse Racing   Horse races are held regularly at the following tracks in the Southeast: **Gowran Park** (Co. Kilkenny, tel. 056/26126), **Wexford Racecourse** (Bettyville, Wexford Town, tel. 053/42307), **Tramore Racecourse** (Tramore, Co. Waterford, tel. 051/81574), and **Clonmel Racecourse** (Powerstown Park, Clonmel, Co. Tipperary, tel. 052/22852).

Dining and Lodging

Dining

*By Georgina
Campbell and
Pat Mackey*

Category	Cost*
Very Expensive	over £20
Expensive	£15–£20
Moderate	£12–£15
Inexpensive	under £12

*per person, excluding drinks and service

Lodging

Category	Cost*
Very Expensive	Over £100
Expensive	£80–£100
Moderate	£60–£80
Inexpensive	under £60

*double occupancy

Highly recommended restaurants and hotels are indicated by a star ★.

Borris

Dining and Lodging   **Step House.** This late-Georgian house on the banks of the River Barrow is the perfect setting for Irish country-house cuisine. Drinks are served beside an open fire in the chintz-draped sitting room before dinner in the equally cozy, candle-lighted dining room. The food is seasonal: Local pheasant and wild duck are on the menu in winter, and local salmon, mussels, and prawns are served in summer. A Continental influence is evident in appetizers like mussels stuffed with garlic butter, and main courses tend to be simple: poached wild salmon hollandaise for example. When it comes to dessert, don't miss their incredible house special, a chocolate *gâteau* composed of meringue, chocolate mousse, sponge, and chocolate *ganache*—it's so complicated, it takes two days to make! There's a casual, less expensive cellar bistro/bar as well, where you can dine in the courtyard in fine weather. There are also 5 rooms with bath *(Inexpensive). Co. Carlow, tel. 0503/73401. Reservations advised. Dress: casual but neat. MC, V. No lunch Tues. and Wed., closed Mon. and Feb. Restaurant Expensive; bistro Moderate.*

Cahir

Lodging   **Kilcoran Lodge.** This handsome 19th-century house sits amid beautiful countryside 6 km (4 mi) outside Cahir beneath the Galtee Mountains on the main Cork–Dublin (N8) road. Rooms facing the front sport the best views of the beautiful heather-covered slopes. Guest rooms are pleasant and have Victorian-style furnishings and comfortable beds. The furnishing in the public areas is discreet and stately, and the entire hotel wears the ambience of a country manor house. *Co. Tipperary, tel. 052/41288. 23 rooms with bath. Facilities: restaurant, pool, health club, nearby fishing and horseback riding. AE, DC, MC, V. Expensive.*

Carlow

Lodging **Royal Hotel.** The Royal is located in the center of town; while this may be convenient, you may also find the busy traffic around the building to be a bit distracting. The lobby and public spaces are decorated with wood trim and heavy, Victorian-style furniture covered with floral prints. Comfortable guest rooms are decorated in a similar fashion. *8–13 Dublin St., Co. Carlow, tel. 0503/31621. 32 rooms with bath. Facilities: restaurant, cable TV. AE, DC, MC, V. Moderate.*

★ **Seven Oaks.** This handsome hotel is in a quiet suburb on the outskirts of town, just a 10-minute ride from the Carlow train station. The building, which was built at the turn of the century, has been recently renovated, and you'll find that the guest rooms in the new section are more spacious than the older ones. The bright, airy public space is filled with modern furniture and plenty of cut glass, which accents the charming rural decor. Guest rooms are also filled with modern furnishings, but again the rural motif is carried throughout with hunting prints and a floral decor. *Athy Rd., Co. Carlow, tel. 0503/31308. 16 rooms, 12 with bath. Facilities: restaurant, bar, cable TV. AE, DC, MC, V. Moderate.*

Cashel

Dining **Chez Hans.** This small, converted Victorian church at the foot of the Rock of Cashel oozes Old World charm: Dark wood and tapestries provide an elegant background for tables dressed in beige linen, Traditional French cuisine with a hint of nouvelle has been adapted to take advantage of fresh Irish ingredients. Specialties include roast rack of spring lamb with a fresh herb crust and tarragon sauce, and free-range hot chicken, lightly smoked and served with a yogurt, apple, and Clonmel cider sauce. Steaks are always excellent here, as is the fish. Owner-chef Hans Matthia has compiled an unusual list of 11 house wines, including two exclusive whites from his sister's vineyard in Germany. *Rockside, tel. 062/61177. Reservations required. Dress: casual but neat. No credit cards. Dinner only; closed Sun., Mon., Dec. 25–26, and the first 3 weeks of Jan. Very Expensive.*

Dining and Lodging **Cashel Palace.** Located dramatically at the foot of the Rock of Cashel, this 18th-century bishop's palace is an exquisite accommodation.
★ The redbrick-and-stone manor house is set back from the street in its own garden, so despite its central location it is quite tranquil. The public rooms, paneled in pine and filled with Queen Anne antique furniture, are dominated by twin marble fireplaces and carved wood pillars. Perhaps the most striking feature is the sweeping, intricately carved red-pine staircase leading up to the second floor. The richly decorated guest rooms are equally luxurious, filled with four-poster canopied beds and antiques. Request a room facing the back so that

you can enjoy the breathtaking view of the Rock of Cashel rising up behind the hotel. The Four Seasons restaurant in the hotel is an elegant dining room done in rich floral drapery, Waterford glass, and formal table settings. The menu here relies heavily on game in season, local lamb and beef, and fresh fish, while the less formal basement restaurant serves simple, light meals all day. *Main St., Co. Tipperary, tel. 062/61411. 17 rooms, 3 suites, all with bath. Facilities: 2 restaurants, bar, gardens, fishing, conference facilities. AE, DC, MC, V. Very Expensive.*

Clonmel

Lodging **Knocklofty House.** This large Georgian mansion, once the home of the earls of Donoughmore, is set on 159 acres of parkland on the banks of the River Suir 8 km (5 mi) outside town on the Ardfinnan road. Guest rooms, particularly those in the front, have fine views of the surrounding countryside. The oak-paneled public spaces are decorated with antique furniture from the Georgian period, giving the impression of a manor-house setting. Guest rooms also are done in antiques, with lovely Oriental carpets. *Co. Tipperary, tel. 052/38322. 15 rooms with bath. Facilities: restaurant, 24-hr room service, tennis courts, pool, gym, sauna, Jacuzzi, riding facilities, clay pigeon shooting, private river fishing. MC, V. Very Expensive.*
Minella Hotel. This bow-fronted Georgian manor hotel is found in a quiet neighborhood on the banks of the River Suir. The rooms afford fine views of the river, particularly those in the front and on the east wing. Old World charm is communicated through the comfortable Victorian furnishings and walls decorated with hunting prints. The dining room is oak-paneled. *Coleville Rd., Co. Tipperary, tel. 052/22388. 45 rooms with shower. Facilities: restaurant, cable TV, 24-hr room service, fishing. AE, DC, MC, V. Expensive.*

Dungarvan

Lodging **Clonea Strand Hotel.** This unpretentious, family-run hotel is located on a scenic stretch of Waterford coastline overlooking Clonea Beach, about 3 km (2 mi) outside Dungarvan. The hotel has direct access to a safe swimming beach. The rooms are comfortable and bright, with plenty of modern, natural-wood furnishings. Amenities include coffee/tea-making facilities and hair driers. *Clonea, Co. Waterford, tel. 058/41277. 35 rooms with bath. Facilities: restaurant, cable TV, pool, sauna, gym, bowling alley, shore fishing. AE, DC, MC, V. Moderate.*

Dunmore East

Dining **The Ship Restaurant.** Dinner is always delicious in this bar/restaurant found in a 19th-century house overlooking the bay. The dining room is casual and easygoing, with simple, sturdy furnishings; dark wood walls; and a nautical theme. The food is an imaginative mixture of French and Irish influences, and the emphasis is on fresh local seafood. Start off, perhaps, with deep-fried pastry parcels stuffed with fresh crabmeat, or pan-fried prawns with a lemon, verbena, and thyme mousseline. Entrées include grilled or pan-fried black sole, or kebabs of fresh prawns and scallops pan-fried in a chive and hyssop butter. Desserts, such as a chocolate boat filled with white-chocolate mousse on a raspberry *coulis*, are tempting, and there's a good selection of Irish farmhouse cheeses. *Tel. 051/83141 or 051/83144. Reservations accepted. Dress: casual. No lunch; closed Sept.–May, Sun. and Mon. MC, V. Moderate–Expensive.*

Glen of Aherlow

Lodging **Aherlow House Hotel.** Set in the middle of a tranquil forest 6½ km (4 mi) outside of Tipperary Town, this simple, rustic hotel was once a hunting lodge. Antique furniture and plenty of pine trim complete the country atmosphere. Guest rooms are modern, beds comfortable, and decor attractive. Ask for a room with a view of the Galtee Mountains. *Co. Tipperary, tel. 062/ 56153. 10 rooms with bath. Facilities: fishing, pony trekking. AE, DC, MC, V. Inexpensive.*

Gorey

Dining **Marlfield House Hotel.** A conservatory and an abundance of greenery create a light and airy garden atmosphere in this Regency-period house. Tables in this stylish restaurant are impeccably dressed with white linen, gleaming glasses, silver, and fresh flowers. The sophisticated cuisine is classical with modern leanings, and great emphasis is placed on the use of fresh local ingredients. Dishes include salade *tiède* made with a selection of salad greens and lambs' sweetbreads, duck livers, prawns or mussels, and wild local salmon served with a sorrel or watercress sauce. Chocolate is a specialty, and elegant desserts might combine white-chocolate mousse with dark-chocolate sauce. *Courtown Rd., Co. Wexford, tel. 055/21124. Reservations required. Jacket and tie suggested. AE, DC, MC, V. Closed Dec. Very Expensive.*

Kilkenny Town

Dining and **Lacken House Guesthouse and Restaurant.** This well-known
Lodging restaurant is in the cellar of a Georgian house on the edge of Kilkenny. Owner-chef Eugene McSweeney and his wife Breda have maintained the period character of the house, using traditional furnishings throughout. Formally dressed waiters serve international dishes made with fresh local ingredients. Baked crab *gâteau* is a typical appetizer—crabmeat blended with a sole mousse, then baked in a *dariole* mold, turned out, and served with an herb and cream sauce. Salmon from the nearby River Nore is the star of the menu in dishes such as cutlet of Nore salmon with a galette of potato and celeriac served with sage butter sauce. For dessert try the homemade ice creams. (There are also 8 rooms with bath [inexpensive].) *Dublin Rd., tel. 056/61085 or 056/65611. Reservations advised. Dress: casual but neat. AE, DC, MC, V. No lunch; closed Sun., Mon., and one week at Christmas. Moderate–Expensive.*

Lodging **Butler House.** This elegant Georgian house, an integral part of the Kilkenny Castle complex, once belonged to the earls of Ormonde. It is now open to guests under the management of the Kilkenny Civic Trust. The best approach is through the crafts workshops opposite the castle and into its old-style walled back garden. Rooms are all decorated in good, modern taste, with plain oatmeal-colored carpets, off-white woolen spreads, large potted plants, and contemporary prints. Ask for a room with a bow window overlooking the garden and castle; those facing Patrick Street are noisier and generally smaller. *16 Patrick St., Kilkenny, tel. 056/22828. 13 rooms with bath. Facilities: evening meal (high season only), wine license, TV and direct dial phones in rooms. AE, DC, MC, V. Moderate.*

★ **The Newpark Hotel.** Set back from the road in the rural suburbs of Kilkenny Town, this hotel is a popular base for businesspeople, tour groups, and independent travelers. At its core is a Victorian house, now surrounded by modern extensions. All the guest rooms are modern, bright, and airy, though you'll find that those in the rear have the best views. They are decorated in soft pastel colors and are brightened by floral-patterned drapes. The public spaces in the hotel are done in a country style and are accented with comfortable pine furnishings. *Castlecomer Rd., Co. Kilkenny, tel. 056/22122. 60 rooms with bath. Facilities: restaurant, pool, Jacuzzi, steam room, gym, 2 tennis courts, cable TV, 24-hr room service. AE, DC, MC, V. Moderate.*

Leighlinbridge

Dining
The Lord Bagenal Inn. This famous old pub beside the River Barrow is today a bar/restaurant with open fires and warm lighting. The bar menu is a basic selection of steaks, fresh fish, and some international dishes like chicken Kiev and spare ribs with sweet and sour sauce. The French-style restaurant's menu changes weekly and is considerably more sophisticated. A typical menu might include a homemade soup, avocado pear with prawn dressing, tournedos steak with *chasseur,* or poached or grilled salmon steak served with hollandaise or lime butter sauce. *Main St., Leighlinbridge, Co. Carlow, tel. 0503/ 21668. Reservations advised weekends. Dress: casual. DC, V. No dinner Sun. or Mon. Closed Dec. 25 and Good Friday. Moderate.*

Rosslare

Lodging
★ **Kelly's Strand.** Owned and run by the Kelly family since 1895, this hotel is a traditional weekend retreat. The on-premises recreational facilities are extensive, including tennis and squash courts, pools, saunas, a golf course, and a health club—not to mention the beach and another golf course nearby. Guest rooms are done in comfortable, rustic decor, and those facing the front have lovely sea views. The lobby and public spaces employ cane furniture and pastel shades to set a relaxed atmosphere. *Co. Wexford, tel. 053/32114. 91 rooms with bath. Facilities: restaurant, solarium, tennis, squash, indoor and outdoor heated pools, croquet, jogging track, health club, saunas, cable TV, 24-hr room service. MC, V. Closed early Dec.–Feb. 28. Moderate.*

The Cedars Hotel. With its new recreation center and recent refurbishment, The Cedars is a good bet for a seaside escape. Located in a quiet area near the beach, life here is cool, fresh, and relaxing. Public spaces are decorated with cane furniture, while guest-room pieces are more modern. The rooms pick up the beach atmosphere with their bright drapery and yellow, white, and blue color scheme. *Co. Wexford, tel. 053/32124. 34 rooms with bath. Facilities: restaurant, leisure center. AE, DC, MC, V. Moderate.*

Rosslare Harbour

Lodging **Great Southern Hotel.** Part of a popular Irish hotel chain, the Rosslare Great Southern is located on a rise overlooking the harbor, just a few minutes' walk from the ferry port. It's a modern two-story hotel—a stark, unimaginative structure on the outside. Its recently renovated interior is more cheerful, with a bright color scheme of blue, green, and white. The comfortable, modern guest rooms are done in a floral decor, and those facing the rear have views of the sea. *Co. Wexford, tel. 053/ 33233. 99 rooms with bath. Facilities: restaurant, bar, tennis, nearby golf, health club, saunas, pool, snooker room, children's playground, conference rooms, live entertainment during summer, cable TV, 24-hr room service. AE, DC, MC, V. Closed Jan.–Apr. Moderate.*

Hotel Rosslare. This historic old hotel (with a totally modern facade) is located at the top of a cliff overlooking Rosslare Bay and the ferry port below. Cheery and bright, the spacious public rooms are done in restful pastel shades. Guest rooms have modern, functional furniture and floral decor. Bedrooms have balconies, and those at the rear have the best sea views. Traditional Irish music is heard live here on summer evenings. *Co. Wexford, tel. 053/33154. 25 rooms, 22 with bath. Facilities: restaurant, bar, beer garden, squash court, billiard room, saunas, nearby beach and golf. AE, DC, MC, V. Moderate.*

Tuskar House Hotel. Found in a quiet area near the ferry port, this small, family-run hotel promises simple pleasures: comfortable rooms and good views of the sea (especially from the rear). The ambience of the public rooms is defined by lots of polished pine, glass, and greenery. In the guest rooms, you'll find functional, modern furniture and a bright, cheery decor. *St. Martin's Rd., Co. Wexford, tel. 053/33363. 20 rooms with bath. Facilities: restaurant. AE, DC, MC, V. Inexpensive.*

Thomastown

Dining and Lodging **Mount Juliet.** One of Ireland's newest luxury hotels, this imposing Georgian mansion is situated within a walled estate of 1,400 acres on the River Nore (17 km/11 mi south of Kilkenny City on the N9). The house has been sumptuously refurbished and incorporates many of the original features, including finely stuccoed ceilings, marble mantelpieces, and carved door trims. Its claim to be "a haven of tranquility" is all too true, but unless you are keen on the outdoor life, its rarified exclusivity and its isolation could quickly become tedious. The two great attractions here are horseback riding on the extensive trails within the estate (which is shared with the Ballyinch Stud) and golfing on the Jack Nicklaus–designed parkland course, which was inaugurated in 1991. The Lady Helen McAlmont Restaurant, a stately room in Wedgwood blue and white, its tables adorned with crystal, silverware, and fine linen, serves haute cuisine with Franco-Irish touches from succulent local produce. Bedrooms are large and individually decorated, with mahogany furniture, super-king-size beds, original fireplaces, and well-appointed bathrooms; all the rooms have peaceful views of the estate. *Co. Kilkenny, tel. 056/24455. 32 rooms with bath. Facilities: 2 restaurants, 2 bars, clay pigeon shooting, fishing, hunting, tennis, croquet, cricket, archery, 18-hole golf, equestrian center, riding trails. AE, DC, MC, V. Very Expensive.*

Waterford City

Dining **Dwyers of Mary Street.** This unusual restaurant is situated in an old Royal Irish Constabulary barracks (the original bars are still on the downstairs windows). The pink, green, and cream color scheme is pretty and fresh, original paintings grace the walls, and the furnishings are a pleasing mixture of styles—antiques are offset by modern touches, such as Bauhaus chairs. The cuisine is French-influenced country house, and the menu changes every two weeks. A typical meal might begin with puff pastry pies stuffed with black pudding and apple and served with an apple and cider sauce, followed by brochette of lamb (noisettes of lamb served with a red-currant and mint sauce) and seasonal vegetables. Finish with brown bread ice cream—homemade ices are one of chef and co-owner Martin Dwyer's specialties. *Mary St., tel. 051/77478. Reservations advised. Dress: casual. AE, MC, V. Lunch by arrangement only. Closed Sun. in winter, 7 days in Nov. and at Christmas (call ahead for exact dates). Moderate.*

Dining and **Waterford Castle.** If you've always dreamed of staying in a cas-
Lodging tle during your visit to Ireland, here's your opportunity. This
★ luxury hotel occupies a genuine stone castle built by the Fitzgerald family in the 17th century. It's located on a 300-acre island in the River Suir, 3 km (2 mi) outside Waterford City, and can be reached only by car ferry. The main hall and drawing room are impressive, filled with ornate antique furniture and tapestries—be sure to notice the fine oak paneling and the great stone fireplace. The guest rooms are quite luxurious, featuring four-poster beds and a lavish decor. The traditional atmosphere in the Leinster Room restaurant is set by the ornate plastered ceiling, the oak furniture, and the deep burgundy Donegal carpet. The cuisine here is also traditional—country-style dishes include poached salmon, asparagus served in puff pastry, and bread and butter pudding. *The Island, Ballinakill, Co. Waterford, tel. 051/78203. 19 rooms with bath. Facilities: restaurant, tennis, 18-hole golf course, pool, horseback riding, fishing, cable TV, 24-hr room service. AE, DC, MC, V. Very Expensive.*

Lodging **Jury's Hotel.** Found on 35 acres of quiet parkland high above the River Suir, Jury's is a stylish modern hotel. All the rooms face south, toward Waterford City, and have panoramic views of the harbor and the surrounding countryside. The large foyer is impressive, with marble and brass trim, and the lobby seating is quite comfortable. Guest rooms are done in bright, pleasant colors, and the furniture is modern and functional. The leisure complex is extensive. *Ferrybank, Co. Waterford, tel. 051/32111. 100 rooms, 4 suites, all with bath. Facilities: restaurant, tennis courts, health club, saunas, Jacuzzis, pool, cable TV, 24-hr room service. AE, DC, MC, V. Expensive.*

The Granville Hotel. Located in the center of the city just five minutes by taxi from the train station, this was the birthplace of the Irish-American Civil War hero and Montana governor Thomas Francis Meagher. Though it was built in the early 19th century, the building was recently renovated. The country-manor decor of the public area is emphasized by the use of hunting prints, wood paneling, tapestries, and archways. Guest rooms are warm, filled with reproductions of Victorian furniture and plenty of wood trim. Rooms in the front, and those found over the dining room, may be a bit noisy. *Meagher Quay,*

Co. Waterford, tel. 051/55111. 74 rooms with bath. Facilities: restaurant, health club, saunas, fishing, pony trekking, cable TV, 24-hr room service. AE, DC, MC, V. Moderate.

★ **The Tower Hotel.** This hostelry is right on The Mall, a quiet section of the city just 10 minutes from the train station by cab. The public rooms have recently been refurbished; they are filled with plenty of fresh flowers and greenery and accented with warm, polished wood trim. The bright, airy guest rooms are comfortable, with modern, functional furniture and a floral decor. Rooms in the rear have good views of the river. *The Mall, Co. Waterford, tel. 051/75801. 125 rooms with bath. Facilities: restaurant, cable TV, 24-hr room service. AE, DC, MC, V. Moderate.*

★ **Diamond Hill Country House.** This creeper-covered modern guest house is found just 5 km (3 mi) from Waterford City in a quiet cul-de-sac off the Waterford–Rosslare road. Its owners have won several awards for both the fine Irish breakfasts served here and the lovely gardens that surround the house. The country-house decor in the public spaces is comfortably accented with tweed fabrics, tapestries, and plenty of greenery. Bedrooms are bright and airy and are filled with modern furniture. *Slieverue, Co. Waterford, tel. 051/32855. 10 rooms with shower. Facilities: dining room, wine bar, crafts shop, gardens. MC, V. Inexpensive.*

Wexford Town

Lodging **The Talbot Hotel.** In spite of being an unattractive pink six-story building on a busy main road, this establishment is a firm favorite with many regular visitors to the southeast—and with tour-bus companies. The public rooms are dimly and artificially lit at all times, but always lively. The hotel features regular live entertainment, especially during the summer, and a well-equipped recreation center. You'll find that the guest rooms are modern and decorated with Irish country-style furniture and a floral color scheme. Rooms that face front and rooms found over the ballroom can be noisy. *Trinity St., Co. Wexford, tel. 053/22566. 99 rooms with bath. Facilities: restaurant, pool, squash courts, health club, saunas, cable TV, 24-hr room service. AE, DC, MC, V. Moderate.*

White's Hotel. Housed in a historic 19th-century building fronted by a modern conservatory, this property is a friendly, convivial place conveniently located in the center of town. Its numerous old-fashioned passageways, brass trim, and red velvet decor combine with candlelight and roaring log fires to create a warm ambience. The country-style guest rooms are furnished with Victorian reproductions. Those found in the new addition to the hotel are more spacious. *George's St., Co. Wexford, tel. 053/22311. 82 rooms with bath. Facilities: restaurant, cable TV, 24-hr room service, nearby fishing and pony trekking. AE, DC, MC, V. Moderate.*

Dining and Lodging ★ **Ferrycarrig.** A pleasant alternative to Wexford town center is provided by this modern low rise (3 km/2 mi outside town on the N11 Enniscorthy road) on the banks of the River Slaney. Rooms are identically furnished, with relaxing pastel blue or pink color schemes and light-wood trim; they all overlook the well-kept riverside gardens. The restaurant, in a light and airy conservatory extension, is renowned locally for its fine cuisine and high standard of service. A singer and pianist entertain at dinner, which is worth lingering over. Typical dishes include boned guinea fowl with a fresh cranberry and orange sauce or poached turbot in a tomato and cucumber vin blanc sauce, surrounded by fresh mussels. *Ferrycarrig Bridge, Co. Wexford, tel. 053/22999. 40 rooms with bath. Facilities: restaurant, bar, tennis, fishing. AE, DC, MC, V. Expensive.*

The Arts and Nightlife

The Arts

Entertainment in the Southeast is largely confined to the tourist hotels during the summer. These programs of largely Irish entertainment are sponsored by the **Comhaltas Ceoltoiri Eireann (Irish Cultural Association,** 32 Belgrave Sq., Dublin, tel. 01/800295) for visitors. Live entertainment is held Tuesday through Sunday at 9 PM between mid-June and mid-September at their regional center, the **Bru Boru Heritage Center** (Cashel, Co. Tipperary, tel. 062/61122) at the foot of the Rock of Cashel. Folk singing, story-telling, and dance are enjoyed Tuesday through Saturday, and there are informal music sessions on Sunday nights. There is a *ceili* (Irish dance) held nightly during the summer at the Irish-language college, **Colaiste na Rinne,** located at Ring in County Waterford (tel. 058/46104). One special performance you won't want to miss is that of the local mummers in County Wexford. Mumming, which combines a style of intricate wooden-sword dancing with spoken verse and incantations, was introduced into County Wexford in the 17th century by shipwrecked sailors from Cornwall, who could trace the dance back to their Moorish origins in North Africa. Contact the Wexford Tourist Information Office (tel. 053/23111) for further information.

Culture buffs won't want to miss the **Garter Lane Arts Centre** (O'Connell St., Waterford, tel. 051/55038), the largest such cultural center in Ireland. Call ahead for a schedule of upcoming concerts, exhibits, and theater productions at the center.

A number of popular cultural festivals are held in the Southeast on an annual basis. The **Waterford International Festival of Light Opera** (tel. 051/74402), the only competitive event of its kind, is a great draw for amateur musical societies from throughout Ireland and Great Britain. The festival runs for 17 nights every September at the Theatre Royal (The Mall, Waterford).

Also worth investigating is the **Wexford Opera Festival** (tel. 053/22141). For more than 30 years this season of professional operatic productions by famous artists from around the world has been held every October at the Theatre Royal in Wexford. Lastly, the **Kilkenny Arts Week** held in late August is a series of classical music performances, concerts, and readings at halls throughout Kilkenny. For more information, contact the Kilkenny Tourist Information Office (*see* Important Addresses and Numbers in Essential Information, above).

Nightlife

The neighborhood pub is an integral part of Irish life, and travelers who take time to visit some of them will be granted an unvarnished look at Ireland's people—not to mention one of Ireland's favorite pastimes. Wander in, ask the bartender to draw you a pint of Guinness, and strike up a conversation. The stories and local color you'll glean from a chat with your neighbor at the bar are sure to enrich your impressions of Ireland.

While you're traveling through the Southeast, there are a few establishments in particular that you might seek out for their fine entertainment. In County Wexford's Rosslare, visit the **Portholes Bar** at the Hotel Rosslare (Rosslare Harbour, tel. 053/33110) for lively traditional Irish music most evenings during the summer. **T&H Doolan's Bar** (George's St., tel. 051/72764) in Waterford City is another pub that hosts good traditional Irish music most summer nights and on weekends year-round. Also, the **Seanchie Pub** (Ballymacart, Ring, Co. Waterford, tel. 058/46285) is an award-winning place that features traditional music and dancing in the courtyard on Sundays during the summer.

Winner of the National Bar Catering and Pub of the Year Award on a number of occasions, **Langtons Bar** (69 John St., Kilkenny, tel. 056/65133) boasts old-style decor with an emphasis on sports memorabilia. Bar food, snacks, and full lunch or dinner are available.

7 The Southwest

Cork City, Killarney,
The Ring of Kerry, Dingle

By Alannah Hopkin

A resident of Kinsale, Alannah Hopkin is the author of several books, including The Living Legend of St. Patrick *and* Inside Cork.

Cork, Kerry, Limerick, and Clare—the sound of these Southwest Ireland county names has an undeniably evocative Irish lilt. A varied coastline, spectacular scenery (especially around the famous lakes of Killarney), and a mild climate have long attracted visitors to this region. Although the Southwest contains Ireland's second and third largest cities—Cork and Limerick—its most notable attractions are rural: miles and miles of pretty country lanes meandering through rich but sparsely populated farmland. Even in the two main cities the pace of life is perceptibly slower than in Dublin. To be in a hurry in this region is to verge on demonstrating bad manners. It was probably a Kerryman who first remarked that when God made time, he made plenty of it.

As you look over thick fuchsia hedges at thriving dairy farms or stop off at a wayside restaurant to sample the region's seafood and locally raised meat, it is hard to imagine that some 135 years ago this area was decimated by famine. Thousands perished in the fields and the workhouses, and thousands more took "coffin ships" from Cobh in Cork Harbour to the New World. Between 1846 and 1849 the population of Ireland fell by an estimated 2½ million. Many small villages in the Southwest were wiped out. The region was battered again in the civil war that was fought with intensity in and around "Rebel Cork" between 1919 and 1921. Economic recovery only began in the late '60s, which led to a boom in hotel construction and renovation—not always, alas, in the style most appropriate to the area.

Outside of Killarney and Shannon, tourist development remains fairly low-key. The area is trying to absorb more visitors without losing too much of what attracts them in the first place: uncrowded roads, unpolluted beaches and rivers, easy access to golf and fishing, and unspoiled scenery where wildflowers, untamed animals, and rare birds (which have all but disappeared in more industrialized European countries) still thrive.

South of the city of Cork, the main business and shopping town of the region, the resort town of Kinsale is the gateway to a relatively unspoiled coastline containing Roaring Water Bay, with its many islands, and the magnificent natural harbor, Bantry Bay. The southwest coast of the region is formed by three peninsulas: the Beara, the Iveragh, and the Dingle; the road known as the Ring of Kerry makes a complete circuit of the Iveragh Peninsula. Killarney's sparkling blue lakes and magnificent sandstone mountains, inland from the peninsulas, have a unique and romantic splendor, though the area in July and August is packed with visitors. Around the Shannon estuary a traveler moves into "castle country," littered with ruined castles and abbeys as a result of Elizabeth I's attempt to subdue the old Irish province of Munster in the 16th century. Limerick City, too, bears the scars of history from a different confrontation with the English, the Siege of Limerick, which took place in 1691.

Although the Southwest offers several sumptuous country-house hotels, it is basically an easygoing, unpretentious region, where informality and simplicity are the keynotes of hospitality. As in the rest of Ireland, social life centers around the pub, and a visit to your "local" is the best way to find out what's going on. Local residents have not lost their natural curiosity about "strangers," as visitors are called. You will frequently be asked, "Are you enjoying your holiday?" "Yes" is not a good enough answer: What the locals are really after is your life story.

Essential Information

Important Addresses and Numbers

Tourist Information The Irish Tourist Board provide a free information service; their Tourist Information Offices (TIOs) also sell a selection of tourist literature. For a small fee they will book accommodations anywhere in Ireland. TIOs are located in the following places:

Cork City (Grand Parade, tel. 021/273251). **Killarney** (Town Hall, tel. 064/31633). **Limerick** (The Granary, Michael St., tel. 061/317522). **Shannon Airport** (tel. 061/61664). **Skibbereen** (Town Hall, tel. 028/21766). **Tralee** (Ashe Memorial Hall, tel. 066/21288). Open weekdays 9–6; Sat. 9–1.

Bantry (tel. 027/50229). **Clonakilty** (tel. 023/33226). **Cork Airport** (tel. 021/964347). **Dingle** (tel. 066/51188). **Kenmare** (tel. 064/41233). **Kinsale** (tel. 021/772234). **Youghal** (tel. 024/92390). Open weekdays 9–6; Sat. 9–1, July–August only.

Emergencies **Police, Fire,** and **Ambulance:** all areas, tel. 999, toll free.

Doctor/Dentist **Southern Health Board** (tel. 021/545011).

Pharmacies **Cork: Hamilton Long** (66 Patrick St., tel. 021/270548). **Killarney: P. O'Donoghue** (Main St., tel. 064/31813). **Limerick: Roberts James** (105 O'Connell St., tel. 061/44414).

Arriving and Departing by Plane

Airports and Airlines The Southwest has two international airports: Shannon in the West, and Cork on the Southwest coast. **Shannon Airport** (tel. 061/61444), situated 26 km (16 mi) west of Limerick City, is the point of arrival for all transatlantic flights; it also serves some flights from the United Kingdom and Europe. **Cork Airport** (tel. 021/313131), which is located 5 km (3 mi) south of Cork City on the Kinsale road, is used primarily for flights to and from the United Kingdom. Most U.K. flights to the Continent are routed via Dublin, apart from holiday charters. Regular 30-minute internal flights are scheduled between Shannon and Dublin, Shannon and Cork, and Cork and Dublin. **Kerry County Airport** (tel. 066/64350) at Farranfore, 16 km (10 mi) from Killarney, mainly services small planes, but it is gradually increasing its commercial traffic with a daily flight from Dublin and London.

Flights from North America **Aer Lingus** offers direct flights to Shannon Airport from New York. Aer Lingus also provides direct flights to Shannon from Chicago and Boston. **Delta** has direct flights to Shannon from Atlanta. A number of charter flights also operate from the United States and Canada May–September; contact your travel agent and local newspapers for further details.

Flights from the United Kingdom **Aer Lingus** and **Ryanair** offer direct flights to Shannon and Cork City from most major U.K. airports. Ryanair also provides a daily flight from Stansted to Kerry.

Between Airports **By Bus.** From **Shannon Airport,** Bus Éireann (tel. 061/61311)
and Major Cities runs a regular bus service to **Limerick City** between 8 AM and
midnight. The ride takes about 40 minutes and costs £3.

A bus service runs between **Cork Airport** and the **Cork City Bus
Terminal** (Parnell Pl., tel. 021/506066) every 30 minutes, on the
hour and the half hour. The ride takes about 10 minutes and
costs £1.50.

By Taxi. Taxis can be found outside the main terminal building
at the Shannon and Cork airports. The ride from Shannon Airport to Limerick City costs about £16; from Cork Airport to
Cork City costs about £4.

Arriving and Departing by Other Transportation

By Ferry/Car From the United Kingdom, the Southwest has two ports of entry: Rosslare (in County Wexford) and Cork City. (*See* Chapter
6 for Rosslare ferry details.) From Rosslare Harbour by car,
take the N25 to Cork (208 km/129 mi) and allow 3½ hours for the
journey. You can pick up the N24 in Waterford for Limerick
City (211 km/131 mi), which also takes about 3½ hours.

By Ferry/Bus Train connections between Rosslare Harbour and Cork City,
Limerick City, or Tralee all involve changing at Limerick Junction, so the journey time is usually longer than by car or bus. It
is quicker and cheaper, if less comfortable, to use the long-distance buses that service the ferries. **International Express
Supabus** leaves London's Victoria Coach Station daily and travels overnight via Bristol to Fishguard, then on to Cork, Killarney, and Tralee. Timetables can be obtained from any National
Express Coach Station or by calling Supabus (tel. 071/730–
3499). An Irish company, **Slattery's** (tel. 071/482–1604), also
runs a bus service from London to Cork and Tralee. The journey to Cork via Rosslare by bus and ferry is an arduous one of
about 18 hours.

Swansea–Cork Ferries (tel. 0792/456116) operates a 10-hour
crossing between the two ports on a comfortable, well-
equipped boat. Supabus (*see* above) will get you to the Swansea
ferry from anywhere in the United Kingdom.

By Car The main driving access route from Dublin is the N7, which
goes direct to Limerick City (192 km/120 mi); from Dublin, pick
up the N8 in Portlaoise for Cork City (257 km/160 mi). The journey time between Dublin and Limerick runs just under three
hours; between Dublin and Cork takes about 3½ hours.

By Train From Dublin Heuston Station (tel. 01/366222), the region is
served by three direct rail links to Limerick City, Tralee, and
Cork City. Journey time from Dublin to Limerick is 2½ hours;
to Cork, 2¾; to Tralee, 3¾. For passenger inquiries: in Limerick, tel. 061/31555; in Cork, tel. 021/506766; in Tralee, tel. 066/
21211.

By Bus Bus Éireann operates Expressway services from Dublin to
Limerick City, Cork City, and Tralee. Add approximately one
hour to the journey time by train. Most towns in the region are
served by the provincial Bus Éireann network (tel. 01/302222 in
Dublin, 061/313333 in Limerick, 021/506066 in Cork, and 066/
21211 in Tralee).

Getting Around

By Car A car is the ideal way to explore this region, packed as it is with scenic routes, attractive but remote towns, and a host of out-of-the-way restaurants and hotels that deserve a detour. The roads are generally small, two-lane affairs (one in each direction). You will find a few miles of two-lane highway on the outskirts of Cork City, Limerick City, and Killarney, but much of your time will be spent on roads so narrow and twisty that it is not advisable to exceed 40 mph.

Getting around the Southwest is every bit as enjoyable as arriving, provided you set out in the right frame of mind—a relaxed one. There is no point in imposing a rigid timetable on your journey when you are visiting one of the last places in Western Europe where you are as likely to be held up by a donkey cart, a herd of cows, or a flock of sheep as by road construction or heavy trucks.

Car Rentals All the major car rental companies have desks at Shannon and Cork airports:

Shannon Airport: Avis (tel. 061/61643), **Dan Dooley** (tel. 061/61098), **Hertz** (tel. 061/61639), **Irish Car Rentals** (tel. 061/62649), and **Murray's Europcar** (tel. 061/61618).

Cork Airport: Avis (tel. 021/965321), **Hertz** (tel. 021/965849), **Johnson & Perrott** (tel. 021/963133), **Kenning Car Hire** (tel. 021/276611), and **Murray's Europcar** (tel. 021/966736).

In Killarney, try **Killarney Autos Ltd.** (tel. 064/31355).

By Train The rail network, which covers only the inner ring of the region, is mainly useful for moving from one touring base to another. Except during the peak season of July and August, only four trains a day run between Cork (or Limerick) and Tralee. More frequent service is offered between Cork City and Limerick City, but the ride involves changing at Limerick Junction—as does the journey from Limerick to Tralee—to wait for a connecting train. Be sure to ascertain the delay involved in the connection. (For passenger inquiries, *see* Arriving and Departing by Train, above.) The journey from Cork to Tralee takes 2¼ hours; from Cork to Limerick, about 2–2½ hours; from Limerick to Tralee, 3–3½ hours.

By Bus The provincial bus service, which is cheaper and more flexible than the train, serves all the main centers in the region. Additional services are available during the peak summer season. Express services are available between Cork City and Limerick City (twice a day) and between Cork and Tralee (high season only), and between Killarney, Tralee, Limerick, and Shannon (once a day; twice in peak season).

If you plan to travel extensively by bus, a copy of the Bus Éireann timetable (45p from bus terminals) is essential. As a general rule, the smaller the town, and the more remote, the less frequent its bus service. For example, Kinsale, a well-developed resort 29 km (18 mi) from Cork, is served by at least five buses a day, both arriving and departing; Castlegregory, a small village on the remote Dingle Peninsula, has bus service only on Fridays.

The main bus terminals are at Cork (Parnell Pl., tel. 021/506066); Limerick (tel. 061/313333); and Tralee (Casement Station, tel. 066/21211).

Guided Tours

Orientation Tours **CIE,** part of the state-run public-transport network, offers a range of day and half-day guided tours from June to September. They can be booked at the bus stations in Cork or Limerick or at any Tourist Information Office (*see* above). A full-day tour costs £10; half-day, £6.50, exclusive of meals and refreshments.

Because distances are not great within the region, Blarney Castle, Killarney, Dingle, and Kinsale can all be visited on a full-day or half-day tour from either Cork City or Limerick City. From Cork, CIE offers orientation tours of the city and excursions to Youghal, Mitchelstown Caves, Gougane Barra National Park, and West Cork, as well as the previously mentioned destinations. No city tours of Limerick are available, but this is the area to take a castle tour and visit some of the Shannon's magnificent castles. CIE also offers overnight stays in a range of 25 destinations, including Killarney, Cork, and Kinsale. The tours are an excellent value at £27.50 for transport and bed-and-breakfast in a grade-A hotel (based on double occupancy).

Full-day and half-day coach tours of Killarney and the Shannon region (during mid-June–September only) are organized by **Gray Line Shannonway Tours** (Limerick Ryan Hotel, Ennis Rd., Limerick, tel. 061/32621). **Shannon Castle Tours** (Limerick, tel. 061/61788) will escort you to an "Irish Night" in Bunratty Folk Park or take you to a medieval banquet at Bunratty or Knappogue Castle; although the banquet isn't authentic, it is a boisterous occasion that is full of goodwill.

Foremost among the Killarney tour operators is **Destination Killarney** (Scott's Gardens, Killarney, Co. Kerry, tel. 064/32638). Besides offering day and half-day tours of Killarney and Kerry by coach or taxi, the group will prearrange your visit, lining up accommodations, entertainment, special-interest tours, and sporting activities in one package.

A full-day (10:30–5) tour costs about £10 per person, excluding lunch and refreshments. The Killarney Local Circuit tour is an excellent half-day orientation. The unique and memorable Gap of Dunloe tour at £19 includes a coach, boat trip, and horseback ride through the Gap. More conventional day trips can also be made to the Ring of Kerry, the Loo Valley, and Glengarriff; the city of Cork and Blarney Castle; Dingle and Slea Head; and Caragh Lake and Rossbeigh.

The following companies will also organize day and half-day trips by coach or taxi: **Deros Tours** (Main St., tel. 064/31251), **Killarney & Kerry Tours** (Innisfallon, 15 Main St., tel. 064/33880), and **Castlelough Tours** (High St., tel. 064/32496).

Jaunting cars (pony and trap) that carry up to four people can be hired at a stand outside Tourist Information Offices. They can also be found at the entrance to Muckross Estate and at the Gap of Dunloe. A ride costs between £10 and £24, negotiable with the driver, depending on time (1–2 hours) and route. To pre-book a jaunting car, try **Counihan's** (tel. 064/31874).

Special-Interest Tours Special-interest tours of the region for small or large groups can be prearranged with Valerie Fleury of **Discover Cork** (Belmont, Douglas Rd., Cork, tel. 021/293873). Half-day and full-day tours are individually planned to satisfy each visitor's needs.

Walking Tours **Tourist Trails,** which allow the visitor to follow a signposted route while reading an accompanying booklet (75p), have been set up in Cork City, Limerick City, Youghal, Kinsale, and Killarney Town. Booklets can be purchased at local Tourist Information offices. History buffs should inquire at TIOs for details of guided walking tours, which are organized during the summer by local volunteers.

Exploring the Southwest

If you have only three or four days in the Southwest, you might consider skipping the cities and concentrating on the coast and the mountains. For a short visit, it makes sense to base yourself in Killarney. Reserve one day for an old-style trip through the Gap of Dunloe and the lakes by jaunting car and rowboat. If you have a car, several other attractions can be explored in a day.

If, on the other hand, your schedule allows a week or 10 days in the region, you might want to spend a night or two in the Cork City vicinity (taking in Blarney Castle and Cobh), a night in Kinsale, a night in a country-house hotel (such as the Park at Kenmare or Longueville House at Mallow), and two or three nights in Killarney. Then head west to the Ring of Kerry and the Dingle Peninsula if the weather is good, or north toward Limerick and the Shannon castles if it is not. But don't let passing showers deter you too much. In Killarney, especially, light showers are part of the experience and seldom last long; they can be followed within minutes by brilliant sunshine.

Highlights for First-time Visitors

Blarney Castle (*see* Tour 1)
Bunratty Castle and Folk Park (*see* Tour 4)
Connor Pass (*see* Tour 3)
Craggaunowen Project (*see* Tour 4)
Gap of Dunloe (*see* Tour 3)
Garnish Island (*see* Tour 2)
Great Blasket Island (*see* Tour 3)
Kinsale (*see* Tour 2)
Skellig Islands (*see* Tour 3)
Slea Head (*see* Tour 3)

Tour 1: Cork City and Environs

Numbers in the margin correspond to points of interest on the Southwest and Cork City maps.

① **Cork,** the major metropolis of the south, is Ireland's second-largest city. Its official population of 138,500 is misleadingly low because it doesn't include the many Corkonians who prefer to live outside the city limits, in pleasant rural areas 10 or 15 minutes' drive from town. In 1185, the city received its first charter from Prince John of Norman England. Major development occurred during the 17th and 18th centuries with the expansion of the butter trade, and many attractive Georgian-

Tuamgraney

Ennis
Quin
**Craggaunowen
Project** 85

Killaloe

Nenagh

N7

N62

**Knappogue
Castle** 84

TIPPERARY

Shannon

Bunratty Castle 83
Plassey 82

Thurles

N18

River Shannon

N75

Limerick 81

Foynes

Askeaton

R521

LIMERICK

N20

N24

R497

N8

Cashel

Adare 80

Rathkeale 79

Croom

Holycross

N74

Tipperary

N21

Newcastle
West

N20

Kilmallock

Kilfinnane

Cahir

N24

Milford

Clogheen

R576 R579

Mitchelstown

WATERFORD

Kanturk

Castletownroche

N8

N72

Lismore

N72

N72

Mallow

Fermoy

River Blackwater

Dungarvan

CORK

N20

N8

Rathcormac

Youghal

Blarney 22

R579

R617

Cork City 1 — 21

N25

Midleton

Macroom

N22

Fota
Island

23 **Fota Demesne**

Shanagarry

24 **Cobh**

Cloyne

Ballycotton

R600

Cork
Harbour

Dunmanway

N71

Bandon

25 **Kinsale**

Celtic Sea

R600

26 **Charles Fort**

Timoleague 27

Clonakilty

Courtmacsherry

N71 R597 N71

Ross Carbery

28

Glandore

KEY
— Rail Lines
⛴ Ferry

N

0   20 miles

0   30 km

238

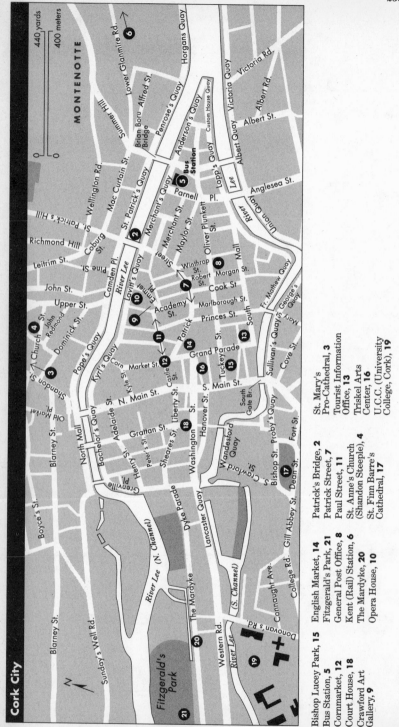

style buildings with wide bow-fronted windows were constructed during this time. Cork gets its name from the Irish (Gaelic) word *corcaigh*, which means "marshy place." When the marsh was drained, the River Lee was divided into two streams that now flow through the city, leaving the main business and commercial center on an island. As a result, the city features a number of bridges and quays, which, although initially confusing, add greatly to the port's unique character.

"Rebel Cork" emerged as a center of the nationalist Fenian movement in the 19th century. The city suffered great damage during the civil war in the early '20s, when much of its center burned. Dogged by economic slumps throughout this century, Cork is only now regaining some of its former glory through sensitive commercial development and an ongoing program of inner-city renewal. It is still something of a ghost town after 6 PM, when the business community has gone home.

Cork's main attractions are best visited on foot. Patrick Street is the main thoroughfare; it's helpful to start at **Patrick's Bridge.** Look across the river to Patrick's Hill, where tall Georgian houses have mostly been converted to consulting rooms for doctors. The hill is so steep that steps are cut into the pavement. The slopes of the hilly north city are dominated by the tower of **St. Mary's Pro-Cathedral** and the Shandon Steeple with its four-sided clock. If you're interested in tracing Cork ancestors, the presbytery at St. Mary's has records of births and marriages dating from 1784. *Cathedral Walk. Admission free. Open daily 9–6.*

The Bells of Shandon were immortalized in an atrocious but popular 19th-century ballad of that name. The pepper-pot **Shandon Steeple** belongs to **St. Anne's Church** on Church Street, a three-minute walk downhill (toward the city center) from the Pro-Cathedral. Visitors who are prepared to climb the 120-foot tower can have the bells rung out over Cork at their request. *Admission: £1, £1.50 with bell tower. Open May–Oct., Mon.–Sat. 9:30–5; Nov.–Apr., 10–3:30.*

From Patrick's Bridge, you can't quite see the **bus station;** still facing the river, it is one block downstream on the right. The Brian Boru Bridge, in front of the bus station, leads to **Kent (Rail) Station,** which is north of the river two blocks to the right.

Turn your back on the river and head up **Patrick Street.** On the left is **Merchant's Quay,** where tall ships that once served the butter trade used to load up before heading downstream to the open sea. The design of the large, £30 million shopping center on the site (built in 1989) evokes the warehouses of old. **Roches Stores,** on the left, is the largest department store in town; **Cash's,** next door, is the most upscale.

Turn left into Winthrop Street, a pedestrian mall, which leads to the **General Post Office,** a neoclassical building with an elegant colonnaded facade, built on the site of the Theater Royal. It reopened in 1989 after major refurbishment. The post office is located on Oliver Plunkett Street, a busy narrow road known for its fashion boutiques and jewelry stores.

Time Out Resist the temptation to nip in to McDonald's on Winthrop Street; try the **Long Valley** instead. This friendly old bar, popular with artists, writers, students, and other eccentrics, serves tea, coffee, and pints as well as enormous sandwiches filled with salad and home-cooked meat.

Continue around the graceful curve of Patrick Street—and don't forget to look up. Above some of the standardized plate-glass and plastic shop facades are examples of the bow-fronted Georgian windows that are so typical of old Cork. Cross the street in front of **Penney's** and take Academy Street, which
9 leads to the **Crawford Art Gallery.** Here you'll find an excellent collection of landscape paintings depicting Cork in the 18th and 19th centuries. Look out for the work of Nathaniel Grogan (1740–1807). The gallery also mounts adventurous exhibitions by contemporary artists from Ireland and abroad; its cafeteria is one of the best places in town for a light lunch or a tasty home-baked cake. *Emmet Pl., tel. 021/273377. Admission free. Open weekdays 9–5, Sat. 9–1.*

10 The **Opera House,** an unfortunate concrete building dating from the '60s, is on the left of the Crawford, but turn right out
11 of the front door instead, crossing into the pedestrianized **Paul Street** area whose development has transformed the city center. The piazza is a popular place for street theater and entertainment. The shops here offer the best in modern Irish design—from Donegal tweeds to hand-blown glass.

If you follow Paul Street in a westerly direction from the
12 Crawford Art Gallery, you'll reach the **Cornmarket,** once the site of a thriving outdoor market. This area has dwindled to a few secondhand clothes dealers, but the shops alongside are worth checking for antiques. Turn left at the crossroads at Paul
13 Street for the Grand Parade, where you will find a **Tourist Information Office** (TIO) at the far end on your left-hand side. *Tourist House, Grand Parade, tel. 021/273251. Open weekdays 9–6, Sat. 9–1.*

If you're curious about food and not squeamish at the sight of it "in the raw," turn right out of the TIO, cross Oliver Plunkett
14 Street, and explore the **English Market.** Note the elaborate Victorian cast-iron construction and the old-fashioned displays of fresh country produce, the styles virtually unchanged since the turn of the century. The stall by the door sells a Cork specialty, tripe (cow's intestines) and drisheen (blood sausage). *Open weekdays 9–5:30, Sat. 9–1.*

Cross the Grand Parade by its central fountain and take a stroll
15 through the green space opposite, **Bishop Lucey Park.** Here you'll see works by contemporary Cork sculptors on permanent exhibition. Turn right at the top into South Main Street. The
16 **Triskel Arts Center** is signposted down an alley on the right. It has a small auditorium, a coffee shop, and interesting exhibitions of contemporary arts and crafts. *Tobin St., tel. 021/ 272022. Admission free. Open weekdays 11–6, Sat. 11–5, and during advertised performances.*

If churches take your fancy, you will want to make a detour to
17 **St. Finn Barre's Cathedral.** Turn left out of Bishop Lucey Park and cross the river at South Gate Bridge, turning right onto Proby's Quay. Pause awhile on the quay to savor the atmospheric views of the old quays from what was once the entrance to medieval Cork. The three spires of the 19th-century Gothic cathedral are visible up ahead on Bishop Street. St. Finn

Barre, the founder of Cork, established a monastery on this site around AD 650. The present cathedral belongs to the Church of Ireland. *Admission free. Open daily 9–6.*

Retrace your steps down South Main Street to the busy crossroads at Washington Street. The imposing classical portico across the road belongs to the **Court House,** which dates from the 1830s and is still in use today.

From here, some may prefer to take a No. 5 bus to the Mardyke instead of walking. It is about a mile to the left up Washington Street and the Western Road. Alight near the Doric-porticoed gates of the University College campus.

U.C.C., as **University College, Cork,** is known, has about 7,000 students. The main quadrangle is a fine example of 19th-century university architecture in the Tudor Gothic style, reminiscent of many an Oxford or Cambridge college. Several ancient Ogham stones (pre-Christian standing stones featuring an early form of writing) are on display, as well as occasional exhibitions of archival material from the old library. The Honan Collegiate Chapel, to the east of the quadrangle, was built in 1916 and modeled on the 12th-century Hiberno-Romanesque style (which is best exemplified by the remains of Cormac's Chapel at Cashel; *see* Tour 3 in Chapter 6). The college chapel contains stonework, textiles, and stained glass executed earlier this century by craftsmen of the Irish revivalist school. *Tel. 021/276871. Admission free. Open weekdays 9–5, but phone ahead during school vacations.*

One block across Western Road beyond the campus entrance is **The Mardyke,** a popular riverside walk where cricket is played on summer weekends. It leads to **Fitzgerald's Park,** where a Georgian mansion, the **Cork Public Museum,** houses a well-planned exhibit of Cork's history from ancient times to the present day. *Tel. 021/270679. Admission free. Open weekdays 11–1 and 2:15–5, Sun. 3–5. Closed Sat. and bank holidays.*

Blarney *Numbers in the margin correspond to points of interest on the Southwest map.*

Blarney, which is located 8 km (5 mi) northwest of Cork City on the R617, is a small community built around a village green dominated by the **Blarney Castle** to the north. In the peak season of July and August, or if en route to Killarney, follow the signposts off the main N22 Killarney road at Carrigrohane to avoid inner-city traffic tie-ups. Most first-time visitors wish to make the trip to Blarney Castle so they may acquire the "gift of the gab" by kissing its famous, lipstick-besmeared stone. Frankly, this is all a lot of blarney, but the kiss itself does make a good photograph.

To reach Blarney Castle, you'll need to climb 127 steep steps to the battlements. Expect a line from mid-June to September 1; while you wait, you can admire the views of the thickly wooded River Lee valley below. The ruined central keep is all that's left of this mid-15th-century MacCarthy stronghold. The efforts of Cormac MacCarthy to smooth-talk Elizabeth I of England gave the English language the term "blarney" to describe flattering and cajoling conversation. To kiss the stone, you must lie down on the battlements, hold on to a guard rail, and lean your head way back. It's good fun and not at all dangerous.

Visitors can also take pleasant walks around the castle grounds; Rock Close contains oddly shaped limestone rocks landscaped in the 18th century and a grove of ancient yew trees that is said to have been the center of Druid worship. *Blarney Castle, tel. 021/385252. Admission: £2.50 adults, £1.50 senior citizens, £1 children. Open May, Mon.–Sat. 9–7; June–July, 9–8:30; Aug., 9–7:30; Sept., 9–6:30; May–Sept., Sun. 9:30–5:30; off-season, Sun. 9:30–sundown.*

Blarney Castle House, which is located next door to the Castle, was recently reopened to the public. Built in 1784 in the style of a Scottish baronial mansion, the three-story gray stone building has picture-book turrets and fancy stepped gables. The interior features a fine stairwell and numerous family portraits. *Tel. 021/385252. Admission: £2 adults, £1.50 senior citizens, £1 children. Open June–mid-Sept., Mon.–Sat. noon–6.*

Blarney also probably has more crafts shops than anyplace else in Ireland. Most of these stores are concentrated on the south and west of the village green, a two-minute walk from the castle. A shopping visit here can be used profitably for price comparison and bargain hunting; in spite of appearances, these shops, in general, will not rip you off.

Time Out Instead of braving Blarney's overcrowded bars and restaurants, take a break at the **Angler's Rest** (Leemount, Carrigrohane, tel. 021/871167), a delightful riverside inn with garden tables in the summer and a good choice of bar food. It is midway between Blarney and Cork, off the main N22 Killarney Road on the R579.

Cork Harbour–
Fota Island
and Cobh

To explore Cork Harbour, follow the signposts for Waterford on the N25 along the banks of the River Lee. Alternatively, a suburban rail service from Kent Station (tel. 021/504422 for timetable) has stops at Fota Island and Cobh (pronounced "Cove"), and it offers better harbor views than the road.

The turreted building on the opposite side of the Lee just outside town is **Blackrock Castle.** This 16th-century fortification was rebuilt in the 19th century and is now a restaurant and bar (tel. 021/357414). Shortly after you get a glimpse of Blackrock, the road leaves the river. The turning for Fota Island and Cobh (R624) is clearly signposted off the N25 on the right-hand side about 8 km (5 mi) outside town. Turn right again at the gate **㉓** lodge of the huge **Fota Demesne,** on Fota Island.

The estate's 70-acre **Fota Wildlife Park** serves as an important breeding center for cheetahs and wallabies. It also contains free-ranging monkeys, zebras, giraffes, ostriches, flamingos, emus, and kangaroos. *Tel. 021/812678. Admission: £2.50 adults, £1.25 children and senior citizens. Car park £1.25 per car for all amenities. Open Apr. 7–Oct. 31, Mon.–Sat. 10–6, Sun. 11–6.*

Turn right out of Fota and continue south on the R624 to Cobh. Fota Island is linked to Great Island by Belvelly Bridge. A signpost to the left here provides an interesting detour to **Barryscourt Castle,** a 13th-century structure, complete with courtyard and flanking towers, which is currently being restored. *Carrigtwohill, tel. 021/883864. Admission free. Open Apr.–Oct., daily 10:30–6:30. Guided tours of castle keep are subject to work in progress.*

24 Cobh itself faces the open sea, which is some 8 km (5 mi) down the harbor at Roches Point. Both **Cobh** (previously known as Queenstown) and **Roches Point** are familiar landmarks for the many generations who left the port of Cork on immigrant ships for the New World. For a sense of their experience, and the best view of Cobh and St. Colman's Cathedral, an imposing 19th-century Gothic construction made of granite, take a one-hour harbor tour from Kennedy Pier. *Marine Transport, tel. 021/ 811485. Cost: £2 adults, £1 children. May–Sept., 10, 11, noon, 1:30, and 2:30.*

A new (1993) heritage center, **The Queenstown Project,** in the old railway station, re-creates the experience of emigrants who left Cobh between 1750 and the mid-20th century. It also tells the stories of the great transatlantic liners, including the *Titanic,* whose last port of call was Cobh, and the *Lusitania.* The *Lusitania* was sunk by a German submarine off this coast on May 7, 1915, with the loss of 1,198 lives. Many of the victims are buried in Cobh, with a memorial to them on the local quay. *Tel. 021/813612. Admission: £3.50 adults, £2 children and senior citizens. Open Apr.–Sept., Mon.–Fri. 9:30–7:30, weekends 10–7; Nov.–mid-Jan., daily 10–5.*

Tour 2: Kinsale to Glengarriff

This tour takes you on a meandering scenic drive of about 136 km (85 mi) around the unspoiled coast of West County Cork. It starts at the historic old port of Kinsale and travels through a variety of seascapes to the lush vegetation of Glengarriff. The drive from Kinsale to Glengarriff can take about two hours nonstop, but the whole point of taking this tour is to linger anywhere that takes your fancy. The tour is most enjoyable between May and October, when the weather is still warm enough to explore the area on foot.

25 **Kinsale** is 29 km (18 mi) from Cork City past the airport on the R600. This exceptionally beautiful town is built on the slopes of Compass Hill at the top of a wide fjordlike harbor. Its steep narrow streets and tall slated houses feature a Spanish accent that can be traced back to the Battle of Kinsale in 1601, when the Irish and Spanish joined forces here to fight the English— and lost. Subsequently an important fishing port, with the significant presence of a British army and navy, the town today attracts yacht owners and deep-sea anglers. It is also well-known for its many fine restaurants, which definitely make a visit here worthwhile.

A signposted walking tour of the town, with an accompanying booklet (75p from the Kinsale Tourist Information Office or Boland's on Pearse St.), will familiarize you with its interesting and varied history. Visit the **museum** in the town's 17th-century Dutch-style courthouse for more insight into the past, and take a look at its fascinating collection of cuttings and memorabilia from the wreck of the *Lusitania* (*see* Cobh, above). The museum staff will also give you details of free guided walks that take place regularly in the summer, or by appointment for groups. *The Old Courthouse, Market Pl., tel. 021/772044. Admission: 30p. Open Mon.–Sat. 11–5, Sun. 3–5.*

Leave the town center and return to the point where the main road from Cork City enters Kinsale. Follow the signpost at the **26** water's edge to Summer Cove and **Charles Fort.** This structure was built in the wake of the defeat of the Spanish and Irish forces, on the harbor shore 3 km (2 mi) east of town. If the sun is shining, take the footpath that is signposted Scilly Walk; it winds along the edge of the harbor under tall overhanging trees and then through the village of Summer Cove. Charles Fort is one of the best preserved "star forts" in Europe, enclosing some 12 acres on a cliff top. It will remind some of Fort Ticonderoga in New York. In its heyday, it had a population of 2,000; it was in use until 1920, when it was burned out by the Irish Republican Army. *Tel. 021/772684. Admission: £1 adults, 40p children and senior citizens. Open mid-June–mid-Sept., daily 10–6:30; mid-Apr.–mid-June, Tues.–Sat. 10–5, Sun. 2–5. Guided tours on request. Mid-Sept.–mid-Apr., weekdays 8–4:30, except public holidays. No guides off-season.*

Time Out The **Spaniard Inn** (tel. 021/772436) looks over the town and harbor from a hairpin bend on the road to Charles Fort. Inside, sawdust-covered floors and a big open fire make this anglers' bar a cozy spot in the winter. In the summer, you can take a pint to the sunny veranda and watch the world go by on land and sea.

Next, leave town through its center by following the quays and drive west along the Bandon River toward the bridge. The route is signposted to **Ballinspittle** (R600). This grotto with a large statue of the Virgin Mary had a moment of fame in the summer of 1985 when tens of thousands saw the statue move nightly. Fundamentalists smashed the effigy, and its replacement remains immobile, although the pious still stop here.

(If the sun is shining, you may wish to take a brief detour from Ballinspittle village. Follow signposts for the **Old Head of Kinsale** and walk out the headland to enjoy the sea views from the lighthouse.)

The main route takes you through **Garretstown Woods** (signposts for Clonakilty on the R600), which are carpeted with wild bluebells in April; then pass the edge of Courtmacsherry Bay, running alongside a wide saltwater inlet that teems with curlew, plover, and other waders.

Time Out The **Pink Elephant** (Harbour View, Kilbrittain, tel. 023/49608) is an irresistible stopping place in good weather—a pink-painted, moderately priced bar and restaurant with sweeping sea views on its own grounds high above Courtmacsherry Bay. The bar serves soup and sandwiches on homemade brown bread; the restaurant features plain home cooking, including roast or grilled meat and a daily vegetarian special.

The pretty village of multicolored cottages glimpsed across the water is **Courtmacsherry**, where sandy beaches make it a popular holiday resort. It can be reached by following the signposts from Timoleague.

(27) The R600 continues west to the head of the saltwater inlet (*see* above) and the village of **Timoleague**, which is dominated at the water's edge by a striking ruined abbey. Built in the mid-13th century, it is one of the best-preserved early Franciscan friaries in Ireland. You walk around the back to find the entrance gate. The abbey was sacked by the English in 1642, but like many ruins of its kind, it was used as a burial place until recent times. Ignoring the graves, you can trace the ground plan of the old friary—the chapel, refectory, cloisters, and wine cellar. At one time the friars were famous wine importers.

Timoleague Castle Gardens are signposted in the village. Although the castle is long gone—it has been replaced by a modest early 20th-century house in gray stone—the original gardens have survived. Palm trees and other frost-tender plants flourish in the mature shrubbery; there are two large, old-fashioned walled gardens, one for flowers and one for fruits and vegetables. *Tel. 023/46116. Admission: £1.20 adults, 60p children. Open Easter weekend and mid-May–mid-Sept., daily noon–6.*

The R600 now runs inland to **Clonakilty,** a small market town where many of the shops and businesses have abandoned chrome and plastic materials for traditional hand-painted signs and wooden facades—to very charming effect. Many fine sandy beaches are located nearby; the best of them are found at Inchydoney, which is 3 km (2 mi) outside of town.

This area is the heart of West County Cork, where small, twisted roads are overhung by tall hedges of *Fuchsia magellanica*. Originally imported as a garden shrub in the mid-19th century, it quickly adapted to the balmy sea air and is widely regarded as a weed used here for hedging—albeit a beautiful one with its delicate, drooping mauve-and-red trumpeted flowers. In June, the hedges are offset by tall purple foxgloves, and in August and September by bright purple heather.

The R600 joins the sea again at Rosscarbery, where you leave the main road by turning left at the signpost for Glandore at the end of the causeway. Glandore and Union Hall are twin fishing villages on either side of the landlocked Glandore harbor. ㉘ **Glandore,** with its steep hill and pretty church, is the more charming of the two; it is a popular spot for visitors from the United Kingdom and Germany. Glandore's influx of affluent visitors and expensive yachts has not been shared in **Union Hall,** where simple fishing trawlers still tie up at the quay.

Now you are truly in the back of beyond, where the tiny roads ㉙ are without route numbers. However, **Castletownshend** is clearly signposted from Union Hall via Rineen. Castletownshend's main street runs steeply down a hill to the sea. It has an unusual number of graciously designed large stone houses, mostly dating from the mid-18th century when it was an important trading center. Nowadays, this deliciously sleepy place comes alive in only July and August, when the activity centers on the waters of its sheltered harbor. It was the home of Edith Somerville and Violet "Martin" Ross, authors of the humorous "Resident Magistrate" (R.M.) stories, which in a good-natured manner show the differences between the British and the Irish ways of thinking; the stories were very popular during the early 20th century. The writers' graves can be visited by climbing the 52 steep steps to the cliff-top St. Barrahane's Church; the view is well worth the effort.

Time Out The place to go for a pint and a sandwich in Castletownshend is **Mary Ann's** (tel. 028/36146), one of the oldest bars in the country, whose low-beamed interior is frequented by a very friendly mix of visitors and locals. Writer Edna O'Brien claims that it is her favorite pub in the whole world.

You have only one way out of Castletownshend: the way you came in, up the hill, after which you take the Skibbereen road (the R596). If you have time for a side trip to Sherkin Island or Cape Clear Island, take the Baltimore road (the R595) by turn-

㉚ ㉛ ing left at the entrance to Skibbereen. **Baltimore,** once a small fishing village, is now a popular sailing center. **Sherkin Island** is only a 10-minute ferry trip from Baltimore (7 ferries are scheduled daily; call 028/20125 for times). The island, with a population of 90, offers several safe sandy beaches and abundant wildlife.

㉜ Cape Clear Island is part of the West Cork Gaeltacht (Irish-speaking area). The ferry to the island takes about an hour (cost: £6 round-trip; call 028/39119 for sailing times), and it's exciting to watch the skipper thread his way through the many rocks and tiny islands of Roaring Water Bay. You have excellent views of the Fastnet Rock Lighthouse, focus of the famous yachting race. Cape Clear can be explored on foot in about an hour, but bird-watchers will want to stay longer. It is the southernmost point of Ireland, and its observatory is famous for records of rare songbird migrants. Large flocks of ocean-going birds can be seen offshore in the summer.

Baltimore, like Castletownshend, is the end of the road, and the visitor must double back to **Skibbereen,** a busy but uninteresting market town. From here take the N71 to Bantry. If you still have an appetite for lovely coastal villages, take a detour at Ballydehob on the R592 to Schull, then the R591 to Goleen and Crookhaven, returning to Bantry through Durrus.

㉝ On the right-hand side of the road as you enter **Bantry,** you will see the porticoed entrance to **Bantry House.** This magnificent mansion, set in Italianate gardens and overlooking the sea, was built in the mid-18th century. Giving the house a baroque, Continental air is an extensive art collection (including exquisite 18th-century tapestries and furniture) acquired by the second earl of Bantry during his European grand tour. Some of the rooms are now a little shabby, but the beauty of the location compensates for the lack of polish. Climb to the top of the rear garden for the best views. *Tel. 027/50047. Admission: £2 adults, £1.50 senior citizens, 50p children. Open daily 9–6; till 8 on long summer evenings.*

It is not the town of Bantry that the balladeers celebrate, as a quick glance will confirm, but the glorious sweep of **Bantry Bay,** which is on your left as you climb out of town on the N71. This is a starker, more magnificent prospect than any encountered so far, and the sparse, windswept vegetation gives an idea of what the wet and windy winters are like on the more exposed part of this coast.

㉞ The descent into wooded, sheltered **Glengarriff** reveals yet another kind of landscape: It is mild enough down here for subtropical plants to thrive. You are also back on the beaten track with crafts shops, tour buses, and boatmen soliciting your business by the roadside. Do not ignore the boatmen: They can row

㉟ you over to **Garnish Island,** about 10 minutes offshore, which features beautiful formal Italian gardens, shrubberies with rare subtropical plants, and excellent views from the strange Grecian temple. (The boat trip is subject to negotiation—expect to pay about £4 round-trip.) *Tel. 027/63040. Admission £1.50 adults, 50p senior citizens and children. Open July–*

Aug., Mon.–Sat. 9:30–6:30, Sun. 11–6; Apr.–June and Sept., Mon.–Sat. 10–6:30, Sun. 1–6; Mar. and Oct., Mon.–Sat. 10–4:30, Sun. 1–5. Last landings 1 hour before closing.

Tour 3: Killarney, the Ring of Kerry, and the Dingle Peninsula

Killarney, one of the region's most attractive locales, is a year-round, all-weather destination. Because of the area's topography, rain seldom lasts long among the mountains, and the passing showers, which can be watched approaching over the lakes, actually add to your enjoyment of the ever-changing scenery. However, rain can spoil the drive around the Ring of Kerry, blocking views across the water to the Beara Peninsula in the east and the Dingle Peninsula in the west. Dingle is also notorious for its heavy rainfall and an impenetrable sea mist that can strike at any time of year. If it does, sit it out in Dingle Town or the village of Dunquin, and enjoy the friendly bars, cafés, and crafts shops.

Killarney The lakes and mountains of **Killarney** are perhaps the most cel-
36 ebrated—and the most commercialized—attractions in Ireland. Killarney's heather-clad mountains, lush subtropical vegetation, and deep-blue lakes dotted with wooded isles have left a lasting impression on innumerable visitors, beginning in the 18th century with the English traveler Arthur Young and Bishop Berkeley. Travelers in search of the natural beauty so beloved by the Romantic movement began to flock to the Southwest, among them writers Sir Walter Scott and William Thackeray. By the mid-19th century, Killarney's stunning scenery was considered as exhilarating and awe-inspiring as anything in Switzerland or England's Lake District.

The lives of Kerry's impoverished natives were transformed by the influx of affluent visitors that followed the 1854 arrival of the railway, and the locals became adept at inventing apocryphal legends and farfetched stories to impress the vacationers.

It is the combination of wild mountain scenery and lush subtropical vegetation that attracts today's visitors. The vegetation is splendid at any time of year. The red fruits of the Mediterranean strawberry tree *(Arbutus unedo)* are at their height in October and November. Also at that time, the bracken turns rust, contrasting with the many evergreens. In late April and early May, the purple flowers of the rhododendron *ponticum* put on a spectacular display. (This Turkish import has adapted so well to the climate that its vigorous growth threatens native oak woods, and many of these purple plants are being dug up by volunteers in a belated effort to control its spread.)

Numbers in the margin correspond to numbered points of interest on the Killarney Area map.

37 **Killarney Town,** on a flat plain more than a mile from the lakes, is best regarded as a necessary evil in which little time should be spent. Overcrowded in July and August with Irish and European visitors, the peak season for Americans is September and October. At other times of year, particularly from November to mid-March, when most of the hotels are closed, the town is quiet to the point of being eerie. Given the choice, go to Killarney in April, May, or early October.

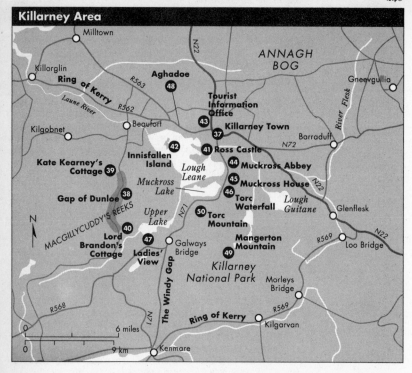

Killarney Area

Milltown

Killorglin

Ring of Kerry

Laune River

R563

Aghadoe
48

N22

ANNAGH
BOG

Gneevgullia

Kilgobnet

Beaufort

R562

Tourist
Information
Office

43

37 Killarney Town

River Flesk

Barraduff

N72

42 Innisfallen
Island

41 Ross Castle

44 Muckross Abbey

Kate Kearney's
Cottage **39**

Lough
Leane

Muckross
Lake

45 Muckross House

46 Torc
Waterfall

Lough
Guitane

Glenflesk

N22

Gap of Dunloe **38**

MACGILLICUDDY'S REEKS

N

Upper
Lake

N71

50 Torc
Mountain

R569

N22

Loo Bridge

Lord
Brandon's
Cottage

40

47
Ladies'
View

Galways
Bridge

Mangerton
Mountain

49

Killarney
National Park

Morleys
Bridge

R568

The Windy Gap

N71

Ring of Kerry

R569

Kilgarvan

0   6 miles

0   9 km

Kenmare

Limiting your time in Killarney should enable you to fit the Gap
of Dunloe and the Lower Lake into your itinerary. To reach the
38 **Gap of Dunloe,** drive west 7 km (4½ mi) from Killarney on the
Beaufort road, Route R562, and follow the signs another 2½ km
39 (1½ mi) to the Gap. You are advised to wait until you reach **Kate
Kearney's Cottage** before hiring a jaunting car (pony and trap)
or pony. Kate was a famous beauty who sold moonshine to visitors from her home, contributing greatly, one suspects, to
their enthusiasm for the scenery.

Time Out **Kate Kearney's Cottage** (tel. 064/44116) is now, appropriately
enough, a pub. It's a good place to pause for a glass of Irish coffee.

The trip through the Gap of Dunloe takes about 90 minutes.
The road stretches for 6½ km (4 mi) between MacGillicuddy's
Reeks (to the west) and the Purple Mountains. If you are on an
organized tour, you can walk or ride (on a pony or in a jaunting
car) all the way through to Lord Brandon's Cottage at the head
of the Upper Lake and continue by boat. Although cars are
banned from the Gap, the first 3 km (2 mi) are busy with horse
and foot traffic in the summer, much of which turns back at the
halfway point. Five small lakes are strung out beside the road,
and massive glacial rocks form the side of the valley, creating
strange echoes. (Test it out by giving a shout.) Parking is available near Kate Kearney's Cottage and Lord Brandon's Cottage.

At the head of the Gap, the **Upper Lake** comes into view, with the Black Valley stretching into the hills at the right. From **40** **Lord Brandon's Cottage,** a tea shop serving soup and sandwiches (open Easter–Sept., 10–dusk), a path leads to the edge of the lake, and the journey is continued by rowboat. It is an old tradition for the boatman to carry a bugle and illustrate the echoes. Look out for caves on the left-hand side when passing through the narrow Middle Lake. The boat passes under Brickeen Bridge and into the **Middle Lake,** where 30 islands are steeped in legend, much of which, no doubt, will be recounted by your boatman.

41 The journey ends at **Ross Castle** (closed indefinitely for restoration but worth admiring from the outside), a 14th-century **42** stronghold. You can take yourself to **Innisfallen Island** by hiring a rowboat at Ross Castle (cost: £1.50 per hour), or you can join a cruise in a covered, heated launch (cost: £4, also from Ross Castle). The romantic ruins on the island date from the 6th or 7th century. Between 950 and 1350 the *Annals of Innisfallen* were compiled here by the monks. (The book survives in the Bodleian Library in Oxford.) The launch and castle may be reached by car.

Another popular excursion from Killarney is a half-day trip to Muckross Abbey, Muckross House and Estate, and the Torc Waterfall. Cars are not allowed to tour the grounds of the estate, but a car park is located at the house. Some people choose to make the whole trip by jaunting car, hiring one at the stand **43** near the **Tourist Information Office** (TIO) in Killarney. (The cost of a jaunting car is £10–£24, negotiable with the driver, for up to four people. Get an estimate from the TIO.) To save time and money, drive the 4 km (2½ mi) to Muckross Abbey on the N71 Kenmare road, and pick up a jaunting car there. Or, hire a bicycle in town, pack a lunch, and make a day of it.

Though it was completely wrecked by Oliver Cromwell's British troops in 1652, the 15th-century Franciscan **Muckross Ab-** **44** **bey** is still amazingly complete, although roofless. An ancient yew tree rises above the cloisters and breaks out over the abbey walls. Three flights of stone steps allow access to the upper floors and living quarters, where you can visit what was once their dormitory, kitchen, and refectory. *Admission free. Open daily daylight hours.*

45 **Muckross House,** a 19th-century Elizabethan-style manor, is about 1.6 km (1 mi) farther west on the N71; it now houses the Kerry Folklife Center, where blacksmiths, weavers, basket makers, and potters demonstrate their crafts. One exhibit illustrates Kerry's musical and poetic past, and another deals with antique farm tools and machinery—some of which are still in use on the smaller farms of Kerry. The informal grounds here are noted for their rhododendrons and azaleas, the water garden, and the outstanding limestone rock garden. *Tel. 064/ 31440. Admission: £2 adults, £1 children, gardens free. Open Mar. 17–June 30 and Sept.–Oct., daily 9–6; July–Aug., daily 9–7; rest of year, daily 11–5.*

Another 1.6 km (1 mi) west on the N71 (7 km/4½ mi from Killar- **46** ney) is the **Torc Waterfall,** which is about a 10-minute walk from the car park. After your first view of the roaring cascade, it's worth the climb up a long flight of stone steps to the second, less-frequented clearing. If the weather is fine, return to your

④⑦ car and drive on west to **Ladies' View,** a panoramic vista. The N71 continues to Kenmare, from where you can complete the circuit by taking the shorter but very narrow Windy Gap route, or make a wide sweep via Kilgarvan on the R569 and N22, driv-
④⑧ ing back through the town to **Aghadoe,** 5 km (3 mi) outside Killarney on the R562 Beaufort–Killorglin road. Here is another remarkable view of the Lower Lake with Innisfallen Island in the distance and the Gap of Dunloe away to the west. Stand beside Aghadoe's 12th-century ruined church and round tower and watch the shadows creep across the lake at dusk.

The Mangerton walking trail is reached by turning left off the N71 midway between Muckross Abbey and Muckross House (following signposts). On foot you'll reach the summit of
④⑨ **Mangerton Mountain** (748 meters/2,756 feet) in about two
⑤⓪ hours—less should you choose to hire a pony. **Torc Mountain** (537 meters/1,764 feet) can also be reached off Route N71; it is a satisfying 1½-hour climb. Do not attempt either in misty weather. The Kerry Way, a long-distance walking route, passes through the **Killarney National Park** on its way to Glenbeigh (detailed leaflet from TIO). For the less adventurous, four safe and well-signposted nature trails of varying lengths are available in the National Park. Try Arthur Young's Walk (4 km/2½ mi); it passes through old yew and oak woods frequented by Sika deer.

From May to September, Killarney offers visitors a lively nightlife, including discos, Irish cabarets, and singing pubs— the latter are a local specialty with a strong Irish-American flavor. But the real pleasure of Killarney is outdoors. Its mild, totally unpolluted air smells of damp woods and heather moors. Few people feel they have exhausted the area's natural resources in one visit. Most leave with the intention of one day returning to find the fascinating shifts of light, the varied scenery, and the peaceful solitude as seductive as ever.

The Ring of Kerry *Numbers in the margin correspond to points of interest on the Southwest map.*

Because most tour buses travel the Ring of Kerry counterclockwise, we recommend that independent travelers take it clockwise, starting at Kenmare. This is equally convenient for those approaching from Glengarriff (on the N71) and Killarney (also on the N71). The trip covers 176 km (110 mi) on the N70 (and briefly the R562) if you start and finish in Killarney; the journey will be 40 km (25 mi) shorter if you only venture between Kenmare and Killorglin; from this latter point, people often choose to travel on to the Dingle Peninsula without returning to Killarney. Allow at least one full day for the Ring—and pray for sunshine, which makes all the difference.

⑤① **Kenmare** is a small market town at the head of the sheltered Kenmare River estuary and a popular touring base.

As you drive down the Iveragh Peninsula, the Beara Peninsula and its blue-gray mountain ranges, the Caha and the Slieve Miskish, are across the water to the south. The village of
⑤② **Sneem** (from the Irish *an tSnaidhm*—the knot), on the estuary of the Ardsheelaun River, is one of the prettiest in Ireland, although its village green is atypically English-style. Look for "the pyramids" (as they are known locally) beside the parish church. These 40-meter (12-foot) tall traditional stone structures with stained-glass insets look as though they have been

here forever. In fact, the sculpture park was completed in 1990 to the design of the Kerry-born artist, James Scanlon, who has won international awards for his work in stained glass. 3.2 kilometers (2 miles) south is the beautiful hotel and wooded estate of **Parknasilla.** The road then runs inland for a few miles before emerging at the coast again at **Castlecove.**

53 **Staigue Fort,** signposted 4 km (2½ mi) inland at Castlecove, is one of the finest examples of an Iron Age stone fort in Ireland. Approximately 2,500 years old, this structure made from local stone is almost circular and about 23 meters (75 feet) in diameter, with only one entrance, on the south side. Between the Iron Age (from 500 BC to the 5th century AD) and early Christian times (6th century AD), such "forts" were, in fact, fortified homesteads within which several families of one clan and their cattle lived. The walls at Staigue Fort are almost 4 meters (13 feet) wide at the base, 2 meters (7 feet) at the top; they still stand at 5½ meters (18 feet) on the north and west sides. Within the walls stairs lead to narrow platforms on which the lookouts stood. (Private land must be crossed to reach the fort, and a nominal "compensation for trespass" is often requested by the landowner.)

54 Beyond the next village, **Caherdaniel,** is **Derrynane House.** This home once belonged to the famous politician Daniel O'Connell (1775–1847), "The Liberator," who campaigned for Catholic Emancipation (the granting of full rights of citizenship for Catholics), which became a reality in 1828. The house with its lovely garden and 320-acre estate now forms **Derrynane National Park.** The south and east wings of the house are open to visitors and still contain much of the original furniture and other items associated with O'Connell. *Derrynane House: tel. 0667/5113. Admission: £1 adults, 30p children and senior citizens. Open mid-June–Sept., daily 10–1 and 2–7; Oct.–mid-June, Tues.–Sat. 10–1 and 2–5, Sun. 2–5. Park: admission free, open all year.*

55 The village of **Waterville,** which is 5 km (3 mi) north, is famous for game fishing and its 18-hole championship golf course. Salmon and trout fishing are excellent at nearby Lough Currane.

Time Out **The Smuggler's Inn,** situated on a mile-long sandy beach, is a small, family-run guest house and restaurant with a good reputation for seafood. This is an ideal spot for a leisurely lunch or a quick pint and a sandwich. *Cliff Rd., Waterville, tel. 0667/4330. Closed Nov. 3–Feb. 15.*

Just outside Waterville, a scenic detour is signposted from the main Ring to Ballinskelligs, an Irish-speaking area with a fine **56** sandy beach, and **Valentia Island.** Some of the romance of visiting an island has been lost since Valentia was connected to the mainland by a road bridge in 1971. The island still gives its name to weather reports, but the station that monitors the Atlantic weather systems has now moved onto the nearby mainland.

The Skellig Experience, situated where the road bridge joins Valentia Island, it contains exhibits on local bird life, the history of the lighthouse and keepers, and the life and work of the early Christian monks. There is also a 15-minute audio-visual show that allows you to "tour" the monastery without leaving dry land. If, however, you're keen on seeing the Skelligs up-close (landing is prohibited without a special permit), you can take a one-and-a-half-hour guided cruise with author and Skellig expert, Des Lavelle. Little Skellig is breeding ground of over 20,000 pairs of gannets, and Puffin island to the north has a large population of shearwaters, storm petrel, and puffins. Photographers will love the boat trip, but sailors are warned that these are choppy waters at the best of times. *Valentia, Co. Kerry., tel. 064/31633. Admission to center only: £3 adults, £1.50 children. Admission to center and cruise: £15 adults, £8 children. Open 9:30–5, April–June and Sept.; 9:30–7 July and Aug. Phone to confirm cruise times or ask at Killarney TIO.*

⑤⑦ From Valentia, you'll see the conical-shaped **Skelligs** rising 217 meters (700 feet) out of the Atlantic. The larger rock, Skellig Michael (or the Great Skellig), which has the remains of a settlement of early Christian monks, is reached by climbing 600 increasingly precipitous steps. In spite of one thousand years' battering by Atlantic storms, the church, oratory, and beehive-shaped living cells are surprisingly well-preserved.

Because of the ever-increasing stream of tourist traffic, the rock of this impressive archaeological site has been subjected to serious erosion, and local boatmen have been asked to limit landings. Because the other rocks are nature reserves (on which landing is forbidden without a special permit), a round-trip by boat can still be an interesting and rewarding experience, even without landing. Little Skellig has some 20,000 pairs of nesting gannets, and Puffin Island to the north is also a nature reserve with a large population of shearwaters, storm petrels, and about 7,000 pairs of puffins. Boats leave from Knightstown Harbour on Valentia, Ballinskelligs Pier, and Cahirciveen (*see* below). Landing is, in any case, only possible in the very calmest of weather. If you are absolutely determined to land on Skellig Michael, and are prepared to wait for the right weather conditions, contact Des Lavelle (tel. 0667/6124). Expect to pay about £12 per head for a half-day look-see cruise—and bad sailors take warning, these waters are exceedingly choppy at the best of times.

⑤⑧ The main road, the N70, is joined again just outside **Cahirciveen** (accent on the last syllable: Cah-her-sigh-*veen*), the main market town and shopping center for South Kerry, situated at the foot of Bentee Mountain. The impressive church that dominates the main street was built in 1888 to honor the local hero, Daniel O'Connell (*see* Derrynane House, above). Following the tradition in this part of the world, the town's modest terraced houses are painted in different colors—the brighter the better. The same sign-writers who recently transformed Kenmare with their old-fashioned hand-painted signs have been at work here, too.

The road from Cahirciveen to Glenbeigh is one of the highlights of the Ring. To the north is Dingle Bay and the jagged peaks of the Dingle Peninsula, which will, in all probability, be shrouded in mist. If they are not, the gods have indeed blessed your journey. The road runs close to the water here, and beyond Kells it climbs high above the bay, hugging the steep side of Drung Hill before descending to Glenbeigh. Note how different the stark character of this stretch of the Ring is from the gentle, woody Kenmare Bay side.

59 **Glenbeigh** is a popular holiday base, offering excellent hiking in the Glenbeigh Horseshoe, as the surrounding mountains are known, and exceptionally good trout fishing on Lough
60 Coomasaharn. **Rossbeigh,** which is 3 km (2 mi) away, has about 3 km (2 mi) of soft yellow sandy coastline backed by high dunes. It faces Inch strand, a similar formation across the water on the Dingle Peninsula.

A signpost to the right just outside Glenbeigh points to **Caragh Lake,** another tempting side excursion to a beautiful expanse of water set among gorse-and-heather-covered hills and majestic mountains. The road encircles the lake, hugging the shoreline much of the way.

61 **Killorglin,** which is perched atop a hill 9½ km (6 mi) beyond Glenbeigh, is the scene of the famous Puck Fair, a three-day stint of merrymaking that takes place during the second weekend in August. A large billy goat with beribboned horns, installed on a high pedestal, presides over the fair. The origins of the tradition of King Puck are lost in time. Though some horse-, sheep-, and cattle-dealing still occurs at the fair, the main attractions these days are free outdoor concerts and extended drinking hours. The crowd is predominantly young and invariably noisy, so avoid Killorglin at fair time if you've come for peace and quiet. On the other hand, if you intend joining in the festivities, be sure to book accommodations well in advance.

The Dingle Peninsula The landscape here is formed by rugged mountains and cliffs, interspersed with softly molded glacial valleys and lakes. The peninsula is outlined by long sandy beaches and rocky cliffs pounded by the Atlantic Ocean. On the coastal plains, dry stone walls enclose small, irregular fields. The whole area is exceptionally rich in antiquities, especially prehistoric and early Christian remains. The tip of the peninsula—**Corca Dhuibhne (Corcaguiny)**—is officially a Gaeltacht (or area of Irish [Gaelic] speakers), although like all Gaeltacht communities, it is bilingual nowadays; English is the second language.

The peninsula can be covered in a long day trip of about 160 km (99 mi). From Tralee, Killarney, or Killorglin, head for Castlemaine, and take the coast road (the R561 and R559) to the town of Dingle via Inch. If mist or continuous rain is forecast, postpone the trip until visibility improves.

The head of Dingle Bay is cut off by two sand spits that enclose Castlemaine Harbour. The sand spit on the Dingle side forms
62 the sheltered seaside resort **Inch,** which has a 6½-km- (4-mi-) long sandy beach backed by dunes.

63 **Annascaul,** which is 8 km (5 mi) down the coast road from Inch, near the junction of the Castlemaine and Tralee roads, was an important livestock center until the 1930s. This explains why such a small village has such a wide street (cattle trading was carried out in the streets), and also why it boasts so many pubs for so few residents.

Time Out Photographers will be tempted to snap **Dan Foley's** (tel. 066/57257) flamboyantly painted pub. Wander in for a pint, and have a chat with Dan, who is also a magician, a farmer, and an expert on local history.

64 **Dingle,** the chief town of the peninsula, marks the start of the Irish-speaking area. It is backed by mountains and faces a shel-

tered harbor. In the summer months, its year-round population
of 1,400 is doubled by visitors. Dingle offers a good selection of
crafts shops and restaurants, but since 1985 its main attraction
has been a very friendly and entertaining bottle-nosed dolphin
who has taken up residence in the harbor. The Dingle dolphin,
or Fungie, as some people call him, will play for hours with
swimmers (a wet suit is essential) and scuba divers, and he follows local boats in and out of the harbor. Being wild, it is impossible to predict whether he will stay, but boatmen have become
so confident of a sighting that they offer trippers their money
back if Fungie does not appear. Boat trips (cost: £5 adults, £2
children) leave the pier hourly in July and August between 11
and 6, weather permitting. At other times, call David Donegan
at 066/51720.

Time Out   Dingle has a wide choice of pubs, but **O'Flaherty's** (Bridge St.
at the entrance to the town, tel. 066/51461) is something special. This simple stone-floored bar is a mecca for traditional musicians. Spontaneous music sessions occur most nights in July
and August, less frequently at other times. Even without music, this pub provides a good spot to compare notes with fellow
travelers.

65 **Ventry,** the next town along the coast, has a long sandy beach
with safe bathing and ponies for hire. Between Ventry and
Dunquin, you'll find several interesting archaeological sites on
the spectacular cliff-top road along Slea Head. After you pass
between two tall hedges of fuchsia bushes about 6 km (3½ mi)
66 outside Ventry, the Iron Age promontory fort, **Dunbeg,** can be
seen on the left below the road. A fortified stone wall cuts off
the promontory, and the landward side is protected by an elaborate system of earthworks and trenches. Within the enclosure
is a ruined circular building, with walls up to 6.35 meters (22
feet) wide. Unlike Staigue Fort on the Ring of Kerry, this was
not a homestead but was probably used as a refuge in times of
danger. *Freely accessible; follow signposts across fields.*

If you continue west along the coast road, you'll see signs indicating "Prehistoric Beehive Huts"—*clocháns* in Irish. These
cells are built of unmortared stone on the southern slopes of
Mt. Eagle. In the early Christian period, they were used by
hermit monks. Some 414 of these huts exist between Slea Head
and Dunquin.

The view of the Blasket Islands and the Atlantic Ocean from
67 the top of the towering cliffs of **Slea Head** stops most visitors in
their tracks. The long sandy strand below, Coumenole, looks
beautiful and sheltered, but swimming here is dangerous. This
treacherous stretch of coast has claimed many lives in ship-
wrecks—most recently in 1982 when a large cargo boat, the
Ranga, foundered on the rocks and sank. In 1588, four ships of
the Spanish Armada were driven through the Blasket Sound;
two made it to shelter, and two sank. One of these, the *Santa
Maria de la Rosa,* was found only recently; it is currently being
excavated by divers in the summer months.

68 The largest of the **Blasket Islands** visible from Slea Head, the
Great Blasket, was inhabited until 1953. The Blasket islanders
were great storytellers, and were encouraged by scholars of
the Irish language to write their memoirs. *The Islandman,* by
Tomás O Crohán, gives a vivid picture of a hard way of life.

You've Let Your Imagination Go, Now Get Up And Follow Your Dreams.

For The Vacation You're Dreaming Of, Call American Express® Travel Agency At 1-800-YES-AMEX.*

American Express will send more than your imagination soaring. We'll fly you, sail you, drive you to any Fodor's destination and beyond. Because American Express believes the best vacations happen from Europe to the Orient, Walt Disney® World to Hawaii and everywhere in between.

For dependable service, expert advice, and value wherever your dreams take you, call on American Express. After all, the best traveling companion is a trustworthy friend.

AMERICAN EXPRESS Travel Agency

It's easy to recognize a good place when you see one.

American Express Cardmembers have been doing it for years.

The secret? Instead of just relying on what they see in the window, they look at the door. If there's an American Express Blue Box on it, they know they've found an establishment that cares about high standards.

Whether it's a place to eat, to sleep, to shop, or simply meet, they know they will be warmly welcomed.

So much so, they're rarely taken in by anything else.

Always a good sign.

"Their likes will not be seen again" as O Crohán's catchphrase puts it. The smaller Blasket, Inishvickillane, is owned by Charles J. Haughey (the Irish prime minister until 1992)—known locally as "Charlie"—who traditionally inaugurates the Dunquin Regatta on every August Bank Holiday.

69 **Dunquin** was once the mainland harbor for the islanders. No scheduled ferry service is available; inquire in Dunquin in June, July, and August for boats heading to Great Blasket during the day, depending on the weather (no phone available for the boats). At the pier (signposted from the main road), you will see curraghs (open fishing boats traditionally made of animal hide stretched over wooden laths and tarred) stored upside down. These light canoes (covered in canvas nowadays) are walked to the sea on the heads of three or four men, their legs beneath making each boat look like an enormous black insect. Similar boats are used in the Aran Isles, and when properly handled they prove extraordinarily seaworthy. The pier is surrounded by cliffs of colored silurian rock, which is more than 400 million years old and rich in fossils.

Dunquin is at the center of the Gaeltacht, and it attracts many students of Irish language and folklore. It will be familiar to film buffs, as it was around here that *Ryan's Daughter* was filmed by David Lean in 1969. The movie production gave tourism its first major boost in the area, and its shooting is recalled with affection. The ruins of the film's schoolhouse can be found about ⅘ km (½ mi) outside Dunquin. You will notice that some of its cut-stone features are actually made of fiberglass. Ask for directions to the building at Kruger's Pub.

Time Out **Kruger's Pub,** well signposted in the town, is the main social center of Dunquin. It has always been frequented by artists and writers—including Brendan Behan—and still is.

Between Dunquin and Ballyferriter the road skirts **Clogher Strand;** this is not a safe spot to swim, but it's a good place to watch the ocean pounding dramatically on the rocks when a storm is approaching or a gale is blowing. Overlooking the beach is Louis Mulcahy's pottery studio. Mulcahy is one of Ireland's leading ceramic artists, producing large pots and urns that are both decorative and functional; he has trained several local people to work in the studio. Visitors are welcome to watch the work in progress and to buy items at workshop prices. *Clogher Strand, tel. 066/56229. Open daily 9:30–6.*

70 **Ballyferriter,** another Irish-speaking town, is mainly a holiday village and a popular center for self-catering vacationers, many of them German or Dutch. Like much of the peninsula, this area is great for walking. A footpath off the road north out of Ballyferriter, signposted Béal Bán, will lead you past a long **71** sandy beach to **Dún an Óir** (the walk is about 2½ km/1½ mi). To reach this former fort by car, take the Dunquin road and turn right after about ⅘ km (½ mi), following signposts. The site was originally an Iron Age promontory fort, within which an invasion force of about 600 Spaniards and Italians built another fort in 1580. They came to support the Catholic Irish against the Protestant English. The English successfully bombarded the fort from land and sea, and they then slaughtered all survivors, including many innocent local inhabitants. Dún an Óir—which means "fort of gold" in Irish—is now largely obliterated, but folk memory of the massacre is so strong that a memorial was erected on the site in 1980. *Freely accessible.*

Return to the main road and go back through Ballyferriter, following signs for Ballydavid, to visit two of the many important early Christian sites in the area. **Gallarus Oratory,** on the right-hand side of the main road, is one of the best preserved early Christian churches in the country, dating from the 7th or 8th century. Note the ingenious use of corbeling—successive levels of stone projecting inward from both side walls until they meet at the top to form an unmortared roof. The structure is still watertight after more than a thousand years. *Freely accessible.*

Kilmakedar Church, which is 3 km (2 mi) northeast of Gallarus, is one of the finest examples of Romanesque (Early Irish) architecture surviving. Although the Christian settlement dates from the 7th century, the present structure was built in the 12th century. Note how the native builders integrated foreign influences with their own local traditions, keeping the blank arcades and round headed windows, but using stone roofs, sloping doorway jambs, and weirdly sculpted heads. Ogham stones and other interestingly carved, possibly pre-Christian stones can be examined in the churchyard. *Freely accessible.*

From Kilmakedar, return to Dingle on the well-signposted main road, then head north across the **Connor Pass,** a mountain route that passes over the center of the peninsula and offers magnificent views of Brandon Bay, Tralee Bay, and the beaches of North Kerry, with Dingle Bay in the south. It was from Brandon Bay that Brendan the Navigator (AD 487–577) is believed to have set off on his famous voyages in a specially constructed curragh. On his third trip it is possible that he reached Newfoundland or Labrador, then Florida. He was the inspiration for many voyagers, including Christopher Columbus.

The summit of **Mt. Brandon** (953 meters/3,127 feet) is away on the left as you cross the Connor Pass, and is accessible only to walkers. Do not attempt the climb in misty weather. The easiest way to make the climb is to follow the old pilgrims' path, the Saint's Road; it starts at Kilmakedar Church and rises to the summit from Ballybrack, which is the end of the road for cars. At the summit, visitors will reach the ruins of an early Christian settlement. The top can also be approached from a path that starts just beyond Cloghane (signposted left on descending the Connor Pass); this latter climb is longer and more strenuous.

The main road to Tralee is signposted right at Kilcummin, and runs just inland of Brandon Bay and Tralee Bay, giving glimpses of the latter's long sandy beach at Camp. One approaches Tralee across an uninteresting plain, distinguished only by the black and white sails of the newly restored windmill at **Blennerville.** *Tel. 066/21064. Admission: £1.50 adults; 50p children. Open Apr.–Oct., daily 10–5.*

Tour 4: North Kerry and Shannonside

Because of their proximity to Shannon Airport, the gateway to Ireland for transatlantic visitors, North Kerry and Shannonside have many more formally organized attractions than the rest of the Southwest. For the visitor, the area's well-restored castles help compensate for the lack of dramatic scenery. This tour takes in the north of County Kerry, the city of Limerick, and those parts of counties Limerick and Clare that border the estuary of the River Shannon.

77 **Tralee** is County Kerry's largest town, with a population of about 16,500. This busy yet unprepossessing place has long been associated with the popular Irish song "The Rose of Tralee," the inspiration for the annual Rose of Tralee International Festival. Irish communities from around the world send young women to join native Irish competitors; one of them is chosen as the "Rose of Tralee." Festival week, the last in August, attracts musicians and entertainers from all over the country, and it coincides with a horse race, so the town is always packed with people. Tralee is also the home of **Siamsa Tíre**—the folk theater of Ireland; it is worth stopping here to catch one of the theater's lively and colorful productions (*see* The Arts, below).

From Tralee, you can take the N69 road, which runs along a plain at the base of the Stack's Mountain, for 27 km (16 mi) to **Listowel**, a small, sleepy market town that only really comes alive for its horse race during the third week of September.

Time Out Writer **John B. Keane** (author of *The Field*, which was recently made into a film starring John Hurt and Richard Harris) owns and runs the bar that bears his name in the town center. As one would expect, Keane is a great raconteur.

A detour to the left at Listowel on the R553 will take you to the seaside resort of **Ballybunion,** famous for its long sandy beach and championship golf course. The main route along the N69 leads to **Tarbert** (18 km/11 mi) on the Shannon estuary. This is the terminus for the ferry to Killimer in West Clare, a convenient 20-minute shortcut if you're heading for the west of Ireland. The **Shannon**, with a length of 273 km (170 mi), is the longest river in Ireland or Britain. The magnificent estuary, in front of you at this point, stretches westward for a further 96 km (60 mi) before reaching the sea.

78 The N69 continues up the Shannon estuary to **Glin** (5 km/3 mi) and the first of several castles on the itinerary. A Fitz-Gerald castle at Glin, right on the banks of the Shannon, has been standing here for more than 700 years. The present knight of Glin, Desmond Fitz-Gerald, is a keen campaigner for the Irish heritage, and a well-known figure in the country's artistic circles. The current castle dates only from 1785; crenellations and Gothic details were added to the house in the 1820s to make it look more like an ancestral home. The neoclassical hall features elaborate plasterwork with a ceiling painted in the original red and green; the hall opens onto an imposing double staircase. The house also has a unique collection of 18th-century Irish furniture. *Tel. 068/34173. Admission: £2 adults, £1.50 children. Open May 1–June 4, daily 10–noon and 2–4; other times by appointment.*

Foynes, which is 9 km (5½ mi) up the N69, was the landing place for transatlantic air traffic in the 1930s and '40s. The famous flying boats landed here to refuel before heading on to their European destinations, carrying a diverse range of people, from celebrities to refugees. The town's new museum, which is a must for aviation buffs, recalls the recent history of flying with a range of exhibits and an audiovisual show. *Tel. 069/*

65416. Admission: £1.70 adults, £1 children. Open July 8–Oct. 29, Mon.–Sat. 10–6; Sun. 2–7.

The N69 continues to Limerick through **Askeaton,** where the ruins of a 15th-century Desmond stronghold almost cover a rocky islet on the River Deel. On the banks of the river are the well-preserved ruins of a 15th-century Franciscan friary. *Freely accessible.*

Just beyond Askeaton, turn right on the R518 for Rathkeale and Adare. **Castle Matrix,** in **Rathkeale,** dates from 1440, when it was in possession of the earls of Desmond. Confiscated by Elizabeth I, the castle served as a meeting place for the poet Edmund Spenser and Walter Raleigh when they were young and not yet famous. Raleigh subsequently brought the first potato tubers from North Carolina to Castle Matrix, from where they were distributed throughout south Munster (the old provincial name for the region). In 1962, the late Colonel Sean O'Driscoll, an American architect, bought Castle Matrix and restored it. The library, which serves as the headquarters of the Irish Heraldry Society, has an interesting collection of documents relating to the "Wild Geese," Irish mercenaries who served in European armies in the 17th and 18th centuries. *Tel. 069/64284. Admission: £2 adults, £1 children. Open May 15–Sept. 15, Sat.–Tues. 1–5.*

Adare is a lovely village with several thatched cottages amid wooded surroundings on the banks of the River Maigue. The village is also rich in ruins; on foot, you can locate the remains of two 13th-century abbeys, a 15th-century friary, and the keep of a 13th-century Desmond castle.

Beyond Adare, the N21 merges with the N20, which goes straight to the center of **Limerick** (16 km/10 mi), the third-largest city of the Republic, with a population of about 65,000. Oddly enough, no connection at all exists between the city and the facetious five-line verse form known as a limerick.

Like most Irish coastal towns, Limerick was originally a 9th-century Danish settlement. In 1691, the Irish retreated to the walled city of Limerick after the Battle of the Boyne. They were besieged by William of Orange, who made three unsuccessful attempts to storm the city but then raised the siege and marched away. A year later, another of William's armies overtook the city for two months, and the Irish opened negotiations. The resulting Treaty of Limerick was never ratified—it guaranteed religious tolerance—and 11,000 men of the Limerick garrison joined the French army rather than fight in a Protestant "Irish" army. These events and other colorful episodes from Limerick's history are the subject of a 45-minute *son et lumière* show at **St. Mary's Cathedral** on Bridge Street. The cathedral itself, once a 12th-century palace, features pilasters and a rounded Romanesque entrance that were part of the original structure. Take a close look at the grotesque black oak carvings on the 15th-century misericords in the choir stalls. *Admission to show: £2.50. June 10–Sept. 15, nightly at 7 and 9:15. No advance booking needed.*

Nicholas Street, behind the cathedral, leads to Castle Street and the entrance to **King John's Castle,** built by the Normans in the 13th century. Its north side still bears traces of the 1691 bombardment. If you climb the drum towers, you'll have a good view of the town and the Shannon. *Tel. 061/312344. Admission:*

80p adults, 30p children. Open mid-June–mid-Sept., daily 10–6.

The old part of Limerick is located in this area around the cathedral and the castle, dominated by mid-18th-century buildings with fine Georgian proportions. One of these structures, The Granary, built in 1774 for grain storage, is now the **Tourist Information Office** (Michael St., tel. 061/317522). The main shopping area, which consists mostly of modest chain stores, lies a 3- or 4-minute walk to the south on O'Connell Street.

Time Out Just off O'Connell Street, on Honan's Quay, is the **Riverrun Gallery** (tel. 061/40277), which specializes in exhibits of contemporary Irish art; it also has a very pleasant restaurant that serves tasty, healthy, home-cooked food. *Open Mon.–Sat. 10–5:30.*

㉘ Limerick's university grounds are situated at **Plassey** on the outskirts of the city. The drive there is worth taking (5–10 minutes on the Ring Road signposted Dublin N7) to visit the **Hunt Museum,** located on this small, but nicely landscaped campus. The museum contains the finest collection of Celtic and medieval treasures outside the National Museum in Dublin. European objets d'art are featured, as well as ancient Irish metalwork. *Tel. 061/333644. Admission: £1.30 adults, 60p children. Open May–Sept., daily 9:30–5.*

The N18 between Limerick and Shannon Airport is one of the best stretches of road in Ireland—but visitors will soon discover that four-lane highways are quite rare. Shannon Airport is located 16 km (10 mi) from Limerick. On the road to the airport is **Bunratty Castle and Folk Park** (16 km/10 mi west of Limerick), one of those rare attractions that appeals to all age groups and manages to be both educational and fun.

㉙ **Bunratty Castle,** built in 1460, has been fully restored and decorated with 15th- to 17th-century furniture and furnishings. It gives a wonderful insight into the life of those times. As you pass under the walls of Bunratty, look for the three "murder holes," which allowed defenders to pour boiling oil on attackers below. *Tel. 061/361511. Admission: £3.10 adults, £1.60 children. Open daily 9:30–5:30 (last admission 4:30). Medieval banquets are held here twice nightly (see Nightlife, below).*

Bunratty Folk Park in the castle grounds, which re-creates a 19th-century village street, has examples of the traditional rural housing of the region. The park is every bit as quaint as some first-time visitors expect all of modern Ireland to be. The exhibits include a working blacksmith's forge; demonstrations of flour milling, bread making, candle making, thatching, and other traditional skills; and a variety of farm animals in reconstructed small holdings, complete with farmyard smells. An adjacent museum of agricultural machinery cannot compete with the furry and feathered live exhibits. *Tel. 061/361511. Admission: £2.40 adults, £1.20 children. Open daily 9:30–7.*

Time Out No visit to Bunratty is complete without a drink in **Durty Nelly's** (tel. 061/364072) next door, a famous Old World pub that has inspired imitations around the world.

Shannon Airport is signposted to your left shortly after Bunratty, but if you have time before leaving, we suggest turning right at this crossroads. Take the R471 to Sixmilebridge and then turn left on to the R462 and left again at Kilmurry to the R469 for Quin and two more attractions.

84 **Knappogue Castle** at Quin is a 15th-century MacNamara stronghold that has been extensively restored and furnished in the 15th-century style. The castle, which is also a venue for medieval-style banquets, looks spectacular when floodlit. *Tel. 061/71103. Admission: £1.90 adults, £1.15 children. Open May–Sept., daily 9:30–5:30.*

85 Signposted off the road back to Sixmilebridge about 10 km (6 mi) from Quin is the **Craggaunowen Project.** Craggaunowen Castle, a 16th-century tower house, has been restored with furnishings from the period. Especially notable are the two authentic replicas of early Celtic–style dwelling places that have been constructed on the castle grounds. On an island in the lake, reached by a narrow footbridge, is a clay-and-wattle *crannóg,* a fortified lake dwelling; it resembles what might have been built in the 6th or 7th century when Celtic influence was still predominant in Ireland. The reconstruction of a small ring fort shows how an ordinary farmer would have lived in the 5th or 6th century, at the time when Christianity was being established. Tools, cooking utensils, and a cooking pit are featured in this peaceful, open-air exhibit. The two forts are "inhabited" by lively, articulate students, who will answer all your questions about life in the Bronze Age (2000 BC–500 BC) and the Iron Age (500 BC–AD 450). It is a strange experience to walk across the little wooden bridge above reeds rippling in the lake into Ireland's Celtic past as a jumbo jet passes overhead on its way into Shannon Airport—1,500 years of history compressed into an instant. *Tel. 061/72178. Admission: £2.25 adults, £1.30 children. Open May–Sept., daily 10–6.*

Off the Beaten Track

Anne's Grove Gardens, near Castletownroche in north County Cork (midway between Mallow and Fermoy on the N72), were inspired by the ideas of William Robinson, a 19th-century gardener who favored naturalistic planting. Exotic foliage plants border paths winding down to the river; magnificent magnolias and vast numbers of naturalized primulas are among the plants on view. *Tel. 022/26145. Admission: £1.80 adults, £1 children and senior citizens. Open Easter–Sept., weekdays 10–5, weekends 1–6.*

The Beara Peninsula is the one part of the Southwest that most visitors leave out. For a wonderful scenic drive that will take a whole day, turn left at Glengarriff and head south on R572 along the peninsula's edge. You'll have views across Kenmare Bay to the Sheep's Head Peninsula. Pass through Castletownbere, stopping just beyond it at the ruins of **Dunboy Castle and House** (open Easter–Oct., daily 10–7). Then follow signposts for **Dursey Island,** a bird-watcher's paradise, which is still inhabited, but only accessible by cable car. (Cost: 50p. Open Mon.–Sat. 9, 11, 2:30, and 5; July–Aug., also 7 PM and 8 PM. For Sunday times, tel. 027/73016.) Return via **Allihies,** where a detour takes you along a precipitous but breathtaking coastal road to **Eyeries,** and then up the edge of the Kenmare River to Kenmare.

Riverstown House, which is located 6 km (4 mi) from Cork on the Dublin road (N20), has been restored with the help of the Georgian Society. It is mainly noted for allegorical plasterwork carried out by the Italian Francini brothers in 1734 and the rococo flowers and foliage adorning the dining room walls. The house is attractively furnished with period furniture. *Tel. 021/ 821205. Admission: £1.50. Open May–Aug., Thurs.–Sat. 2–6; other times by appointment.*

Shopping

Shopaholics risk severe withdrawal symptoms in the Southwest. Outside Cork City, visitors are faced mostly with crafts and sweaters, and most tourist-oriented crafts shops carry the same lines. The suggestions below should help you to find something a little different. (All shops are in Cork City unless otherwise stated.)

Specialty Stores

Antiques For country-style furniture, try **The Pine Pitch** (Emmet Pl., tel. 021/273131) or **Pinnacle** (44 MacCurtain St., tel. 021/ 503919). For Georgian and Victorian furniture and objects, go to **Monica's** (24 Oliver Plunkett St., tel. 021/271118). Interesting jewelry, Victoriana, and period clothes can be found at **Victoria's** (2 Oliver Plunkett St., tel. 021/272752). For general bygones and curiosities, try **O'Regan's Antiques** (3 Paul Lane, tel. 021/272902) beside the City Center Car Park and also at Pope's Quay. In Killarney, have a look at **J. O'Leary** (32 Main St., no tel.).

Clothing Oliver Plunkett Street and the Paul Street area remain the best bets for clothing in Cork. Try **Richard Alan** (63 Oliver Plunkett St., tel. 021/273759), **Monica John** (13 French Church St., tel. 021/271399), or **Gilmani** (Savoy Centre, Patrick St., and Glengarriff Rd., Bantry, tel. 027/50684) for sophisticated and expensive styling. Younger and cheaper fashions can be found at **Red Square** (8 Paul St., tel. 021/271716) and **Moderne** (89 Patrick St., tel. 021/270266).

Rainwear **The House of Donegal** (6 Paul St., tel. 021/272447) carries classic rainwear for men and women that should last a lifetime. For more casual weatherproof clothing, try **The Tack Room** (Academy St., tel. 021/272704); for inexpensive rainwear, go to **Penney's** (27 Patrick St., tel. 021/271935) or the main street "drapery store" in any small town.

Sportswear **Matthews** (Academy St., tel. 021/277633) and **Great Outdoors** (23 Paul St., tel. 021/276382) cater to most needs.

Tweeds The best tweed comes from Donegal, and the **House of Donegal** (6 Paul St., tel. 021/272447) features a good stock of it. The shop sells both men's and women's ready-to-wear and made-to-measure, which they will ship home to you.

Crystal **Cash's** (18 Patrick St., tel. 021/276771) has a good selection of Waterford glass, as does **Blarney Woolen Mills** (Blarney, tel. 021/385280). For striking modern uncut crystal, try the **House of James** (10 Paul St., tel. 021/272324).

Irish Crafts For the very best in modern design, check out the **House of James** (10 Paul St., tel. 021/272324). This shop carries Stephen

Pearce's tableware and bowls; you can also take a trip to his studio and buy at workshop prices (Kilmahon, Shanagarry, near Cloyne, Co. Cork, tel. 021/646807). **Blarney Woolen Mills** (Blarney, tel. 021/385280) has the largest stock and the most turnover of crafts in the country. The mills sell everything from Irish-made high fashion to Aran handknits to leprechaun key rings. They also have an outlet in Killarney (10–11 Main St., tel. 064/33222). **Boland's** (Pearse St., Kinsale, tel. 021/772161) features some unusual items, including exclusive sweaters, designer rainwear, and linen shirts. **Keane on Ceramics** (Pier Rd., Kinsale, tel. 021/772085) is a gallery that represents the best of the southwest's ceramic artists. Lisbeth Mulcahy at **The Weaver's Shop** (Green St., Dingle, tel. 066/51688) sells outstanding handwoven, vegetable-dyed woolen wraps, mufflers, and skirt lengths. **Louis Mulcahy**'s pottery (at Clogher, near Dingle, tel. 066/56229) sells tableware and decorative bowls and urns. **Peter Wolstenholme** (Pottery Workshop, Courtmacsherry, Co. Cork, tel. 023/46239) produces decorated tableware and witty ceramic objects. The most reliable crafts shops in Killarney are located on Main Street and High Street; they all carry a standard range of crystal, handknits, T-shirts, sweatshirts, and tweed hats.

Sports and Fitness

Outdoor activities are very much a way of life in the Southwest, and, like everything else around the region, such activities are undertaken casually and informally, with a minimum of organization.

Participant Sports

Bicycling   Bicycles can be hired by the day or the week. Distances may look small on the map, but hills can be steep. Except on the hottest summer days, you're advised to carry a light waterproof jacket. Traffic is usually light, especially if you seek out alternatives to the National routes (N-numbered roads). Tours 2, 3, and 4 in this chapter are all suitable for cyclists. The Irish Tourist Board publication *Cycling Ireland* (cost: £2) suggests six other bicycling circuits that can be made in the region.

For bicycle rentals, expect to pay about £6 per day, or £25 for seven days, with a £30 refundable deposit. Bicycles may be rented at the following establishments. **Blarney: Tony McGrath** (Stoneview, tel. 021/385658); **Cork: Cycle Center** (Kyle St., tel. 021/276255); **Dingle: John Moriarty** (Main St., tel. 066/51316); **Killarney: O'Callaghan Bros.** (College St., tel. 064/31465); **Limerick: Limerick Sports Store** (10 William St., tel. 061/45647); **Skibbereen: N.W. Roycroft** (Ilen St., tel. 028/21235); **Tralee: J. Caball Himself Ltd.** (Staughton's Row, tel. 066/21654).

Fishing   The deep-sea fishing season runs from April to October. Boat rental costs about £18 per person per day. Shore fishing is available all along the coast, from Cobh in the east to Foynes in the west. The whole region offers excellent opportunities for lake and river fishing, although most anglers head for Waterville or Killarney. Boats can be hired at Ballycotton, Cork Harbour in Cobh, Midleton, Passage West, Crosshaven, Kinsale, Courtmacsherry, Clonakilty, Castletownshend, Valentia Island, Fenit, and Dingle. Your hotel or the local tourist information office can suggest places that rent boats. The latter will also recommend locations for coarse and game fishing. Fishing tackle, bait, and licenses can be obtained at **The Cycle Center** (Thomond Shopping Center, Roxboro, Limerick, tel. 061/44900), **O'Neill's** (Plunkett St., Killarney, tel. 064/31970), and **T.W. Murray** (87 Patrick St., Cork, tel. 021/271089).

Golf The Southwest offers a great variety of 18-hole courses, many of them world-famous championship clubs set amid wonderful scenery. Greens fees average around £18 for a full day. Professionals charge about £12 for 30 minutes of instruction. Bring your own clubs: They are not generally available for rental, and not all courses provide golf carts.

Cork Golf Club at Little Island is considered to be the most challenging in the county. The clubs in Waterville and Ballybunion in County Kerry are tricky but highly praised seaside links. Killarney Golf and Fishing Club is unsurpassed for its lake and mountain scenery. Because some clubs cannot welcome visitors on weekends or on competition days, it is best to phone ahead. The following is a selection of the available 18-hole courses.

Cork City: Douglas Golf Club (Douglas, tel. 021/895297); **Cork Golf Club** (Little Island, tel. 021/353451); **Harbour Point Golf Club,** (Clash Rd., Little Island, tel. 021/353094); **Monkstown Golf Club** (Parkgarriffe, Monkstown, tel. 021/841376); **Muskerry Golf Club** (Carrigrohane, near Blarney, tel. 021/385297). **County Cork: Mallow Golf Club** (Ballyellis, Mallow, tel. 022/21145); **Youghal Golf Club** (Knocknaveny, Youghal, tel. 024/92787). **County Kerry: Waterville Golf Club** (Ring of Kerry, tel. 0667/4133); **Killarney Golf and Fishing Club** (Killorglin Rd., Killarney, tel. 064/31242); **Tralee Golf Club** (Barrow, Ardfert, Tralee, tel. 066/36379); **Ballybunion Golf Club** (Ballybunion, tel. 068/27146). **Shannon: Shannon Golf Club** (near Shannon Airport, Co. Clare, tel. 061/61020).

Health and Fitness Clubs Leisure centers are a new but fast-growing phenomenon in the region, and facilities are constantly being upgraded. Most hotels like to reserve their facilities for guests and local club members. Exceptions are listed below. Expect to pay up to £4 for the use of the pool, about £6 if access to a sauna and a gymnasium is included in the price. Aerobics classes cost about £2 an hour; tennis and squash courts start from £2.50.

Gleneagle Country Club (Muckross Rd., Killarney, tel. 064/31870) provides an indoor pool, a sauna, two tennis courts, and four squash courts.

Jury's Hotel Leisure Center (Western Rd., Cork, tel. 021/507533) has an indoor/outdoor pool, a sauna, a Jacuzzi, two tennis courts, and one squash court open to the public until 5 PM.

Jury's Hotel Leisure Center (Ennis Rd., Limerick, tel. 061/327777) features an indoor pool, a sauna, a Jacuzzi, a steam room, a gymnasium, and one tennis court.

Silver Springs Activity Center (Silver Springs Hotel, Tivoli, Cork, tel. 021/507533) offers an indoor pool, a sauna, a steam bath, a Jacuzzi, two squash courts, and three tennis courts (two indoor, one outdoor and floodlit).

Skellig Hotel (Dingle, Co. Kerry, tel. 066/51144) has an indoor pool, a sauna, and one tennis court.

Westlodge Hotel (Bantry, Co. Cork, tel. 027/50360) has an indoor pool, a sauna, two squash courts, one tennis court, and pitch and putt.

Hiking Two signposted long-distance trails for walkers are available in the region, the **Kerry Way,** which begins in Killarney and loops around the Ring of Kerry (209 km/130 mi), and the **Dingle Way,** which loops from Tralee around the Dingle peninsula (153 km/95 mi). Details on the trails are available on free information sheets from the Irish Tourist Board, Sheet 26C for the Kerry Way and Sheet 26G for the Dingle Way. Other good off-the-highway walks can be found in **Killarney National Park; Gougane Barra** (northeast of Ballylickey off the R584), **Farran** (off the N22 about 10 miles west of Cork City), and **Doneraile Forest** (off the N20 about 5 miles north of Mallow) parks in County Cork; and **Currachase Forest Park** (east of Askeaton off the N69), County Limerick.

Horseback Riding Expect to pay about £6 per hour for a ride, about £9 if lessons are included. Horses and ponies can be hired by the hour at the following places:

County Cork: Hitchmough Riding School (Highland Lodge, Monkstown, near Cork City, tel. 021/371267; **Pinegrove Riding School** (White's Cross, near Cork City, tel. 021/303857). **County Kerry: El Rancho Horse Holidays,** with four- and seven-day treks on Dingle Peninsula (Ballyard, Tralee, tel. 066/21840); **Glenbeigh Riding Stables** (Glenbeigh, Ring of Kerry, tel. 066/68143); **Killarney Riding Stables Ltd.,** with four- and seven-day treks in Killarney National Park, with accommodation (Ballydowney, Killarney, tel. 064/31686). **County Limerick: Clarina Riding Center** (Clarina, tel. 061/301189); **Rathcannon Equestrian Center** (Kilmallock, tel. 063/90557).

Jogging Most people use secondary roads because they have very little traffic, especially before 8 AM. The many long sandy beaches in the region are also popular with runners.

Water Sports
Bare-boat Charters The average cost of a four-berth yacht between 8½ meters and 10½ meters (28 and 35 feet) ranges from £120 per person per week (low season) to £150 (high season). Contact **Yachting International Ireland** (c/o Trident Hotel, Kinsale, Co. Cork, tel. 021/772301) for bare-boat charters and **Rossbrin Yacht Charters** (Rossbrin, near Schull, Co. Cork, tel. 028/37165) for skippered charters.

Boardsailing and Dinghy Sailing The **Oysterhaven Boardsailing Center** (Oysterhaven, near Kinsale, Co. Cork, tel. 021/770738) offers tuition and hire of all equipment, including wet suits, from about £8 per hour. Sailing dinghies as well as sailboards can be hired by the hour (from about £6) or by the day (from about £20) from the following companies, which also offer tuition and residential courses: **Glénans Irish Sailing Club** (head office: 28 Merrion Sq., Dublin, tel. 01/611481) at Castletownbere, Co. Cork; **International Sailing Center** (5 E. Beach, Cobh, Co. Cork, tel. 021/811237); **Baltimore Sailing School** (The Pier, Baltimore, Co. Cork, tel. 028/20141).

Traditional Sailing Cruises along the coast of Kerry and Cork with a skipper and a crew on a traditional 13-meter (42-foot) Galway Hooker for up to six people can be booked at **Teach Dearg Restaurant** (Ballydehob, near Skibbereen, Co. Cork, tel. 028/37282). *Cost:*

£150 per person per week self-catering; £185 per week including meals.

Spectator Sports

Gaelic Games Gaelic football and hurling are fast-moving games that generate great excitement. The county finals are held early July in Cork City at Pairc Ui Chaiomh, but tickets are not easy to come by. Ask about more easily accessible local Gaelic Athletics Association (GAA) events at Tourist Information Offices.

Horse Racing The Southwest is good racing country and the breeding ground for many a National Hunt steeplechase winner. Plenty of small lively meetings provide a good day out. **Killarney** sponsors races that are held during early May and mid-July, **Tralee** has races in late August, and **Listowel** in late September. During the summer, two or three evening meetings a year take place at **Limerick** and **Mallow.**

Road Bowling Quite unrelated to 10-pin bowling, this outdoor sport, unique to Counties Cork and Armagh, is played on quiet stretches of back roads. Two players compete by throwing a heavy iron ball, either underhand or overhand, along the road for a distance of about a mile. The lowest number of throws wins. Betting is complicated and the stakes can be high, which leads to much leaping and cheering, as well as a celebration afterwards in a nearby pub. Ask about bowling in any country pub, or look for listings in the classified ads of Saturday's *Cork Examiner.*

Sailboat Racing Small regattas, consisting of inshore and offshore sailing races, rowing races, swimming races, and local variations, such as curragh racing (Dingle) or salmon-boat racing (Kinsale), take place all along the coast during the summer. These lighthearted events are fun to watch and provide plenty of ad hoc entertainment. Kinsale and Dingle start the season on the August Bank Holiday (the first Monday in August), and Schull, Baltimore, Bantry, Cobh, Glandore, Lough Ine, and Castletownshend share the remaining August weekends. Details are available from local Tourist Information Offices.

Dining and Lodging

Dining

There was a time in Southwest Ireland when diners could choose only between old-fashioned hotel restaurants serving plain roast meat or boiled fish, or unlicensed tea rooms offering a high tea of cold meat, bread and butter, and cakes. Today the dining scene is diverse enough to suit all tastes. This region pioneered a phenomenon known as "the front parlour restaurant," which is typically operated by the owner-chef and his or her spouse. This kind of establishment usually begins in one room in the family home, often a room that was previously a shop or bar. The space is converted into a four- or five-table restaurant, with a small menu featuring fresh local produce cooked Continental style, accompanied by a small selection of wines. If the customer response is good, within a few years more rooms are converted for dining or larger premises are taken.

Most of the leading chefs in the region are French- or Swiss-trained, often having learned their trade in a fine restaurant abroad before setting up business at home. The result has become known as Hiberno-French or Franco-Irish cuisine; traditional Irish dishes are prepared using fresh local produce, influenced by both classical French cooking and nouvelle cuisine techniques.

The outstanding quality of local meat, game, and seafood is enhanced by sauces making subtle use of the rich cream and butter of the region in combination with leeks, mushrooms, sorrel and other herbs, and wines. Salads and vegetables still tend to be a weak point in the meal because most salad ingredients and vegetables must be imported. Similarly, desserts, apart from those making use of fresh cream, are usually disappointing.

Very few restaurants in Southwest Ireland require jacket and tie or fancy dresses at dinner. Unless it is specified below, rest assured that you will feel entirely at ease with your own interpretation of "casual but neat." In July and August and on weekends from May to October, these places operate under considerable pressure, and it is essential to book a table in advance. Be patient with delays and junior front-of-house staff, who are often catering students obtaining their first work experience.

Category	Cost*
Expensive	over £25
Moderate	£15–£25
Inexpensive	under £15

* *per person for appetizer, main course, and dessert, excluding drinks and 10% tip*

Lodging

Accommodations in the Southwest include some of the best country-house hotels in the country, and many more modest establishments with spectacular seaside locations, where you'll receive excellent value. The region also offers reliable modern hotels with unremarkable decor and some delightfully renovated old-fashioned hotels.

Country-house hotels may appear very grand at first sight, but their main aim is to provide a relaxed stay in beautiful surroundings. A good pair of walking boots and a sensible raincoat are more useful here than a formal wardrobe. If you want to dress for dinner, as some people do, then an outfit suitable for a smart lunch in a large city is more than good enough. Elsewhere, informality is the order of the day.

Facilities have improved greatly over the last 10 years, but perhaps not enough to impress some first-time visitors. Only expensive hotels have fitness centers. However, most hotels can organize golf, deep-sea fishing, freshwater angling, and horseback riding. B&Bs are gradually introducing private bathrooms and, in the larger towns, televisions and direct-dial phones in rooms. The absence of a television or phone is indicated under *Facilities* below, as is the absence of an elevator in hotels with more than two stories.

Few hotels have coffee shops, but in general you can order tea or coffee and a sandwich or light snack at the bar. Bear in mind that, if you choose a B&B or guest house without a bar or restaurant, such provisions rest entirely on the goodwill of your host.

Accommodations in West Cork, Killarney, and Dingle are seasonal: Between November and March, choice is very limited. Outside these months, especially from July to mid-October, hotels are busy, so be sure to book well in advance. Hosts in this region are friendly, and there is a lack of cutthroat competition among them: If your first choice is booked up, ask the hotel to recommend some similar lodging nearby.

Category	Cost*
Very Expensive	over £110
Expensive	£80–£110
Moderate	£60–£80
Inexpensive	under £60

All prices are for a standard double room.

Highly recommended restaurants and hotels in a city or town are indicated by a star ★.

Adare

Dining
★ **Mustard Seed.** Fresh flowers adorn the tables of this chic little restaurant in a modest late-Victorian house among the thatched cottages of the village's main street. Chef-owner Dan Mullane's Irish kitchen produces imaginative, healthy cooking with such daily vegetarian specials as nut roast with fresh tomato coulis. Such unusual dishes as shark steak add variety to a menu that also includes roast free-range duckling and roast rack of lamb. *Main St., Adare, Co. Limerick, tel. 061/396451. Reservations advised. AE, DC, MC, V. Wine license only. Dinner only. Closed Sun.–Mon. and Feb. Expensive.*

Lodging
★ **Adare Manor.** This vast Victorian edifice, surrounded by a 1,000-acre riverside estate, is a short walk from the village. Until 1988, this enormous country-house hotel was the home of the earls of Dunraven. Its Gothic interior has vast stone arches, tall mullioned windows, heavy Flemish wood carvings, and elaborately decorated ceilings with hanging crystal chandeliers. Grandeur and opulence reign here on a large scale; it is well worth visiting just for a drink in the Tack Room (with music nightly in the summer) and a peek, if you can't pay the hotel rates. The bedrooms are every bit as splendid as the public rooms: More than 50 of them have individually carved fireplaces, and some of the "staterooms" are bigger than the entire ground floor of an ordinary hotel. All rooms have super-king-size beds, fabulous drapes and carpets, and enormous, mostly Victorian antiques that are painstakingly carved and ornamented. Try room 203 with its elaborate vaulted, molded ceiling, or room 301, which has 15-foot-tall stone-mullioned windows. *Adare, Co. Limerick, tel. 061/396566. 64 rooms with bath. Facilities: indoor pool, sauna, gymnasium, horse riding, fox hunting by arrangement, clay-pigeon shooting, 18-*

hole golf, fishing, 2 bars, restaurant (jacket and tie preferred), helipad. AE, DC, MC, V. Very Expensive.

Dunraven Arms. This two-story Victorian inn in the village center positively oozes Old World charm. Adare is good hunting country, and an equestrian theme pervades the cozy bar and lounges where the dark walls are hung with paintings and prints of horseback riders. The bedrooms, though not large, are comfortably and tastefully decorated with antiques in the traditional style. Try room 6, where Colonel Lindbergh stayed while working on the design of Shannon Airport. *Main St., Adare, Co. Limerick, tel. 061/369209. 45 rooms with bath. Facilities: horseback riding, fox hunting by arrangement, fishing, bicycling, bar, restaurant. AE, DC, MC, V. Expensive.*

Ballylickey

Lodging **Ballylickey Manor House.** This modest 300-year-old white-
★ washed manor house, surrounded by gardens overlooking Bantry Bay, has a sophistication unusual for the area. The ambience here is more country-French than Irish—which can be a plus or a minus, depending on your taste. Four rustic chalets stand around the pool, but the best bet is one of the elegant rooms with bay windows in the main house, which was recently rebuilt and redecorated after a severe fire. The French cuisine in the candlelit restaurant is well above average for the region. *Ballylickey, near Bantry, Co. Cork, tel. 027/50071. 11 rooms with bath. Facilities: heated outdoor pool, fishing on grounds, bar, restaurant. MC, V. Closed Nov.–Mar. Moderate.*

Baltimore

Dining **Chez Youen.** Mr. Youen, an exuberant Breton, owns and runs this small, rustic restaurant where copperware hangs from low beams above a simple tiled floor. It overlooks Baltimore Harbour and Sherkin Island and specializes in the best local seafood, bought directly from the town's fishing fleet. Lobster is available year-round; other treats on the menu include *coquilles St. Jacques* (poached scallops) and *moules marinières* (mussels in white wine). *Baltimore, Co. Cork, tel. 028/20136. Reservations advised on weekends. AE, DC, MC, V. Wine license only. Closed Nov. 1–Dec. 15. Lunch, Easter–Sept. and Sun.; otherwise dinner only. Moderate.*

Bantry

Lodging **Bantry House.** This magnificent mansion overlooking the bay is certainly the best place to stay in town. The Aubusson tapestries and other treasures are kept in the central section of the house, which is open to the public; newly refurbished rooms in both wings are available for bed-and-breakfast. Enjoy the view of Bantry Bay when you wake up—it is breathtaking on a clear day. *Bantry, Co. Cork, tel. 027/50047. 8 rooms with bath. No TV or direct-dial phone in rooms. AE, MC, V. Moderate.*

Caragh Lake

Lodging **Ard na Sidhe.** ("Sidhe" is pronounced *Sheen;* it means "hill of
★ the fairies.") This secluded Edwardian mansion, built in the style of an Elizabethan manor, is low and gabled with casement windows set in stone mullions and gray stone walls covered by

creeper. The attractive large rooms have coordinated carpets and spreads, and lovely floral drapes on the bay windows. Rooms are best in the main building. Antiques and open fires adorn the traditionally furnished lobby and lounges. The hotel also offers delightful, award-winning lakeside gardens. Guests are entitled to use the sporting facilities at the Hotel Europe (*see* Killarney, below) and Dunloe Castle in Killarney. *Caragh Lake, near Killorglin, Co. Kerry, tel. 066/69105. 20 rooms with bath. Facilities: boating and fishing, restaurant, bar. No TV in rooms. AE, DC, MC, V. Closed Oct. 1–Apr. 30. Expensive.*

Castlelyons

Lodging **Ballyvolane House.** Approaching the Southwest from Dublin, Castlelyons is signposted off the N8 in Rathcormac, just south of Fermoy. A true country-house atmosphere pervades this imposing 1728 stone mansion surrounded by extensive gardens, beyond which is a 100-acre dairy farm. The Green family treats guests as friends and gives them the run of the comfortably furnished downstairs rooms. Dinner is served at a large table in the elegant dining room; family silver is set on white napery. The rooms are exceptionally big, sitting areas generous, and decor consists of a rich assortment of antiques and family heirlooms. Both dinner and accommodation must be booked at least 24 hours in advance, but the pre-planning is well worth it. *Castlelyons, Co. Cork, tel. 025/36349. 6 rooms with bath. Facilities: private fishing, horseback riding, wine license only. AE, MC, V. Expensive.*

Clonakilty

Dining **Dunworley Cottage.** Perched on a clifftop about 6 km (4 mi) out-
★ side town (well signposted), this tiny renovated cottage in the middle of nowhere has built up a fanatically loyal clientele. The Swedish chef-proprietor, Katherine Noren, who uses only organically produced meat and vegetables and locally caught fish, prepares all dishes to order; service can be a little slow, but the wait worthwhile. About a third of the menu is vegetarian. Celeriac deep-fried in butter with blue cheese sauce is typical of Katherine's imaginative cuisine; her pan-fried duck in a honey, raisin, and brandy sauce is also recommended. *Dunworley, Butlerstown, near Clonakilty, Co. Cork, tel. 023/40314. Reservations advised. AE, DC, MC, V. Open Wed.–Sun. Closed Oct. 1–Mar. 16. Moderate.*

Cloyne/Midleton

Lodging **Ballymaloe House.** This place is a favorite hideaway for celebrities; although owner Myrtle Allen is too discreet to name any of them, it is well-known locally that Jeremy Irons is a regular guest. Originally the Allen family's home on a 400-acre farm, the rambling house, covered with creeping plants, has been developed into an informal, easygoing hotel over the past 20 years. The rooms here come in all shapes and sizes, but each one is decorated elegantly in variations on the country-house style. There are good options both in the main house and in the courtyard. Myrtle Allen has done much to revitalize Irish cookery, bringing in French undertones and insisting on using only fresh produce; the food at Ballymaloe remains as close as you can get in a restaurant to home cooking. The hotel is just 32

km (20 mi) from Cork City, near the pretty fishing village of
Ballycotton. Drive out and sample the buffet lunch if you're
based in Cork. Turn off the N25 Waterford road at Midleton for
Cloyne, then follow signposts down tiny back lanes for
Shanagarry. The last 2 miles are the trickiest, especially in the
dark. *Shanagarry, Midleton, Co. Cork, tel. 021/652531. 30
rooms with bath. Facilities: outdoor heated pool, tennis court,
deep-sea fishing by arrangement, bar, restaurant (jacket and
tie preferred). No TV in rooms. AE, DC, MC, V. Expensive.*

Cork City

Dining **Arbutus Lodge.** The dining room in this solid Victorian villa is
★ relatively small, ensuring that the highest standards are maintained. The tall ceiling, large bay window, polished mahogany
sideboards, plush velvet chairs, original Irish paintings, and
intricate fresh-flower arrangements on each table evoke the atmosphere of a luxurious private home, providing the ideal setting for a leisurely sampling of French-Irish haute cuisine. An
eight-course "tasting menu" provides a perfect introduction to
the restaurant's special cuisine. Imported ingredients are
avoided as much as possible; local meat, fish, and game, which
are lightly and appropriately sauced and garnished, are highlights. In winter, try the salmis of roast pheasant with lentils;
in summer, the baked sea bass with sea urchin sauce is recommended. Two independent authorities, *The Wine Spectator* and
the *Egon Ronay Guide*, recently declared the wine list here to
be among the best in the world. If your budget is tight, sample
the inexpensive buffet lunch (including tripe and onions, and
beefsteak and kidney pie), which is served in the spacious Gallery Bar with panoramic views of the city. *Middle Glanmire
Rd., Montenotte, Cork, tel. 021/501237. Reservations required.
AE, DC, MC, V. Closed Sun. and Dec. 24–29. Expensive.*

Clifford's. Michael Clifford, once the head chef at the Arbutus
Lodge (*see* above), now runs this small yet very fashionable restaurant on the western edge of the city center near the Jury's
hotel. Although the interior of the Georgian town house has
been modernized, it retains the old cornices and elaborate high
ceilings. The high standard of cooking maintained here offers a
limited number of choices on a fixed-price set menu. House specialties include spinach soup with miniature chicken quenelles
(dumplings), medallions of veal garnished with apples and wal-
nuts, and black sole and prawns in a pepper and lime sauce. *18
Dyke Parade, Cork, tel. 021/275333. Reservations advised.
Jacket and tie required. AE, DC, MC, V. Wine license only.
Closed Sun. and Mon., as well as Sat. lunch. Expensive.*

★ **The Oyster Tavern.** Fully refurbished in 1989, this grand old
Cork eatery, a venerable institution that has served the local
population for more than 200 years, is still a favorite for business lunches and family celebrations. You now enter directly
into the dark-paneled front bar, with the addition of a cocktail
piano that some of the regulars resent. The main attraction of
the Oyster is its traditional Old World atmosphere, redolent of
a Victorian gentlemen's club with its dark woodwork, original
1790s mirrors, red plush upholstery, and waitresses dressed in
black-and-white uniforms. Expect no surprises from the menu,
but savor the exceptional quality of its basic ingredients. *Market Lane (off Patrick St.), Cork, tel. 021/272716. Reservations
advised. AE, DC, MC, V. Closed Sun. and bank holidays.
Moderate.*

Ballymaloe at the Crawford. If you can't get out to the famous country-house hotel (*see* Cloyne, *above*), you can sample Ballymaloe cooking here. The large, airy room was, until recently, an integral part of Cork's municipal art gallery; it retains an artistic air, enhanced by several life-size statues. The food is prepared daily at Ballymaloe, and includes home-grown produce and fresh seafood. Open sandwiches on home-made brown bread are a popular lunchtime choice, and the cakes are also renowned. The evening menu is fashionably light; try seafood in a scallop shell or turkey breast baked with butter and watercress. *Crawford Art Gallery, Emmet Place, tel. 021/274415. Open Mon.–Sat. 10–5, Wed.–Fri. 6:30–9:30. MC, V. Wine license only. Inexpensive–Moderate.*

★ **Halpin's.** By day, this labyrinthine warren of pine booths and tables is a busy self-service restaurant offering an excellent selection of salads, home-baked pizzas, curries, and daily specials. At night, it turns into an intimate waiter-service wine bar, offering the same menu in a more relaxed atmosphere. This establishment is one of the few reputable restaurants in Cork to open on a Sunday evening. *14 Cook St., Cork., tel. 021/271534. Reservations advised lunch and Sat.–Sun. dinner. MC, V. Wine license only. Inexpensive.*

Huguenot. Situated in the fashionable Paul Street area, this restaurant, under new management since 1991, is a pleasant venue for bistro-style French food in relaxed, informal surroundings. The dark, high-ceilinged dining room is dominated by an elaborate carved mahogany fireplace on one side and a bar on the other. Seafood pasta or lamb cutlets in a red wine sauce are served at slightly shabby wooden-topped antique tables by an enthusiastic young staff. *French Church St., Cork, tel. 021/273357. Reservations advised. AE, DC, MC, V. Closed Sun. Inexpensive.*

Lodging **Imperial.** From 1816 until the 1960s, this was Cork's premier hotel. Situated in the heart of the legal and banking district, just around the corner from the smartest shops, the building has an elegant classical facade with pilasters above a generous wrought-iron canopy that distinguishes it from the surrounding offices. The bar and the coffee shop, which are popular meeting places for business executives and affluent shoppers, have been spoiled by overenthusiastic modernization. To savor the Imperial's heritage, ask for an antique-style room with old mahogany furniture and velvet upholstery. The rest of the rooms, in various styles of hotel-modern, are spacious but undistinguished. *South Mall, Cork, tel. 021/274040. 101 rooms with bath. Facilities: 2 bars, 2 restaurants, coffee shop. AE, DC, MC, V. Closed Dec. 24–31. Very Expensive.*

Morrison's Island. Cork's newest hotel opened in 1991 on the riverside, a two-minute walk from the Imperial Hotel. Spacious modern one- or two-bedroom suites with kitchen are furnished with attractive hand-made light oak in a modern design. Polished marble floors and warm terracotta walls enhance the stylish mezzanine-level bar and restaurant overlooking the river. Four penthouses have terrace-views of the city and the river as well. *Morrison's Quay, tel. 021/275858. 40 suites with bath. Facilities: bar, restaurant. AE, DC, MC, V. Very Expensive.*

Silver Springs. Ten minutes outside town on the Dublin–Rosslare approach road, this 1960s glass-and-concrete hotel is set back from the busy main road among extensive lawns. The large and impersonal lodging is favored by tour buses in summer and business travelers in winter. The main recommendation is its recently added fitness center, which is the best in town. The fanciest and largest rooms, decked out in French-boudoir style in pink-and-gray plush, are located in the newest (1988) wing. *Tivoli, Cork, tel. 021/507533. 110 rooms with bath. Facilities: 2 bars, 2 restaurants, sauna, Jacuzzi, gymnasium, steam room, indoor pool, 2 squash courts, 3 tennis courts (1 outdoor, 2 indoor), bowling, 9-hole golf. AE, DC, MC, V. Closed Dec. 25. Very Expensive.*

Jury's. This striking modern smoked-glass and steel structure beside the River Lee is a five-minute walk from the city center and a lively spot, which attracts a young, Yuppie clientele. Its large, open lobby/restaurant area features a waterfall and hanging greenery—some of it plastic. Cork's Bar is popular with the locals at lunch and in the early evening. In the plain yet spacious rooms you'll find quilted spreads, small sofas, and floor-to-ceiling picture windows. Be sure to ask for a room that overlooks the interior patio garden and pool. The hotel's fine classical French restaurant, Fastnet, is the only place in town serving caviar. *Western Rd., Cork, tel. 021/276622. 185 rooms with bath. Facilities: 2 bars, 2 restaurants, sauna, Jacuzzi, gymnasium, indoor/outdoor pool, 2 tennis courts, squash court. AE, DC, MC, V. Closed Dec. 25–26. Expensive.*

★ **Arbutus Lodge.** This two-story Victorian villa is the first choice in Cork for those who like the feeling of staying in a fancy private home; it is only a five-minute drive from the city center (well signposted from St. Luke's Cross) on a hill overlooking the River Lee and the city. The light, airy rooms have been individually decorated with fine antiques and original paintings. The rooms designated as "superior" have vast super-king-size beds (which can unzip into twins on request) and comfortable sofas. Ask for number 14 with its magnificent bay window. The smaller "ordinary" rooms offer their surprises as well: number 9, for instance, has a magnificent carved oak and walnut four-poster bed. The majority of guests are American, often on their third or fourth visit, but the bar and outstanding restaurant (*see* Dining, above) attracts a lively local clientele. *Middle Glanmire Rd., Montenotte, Cork, tel. 021/501237. 20 rooms with bath. Facilities: restaurant, bar. AE, DC, MC, V. Closed Dec. 24–29. Moderate.*

Moore's. An unpretentious establishment on a quiet inner-city stretch of the River Lee, Moore's many ardent fans praise the homey atmosphere and friendly staff. Others complain of the pervasive smell of cooking in the public areas and the twisted narrow corridors that resulted from combining three undistinguished town houses. The cozy rooms have plain carpets and blue patterned drapes and spreads, but they vary greatly in size, shape, and outlook. The best bet is a room with a river view. *Morrison's Island, Cork, tel. 021/271291. 35 rooms with bath. Facilities: bar, restaurant. No elevator. AE, DC, MC, V. Moderate.*

Gabriel House. A four-minute uphill hike from the railroad station, and a seven-minute walk from the bus station, this well-run, large Victorian guest house is as popular as ever. The rooms are small, but they all have pleasant views, nice old sash windows, and floral comforters with matching drapes. Refreshments are available 24 hours a day. Guests are encouraged to make themselves at home in the comfortable television lounge. *Summerhill, St. Luke's, Cork, tel. 021/500333. 20*

*rooms with bath. Facilities: restaurant, TV and direct-dial
phone in rooms. AE, DC, MC, V. Inexpensive.*

★ **Victoria Lodge.** This exceptionally well-appointed B&B, built
originally in the early 20th century as a Capuchin monastery, is
a five-minute drive from the town center; it is also accessible by
several bus routes. Breakfast is served in the spacious old refectory with its polished benches and paneled walls still intact,
and the common room is now a television lounge. The simple,
comfortable bedrooms feature brown chenille spreads, cotton
curtains, and mahogany bureaus. *Victoria Cross, Cork, tel.
021/542233. 22 rooms with bath. Facilities: restaurant, TV and
direct-dial phones in rooms. MC, V. Inexpensive.*

Dingle

Dining **Beginish.** Dingle is an oasis in a culinary desert, although this
★ spot is outstanding by any standard. The small rooms feature
pale green carpeting, fresh flowers on the pink linen tablecloths, and muted classical music. The food is an imaginative
and generous interpretation of French nouvelle cuisine; specialties include brill fillets on leek fondue with white-wine
sauce, and fillet of lamb in phyllo pastry with *duxelles*. The
wine list, with about 100 choices, includes a good selection of
half-bottles. *Green St., Dingle, Co. Kerry, tel. 066/51588. Reservations advised. AE, DC, MC, V. Dinner only. Closed Mon.
and Nov.–Easter. Moderate.*

Doyle's Seafood Bar. This establishment is more of a restaurant
than a bar, but a sandstone-slated floor, rush-seated chairs,
and pine tables create a very casual atmosphere. Because the
seafood is fresh, John Doyle prefers to keep it simple: Fillets of
plaice (flounder) stuffed with crab with prawn sauce is about
the fanciest dish. Crab claws *beurre blanc* and scallops with a
chive butter sauce are more typical options. The menu offers a
good selection of seafood appetizers and irresistible homemade
desserts. Eight very comfortable, moderately priced bedrooms are available in the adjoining town house—as long as you
don't mind the pervasive odor of fish! *John St., Dingle, Co.
Kerry, tel. 066/51174. Reservations advised. DC, MC, V.
Closed Sun. and mid-Nov.–early Mar. Moderate.*

★ **The Islandman.** The front of this dining spot consists of a bar
and a bookshop that blend well with the dark wooden tables,
bentwood chairs, and Tiffany lamps of the small restaurant.
During the day, it is a popular café-bar. The dinner menu,
which caters to more serious eaters, includes roast rack of Kerry lamb with red currant sauce; fresh trout or salmon plainly
broiled; or vegetarian pasta and a side salad. *Main St., Dingle,
Co. Kerry, tel. 066/51803. Reservations advised for dinner.
AE, DC, MC, V. Inexpensive.*

Lodging **Benner's.** An American owner has restored this small town-
★ center hotel to its former glory. It should be made a model for
many similar establishments around Ireland still suffering
from insensitive 1960s modernization programs. All the rooms
are individually furnished with country-style stripped-pine antiques, plain pale cream wool carpets, and light green *eau de nil*
paintwork. Rooms 2 and 3 have pine four-poster beds, but the
largest rooms are 16 and 17 on the third floor. The atmosphere
throughout is cheerful and uncluttered, with plump chintz
sofas in the lobby and well-polished wood paneling on the
ground floor. The front bar has a busy local trade, especially at

lunchtime. *Main St., Dingle, Co. Kerry, tel. 066/51638. 25 rooms with bath. Facilities: 2 bars, restaurant. No elevator. AE, DC, MC, V. Closed Jan.–Mar. 16. Moderate.*

Skellig (Ostan na Sceilge). This is a product of Ireland's 1960s hotel boom, when novelty was prized at any cost. This movement has left us with a two-story concrete-and-glass bedroom section joined to a spaceship-like lobby/bar/restaurant/pool complex meant to recall, of all things, *clocháns*, the local beehive-shape anchorite cells. Be sure to ask for a second-floor bedroom with a sea view—216, 218, 220, and 222 are the best. The hotel is on the water's edge a five-minute walk from town; it is very popular with Irish families—who bring along swarms of children—in July and August. The spacious bar and lounge, which feature exposed stone work and wooden beams, are at their best when crowded and rather eerie when empty. *Dingle, Co. Kerry, tel. 066/51144. 50 rooms with bath. Facilities: bar, restaurant, tennis court, indoor pool, sauna. AE, DC, MC, V. Closed Nov. 11–Mar. 14. Moderate.*

★ **Alpine.** This three-story concrete hotel lacks character, but it compares very favorably to the B&Bs in town, which tend to be small, stuffy, over-furnished, and under-bathroomed. It is just outside town opposite the Skellig (*see* above). The front rooms, with wonderful ocean views, are all plain but clean and have well-appointed bathrooms. *Dingle, Co. Kerry, tel. 066/51250. 14 rooms with bath. No TV or direct-dial phone in rooms. No credit cards. Closed Dec.–Feb. Inexpensive.*

Durrus

Dining **Blair's Cove House.** This restaurant, in the converted stables of
★ a Georgian mansion overlooking Dunmanus Bay, has gleaming silverware, pink napery, and a large crystal chandelier, creating an element of elegance that contrasts sharply with the building's exposed beams and rough stone walls. In summer, you'll dine on the covered, heated terrace overlooking the rose-filled courtyard and fountain. The cuisine is French-Irish (the owners are French) with an emphasis on fresh local produce. Try rack of lamb cooked on the open oak-wood grill, or a seafood special such as monkfish in Pernod sauce. *Blair's Cove, Durrus, Co. Cork, tel. 027/61127. Reservations advised on weekends. MC, V. Wine license only. Dinner only Tues.–Sat.; lunch only Sun. Closed Nov. 1–mid-Mar. Expensive.*

Shiro Japanese Dinner House. One of the biggest surprises of West Cork's culinary world in recent years has been the success of this tiny, 12-seat restaurant, which serves authentic Japanese cuisine in an imposing Edwardian house surrounded by palm trees. The room is decorated with accomplished watercolors by the talented hostess, Tokyo-born Kei Pilz. A fixed-price four-course menu is available with a choice of main dishes such as yakitori (chicken roasted on the spit with a sweet sauce) and tempura (fried fish, squid, vegetables, and prawns). *Ahakista, Durrus, Co. Cork, tel. 027/67030. Advance reservations required. AE, DC, MC, V. Dinner only. Expensive.*

Kanturk

Lodging **Assolas Country House.** This lovely 17th-century manor possesses the air of a dignified family home more than it does a hotel. It is immaculately furnished with period antiques in the individually designed bedrooms. The tableware in the dining room is old Bourke family silver. A large log fire is usually ablaze in the drawing room, where you can join the other guests for a predinner sherry. Both the well-manicured gardens and the cooking here have won awards. Kanturk is known for its good fishing and hunting, and it is located within an hour's drive of Cork, Limerick, and Killarney. *Kanturk, Co. Cork, tel. 029/50015. 9 rooms with bath. Facilities: restaurant (dinner only; jacket and tie required), fishing, tennis court, boating. No TV in rooms. Closed Nov. 1–Mar. 16. Very Expensive.*

Kenmare

Lodging
★

Park Hotel. Formerly a bishop's palace, this establishment is now one of Ireland's premier country-house hotels. Set on extensive grounds with views of the Caha Mountains, the hotel property features terraced lawns that sweep down to the bay. The hotel is a favorite with affluent young executives from Germany and France as well as from Dublin. The thickly carpeted lobby features a black marble fireplace, a tall grandfather clock, and Victorian chaise longues. Sensuous watercolors of Kerry wildlife by Pauline Bewick, a well-known Irish painter who lives nearby, adorn the dining-room walls. The bedrooms are individually designed with late-Victorian furniture faithful to the house's original period; walnut or mahogany bedroom suites have matching wardrobes, chests of drawers, and headboards. A major renovation during the winter of 1990 doubled the size of rooms in the 1950s extension, and introduced stonework to the facade. "Superior deluxe" rooms are the smallest, but big by the standards of other places, with armchairs or sofas in the bedroom area. Park Suite rooms have an entrance hall and a separate sitting area; nine larger suites are also available. All bedrooms have finely equipped bathrooms with glossy Italian marble tiling. Be sure to sample the seafood on the nouvelle-cuisine menu of the renowned restaurant (jacket and tie required). *Kenmare, Co. Kerry, tel. 064/41200. 48 rooms with bath. Facilities: bar, restaurant, fishing, tennis court, horseback riding, golf. TV in rooms on request. DC, MC, V. Very Expensive.*

Sheen Falls Lodge. This rambling hotel opened in 1991 on the site of the former seat of the earls of Kerry. The magnificent setting—between Kenmare Bay and the fall of the River Sheen into the tidal estuary—has 300 secluded acres of lawns, semitropical gardens, and forest. The public rooms feature a mahogany-paneled library with over 1,000 books, mainly of Irish interest, and a billiard room adjacent to the bar. The bedrooms have a combination of new and antique furnishings; they all offer stunning views of either Kenmare Bay or the River Sheen. The restaurant, La Cascade, overlooking the falls, serves classic French cuisine using such local produce as lobster, salmon, oysters, mussels, quail, pheasant, lamb, and beef. Sheen Falls is the latest "in" place among high-flying Dubliners, and no doubt the international jet set will soon follow. *Kenmare, Co. Kerry, tel. 064/41600. 40 rooms with bath. Facilities: bar, restaurant, gym, sauna, steam room, salmon fishing, horseback riding, tennis, croquet, helipad. AE, DC, MC, V. Closed Jan. 1–Mar. 31. Very Expensive.*

Kilfinnane

Lodging **St. Andrew's Villa.** This pleasant B&B is located halfway between Cork and Limerick (R515) on the edge of a small rural
town that does not see many tourists and consequently makes a
big fuss over them. The villa is a modest late-Georgian house, a
home-away-from-home surrounded by gardens in which the
owners, the Nunans, grow their own food. The bedrooms feature Canadian pine trim and pleasant views over the landscaped gardens and lawns. *Mrs. Patricia Nunan, Kilfinnane,
near Kilmallock, Co. Limerick, tel. 063/91008. 4 rooms. Facilities: 2 tennis courts, lunch or dinner on request (BYOB), TV
lounge. No TV or direct-dial phones in rooms. No credit cards.
Inexpensive.*

Killarney

Dining **Panorama.** This vast restaurant in the Hotel Europe, which is a
five-minute drive from town, can seat up to 600 people. All tables enjoy a view of the ever-changing Lower Lake. Wood-
framed carver chairs and large tables draped in pink-and-green
napery furnish the forbiddingly large room; such a large-scale
operation evokes a somewhat anonymous ambience, but the live
entertainment most nights helps to lighten the mood. The cuisine is based on French classical cooking, with Irish variations;
specialties include loin of Kerry lamb with herb stuffing and a
mint-flavored tomato sauce, and turbot poached with julienne
vegetables, mousseline sauce, and boiled potatoes. *Killorglin
Rd., Fossa, Killarney, Co. Kerry, tel. 064/31900. Reservations
advised mid-June–Sept. AE, DC, MC, V. Closed Nov.–Feb.
28. Very Expensive.*

★ **Foley's.** What appears to be a simple front-parlor restaurant
behind a small bar with an open fire is in fact a warren of small
rooms decorated with half-paneled walls, stained glass, and
Tiffany lamps. The food is far superior to the decor; chef Carol
Buckley, daughter of the original owners, trained in a superior
French restaurant, and it shows. Typical dishes include roulade of trout stuffed with prawn mousse and grilled T-bone
steak with garlic butter, accompanied by superb al dente vegetables. The chef's sauces make generous use of superior Irish
cream and butter. The wine list offers over 200 choices, and a
pianist entertains during the summer months. *23 High St., Killarney, Co. Kerry, tel. 064/31217. Reservations advised mid-
June–Sept. AE, DC, MC, V. Moderate.*

Gaby's Seafood. The tiled floors, pine booths, and red gingham
cloths with matching lampshades at this town-center restaurant help create a cheerful, informal bistro atmosphere. The
small dining room is usually crowded because of the good seafood. Try the seafood mosaic (seven or eight kinds of fresh fish
in a cream-and-wine sauce) or lobster Gaby (shelled, boiled in a
cream-and-cognac sauce, and served back in the shell). *17 High
St., Killarney, Co. Kerry, tel. 064/32519. Reservations advised. AE, DC, MC, V. Closed Mon. lunch, Sun., and mid-
Dec.–mid-Mar. Moderate.*

Sheila's. Sheila's has fed the people of Killarney and its visitors
for more than 30 years, and it was recently handed down from
mother to daughter. Situated in the town center, it is brightly
lighted and simply furnished with stripped pine tables and red
paper mats. The unpretentious menu features such Irish specials as corned beef with cabbage and Irish stew (Kerry lamb

stewed with barley, carrots, onion, and potatoes). In a town bedeviled by tourist traps, this friendly spot offers excellent value for the money. *75 High St., Killarney, Co. Kerry, tel. 064/31270. Reservations advisable in high season. Wine license only. MC, V. Inexpensive.*

Lodging   **Europe.** The combination of a secluded lakeside location (a five-minute drive from town) and luxurious but unfussy decor gives this modern five-story hotel the edge over its competitors. Almost all the bedrooms feature solid pine trim, a lake view, and a private balcony. The spacious lounges and lobbies are rather large and impersonal, but they do have picture windows overlooking the lake and mountains and an imaginative display of old carved timber and valuable antiques. The sports facilities, including an Olympic-size pool, are among the best and most up-to-date in the district. *Killorglin Rd., Fossa, Killarney, Co. Kerry, tel. 064/31900. 176 rooms with bath. Facilities: indoor pool, sauna, gymnasium, tennis court, fishing, horseback riding, 2 restaurants, 2 bars. AE, DC, MC, V. Closed Nov.–Feb. Very Expensive.*

Killarney Great Southern. Built in 1854 just across from the railway station, this three-story building covered with creeping plants is a relic of a past age. In the main section, the high-ceilinged bedrooms feature tall Georgian-style windows and some antiques; rooms in the new wing lack character by comparison, but they all have garden views. The lobby is ennobled by Grecian pillars and large gilt mirrors; blue velvet armchairs surround an open fire. The Victorian-style cocktail bar, a total anachronism, has Persian rugs on its stripped-pine floor, spoon-back bar stools, and an open fire, but it is typical of the slightly faded elegance and informal atmosphere of this much-loved institution. *Killarney, Co. Kerry, tel. 064/31262. 180 rooms with bath. Facilities: indoor pool, sauna, tennis court, 2 restaurants, bar. AE, DC, MC, V. Closed Jan. and Feb. Very Expensive.*

★ **Cahernane.** This 1887 lakeside mansion, set in secluded grounds only a five-minute drive from town, was once the country retreat of the earls of Pembroke. The lobby, with its heavily carved wooden staircase and ornate fireplace, and the lounge, with its shabby Leatherette bucket chairs, retain the slightly gloomy atmosphere of a Victorian hunting lodge. The 12 rooms in the main house offer paneled ceilings, solid teak doors, creaking floorboards, and polished mahogany wardrobes as big as many a modern hotel bedroom. Try room 23 on the third floor, which has an extraordinary window overlooking the lake. The well-concealed modern section, whose bedrooms feature strident purple-and-black contemporary decor, have less charm than the older rooms. *Muckross Rd., Killarney, Co. Kerry, tel. 064/31895. 50 rooms with bath. Facilities: tennis court, 9-hole golf, croquet, horseback riding, 2 restaurants, bar. No TV or direct-dial phones in rooms; no elevator. AE, DC, MC, V. Closed Nov. 1–Feb. Expensive.*

Gleneagle. This lodging will appeal to sociable people who enjoy plenty of action but are unperturbed by bizarre decor; the main house and its three modern bedroom extensions combine clashing decorating styles and an apparently random selection of carpets and drapes. The hotel is on the main road to Kenmare, about a five-minute drive from town. It is popular with both Irish and American visitors, and serves mainly a younger crowd. Evening entertainment includes live music at the Eagles Whistle Singing Pub and, during mid-June through September, disco music and top Irish cabaret acts at the Wings Nightclub. Ask for a bedroom in the newest wing, which has a lake view; the rooms are the largest in the hotel, and all have private balconies. *Muckross Rd., Killarney, Co. Kerry, tel. 064/31870. 155 rooms with bath. Facilities: 2 tennis courts, 4 squash courts, practice golf, sauna, indoor pool, bar, restaurant, nightclub. TV in rooms on request. AE, DC, MC, V. Expensive.*

★ **Kathleen's Country House.** Situated on the Tralee road a mile outside town, this imaginatively designed two-story guest house, incorporating traditional slate walls and roofing and large, modern windows, was built in 1979 to owner/manager Kathleen O'Regan-Sheppard's exacting specifications. The rooms are relatively spacious, light, and airy, with wooden trim, bright floral comforters, and matching floral curtains. Everything is spotlessly clean. The small second-floor lounge offers pleasant views of the wooded valley and Killarney Town below. The restaurant serves only fresh produce and organic vegetables. *Tralee Rd., Killarney, Co. Kerry, tel. 064/32810. 15 rooms with bath. Facilities: restaurant (no smoking) for dinner only. Wine license only or BYOB, horseback riding. No credit cards. Moderate.*

Lake. Set well back from the main road opposite the Gleneagle, this vast 1820s house is a mildly eccentric place with a glorious location and excellent lake views. It appeals mainly to visitors from the United Kingdom and Germany. The authentic Victorian decor of the lobby, stairs, and corridors, including heavy wooden banisters and high ceilings, is diminished by the ill-chosen modern furniture, such as plastic stacking chairs in the restaurant and cheap cane tables and chairs in the sun lounge. Try room 169, which offers polished mahogany furniture and a lake view. Rooms in the new wings have stripped oak trim and pretty print drapes, but you still reach them via long creepy corridors. *Muckross Rd., Killarney, Co. Kerry, tel. 064/31035. 65 rooms with bath. Facilities: tennis court, fishing, bar, restaurant. TV in rooms on request. No elevator. AE, DC, MC, V. Closed Dec.–Mar. Moderate.*

★ **Arbutus.** Run by the friendly Buckley family since it was built more than 60 years ago, this is a good budget hotel in the town center; it is a short step from the bus and train station and a three-minute walk from the main shopping and dining area. The lobby has an open fire, and the bar is popular with locals. The rooms in the new second-story section are recommended for the space and recent furnishings. *College St., Killarney, Co. Kerry, tel. 064/31037. 36 rooms with bath. Facilities: bar, restaurant. No elevator. AE, DC, MC, V. Inexpensive.*

East Avenue. This centrally located mock-timber building dating from 1978 offers a better degree of comfort and cleanliness than many other older hotels nearby. It also has conference and banquet facilities for up to 300 people and holds popular disco evenings every weekend. The cheerful rooms offer gray, blue, and pink decor and white woodwork; the quietest ones are situated in the new (1989) section, which has been well soundproofed. *East Ave., Killarney, Co. Kerry, tel. 064/32522. 25 rooms with bath. Facilities: 3 bars, restaurant (lunch, summer only), disco; no TV or direct-dial phones in rooms. AE, DC, MC, V. Inexpensive.*

Linden House. On a busy road just off the main street, this family-run guest house is a plain, functional 1960s suburban home with uninspired olive-green drapes and carpeting and plywood decor; however, it offers an excellent value among the more inexpensive hotels. Its clientele consists mainly of independent travelers from Ireland, Europe, and the United States. The quietest rooms are located in the back. The optional evening meal is a substantial, home-cooked affair. *New Rd., Killarney, Co. Kerry, tel. 064/31379. 20 rooms with bath. Facilities: restaurant (wine license only) for dinner only. V. Closed Dec. and Jan. Inexpensive.*

Killorglin

Dining   **Nick's Seafood and Steak.** Owner/chef Nick Foley trained as a veterinary surgeon but finds life in the kitchen more congenial. The old stone town house has a bar-cum-dining room at street level and a quieter dining room on the floor above. Seasonal specials include seafood and game; Foley is known for his cockle-and-mussel soup. In winter, sample the haunch of Kerry venison in red-wine and juniper sauce. All vegetables are grown locally. *Main St., Killorglin, Co. Kerry, tel. 066/61219. Reservations advised. DC, MC, V. Bar food only at lunch. Closed Dec. 24–26. Moderate.*

Kinsale

Dining   **Blue Haven.** This tastefully decorated old town house has received international acclaim for its seafood. Inexpensive bar lunches are served in the lounge bar, the patio, and the conservatory, which are all decorated with swagged curtains, hanging plants, and nautical brass. The quiet, pastel-colored restaurant overlooks a floodlit garden whose fountain is adorned by cherubs. For dinner, choose between something traditional, such as lobster thermidor or beef *en croute,* or something more unusual, such as the chef's special seafood chow mein. There are also 10 moderately priced guest bedrooms. *3 Pearse St., Kinsale, Co. Cork, tel. 021/772209. Reservations advised. AE, DC, MC. Expensive.*

★   **The Vintage.** This charming, front-parlor restaurant, hidden away in a narrow back street one minute from the center of town, is the outstanding one of its kind. It is patronized equally by discerning locals and celebrities. The original front room has been extended without losing the impression that you are dining in a chic, antique-filled private home. The Swiss-trained owner, Michael Riess, is personally responsible for what comes out of the kitchen, while his Irish wife, Marie, tends the front of the house. Hot oysters in a sauce of dry white wine, cream, and sorrel, and guinea fowl with red cabbage and apples are among the unusual specialties on the sophisticated international menu. *Main St., Kinsale, Co. Cork, tel. 021/772502. Reservations advised. AE, DC, MC, V. Dinner only. Closed Sun. in winter, 2 weeks in Nov., 3 weeks in Jan.–Feb. Expensive.*

Jim Edwards. One of the most succesful pub/restaurants in Ireland, this place is renowned for the quality of its steaks and seafood. The restaurant is unpretentiously decorated with dark wood tables, dark-green place mats, and red carpets and drapes. The staff, under the personal supervision of the owner and his wife, is friendly and efficient. Portions tend to be exceptionally generous, and children are welcome. Recommended dishes include the fricassee of seafood and the succulent chargrilled local steak fillet. (The separate bar serves inexpensive fare.) *Market Quay, Kinsale, Co. Cork, tel. 021/772541. Reservations advised weekends and summer. AE, DC, MC, V. Closed Tues. dinner, mid-Nov.–mid-Mar. Moderate.*

Max's Wine Bar. More a small, chic restaurant than a wine bar, this establishment is run impeccably by owner Wendy Tisdall. In the low-beamed main room is a variety of small antique tables with equally varied chairs and benches. At the back is a small, flower-filled conservatory. Most menu choices can be ordered as either starters or main courses. Salads, which are not generally taken seriously in the southwest, are especially good here, as is the home-made soup. Mussels in garlic breadcrumbs and salmon in sorrel sauce are among the seafood choices. *Main St., Kinsale, Co. Cork, tel. 021/772443. Reservations advised PM. MC, V. Closed Nov. 1–Dec. 7 and Dec. 24–Feb. 28. Moderate.*

Lodging **Acton's.** Kinsale's biggest hotel is constantly being renovated but never seems to get it right. It has an ideal seafront location on the town pier, but be sure to specify a room with a sea view: The other side overlooks a noisy back street. Although the rooms offer the typical comforts of a modern hotel, they tend to be a bit cramped. The bar and lobby are subject to invasions from conference groups, bus tours, and weddings, as well as jazz buffs attending the very popular Sunday-brunch jazz sessions. *Pier Rd., Kinsale, Co. Cork, tel. 021/772135. 55 rooms with bath. Facilities: indoor pool, sauna, gymnasium, bar, restaurant. AE, DC, MC, V. Expensive.*

★ **Scilly House.** Californian Karin Young has turned this lovely Georgian house set in an acre of mature gardens into a country inn, right on the edge of town opposite the Spaniard Inn. All the rooms offer wonderful views of the town, the harbor, and Charles Fort. They feature colonial furniture and old American quilts on the walls alongside Karin's watercolors. All the rooms are clean and fresh, with a restrained pink-and-white floral motif. In the evenings, host Bill Skelly often leads a sing-along around the grand piano in the library. *Scilly, Kinsale, Co. Cork, tel. 021/772413. 7 rooms with bath. Facilities: wine bar, evening meal by arrangement. Wine license only. MC, V. Closed mid-Nov.–early April. Moderate.*

Trident. This modern low rise on the water's edge is popular with visitors who come to Kinsale for deep-sea fishing—mainly all-male Dutch or English groups. The cinderblock modern rooms feature tweed curtains and drapes and large windows overlooking the inner harbor. The Fisherman's Bar is a congenial spot for conversation between the locals and visiting anglers. *Pier Head, Kinsale, Co. Cork, tel. 021/772301. 46 rooms with bath. Facilities: restaurant, bar, deep-sea fishing. AE, DC, MC, V. Moderate.*

White House. Six comfortable bedrooms are available above this popular bar/restaurant in the town center. They all feature brass bedsteads, matching pink-and-white comforters and curtains, and pine bathroom trim. The friendly atmosphere and good value make it a popular place with those in the know, so you'll need to book well in advance for weekends and the summer. *Pearse St., Kinsale, Co. Cork, tel. 021/772125. 6 rooms with bath. Facilities: bar, restaurant. MC, V. Inexpensive.*

Limerick

Dining **De la Fontaine.** Only a discreet black awning indicates the existence of this restaurant, which sits atop a former warehouse in the city center, a short walk to the east of O'Connell Street (turn right onto Roches Street). It offers both a cozy ambience and authentic French "cuisine moderne." The dining room, graced with pretty floral napery and heated by a glowing gas fire, has a high-pitched oak-beamed ceiling. The cooking is chef/owner Alain Bras's interpretation of nouvelle cuisine; recommended dishes include marinated salmon with dill and chicken breast stuffed with a julienne of vegetables in orange and Dubonnet sauce. The restaurant also offers a good wine list. *12 Gerald Griffin St., Limerick, tel. 061/44461. Reservations advised. Wine license only. V. Closed Sun. Moderate.*

Jasmine Palace. Since opening in 1988, this Cantonese restaurant has become one of the most fashionable in town with both old and young sophisticates, possibly because it's the only decent place where you can eat late (last orders at midnight). The large upper-floor room on the busy main street is furnished with a plush carpet, generous-size tables, and divisions of potted plants to create some privacy amid the busy surroundings. Besides the usual fixed-price dinners, the restaurant offers an excellent sizzling chicken and a very good Cantonese roast duck. *O'Connell Mall, O'Connell St., Limerick, tel. 061/412484. Reservations advised. AE, DC, MC, V. Wine license only. Moderate.*

Lodging

★ Jury's. Built around a garden overlooking the Shannon, this modern steel-and-glass hotel offers a quiet location only a four-minute walk from the traffic-filled city center. The bright, airy lobby and lounges are decorated with hanging greenery. Limericks Bar is a popular meeting place for local Yuppies. Although the rooms have painted concrete walls, they are all spacious and feature floor-to-ceiling picture windows overlooking either the interior garden or the river. *Ennis Rd., Limerick, tel. 061/327777. 95 rooms with bath. Facilities: indoor pool, sauna, Jacuzzi, steam room, gymnasium, tennis court, fishing, bar, coffee shop, restaurant. AE, DC, MC, V. Expensive.*

George. Founded in 1820 as the Royal George, this unpretentious hotel is a landmark in Limerick's city center, although its facade has been brutally modernized. It is probably best known these days for the Glory Hole Pub, which presents Irish music nightly. Rooms have also been modernized, but in a more tasteful way than the facade; they are plain but comfortable with white melamine trim. *O'Connell St., Limerick, tel. 061/414566. 54 rooms with bath. Facilities: 2 restaurants, 2 bars, nightclub. AE, DC, MC, V. Moderate.*

★ Glentworth. A large glass sun lounge dominates the facade of this modern city-center hotel just one block away from O'Connell Street. It is a friendly, practical place to stay, only a few minutes' walk from the bus and rail stations. The Music Bar and Niteclub attract a lively young crowd. Guests can use sporting facilities (swimming, tennis, a gym) at the nearby Thomond College on request. The rooms, decorated in unadventurous tones of beige, are a little small, but they are more than adequate for the price range. *Glentworth St., Limerick, tel. 061/413822. 61 rooms with bath. Facilities: 2 restaurants, 3 bars, nightclub. AE, DC, MC, V. Inexpensive.*

Mallow

Lodging Longueville House. A large early 18th-century house with Victorian wings and a magnificent conservatory, Longueville is an imposing edifice from the outside, with symmetrical two-story wings flanking the classic three-story central section featuring a porch supported by four pillars. The vast drawing rooms overlook the tranquil lawns of the estate (which is on the Blackwater River); they are decorated with large gilt-framed mirrors and oil paintings, and have a stately elegance. The bedrooms are comfortable and filled with antiques; the best rooms are the high-ceilinged ones on the first-story front. The President's Room restaurant serves highly acclaimed French-Irish cuisine. In summer it is possible, weather permitting, to dine in the magnificent conservatory. Don't forget to sample a glass of fruity white wine from the Longueville vineyard, which is believed to be the only commercial vineyard in Ireland. Mallow is at the crossroads of the Cork–Limerick and Waterford–Killarney roads, within an hour's drive of all four towns. *Mallow, Co. Cork, tel. 022/47156. 16 rooms with bath. Facilities: fishing, restaurant (jacket and tie required), bar. AE, DC, MC, V. Closed Dec. 21–Mar. 1. Very Expensive.*

Parknasilla

Lodging **Parknasilla Great Southern.** A porter in a frock coat and striped gray pants typifies the elegant and slightly stuffy turn-of-the-century atmosphere of this grand old hotel. Previous guests include General de Gaulle, Princess Grace, and George Bernard Shaw, who wrote much of *Saint Joan* while staying here. Although some rooms are a bit plain, they have been tastefully decorated in soft pinks and blues. The sheltered coastal location and excellent sporting facilities make it an ideal retreat. *Parknasilla, near Sneem, Co. Kerry, tel. 064/45122. 85 rooms with bath. Facilities: bar, restaurant (jacket and tie required), tennis court, indoor saltwater pool, sauna, horseback riding, sailing, windsurfing, waterskiing, fishing, golf. AE, DC, MC, V. Closed Nov.–mid-Mar. Very Expensive.*

Quin

Lodging **Ballykilty Manor.** A modest Georgian house on 50 acres along the River Rine, this is a handy stopover if you're heading for or returning from the west. It is located 16 km (10 mi) from Shannon and 10 km (6 mi) from Ennis. The renovated rooms feature some antique pieces; ask for a room at the front of the house overlooking the lawn and the ruins of 15th-century Quin Abbey. *Quin, Co. Clare, tel. 065/25627. 11 rooms with bath. Facilities: restaurant, bar, fishing, pitch and putt, horseback riding and hunting by arrangement. AE, DC, MC, V. Moderate.*

Shannon

Lodging For lodging convenient to Shannon Airport, *see* also listings for Adare, Limerick, and Quin, above, and Ennis and Newmarket-on-Fergus, Chapter 8.

Shannon Great Southern. This pleasant modern low rise is conveniently located just across from the main terminal at Shannon Airport, making it an ideal first or last stopping place for transatlantic travelers. Try an Irish coffee in the circular bar overlooking the river; the drink was invented at Shannon Airport to fortify passengers on the fueling stopover that was inevitable in the early days of aviation. The bland yet comfortable rooms have unexceptional contemporary hotel decor. *Shannon Airport, Co. Clare, tel. 061/61122. 118 rooms with bath. Facilities: restaurant, bar. Moderate.*

Skibbereen

Dining　**West Cork Hotel.** Sometimes, plain cooking (just like Ma's) is just what you're in the mood for; this busy, family-run hotel is the place to find it. Forgive the vagaries of the decor, which range from fake Louis XV to nondescript modern, and concentrate on the vast portions of roast meat, potatoes, and vegetables, which are served by attentive waitresses. At dinner, hearty eaters will enjoy the mixed grill. *Bridge St., Skibbereen, Co. Cork, tel. 028/21277. Reservations advised for parties of more than 4. AE, DC, MC, V. Inexpensive.*

Tralee

Dining　**Chez Jean Marc.** Aiming for Parisian sophistication in the depths of Kerry is not easy, but this chef's generous interpretation of nouvelle cuisine comes fairly close. The small, cozy room features a pastel pink-and-green decor and an open fire. Some recommended specialties are duck off the bone in caramel and sherry sauce, and Dover sole fillets with crab and salmon mousse in a creamy Riesling sauce. *29 Castle St., Tralee, Co. Kerry, tel. 066/21377. Reservations advised. Dinner only; closed Sun. DC, MC, V. Moderate.*

★　**Skillet.** This is a friendly, relaxed bistro, with contemporary paintings, low beams, and red-and-white-check place mats. Backpackers and a generally young crowd are attracted by the generous portions and the low prices. Vegetarian lasagna and pan-fried trout with almonds are regular favorites. *Barrack La., Tralee, Co. Kerry, tel. 066/24561. No reservations necessary. Closed Sun. MC, V. Inexpensive.*

Lodging　**Ballyseede Castle.** Located 3 km (2 mi) east of Tralee on the main Killarney road, this former Fitzgerald Castle is approached through an impressive granite gateway. Within easy reach of four of the best courses in the region, it's popular with golfers. Victorian additions complement this imposing three-story castle. The individually decorated rooms have been generously furnished with antiques and two magnificent drawing rooms with ornamental plasterwork and marble fireplaces complete the picture. Try the Yeats room, which is one of the fanciest. *Tralee, Co. Kerry, tel. 066/25799. 13 rooms, 10 with bath. Facilities: restaurant, bar. No TV in rooms. AE, MC, V. Expensive (Moderate, if you take a room without bath).*

Brandon. This five-story modern hotel in the center of town is not especially exciting, but it is the only place in Tralee with a pool and a fitness center, and, unlike some of its competition, it's clean and well-run. The decent-size rooms are furnished plainly, with uninspiring urban views. The restaurant is reputable. Rates shoot up during the Rose of Tralee Festival (late August) and the Listowel races (third week in September). *Princes St., Tralee, Co. Kerry, tel. 066/23333. 154 rooms with bath. Facilities: indoor pool, sauna, steam room, gymnasium, restaurant, 2 bars. AE, DC, MC, V. Expensive.*

Waterville

Dining　**The Huntsman.** Locals agree that this is the best eatery in town, in spite of the overwhelming bordellolike decor: bright-red carpets, red chairs, and lampshades that tint the light red as well. The specialty here is fresh, plainly cooked fish: lobsters from the tank broiled and served with roe, salmon hollandaise, and scampi Newburg. *Waterville, Co. Kerry, tel. 0667/4124. Reservations advised. AE, DC, MC, V. Open daily until the end of Oct.; weekends only off-season. Moderate.*

Lodging　**Butler Arms.** The white castellated towers at the corners of this imposing but architecturally undistinguished hotel provide a familiar landmark on the Ring. The building has been in the same family for three generations; it has a regular clientele, predominantly male, who come back year after year for the excellent fishing and/or golf facilities nearby. It was a favorite base for Charlie Chaplin. Although the accommodations are neither smart nor chic, the solid comfort of the rambling old lounges with open turf fires is highly conducive to both conversation and relaxation. *Waterville, Co. Kerry, tel. 0667/4144. 27 rooms with bath. Facilities: restaurant, 2 bars, tennis court, deep-sea and freshwater angling, horseback riding. AE, DC, MC, V. Closed Oct. 12–Easter. Expensive.*

The Arts and Nightlife

The Arts

Arts Centers/　Some of Ireland's finest contemporary painters live and work in
Galleries　the Southwest—Pauline Bewick, Tim Goulding, Cormac Boydell, Barrie Cooke, and Maria Simonds-Gooding among them—but they often choose to exhibit mainly in Dublin and abroad. You may find some of the above artists' prints at the places mentioned below, but the bulk of the work on display is priced moderately and by lesser-known local artists, some of whom, no doubt, have a big future.

Cork Arts Society (16 Lavitt's Quay, Cork, tel. 021/277749) has a representative selection of fairly conservative oils and watercolors by local artists, all of which are for sale. For more adventurous work in all media, take a look at the **West Cork Arts Center** (North St., Skibbereen, tel. 028/22090), where works are also for sale. In Limerick, don't miss the **Riverrun Gallery** (Honan's Quay, tel. 061/40277), probably Ireland's leading provincial commercial gallery. Offbeat exhibits can also be found at the **Triskel Arts Center** (Tobin St., off S. Main St., Cork, tel. 021/272022) and the **Belltable Arts Center** (69 O'Connell St., Limerick, tel. 061/319866). **J & R Forrester** (83 N. Main St., Bandon, tel. 023/41360) has a small gallery above its crafts shop showing well-selected, reasonably priced works.

A thriving community of ceramic artists resides in the Southwest (*see* Shopping, Irish Crafts, above). For a list and location map of potters who welcome visitors, drop in at or phone **J & R Forrester** (*see* above).

Film　Aside from the Cork Film Festival in Cork City, held annually in mid-September (details from the **Triskel Arts Center,** *see* Arts Centers/Galleries, above), the Southwest is not a good place for movie buffs. Such screens as there are are dominated

by movies for the teenage market. If you want to catch up on
the latest horror films, check the listings in the *Cork Examiner*
or the *Limerick Leader*.

Theater   **Cork Opera House** (Lavitt's Quay, Cork, tel. 021/270022) is the
city's major hall for touring productions and variety acts.
Smaller productions are staged at the **Everyman Palace**
(MacCurtain St., Cork, tel. 021/501673), where the ornate Victorian interior has recently been restored.

The **Triskel Arts Center** in Cork and the **Belltable Arts Center** in
Limerick (*see* Arts Centers/Galleries, above) have small audi-
toriums for one-person shows and experimental works.

In Tralee, try to catch the **National Folk Theater of Ireland
(Siamsa Tíre)**. Language is no barrier to this colorful entertainment, which re-creates traditional rural life through music,
mime, and dance. *Godfrey Pl., Tralee, tel. 066/23055. Admission: £4 adults, £3 children. Shows July–Aug., Mon.–Sat.;
May, June, and Sept., every Tues. and Thurs. at 8:30.*

Nightlife

Medieval Banquets   Most first-time visitors will not want to miss the medieval banquets held at the Bunratty and Knappogue castles. Both events
cater largely to overseas visitors, many of them on organized
tours; they will have little appeal for independent travelers in
search of "the real Ireland." Medieval banqueting may not be
authentic, but it is fun. At Bunratty, you'll be welcomed by
Irish colleens in 15th-century dress who bear the traditional
bread of friendship; you are led off to a honey-and-mead reception. Before sitting down at the long tables in the candlelighted
great hall, you don a bib: You'll need it, because you'll be eating
the four-course meal medieval style—with your fingers! The
serving wenches take time out to sing a few ballads or pluck the
strings of a harp. This warmhearted evening of Irish hospitality can be taken in the lighthearted spirit in which it is offered.
These banquets are so popular that they must be booked as far
in advance as possible. *Bookings for both Bunratty and
Knappogue can be made by calling 061/360788. Tickets, including four-course meal, wine, mead, and entertainment:
£27.90. Nightly (subject to demand) at 5:45 and 8:45.*

If you can't get a place for a banquet, the next best thing is a
Ceilí at Bunratty Folk Park; this program features traditional
Irish dance and song and a meal of Irish stew, soda bread, and
apple pie. *Tel. 061/360788. Cost: £22.90, including wine. May–
Sept., 5:45 and 9 PM.*

Pubs, Cabarets,   Pub entertainment is the key to the Southwest's nightlife and
and Discos   offers better value, variety, and authenticity than the package
market–oriented Irish cabaret options. If the music is in the
main bar, you'll seldom have to pay a cover charge. Dancing to a
fully amplified band in a room adjacent to the bar costs anywhere from £1.50 to £8, depending on the performers. During
mid-June through September, you'll find musical entertainment most nights; during other seasons, Thursday through
Sunday are the busiest times. Dingle is the best place in the region for traditional Irish music; elsewhere, pubs and clubs offer
a mix of traditional, Irish, and folk ballads; country and rock
classics; and a touch of New Orleans jazz in Cork and Kinsale.
Spontaneous music sessions can take off at any time, especially

on the Dingle Peninsula; elsewhere, performances usually begin around 9. Discos and nightclubs are usually attached to hotels or bars; they are open from 10:30 PM until 1 or 2 AM. Expect to pay a £2.50–£5 cover fee.

Cork City **Mojo's** (George's Quay, tel. 021/311786) specializes in live rhythm and blues; **De Lacy House** (74 Oliver Plunkett St., tel. 021/270074) attracts a young crowd for rock and folk gigs. Live music (rock and nostalgia) is featured at **Rearden's Mill** (25 Washington St., tel. 021/27169). The **Stradbally Village** (Grand Parade Hotel, tel. 021/274391) offers traditional music and dancing nightly in an indoor reconstructed village. In the same hotel, you'll find live rock music at **Chandra's Nightclub.** **Mangan's Brasserie** (Carey's La., tel. 021/276531) is the leading night spot for the over-25s to wine, dine, and dance.

County Cork Kinsale and Clonakilty are the liveliest towns for nightlife. Check out the **Spaniard Inn** (Scilly, tel. 021/772436) for live rock and folk groups. **The Shanakee** (Market St., Kinsale, no tel.) is renowned in the area for nightly sing-alongs and ballad sessions; dancing workshops are given every Thursday. The **Bacchus Brasserie** (Guardwell, tel. 021/772382) offers dining and dancing to the over-25s. Jazz buffs will enjoy **Creole** (Pearse St., Kinsale, tel. 021/774109), which features live New Orleans jazz sessions in summer.

Tigh de Barra in Clonakilty (Pearse St., tel. 023/33381) is a focal point for West Cork's traditional musicians, many of whom live in the nearby Irish-speaking area. **Dunmore House** (Muckross, Clonakilty, tel. 023/33352) features local artists in cabaret on Tuesdays and a family night with dancing and talent competitions on Thursdays, July to September.

Killarney Singing bars are popular in Killarney, where a professional leads the singing and encourages audience participation and solos. Try **The Laurels** (Main St., tel. 064/31149). Killarney is strict on "Over 21s, Neat Dress Essential," and this is the rule at the **Kenmare Rooms** in the East Avenue Hotel (East Ave., tel. 064/32522), which offers a live cabaret with big names in the summer. The charge here includes admission to **Revelles Disco. Scott's Hotel Gardens** (College Rd., tel. 064/31060) and **Gleneagles** (Muckross Rd., tel. 064/31870) are the summer hot spots, offering big-name cabaret acts, singing bars, and discos.

Kerry Try the **Kingdom Bar** (Kenmare, tel. 064/41361) for traditional music; for folk music, head for the **Strand Hotel** (Waterville, tel. 0667/4248). Just about every bar on the Dingle Peninsula offers music every night in July and August—or so it seems, if you're looking for a quiet one! **O'Flaherty's** (Bridge St., Dingle, no tel.) is a fine place for traditional music. For sing-along and dancing, try **An Reált—The Star Bar** (The Pier, Dingle, no tel.). In Tralee, ballad sessions are more popular than traditional Irish music. If you're looking for the latter, call 066/25965—the *seisún* (having a good time) hotline—which will tell you where the action is. For ballad sessions, check out **Kirby's Brogue Inn** (Rock St., no tel.) and **Jim's Cottage Bar** (Edward St., no tel.). **Horan's Hotel** (Clash St., tel. 066/21933) has disco music and cabaret acts nightly during July and August, on weekends only during the off-season.

Limerick **Foley's Bar** (Lower Shannon St., tel. 061/48783) has a ballad or traditional session every night except Wednesday. Traditional music is featured at **Nancy Blague's Pub** (19 Denmark St., tel.

519 M.P.H.

190 M.P.H.

75 M.P.H.

0 M.P.H.

WE LET YOU SEE EUROPE AT YOUR OWN PACE.

Regardless of your personal speed limits, Rail Europe offers everything to get you over, around and through anywhere you want in Europe. For more information, call your travel agent or **1-800-4-EURAIL.**

Rail Europe

061/46327) on Tuesday and Sunday. The **Glory Hole Bar** (George Hotel, O'Connell St., tel. 061/44566) has sessions every night, and there is late-night disco at **Tropics** (also in the George Hotel) Friday through Sunday. More nighttime entertainment can be found weekends at **Whispers Nightclub** (Cruise's Royal Hotel, O'Connell St., tel. 061/44977).

8 The West

Cliffs of Moher, The Burren,
Galway City, County Mayo

*By Alannah
Hopkin*

As any Dubliner will tell you, the West is distinctively different from the rest of Ireland. Within Ireland, the West refers to the region that lies west of the River Shannon; most of this area falls within the old Irish province of Connaught. The coast of this region is situated at the western extremity of Europe, facing its nearest neighbors in North America across 3,200 km (2,000 mi) of Atlantic Ocean. While the East, the Southwest, and the North were influenced by either Norman, Scots, or English settlers, the West escaped systematic resettlement and, with the exception of the walled town of Galway, remained purely Irish in language, social organization, and general outlook for far longer than the rest of the country. The land in the West, predominantly mountains and bogs, did not immediately tempt the conquering barons. Oliver Cromwell was among those who found the place thoroughly unattractive, and he gave the Irish chieftains who would not conform to English rule the choice of going "to Hell or Connaught."

It was not until the late 18th century, when better transport improved communications, that the West started to experience the so-called foreign influences that had already Europeanized the rest of the country. The West was, in effect, dragged out of the 16th century and into the 19th. You will notice that all buildings of interest in the region date either from before the 17th century or from the late 18th century onwards.

Today, many people maintain that the West is the most typically Irish part of the country. It features the highest concentration of Irish-speaking communities and the best traditional musicians in the Republic. Many residents still live on small farms rather than in towns and villages (towns were unknown in pre-Christian Irish society); especially in winter, the smell of turf fires still pervades the region.

As in the Southwest, the population of the West was decimated by famine in the mid-19th century and by mass emigration from then until the 1950s. A major factor in the region's recovery from economic depression has been the attraction to visitors of its sparsely populated mountain landscape and long, indented coastline with its many lakes and rivers. Tourism's development, however, has been mercifully low-key. Apart from a seaside promenade and fun palace at Salthill, just outside Galway, the area has seen no major investment in public amenities. Instead, additional land has been acquired for the Connemara National Park. Despite the sufficient number of top-class accommodations and the many charmingly converted country-house hotels, nothing intrudes on the simple attractions of the region's rugged, unspoiled countryside. The existence of some of the best angling in Europe on the West's rivers, lakes, and seas accounts for many regular visitors. Most holiday cottages are built according to the model of the traditional thatched cabin. The residents of the West have encouraged the revival of such cottage industries as knitting, weaving, and woodworking; the provision of bed-and-breakfast in existing homes; and informal sessions of traditional music in small bars. The lack of razzmatazz makes the West an ideal destination for travelers on a tight budget. The place comes alive between June and September. April, May, and October are good times for an off-peak visit. Outside these months many places will be closed; nightlife options and restaurant choices become limited. During the winter, weather can be harsh, with gales and rain sweeping in day after day from the Atlantic.

Essential Information

Arriving and Departing by Plane

Airports and Airlines The West's most convenient international airport is **Shannon** (tel. 061/61444), 25 km (16 mi) east of Ennis in the Southwest (*see* Essential Information, Chapter 7). **Carnmore Airport** (tel. 091/52874), near Galway City, and **Horan International Airport** (tel. 094/67222), at Knock in County Mayo, are used mainly for internal fights, with steadily increasing U.K. traffic. A small airport for internal traffic only is also located at **Knockrowen**, Castlebar, in County Mayo (tel. 094/22853). Flying time from Dublin is 25–30 minutes to all airports.

Flights from the United States No scheduled flights run from the United States to Galway or Knock; use Shannon Airport (*see* Essential Information, Chapter 7).

Flights from the United Kingdom **Aer Lingus** offers daily flights from London's Heathrow Airport to Galway and Knock via Dublin; the trip takes about two hours. **Ryanair** has at least one flight a day to Galway from London's Stansted Airport; flying time is 70 minutes. The company also flies to Knock once a week from Birmingham, Coventry, and Bradford and daily from London's Luton Airport; flying time is 80 minutes.

Between the Airport and the Cities Carnmore Airport is located 6½ km (4 mi) from Galway City. No regular bus service is available from the airport to Galway, but most flight arrivals are taken to Galway Rail Station in the city center by an airline courtesy coach. Inquire when you book. A taxi from the airport to the city center costs about £7.

If you're flying from Dublin to Horan International Airport in Knock, you can pick up your rental car at the airport. Otherwise, inquire at the time of booking about transport to your final destination: no regular bus service is available from Horan International Airport.

Arriving and Departing by Car, Train, and Bus

By Car Leave Dublin by the N4, picking up the N6 in Kinnegad for Galway City. The 204-km (127-mi) journey between Dublin and Galway takes about three hours. From Cork City take the N20 through Mallow and the N21 to Limerick City, picking up the N18 Ennis–Galway road in Limerick. The drive from Cork to Galway lasts 209 km (130 mi) and takes about three hours.

From Killarney the shortest and most pleasant route is the N22 to Tralee, then the N69 through Listowel to Tarbert and the ferry across the Shannon Estuary to Killimer in County Clare, joining the N68 in Kilrush, and then picking up the N18 in Ennis. The drive from Killarney to Galway lasts 193 km (120 mi) on this route and takes just under three hours. The ferry leaves Tarbert every hour on the half hour and takes 20 minutes, avoiding a 104-km (65-mi) detour through Limerick City. It costs £6 one-way, £10 round-trip. (Ferries return from Killimer every hour on the hour.)

By Train Galway City, Westport, and Ballina are the main rail stations in the region. For County Clare, travel from Cork City, Killarney Town, or Dublin's Heuston Station to Limerick City (tel. 061/315555) and continue the journey by bus.

Trains for Galway, Westport, and Ballina leave from Dublin's Heuston Station (tel. 01/366222). The journey time to Galway is three hours; to Ballina 3¾ hours; and to Westport 3½ hours. For train passenger inquiries, call 091/62141 in Galway, 096/21011 in Ballina, 098/25253 in Westport.

By Bus **Bus Éireann** operates a variety of Expressway services into the region from Dublin, Cork City, and Limerick City to Ennis, Galway City, Westport, and Ballina, the principal depots in the region. Expect bus rides to last about one hour longer than the time by car.

For bus passenger inquiries, call 01/366111 in Dublin, 021/506766 in Cork, and 061/313333 in Limerick.

Getting Around

A car is essential in the West, especially during September through June. Although the main cities of the area are reached easily from the rest of Ireland by rail or bus, transport within the region is sparse and badly coordinated. If a rental car is out of the question, your best option is to make Galway your base and take day tours (available mid-June–Sept.) west to Connemara and south to the Burren, and a day or overnight trip to the Aran Islands. It *is* possible to explore the region by local and intercity bus services, but you will need plenty of time.

By Car The West has good, wide main roads (National Primary Routes) and better-than-average local roads (National Secondary Routes), both known as "N" routes.

However, if you stray off the beaten track on the smaller Regional ("R") or unnumbered routes, particularly in Connemara and County Mayo, you may encounter some hazardous mountain roads. Narrow, steep, and twisty, they are also frequented by untended sheep, cows, and ponies grazing "the long acre" (as the strip of grass beside the road is called) or simply straying in search of greener pastures. If you find a sheep in your path, just sound the horn and the creature will scramble away. A good maxim for these roads is "You never know what's around the next corner." Bear this in mind, and adjust your speed accordingly. Hikers and cyclists constitute an additional hazard on narrow roads in the summer.

Within the Connemara Irish-speaking area, road signs will be in Irish only. The main signs to recognize are Gaillimh (Galway), Rós an Mhíl (Rossaveal), An Teach Doite (Maam Cross), and Sraith Salach (Recess). A good touring map, available locally through newsagents and Tourist Information Offices, will give both Irish and English names where needed.

If you haven't already picked up a rental car at Shannon Airport (*see* Getting Around by Car, Chapter 7), try the following:

Galway City and Vicinity: Avis (tel. 091/68901), **Budget** (tel. 091/66376), **Hertz** (tel. 091/61837), **Johnson and Perrott** (tel. 091/68873), and **Murray's** (tel. 01/62222).

Horan International Airport, Knock: Avis (tel. 094/67252), Murray's (tel. 01/681777), and South County Self Drive (Thrift Rent-a-Car, tel. 01/806005).

By Train Rail transportation is not good within the West. The major destinations of Galway City and Westport/Ballina are situated on different branch lines. Connections can only be made between Galway and the other two cities by traveling inland for about an hour to Athlone (for inquiries, *see* Arriving and Departing by Train, above).

By Bus In July and August, the provincial bus service is augmented by daily services to most resort towns. Outside these months, many coastal towns receive only one or two buses per week. Bus routes are often slow and circuitous, and service can be erratic. A copy of the Bus Éireann timetable (45p from any station) is essential. The main bus stations are located at Ennis (tel. 065/ 24177), Galway City (Ceannt Station, tel. 091/62131), Westport (Railway Station, tel. 098/25253), and Ballina (tel. 096/21657).

By Ferry to the Aran Islands From mid-May to early September, a ferry departs from Galway City Docks at 9:30, 1:30, and 6:30. This ride is the longest sea crossing available—about 48 km (30 mi)—and takes about three hours. It costs £15 round-trip and can be booked at the Aran Ferries desk in the Tourist Information Office (TIO, Victoria Pl., Eyre Sq., tel. 091/63081). The TIO will also arrange bed-and-breakfast accommodations on the islands.

Most people opt for the one-hour crossing (about 16 km/10 mi) from Rossaveal, which is located 32 km (20 mi) west of Galway by car. This ride costs £12 round-trip. The boat ride is arranged by Island Ferries, which has a booking office opposite the TIO on Victoria Place in Galway City (tel. 091/61767). The company provides a coach connection from Galway to Rossaveal. Car parking is free on the quay at Rossaveal. Five sailings a day from Rossaveal are scheduled during the summer months (weather permitting) at 10:30, 12:30, 1:30, 6, and 6:30. Bicycles are transported free, and price discounts are available for families, students, and groups.

If you are heading for Inishere, the smallest island, the shortest crossing is from Doolin in County Clare (*see* Tour 1, below).

Frequent interisland ferries are available in summer months, but tickets are not transferable, so ask the captain of your ferry about his interisland schedule if you plan to visit more than one island; otherwise, your trip can become expensive.

By Plane to the Aran Islands Aer Arann (tel. 091/55437) offers four flights daily on weekdays, and two flights on Saturday and Sunday during July and August. The flights call at all three of the Aran Islands and leave from Connemara Airport (tel. 091/93034) near Galway. The flight takes about 6 minutes and costs £25 round-trip.

For £24, you can fly one-way and travel one-way by boat from the Galway City docks. Ask about other special offers at the time of booking.

Important Addresses and Numbers

Tourist Information The Irish Tourist Board provides free information service, tourist literature, and an accommodations booking service at its Tourist Information Offices (TIOs).

Main Offices **Ennis** (tel. 065/28366), **Galway City** (Victoria Pl., Eyre Sq., tel. 091/63081), **Horan International Airport, Knock** (tel. 094/67247), and **Westport** (tel. 098/25711). These offices are open all year weekdays 9–6 and Saturday 9–1.

Other Offices **Achill** (tel. 098/45384), **Aran Islands (Inishmore)** (tel. 099/61263), **Ballina** (tel. 096/70848), **Castlebar** (tel. 094/21207), **Clifden** (tel. 095/21163), **Cliffs of Moher** (tel. 065/81171), **Kilkee** (tel. 065/56112), **Kilrush** (tel. 065/51047), **Lahinch** (tel. 065/81474), **Lisdoonvarna** (tel. 065/51577), **Salthill** (Galway City, tel. 091/63081), and **Thoor Ballylee** (near Gort, tel. 091/31436). These offices are open July and August only, weekdays 9–6 and Saturday 9–1.

Emergencies **Police, fire,** and **ambulance** in all areas: dial 999 toll-free.

Doctors and Dentists **County Clare: Mid-Western Health Board** (tel. 061/316655); **Counties Galway and Mayo: Western Health Board** (tel. 091/51131).

Pharmacies **Galway: Matt O'Flaherty** (39 Eyre Sq., tel. 091/62927). **Westport: O'Donnell's** (Bridge St., tel. 098/25163).

Guided Tours

Orientation Tours The only full- and half-day guided tours in the region start from Galway. **CIE** offers a choice of full-day tours covering Connemara, the Burren and the Atlantic coast, Westport and Achill Island, Carraroe, and South Connemara (cost of all tours: £9 adults, £4.50 children), and half-day tours to Cong or South Connemara (cost: £6 adults, £3 children). Tours run from mid-June to early September only, with the widest choice available between mid-July and mid-August. Book in advance at Galway City's Ceannt Railway Station (tel. 091/62141) or the Salthill Tourist Information Office (tel. 091/63081), which also serve as departure points.

Galway Tours runs a day tour through Connemara and County Mayo, and another to the Burren in July and August and on certain bank holiday weekends. Tickets can be booked at the Tourist Information Office in Galway City (Victoria Pl., Eyre Sq., tel. 091/63081).

Walking Tours Galway City's **Tourist Information Office** (Victoria Pl., Eyre Sq., tel. 091/63081) has details of walking tours of Galway, which are organized on an occasional basis.

Exploring the West

Allow at least four days for exploring the region, and six days if you aim to visit the Aran Islands and/or Achill Island. Although distances between sites are not great, most of the tours in this chapter use the scenic but slower national secondary routes, on which covering 80 km (50 mi) to 112 km (70 mi) a day is a comfortable target.

Highlights for First-time Visitors

The Burren (*see* Tour 1)
Clifden (*see* Tour 3)
The Cliffs of Moher (*see* Tour 1)

Connemara National Park (*see* Tour 3)
Dun Aengus, Inishmore (*see* Tour 2)
Kylemore Abbey (*see* Tour 3)
Salmon Weir Bridge (*see* Tour 2)
Westport, Clew Bay (*see* Tour 3)

Tour 1: The Burren and Beyond— West Clare to South Galway

Numbers in the margin correspond to points of interest on the West map.

❶ Start in **Ennis,** the county town of County Clare, 25 km (16 mi) west of Shannon Airport on the main road (the N18) to Galway. **Ennis,** a pleasant if physically unremarkable town, is a major crossroads and a convenient stop between the West and the Southwest. It has always fostered traditional music, especially fiddle playing and step dancing (a kind of square dance). The Fleadh Nua festival in Ennis at the end of May attracts both performers and students of Irish music, who sing and dance in a series of concerts, workshops, and lectures.

Two statues in town bear witness to the role the people of Ennis have played in Irish democracy. On a tall limestone column above a massive pediment in the town center stands a statue of Daniel O'Connell (1775–1847), "The Liberator" (*see* Tour 3, Chapter 7), who was a member of Parliament for County Clare between 1828 and 1831, the time at which he was instrumental in bringing about Catholic Emancipation. Outside the Courthouse (in the town park, beside the River Fergus, on the west side of Ennis) stands a larger-than-life bronze statue of Eamon De Valera (1882–1975), who successfully contested the election here in 1917 that launched his political career. Although De Valera was born in the United States, his maternal forebears were from County Clare. He was the dominant figure in Irish politics during this century, serving as prime minister for most of the years from 1937 until 1959, when he resigned as leader of Fianna Fáil, the party he founded; he went on to serve as president until 1973.

From Ennis, the main tour heads for the coast, which has been a playground for many generations of Irish people. If the season or the weather does not favor relaxing on sandy beaches and playing 18-hole golf courses, we suggest you take a shortcut, leaving Ennis on the N85 and joining the tour again at Lahinch, which is 32 km (27 mi) from Ennis.

The main route follows the N68 from Ennis to Kilrush (43 km/27 mi). (Those crossing from County Kerry by the Tarbert–Killimer ferry can join the tour at Kilrush, 5 km/3 mi west of Killimer.) The N68 is a good stretch of relatively straight two-lane highway passing through a thinly populated region of small farms. Many visitors remark on the smallness of the farms in the West, the great majority being between 30 and 100 acres, and some no more than small holdings. In order to make a living, most of these farmers or their spouses (in some cases both) have a second job, such as fishing, running a B&B, or working seasonally. The rest rely on government subsidies or unemployment benefits, but few of them would trade their lives in Western Ireland for more lucrative pursuits elsewhere.

Kilrush is a small market town based on a formal layout dating, like most towns in West Clare, from the mid-19th century. Streets radiate from a large central square, the widest one leading to the harbor and the docks. This plan creates the impression that the town (pop. 3,000) is bigger than it actually is. You'll find pleasant walks and picnic tables in the **Kilrush Woods,** a mature, freely accessible 420-acre forest on the east side of town.

Kilkee, which is 12 km (8 mi) west of Kilrush on the N68, is a popular holiday resort with safe bathing both in the waters along its long sandy beach and in deep rock pools known as Pollock holes, which remain full at low tide. The latter attract scuba divers as well as swimmers. From Kilkee, you can take an excursion to Loop Head Lighthouse on the R487 (about 38 km/24 mi round-trip). Loop Head is at the northern tip of the mouth of the Shannon, the very end of its long estuary.

The main route heads north up the coast on the N67. Sandy beaches and more Pollock holes can be found by taking a left off the main road at any sign that indicates "Strand" and traveling for about 2½ km (1½ mi). The shortcut joins the main tour on the N67 at **Lahinch,** another resort village, which has two 18-hole golf courses. From here, take the R478 for the Cliffs of Moher. For the first time on this coast, the road narrows and starts to climb. It twists past small whitewashed farms and green fields with glimpses of the sea on the horizon.

② The best way to appreciate the magnificent **Cliffs of Moher** is to walk the short distance from the car park to O'Brien's Tower, which is located at the cliffs' highest point. The car park is a favorite spot of performers, and if you're lucky you will find some free entertainment—perhaps step dancers, fiddle players, or even a one-man band. Next to the car park, take a look at the Visitor Center, at which leaflets explain various aspects of the cliffs' natural history, and visitors enjoy a crafts shop and tea room. *Visitor Center, tel. 065/81565. Admission free. Open Mar.–Oct. 26, daily 10–6.*

The cliffs rise vertically along 8 km (5 mi) of coastline, at some points towering 185 meters (600 feet) above the sea. The stratified deposits of five different rock layers can be seen in the striations of the cliff face. The shelves of rock on the cliffs are home to numerous sea birds, including a large colony of puffins. On a clear day the Aran Islands and the mountains of Connemara are visible to the north, while the lighthouse on Loop Head and the mountains of Kerry may be seen to the south.

Follow the R478 from the cliffs inland toward Lisdoonvarna. A detour, signposted on the left as "Roadford/Doolin" on the **③** R479, is a must for music lovers. **Doolin,** a tiny village consisting almost entirely of B&Bs, hostels, and pubs, claims three of the best pubs in Ireland for traditional music (*see* Nightlife, *below*). This village is a magnet for young musicians, some of whom camp out here for the whole summer learning from the resident virtuosos.

On Doolin Pier, about 1½ km (1 mi) outside the village, local fishermen sell their catch fresh off the boat—lobster, crayfish, salmon, and mackerel. From mid-March until October (weather permitting), a regular ferry service takes visitors for a 30-minute ride to Inisheer, the smallest of the Aran Islands (*see*

Tour 2, *below*). *Ferry, tel. 065/77086. Cost (round-trip): £12 adults, £6 children. Over 10 sailings daily mid-Mar.–Oct.*

4 Retrace your route to the R478 and turn left for **Lisdoonvarna,** a spa town featuring several sulfurous and iron-bearing springs with radioactive properties, all containing iodine. The town grew up in the late 19th century to accommodate visitors who wished to "take the waters." Its buildings reflect a mishmash of mock-architectural styles: Scottish baronial, Swiss chalet, Spanish hacienda, and American motel. Lovers of kitsch will find the town delightful, while others may condemn it as tacky.

Lisdoonvarna is the traditional vacationing spot for the West's bachelor farmers, who used to congregate here at harvest time in late September with the vague intention of finding wives. (Irish farmers are notoriously shy with women and reluctant to marry, often postponing the event until their mid- or late-fifties.) This tradition has been resurrected as the Matchmaking Festival, which takes place in Lisdoonvarna during late September and early October. Middle-aged singles dance to the strains of country-and-western bands, and a talent contest is held to find the most eligible bachelor. An increasing number of women from the United States are trying their luck at the festival and are all but guaranteed a good time, if not a husband. By contrast, in July and August, the town is a favorite holiday spot with the Irish under-thirties, who dance the night away in a more contemporary style.

Lisdoonvarna Spa and Bath House has been renovated and is worth a visit if you're curious about health cures. The water offered here for drinking contains iron and magnesia and tastes quite as vile as does most spa water. The bathing water can be enervating but is comparatively pleasant. Electric sulfur baths, massage, and wax baths are available, as well as a sauna and a solarium. The spa complex is on the edge of town in an attractive parkland setting. *Tel. 065/74023. Admission free to complex. Sulfur baths: £5 (book in advance). Open early June–early Oct., daily 10–6.*

Lisdoonvarna is situated in the heart of **The Burren,** and as you travel 16 km (10 mi) north on the N67 toward Ballyvaughan, the landscape becomes rockier and stranger. Instead of Irish green, gray is the prevailing color. The word Burren means "great rock." The Burren consists of fissured limestone known as *karst,* which is exposed in great irregular slabs with deep cracks between them known as pavements. This plateau appears, from a distance, so dry that nothing could grow on it, and its landscape reminds many visitors of the surface of the moon. In fact, underneath the rough, scarred surface of the Burren are spectacular caves, streams, and potholes. "Turloughs"—seasonal lakes that disappear in dry weather—appear on the plateau's surface. In the cracks of the rocks, an amazing variety of wildflowers and plants can be found, which are at their best from mid-May to mid-June. Botanists are particularly intrigued by the cohabitation of Arctic and Mediterranean plants. Many of these plants are so tiny as to be invisible from the car window, so make a point of exploring some of this rocky terrain on foot.

Just outside Ballyvaughan, you'll see a signpost to the right for **5** the **Ailwee Cave,** the only such chamber in the region accessible to those without spelunking expertise. This vast 2-million-year-old cave is illuminated for about 1,000 meters (3,300 feet) and contains an underground river and waterfall. *Tel. 065/ 77036. Admission: £2.70 adults, £1.40 children. Open mid-June–Sept. 1, daily 10–7; Sept. 2–Nov. 1, daily 10–6.*

6 From the cave, return to the R480 and continue south, taking a right after about 16 km (10 mi) on to the R476 for **Kilfenora.** Here, the tiny **Burren Display Center,** a modest audiovisual display with additional exhibits, explains all you'll want to know about The Burren's geology, flora, and archaeology. *Tel. 065/ 88030. Admission: £1.70 adults, £1 children. Open June–Aug., daily 9:30–7:30; Mar. 9–May 31 and Sept.–Oct., daily 10– 5:30.*

Have a look at the tiny church beside the Display Center before leaving. The ruins of a small 12th-century church, once the **Cathedral of St. Fachan,** have been partially restored as a parish church. There are some interesting carvings in the roofless choir, including an unusual life-size skeleton. In a field about 50 meters (165 feet) to the west of the ruins is an elaborately sculpted high cross that is worth examining even though parts of it are badly weathered.

7 Retrace your route on the R476, carrying on for about 16 km (10 mi) to **Corofin.** Here, those in search of their Irish roots will want to visit the **Clare Heritage Center,** which offers a genealogical service and do-it-yourself advice. It also features a display on the history of the West of Ireland in the 19th century, covering culture, traditions, emigration, and famine, as it exposes some grim statistics. In 1841, for example, the population of County Clare was 286,394. Fifty years later, famine and emigration had reduced this number to 112,334, and the population continued to decline, reaching an all-time low of 73,597 in 1956. (It is now heading for the 90,000 mark.) *Tel. 065/27955. Admission: £1.50 adults, 50p children. Open Apr.–Oct., daily 10–6; Nov.–Mar., weekdays 9–5.*

Another site in Corofin that should appeal particularly to archaeology buffs is the **Dysert O'Dea Castle Archaeology Center,** a 15th-century castle on the edge of town, with an exhibition on the antiquities of The Burren. Twenty-five monuments stand within a 1½-km (1-mi) radius of the castle; these date from the Bronze Age to the 19th century, and all of them are described at the center. *Tel. 065/27722. Admission: £1.50 adults, 50p children. Open May–Sept., daily 10–7.*

8 From Corofin, leave The Burren by taking the R460 north for 24 km (15 mi) to Gort; turn left (north) on to the N18. In the center of **Gort** (a dull little town), look out for a sign on the right for **Thoor Ballylee.** Admirers of the poet W.B. Yeats (1865– 1939) will want to take the detour 5 km (3 mi) up the N66 to visit the Norman tower that Yeats bought as a ruin in 1916 for the sum of £35. He repaired it and lived there intermittently until 1929. This handsome stone building beside a tranquil mill stream is now fully restored with Yeats's original decor and furniture. An audiovisual display is available on the Nobel Prize–winning poet and his works. *Tel. 091/31436. Admission: £1.50 adults, 50p children. Open May–Sept., daily 10–6.*

Return to the N18 and continue north for Galway City. Just outside Gort on the left-hand side is **Coole Park,** former location of the home of Yeats's patron, Lady Augusta Gregory (1859–

1932). Once a center for the Irish literary revival, the house fell derelict after her death and was demolished in 1941. The park is now a national forest and wildlife park, with picnic tables. The only reminder of its literary past is the Autograph Tree, a copper beech on which many of Lady Gregory's famous guests carved their initials, including George Bernard Shaw, Sean O'Casey, and Douglas Hyde, the first president of Ireland. *No phone. Car park: £2. Open daily 10–dusk.*

As the road runs farther north you will see fields hedged by dry stone walls made of gray boulders piled on top of one another; mortar is not used in the walls' construction. They are a typical feature of the West of Ireland, as are the long evenings caused by the sun slowly sinking over the Atlantic on the western horizon. As you approach Galway City you will catch an occasional glimpse of the sea on your left. This is Oyster Country, where the famous Galway oyster grows.

⑨ Clarinbridge, 19 km (12 mi) south of Galway City, is the place to stop and sample these shellfish, if there is an "R" in the name of the month of your travels. The new oyster season is launched with an Oyster Festival, a must for mollusk eaters, held annually in and around the town on the last weekend in September. From Clarinbridge, follow the signs for Galway City, which will take you to Eyre Square. Expect a few delays along the way in July and August, when traffic is at its peak.

Tour 2: Galway City and the Aran Islands

⑩ Many Irish people consider **Galway** to be the best city in the Republic. This compact, lively, and informal place possesses a distinctive cosmopolitan charm. Good road and rail links with the capital make Galway and the surrounding region a favorite weekend destination for jaded Dubliners. The city, which has always attracted writers and artists, features two small but internationally acclaimed theater companies (*see* The Arts and Nightlife, below). Its university is a center for Gaelic culture, where many students take their degrees in the Irish language. Galway's predominantly young and well-educated population has attracted several multinational companies to its industrial estates, and the town positively buzzes with energy.

Galway is the largest city in the West of Ireland, with about 37,000 residents; it is situated at the head of Galway Bay, where the River Corrib flows from the Lough down to the sea. Across the wide entrance to Galway Bay lie the three Aran Islands with their distinctive Irish-speaking communities. Galway has always been the chief trading post for the islands, and it is the most practical place from which to organize an excursion to them. If you can possibly make time for even a day trip by air to one of these islands, it will be a unique experience and a topic of conversation long after your visit to Ireland is over. Such a trip will also greatly enhance your understanding of Irish folkways and Gaelic culture.

Galway celebrated the 500th anniversary of its charter as a city in 1984 with a great display of civic pride, which has scarcely abated in the intervening years. The people here have plenty to be proud of. In the early 1980s, Galway was the first city in Ireland to discourage bland, international-style neon and plastic commercial signs and facades by reviving the old Irish tradition of hand-painted wooden shop signs with Gaelic lettering.

The city has been further enhanced by the installation of well-designed modern sculptures, floral hanging baskets, and window boxes.

The founders of Galway were Anglo-Normans who arrived in the mid-13th century and fortified their settlement against "the native Irish," as local chieftains were called. Galway became known as the City of the Tribes because of the dominant role in public and commercial life of the 14 families who founded it. Their names are still common in Galway and elsewhere in Ireland and recur regularly in any account of Irish history and culture: Athy, Blake, Bodkin, Browne, D'Arcy, Dean, Font, French, Kirwan, Joyce, Lynch, Morris, Martin, and Skerret.

Numbers in the margin correspond to points of interest on the Galway City map.

Old Galway is best explored on foot—indeed, in July and August, when the tourist season is at its peak and traffic on its narrow streets becomes heavy, walking is virtually the only way to get around. The major point of orientation for the visitor is **Eyre Square,** the center of the city. The square is dominated on its southeast side by the solid four-story limestone facade of the **Great Southern Hotel** (Eyre Sq., tel. 091/64041), built to coincide with the arrival of the railway in the mid-19th century. The bus station and Ceannt Rail Station are just behind the hotel on Station Road, on the left-hand side as you face the hotel. **The Tourist Information Office** is located on Victoria Place on the right-hand side of the hotel. *Tel. 091/63081. Open weekdays 9–6, Sat. 9–1.*

The grassy central area of Eyre Square is known as **Kennedy Park,** in honor of John F. Kennedy, who visited the city in 1963, five months before his assassination. The park is dominated by a beautiful 6-meter (20-foot) steel sculpture, which stands in the midst of a fountain pool. The work, installed in 1986, takes the form of brown sails that are seen on the traditional sailing boats, known as Galway hookers; these boats were used until the early part of this century to carry turf, provisions, and cattle across Galway Bay and out to the Aran Islands. The genial stone figure with a pipe, seated beside the steel sculpture, is Padraic O'Conaire, a pioneer of the Irish-language revival at the turn of the century. So ascetic was this great storyteller that when he died in a Dublin hospital in 1928 his only possessions were his pipe, his tobacco, and an apple. The monument beside the park fountain, known as the Browne Doorway, was taken in 1905 from a town house belonging to the family of that name. This doorway features the 17th-century coats of arms of both the Browne and Lynch families. Keep an eye out for similar if less elaborate versions of the entranceway as you walk around the old part of town. The bronze cannons in Kennedy Park were presented at the end of the Crimean War to the Connaught Rangers, recruits to a famous regiment of the British army from the West of Ireland.

Leave Eyre Square by Williamsgate, which is a small street on your left as you stand at the top of the square with your back to the Great Southern Hotel. The **General Post Office** is located on Eglinton Street, the first street off Williamsgate to your right. Next, continue straight ahead down William Street to **Lynch's Castle,** now a branch of the Allied Irish Bank, on the corner of Shop Street. This edifice is the best remaining example of a

Galway City

Claddagh, **16**
Collegiate Church of
St. Nicholas, **14**
Eyre Square, **11**
Lynch's Castle, **12**
Lynch Memorial
Window, **13**
Salmon Weir
Bridge, **17**
Spanish Arch, **15**
University College, **18**

merchant's town-castle; a number of these fortified houses were inhabited by the leading families of Galway in the 16th and 17th centuries. Lynch's Castle features decorative details on its stone lintels that are usually found only in southern Spain; the building serves as a reminder of the close trading links that once existed, in the 16th and 17th centuries, between Galway and Spain.

To visit two of Galway's more famous sights, turn right at Lynch's Castle into Abbeygate Street, then take the first left, **13** at Market Street. Here you will find the **Lynch Memorial Window** embedded in a stone wall above a built-up Gothic doorway. At this spot, according to legend, James Lynch FitzStephen, mayor of Galway in the early 16th century, condemned his son to death after he had confessed to murdering a Spanish visitor. When no one could be found to carry out the execution, Judge Lynch hanged his son himself before retiring into seclusion.

Market Street leads to Lombard Street and the entrance to the **14** **Collegiate Church of St. Nicholas,** which was built by the Anglo-Normans in 1320 and enlarged in the 16th century. The church contains many fine carvings and gargoyles dating from the late Middle Ages. According to legend, Columbus once prayed here, because Galway was his last port of call before setting off on his voyage to discover the New World. The story, of course, is impossible to prove; but it's not totally implausible. On Saturday mornings, a traditional street market, held in the shadow of the church, enlivens the already busy city center. *Admission free. Open daily 8–dusk.*

If a browse around the shops is more enticing than the two previously mentioned attractions, continue from Lynch's Castle straight (south) down **Shop Street, High Street,** and **Quay Street,** investigating also the alleys and lanes on your left. (The same area can be reached from the Collegiate Church of St. Nicholas by following Lombard Street as it continues into Cross Street, where it finally meets the junction of Quay Street and High Street.) This section of town is considered the heart of fashionable Galway; here visitors will find all the city's best restaurants, bars, boutiques, art galleries, and crafts, antiques, and book shops. This vibrant part of town, with narrow winding streets, brightly painted shops, and unconventionally dressed locals, charms both tourists and residents.

Time Out **Noctan's** (or **Tig Neactain,** to Irish speakers; 17 Cross St., tel. 091/66172) is a bar with old-fashioned partitioned snugs, on the corner of Quay Street and Cross Street. It serves an excellent and inexpensive selection of imaginative bar food at lunchtime. Actors, writers, artists, musicians, and students come here often; although it can be noisy, it is the city's "in" place to meet and to find out what's happening locally in the arts.

Leave the maze of streets on Galway's Left Bank by walking downhill toward the River Corrib. Ignore the bridge straight ahead (which leads to the nearby modern seaside resort, Salthill) and turn left toward the **Spanish Arch,** which is visible **15** at the far side of the car park. This structure, another reminder of Galway's past links with Spain, was built in 1594 to protect the quays where Spanish ships unloaded cargoes of wines and brandies. Beside the arch is the **Galway City Museum,** which contains an interesting selection of material relating to local history. *No tel. Admission: 50p adults, 30p children. Open June–Aug., daily 10–1 and 2–5.*

(16) In this part of the city, the **River Corrib** is famous for its large population of mute swans. Pause and admire these stately birds while looking across the estuary to the **Claddagh** on its west bank. This district was once an Irish-speaking fishing village outside the walls of the old town, which retained its own strong, separate identity until early this century. Unfortunately, the Claddagh's traditional thatched cottages were replaced by a conventional housing plan in the 1930s, and not much remains today of its unique traditions besides a piece of jewelry called the Claddagh ring, featuring two hands clasped in friendship around a heart. It is still used by many Irish people as a wedding ring. Reproductions in gold or silver are favorite souvenirs of Galway.

(17) A riverside walk from O'Brien's Bridge to the **Salmon Weir Bridge** is signposted upriver from the Spanish Arch. In season—from mid-April to early July—shoals of salmon are visible from the bridge, lying in the clear river water before making their way upstream to the spawning grounds of Lough Corrib. This view is one of the most popular and memorable sights in Galway.

Galway's **Catholic Cathedral,** on an island forming the west bank of the River Corrib beside the Salmon Weir Bridge, was dedicated by Cardinal Cushing of Boston in 1965. The building features cut limestone with Connemara flooring, a copper dome, and all manner of expensive ornamentation. The 1960s was not a good period for Irish architecture, and its indelicate design lacks divine inspiration.

(18) If an excursion to the campus of **University College** interests you, follow University Road to the west of the cathedral back on to the mainland, turning right into the quadrangle at the second corner after about ½ km (¼ mi). The pleasant Tudor-Gothic–style quadrangle was completed in 1848, three years after the founding of the university. Its library boasts an important archive of Celtic-language materials, and it also hosts courses in July and August in Irish studies for overseas students.

The Aran Islands *Numbers in the margin correspond to points of interest on the West map.*

For details on getting to the Aran Islands, *see* Getting Around in Essential Information, above.

Something very special about small inhabited islands creates a magnetic attraction for certain travelers. In the case of the
(19) **Aran Islands,** the attraction is enhanced by their geography—the same weird limestone rock that is found on The Burren (*see* Tour 1, above), lifted in great ramparts against the pounding Atlantic Ocean—and their Irish-speaking inhabitants, who have inherited the lands and traditions of a hardy, plain-living fishing and farming folk. All islands have their idiosyncrasies, but the Aran Islands are more unusual than most.

Over the years they have attracted a number of writers and artists, including J.M. Synge (1871–1909), who learned Irish on Inishmaan and wrote his play *Riders to the Sea* about its people. The film *Man of Aran*, made on Inishmore in 1932 by the American director Robert Flaherty, is a classic documentary recording the islanders' dramatic battles with sea and storm. Since those days the islanders have benefited enormously from 20th-century progress; they now have multichannel television, a daily air service to Galway (subsidized by the government), outboard motors on their currachs, and all the modern conveniences in their homes. Yet these island folk retain a certain distinctness from the mainland people, preferring a simpler kind of home decor, very plain food, and a strong sense of community. Crime is virtually unknown on the islands; you will find no locks on the doors of your B&B, and its front-door latch is left permanently open. Many of the islanders have sampled life in Dublin or the cities of the United Kingdom and the United States, but they often return home by choice, some of them in time to raise their families on the islands, where the population remains stable.

Inishmore, the largest of the islands, with a population of 900, and the closest to the Connemara coast, is also the most commercialized, its appeal slightly diminished by the existence of some road traffic. In the summer, ferries arriving at **Kilronan,** its main village and port, are met by minibuses and pony and cart drivers, all anxious to show visitors "the sights." For the energetic, the best way to see the island is by bicycle. (Bring your own or hire one from the shed on the quay—no telephone.) The island is more than 8 km (5 mi) long and about 3 km (2 mi) wide at most points, with an area of 7,640 acres, making it just a little too large to explore comfortably on foot in a day.

Leaving Kilronan, you will notice the tall, dry (unmortared) stone walls, enclosing diminutive fields, which are a feature of the islands. The stone walls enabled the farmers to clear the land of rocks, while at the same time they created a buffer against the Atlantic gales. The farmers then had to "manufacture" soil by combining sand and rotted seaweed—the only available materials. As the road climbs the hill beyond Kilronan, you have access to panoramic views of the Connemara coast. Footpaths lead across the fields to both stony and sandy beaches, most of them contained in small deserted coves.

The main attraction on Inishmore is **Dun Aengus,** one of the finest prehistoric monuments in Europe, dating from about 2000 BC. The fort is situated spectacularly on the edge of a 90-meter- (300-foot-) high cliff overlooking a sheer drop. The defenses consist of three rows of concentric circles, but who were defending themselves against whom is a matter of conjecture. Visitors have a great view of the island and the Connemara coast from the innermost rampart. *Admission free. Freely accessible.*

Inishmaan, the middle island in both size and location, has a population of about 300 and can be comfortably explored on foot—in fact, you have no alternative! This island features several antiquities—Conor Fort, a smaller version of Dun Aengus; the ruins of two early Christian churches; and a chamber tomb known as the Bed of Diarmuid and Grainne, dating from about 2000 BC. Visitors can also take wonderful cliff walks above secluded coves.

On Inishmaan, the traditional Aran lifestyle is most evident. Until the mid-1930s or so, the women of Aran dressed in thick red woolen skirts to keep out the Atlantic gales, while the men wore collarless jackets, baggy trousers made of homespun tweed with *pampooties* (hide shoes without heels, suitable for walking on rocks), and a wide hand-plaited belt called a *crios* (pronounced "krish"). Most islanders still don the famous hand-knitted Aran sweaters, with their intricate designs and symbols, though nowadays they accompany them with jeans and sneakers. The origins of these designs gives an idea of the hardships endured by the islanders down the years: A body lost at sea could be identified by the pattern on its sweater, as each district had its own pattern. Often this design was the only means of identification.

It is possible to explore **Inisheer,** the smallest and flattest of the islands, on foot in an afternoon, though if the weather is fine you may be tempted to linger on the long sandy beach that lies between the quay and the airfield. In the summer, Inisheer's population of 300 is augmented by high school students from all over Ireland attending its language school. Only one stretch of road, about 450 meters (500 yards) long, links the airfield and the village.

The **Church of Kevin,** signposted to the southeast of the quay, is a small early Christian church that gets buried in sand by the storms every winter. Every year the islanders dig it out of the sand for the celebration of St. Kevin's Day on June 14. A pleasant walk through the village takes you up to **O'Brien's Castle,** a ruined 15th-century tower open free to the public, which sits on top of a rocky hill—the only hill on the island.

Nature lovers will enjoy a ramble to "the back of the island," as its uninhabited side facing the Atlantic is called. No beaches can be found on the back of the island, but people do swim off the rocks. It is worth making a circuit of the island to get a sense of its unique tranquillity. A maze of footpaths runs between the high stone walls that divide the fields. On Inisheer, the fields are so small that they can support only one cow each, or two to three sheep. Those that are not cultivated or grazed turn into natural wildflower meadows between June and August, overrun with harebells, scabious, red clover, ox-eye daisies, saxifrage, and tall grasses. It seems almost a crime to walk here—but who can resist taking a rest in the corner of a sweet-smelling meadow on a sunny afternoon, sheltered by high stone walls with no sound but the larks above and the wind as it sifts through the stones? These singular moments make a visit to the Aran Islands worthwhile.

Tour 3: Through Connemara and County Mayo

Numbers in the margin correspond to points of interest on the West map.

Connemara is the name given to the western part of County Galway, which lies between Lough Corrib and the Atlantic. Its moorland is dominated by the Maamturk Mountains and the Twelve Bens range to the north and is fringed by a deeply indented Atlantic coastline with innumerable creeks, bays, and small harbors. Population in this area is sparse, even on the lowland plains, which are mainly bog. Connemara National Park, in the north of the region, covers some 4,900 acres.

Two main touring routes—inland and coastal—lead through Connemara. Those who have traveled out from Galway City to Rossaveal on the R336 coastal route through Salthill, Barna, and Spiddle will have noticed how this, once one of the most impressive and unspoiled coastal roads in Ireland (and in an Irish-speaking area), has been scarred by ill-sited and badly designed bungalows. The majority of traditional thatched cabins in the West are holiday homes; local residents prefer to live in garish concrete one-story homes—a strident Spanish hacienda style, totally out of keeping with the local climate, is particularly favored. These new buildings are deplored by most visitors, including leading architects and environmentalists, but are stoutly defended by the bungalow-dwellers themselves. To avoid a second look at these eyesores, those starting from Rossaveal should follow the continuation of the R336 northwards to Maam Cross, joining this tour there on the N59.

If you start from Galway City, get on the well-signposted outer-ring road and follow signs for the N59—Moycullen, Oughterard, and Clifden—the inland Connemara route.

After about 32 km (20 mi), just past the village of Rosscahill, look for a signpost on the right side to **Aughnanure Castle.** This six-story stone tower house was built in the 16th century by the O'Flahertys, a ferocious Irish clan who frequently raided Galway City. The large square building stands beside the River Drimneen in the midst of a field often grazed by sturdy Connemara ponies—a local breed whose shaggy good looks and strong character have made them world famous. *No tel. Admission: 60p adults, 25p children and senior citizens. Open mid-June–mid-Sept., daily 10–6. Key with caretaker rest of year.*

20 Return to the main road and continue on the N59 to **Oughterard** (pronounced "Ook-ter-ard"), a small and pretty village close to the shore of **Lough Corrib.** The lough is signposted to the right in the village center, less than 1½ km (1 mi) up the road, which explains why Oughterard is one of Ireland's leading angling resorts. In the summer from mid-June to early September, local boatmen offer trips on the lough, which has several islands. It is also possible to take a boat trip to **Cong** on the other side of the lough. This unusual village of small Gothic-style cottages was the location of the John Ford movie *The Quiet Man*, starring John Wayne, which was filmed in 1951. The boat docks beside Ashford Castle, now a luxury hotel where President Reagan stayed during his visit in 1984. **Inchagoill Island** (the Island of the Stranger), midway between Oughterard and Cong, is a popular destination for a half-day trip; it features several early Christian church remains. *Cost of boat rides subject to negotiation—expect to pay about £6 per person.*

Pick up the N59 again in Oughterard, where it continues west beside a string of small lakes. The sudden appearance of their shining blue water reflecting the blue sky is a typical **21** Connemara sight on a sunny day. **Maam Cross** (where the Rossaveal road joins this tour) is literally just a crossroads, apparently in the middle of nowhere. It was once an important meeting place for the people of north and south Connemara, and is still the location of a big monthly cattle fair. Walkers will find wonderful views of Connemara by heading for any of the local peaks visible from the road.

Between Maam Cross and Recess (a distance of 16 km/10 mi), you will find some of the best scenery in Connemara. A short walk to either side of the main road will lead you to the shores of one of the many small loughs in the area: Stop and linger if the sun is out—even intermittently. It is the quality of the light filtering through the clouds that gives such splendor to the distant, dark-gray mountains and creates fascinating patterns on the brown-green moorland below. In June and July, the light lasts in the sky until almost 11, and it is worth taking a late-evening stroll to observe the sun's reluctance to set.

If the weather is allowing the light to play its tricks, try to take a 26-km (16-mi) detour to the left about 3 km (2 mi) beyond Recess, following signposts for Cashel Bay (first right on the R340, second right on the R342) and then Ballynahinch (third right on the R341). If it is raining, however, stay on the main road for 19 km (12 mi) from Recess to Clifden.

㉒ Cashel Bay is a quiet, extremely sheltered angling center at the head of Bertraghboy Bay. General de Gaulle is among the many people who have sought seclusion here. Take it easy on the narrow mountain roads—stray sheep and bolting Connemara ponies are regular hazards, along with cyclists and reckless local drivers. The final turn on to the R341 takes you along the shores of **Ballynahinch Lake** and into more wooded country. Woodland in this part of the world indicates the proximity of a "big house" whose owner can afford to plant trees for pleasure and prevent them from being cut down for fuel. You will see a sign on the left-hand side for **Ballynahinch Castle,** now a small hotel but once the home of the Martin family, one of whom, Richard Martin (1754–1834), known as Humanity Dick, was the founder of the Royal Society for the Prevention of Cruelty to Animals.

Time Out Drive through the gates of **Ballynahinch Castle** (Ballinafad, Co. Galway, tel. 095/31006) and slowly up its well-kept driveway. Nonresidents are welcome here, and the **Fisherman's Bar** in the castle basement serves inexpensive bar lunches year-round. You can also take scenic walks through the woodlands by the lake on the castle's 350-acre estate.

㉓ A left turn back onto the N59 will take you for 16 km (10 mi) to **Clifden,** far and away the prettiest "town" in Connemara. In most places, Clifden, with 1,381 residents, would be called a village, but out here it is looked on as something of a metropolis. Clifden offers a good selection of small restaurants, lively bars with music most nights in the summer, some very pleasant accommodations, and excellent walks. These features, as well as its location between the mountains and the sea, have made it a popular base for touring Connemara by car.

The town, perched high above Clifden Bay with its back to the mountains, has a profile enhanced by the tapering spires of its two churches. At first glance, however, it does not appear to lie beside the sea at all. The seashore is, in fact, best discovered on foot, by taking a short (2 km/1¼ mi) walk along the quay road through the grounds of the ruined **Clifden Castle.** The castle was the home of John D'Arcy, who founded the town in 1815, giving it its distinctive layout of a wide main street on a long ridge with a parallel street below it. The town is sleepy out of season but teems with visitors in July and August, when the **Clifden Connemara Pony Show** (equestrian events and sales accompanied by exhibits of Irish arts and crafts) is a main attraction.

To appreciate Clifden's almost Alpine location, take the aptly named **Sky Road**, signposted at the west end of town, a high narrow circuit of about 5 km (3 mi) via Kingstown; you'll enjoy the breathtaking scenery above the precipitous shores of Clifden Bay.

Time Out Try the **D'Arcy Inn** (Main St., tel. 095/21450), a Tudor-style bar in the center of town, for a quick pub lunch or a light evening meal. Inexpensive, plain Irish fare—Irish stew or poached salmon, accompanied by plenty of spuds—is served either in the upstairs restaurant or in a small room at the back of the bar.

Next, continue on the N59 from Clifden toward Letterfrack (14 km/9 mi) through the **Inagh Valley,** which is flanked by two impressive mountain ranges with distinctive conical-shape peaks, which rise almost directly to over 600 meters (1,968 feet) without any foothills.

Kylemore Valley, between the Twelve Bens and the Dorruagh Mountains, the latter naturally forested, is one of the more conventionally beautiful stretches of road in Connemara. The road passes over three lakes; if you have not already stopped at the

㉔ sign for **Kylemore Abbey,** you will certainly do so ¾ km (½ mi) later to look back at this fantastic turreted gray-stone building, which is visible across a reedy lake with a backdrop of wooded hillside. The abbey was built as a private home in 1864 by Mitchell Henry, a member of Parliament, and is now a convent of Benedictine nuns, who run a girls' boarding school here. The location is sheer heaven, almost enough to tempt one to take up the religious life.

The nuns welcome visitors to their well-stocked crafts center and simple cafeteria, and the grounds are freely accessible most of the year. Ask at the crafts shop for directions to the Gothic Chapel, a tiny replica of Norwich Cathedral built by Mitchell Henry on the abbey grounds. *Tel. 095/41113. Admission free. Crafts shop open Mar. 17–Nov. 1, daily 10–6; cafeteria open Easter and May–Oct. 15, daily 10–6; grounds open Feb.–Dec. 24, daily 10–6.*

About 8 km (5 mi) beyond Kylemore, signposted in the village

㉕ of **Letterfrack,** is the **Connemara National Park Visitor Center.** Drop in for details of the many excellent walks and beaches in the area. Some of the shorter (under 2 km/1¼ mi) walks can be followed from the main road on carefully laid-out gravel paths, though most visitors will want to venture farther afield. *Tel. 095/41054. Admission free. Car park: £1. Open Apr.–Oct., daily 10–6.*

Beyond Letterfrack the road travels for some miles alongside

㉖ **Killary Harbour,** a narrow fjordlike inlet that runs for 16 km (10 mi) between the mountains, with its northern shore located in County Mayo. The harbor offers an extremely safe anchorage, 13 fathoms (78 feet) deep for almost its entire length and sheltered from storms by mountain walls. The rafts floating in Killary Harbour belong to fish-farming consortia who are artificially raising salmon and trout in cages beneath the water. This is a matter of some controversy all over the West, with some people fearing the long-term effect of pollution from certain fish-farming practices on wild salmon and trout, and others welcoming the employment opportunities.

At **Leenane,** another tiny village, we leave Killary Harbour and County Galway to head up into County Mayo. If the weather is good and you're seeking more mountain scenery, take a detour to the left about 1½ km (1 mi) beyond Leenane on the R335, through the Doolough Valley between Mweelrea Mountain and the Sheeffry Hills and on to Westport via Louisburgh. Many lovers of the West claim that this section is the region's most impressive and unspoiled stretch of scenery. It will add about 24 km (15 mi) to your journey. Otherwise take the N59 from Leenane direct to Westport, a distance of 32 km (20 mi).

㉗ Look out on either road for the great bulk of **Croaghpatrick,** a 762-meter (2,500-foot) mountain with a conical tip. On clear days a small white building is visible at its summit; a wide path ascends to it. The latter is the Pilgrim's Path, which about 25,000 people, many of them barefoot, follow each year in order to pray to St. Patrick in the oratory on its peak. The traditional date for the pilgrimage is the last Sunday in July, but the climb can be made in about three hours (round-trip) on any fine day and is well worth it for the magnificent views of the islands of Clew Bay. The climb starts at **Murrisk,** a village about 8 km (5 mi) outside Westport on the R335 Louisburgh road.

㉘ **Westport** is by far the most attractive town in County Mayo, situated on an inlet of Clew Bay, a wide expanse of sea dotted with islands and framed by mountain ranges. It is unusual in that it was planned by an architect, James Wyatt, in the late 18th century when he was employed to finish nearby Westport House (*see* below). Streets radiate from the central Octagon, and a charming riverside mall is lined with tall lime trees. The town remains a popular fishing center and has several good beaches close by. An old-fashioned farmers' market is held on Thursday mornings on the Octagon; work clothes, harnesses, tools, and children's toys are for sale. You will discover some equally old-fashioned shops—ironmongers, drapers, and the like—by wandering around the streets that lead to the Octagon.

Time Out For something a little different along picnic lines, try the take-outs offered at the inexpensive German-owned **Continental Cafe** (High St., Westport, no tel.), or sit at an outside table on the sidewalk and sample the home-baked goods, soups, and salads. Health-food lovers will regard this place as an oasis in the wilderness.

The Quay is clearly signposted from the Octagon, about 2 km (1¼ mi) outside town. Visitors will find some good bars down here, as well as a choice of decent restaurants (*see* Dining, below). The main attraction on the Quay is **Westport House,** a stately home built on the site of an earlier castle and completed in 1788 by architect James Wyatt for the marquess of Sligo. The rectangular three-story house is furnished with late-Georgian and Victorian pieces. Family portraits by Opie and Reynolds, old Irish silver, and a collection of old Waterford glass are all on display. The home is situated superbly beside a lake with a small formal garden. However, its charm is sadly diminished for some visitors by rampant commercialization that extends even to video games in the old dungeons, which belonged to the earlier castle. The once tranquil grounds have given way to a small amusement park for children and a children's zoo. Sensitive souls should try to arrive early, when it is less likely to be busy. *Tel. 098/25430. Admission: £4.50 adults, £1.75 children.*

Open mid-May–May 31 and Aug. 26–mid-Sept., Mon.–Sat. 2–5; June 1–29, Mon.–Sat. 2–6; June 30–Aug. 25, Mon.–Sat. 10:30–6; mid-May–mid-Sept., Sun. 2–6.

If the weather does not favor a visit to **Achill Island,** which offers cliff walks, sandy beaches, and deep-sea fishing, take the N60 from Westport House to Castlebar, the inland county seat, then the N5 to Ballavary, the N58 to Foxford, and the N57 to Ballina. The total drive from Westport House to Ballina is 50 km (31 mi).

For Achill Island, take the N59 to **Newport,** a pleasant village on the Beltra River, which is popular from March to September with salmon fishermen. The N59 follows the shores of Newport Bay (the northern shore of Clew Bay) to **Mulrany,** where the R319 branches off to the left for Achill.

㉙

㉚ **Achill Island** is one of those places that can be heaven on earth in good weather because of its splendid scenery. Accommodations and facilities, however, are very basic, so if the weather is too cold or wet to enjoy the outdoors, you'll probably be bored. A short causeway leads from the mainland to Achill Sound, the first village on the 147-sq-km (57-sq-mi) island. Achill, the largest island off the Irish coast, is mainly bogland and wild heather. The main road runs through rhododendron plantations to Keel, which has a 3-km (2-mi) beach with amazing cathedral-like rock formations in the cliffs at its east end. Alternatively, take the longer scenic route signposted "Atlantic Drive." Until a few years ago, the people of Achill made a very poor living. Even as recently as the 1960s, some families were reliant on "remittances" from family members who had emigrated to the United States or England. Tourism has improved things, as has the establishment of cottage industries (mainly knitting) and shark fishing, which is popular from April to July.

To reach Ballina, retrace your steps to Mulrany and turn left onto the N59. The road runs for about 24 km (15 mi) across desolate, almost uninhabited bog, some of which has had its turf cut away down to rock level by successive generations' searching for fuel. The road then takes a right at Bangor across another long (32-km/20-mi) stretch of bog to Ballina.

㉛ **Ballina,** with a population of about 7,500, is the largest town in County Mayo and has quite a bit of light industry. Fishing for salmon and trout on the River Moy and nearby Lough Conn is its chief attraction. The town center is untidy and generally uninteresting; unless you plan to stay here for the fishing, you will probably want to drive straight through Ballina and continue for 59½ km (37 mi) on the N59 to Sligo Town.

Off the Beaten Track

While in Galway City, admirers of the writer James Joyce (1882–1941) will want to visit **Nora Barnacle House,** home of his Galway-born wife. The building is located in Bowling Green, adjacent to the Collegiate Church of St. Nicholas (*see* Tour 2: Galway City and the Aran Islands, above). Joyce stayed in the house many times. It contains memorabilia of the Barnacle family and papers relating to Joyce. *No tel. Admission: suggested voluntary donation of at least £1. Open weekdays 10–5.*

A **Corrib Cruise** from Wood Quay at the Galway City Docks is a lovely way to spend a fine afternoon; it makes a welcome change from the car if you're touring. It lasts 1½ hours and travels 8 km (5 mi) up the River Corrib and about 6 km (3½ mi) around Lough Corrib. *Tel. 091/63081; ask for Aran Ferries. Cost: £4 adults, £2 children. Cruises May–Sept., daily at 3, July– Aug., daily at 1 and 4:30.*

If you like small, peaceful islands, take a trip to **Inishbofin,** which is 12 km (7½ mi) off the coast of Connemara. The island is about 6 km (3½ mi) by 8 km (5 mi), and has a population of 180. Cliffs, sandy beaches, small lakes, and a sheltered harbor are its main attractions. Inishbofin is popular with walkers, botanists, and naturalists. The Galway City Tourist Information Office (tel. 091/63081) will book your lodging on the island. Ferries (tel. 095/45806 for times and prices) leave daily from Cleggan, a small fishing village near Clifden, 1½ hours from Galway City.

Shopping

Shoppers hunt for crafts, Irish-made clothing, jewelry, antiques, and memorabilia in the West. The major shopping areas are Galway City and Ennis, and their most interesting shops carry the above-mentioned items. Connemara offers a large concentration of crafts shops; it is the best place in Ireland to buy an Aran sweater—either a traditional off-white design, or plain linen and cotton Aran-style knits in jewellike red, green, or blue.

Galway City is the place to buy a Claddagh ring (*see* Tour 2: Galway City and the Aran Islands, above). On the Aran Islands, sally rods are woven into attractive baskets (once used for potatoes or turf); colorful woven belts, known as **críoses** (pronounced "krishes"), are hand-plaited from strands of wool. Handwoven woolen or mohair shawls or rugs provide an affordable touch of luxury. Musical instruments, traditionally made furniture, Connemara marble jewelry, modern lead crystal, batik, handmade beeswax candles, tweed place mats, and dried flower arrangements are among the many other attractive and interesting items—apart from tweeds and sweaters—to be found in the West. The majority of crafts shops mentioned below will mail items for overseas visitors.

County Clare (West)

Doolin **Crafts Gallery and Workshop** (beside the cemetery and church, tel. 065/74309) carries only Irish-made goods, including sweaters, modern lead crystal, linen, lace, and tweed. A jeweler's workshop and a resident batik maker are also available.

Ennis **The Belleek Shop** (36 Abbey St., tel. 065/29607) carries Belleek china, Waterford crystal, and Donegal Parian china, as well as Lladro, Hummel, and other collectible china. **Flax In Bloom** (Abbey St., tel. 065/20833) offers women's and teenagers' fashions with an emphasis on Irish design and classic fabrics. **The Sweater Shop** (41 O'Connell St., tel. 065/20950) sells designer knitwear. At **Clare Business Center** (Francis St., tel. 065/ 20166) you'll find Peadar O'Loughlin, violin maker; Rosemary Cullen, jewelry maker; Bridin Twist, dress designer; and Patchouli, which sells patchwork rugs and hangings. **Fancy**

That (11 Abbey St., tel. 065/28887) stocks Irish Dresden, Royal Winton, Stephen Pearce pottery, porcelain dolls, prints, and original paintings. Stop off at **Honan Antiques** (Abbey St., tel. 065/28137) for Victorian items and mementos.

Lahinch **Design Ireland** (tel. 065/81480) is a small shop that carries Irish-made goods, including sweaters, linen, tweed, and other fine gift items.

County Galway

Clifden **Millar's Connemara Tweeds** (Main St., tel. 095/21038) is a general crafts and art gallery with a good selection of traditional tweeds and handknits. **The Celtic Shop** (tel. 095/21064) features good-quality general crafts. **Fire and Fleece** (tel. 095/35955) carries designer knitwear.

Galway City **Browne Doorway** (17 Eyre Sq., beside the Great Southern Hotel, tel. 091/65757) stocks general crafts and gift items. Try **House of James** (Castle St., tel. 091/67776) for the best in modern household items, as well as high-fashion (Irish-made) clothing. Browse in **Treasure Chest** (William St., tel. 091/67237) for china, crystal, gifts, and classic clothing. **Padráic O'Máille** (Dominick St., tel. 091/62696) carries Aran sweaters, handwoven tweeds, and classically tailored clothing. Stop at **T. Dillon & Sons** (William St., tel. 091/61317) for jewelry; the store claims to be the original maker of the Claddagh ring. **Kenny's Bookshop** (High St., tel. 091/62739) offers five floors of books of Irish interest, mainly secondhand and antiquarian, as well as prints, maps, and a small art gallery.

Kylemore **Kylemore Abbey** (tel. 095/41113) sells sweaters, gifts, and general crafts items.

Letterfrack **Connemara Handcrafts** (tel. 095/41058) is a large roadside shop with an extensive selection of crafts and women's fashions made by Avoca Handweavers.

Recess **Joyce's** (tel. 095/34604) is a roadside shop carrying an imaginative selection of modern ceramics, handwoven shawls, and other good-quality crafts, in addition to books of Irish interest and a gallery of original paintings and small sculptures.

Spiddle **Mairtín Standún** (tel. 091/83108), a family-run drapery store, has expanded into a well-stocked crafts shop specializing in local handknits and tweeds.

County Mayo

Ballina **De Danaan Antiques** (Teeling St., tel. 096/21063) stocks old and antique country pine furniture. Try **Maguire Martin Showrooms** (Tone St., tel. 096/22598) for Victorian and Edwardian furniture, porcelain, paintings, and memorabilia. **Victorian Village Antiques** (Pearse St., tel. 096/22127) carries Victorian furniture and bric-a-brac.

Foxford **Woolen Mills and Craft Shop** (tel. 094/56104) is a factory outlet for top-quality blankets, rugs, and tweeds.

Westport **O'Reilly and Turpin** (Mill St., no tel.) features knitwear, handwoven items, and pottery. Stop at **John O'Brien** (Shop St., tel. 098/25169) for tweeds, Aran sweaters, and Irish linen. **Westport Antiques and Art Center** (Lodge Rd., tel. 098/26132) offers pine and country furniture and mementos.

Sports

Participant Sports

Bicycling Bicycles can be rented by the day or by the week. Traffic is generally light on roads other than the national primary routes, but bear in mind that this is a very hilly region. All Tourist Information Offices in the West provide lists of suggested cycle tours. The Irish Tourist Board publishes a leaflet, *Cycling Ireland* (£2), that describes four circuits in the West.

Bicycle Rentals **County Clare—Doolin: Mrs. Josephine Moloney, The Horse Shoe** (tel. 065/74006); **Ennis: Michael Tierney** (17 Abbey St., tel. 065/29433); **Kilfenora: Lynch & Howard** (tel. 065/84079); **Kilkee: Williams Ltd.** (Circular Rd., tel. 065/56041).

County Galway—Clifden: John Mannion (Railway View, tel. 095/21160); **Galway City: Europa Bicycles** (Hunter's Building, Earl's Island, tel. 091/63355); **Round the Corner** (Queen St., Victoria Pl., Eyre Sq., tel. 091/66606); **Renvyle: Gerard Coyne** (Tullycross near Letterfrack, tel. 095/43450).

County Mayo—Achill Island: Achill Sound Hotel (tel. 098/45245); **O'Malley's Island Sports** (Keel P.O., tel. 098/43125); **Ballina: W.J. Kearney** (Abbey St., tel. 096/21249); **Cong: O'Connor's Garage** (tel. 092/46008); **Westport: J.P. Breheny & Sons** (Castlebar St., tel. 098/25020).

Board Sailing and Dinghy Sailing **Galway Sailing Center** (Rinville, Oranmore, tel. 091/94527) offers dinghy sailing and board sailing on Lough Corrib or on coastal waters. Instruction is also available. **Little Killary Adventure Center** (Salruck, Connemara, Co. Galway, tel. 095/43411) provides sailing and windsurfing instruction on sheltered coastal waters. One- and two-week courses in sailing and board sailing are available at the **Glénans Center,** based on an otherwise uninhabited island in Clew Bay near Westport. Contact the Center's head office (28 Merrion Sq., Dublin, tel. 01/611481).

Fishing Game fishing for wild Atlantic salmon, wild brown trout, and sea trout is one of the main attractions of the West. The salmon and brown trout season runs from March through September, closing earlier in some waters. Generally, fishing is at its best between mid-May and mid-June. The sea trout season starts in late May and also ends at the end of September. Details of the numerous fisheries in the area are available from the local Tourist Information Offices, or consult the Irish Tourist Board leaflet *Angling Ireland* (£1.80). Similar leaflets are available on coarse angling and sea angling.

Shore fishing is available all along the coast. Boats can be hired from April to October for deep-sea fishing (about £15 per person per day) from the following ports: **County Clare:** Doonbeg, Liscannor, Ballyvaughan; **County Galway:** Roundstone, Clifden, Cleggan, Inishbofin Island; **County Mayo:** Westport, Ballina, Belmullet, Killala.

Fishing tackle, bait, and licenses can be obtained at **Freeny's** (High St., Galway City, tel. 091/62609), **Murt's** (7 Daly's Pl., Wood Quay, Galway City, tel. 091/61018), **John Walkin** (Tone St., Ballina, Co. Mayo, tel. 096/22442), and **Patrick Kelly** (Bridge St., Lower Westport, Co. Mayo, tel. 098/25982).

Fitness Clubs Only two hotels in the region allow nonresidents to use their fitness facilities.

The **Connemara Gateway** has an unusual indoor pool beneath a glass-topped dome. *Oughterard, Co. Galway, tel. 091/82328. Admission: £3 adults, £2 children; sauna £2, tennis court £1. Open daily 10–8.*

The **Downhill Hotel** features a sports complex with a 12-meter (39-foot) indoor oval pool, a sauna, a Jacuzzi, a gym, two squash courts, and three tennis courts. *Ballina, Co. Mayo, tel. 096/ 21033. Admission: £4 per day for use of all facilities. Open weekdays 3–11, Sat. 10–9, Sun. 10–7.*

Golf The West features some of the most challenging and ruggedly scenic courses in the country. Greens fees vary from £6 for a nine-hole course to £35 for a championship course, averaging about £15 per round for 18 holes. Courses are geared to visitors and are generally uncrowded, but it is always advisable to call beforehand.

County Clare The championship course at **Lahinch Golf Club** (Lahinch, tel. 065/81003) offers challenging links following the natural contours of the dunes. The 6,186-meter (6,702-yard) course has hosted many great golfing occasions since it opened in 1892. The new Lahinch course, known as the **Castle Course** (same tel.), offers a more carefree round of seaside golf, with shorter holes than the championship course. **Dromoland Golf Course** (Newmarket-on-Fergus, tel. 061/71144) is one of the most scenic in the country, set in a 700-acre estate of rich woodland in the grounds of the Dromoland Castle Hotel. It has a natural lake that leaves little room for error on a number of holes. **Ennis** features an 18-hole parkland course (Drumbiggle Rd., tel. 065/24074) overlooking the town. Exhilarating nine-hole courses overlook the sea at **Spanish Point** (Miltown Malbay, tel. 065/84198), **Kilrush** (Ennis Rd., tel. 065/51138), and **Kilkee** (East End, tel. 065/56048).

County Galway The **Connemara Golf Club** (Ballyconneely, near Clifden, tel. 095/21153), which opened in 1973, is situated on a dramatic stretch of Atlantic coastline; the course measures 6,560 meters (7,107 yards), and its par of 72 is rarely matched. The **Galway City Golf Club** (Blackrock, Salthill, tel. 091/22169) is situated inland, although some of the fairways run close to the ocean. **Oughterard Golf Club** (tel. 091/82131) features a parkland course suitable for novices and those who wish to improve their games. **Tuam** (Barnacurra, tel. 093/24354) and **Ballinasloe** (Rosgloss, tel. 0905/42126) also offer 18-hole courses.

County Mayo **Westport Golf Club** (Carrowholly, tel. 098/25113), beneath Croughpatrick Mountain, overlooks Clew Bay; designed by Fred Hawtree in the early 1970s, it has twice been the venue for the Irish Amateur Championship. **Castlebar Golf Club** (Rocklands, tel. 094/21649) is a moderately challenging parkland course. Nine-hole courses are located at **Achill** (tel. 098/ 43202), **Ballina** (tel. 096/21050), and **Mulrany** (tel. 098/36262).

Hiking The West features excellent hiking country, although as yet there are only two signposted trails. **The Burren Way** runs from Ballinalacken, just north of Doolin, to Ballyvaughan on the shores of Galway Bay, a distance of about 20 km (12½ mi). The trail runs through the heart of the limestone landscape of The Burren, with ever-changing views of the Aran Islands and Galway Bay. The 73-km (45-mi) **Western Way** extends from Oughterard on Lough Corrib through the mountains of Connemara and South County Mayo past Killary Harbour to Westport on Clew Bay; this trail includes some of the finest mountain and coastal scenery in Ireland. For other routes, consult *Irish Walk Guides—The West*, a pamphlet available at local Tourist Information Offices.

Horseback Riding Horses and ponies can be hired by the hour. Expect to pay about £6 for a hack, and about £9 if instruction or the use of indoor facilities is included.

County Clare **Clonmore Riding Center** (Clonmore Lodge, Quilty, tel. 065/87020) offers trekking and residential riding vacations.

County Galway **Aille Cross Equestrian Center** (Aille Cross, Loughrea [near Athenry], tel. 091/41216) features trekking, trail riding, and hunting. **Cashel House Hotel Riding Center** (Cashel, Connemara, tel. 095/31001) offers scenic treks. **Errislannan Manor Connemara Pony Stud and Riding Center** (Clifden, Connemara, tel. 095/21134) provides mountain treks, instruction, and courses for children. **Hazelwood House and Stables** (Creganna, Oranmore [near Galway City], tel. 091/94275) also offers trekking.

County Mayo **Claremorris School of Equitation** (Lisduff, Claremorris, tel. 094/71684) features show jumping and forest riding. **Drummindoo Stud and Equitation Center** (Castlebar Rd., Westport, tel. 098/25616) welcomes beginners and children.

Tennis The West isn't a popular place for playing tennis because of its wet and windy climate. Some hotels have one or two courts (*see* Lodging, below). Nine courts at the **Galway Lawn Tennis Club** (Threadneedle Rd., Salthill, tel. 091/22353) are available to nonmembers at £4 per hour. Nonmembers can also use the facilities at the **Tennis and Badminton Club** (Ennis, Co. Clare, tel. 065/21430). A public court is situated on Newport Road in Westport in County Mayo, and four public courts may be found in Ballina beside the River Moy on the N59 Sligo road.

Yacht Charters **Connemara Yacht Charters** (Drinagh Harbour, Errislannan, Clifden, Co. Galway, tel. 095/21332) has one five-berth cruiser available. Michael Clarke of **Western Ocean Yacht Charters** (5 New Docks, Galway City, tel. 091/65589) operates skippered charters along the Connemara coast.

Spectator Sports

Hooker Racing No longer used as working boats to carry turf and provisions, a small fleet of hookers is maintained and raced by enthusiasts. These solid, heavy broad-beamed sailing boats with distinctive gaff-rigged brownish-red sails participate in frequent races on Galway Bay in July and August. The main events take place in Carraroe in County Galway on the last weekend in July, and in Kinvara in County Galway (on the opposite southern shore of Galway Bay) on the third weekend in August.

Horse Racing Many small events are held throughout the year in the West, including trotting races, pony races, beach derbies, and the like. Local Tourist Information Offices can provide details. The main event is the **Galway Races,** which start on the last Monday in July and continue until the following Saturday. This boisterous, full-scale festival attracts a massive crowd; all manner of sideshows are set up, featuring entertainers, card sharps, Gypsy fortune-tellers, rifle ranges, and open-air concerts.

Dining and Lodging

Dining Because the West has a brief high season—from mid-June to early September—and a quiet off-season, it does not offer as big a choice of small owner-operated restaurants as other parts of Ireland. Often the best place to eat is a local hotel—Sheedy's Spa View in Lisdoonvarna, for example, which has one of the few excellent chefs in County Clare, or Rosleague Manor in Letterfrack. Hotel dining is described in Lodging, below.

The dominant style of cuisine in the West is best described as "country-house cooking"; it relies on dishes that could be prepared by an enthusiastic host for a private dinner party at home—for instance, homemade pâté or seafood cocktail, followed by tournedos or salmon hollandaise, and chocolate mousse for dessert. Even at Drimcong House (near Galway City), home of one of Ireland's most acclaimed chefs, the emphasis is on fresh local produce prepared in relatively simple ways, albeit with the perfection that only a master can achieve.

Restaurants in this region are less expensive than elsewhere and portions are extremely generous. You'll find it hard to stick to a diet here and salads and fresh fruit are scarce. But the quality of the meat (especially spring lamb, steak, chicken, and duck) and the seafood (especially oysters, salmon, and sea trout) is truly outstanding. Lobster, crayfish, crab, scallops, and mussels are available throughout the summer. Galway Bay's famous oysters are at their best when there is an "R" in the month; the oyster season officially runs from September to late April.

The majority of restaurants in the West are happy with a "casual but neat" appearance, so dress code is not indicated. Exceptions are the grander (i.e., Moderate and Expensive) country-house hotels, where any man in the cocktail bar or dining room after 7 PM should wear a jacket and tie.

Category	Cost*
Expensive	over £20
Moderate	£15–£20
Inexpensive	under £15

*per person for appetizer, main course, and dessert, excluding drinks and 10% tip

Lodging The West features some of Ireland's best country-house and castle hotels, some distinguished regular old and new hotels, and a good choice of inexpensive B&Bs. Ashford and Dromoland Castles are undoubtedly the star of the region, but lesser-known (and less expensive) places such as Ballynahinch Castle and Cashel House Hotel, both in Connemara, offer similar comfort on a smaller, more intimate scale.

The region is short on moderately priced hotels (particularly Galway City), but to compensate, there are wonderful bargains in the lower price range. One of the great attractions of staying in the West, whatever the price range, is the restful atmosphere of so many of the hotels and guest houses, often situated in the middle of a large private estate beside a lake or river, overlooking the sea or distant mountains.

Accommodations are busy July and August, and the best places also get full in May, June, and September, particularly on weekends. Book well in advance. Many visitors enjoy outdoor activities, such as fishing, golfing, walking, and horseback riding; facilities for other sports, such as tennis courts or indoor pools, are scarce. So are television sets in bedrooms, even in upscale hotels. Rooms also do not always have direct-dial phones.

Category	Cost*
Very Expensive	over £100
Expensive	£75–£100
Moderate	£50–£75
Inexpensive	under £50

All prices are for a standard double room, excluding service.

Highly recommended restaurants and hotels are indicated by a star ★.

Achill Island

Lodging **Ostan Gob A'Choire (Achill Sound Hotel).** This small waterside hotel is in the first village you approach arriving from the mainland. The solid two-story town house has a brick-and-plate-glass bedroom extension. All bedrooms offer a sea view, but the nicer ones, with tweed curtains and reproductions of Georgian furniture, are located in the old building. The smaller new rooms are already a little worn, but they are spotlessly clean and have pleasant views of the sound. *Ceilís* (Irish dancing and song) are staged in the bar most weekends. *Achill Sound, Co. Mayo, tel. 098/45245. 36 rooms with bath. Facilities: bar, restaurant. V. Closed Oct.–Mar. 22. Inexpensive.*

The Aran Islands

Inishmaan has no hotels, and the other islands have only one each. However, you'll find no shortage of B&Bs on the islands—most of them in simple family homes—even at peak times. The best way to book is through the Galway City Tourist Information Office (Victoria Pl., Eyre Sq., Galway, tel. 091/630081). Each island has at least one restaurant with a wine license that serves plain home cooking. Most B&Bs will provide a packed lunch and an evening meal (called high tea) on request.

Inisheer **Hotel Inisheer.** This pleasant modern low-rise in the middle of
Lodging the island's only village is located a few minutes' walk from the quay and the airstrip. The simple whitewashed building with a slated roof and half-slated walls offers bright, plainly furnished rooms. A section of five rooms was added in 1990; they are slightly larger than the other 10 rooms. The restaurant (open to nonresidents) is the best bet on the island, although most of the food is imported frozen. *Lurgan Village, Inisheer, Aran Islands, Co. Galway, tel. 099/75020. 15 rooms, 5 with bath. Facilities: bar, restaurant. No TV or direct dial in rooms. DC, MC, V. Closed Oct. 1–Easter. Inexpensive.*

Inishmore
Lodging

Johnston Hernon's Kilmurvey House. Situated in the island's second village about 6½ km (4 mi) from the quay and the airport (accessible by minibus), this rambling stone 200-year-old farmhouse, is the first choice of many visitors (about 60% of them American) to the island. Four large rooms in the old house are furnished with hand-me-downs, and four modern rooms in a new extension have built-in furniture. *Kilmurvey, Inishmore, Aran Islands, Co. Galway, tel. 099/61218. 8 rooms. Facilities: restaurant with wine license, residents only. No TV or direct dial in rooms. No credit cards. Closed Oct.–Apr. Inexpensive.*

Ballina

Dining

Tullio's. This restaurant is part of a smart Victorian pub in the town center. The fin de siècle art-nouveau decor features an elaborate etched stained-glass window, a molded plaster ceiling, striped moiré wallpaper, a dark-green Turkish carpet, brass oil lamps, and well-upholstered velvet chairs. Cheerfully elegant rather than formal, the brightly lighted dining room with lively background music is frequented by Ballina's businesspeople and vacationing anglers. Dishes combine traditional French and Italian cuisines and come in very generous portions. Half duckling à l'orange, turbot Veronique (served with grapes in a sauce), and *escalope milanese* are among the extensive à la carte choices, but if you're really hungry, go for the five-course set menu. *Pearse St., Ballina, Co. Mayo, tel. 096/21890. Reservations advised weekends. MC, V. Moderate.*

Lodging

Mount Falcon Castle. This rambling Victorian Gothic countryhouse 5 km (3 mi) outside town is within easy reach of several beautiful small beaches. Owner-manager Constance Aldridge is renowned for putting guests at ease and encouraging them to mingle. Children are especially welcome. An excellent holiday base, the hotel features good walks and salmon fishing on the River Moy within the extensive grounds, with horseback riding, sea fishing, and golf nearby. Rooms are furnished comfortably with a mix of antiques and heirlooms, and overlook the wooded grounds. Local produce is usually served, and the country-style home-cooking has a fine reputation. *Ballina, tel. 096/21172. 10 rooms, 8 with bath. Facilities: tennis, fishing, restaurant (wine license only). No TV or phone in rooms. AE, DC, MC, V. Closed Feb. 1–Easter. Expensive.*

Downhill Hotel. Delightfully situated on 40 wooded acres beside a gushing tributary of the River Moy (just off the N59 Sligo road), this hotel is a popular spot with anglers and outdoor types. The late-Victorian main house feels a little gloomy downstairs, but it is comfortable. Rooms in the new wing tend to be smaller than those in the main house, but the former have good views of the river across the garden. Rooms in the main house feature Georgian-style furniture with tastefully coordinated quilts and drapes. The sporting facilities are the best for miles. *Ballina, Co. Mayo, tel. 096/21033. 52 rooms with bath. Facilities: indoor heated pool, gym, sauna, Jacuzzi, solarium, 2 squash courts, snooker, 3 tennis courts, fishing, 2 bars, restaurant. AE, DC, MC, V. Expensive.*

Ballyvaughan

Dining
★

Claire's. Look for a crafts shop with the name Manus Walsh over the door. He's Claire's husband, and her pretty little res-

American Express offers Travelers Cheques built for two.

American Express® Travelers Cheques *for Two*. The first Travelers Cheques that allow either of you to use them because both of you have signed them. And only one of you needs to be present to purchase them.

Cheques *for Two* are accepted anywhere regular American Express Travelers Cheques are, which is just about everywhere. So stop by before your next trip and ask for Cheques *for Two*.

 Travelers Cheques

2½ Hours
VHS-C

2½ Hours
8mm

SONY

Pack Wisely.

Given a choice, the seasoned traveler always carries less.
Case in point: Sony Handycam® camcorders, America's most
popular. They record up to 2½ hours on a single tape.
VHS-C tapes record only 30 minutes.* And why carry five tapes
when you can record everything on one? Which brings us
to the first rule of traveling: pack a Sony Handycam camcorder.

Over 1500 Great
Weekend Escapes...

in Six Fabulous Fodor's Guides to
Bed & Breakfasts, Country Inns, Cottages,
and Other Weekend Pleasures!

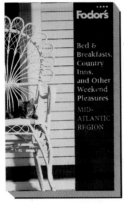

**The
Mid-Atlantic
Region**

**The
South**

**New
England**

**The
West Coast**

**England
and
Wales**

Canada

Fodor's
Where the best memories begin

taurant, overlooking a leafy garden, is behind his shop. This dining spot has pine walls covered with greenery and batiks, rush-seated pine chairs, and a bright yellow candle in a bottle on each table. You can taste the freshness in the simple but imaginatively prepared food, including such entrées as panfried plaice with orange butter, and sirloin steak with Irish whiskey mustard sauce. *Ballyvaughan, Co. Clare, tel. 065/ 77029. Reservations advised. MC, V. Wine license only. Open May–Sept., dinner only. Moderate.*

Lodging
★
Gregan's Castle Hotel. This quiet, well-run large Victorian country house, surrounded by award-winning gardens, is located at the base of the aptly named Corkscrew Hill (on the N67, midway between Ballyvaughan and Lisdoonvarna) and overlooks the gray mountains of The Burren and Galway Bay. All bedrooms are individually furnished with Georgian and Victorian antiques and William Morris wallpaper; older ones feature molded plaster ceilings. The spacious new rooms on the ground floor have private patio gardens but lack the splendid views of the first-floor rooms. *Ballyvaughan, Co. Clare (via Galway), tel. 065/77005. 22 rooms with bath. Facilities: croquet, bar, French restaurant (jacket and tie preferred). No TV in rooms. MC, V. Closed Nov.–mid-Mar. Expensive.*

Cashel Bay

Lodging
★
Cashel House. This place has more antiques and curios per square foot than any other hotel in Ireland. Dermot McEvilly claims that he acquired his extensive collection when it was cheaper than buying new pieces; you'll admire the intricately carved oak tables, Biedermeier bureaus, gilt mirrors, Georgian bookcases, ormolu clocks, and other knickknacks scattered liberally around the lobby, lounge, library, and downstairs corridors. A favorite hideaway for sophisticated French and American guests, as well as Ireland's elite, this luxurious country house also features an award-winning 50-acre garden of exotic flowering shrubs, woodland walks, and Connemara ponies grazing out back. Bedrooms are furnished with a generous mix of antiques and curios and have king-size beds, which are canopied in the 13 minisuites. Each room overlooks a stretch of the richly planted garden and has plain wool carpets, pink-and-green drapes and spreads, and brass bedside lamps. For a sea view, ask for a front room. *Cashel Bay, Co. Galway, tel. 095/31001. 28 rooms with bath. Facilities: horseback riding, tennis court, private beach, bicycle rental, fishing. AE, DC, MC, V. Very Expensive.*

Zetland. This mid-Victorian hunting lodge was built for the earl of Zetland and is on a hill overlooking the secluded Cashel Bay. The hotel is popular with anglers, hunters, and townsfolk in search of a rural retreat. Bedrooms are decorated in floral chintz and overlook the garden. The "minisuites" with a sea view in the old house are twice as large as the other rooms and are furnished with late-Victorian antiques. Your best bet is one of the middle-grade "superior" rooms in the converted coach house: all offer sea views, highly polished mahogany antiques, velvet armchairs, and fully tiled bathrooms with decorated washbasins. *Cashel Bay, Co. Galway, tel. 095/31111. 19 rooms with bath. Facilities: fishing, shooting, horseback riding, tennis, bar, restaurant. AE, DC, MC, V. Closed Nov.–Easter. Very Expensive.*

Clarinbridge

Dining **Paddy Burke's.** Once a simple village bar on the main Ennis–
Galway road, this long, low-ceilinged, 200-year-old thatched
cottage, divided into three separate eating areas, is now a
world-famous seafood restaurant. The bar itself verges on din-
gy; ask for a table in the restaurant's adjoining room, furnished
with oak-topped tables and solid chairs. Copper pans and
sporting prints adorn the walls. Oysters are a specialty; if
they're not in season, try king scallops Mornay or monkfish in a
garlic, cream, and white-wine sauce. *Clarinbridge, Co. Galway, tel. 091/96107. Reservations advised; essential in July
and Aug. MC, V. Moderate.*
Moran's Oyster Cottage. Signposted off the main road on the
south side of Clarinbridge, this waterside thatched cottage,
the home of the Moran Family since 1760, houses a simply furnished restaurant at the back that serves only seafood. If oysters are not in season, try the seafood special (smoked salmon,
crab, prawns, and crab claws with homemade brown bread) or a
bowl of garlic mussels. *The Weir, Kilcolgan, Co. Galway, tel.
091/96113. Reservations advised. AE, MC, V. Inexpensive.*

Clifden

Dining **Doris's.** Owned and run by a young German couple, this establishment occupies two small floors of one of the oldest houses in
town. At this restful place with plain white walls, lots of natural wood, tweed drapes, and dark-red carpets and napery,
you'll find upstairs both a harpist (most evenings) and an open
turf fire. Doris describes her cuisine as Mediterranean, but the
menu also reveals some Asian influence: vegetable pilaf and
grilled pork are both served, along with Andalusian chicken
salad, *tournedos à la chasseur* (filet mignon with a tomato, onion, and pepper sauce), and a good selection of seafood.
*Clifden, Co. Galway, tel. 095/21427. Reservations advised
weekends and July–Aug. AE, DC, MC, V. Closed Oct. 1–Mar.
1. Moderate.*

Lodging **Abbeyglen Castle.** Perched on a hilltop about 1 km (½ mi) outside Clifden overlooking the town and bay, this white-turreted
fake castle (the crenellations were added only a few years ago)
on 12 acres of steep grounds provides a stunning view over the
church spires of Clifden to mountains, lakes, and the sea. A
large dining room looks out to the wonderful view. Try to get a
front room; the back rooms face an overgrown garden. Bedrooms are comfortable, with side tables and matching chintz
spreads and drapes, but in some rooms the modern veneered
furniture shows signs of wear. The bar is a lively and romantic
spot on summer evenings. *Sky Rd., Clifden, Co. Galway, tel.
095/21201. 46 rooms with bath. Facilities: outdoor heated pool,
tennis court, pitch-and-putt, sauna, solarium, snooker, helipad, bar, restaurant. AE, DC, MC, V. Closed Jan. Expensive.*

★ **Rock Glen Manor House.** Cross the bridge at the west end of
town and go 2½ km (1½ mi) down the Roundstone road (the
R341) to find this beautifully converted shooting lodge, built in
1815. On windy days, a tiny Connemara pony, Gregory, stands
sentinel at the entrance gates and enjoys the breeze. Riding
boots and tennis rackets in the hall make this feel more like a
private home than a top-class hotel, as does the warm welcome
from owner-manager Evangeline Roche. The ground floor is

generously furnished with Victorian antiques; the large sunny drawing room, with plump white armchairs, magazines, books, and board games, offers a turf fire. Rooms vary in size and appeal; the best are situated on the first-floor front with sea views, but all the rooms are nicely furnished in the Georgian style, with fluffy mohair or chintz bedspreads, brass curtain rods and bedside lamps, and fully tiled bathrooms. Small-paned teak windows provide restful scenic views. Most guests are fly/drive tourists and others who appreciate the sedate and leisurely atmosphere of traditional country life that has been carefully re-created here. The Victorian-style restaurant, which serves fresh local produce, is worth a visit. *Clifden, Co. Galway, tel. 095/21035. 29 rooms with bath. Facilities: snooker, tennis court, bar, restaurant (dinner only). AE, DC, MC, V. Closed Nov.–Feb. Moderate.*

Dun Aengus. A B&B only a few minutes up the road from the Abbeyglen, this is the highest house in Clifden, with a positively vertiginous view over the bay and town which has to be seen to be believed. The large modern building has a weather-slated roof and a top story above the whitewashed ground floor. Simply fitted rooms are decorated with modern pine and candlewick spreads, and they have fully tiled bathrooms. Rooms numbered 1 to 4 share the singular view, as does the breakfast room. *Mrs. M. Ryan, Dun Aengus, Sky Rd., Clifden, Co. Galway, tel. 095/21069. 6 rooms with bath. Facilities: snooker, TV lounge (no TV or direct dial in rooms). Evening meal June–Aug. (BYOB). No credit cards. Inexpensive.*

Cong

Lodging **Ashford Castle.** This American-owned and -managed large gray-stone turreted castle on the edge of Lough Corrib, surrounded by neatly manicured lawns and gardens, will fulfill every first-time visitor's dream of a genuine Irish castle. The high-ceilinged interior is lavishly furnished with priceless antiques and top-quality reproductions. Large 19th- and 20th-century oil paintings in gilt frames hang from the castle's carved stone walls above polished wood paneling, illuminated by crystal chandeliers. However, as old hands will tell you, the place is a far cry from the unpredictable charms of the "real Ireland." The only Irish people you'll meet here, apart from the staff, are the gold Rolex set. The bedrooms in the discreetly added new wing are disappointingly like any other luxury hotel rooms; although they're beautifully furnished in the Georgian style, they have low ceilings and are boxy. Among the 20 "deluxe" rooms and six suites are the sunny ground-floor rooms occupied by President Reagan on his 1984 state visit; they still feature the extra-long bed especially made for him, and gold bath taps. "Deluxe" rooms have wonderful views of the river, lake, or gardens, generous sitting areas, heavily carved antique furniture, and extra-large bathrooms. The suites are vast and faultless, furnished with Georgian antiques and blissfully comfortable. *Cong, Co. Mayo, tel. 092/46003. 82 rooms with bath. Facilities: fishing, 9-hole golf, horseback riding, jaunting car, 2 tennis courts, clay-target shooting, 2 bars, 2 restaurants. AE, DC, MC, V. Very Expensive.*

Ennis

Lodging **The Old Ground.** This rambling creeper-clad building in the town center, dating from the early 18th century and much added to over the years, is a comfortable, well-established hotel that has retained its past elegance. The lodging serves as a popular base for Americans, especially golfers. The old house's attractive bedrooms offer pine bedheads, brass bedside lights, and candy-striped wallpaper. Some rooms overlook the busy main street, so try to get one facing the gardens. Smaller rooms in the new wing have the same tasteful combination of pine and brass. Be sure to look at the lovely old silver and the large Georgian sideboards in the dining room. *Ennis, Co. Clare, tel. 065/ 28127. 60 rooms with bath. Facilities: bar, restaurant. AE, DC, MC, V. Expensive.*
West County. A striking glass conservatory runs the length of the facade of this modern low-rise hotel on the edge of town (on the N18 Limerick road). It's a lively place, geared to the tour-bus trade, yet its roomy, pleasantly decorated public area can handle the crowds. Bedrooms feature wood-veneer furniture, speckled carpet, and floral drapes and spreads. The best rooms are located at the front overlooking the gardens; the rest have a view of the car park. *Ennis, Co. Clare, tel. 065/28421. 109 rooms with bath. Facilities: snooker, minigym, sauna, fishing, 2 bars, 2 restaurants, nightclub with live entertainment. AE, DC, MC, V. Moderate.*

Fanore

Dining **Admiral's Rest.** You can guess from the nautical bric-a-brac on view that this place belongs to a retired naval man—one John Macnamara, who is an expert on The Burren's wildlife. (Ten inexpensive B-&-B rooms are available in the next-door bungalow.) The restaurant is housed in a modernized cottage on the coast road between Lisdoonvarna and Ballyvaughan, just across the road from the sea, which is visible through the large oval windows. Decor is rugged but stylish, including varnished stone floors, stone-topped tables, *sugán* (rope-seated) chairs, an open wood and turf fire, and posies of wildflowers on the tables. Seafood, such as lobster, mussels, or crab claws in garlic butter, is the mainstay of the simple menu, but you can also order a grilled T-bone steak, Irish stew, or a spicy vegetarian salad. *Fanore (near Ballyvaughan), Co. Clare, tel. 065/76105. Reservations advised. Wine license only. AE, MC, V. Closed Nov.–Easter. Inexpensive.*

Galway City

Dining **Drimcong House.** To reach this exceptional country-house res-
★ taurant 19 km (12 mi) out of town on the N59 Oughterard/ Clifden road, drive through the village of Moycullen; you'll see the driveway on your right. Gerry Galvin, the owner-chef, is one of the best cooks in Ireland. His wife Marie supplies the kitchen with herbs and unusual vegetables, all organically grown on the Galvins' land and virtually unavailable elsewhere in the West. The restaurant is housed in a modest, symmetrical two-story farmhouse, probably dating from the late-17th century. Leather place mats are set on solid oak tables, and the dining room is decorated with prints, cartoons, and original paintings by contemporary Irish artists. Gerry's cooking is dis-

tinguished by its simplicity; the exceptional menu might include hot oyster broth; monkfish marinated in olive oil and spring herbs, and then panfried and served on a leek sauce; or rack of Connemara lamb with an herby port-wine sauce. *Moycullen, Co. Galway, tel. 091/85115. Reservations advised. AE, DC, MC, V. Open Tues.–Sat. dinner only. Closed Christmas–mid-Mar. Expensive.*

Malt House. A small, busy bar in an alley off High Street in old Galway's center adjoins this restaurant's small ground-floor dining room, with a large bay window, a beamed roof, and rough cast walls. Tables are fairly close together, but nicely set with pink and green napery. Popular with locals on special occasions as well as with visitors, the lively spot specializes in seafood prepared in the classic French style; good choices are lobster, scallops, and the house special, prawns supreme in garlic cream. Other recommended dishes include boned duckling Gascony, served with potato stuffing and cherry sauce, or veal St. Augustine, made with cranberry sauce topped with pear and blue cheese. (A simpler, inexpensive menu featuring steaks and seafood is available at the bar.) *Olde Malte Arcade, High St., Galway, tel. 091/67866. Reservations advised. AE, DC, MC, V. Closed Sun. Expensive.*

Oyster Room. The main restaurant of the Great Southern Hotel, this establishment is by far the most formal eatery in Galway, a city noted for its easygoing informality. The high-ceilinged connecting rooms off the lobby are suitably hushed, decorated in pale pink and green tones and featuring thick carpets, elegantly draped windows, tall gilt mirrors, and brass lamps. Tables with comfortable velvet-upholstered chairs are well spaced. The conservative French-Irish cuisine showcases the local seafood. Specialties include breast of chicken, stuffed with white crabmeat in Noilly Prat sauce and garnished with crab claws, and fresh Corrib salmon, served with fish and spinach mousse and baked in phyllo pastry. *Great Southern Hotel, Eyre Sq., Galway, tel. 091/64041. Reservations advised. Jacket and tie required. AE, DC, MC, V. Expensive.*

★ **Noctan's.** A small menu (with a choice of three fish and three meat dishes and one vegetarian main course, as well as appetizers and desserts) is served in the first-floor room above one of the most famous bars in the old town's Left Bank. The Swiss chef describes his cooking as *cuisine du marché*—the dishes offered are determined by that morning's marketing. Fillet of salmon Florentine, served with spinach in a cream sauce, and steak fillet Marianne, which is grilled and finished with brandy, are local favorites. The mildly bohemian ambience is created by an open fireplace, filled with dried grasses in the summer, and a tiny red-walled corner room, which is decorated with old theatrical prints. An odd assortment of Victorian chairs surround the different-size tables, which are likely to be occupied by leading lights in Galway's thriving performing arts and visual arts scenes. *17 Cross St., Galway, tel. 091/66172. Reservations advised. MC, V. Dinner only. Closed Sun.–Mon. Moderate.*

The Brasserie. French in ambience and decor, American in cuisine, this cheerful place—with bright red bentwood chairs, apple-green walls, and floral oilcloth on the tables beneath a brass ceiling fan—is situated right next door to the Taibhdhearc Theater and a stone's throw from the Druid Theater. The restaurant is known for its barbecued ribs. Tacos, pizzas, chicken Kiev, and steak are the alternatives, and the menu has a good selection of waffles and homemade ice cream. Service is friendly and informal, and the piped music is muted. *Middle St., Galway, tel. 091/61610. Reservations advised weekends. AE, MC, V. Closed Sun. and public holidays. Inexpensive.*

Conlon's. Known for its low prices and very fresh fish, this old Galway institution is located just off Eyre Square opposite the General Post Office. The upstairs area is mainly for takeout; the simple, café-style restaurant in the basement features a tiled black-and-white floor, wood-paneled walls, and plastic-topped tables. Start with the famous chowder, followed by breaded strips of assorted fish, smoked haddock, or cod Mornay, all of them served with either chips or salad. This is also one of the cheapest and most reliable places in the area to eat oysters in season. *Eglinton St., Galway, tel. 091/62268. Wine license only. No reservations. No credit cards. Inexpensive.*

Lodging **Ardilaun House.** This lovely 19th-century house lies at the end
★ of a tree-lined avenue in a quiet suburb, midway between the city center and the Salthill promenade—about five minutes' drive from both. The peaceful public rooms overlooking the gardens have open fires in the large marble chimneypieces, fresh flower arrangements, and Regency-style furniture. The original house has been discreetly extended to allow for additional lodging space. The individually designed bedrooms feature a pink, gray, or green color scheme and Irish-made mahogany furniture with brass trim. All the fully tiled bathrooms have heated towel racks and marble sinks. For views of the bay, book a top-floor even-numbered room. Other rooms, which are just as pleasant, overlook the flower garden, shrubberies, and a fountain. *Taylor's Hill, Galway, tel. 091/21433. 91 rooms with bath. Facilities: restaurant, 3 bars, sauna, tennis, gym, Jacuzzi. AE, DC, MC, V. Expensive.*

★ **Galway Great Southern.** Built in 1845 to coincide with the arrival of the railway in the area, this imposing limestone-faced hotel overlooking the main square is still the best address in town. As soon as you walk into the large, thickly carpeted lobby through heavy glass-paneled wooden doors with large brass handles, you know that you've arrived at one of Europe's grandest old-fashioned hotels; this solid and luxurious establishment retains a great sense of tradition. Rooms are fairly big and combine the best of old and new, with tall ceilings and windows, tastefully muted coordinated color schemes, and Georgian-style tables and chairs. Ask for a back room on the fifth floor if you want a view of Galway Bay. It's worth visiting the rooftop swimming pool to enjoy an extraordinary panorama of the city and Galway Bay. In the evening, guests can sample French-Irish cuisine at the formal Oyster Room (*see* Dining, above) or have a drink in the lobby at the charming Railway Bar and Lounge. *Eyre Sq., Galway, tel. 091/64041. 120 rooms with bath. Facilities: indoor heated pool, sauna, plunge pool, restaurant, 2 bars. AE, DC, MC, V. Expensive.*

Galway Ryan. A number of modern low-rise hotels dating from the late '60s are situated on the outskirts of Galway, and the Ryan is the most attractive of these. Located 5 km (3 mi) from the city center, on the Ring Road, the hotel enables you a quick getaway from Galway during the morning rush hours. The public rooms are spacious and well-lighted but have anonymous modern decor. Each large bedroom, decorated in gray and beige tones, features a sitting area and a window the length of one wall that overlooks the hotel gardens. *Dublin Rd., Galway,* *tel. 091/53181. 96 rooms with bath. Facilities: bar, restaurant. AE, DC, MC, V. Expensive.*

Skeffington Arms. The Skeff, on the west side of Eyre Square, attracts a loyal clientele who like its central location and the history that still pervades this shabby Victorian landmark after innumerable refurbishments (most recently in 1989). The large, modernized bar on the ground floor is popular with both young and old. Guests approach rooms up a wide, top-lighted stairway, a relic of the Skeff's Victorian heyday. All bedrooms feature plain woolen carpets and floral drapes as well as odd bits of old furniture. The best and most spacious rooms are Nos. 3, 4, 6, and 10, overlooking the square. *28 Eyre Sq., Galway, tel. 091/63173. 22 rooms with bath. Facilities: 2 bars, 2 restaurants. AE, MC, V. Closed Dec. 24–26. Moderate.*

Anno Santo. Situated 300 meters (320 yards) from the sea on a residential road in Salthill (about an eight-minute drive from the city center), this small hotel has been run by the Vaughan family since 1950. A two-story bedroom wing has been added to the original, rather overdecorated bungalow. The upstairs rooms are smaller but brighter than the downstairs ones. Carpets with dizzying designs, plywood headboards and closets, and white candlewick spreads will not win any design awards, but the bedrooms are spotlessly clean. Guests of all nationalities stay here, and the Vaughans are friendly and full of helpful touring advice. *Threadneedle Rd., Salthill, Galway, tel. 091/23011. 14 rooms with bath. Facilities: bar, restaurant. AE, DC, MC, V. Closed Dec. 24–Jan. 7. Inexpensive.*

Kilkee

Dining **Manuel's Seafood.** About 1½ km (1 mi) north of Kilkee, this modern restaurant, perched on a hill, looks out across fields to Kilkee Bay. Manuel (Irish-born of Italian descent) waits tables and his German wife, Doris, cooks. Rustic pine tables and tweed-seated chairs stand on a gaily tiled floor; the walls are adorned with scallop shells and dried shellfish. The menu includes black sole grilled on the bone, lobster Thermidor, garlic chicken breasts, and a vegetarian daily special. *Corbally, Kilkee, Co. Clare, tel. 065/56211. Reservations advised weekends and June–Aug. Wine license only. DC, MC, V. Dinner only. Closed mid-Sept.–Easter. Moderate.*

Knockferry

Lodging **Knockferry Lodge.** A half-hour drive from Galway City (21 km/13 mi—turn right off the N59 in Moycullen), this is an excellent base for visiting the city as well as Lough Corrib and Connemara. Owners Des and Mary Moran encourage visitors to this secluded fishing lodge on the lake to stay more than one night—the longer you stay, the lower the rate. The Morans like to share their local knowledge with guests and encourage them to get to know each other around the turf fire after dinner. Bedrooms are pretty and simple, with modest antiques, Laura Ashley curtains and drapes, and hanging ferns in the half-tiled bathrooms. *Roscahill, Co. Galway, tel. 091/80122. 10 rooms with bath. Facilities: fishing (boats for hire), billiards, bar, restaurant (wine license only). No TV or direct-dial phones in rooms. MC, V. Closed Nov.–Apr. Inexpensive.*

Lahinch

Lodging **Aberdeen Arms.** This beautifully refurbished Victorian seaside
★ hotel is a model of its kind, offering elegance and comfort in a
friendly, easygoing setting. It is popular with golfers, and humorous golfing prints hang on the dark-paneled walls of the bar
and grill room. Ask for one of the new rooms that face the sea
and feature spectacular skylights and windows. All rooms are
large and tastefully decorated with built-in, cream-colored
melamine closets, plain carpets, and matching cream floral
drapes and spreads; some offer Georgian-style tables and
chairs. The main dining room offers an excellent and varied
menu of French-Irish cuisine; the hotel also serves one of the
best breakfasts in the county. *Lahinch, Co. Clare, tel. 065/
81100. 55 rooms with bath. Facilities: snooker, minigym, sauna, Jacuzzi, 10 tennis courts, horseback riding, 2 restaurants,
2 bars. AE, DC, MC, V. Moderate.*

Letterfrack

Lodging **Rosleague Manor.** This pink, creeper-clad, two-story Georgian
house stands amid wooded grounds overlooking Ballinakill Bay
and the mountains of County Mayo and Connemara. The clutter
of walking and shooting sticks beneath the grandfather clock
in the hall sets the tone of this fairly informal small country-
house hotel. The best rooms are located on the first-floor front,
overlooking the bay. All the solidly comfortable bedrooms are
furnished with well-used Victorian and Georgian antiques,
fourposters or large brass bedsteads, and drapes that match
the William Morris wallpaper. The expensive, award-winning
restaurant features seafood and homegrown vegetables. *Letterfrack, Co. Galway, tel. 095/41001. 13 rooms with bath. Facilities: tennis court, sauna, bar, restaurant. No TV in rooms.
MC, V. Expensive.*

Lisdoonvarna

Lodging **Ballinalacken Castle.** This is not a castle but a sprawling Victorian lodge with bow windows that stands beside the 16th-
century O'Brien castle ruins. Located on a hill, 4 km (2½ mi)
outside Lisdoonvarna, it commands a panoramic view of the
Atlantic, the Aran Islands, and, across Galway Bay, the
Connemara Hills; the hotel is surrounded by 100 acres of wildflower meadows. The interior is much less impressive, yet the
room rates are reasonable. Bedrooms come in all different
shapes and sizes; some have marble fireplaces and high ceilings, and all have splendid views. The furniture throughout the
lodge is a haphazard mix of hand-me-downs, modern stuff, lovely old Irish oak, and sumptuous inlaid bureaus. *Lisdoonvarna,
Co. Clare, tel. 065/74025. 6 rooms, 4 with bath. Facilities: bar,
TV lounge (no TV or direct-dial phones in rooms). No credit
cards. Closed early Oct.–May. Inexpensive.*
Sheedy's Spa View. Originally a 17th-century farmhouse, this is
now a small, friendly hotel that has belonged to the Sheedy
family since 1855. It is only a short walk from both the town
center and the spa wells. Rooms are well cared for, simple, and
spotlessly clean; most of them offer a Georgian-style coffee table and chairs. The award-winning, moderately priced Orchid
Room restaurant serves an outstanding five-course set menu
featuring French-Irish cuisine prepared by Patsy Sheedy and

her internationally trained son, Frankie. *Lisdoonvarna, Co. Clare, tel. 065/74026. 11 rooms with bath. Facilities: bar, restaurant (dinner only, bar food at lunch), tennis court, TV lounge. No TV in rooms. AE, DC, MC, V. Closed Oct.–mid-Mar. Inexpensive.*

Mulrany

Lodging **Mulrany Bay Hotel.** Midway between Westport and Achill Island, overlooking the north shore of Clew Bay, this rambling old hotel was built in the 1890s and, frankly, has seen better days. However, the sea view and 100 acres of wooded gardens are ample compensation for the garish carpets and tatty modern furniture downstairs. It's a characterful place that appeals to individualists, including the late John Lennon, who stayed in the Lennon Suite—a suitably weird set of rooms up in the eaves—in 1968. Ask for a front room with a bay window—No. 104, for example—or, failing that, any room in the old house, most of which have floral duvets and modern veneered furniture with small sitting areas. Smaller, darker rooms in the new wing are used only in July and August. *Mulrany, Co. Mayo, tel. 098/36222. 39 rooms with bath. Facilities: sauna, yoga room, snooker, bar, restaurant. No TV in rooms. AE, DC, MC, V. Closed Nov.–mid-Mar. Moderate.*

Newmarket-on-Fergus

Lodging **Dromoland Castle.** Situated 13 km (8 mi) from Shannon and 9½ ★ km (6 mi) from Ennis, this luxury hotel is a popular first stop with affluent American and French visitors. The original 16th-century O'Brien castle was pulled down early in the 19th century and replaced with an impressive turreted Gothic-style stone building that is now the hotel. The castle stands beside a lake, surrounded by well-landscaped formal gardens in their own neatly kept park. The hotel interior was recently given a face-lift by New York interior decorator Carlton Varney. Wide, thick-carpeted corridors are flanked by stone walls graced with large ancestral portraits. Bedrooms overlook the old Queen Anne stable yard and feature Regency-style furniture and a pleasant pink or green color scheme. A cut-glass decanter of complimentary sherry awaits guests in every room. The vast suites have ruched drapes on the tall windows, great views over the park, and antiques, many of them Irish-Georgian. *Newmarket-on-Fergus, Co. Clare, tel. 061/368144. 73 rooms with bath. Facilities: 18-hole golf course, lake fishing, bicycles, shooting (Nov.–Jan.), 2 tennis courts, billiards, horseback riding. AE, DC, MC, V. Very Expensive.*

Newport

Lodging **Newport House.** This Georgian mansion is strictly for those who will feel at ease in a rather grand and elegant private home. The handsome creeper-covered building beside the Newport River dominates the little town. Beyond a small, tidy lobby are spacious reception rooms furnished with gilt-framed family portraits, Regency mirrors and chairs, handwoven Donegal carpeting, and crystal chandeliers hanging from ornate stucco ceilings. The sweeping staircase, top-lighted by a lantern and a glass dome, leads to an airy gallery and the bedrooms. These are bright and less elaborate than the public rooms, with pretty chintz drapes and a mix of Victorian antiques and merely old furniture. Most bedrooms have sitting areas and good views of the river and gardens; others have such compensations as the enormous Jacobean four-poster in room No. 10. *Newport, Co. Mayo, tel. 098/41222. 19 rooms with bath. Facilities: fishing, horseback riding, snooker, bar, restaurant. No TV in rooms and no TV lounge. AE, DC, MC, V. Closed Oct.–mid-Mar. Expensive.*

Oughterard

Lodging **Connemara Gateway.** An adventurously designed modern low-rise building with traditional gray slated roofs above white-washed walls, this hotel, about 1 km (½ mi) outside the village on the Galway side of the N59, combines the best of old and new. The traditional Irish cottage is the theme of the lobby and the bar, both of which are decorated with wooden and cast-iron artifacts, old country pine furniture, and chintz sofas. The modern room furnishings are enhanced by floral wall panels, matching floral drapes, and fluffy mohair coverlets; all bedrooms have small sitting areas beside the large teak framed windows affording views of the gardens and the distant hills. The plentiful tour-bus trade does not spoil its carefully fostered charm. *Oughterard, Co. Galway, tel. 091/82328. 62 rooms with bath. Facilities: fishing, indoor heated pool, sauna, tennis court, bar, restaurant. AE, DC, MC, V. Expensive.*

★ **Currarevagh House.** Turn right in the village square and follow the twisting road signposted "Lakeshore" for about 6 km (4 mi) to find this very special, secluded place, pronounced "Currareeva." It's a genuine, unspoiled, old-fashioned country house in which breakfast is still laid out Edwardian buffet–style on the dining room sideboard and the afternoon tea ritual is observed in the drawing room. A terrifying tiger skin hangs on the staircase, and other stuffed hunting trophies jump out at you from the dark wood paneling. Magnificent displays of fresh flowers, gathered from the 150 wooded acres, adorn the lobby and sitting rooms, where plump white armchairs tempt you to a seat in front of marble fireplaces with open turf fires. Rooms are furnished with modest antiques and family hand-me-downs (successive generations of the Hodgson family have lived here since they built the house in 1846). All bedrooms in the main house have different, slightly haphazard color schemes; the front ones overlook Lough Corrib, while others offer an equally pleasant view of the gardens (including rhododendrons, azaleas, camellias, and hydrangeas) and the mountains. The bedrooms in the new wing blend in successfully with the old house. They are more conventionally furnished, with built-in furniture in dark polished wood, and overlook both the lake and the garden. *Oughterard, Co. Galway, tel. 091/82312. 15 rooms with bath. Facilities: fishing (boats for hire), tennis court, private beach (lakeside), croquet, TV room, bar, restaurant. No TV or direct dial phones in rooms. No credit cards. Closed Oct.–Easter except for parties of more than 8. Expensive.*

Recess

Lodging **Ballynahinch Castle.** Turn left off the N59 at the sign for the
★ castle between Recess and Clifden, and after about 3 km (2 mi) look out for a fairy-tale green-and-white-painted gate lodge on the right. The castle is really a large house built in the late 18th

century, on the site of an O'Flaherty castle beside the Ballynahinch River; it's a favorite retreat of statesmen and movie stars—including ex–U.S. President Gerald Ford and actor Alec Guinness. Visitors can walk in the property's 40 wooded acres, and they have access to excellent fishing and shooting facilities. Ballynahinch achieves great comfort without ostentation; the tiled lobby with Persian rugs, for example, has two inviting leather chesterfields in front of an open fire. The wide corridors, carpeted in Turkish red, feature prints and old photos of Connemara on the walls. The biggest bedrooms, in the discreetly added new ground-floor wing, have four-poster beds, Georgian-style mahogany furniture, and floor-to-ceiling windows overlooking the river. Rooms in the old house are equally comfortable and quiet (they do not have televisions). *Ballinafad, Recess, Co. Galway, tel. 095/31006. 28 rooms with bath. Facilities: fishing, shooting, tennis court, croquet, bar, restaurant. AE, DC, MC, V. Expensive.*

Westport

Dining **The Asgard.** This restaurant is situated in a small room above a pub, but it has its own separate entrance and a small anteroom with an open fire for pre-dinner cocktails. White damask napery covers the tables in the red-carpeted and red-draped dining room, which is decorated with large nautical prints and cooled by a brass ceiling fan. Service is friendly and professional. Cream of nettle soup, roast stuffed duckling with orange sauce, and fillet of sole vermouth are typical items on the menu of this popular and reliable eatery. *The Quay, Westport, tel. 098/25319. Reservations advised. Dinner only (award-winning, inexpensive bar food at lunch). AE, DC, MC, V. Moderate.*

Quay Cottage. A tiny waterside cottage has been gutted and cleverly converted into an atmospheric, informal wine bar and shellfish restaurant. Fishing nets, glass floats, lobster pots, and greenery hang from the high-pitched roof with exposed beams. All manner of nautical bric-a-brac also decorates the place. The dining room features rush-seated chairs at the polished oak tables and an open fire on evenings and rainy days. The lively place attracts a youngish crowd, in search of a good time as much as of good food. Try the chowder special (a thick vegetable and mussel soup), garlic butter crab claws, or a half-pound steak fillet, and be sure to sample the homemade brown bread. *The Quay (beside Westport House), Westport, tel. 098/26412. Reservations advised evenings and Sunday lunch. Wine license only. AE, MC, V. Closed Jan. 1–Feb. 1. Moderate.*

Lodging **Hotel Westport.** This glass and aluminum hotel, a five-minute walk from the town center, is quiet and convenient, surrounded by lawns and overlooking the grounds of Westport House. The lobby, bar, and restaurant, decorated in an art-nouveau style, have heavy mahogany and stained-glass partitions. All bedrooms in the two-story bedroom wing are identical but pleasant, with Georgian-style mahogany bureaus and tables, off-white floral comforters, and fully tiled bathrooms. *Westport, Co. Mayo, tel. 098/25122. 49 rooms with bath. Facilities: bar, restaurant (dinner only). AE, DC, MC, V. Moderate.*

Olde Railway Hotel. By far the best bet in the town center, this Victorian railway hotel offers both character and comfort.

Fishing trophies, Victorian plates, framed prints, and water-colors brighten up the solidly furnished lobby and lounge. A mix of Victorian and old pieces furnishes the individually decorated bedrooms. Room No. 209 features a heavy Victorian bed and a river view. No. 114 has a Victorian chaise lounge and a large Georgian wardrobe. Some rooms, such as No. 109, have simpler, white-painted furniture. All the bedrooms are sunny, with ruched Austrian blinds. The front bar can be lively with good, inexpensive lunches and live music in the evening during tourist season and weekends. *The Mall, Westport, Co. Mayo, tel. 098/25166. 20 rooms with bath. Facilities: fishing, restaurant (dinner only), 2 bars. AE, DC, MC, V. Moderate.*

The Arts and Nightlife

The Arts

Visual Arts/ Galleries Although many painters, sculptors, ceramic artists, weavers, and textile makers are based in the West, no major center exists for exhibiting in the region. Small exhibitions, however, can be found in crafts shops, restaurants, bars, and hotel lobbies during the peak tourist season.

The following small galleries are worth checking out for exhibits of reasonably priced painting, sculpture, stonework, ceramics, prints, wall hangings, and batiks by local artists: **Clifden, Co. Galway: Stanley's** (tel. 095/21039); **Millar's** (tel. 095/21038). **Ennis, Co. Clare: De Valera Library** (tel. 065/21616). **Galway City: Penny's** (High St., tel. 091/62739); **University College** (tel. 091/24411). **Oughterard, Co. Galway: Bridge Cottage Gallery** (tel. 091/82407). **Recess, Co. Galway: Joyce's** (tel. 095/34604). **Spiddle, Co. Galway: Stone Art Gallery** (tel. 091/83355). **Westport, Co. Mayo: Westport Antiques and Art Center** (Lodge Rd., tel. 098/26132).

Theater Galway City has two small but famous theaters. **An Taibhdhearc** (Middle St., tel. 091/62024), pronounced "Awn Tie-vark," was founded in 1928 by Hilton Edwards and Micheal Macliammoir as the national Irish-language theater. It continues to produce first-class shows, mainly of Irish works in both the English and the Irish languages.

The **Druid Theatre** (Chapel La., tel. 091/68617) houses a comparatively young group of actors who have built up an excellent reputation over the past 10 years for adventurous and accomplished productions, mainly of 20th-century Irish and European plays, that travel regularly to the Royal Shakespeare Company's small stage in London.

Nightlife

Pubs are more or less the only form of nightlife around. Most large towns have a disco (usually an annex of a hotel or bar) patronized mainly by the under-thirties on Saturday or Sunday night, starting at about 10:30 and finishing at 1 or 2. In Galway City, the discos are located in the Salthill area. Expect to pay £2.50 to £5 cover charge.

In Ennis, an Irish cabaret evening is presented at the **West County Hotel** (tel. 065/28421) every Tuesday and Friday from early June to late September, with the option of dinner and show (cost: £17.50) or show only (cost: £4.50). Also in Ennis, **Cois Na hAbhna** (tel. 061/71166), a stage show featuring traditional music, song, and dance, takes place at 8:30 PM on Saturdays in June and September, and on Mondays, Thursdays, and Saturdays in July and August.

Pubs Traditional-music performances can take place spontaneously, but the pubs listed below have built up a reputation for music, and they foster it by engaging professional musicians to play for at least part of the evening. Such music sessions usually start at about 9:30. Saturday and Sunday are the busiest nights, but in July and August many of these places have music every evening. In general (unless there's a special big-name act), there's no admission charge for these sessions. If you're really enjoying yourself, it is good form to ask the barman to take drinks to the musicians, or do it yourself during the breaks.

Traditionally, all those present at a spontaneous session pay their dues by contributing to the entertainment in turn. In the larger pubs, it is impossible to observe this custom; instead, each musician, as in a jazz session, will take a solo turn. But if you're privileged enough to be included in a small session, try to have someone in your group ready to sing, play music, or tell a good joke. Your participation is an excellent way to make friends. The following places all feature traditional and folk music unless otherwise indicated:

County Clare **Ballyvaughan: Monk's Pub** (no phone). **Burren: Linnane's Pub** (New Quay, tel. 065/78120). **Doolin: Gus O'Connor's** (tel. 065/74168); **McDermott's** (no phone); **McGann's** (tel. 065/74133). **Ennis: Brandon's** (70 O'Connell St., tel. 065/28133); **Brogan's** (24 O'Connell St., tel. 065/29859); **Patrick's Pub** (Market St., tel. 065/28747). **Ennistymon: Nagle's** (Main St., tel. 065/71606). **Kilfenora: Vaughan's Pub** (no phone). **Lahinch: O'Dwyer's 19th** (no phone). **Lisdoonvarna: The Roadside Tavern** (no tel.).

County Galway **Aran Islands: American Bar** (Kilronan, Inishmore, tel. 099/61130). **Clifden: Abbeyglen Castle Hotel** (tel. 095/21070). **Letterfrack: The Bard's Den** (tel. 095/41042). **Galway City: Sally Long's Music Bar** (rock and disco; tel. 091/65756); **The Quays** (Quay St., tel. 091/61777); **Noctan's** (Cross St., tel. 091/66172); **Garravanes** (Shop St., no phone); **Murray's Piano Bar** (cocktail music, Hotel Salthill, Salthill, tel. 091/22448). **Oughterard: Faherty's** (tel. 091/82194).

County Mayo **Achill Island: Alice's Harbor Inn** (Achill Sound, tel. 098/45138); **Achill Sound Hotel** (tel. 098/45245). **Ballina: Downhill Hotel** (tel. 096/21033). **Claremorris: Dalton Inn** (live rock, folk, and disco; tel. 094/71408). **Mulrany: Campbell's Tavern** (tel. 098/36234). **Westport: Ardmore Pub** (The Quay, no tel.); **Hogan's** (The Octagon, no tel.).

9 The Northwest

Yeats Country, Donegal Bay, the Northern Peninsulas

By Andrew Sanger

British travel writer Andrew Sanger is the author of several popular guidebooks; he contributes frequently to several publications, including The Guardian, The Daily Telegraph, and The Sunday Times.

In the wild wet grass-and-heather hills of Donegal, Leitrim, and Sligo, the three counties in the remote Northwest, you'll find some of Ireland's most majestic scenery. Cool, clean waters from the roaring Atlantic Ocean slice the landscape into long peninsulas of breeze-swept rocky crests, each one remote from the next. The lower country, at least where it is covered by layers of moist bog, cuts open to reveal dark brown peat underneath; although this area may be thought less pretty than the rest of the region, it has a haunting, lonely appeal.

Tucked into the folds of the Northwest's hills, modest little market towns and unpretentious villages with muddy streets go about their business quietly. In the squelchy peat bogs, cutters working with long shovels pause to watch and wave as you drive past. Remember to drive slowly along the country lanes, for around any corner you may find a whitewashed thatched cottage with children playing outside, a shepherd leading his flock, or a bicycle-riding farmer wobbling along in the middle of the road.

Keep in mind, though, that the whole region—and County Donegal in particular—attracts a good share of visitors during July and August; this is a favorite vacation area for people who live in nearby Northern Ireland. To be frank, a few places are quite spoiled by popularity with tourists and careless development. The Rosses Peninsula on Donegal's west coast, still sometimes described as beautiful, is marred by too much building. Bundoran, on the coast between Sligo Town and Donegal Town, a cheap-and-cheerful family beach resort full of so-called "Irish gift shops" and "amusement arcades," is another place to pass by rather than visit. On the whole, though, the Northwest is big enough, untamed enough, and grand enough to be able to absorb all of its summer (and weekend) tourists without too much harm.

Something in the turbulent Atlantic air blows over these hills—a sense that the past is not so far away, a lilting half-heard Celtic tune that soothes the soul yet fires the imagination. County Donegal has the country's largest Gaeltacht (Irish-speaking area). Driving in this part of the country, you'll be amused, frustrated, and delighted by turns whenever you come to a crossroads: Signposts show only the Irish place names, often so unlike the English versions as to be completely unrecognizable. All is not lost, however—any good map generally gives both the Irish and the English names, and locals are usually more than happy to help out with directions (in English), sometimes with a yarn thrown in. County Donegal was part of the near-indomitable ancient kingdom of Ulster, which was not conquered by the English until the 17th century. By the time they were driven out in the 1920s, the English had still not eradicated rural Donegal's Celtic inheritance.

If the whole of Ireland is a land of seemingly infinite diversity, in the Northwest even the air, the light, and the colors of the countryside change like a kaleidoscope. Look once, and scattered snow-white clouds are flying above tawny-brown slopes. Look again, and suddenly the sun has brilliantly illuminated some magnificent reds and purples in the undergrowth. The inconstant skies brighten and darken at will, bringing out a whole spectrum of subtle shades within the unkempt gorse and heather, the rocky slopes merging into somber peat and grassy meadows of scintillating green.

Not only close to the bracing ocean shore but also farther inland, water in all its forms dominates the Northwest; countless lakes, running streams, and rivers wind through lovely pastoral valleys. Be prepared for plenty of rainfall as well; don't forget to carry a raincoat or umbrella—although, as a kind local may inform you, the "brolly" acts purely as a talisman: "For it's only when you *don't* have it with you that the rain will really come down" is a piece of local wisdom.

Essential Information

Arriving and Departing by Plane

Airports The principal international air arrival point to the Northwest is the tiny airport at Charlestown, near Knock. Usually known simply as **Knock Airport,** the official name is **Horan International Airport** (tel. 094/67222). **Eglinton Airport** (tel. 0504/810784), at Derry City, a few miles over the border, receives flights from the U.K. airports of Manchester and Glasgow and from Dublin. Eglinton is a particularly convenient airport for reaching northern County Donegal. Small local airfields are also located at **Carrickfinn** (tel. 075/48232) near Dungloe and **Sligo Airport** (tel. 071/68280 or 071/68318) at Strandhill, 8 km (5 mi) from Sligo Town.

Airlines from the United Kingdom **Ryanair** offers flights daily to Knock Airport from London and other British and Irish airports. **Aer Lingus** has direct flights daily to Knock Airport, Eglinton Airport, and Sligo Airport from Dublin. **Loganair** provides direct flights daily to Eglinton Airport from Manchester and Glasgow, and to Carrickfinn Airport near Dungloe (four flights weekly) from Glasgow.

Between the Airports and Your Destination
By Car For car renters, Knock Airport is convenient—just 54½ km (34 mi) south of Sligo Town; a car rental desk is located at the airport. You can also pick up rental cars at Sligo and Eglinton (Derry) airports.

By Bus If you aren't driving, Knock Airport becomes less attractive, as you'll have no easy public transportation link to your destination, except the once-a-day (in season) local bus to Charlestown (11 km/7 mi away). Nor can you rely on catching a bus at the smaller airports, except at Sligo Airport, where buses run from Sligo Town to meet all flights.

By Taxi Cabs sometimes stand waiting outside Knock Airport to meet incoming flights, but passengers arriving at the other airports may have to phone a local taxi company. Phone numbers of taxi companies are available from airport information desks and are also displayed beside pay phones inside the airport terminals.

Arriving and Departing by Car, Train, and Bus

By Car Sligo, the largest town in the Northwest, is relatively accessible on the main routes. The N4 travels the 224 km (140 mi) direct from Dublin to Sligo, but you need to allow at least four hours for this journey. The N15 continues from Sligo Town to Donegal Town and proceeds from Donegal Town to Derry City, just over the border in the province of Northern Ireland. The best approach for anyone driving up from the West and the Southwest is on the N17, connecting Sligo to Galway.

By Train Sligo Town is linked by a direct train line to Dublin. From Dublin three trains a day are available, and the journey takes 3 hours and 20 minutes. The trip costs £26 one-way, £28 round-trip (valid up to four days), and £34.50 round-trip (valid up to one month). The train stops at Ballymote (20 minutes from Sligo), Boyle (40 minutes), and Carrick-on-Shannon (50 minutes). However, if you want to get to Sligo Town by rail from other provincial towns, you'll be forced to make some inconvenient connections and take roundabout routes. The rest of the region has no railway services. Contact **Irish Rail** (tel. 01/366222).

By Bus **Bus Éireann** (tel. 01/366111) can get you from Dublin to Sligo Town in four hours for £7.50 one-way, £10 round-trip. Three buses a day from Dublin are available. Another bus route, three times a day from Dublin, gets to Letterkenny, in the heart of County Donegal, in 4¼ hours, via a short trip across the Northern Ireland border, for £10 one-way, £13 round-trip. Other Bus Éireann services connect Sligo Town to other towns all over Ireland; for these connections, call 071/2152.

Getting Around

By Car
Driving Roads are uncongested, but in some places they are in a poor state of repair. In the Irish-speaking areas, signposts are written only in the Irish (Gaelic) language, which can be confusing. You need to prepare beforehand for this by checking the Irish names of places on your route.

Car Rentals You can rent a car in Sligo Town from **O'Mara** (tel. 071/44068), or at Sligo Airport from **Johnson & Perrott** (tel. 071/68280). At Knock Airport, cars may be rented from **Avis** (tel. 094/67252). A medium-size four-door costs around £40 per day with unlimited mileage (inclusive of insurance and taxes), or around £240 per week. Avis rentals tend to be a little more expensive than other companies'. If you're planning to tour mostly northern County Donegal, you may find it more convenient to rent a car in Derry City from **Hertz** (tel. 0504/360420). If you're planning to take a rental car across the border to Northern Ireland, inform the company in advance and check the insurance position.

By Bus **Bus Éireann** services operate out of Sligo Town (tel. 071/60066) and Letterkenny (tel. 074/21309) to destinations all over the region, as well as to other parts of Ireland. From Sligo Town, you can reach almost any point in the region for under £10. Several other local bus companies link towns and villages in the Northwest, including **Funtrek** (tel. 01/730852) and **McGeehans** (tel. 075/46101).

Important Addresses and Numbers

Tourist
Information The main visitor information center for the whole Northwest region is the Tourist Information Office (TIO) in **Sligo Town** (Áras Reddan, Temple St., tel. 071/61201). Sligo is in the extreme south of the region; if you are traveling in County Donegal in the North, try the TIO at **Letterkenny** (Derry Rd., tel. 074/21160) in a small chalet-type modern building about 1.6 km (1 mi) out of town. Both TIOs are open year-round: Sept.–May, weekdays 9–1 and 2–5; June, Mon.–Sat. 9–1 and 2–6; July–Aug., Mon.–Sat. 9–8, Sun. 10–2.

The following TIOs are open only during the summer months (usually the first week in June to the second week in September):

Bundoran, County Donegal (Main St., tel. 072/41350).

Carrick-on-Shannon, County Leitrim (on the river quay, tel. 078/20170). Information for County Leitrim and its county town.

Donegal Town, County Donegal (Quay St., tel. 073/21148).

Dungloe, County Donegal (in the village center, tel. 075/21297).

Emergencies   Call 999 for **police, fire,** or **ambulance** services.

Main Police   **Carrick-on-Shannon** (tel. 078/20021), **Donegal Town** (tel. 073/
Stations   21021), **Letterkenny** (tel. 074/22222), and **Sligo Town** (tel. 071/42031).

Hospitals   **Letterkenny General Hospital** (High Rd., Letterkenny, Co. Donegal, tel. 074/22022) and **Sligo General Hospital** (Dromahair Rd., Sligo Town, Co. Sligo, tel. 071/42161).

Guided Tours

In July and August, walking tours of Sligo Town depart twice daily from the Tourist Information Office at 11 AM and 7 PM. They are free and last about 1 to 1½ hours. However, the guides are generally students, so a tip of 50p or £1 is welcome. For a friendly, relaxed minibus tour of the area with a knowledgeable guide, call **John Houze** (tel. 071/42747) for his tour around Lough Gill (cost: £5 adults, £2.50 children under 16) and his tour north of Sligo Town to Drumcliff, Lissadell House, and Creevykeel (cost: £6 adults, £2.50 children under 16). **Bus Éireann** (tel. 071/60066 in Sligo, 074/21309 in Letterkenny) offers useful budget-priced one-day guided coach tours of the Donegal Highlands and to Glenveagh National Park. These tours start from Bundoran, Sligo Town, Ballyshannon, and Donegal Town.

Exploring the Northwest

Highlights for First-time Visitors

Ardara (*see* Tour 2)

Donegal Town (*see* Tour 2)

Glenveagh National Park (*see* Tour 3)

Grianan Ailigh, for the view of Lough Swilly (*see* Tour 3)

Lough Gill (*see* Tour 1)

Sheephaven Bay, from Rosguill Peninsula to Horn Head (*see* Tour 3)

Tour 1: Yeats Country—Sligo Town and Environs

Numbers in the margin correspond to points of interest on the Yeats Country and Around Donegal Bay and the Sligo Town maps.

This tour, which covers the most accessible part of the Northwest, visits a pleasant, peaceful countryside of lakes, farms, and woodland on the border of Counties Sligo and Leitrim. If you are familiar with the romantic poems of W. B. Yeats, it will undoubtedly bring to mind some of his best writing. Yeats knew intimately all these villages and landscapes and eloquently celebrated many of them in verse. Often on this route, you'll have glimpses of "bare Ben Bulben's head," as he called flat-topped Ben Bulben Mountain, which looms over the western end of the Dartry range.

1 Begin this tour at **Sligo Town,** although you may not be staying in the town itself; the most interesting accommodations are located a few miles out. This busy marketplace is very much the region's principal community. With a population of about 17,000 inhabitants, it is the only sizable town in the whole of Northwest Ireland. Sligo is centered around two bridges across the River Garavogue, and its name in Irish, Sligeach, means "place of shells." This lovely riverside location, squeezed onto a patch of land between Sligo Bay and Lough Gill, often became a battleground in its earlier days. The community was attacked by Viking invaders in the 9th century and, later, by a succession of rival Irish and Anglo-Norman conquerors. In 1245, Sligo was fortified by the most successful of these victors, Maurice FitzGerald, earl of Kildare, although nothing is left now of his medieval castle.

Modern-day Sligo offers visitors only modest sights, but it does deserve a stroll, especially because of its close associations **2** with W. B. Yeats and his talented family. At the **Yeats Memorial Building** beside Hyde Bridge, an annual Yeats Summer School is conducted every August—guest speakers are invited to lecture on the world-renowned poet and his contemporaries. During the rest of the year, occasional exhibitions and other lectures on the writer are held in the area.

Yeats's brother, Jack, was a famous painter in his day; he once said, "I never did a painting without putting a thought of Sligo in it." Yeats's father, John, had a considerable reputation as a portraitist. Many of the works of these two artists, including portraits of W.B., are displayed with paintings by other Irish **3** artists at the **Sligo County Library and Museum,** on Stephen Street. Several pictures with connections to the Yeats family were donated by a New York stockbroker, James A. Healey, whose mother emigrated to the United States in 1884. Other items at the museum that can be seen on request are a collection of Yeats's first editions and such intriguing memorabilia as the author's personal letters and the Irish tricolor flag that draped his coffin when he was buried at nearby Drumcliff. *Stephen St., tel. 071/2212. Admission free. Library open Tues.–Sat. 10–1 and 2–5, and also 7–9 on Tues. and Thurs. Museum open June–Sept., Tues.–Sat. 10:30–12:30 and 2:30–4:30.*

To find Sligo's only existing relic of the Middle Ages, walk down Bridge Street, nearly opposite the library and museum. Cross the river and turn left into Abbey Street, and here you'll find **4** the rather forlorn ruins of the **13th-century Abbey,** built for the Dominicans by Maurice FitzGerald. After a fire in 1414, it was extensively rebuilt, only to be destroyed again by Cromwell's Puritans in 1641. Some fine stonework remains, especially in the 15th-century cloisters. *Admission free. Usually open—if*

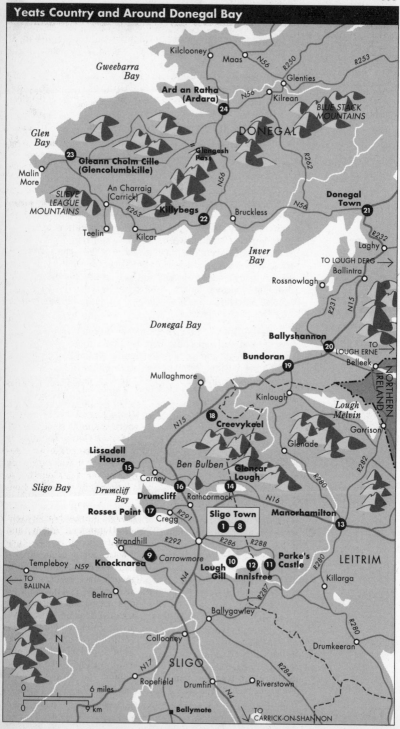

Yeats Country and Around Donegal Bay

Sligo Town

not, key with caretaker (currently Mr. A. McGuinn, 6 Charlotte St.).

Retrace your steps, turning left into Teeling Street to see the **❺ Courthouse.** Compared with the generally simple style of most Irish country architecture, this Victorian Gothic building is distinctly elaborate with its flamboyant, turreted Gothic exterior; it is not open to casual visitors. After it was built, the structure became a symbol for English power. The Courthouse takes its inspiration from the much larger Law Courts in London.

Continue beyond the Courthouse into Old Market Street right **❻** onto High Street, passing the new **Dominican Abbey,** and left onto Church Street. At the end of Church Street, turn right onto Charles Street. You will notice along these streets that Sligo has numerous churches of all denominations. Presbyterians, Methodists, and even Plymouth Brethren are represented here, as well as Anglicans (Church of Ireland) and, of course, Roman Catholics. According to the Irish writer Sean O'Faolain, "The best Protestant stock in all Ireland is in Sligo." The Yeats family were part of that stock. At the end of Charles Street, turn left onto John Street. If the door is unlocked, step **❼** inside little **St. John's Cathedral** (Church of Ireland) on John Street. Admire its handsome square tower and fortifications; in the north transept you'll find a memorial to Susan Mary Yeats, mother of W.B. and Jack. *Admission free. No set hours.*

Next door is the larger and newer Catholic church. Walk round into Temple Street where you'll find the church's entrance and

8 County Sligo's **Tourist Information Office,** useful for the whole of the Northwest. It's located in the same building as the **Hawkswell Theatre,** an unattractive '60s low-rise on the corner of Charles Street.

Time Out One of Sligo's best pubs is **Hargadon's** (O'Connell St.), an atmospheric old place with cozy private snugs (rooms)—try the fine sandwiches, cakes, and coffee. On the same street nearby, **Beezie's** (tel. 071/45239) is a lively, popular bar and restaurant serving reasonably priced "Tourist Menu" meals (typical Irish meat dishes with two vegetables).

Numbers in the margin correspond to points of interest on the Yeats Country and Around Donegal Bay map.

9 Rising to the west of Sligo is **Knocknarea** (328 meters/1,083 feet), the "cairn-heaped grassy hill" that once caught Yeats's imagination. To drive out for a closer look at this flat mountain not unlike Ben Bulben, take the Strandhill road out of town (the R292; it goes due west, following Sligo Bay). After 8 km (5 mi), a left turn brings you closer to the hilltop, though you will have to get out and walk to reach the summit, where you will have a good view of the mountains of Counties Donegal and Sligo. The huge cairn at its summit, a heaped-stone monument made with 40,000 tons of rock, is traditionally believed to commemorate "passionate Maeve," as Yeats called her, a 1st-century AD Celtic queen of Connaught who is the heroine of many Irish legends. Archaeologists argue, though, that the cairn is more likely a 3,000-year-old tomb.

Strandhill, at the foot of Knocknarea, is an unremarkable seaside resort, though it does have a good sandy beach and one unusual attraction called Dolly's Cottage, a typical 19th-century rural dwelling that serves now as a folk museum in which members of the Irish Countrywomen's Association sell their homemade wares. Some evenings, folk music sessions are held here. *Admission free. Open July–Aug., daily 3–5.*

A short drive southeast of Knocknarea is **Carrowmore,** a site where several megalithic remains cover a broad area. Unfortunately, many have been badly damaged, but this is Ireland's largest single group of Stone Age monuments. Most are communal tombs dating back to 4000 BC. You can reach Carrowmore on the minor road back to Sligo Town. The whole trip around Knocknarea and back into town is about 16 km (10 mi).

10 Next, head from Sligo Town toward the shores of beautiful, gentle **Lough Gill.** To leave Sligo, get onto Stephen Street and take the N16 out of town (signposted to Manorhamilton and Enniskillen). Turn right almost at once onto the R286. Within minutes you will find some gorgeous views of the lake so adored by the young Yeats. In fact, Lough Gill in Irish means simply "Lake Beauty." The legend is (there would have to be a legend about such a place) that the bell from Sligo's Abbey lies at the bottom of the lake and those who are without sin can hear it pealing. No one has ever reported hearing it.

11 As the road dips down to the lake, it changes to R288, where you'll soon encounter **Parke's Castle,** on the right as the road dips down. This sturdy fortified house was constructed in the 17th century by an English gentleman settler who needed the strong fortifications to defend himself against a hostile populace. What made relations worse is that he obtained his building materials mainly by dismantling a historic fortress on the site, which had belonged to the clan leaders of the O'Rourkes of Breffni (this district used to be called Breffni). The entrance fee includes a short video show on the castle and local history. A snack bar is available. *Tel. 071/64149. Admission: £1. Open June–Sept., daily 9:30–6:30; Apr.–May and Oct., daily 10–5.*

About 1.6 km (1 mi) farther, the road twists away from the lake, following the River Bonet toward Dromahair. Just at the edge of the village, you can pause first to ponder the story behind **The Old Hall,** a fine riverside mansion on the river's right bank (signposted; not open to visitors). It was built in 1626 for another unwelcome English landowner, Sir William Villiers, who constructed his house from stones taken from the ruins of an important O'Rourke castle that stood right next door. In that old fort, in the year 1152, Tiernán O'Rourke lived with his pretty wife, Dervorguilla, until one day their castle was attacked by Dermot MacMurrough, king of Leinster, who managed to persuade Dervorguilla to run away with him. O'Rourke was furious and formed an alliance with all the other Irish chieftains to bring MacMurrough to justice.

O'Rourke did get his wife back, but MacMurrough then sought help from the Plantagenet king of England, Henry II, who sent one of his best men, Strongbow, to fight beside MacMurrough against the Irish kings. And so began the Anglo-Norman invasion of Ireland, the start of the long effort by England to conquer the Irish.

On the other side of the River Bonet stand the handsome remains of **Creevelea Abbey,** reached by a few minutes' walk along a footpath. In fact not an abbey but a friary, Creevelea was founded for the Franciscans in 1508 by a later generation of O'Rourkes. It was the last Franciscan community to be founded before the suppression of the monasteries by England's King Henry VIII. Like many such ruined abbeys, the place still has religious meaning for the local people, who treat it with reverence. One curiosity of this abbey is the especially large south transept; notice, too, its endearing little cloisters, with well-executed carvings on the pillars of St. Francis of Assisi. *Signposted at Dromahair. Admission free. Accessible all day.*

Real Yeats fans will want to cast eyes on nearby Innisfree, the "Lake Isle" around which the poet weaved his enticing imagery:

> "I will arise and go now, and go to Innisfree . . .
> And live alone in the bee-loud glade. . . .
> I hear lake water lapping with low sounds by the shore;
> While I stand on the roadway, or on the pavements grey,
> I hear it in the deep heart's core."

To reach Innisfree, drive through the little village of **Dromahair** to take the R287, the minor road that heads back along the south side of Lough Gill toward Sligo Town. Turn right at a small crossroads, after two or three miles, where signposts ⑫ point to **Innisfree** (pronounced *Inish Free*). A little road leads another couple miles down to the lakeside, where you can see the island just offshore. The small tree-covered island is not the haven of peace that it must have been when Yeats wrote those words—excursions arrive by boat from Sligo Town, and visitors traveling by car turn up throughout the day.

A little beyond the Innisfree turnoff lies **Dooney Rock,** across the water on the southwestern end of the Lough Gill; this is where the poet daydreamed, contemplated the lake's islands, and imagined a fiddler on the rock who made "folk dance like a wave of the sea."

Come back along the R287 toward Dromahair, but instead of turning into the village, continue driving (the road number changes to R280) toward **Manorhamilton.** This small rural town was built in the 17th century for the Scottish Planter (colonist settling on Irish lands confiscated from Catholic owners) Sir Frederick Hamilton. Sir Frederick had been given the local manor house by Charles I of England (hence the town's name). The manor itself is now an ivy-covered ruin, and there's not much to see here. The surrounding scenery, however, is superb. Take the N16, signposted to Sligo Town, for about 9½ km (6 mi) until you reach the little turning that heads right to **Glencar Lough.** The turn is signposted "waterfall," and you'll discover several waterfalls here, with a parking lot and footpath leading to one of the highest. The lake is fed by the River Drumcliff and other streams at the foot of the Dartry Mountains: "Where the wandering water gushes/ From the hills above Glen-Car," as Yeats saw it.

Stay on Lough Glencar's right bank, and you'll reach a fork in the road: a left heads back to the N16 and Sligo Town, a right weaves across the country toward the N15 and the villages of Drumcliff and Carney. You want to take the right, but even if you miss it, almost any other right turn off the N16 will lead you in the same direction.

Next, stop at **Lissadell House** (signposted from the N15), near Carney, beside the Atlantic waters of Drumcliff Bay. This impressive aristocratic residence has belonged to the distinguished Gore-Booth family since it was built in 1834. The family became good friends of W. B. Yeats, who recalled seeing the house often as a child from his grandmother's carriage. Later, in 1894, he was invited to visit the house and acquainted with the two Gore-Booth daughters, Eva and Constance. He recalled their meeting in verse: "The light of evening, Lissadell,/ Great windows open to the south,/ Two girls in silk kimonos." Eva became a poet, while sister Constance went on to lead a dramatic political life as a fiery Irish nationalist, taking a leading role in the 1916 Easter Rising against the British.

Lissadell House is now open to the public, with tours of the house, a crafts shop, and refreshments. A copy of Yeats's poem "In Memory of Eva Gore-Booth and Con Markievicz" is displayed on a sign beside the main gate at the entrance, and aficionados of all things Yeatsian will find the house interesting if only for the associations with the poet. Others may prefer to wander the grounds. The interior is typical of 19th-century aristocratic country homes. The woods of the Lissadell estate have become a forestry and wildlife reserve—a fine place for bird-watchers, it serves as a home to Ireland's largest colony of the barnacle goose, along with several other species of wildfowl. *Tel. 071/63150. Admission: £2 adults, 50p children. Open June–Sept., Mon.–Sat. 10:30–12, 2–4:30.*

Double back from Lissadell, through Carney, in the direction of Drumcliff. Just north of Carney, by the way, the legendary

Battle of the Book took place in AD 561, one of the earliest and most acrimonious cases in the whole history of copyright law.

St. Columba, a recluse and missionary who established Christian churches and religious communities in Northwest Ireland, is thought to have been the founder of a monastic settlement around 575 at **Drumcliff,** east of Lissadell and Carney on the N15. The monastery flourished for many centuries, but all that is left of it now is the base of a Round Tower and a richly carved High Cross dating from around 1000. These remains stand close together by the road. More notable now is the fact that W. B. Yeats lies buried with his wife, Georgie, in an unpretentious grave in the grounds of Drumcliff's plain and simple Protestant church, opposite the High Cross. Yeats actually died on the French Riviera in 1939; it took almost a full decade for his body to be brought back to Drumcliff in accordance with his wishes. In the poem "Under Ben Bulben," he spelled out not only where he was to be buried but also what should be written on the tombstone: "Cast a cold eye/ On life, on death./ Horseman, pass by!" Today you can stand in the churchyard and read those words cut into the gray headstone. It is easy to see why the curious, flat-topped Ben Bulben (536 meters/1,730 feet) made such an impression on the poet; the mountain gazes calmly down upon the small rural church, and at the same time it faces the mighty Atlantic.

Before returning to Sligo Town, for another sight of the Atlantic breakers you can turn right off the N15 at Rathcormack and take a trip, via Gregg, out to **Rosses Point,** where Yeats and his brother, Jack, often stayed during their summer vacations. This popular seaside and leisure area with good safe sandy beaches and fine views is around 6 km (4 mi) from the N15 and is clearly signposted. Two popular sportsmen's havens, the County Sligo Golf Club and the Sligo Yacht Club, are also located here. From Rosses Point, the drive is just 8 km (5 mi) straight back to Sligo Town on the R291.

Tour 2: Around Donegal Bay

The soaring Donegal hills beckon from the horizon as you travel north to Donegal Town from Sligo Town. The rolling coastal fields break open here and there to give startling views across the waters of Donegal Bay. The whole stretch from Sligo Town to Donegal Town has become the Northwest's most popular vacation area, but this is certainly no French Riviera. You'll pass a few small and unremarkable seashore resorts, and, in some places, you may find that haphazard and fairly tasteless construction detracts from the scenery. In between these minor resort developments, the traveler encounters wide-open spaces free of traffic and full of fresh air. The most interesting part of this tour lies on the north side of the bay—all that rocky indented coastline due west of Donegal Town. That's where you'll breathe a sigh of relief and enter the true away-from-it-all world of County Donegal.

Take the N15 from Sligo Town in the direction of Donegal Town. The whole County Sligo coastal region is dotted with numerous prehistoric sites; 16 km (10 mi) after you pass Drumcliff (*see* Tour 1, *above*), you'll reach, at **Creevykeel,** one of Ireland's best megalithic court-cairns. The site (signposted) lies off the road, just beyond the edge of the village of Cliffony. You'll see a burial area and an enclosed open-air "court" where rituals were performed around 2500 BC.

Here you're crossing the county line into Donegal, but the first town reached could hardly be less typical of the area. **Bundoran** is one of Ireland's most popular seaside resorts, yet it remains remarkably unsophisticated, with little to offer except a long seafront development favored by Irish and Northern Irish family vacationers. While its souvenir shops and amusement arcades are not very appealing, it does have certain attractions. You'll find first-class golf facilities available on the edge of town at Aughrus Head, as well as horseback riding, and good fishing is 6½ km (4 mi) away at **Lough Melvin.** North of the town center you'll find another handsome beach at Tullan Strand, washed by the kind of waves that thrill surfers. Between the main beach and Tullan, some weird cliffside rock formations have been sculpted by the Atlantic's power. Something of a local spectacle, these natural creations have been given whimsical names such as the Fairy Bridges, the Wishing Chair, and the Puffing Hole (this last one blows wind and water from the waves pounding below).

Continue on the N15 for another 6½ km (4 mi) to reach **Ballyshannon,** which rises gently from the banks of the River Erne. On the left-hand side of the road as it reaches the town, you'll see the factory of **Donegal Parian China** (tel. 072/51826), which produces exquisite chinaware and porcelain. Stop at the factory for one of the free 15-minute tours that are given all day from May to September. (You may be more familiar with chinaware from the older **Belleek Pottery** [tel. 0365/65501], which straddles the Republic–Northern Ireland border 6½ km/4 mi away. Both companies produce a delicate cream-colored pottery of great value and elegance.)

Lough Erne marks an ancient frontier, and the Ballyshannon River crossing was for centuries the gateway into the Ulster region. Through the medieval period Ballyshannon was the southern stronghold of the O'Donnell clan, whose lands eventually became County Donegal. Today, Ballyshannon is a peaceful little town with mountain views; the surrounding area offers great opportunities for anglers because the local river and estuary are both teeming with fish. The town was also the birthplace of the prolific Irish poet William Allingham. Each year in early August, the normally quiet village springs to life with a grand festival of folk and traditional music (*see* The Arts and Nightlife, below).

Time Out   In its triangular central area, Ballyshannon has several bars and places to grab a snack. The biggest and most popular pub is the green-shuttered **Seán Óg's,** which serves light Irish meals all day and features traditional music in the evenings.

Stay on the N15 toward Donegal Town, 21 km (13 mi) away. About a mile before you arrive in town, a sign on the right points to **Donegal Craft Village** (shops are usually open 9 to 5), rather a grand name for a small roadside complex of new crafts shops. You can shop for imaginative pottery, handwoven goods, and ceramics and stop off at a coffee shop that sells snacks. Then continue on into **Donegal,** turning past the town's small harbor amid trees on the edge of Donegal Bay. Here you'll find a view across the water, with its tiny islands and wooded banks, that is tranquil and delightful. The road brings you into a triangular main area called the Diamond (a common name for the central square of a former Plantation town). Donegal is a small, carefully designed place with a population of fewer than 2,000. Rebuilt in the 17th century, it still preserves a touch of the dignity of that era. Its history actually goes back a lot farther than that Plantation period, when Protestant colonists were planted on Irish property confiscated from their Catholic owners. Donegal was previously known in Irish as *Dun na nGall*, or "Foreigners' Fort." The foreigners in question were Vikings, who in the 9th century set up camp here to facilitate their pillaging and looting. After they had been driven out, the town was taken over by the powerful O'Donnell clan (originally Cinel Conail), who made it the capital of Tyrconail, their extensive Ulster territories.

Near the north corner of the Diamond, clan leader Hugh O'Donnell built **Donegal Castle** (in fact, a fortified tower house rather than a castle) in the 1470s. More than a century later, this structure was the home of his descendant Hugh Roe O'Donnell, who faced the might of the invading English. He was to be the last clan chief of Tyrconail. As the English made steady gains, in 1602 he went to Spain to rally reinforcements from his allies there and died overseas. The Irish faction at Donegal Castle was defeated by English forces and it came into the possession of Sir Basil Brooke. In 1610, he reconstructed the little castle, making it much more lordly and luxurious, and adding the fine Jacobean fortified mansion with towers and turrets that can still be seen today. Inside, there are large ornate fireplaces carved with Brooke's crest, but, due to restoration slated throughout early 1993, the interior of Donegal Castle is closed. *Tirchonaill St. Admission free to view exterior.*

In 1474, Hugh O'Donnell founded a monastery by the waterside of Donegal Town for the Franciscans, but it was partially destroyed by gunpowder in 1601 during a war with English invaders. Despite the damage, it was probably in this monastery that the *Annals of the Four Masters* was written from 1632 to 1636. This important tome chronicles the whole Celtic history and mythology of Ireland from earliest times up to the year 1618. The Four Masters were four monks who believed (correctly, as it turned out) that Celtic culture was doomed after the English conquest, and they wanted to preserve as much of it as they could. At the National Library in Dublin, you may see facsimile pages of the monks' work (the original is kept under lock and key). The monastery's gaunt ruins, impressive more for the location than for what survives of the buildings, can still be seen on the bank of Donegal Bay, just a few paces from the town center and sheltered behind a sea wall. What remains is the choir, south transept, and two sides of the cloisters. *Freely accessible.*

A monument to the Four Masters is situated in the Diamond. Around the three sides of the Diamond, you'll find popular bars, a couple of good old-fashioned hotels, and several shops stocked with high-quality Donegal tweeds and knitwear. Donegal Town has long been one of two principal marketplaces where the county's handicrafts are brought down from the hills to be sold to the rest of the world (the other is the village of Ardara; *see* below). Spinning has almost disappeared now, but handweaving and knitting still contribute to the livelihoods of thousands of country people. In small workshops attached to their rural cottages, they produce top-grade handknits as well as what is regarded as the finest tweed in the world. Donegal Tweed is the name of a universally recognized style of cloth—a sturdy woolen fabric both soft and hard wearing, with distinctive mixed muted colors—that is still at its best when made in these Donegal mountains.

What makes the Donegal area so perfect for tweed making? The natural humidity of the air is important, as is the extremely soft water of the River Eske, which drains off the peat bogs and is used to wash the wool. If you've the time and inclination, and wish to judge the difference in quality, you might find it worthwhile to shop around the region for your handknits and tweed clothes—several village outlets have lower prices than in Donegal Town (*see* Shopping, below).

One well-known shop on the Diamond is **Magee's,** a general clothing store founded in 1866. The original Mr. Magee handed down his business in 1887 to his young cousin Mr. Temple, and the company, now providing suitings to top department stores and clothing manufacturers all over the world, is still owned and run by the Temple family. Much of the stock that carries Magee's label is made in the store's own factory beside the River Eske, only a short walk from the shop. Magee's tweed jackets are said to be among the best in the world, yet they are not expensive if you buy them here. A tour of the weaving factory is fascinating, if a little rushed. You'll see how old-fashioned handwork can be combined with the most modern electronic looms, the two complementing each other. Signs around the factory explain to visitors what is going on. *The Diamond, tel. 073/21100. Free factory tour (lasts around 10 min). No definite times: the first tour starts at about 11, the last at about 3.*

Time Out | If you feel hungry before or after looking at **Magee's,** you won't need to leave the shop to find a bite to eat. The store has its own restaurant on the premises, serving snacks and simple dishes such as baked potatoes, quiches, and salads, or scones and cakes ideal for an inexpensive afternoon tea.

The main road west is the N56, which runs slightly inland from a magnificent shoreline of rocky inlets with great sea views; it's worthwhile turning off the road from time to time to catch a better sight of the coast. About 6½ km (4 mi) out of Donegal Town, the N56 skirts **Mountcharles,** a bleak hillside village that looks back across the bay. Stay on the N56, which takes you through **Bruckless,** where you'll locate a good bed-and-breakfast accommodation, the 18th-century Georgian **Bruckless House** (*see* Dining and Lodging, below). Don't be too impressed by the Round Tower in the churchyard here, which is not an authentic medieval structure but a 19th-century belfry. Soon after Bruckless, the N56 turns inland across the bogs toward Ardara, but this tour stays by the shore.

② The road now becomes the R263, which runs through attractive heathland and wooded hills down to **Killybegs.** This thriving little fishing port takes one by surprise, with its big trawlers from Spain and France moored in its welcoming harbor. Although it is by far the most industrialized place along this coast, the village retains a certain charm because of its waterfront setting. Killybegs also used to serve as a center for the manufacture of Donegal hand-tufted carpets. Examples of this much-sought-after product have found their way into such varied places as the White House and the Vatican.

After Killybegs, the R263 narrows, climbs, and twists, giving even better views of Donegal Bay before descending again into pretty **Kilcar,** a traditional center of tweed making. The next village, signposted by its Irish name **An Charraig (Carrick),** clings to the foot of the Slieve League Mountains, whose color-streaked ocean cliffs are the highest in Ireland and among the most spectacular. To see them, you'll have to do some serious walking on a difficult coastal path, starting out from the Irish-speaking village of **Teelin,** a mile south from Carrick.

After another 8 km (5 mi), crossing barren moorland, the road **㉓** reaches **Gleann Cholm Cille (Glencolumbkille).** This tiny, spread-out hamlet clings to the rockbound harbor of Glen Bay, looking straight out to the pounding Atlantic. The name of this dramatic spot means St. Columba's Glen (or, alternatively, Columba's Glen Church), and the legend is that St. Columba, a Christian missionary (*see* Drumcliff in Tour 1, above), lived here for a while during the 6th century with a group of followers. Some 40 prehistoric cairns are scattered around the village, and these have become connected locally with the St. Columba myths. The **House of St. Columba,** on the clifftop rising north of the village, is a small oratory said to have been used by the saint himself. Inside, stone constructions are supposed to have been his bed and chair. Every year on June 9, starting at midnight, local barefoot people make a two-mile barefoot procession called *An Turas* (the journey) around 15 medieval crosses and ancient cairns, collectively called the Stations of the Cross.

The **Folk Village** near the beach in Glencolumbkille is an imaginative museum of rural life. The exhibit is arranged as a group of traditional-style cottages—representative of three centuries—which are described on a guided tour. The dwellings are true to the old life, with bare earth floors and very basic living conditions. The complex also offers a crafts shop, where high-quality local handmade products can be bought. There's also a tea shop with snacks. *Tel. 073/30017. Admission: £1.50. Open May–Apr., Oct., Mon.–Sat. 10–6, Sun. 12–6. June–Sept., Mon.–Sat. 10–7, Sun. 12–7.*

From Glencolumbkille, if you drive 25½ km (16 mi) up and over the scenic curves of **Glengesh Pass** with a succession of switch-**㉔** backs, you'll go down to the sea again at **Ard an Ratha (Ardara—** say it with the accent on the *last a*). This unpretentious, old-fashioned hamlet of low, pale cottages among the green and brown hills is fortuitously situated at the head of a lovely ocean inlet. For centuries, Ardara has been an important wool-trading center, where great cloth fairs were held on the first of every month. Nowadays, a Weavers' Fair and Vintage Weekend is held only once a year, as near to July 1 as possible, and it has more to do with music, dance, and having fun than with selling homespun. Ardara actually enjoys traditional music all year round; it has a large number of charming and popular pubs, though several seem to be doubling as shops.

Though the cloth fairs have died out, cottage workers in the surrounding countryside still provide Ardara (and County Donegal) with very-high-quality handwoven cloths and, especially, handknits. If you fancy a chunky Aran sweater, you'll find few better or less expensive places to look for one than this area. You'll have several stores to choose from (*see* Shopping, below). During the summer, Ardara attracts quite a large number of visitors and verges on being overcrowded. Yet the tourists make little real impact: Ardara holds loyally to its own traditions and history.

Time Out The long-established **Nesbitt Arms** (tel. 075/41103) in the village center is a reasonable place for a drink and a snack.

The N56, the Donegal coast's narrow and unfrequented "main road," runs through Ardara. Heading south to return to Donegal Bay and Donegal Town (40 km/25 mi), the road runs first across peat bogs—waterlogged grasslands of tawny, tweedy colors ruled across with black lines where the turf has been cut. North from Ardara, the road takes an erratic course up to **Dungloe** (40 km/25 mi), where you can begin the next tour.

Tour 3: Northern Donegal

Numbers in the margin correspond to points of interest on the Northern Peninsulas map.

Traveling on northern County Donegal's country roads, you'll feel that you have escaped at last from all the world's hurry and hassle. True, the county's largest town, Letterkenny, is up here. And Letterkenny, with a population of 6,500, even has a set of traffic lights—the only traffic lights in the whole of the county. For the rest, you'll discover almost nothing but scenery: broad island-studded loughs of deep dark tranquillity; unkempt, windswept, sheep-grazed grasses on mountain slopes; ribbons of luminous greenery following sparkling streams; and the mellow colors of wide bog lands, all under shifting and changing cloudscapes. This tour, apart from Inishowen Peninsula, which is included as a separate excursion at the end, could take anywhere from one day to a week, depending on precisely how low a gear you slip into after a few breaths of Donegal air. You can cut the tour short if necessary, but try your best to catch the rewarding Fanad and Rosguill peninsulas and the drive around Sheephaven Bay.

㉕ We'll start from **Letterkenny;** although it may be the least attractive or interesting place on this whole tour, it is pleasingly down-to-earth. The bustling town center is just a single long street lined with an array of small shops and pubs and dominated by an imposing 19th-century church. The main Donegal **Tourist Information Office**, loaded with maps, literature, and advice, can be found 1.6 km (1 mi) south on the Derry road, N13. *Tel. 074/21160. Open Sept.–May, weekdays 9–5; June, Mon.–Sat. 9–6; July–Aug., Mon.–Sat. 9–8, Sun. 10–2.*

The best thing about Letterkenny is its close proximity to great scenery in every direction. Take the R245 northward out ㉖ of town for 13 km (8 mi) to **Ramelton** (or Rathmelton, though the pronunciation is the same). A handsome little former Plantation town, it climbs uphill from a river harbor close to Lough Swilly. The village was the birthplace of Francis Makemie (1658–1708), who preached here before emigrating and founding the American Presbyterian church. Take the waterside

The Northern Peninsulas

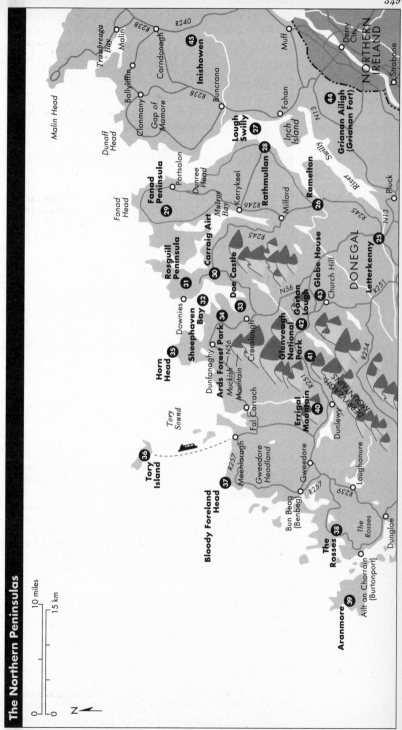

road (the R247), which runs beside one of the loveliest of
27 Donegal's big fjordlike ocean inlets, **Lough Swilly.**

28 After 11 km (7 mi), you'll reach **Rathmullan,** an ancient harbor
village among green fields, with little houses looking across
curving Lough Swilly to the Inishowen hills on the other side.
The view is especially good from the ruins of a 16th-century
Carmelite fortified priory at the top of the village. Rathmullan's modest harbor, below, was once important; here, English naval officers, posing as ordinary merchant seamen,
captured Red Hugh O'Donnell in 1587. They invited him aboard
to taste some of their "cargo of foreign wines," and the sociable
clan leader fell for it. Once on board, he was shipped to impris-
onment in Dublin Castle. After six years he escaped and returned to Donegal with added determination to defend his
homeland—but to no avail. In 1607, Rathmullan's harbor was
the scene of the Flight of the Earls—the great exodus of Ulster
nobility that brought to an end the 13-year war with the English. The million-acre Ulster territories became part of the
English domain, and two years later the Plantation era began,
the root cause of the "Troubles" that are still continuing across
the border in Northern Ireland. This rich history is explained
at Rathmullan's little **Flight of The Earls Heritage Centre**
*Rathmullan, tel. 074/58178. Admission: £1. Open May–Sept.,
Mon.–Sat. 10–6, Sun. 12–6:30.*

The old fort near Rathmullan dock is what remains of a Martello Tower. Six of the towers—fortified defenses built in case
Napoleon's army should invade to support the Irish cause—
were erected around Lough Swilly. Just north of the village,
Rathmullan House (tel. 074/58188) is a top country-house hotel.
It is one of the best accommodations in the Northwest and has
an excellent restaurant (*see* Dining and Lodging, *below*).

Extending north from here is the barren and rock-strewn
29 **Fanad Peninsula.** The signposted **Fanad Scenic Drive** takes you
27 km (17 mi) up beside Lough Swilly to low-lying Fanad Head
at its northern tip, then down again through the tiny resort village of **Kerrykeel,** with views of long and narrow Mulroy Bay
twisting and turning on the other side. If you want to cut the
journey short, you can take the back road direct from
Rathmullen to Kerrykeel for 9½ km (6 mi).

Time Out Passing through Kerrykeel, you might want to take advantage
of its dining spots and bars. **The Village Restaurant** (tel. 074/
50062), a family-run establishment, is the best place around for
good home-cooked meals all day. The menu has plenty of
choices, including three-course lunches at under £8. *Open
June–Sept., daily. Closed the rest of the year Sun., Mon.,
Tues.*

After another 6½ km (4 mi) you'll reach sprawling Milford; turn
30 right onto the R245 to follow Mulroy Bay round to **Carraig Airt
(Carrigart).** The small village, with a lot of charm and many old-
fashioned taverns, gives access via a slender isthmus to
31 **Rosguill Peninsula,** which is extremely beautiful with its rocky
heart and its fringe of sand dunes and beaches. The signposted
Atlantic Drive circles the peninsula. This area is not as far off
the beaten track as you might think; you'll see several caravan
sites and self-catering cottages, popular with visitors from
Northern Ireland. At the little resort of **Downies,** visitors enjoy

a long sandy beach, good fishing, and a chance to buy directly from **McNutts Homespun Tweeds Factory.** Westward are views of the shallow, meandering inlets of **Sheephaven Bay.**

③②

③③ The R245 follows round the sandy shores of the Bay, first running down from Carraig Airt to the imposing waterside **Doe Castle,** a tall weatherbeaten tower at the center of a complex structure enclosed within sturdy defenses. The castle occupies the southern end of Sheephaven Bay, at the foot of **Muckish Mountain** just inland. The building is further protected by the sea on three sides and by a rock-hewn moat on the fourth. Described by attacking English forces in 1587 as "the strongest fortress in all the province," the impressive edifice dates back at least to 1440, when it became the home of MacSweeney Doe, one of the "gallowglasses" (from the Irish *gall o glach*)—foreign mercenaries employed by the O'Donnell clan. Despite the castle's present poor condition, it was still occupied by his descendants until 1890. MacSweeney Doe's curiously carved tombstone is fixed to the southwest tower of the outer wall. *Near Creeslough. Admission free. Usually open. If locked, inquire at caretaker's cottage on approach path.*

③④ You'll pass through adjacent **Creeslough** (pronounced *creeshla*), where the road becomes the N56, to reach **Ards Forest Park** after a couple of miles. Clinging to Sheephaven Bay's southwest shore, the 1,188-acre national park is the former wooded estate of a Capuchin friary; the friary itself is still occupied by the Capuchins. Within the grounds are four prehistoric fortified sites and one dolmen. If the weather is fine, the park's forest trails and picnic sites provide a welcome opportunity to enjoy some air and exercise. *Tel. 074/38021. Admission £1 adults or £3 per family; children under 12 free. Open daily 8 AM–9 PM.*

Another 8 km (5 mi) on the N56 brings you into **Dun Fionnachaid (Dunfanaghy),** a tidy former Plantation village on the very edge of Sheephaven Bay. When the tide goes out, the vast sand flats of Killyhoey Beach are uncovered and the sea recedes into the far distance, but as it rises again the sands are submerged in double-quick time. On the west side of the village, the signpost to **McSwyne's Gun** (McSwyne is the old spelling of MacSweeney) leads to a huge natural blowhole that gives out a deafening bang when the tide rushes in during rough weather.

Time Out In Dunfanaghy, the **Carrig Rua** (tel. 074/36133)—the name's Irish for "red rock"—and **Arnold's** (tel. 074/36208) are both traditional village hotels on Main Street, offering decent unpretentious local fare at about £7 for lunch.

③⑤ A little back road runs from Dunfanaghy up to **Horn Head,** the most spectacular of County Donegal's Atlantic headlands. From its sheer 186-meter (600-foot) cliffs, you have access to great views along the coast to the other headlands ranged one behind the other. And bird-watchers will love it here—the cliffs are home to hundreds of seabirds, including puffin and guillemot.

From this point westward, the terrain is rougher, wilder, and rockier; you're also likely to hear the Irish language being spoken. The N56 reaches round 11 km (7 mi) to **Fal Carrach (Falcarragh),** the site of an Irish-language college.

Another 13 km (8 mi) around the rugged seashore, in good weather, you can catch a ferry from **Meenlaragh** (near Gortahork) to **Tory Island.** Though just 14½ km (9 mi) offshore, Tory is strangely inaccessible; the weather is rarely fair, and the currents are often difficult. Although the island is desolate, rocky, and barren—without a single tree—it has been inhabited since prehistoric times. The local people speak their own Irish dialect and refer to the mainland as "Ireland," considering themselves almost as a separate miniature nation. You'll find medieval and prehistoric relics scattered all over the ocean-battered landscape, notably the **round tower** of pink granite, partly ruined but still with its conical cap poised on the cliffs. At the island's eastern end, **Balor's Fort** is a prehistoric fortress, supposed to have been the residence of Balor, the terrifying one-eyed Celtic god of night and darkness. At the center of the island, the **wishing stones** have the power, it is said, to destroy enemies. Still talked about today is the time, in 1884, when the stones were turned against the British gunboat *Wasp* that came filled with police to collect taxes—which Tory Islanders are unaccustomed to paying. The ship sank, and all but six of the crew were lost. Most of the islanders don't earn enough to pay tax in any case and live simple lives as fishermen. Quite a few, however, have unexpected sidelines as artists, ever since 1968, when the well-known Irish painter Derek Hill chanced to meet islander James Dixon; Dixon felt that he could do a better job of painting than Hill. Many other Tory Island residents thought they could, too, and today the Tory Island artists, depicting their own life and landscape in a naïve style, are widely acclaimed and have exhibited abroad.

Because no accommodation is available on Tory Island, be sure to ask before making the crossing to ensure that a return will be possible the same day. Returning to Meenlaragh on the mainland, you're on the edge of the **Gweedore** headland, which you can follow round on the R257, the coast road. Gweedore is rocky, sparsely covered with heather and gorse, and low-lying until you reach its farthest point, **Bloody Foreland Head.** This dramatic name for once does not recall the slaughter of some historic battle but describes instead the vivid red hues of the gaunt rock face when lighted up at sunset.

Follow the shore road south another 13 km (8 mi) to **Bun Beag (Benbeg)** and **Croithli (Crolly),** at the meeting between Gweedore and the next distinctive headland, **The Rosses.** On both Gweedore and The Rosses, the bleak but dramatic terrain has not benefited from a liberal sprinkling of modern bungalows.

The Rosses, though similar to Gweedore, is more beautiful. The coast road, the R259, struggles over the unbelievably stony and inhospitable landscape, crisscrossed with water channels and strewn with myriad ponds. Yet quite a number of people manage to survive here, many of them Irish speakers. The decline of population and living standards was reversed by Patrick Gallagher (1873–1964), who became known as Paddy the Cope. Son of a poor local family, he left school at 10, went to Scotland as a farmhand, and saved enough money to return home in the 1950s and buy a small holding of his own. Gallagher, affectionately remembered throughout the area, persuaded the citizens around The Rosses to set up cooperatives to bring in new farming methods and machinery, as well as cooperatively owned stores to keep prices down.

Staying on the R259, after 16 km (10 mi) you will reach **Ailt an Chorráin (Burtonport),** which claims to land more salmon and lobster than any other fishing port in Ireland. This village is the departure point for a trip over to **Aranmore,** 6½ km (4 mi) offshore. Aranmore means "big island," and it is indeed the largest and most populous of County Donegal's rocky offshore fragments. The ride out takes 25 minutes and costs £2 (seven crossings daily), but although fairly accessible, the island still feels remote and ungoverned. It has been inhabited for thousands of years—witness the prehistoric fort on its south side—and offers good fishing, as well as striking cliff scenery and views back onto The Rosses.

If you drive 6½ km (4 mi) farther round the coast, the R259 rejoins N56 at **An Clochan Liath (Dungloe),** a pleasant little fishing town regarded as the capital of The Rosses, though you'll find little to do or see here.

Next, start the journey back to Letterkenny. The N56 takes you direct to Croithli (Crolly) in 13 km (8 mi), a quicker journey than going back along the coast road. Stay on the N56 north until you're a couple of miles beyond **Gaoth Dobhair (Gweedore)** village, on the little River Clady, and take the R251 to skirt the south side of **Errigal Mountain** to the village of **Dunlewy,** altogether only about 13 km (8 mi) from Crolly. This whole drive features great scenery, some of the best in County Donegal. Serene Errigal looks especially grand from Dunlewy. The **Lakeside Centre,** or Ionad Cois Locha, on the edge of Dunlewy Lough, is an interesting spot to pause for a look at a reconstructed 19th-century weaver's home where old-style weaving is demonstrated. There's also a café and crafts shop. *Tel. 075/ 31699. Admission free. Open Apr. and May, weekends, June–Sept., Mon.–Sat. 11:30–6, Sun. 12:30–7.*

Follow the R251 round as the road is edged northward by the **Derryveagh Mountains.** After 16 km (10 mi), the road brings you to the main gate of **Glenveagh National Park.** You must leave your vehicle at the entrance; a shuttle bus will take you farther into the park, or you may walk. Also at the gate, you'll see a Visitor Center with a permanent exhibition on the local way of life and on the influence of climate on the park's flora and fauna. The 24,000-acre protected wilderness has a thick carpet of russet-colored heath and dense woodland that rolls down the Derryveagh slopes into the broad open valley of the River Veagh (or Owenbeagh). At the center of the park is the dark and clear **Lough Beagh,** and on a ledge overlooking the long narrow lake stands the elaborately battlemented **Glenveagh Castle,** a most improbable edifice that looks exactly like what it is: a 19th-century folly. For all that, it's actually a grand, luxurious house inside, and its exotic, extensive gardens are also a sheer delight. Beyond the castle, footpaths lead into more remote sections of the park, where you may suddenly chance upon a herd of shy red deer or catch sight of a soaring falcon.

These Glenveagh lands were always known as a remote and beautiful region. They were brought together under single ownership by a ruthless gentleman farmer, John George Adair, who gradually acquired the estate, including its hundreds of poor tenants, between 1857 and 1859. In 1861, he evicted all the tenants without compensation and destroyed their cottages. Adair had the lakeside castle built in 1870, but immediately he went to live in Texas. Adair died in 1885 without returning to Ireland, but his wife, Cornelia, perhaps intrigued by the thought of her husband's castle, crossed the Atlantic to make Glenveagh her home. She lived extravagantly and spent a fortune to make the four different gardens and the walks as lovely as they are today; it was she who planted the luxuriant rhododendrons here. In 1984, the last owner of Glenveagh, U.S. millionaire Henry P. McIlhenny, generously presented the estate to the nation, after years of carefully maintaining and restoring the area. *Glenveagh National Park, Church Hill, Letterkenny, tel. 074/37088 or 074/37090. Admission: £1 adults, 40p children, 70p senior citizens. Several footpaths are available, including Derrylahan Nature Trail, a 1.6-km (1-mi) signposted trail. Guided walks can be arranged. Open Apr. 18–Oct. 26, daily 10:30–6:30 (until 7:30 in June–Aug.); closed Fri. in Apr. and Oct. Guided tours of the castle: £1 adults, 40p children, 70p senior citizens.*

Time Out A cafeteria conveniently located in the park's Visitor Center serves such café food as fish and chips or tea and scones. A full meal will cost you about £5.

㊷ It is 13 km (8 mi) from Glenveagh on the R251 to **Gartan Lough** (close to Church Hill village), although the lake is technically within the national park and is administered partly by the park authorities.

The lake and its surrounding mountain country are marvelously beautiful. St. Columba was supposedly born here in AD 521, and the legendary event is marked by a huge cross (at the beginning of a footpath into the national park). Nearby, you'll find other dubious "relics" of the saint that are popularly believed to possess magical powers, such as the Natal Stone, where he is thought to have first opened his eyes, and the Stone of Loneliness, where he is said to have slept.

㊸ More satisfying is a visit to **Glebe House,** which consists of a fine Regency manor and 25 acres of gardens that are situated on the northwest shore of the lake, just off the R251. The former home of the distinguished artist Derek Hill, it now serves as a remarkable gallery displaying Hill's extensive art collection, which includes works by Renoir and other great Impressionists and Picasso; paintings by Yeats's brother, Jack; and intriguing examples of the work of the Tory Islanders (*see* above). The decoration and furnishings of the house, including original William Morris wallpaper, are worth a look as well. In 1981, Derek Hill handed over this treasure trove of art to the nation. *Church Hill, tel. 074/37071. Admission: £1. Open Easter and May–Oct., Tues.–Sat. 11–6:30, Sun. 1–6:30.*

If you want to learn more about St. Columba and his times, return to the R251 and turn right almost at once onto the R254 in Church Hill. Straightaway you'll arrive at the **Colmcille Heritage Centre.** This exhibition and interpretation center features medieval manuscripts, stained glass, and displays tracing the decline of the Celtic religion and the rise of Irish Christianity. *Gartan, Church Hill, tel. 074/21160. Admission: £1. Open May, Sept.–Oct., Mon.–Sat. 11–6:30, Sun. 1–6:30; June–Aug., Mon–Sat. 10–6:30, Sun. noon–6:30.*

If you stay on the R251, you'll be back in Letterkenny after 16 km (10 mi). One more major peninsula in the region is worth exploring—the huge Inishowen, the most northerly part of Ireland. This grandly wild piece of land remains unspoiled despite a string of small and untempting coast resorts. For the 160-km (100-mi) Inishowen circuit, plus the 64-km (40-mi) round-trip to reach it from Letterkenny, you would need to allow at least a whole day. If time is short, however, you can easily see the best of Inishowen in a much shorter time.

44 If nothing else, visit the Celtic fort **Grianan Ailigh (Grianan Fort)**. Take the main Derry road, the N13, from Letterkenny. After 29 km (18 mi), keep a lookout for signs to Buncrana, because the easy-to-miss sign for the fort is opposite. Instead of turning to Buncrana, take the narrow lane that climbs and turns for more than a mile to reach the fortress, on top of a 251-meter (810-foot) hill. The most striking thing here is the site itself, with an immense panorama of the rolling Donegal and Derry landscape below. To the north, you're given an exquisite aerial view of the Swilly estuary, flowing around Inch Island into Lough Swilly. On either side rise the hills, often partly veiled by mists, of the Fanad and Inishowen peninsulas.

As for the fort, what you'll see is a circular stone enclosure—the diameter is about 23½ meters (76 feet)—that you can enter through a gate (open most of the year). Inside, you'll find further concentric defenses, with passages within the walls and earth ramparts that surround a sturdy central structure. No one knows when Grianan Fort was built, but it was probably an Iron Age fortress: Its position was accurately recorded in the 2nd century AD by the geographer Ptolemy of Alexandria. Later it became the seat of Ulster's O'Neill chieftains and remained so for many centuries, despite serious attempts by their enemies to destroy it, especially in the year 674 and again in 1101. The present-day fortress, however, owes a good deal to overzealous "restoration" in the 1870s; before that, it was in ruins. *Freely accessible.*

Go back to the N13 and cross straight over to take the Buncrana turning. When you meet the R238, another main road coming from Derry City—the town is only 8 km (5 mi) away—turn left. **45** You're now on **Inishowen,** a green pastoral peninsula with a solid mountainous interior, enclosed by Lough Swilly on one side, Lough Foyle on another, and the battering Atlantic to the north. Following the R238, you pass **Fahan,** with its monastic ruins, and **Buncrana,** a popular downscale beach resort much favored by people from Derry City. It has a 14th-century O'Docherty tower that gradually became part of an 18th-century mansion. Shortly after you pass Buncrana, turn left at the fork in the road away from the R238 to stay by the coast, driving past the 19th-century fort on **Dunree Head,** up and over the spectacular viewpoint of the **Gap of Mamore,** and down toward **Dunaff Head,** where Lough Swilly opens into the ocean. Rejoin the R238 at **Clonmany** and take it through **Ballyliffin,** another small resort town with an O'Docherty tower on the beach.

Time Out   Ballyliffin is a convenient place for a snack or meal. Try **The Strand Hotel** (tel. 077/76107), a likable family-run establishment offering well-prepared home-cooked lunches, with a three-course menu for under £9.

By the junction of the R238 and the R240, you'll see a church with a curious remnant of early Christianity against one wall, the decorated 7th-century **Donagh Cross,** accompanied by a couple of pillar stones. The strange carvings on the stones clearly date from a pre-Christian period. Turn the corner into **Carndonagh,** a village featuring several more medieval monastic remains. The road then runs up beside **Trawbreaga Bay,** through picturesque **Malin** village on the waterside up to **Malin Head,** Ireland's most northerly point. Although it does have good views, Malin Head is not as dramatic a spot as some of the other headlands.

Take the signposted route across the peninsula from Malin Head to **Moville,** a sleepy waterside resort on the Lough Foyle side. The drive takes 8 km (5 mi) from here to the peninsula's rocky eastern tip, **Inishowen Head.** On the way, at **Greencastle,** you'll see the fortifications of foreigners who tried to control the nine counties of Ulster: a 14th-century Anglo-Norman fortress and an English fort built five centuries later to defend against French support for the Irish. The drive along the lough shore toward Derry City is attractive but punctuated by small, uninteresting villages whose modernized pubs cater to day (or evening) visitors from Derry. If you want to turn away from Derry toward Letterkenny before reaching the border, take the R239 from **Muff** to **Bridge End,** where, incidentally, you can find one of the most attractive of Ireland's many new Catholic churches.

Off the Beaten Track

Ballymote Start out by traveling about 11 km (7 mi) from Sligo Town south on the N4. Turn right onto the N17 and right again onto an unfrequented minor road, the R293, between meadows and woods for a further 13 km (8 mi) toward **Ballymote,** a most appealing village. Once a place of importance, the formerly imposing castle is now just a ruined shell, and the village is bustling, rustic, and has an extraordinary number of drinking holes—almost every business doubles as a bar! A powerful Anglo-Norman Ulster earl, Richard de Burgo, built the fortress in the 14th century, and for centuries afterward it stood firm against any English conquest of the Northwest. The castle's six towers still stand. Close by is another ruin, that of the Franciscan friary where the *Book of Ballymote* was written in 1391. This tome, now located at the Royal Irish Academy in Dublin, holds tremendous significance to historians, because it enabled them to unravel the secrets of the old Ogham alphabet. This system of writing, with just 20 letters, was inscribed on Celtic standing stones, especially those dating from about the 4th and 5th centuries.

The Leitrim Lakes The hilly landscape of unspoiled County Leitrim is dappled with clean, cool lakes. Anglers love this area because its peaceful waters are filled with fish. Despite a liberal sprinkling of villages, in reality the county is almost uninhabited. Even its largest town, bright and bustling **Carrick-on-Shannon,** has a population of fewer than 2,000 people. The town has plenty of lively bars, and you can hire a boat here to tour the Shannon. From Sligo Town, take the N4 south to Carrick, which is a good base for a quick look around the vicinity. Take the R280 north from the town to **Drumshanbo** at the tip of huge **Lough Allen.** From here, the R208 turns back to **Drumcong** village and the small lakes **Scur** and **St. John.** Where the R208 meets the R202, turn right for Fenagh, and then right again onto the R209 to return along the south side of the lakes into Carrick. If you were to continue beyond Fenagh, you would reach **Mohill**, birthplace of Turlough O'Carolan, the 18th-century blind harpist regarded as the last of the Celtic bards. His most famous composition was adapted for "The Star-Spangled Banner." South of Carrick, labyrinthine back lanes meander across the broad **Shannon** and the lakes—**Boderg, Bofin,** and **Kilglass**— that straddle the river.

Lough Derg   This site is really out of the way, yet tens of thousands determinedly beat a path to this lonely lake, ringed by heather-clad slopes, throughout the period from Whitsunday to the Feast of the Assumption (that is, from June to mid-August). In the center of the lough, Station Island, which is known as St. Patrick's Purgatory, is one of Ireland's most popular pilgrimage sites, even though it is also the most rigorous and austere of such sites in the country. Pilgrims stay on the island for three days, taking no sleep and no food except black tea and dry toast. They walk barefoot around the island, on its flinty stones, to pray at a succession of shrines. The pilgrimage has been followed since time immemorial; during the Middle Ages, it attracted large numbers of devotees from foreign lands.

You can reach the shores of Lough Derg by turning off the main Sligo–Donegal road (N15) in the village of Laghy onto the minor Pettigo road (R232), which hauls itself over the Black Gap and descends sharply into the border village of Pettigo, about 21 km (13 mi) from the N15. From here, take the Lough Derg access road for 8 km (5 mi). *If you would like to know more about St. Patrick's Purgatory in order to become a pilgrim, write: Reverend Prior, Lough Derg, Pettigo, Co. Donegal. Nonpilgrims may not visit the island June–mid-Aug.*

Shopping

The outstanding specialties of the Northwest are high-quality handwoven tweeds and handknits. Smart traditional tweed sports jackets, comfortable yet long-lasting, are one of the best buys. The region is also a good place to purchase Aran sweaters; they are knitted with distinctive crisscross patterns and are made of plain undyed wool. The sweaters are soft but durable. Not so long ago, these warm weatherproof pullovers were worn by every County Donegal fisherman, usually made to a design belonging exclusively to his own family. Patterns are not so restricted now, allowing greater variety in the knitwear, but all the sweaters have that unmistakable Aran look. High-quality machine-made tweeds are also available. All these wool-based items have been made here for centuries, and you'll find that prices are astonishingly low. You'll also want to look out for locally made parian china, a thin, fine, and pale product of very high quality and workmanship. Elaborate flower motifs and a basket-weave design are two distinctive features of this china, which has been a specialty of Belleek, on the Donegal–Fermanagh border, for more than 100 years. In recent years, it has also developed in and around Ballyshannon.

Ardara

This attractive village features several stores that sell handweaving and locally made knitwear. Nowadays the stores usually commission goods directly from cottage out-workers and provide them with the wool and patterns. Prices are about as low as you'll find anywhere. You can get an especially good deal on handsome, chunky Aran handknitted sweaters (£40–£80). You'll find cardigans (similar prices) and scarves (£12) in the same style. You can pick up a pure wool handwoven tweed tie for about £6. A wide choice of ready-to-wear tweeds is carried in all the stores; good-quality tweed sports jackets for women (up to about £80) as well as men (up to £80) are a bargain. The shops here also stock a selection of traditional Irish products from other parts of the country (glassware and linen, for example). The main stores, all recommended, are **Kennedy's** (tel. 075/41106), at the top end of the main street; **John Molloy** (tel. 075/41133), on the Killybegs road; and **C. Bonner & Son** (tel. 075/41196), on Front Street.

Ballyshannon and Belleek

Donegal Irish Parian China (tel. 072/51826), situated just south of Ballyshannon on the N15, is the Republic's largest manufacturer of parian china. A new Visitor Center, opened in 1992, provides information on the manufacturing process. Visitors are welcome to take free 15-minute tours of the workshops (May–Sept., daily 9:30–4:30) and can take advantage of lower factory prices. Traditional methods of manufacture are used, and most of the work is done by hand. The least expensive items (spoons or thimbles) cost around £4. A full tea set starts from £170.

From Ballyshannon, the R230 runs along the south bank of the River Erne toward Belleek. Right beside the Garda (Irish police) checkpoint, 1.6 km (1 mi) before the border to Northern Ireland, you'll find **Celtic Weave China** (tel. 072/51844), a small family business that produces high-quality parian china. The company specializes in the basket-weave design and in elaborate floral decoration, creating many one-of-a-kind pieces on commission for prestigious organizations around the world. A single piece of china will be made to your own specifications if you wish. Extremely delicate-looking handpainted china "flower baskets" are also available (though in fact this type of chinaware is not as fragile as it appears). Most pieces cost under £100.

Continue on the same road into Belleek in Northern Ireland, where **Belleek Pottery** (tel. 0365/65501) stands beside the Erne River. This is the best-known producer of Belleek chinaware. The visitor center here acts as a showroom for the company's wide range of elegant products. Although this is not within the limits of our Northwest region, you'll find Belleek china in the shops of Donegal and Sligo (*see* also Chapter 10).

Donegal Town

Donegal Town has long been the principal marketplace for the region's wool products. There are several smaller shops retailing local handweaving and knits, but the town's principal store is **Magee's** (tel. 073/21100), which occupies a prime position on the Diamond, the town's central area. Look especially for items with Magee's own label; the store has its own factory in town making garments and fabrics for major clothing companies and big-name department stores. Tweed jackets cost around £125 for men and £100 for women; men's suits are priced at £175, and ladies' suits at £185; skirts cost about £50. Aran sweaters are also available from around £80. You can even buy Magee's best-quality tweed by the roll at £16 per yard. For a smart hand-crafted hat of tweed and Irish linen, stroll five minutes up Tirconaill Street, past the castle and the post office, to **Hanna's Hats** (tel. 073/21084). About 1.6 km (1 mi) south of town, right beside the main N15, the **Donegal Craft Village** is a complex of new workshops where you can buy pottery, handweaving, and ceramics from local young craftspeople and watch the items being made.

Kilcar

For a fine selection of handwoven goods and other local crafts, stop off at **Studio** (tel. 073/38194). The store also features a tea shop on the premises.

Sligo Town

For a large selection of handknit and hand-loomed sweaters and all other woolen goods, try **P. F. Dooney & Son** (36 O'Connell St., tel. 071/2274). **Cosgrove's of Sligo** (32 Market St., tel. 071/42809), which retains its original 19th-century shop front, stocks fine foods to satisfy hungry tourists; it also has a crafts section with a selection of pottery, watercolors, and other works by local artists.

Sports

Participant Sports

Bicycling Bicycle rentals are available in **Ardara** from **Donal Byrne** (West End, tel. 075/41156), in **Carrick-on-Shannon** from **Geraghty's** (Main St. tel. 094/31019), in **Donegal Town** from **C. J. Doherty** (Main St., tel. 073/21119), in **Ramelton** from **Hugh Whoriskey** (tel. 074/51022), and in **Sligo Town** from **Gary's Cycles** (Quay St., tel. 071/45418). Many of these rental shops have mountain bikes for cycling in rough hill country. The Northwest is mostly challenging but rewarding cycling country, with some steep climbs and strong winds at times, but with plenty of low-cost accommodations, marvelous scenery, and empty roads. These conditions are perfect for keen cyclists, but others may prefer to use a bike simply for some gentle meandering around a small area.

Bird-watching Bird-watchers have access to a large variety and population of bird life on County Donegal's northern headlands. Most of the bird species are not resident; huge numbers of winter and summer migrants land here. Bird sanctuaries are located on **Inch Island** in Lough Swilly (with a considerable number of whooper swan in the fall), on the **Lough Foyle** shore of Inishowen (with widgeon, waterfowl, and waders in the fall), at **Horn Head** (with Ireland's largest colony of razorbill, as well as puffin and guillemot), and at **Sheskinmore Lough** (with geese, ducks, and waders) near Ardara. The sand and mud flats of **Sligo Bay** attract geese, and in the grounds of **Lissadell House** at Rosses Point, you'll find flocks of barnacle geese. For more information contact the **Irish Wildbird Conservancy** (Southview, Church Rd., Greystones, Co. Wicklow, tel. 01/875759).

Fishing No license is needed for sea fishing or for coarse and pike angling. For game fishing (salmon and sea trout), the license costs £10 for 21 days, or £25 for a full season. Senior citizens are exempt from these costs. The licenses can be obtained for County Donegal from the **Northern Regional Fishery Board** (Ballyshannon, tel. 072/51435) and for Counties Sligo and Leitrim from the **North-Western Regional Fisheries Board** (Ballina, Co. Mayo, tel. 096/22623). Some tackle shops are also permitted to sell licenses.

Tackle Shops **County Donegal: John McGill** (Main St., Ardara); **O'Doherty's** (Main St., Donegal Town); and **Pat Barrett** (Bundoran).

County Leitrim: The Creel or **Geraghty's** (both on Main St., Carrick-on-Shannon) and **Aodh Flynn** (Manorhamilton).

County Sligo: Barton Smith (Hyde Bridge, Sligo Town).

Anglers will find that the best area for brown trout is located around Bundoran, including Lough Melvin. In western County Donegal, you'll have good opportunities for catching sea trout. Plenty of salmon and brown trout live in the rivers of southern County Donegal and northern County Sligo. More brown trout can be found in the loughs near Dunfanaghy in northern County Donegal, near Bundoran on the border of Donegal and Sligo counties, and in the border area of Sligo and Leitrim counties. Pike anglers and coarse anglers can cast their lines in the abundant County Leitrim lakes.

Golf The Northwest has a large number of nine- and 18-hole courses, most in seaside locations, and several of them are world-class. For a full list, you'll need to contact the Irish Tourist Board or local Tourist Information Offices. The Northwest's best 18-hole courses, which all welcome visitors, include **Bundoran Golf Club** (tel. 072/41360), on the cliffs above Bundoran beach; **Donegal Golf Club** (tel. 073/21262), at Murvagh; **County Sligo Golf Club** (tel. 071/77134) at Rosses Point, which has hosted just about every Irish championship; **The North West Golf Club** (tel. 074/61027), near Buncrana on Inishowen Peninsula; **Rosapenna Golf Club** (tel. 074/55301), 24 km (15 mi) northwest of Letterkenny; and **Enniscrone Golf Club** (tel. 096/36297), in the midst of lovely scenery close to the Enniscrone resort on the County Sligo coast about 14½ km (9 mi) north of Ballina. Expect to pay greens fees of around £10–£15 a day.

Hiking Trails in the Northwest provide the experienced walker with challenging opportunities. It helps to be able to read a map, and on high ground you're wise not to take any chances with the weather, which can suddenly become wet and misty. The mountain districts (such as the Blue Stacks, near Donegal Town) offer rough walks with dramatic views. There are long-distance footpaths across County Donegal, in County Leitrim, and around Lough Gill in County Sligo. For information about these walking routes, contact **Field Officer, Long Distance Walking Routes Committee** (Cospoir, 11th Floor, Hawkins House, Dublin 9). Good shorter trails are also accessible, clearly marked within Glenveagh National Park in northwest County Donegal.

Horseback
Riding/Pony
Trekking
For hacking, trekking, and other horseback sport by the hour, the day, or longer periods, contact **Carrigart Riding Stables** (tel. 074/55114), at the foot of the Rosguill Peninsula; **Lenamore Stables** (tel. 077/84022), at Muff on Inishowen Peninsula; **Rockhill Trekking Centre** (tel. 074/50012), at Kerrykeel on the Fanad Peninsula; **Stracomer Riding School** (tel. 072/41787), at Bundoran on the south County Donegal coast; and the **Moneygold Riding Centre** (tel. 071/63337), at Moneygold Grange in County Sligo. Several other establishments offer full riding vacations including lodging, the details are shown in a leaflet from the Irish Tourist Board. For more information, contact **The Association of Irish Riding Establishments** (Mespil Hall, Kill, Co. Kildare, tel. 045/77208 or 045/77299).

Surfing
For **surfing,** head to Strandhill, Rossnowlagh, and Bundoran on the south County Donegal coast (if you need to rent equipment), or to Marble Strand and Rosapenna in north County Donegal (if you have all your own gear). These areas offer excellent conditions for world-class surfing. Ask the **Irish Surfing Association** (Tigh-na-Mara, Rossnowlagh, Co. Donegal, tel. 073/21053) for more specific information.

Dining and Lodging

Dining

By Andrew Sanger and Georgina Campbell

The Northwest is not usually considered a great gastronomic center. You can expect meals to be generally plain and simple, but the servings are generous, with a filling portion of potatoes. Still, the ingredients used in dishes are of good quality and are locally produced. Fish, fresh from the sparkling clean rivers and loughs, could hardly be better. The region has only a few restaurants of distinction. In the rural districts, your best bet is to choose a hotel or guest house that can provide a decent evening meal as well as breakfast.

Category	Cost*
Very Expensive	over £25
Expensive	£15–£25
Moderate	£10–£15
Inexpensive	under £10

*per person for a typical three-course meal, including tax and service but excluding drinks

Lodging

Although the Northwest is a far-flung corner of Ireland, the choice of good bed-and-breakfasts and small hotels in the region is excellent because of the constant influx of visitors, particularly in July and August. The traditional provincial hotels in Sligo Town, Donegal Town, and the small coastal resorts in between have been modernized and equipped with all the necessary comforts, yet they retain the charm that comes with older buildings and their sense of personalized service. However, away from these areas, your options are more restricted, and your best overnight option, with some exceptions, is usually a modest guest house offering bed, breakfast, and an evening meal.

Many of the modern Irish guest houses recommended below are similar to one another in what they have to offer: They are often one-story buildings with undistinguished contemporary furniture and not much character. Many provide peat fires and merely adequate meals. For the most part, however, visitors will find hosts friendly, helpful, and concerned about keeping their properties clean and well-maintained.

A particular pleasure may be gained by staying in an Irish-speaking home. With a little bit of luck, the local Irish Tourist Information Offices can be helpful in making a booking with an Irish-speaking family. In Counties Donegal, Leitrim, and Sligo, you can also stay at some first-class country-house hotels where you are welcomed with gracious professionalism.

Category	Cost*
Very Expensive	over £90
Expensive	£65–£90
Moderate	£45–£65
Inexpensive	under £45

All prices are for a standard double room, including breakfast and tax.

Highly recommended restaurants and hotels are indicated by a star ★.

Ardara

Dining and Lodging

Bay View House. On the outskirts of the village, this modern, well-kept bungalow offers bed and breakfast, as well as a peaceful location with superb sea views. You can relax in front of a peat fire and picture windows in the guest lounge, and enjoy tasty traditional Irish home cooking in the dining room. *Mrs. Bennett, Bay View House, Portnoo Rd., Ardara, Co. Donegal, tel. 075/41145. 7 rooms with shower. Facilities: tea-making equipment in rooms, games room, dining room. Book evening meal before noon. V. Closed Nov. 7–Mar. 1. Inexpensive.*

Greenhaven House. Another good B&B, this establishment is an excellent value for the money. Located only a few minutes from the village, the modern family-run one-story home has its own gardens and marvelous views of the nearby mountains and bay. You'll be warmed by a peat fire in the lounge and wake up to a hearty breakfast. The owners can advise you on shopping for handknits and other items. *Mrs. Eileen Molloy, Greenhaven House, Portnoo Rd., Ardara, Co. Donegal, tel. 075/41129. 6 rooms with shower. No evening meal. No credit cards. Closed Oct.–Feb. Inexpensive.*

★ **Woodhill Guest House.** This spacious home of the Yeats family (no relation to the famous poet) stands on 4 acres of wooded grounds only ½ km (¼ mi) from the village. The residence once belonged to the Nesbitts, former landlords of Ardara. The cream-colored exterior is Victorian, but parts of the interior date back to the 17th century. The fine front public areas feature high ceilings and marble fireplaces; the hall has a lovely round table and stained-glass window. Bedrooms are less grand but large, with superb mountain views. You'll find this an amiable, relaxed place, with frequent Irish folk music sessions presented in the bar. The best feature here is the high-quality home-cooked food. The moderately priced restaurant seats 40 and attracts visitors and locals alike. Cordon bleu à la carte meals, in a French-Irish style, rely upon fresh local ingredients. Typical dishes include salmon with garlic and spinach sauce, accompanied by seasonal vegetables; or rack of lamb with herbs picked from the family garden. The elaborate desserts are all homemade. The breakfast eggs, by the way, couldn't be fresher, because the Yeatses have their own hens. *Mr. and Mrs. Yeats, Woodhill Guest House, Donegal Rd., Ardara, Co. Donegal, tel. 075/41112. 6 rooms with bath. Facilities: restaurant, bar, fishing, clay-pigeon shoots. AE, MC, V. Inexpensive.*

Ballymote

Dining and Lodging ★   **Temple House.** Well off the beaten track, and undoubtedly one of the most unusual B&Bs anywhere, this vast country mansion with a pillared entrance is outwardly gray and austere; the approximately 100 rooms are decorated and furnished in the Georgian and Victorian styles, with highly polished mahogany tables and sideboards, and the original rugs. This is not a country-house hotel but a working organic farm, surrounded by more than 1,000 acres of land. It's been in owners Sandy and Deb Perceval's family since 1665. Within the grounds, you'll find the ruins of the original fortified manor house, built to incorporate a historic Knights Templar castle; guests can also visit formal terraced gardens and a private lake with waterside footpaths. The huge bedrooms feature authentic Victorian curtains, marble-top washstands, polished floorboards, dressing tables, and huge shuttered windows. Deb Perceval prepares a good evening meal, using farm-fresh produce; top-class wines are served. The traditional Irish breakfasts are generous. The Percevals make no pretense of offering modern facilities. Among the six bedrooms, all have hot and cold water but only one has a full private bath. No television is available. *Mrs. D. Perceval, Temple House, Ballymote, Co. Sligo, tel. 071/83329. 6 rooms, 1 with bath. Facilities: boating, shooting, fishing; golfing and horseback riding about 24 km (15 mi) away. AE, V. Moderate.*

Ballyshannon

Dining and Lodging   **Danby House.** On the coast road just 1.6 km (1 mi) out of town, you'll discover this pleasant guest house and restaurant with its own walled gardens. Set on 20 acres of grounds overlooking the Erne estuary of Donegal Bay, the white-and-black building with shuttered windows dates from 1820 and features large, well-proportioned rooms with impressive fireplaces. Bedrooms are furnished with antiques, including mahogany wardrobes, dressing tables, and four-poster beds. Enjoy meals in one of the best French-Irish restaurants (with moderate to expensive meals) in the area. The high-ceilinged dining room, decorated in peach and brown tones, was once a private ballroom; unfortunately, the dim lighting casts a pall over the room. The children of owner-chef Derry Britton serve generous portions of country food, including homegrown vegetables; local free-range duck, prepared in orange and fig sauce; and a variety of seafood, supplied daily from nearby Killybegs. Lobsters are used in an unusual appetizer, and the specialty of the house, pil-pil, consists of lightly grilled prawns served hot in earthenware dishes with lots of garlic, zucchini, shallots, and fresh coriander. *Rosnowlagh Rd., Ballyshannon, Co. Donegal, tel. 072/51138. 5 rooms with bath. Facilities: dining room, bar, fishing, riding (20 stables). AE, MC, V. Inexpensive.*

Bruckless

Dining and Lodging ★

Bruckless House. A two-story 18th-century farmhouse on the north side of Donegal Bay, this unusual B&B stands on 19 acres of woods, gardens, and a meadow where Irish draft horses and Connemara ponies roam. Public rooms have a fine view of Bruckless Bay; their Asian decor reflects years spent in Hong Kong by the owners, the Evans family. The more conventional but comfortable bedrooms share a large bathroom upstairs. Wholesome dinners are prepared with fresh produce from the Evanses' garden, milk and cream from the resident cow, and seafood straight from the bay. Visitors can drive to the nearby Glencolumbkille Folk Museum and Ardara, and along the Donegal coastline. *Mrs. C. J. Evans, Bruckless House, Bruckless, Co. Donegal, tel. 073/37071. 5 rooms, 2 with bath. AE, DC, MC, V. Dinner must be booked by noon. Closed Oct.–Mar. Moderate.*

Castlebaldwin

Dining ★

Cromleach Lodge. Christie and Moira Tighe run this highly regarded restaurant (with excellent accommodations also available), situated on a hillside overlooking Lough Arrow, 5 km (3 mi) off the N4 between Sligo Town and Carrick-on-Shannon at Castlebaldwin. All the windows have panoramic views, making each table in the three small dining rooms equally desirable. An extensive six-course table d'hôte menu is priced according to the choice of the main course, and makes use of fresh ingredients in attractively presented dishes with light sauces. A typical meal could begin with grilled goat cheese, served with salad, followed by a soup such as fresh lobster bisque. Fresh fillet of turbot with chablis and chive sauce and salmon with saffron and lemon sauce are some of the seafood choices. Loin of lamb with rosemary juice and fresh breast of duck with juniper sauce are other favorites. A good choice of desserts includes a selection of fresh fruits individually marinated in different flavored syrups (such as apricots in Grand Marnier or kiwis in lemon and Pernod), a terrine of two chocolates layered with pistachio nuts, a selection of homemade ices, Irish farmhouse cheeses, and homemade petits fours. *Lough Arrow, Castlebaldwin, Co. Sligo, tel. 071/65155. Reservations advised. Dinner Mon.–Sat.; Sun. dinner fortnightly. Closed Dec. 23–31. AE, DC, MC, V. Moderate–Expensive.*

Collooney

Dining and Lodging ★

Markree Castle. Fans of Knockmuldowney House (formerly at Strandhill, west of Sligo Town) will be pleased to learn that this huge, five-story gray stone castle, at the end of a long pot-holed dirt lane, is the family home of Charles Cooper, Knockmuldowney's one-time proprietor. Mr. Cooper and his wife, Mary, are again welcoming bed-and-breakfast guests, and they're also keeping the name Knockmuldowney Restaurant for evening meals. The 17th-century house, situated on a 1,000-acre estate, features fine Edwardian and Victorian mahogany furniture throughout, an oak-paneled hall, and ornate Louis XIV plasterwork in the first-floor dining room. The comfortable bedrooms are furnished in the same rich, heavy period style, but the bathrooms have been modernized; rooms provide garden or river views. The dining room has been restored with 19th-century green and beige decor and plenty of gilding. Mrs. Cooper prepares the delectable French meals with Anglo-Irish touches. Two table d'hôte menus are offered; one is a reasonably priced set five-course menu, and the other has about five choices for each course. Recommended dishes include stuffed mushrooms mornay and Egyptian lemon chicken, which is marinated in garlic, lemon juice, and oil and then baked in butter. Bailey's Blackberry Mist—a mousse made with blackberry puree and Bailey's Irish Cream liqueur—is a favorite dessert, served with homemade biscuits. On Sunday, a traditional lunch is available with a choice of two roasts or fish. Guests will also enjoy afternoon tea with biscuits, banana bread, and fruitcake. *Markree Castle, Collooney, Co. Sligo, tel. 071/67800 (11 km/7 mi south of Sligo Town on the N4). 15 rooms with bath. Facilities: restaurant. AE, DC, MC, V. Expensive.*

Donegal Town

Dining | **Harvey's Point.** This Swiss-owned restaurant and comfortable 20-room hotel is at the foot of the Blue Stack Mountains. One end of the split-level wood-paneled dining room directly overlooks Lough Eske. The establishment features warm peach decor, Tiffany lamps, and locally made granite-top tables. The French cuisine leans toward a nouvelle presentation, with several lobster entrées on the menu; it might be served whole with a choice of two sauces, alongside rice and mussels, or garnished with tomatoes and red cabbage. Fisherman's Platter, a selection of five kinds of fish, is also served with two sauces, and sirloin steak is served with a demiglaze sauce, topped with garlic butter. A special dessert is homemade ice cream with profiteroles and chocolate sauce. *Lough Eske, Donegal, Co. Donegal, tel. 073/22208. Reservations required. Jacket and tie advised. MC, V. Moderate–Expensive.*

Dining and Lodging | **Hyland Central.** Opening onto Donegal's central square, this family-run hotel offers a warm and friendly traditional atmosphere and a good location. Public areas retain a touch of Old World style, but the comfortable bedrooms (some of them quite spacious) lack character, with their rather ordinary modern furniture. Many rooms have a view of lovely Donegal Bay. The large dining room with its efficient staff serves good, filling food. The hotel is a favorite with business travelers, vacationers, and locals who come for a drink or a meal. *The Diamond, Donegal, Co. Donegal, tel. 073/21027. 60 rooms with bath or shower. Facilities: dining room, gardens, indoor pool, solarium, games room. AE, MC, V. Moderate.*

★ **St. Ernan's House.** For a restful stay, it's hard to imagine anything better than this cream-colored, two-story, 19th-century hotel, built by a nephew of the duke of Wellington, on a wooded Donegal Bay island; the house is reached by a causeway only a short distance south of town. Its attractive bedrooms are furnished with antiques and have superb views of the bay. The grand dining room features silk drapes and wallpaper in a green-and-gold Regency stripe pattern. Tables are laid traditionally with white linen, and the entrées make use of fresh local produce, especially fish, prepared in the Irish country-house style. The five-course dinner changes nightly, but a typical menu might include white crabmeat in lime mayonnaise as an appetizer, followed by grilled salmon hollandaise, steamed cod with asparagus tips and Chablis sauce, or baked lamb with rosemary and apricot sauce. Desserts tend to be well-established favorites such as pears Bordeaux (poached in red wine) or crème caramel. *Brian and Carmel O'Dowd, St. Ernan's House, St. Ernan's Island, Donegal, Co. Donegal, tel. 073/21065. 11 rooms with bath. Facilities: dining room (dinner open to nonguests). MC, V. No children under 6. Closed Nov.–Easter. Moderate.*

Dunfanaghy

Dining and Lodging
Arnold's Hotel. A favorite with Irish vacationers, this friendly hotel run by the Arnold family provides unassuming, relaxed accommodations and generous traditional Irish meals. The best rooms overlook the landscaped garden. The Arnolds offer to lead special-interest classes for guests, such as painting and bird-watching. *Main St., Dunfanaghy, Co. Donegal, tel. 074/36208. 34 rooms with bath and shower. Facilities: bar, baby-sitting, games room, tennis. AE, DC, MC, V. Closed Nov.–Mar. Inexpensive.*

Carrig Rua Hotel. On the shore of Sheephaven Bay, this unpretentious, popular two-story white hotel is an ideal base for exploring northern Donegal and Glenveagh National Park. Friendly and modestly priced, the bed-and-breakfast establishment caters to the tastes of Irish family vacationers, especially those from across the border. Children are also made very welcome. The inviting rooms have new furniture and carpeting, and some offer bay views. Meals served here are plain and abundant in the traditional Irish style. *Main St., Dunfanaghy, Co. Donegal, tel. 074/36133. 22 rooms with bath or shower. Facilities: bar, baby-sitting. AE, V. Inexpensive.*

Fahan

Dining
Restaurant St. John's. This restored Georgian house enjoys a lakeside setting. You'll find the atmosphere cozy and old-fashioned, with open fires, pictures of old Derry, and red decor in the dining room, although white Donegal linen is used for tablecloths and napkins. Owner-chef Reg Ryan specializes in uncomplicated home cooking, but he is fastidious about his ingredients and uses only local produce in the peak of its season and homegrown organic vegetables. Homemade bread is baked daily to serve with fresh garden soups and pâtés. The two six-course table d'hôte menus (one moderate, the other expensive) are both a good value. Look for irresistible seafood appetizers, such as hot crab in garlic butter and cream, or monkfish, deep-fried in a very light batter and served with homemade mayonnaise. Fillets of brill with herbs and fennel sauce, or Donegal rack of lamb, served with apple and mint jelly, are typical main courses. Desserts include homemade ice creams and carrageen moss soufflé. *Fahan, Co. Donegal, tel. 077/60289. Reservations advised. Dress: casual. Dinner only. Closed Mon., Christmas*

Day, Good Friday, and 2 wks in Feb. DC, MC, V. Moderate–Expensive.

Letterkenny

Dining   **Carolina House Restaurant.** On the Ramelton Road 2½ kilometers (1½ miles) out of town, you'll find Charles and Mary Prendergast's pleasant eatery. Two four-course prix-fixe meals are offered (coffee and petits fours included). The emphasis is on traditional home-cooked dishes using fresh local meat and fish. Start, for example, with courgette (zucchini) mousse complemented with tomato and basil salad, followed by the seafood chowder. Main courses include trout stuffed with rice, pepper, herbs, and corn. Finish with home-made ice cream. *Loughnagin, Letterkenny, Co. Donegal, tel. 074/22480. Reservations advised. Dress: casual. MC, V. Dinner only. Closed Sun. and Mon. Expensive.*

Dining and Lodging   **Mount Errigal Hotel.** One of County Donegal's smartest and most modern hotels, although not at all posh, this property appeals to both business and family-vacation visitors. Service here is friendly and professional. Private events and conferences are often staged here, and the bar remains a favorite for locals seeking a relaxed night out. The clean and comfortable bedrooms are efficiently arranged, with characterless, pale-colored furnishings. The Glengesh, the hotel's softly lit restaurant, serves popular Irish cooking; it features Edwardian-style brass and glass decor. *Ballyraine, Letterkenny, Co. Donegal, tel. 074/22700. 56 rooms with bath or shower. Facilities: restaurant, 2 lounge bars, disco, games room, facilities for disabled guests, video, sauna, baby-sitting. AE, DC, MC, V. Moderate.*

Rathmullan

Dining   **Water's Edge Restaurant.** Dawn and Kevin Cairns run this restaurant set in a converted row of old cottages on the western shore of Lough Swilly. The cozy, romantic dining spot is two-tiered, with wooden beams, oak tables, deep burgundy-red decor, and linen tablecloths and napkins. The mixed international menu is influenced by the owners' travels but based squarely on fresh local ingredients and seasonal availability; fish is the main strength in summer, while steaks, chicken, duckling, and scallops appear more often in winter. If you like seafood, don't miss the Water's Edge Special, a mixture of fresh fish and shellfish—such as clams, lobster, salmon, and mussels—cooked in white wine and garlic and topped with Roquefort cheese. A popular dessert is Queen Sofia's Delight, a rich meringue-based sweet made with seasonal fruit and fresh cream. *The Ballyboe, Rathmullen, Co. Donegal, tel. 074/58182 or 58138. Reservations advised. Dress: casual but neat. Dinner year-round; light lunches in summer (June–Sept.) only. Closed Christmas Eve. DC, MC, V. Moderate–Expensive.*

Dining and Lodging   ★   **Rathmullan House.** One of Ireland's most enticing and popular country-house hotels, this rambling, cream-colored, two-story mansion, dating from the 18th century, features large bay windows, fine antiques and oil paintings, and prize-winning gardens; its lawns stretch down to a deserted sandy beach. The public areas, including a drawing room, an impressive library, and a coffee room, are the height of elegance, and yet maintain an informal and friendly air. Bedrooms vary from old-fashioned basic to grand, but all of them feature antiques and light-colored wallpaper and curtains. Ask for a room facing Lough Swilly. The light-filled pavilion dining room, with a tented ceiling, has pink and green decor, silk drapes, and views of the gardens and the lake from the windows. Two table d'hôte menus—roasts and seafood with fresh produce—are available in the Irish country-house style. A typical menu might include poached salmon with black butter or roast lamb with herb stuffing and red currant jelly, followed by a sweet dessert or Irish farmhouse cheese. Breakfast, consisting of fresh fruit compotes, carrageen moss pudding, and other hot or cold dishes, is a specialty here. The hotel is well situated for visiting the Donegal coast, Glenveagh National Park, and the Glebe House and Gallery. *Rathmullen, Co. Donegal, tel. 074/58188. 23 rooms, 21 with bath or shower. Facilities: dining room, bar, gardens, heated indoor pool, sauna, steam room, tennis, croquet. No TV in rooms. AE, DC, MC, V. Closed Nov.–Easter. Expensive.*

Fort Royal Hotel. On 18 acres of grounds beside Lough Swilly, this spacious, comfortable hotel, once an aristocratic private home, is a decent, less-expensive alternative to the Rathmullan House (*see* above). It attracts a regular clientele, who enjoy its relaxed professionalism and marvelous location. Rooms are clean and meals are satisfactory. *Rathmullen, Co. Donegal, tel. 074/58100. 15 rooms with bath or shower. Facilities: bar, gardens, golf, tennis, squash. AE, DC, MC, V. Closed Oct.–Mar. Moderate.*

Riverstown

Dining and Lodging
★

Coopershill. A three-story Georgian farmhouse set on 500 acres of private woods and farmland, this fine stone abode has been home to seven generations of the O'Hara family since it was constructed in 1774. It provides an ideal place for a quiet vacation. Large public rooms are furnished with appealing period antiques and overstuffed furniture, and deer heads hang in the vast hallways. The spacious, beautifully furnished bedrooms reflect the same antique style (with no televisions), and most have four-poster or canopy beds. In the tranquil dining room overlooking the woods, Irish-style meals and a wide choice of wines are served by candlelight from a grand sideboard with family silver. The menu, which changes nightly, includes roast beef or lamb, fresh vegetables, and special soups. Guests can walk on the grounds amid undisturbed wildlife. *Coopershill, Riverstown, Co. Sligo, tel. 071/65108. 7 rooms with bath. Facilities: dining room, garden, private fishing, boating. AE, MC, V. Closed mid-Nov.–mid-Mar. Expensive.*

Rossnowlagh

Dining and Lodging

Sand House Hotel. This large modern hotel, located right on Donegal Bay (about 8 kilometers [5 miles] northwest of Ballyshannon), makes a peaceful, well-located base for sightseeing the bay coastline. It has a mock manor-house exterior and access to a 3-km (2-mi) stretch of sand. The renovated, well-kept bedrooms are beautifully decorated with antiques. Choose between a sea view at the front, or back rooms overlooking a golf course. You'll find the staff solicitous and cheerful. The efficient restaurant caters to the plain hearty appetites of Irish vacationers looking for something special.

Fresh seafood, including Donegal Bay oysters and mussels, is the daily specialty, but meat dishes are also given special attention. *Rossnowlagh, Co. Donegal, tel. 072/51777. 40 rooms with bath or shower. Facilities: restaurant, bar, baby-sitting, children's playroom, games room, golf, surfing club, tennis. AE, DC, MC, V. Closed Nov.–Easter. Expensive.*

Sligo Town and Environs

Dining and Lodging

Ballincar House Hotel. In its peaceful 6-acre wooded grounds between Sligo Town and Rosses Point, this out-of-town, leisure-oriented vacation hotel, formerly a private home, is convenient for exploring Yeats Country or the Donegal Bay coast. Its modern bedrooms with private baths and televisions may lack the charm of some other houses in the area, but the restaurant is highly recommended; it specializes in seafood, such as lobster Mornay and salmon. Because of the hotel's popularity, you're advised to reserve rooms well in advance. *Rosses Point Rd., Sligo, Co. Sligo, tel. 071/45361. 20 rooms with bath or shower. Facilities: restaurant, bar, gardens, tennis, sauna, solarium, squash. AE, DC, MC, V. Closed Dec. 23–Jan. 23. Moderate.*

Lodging

Silver Swan Hotel. Standing in the center of town on the Hyde Bridge, this popular hotel and restaurant has an impressive view of the Garavogue River rushing beneath the bridge. Within a rather bland '60s-style exterior, the comfortable mid-range hotel has been recently redecorated and the bedrooms refurnished with pleasing dark-wood modern fittings. All rooms have radio and TV, tea- and coffee-making facilities, garment press, phone, and hair dryer. There's traditional Irish music at the hotel every Wednesday night, and jazz every Sunday morning. *Hyde Bridge, Sligo, Co. Sligo, tel. 071/43231. 35 rooms with bath or shower. Facilities: restaurant, bar. AE, MC, V. Expensive.*

Sligo Park Hotel. A mile out of town on the N4 (the main Dublin road), this modern, well-run property has recently undergone extensive upgrading, with the addition of a heated pool, a well-equipped gym, and a billiards room. Its predictable, reliable comforts (private baths, phones, and televisions in each room) appeal to business travelers, but it also makes a reasonable base for visitors to Yeats Country. Bedrooms, too, have been refurbished, and a new bar added, making this probably the best hotel in Sligo Town. The hotel offers dancing and piano entertainment on some evenings. *Pearse Rd., Sligo, Co. Sligo, tel. 071/60291. 62 rooms with bath or shower. Facilities: restaurant, bar, gardens, secretarial services, laundry services, gym, heated swimming pool, tennis courts, room service. AE, DC, MC, V. Moderate.*

The Arts and Nightlife

The Arts

The rustic and underpopulated Northwest features few serious arts activities and events. If you're in the right place at the right time, however, you can attend or participate in several entertaining festivals. Ask at the Irish Tourist Board Information Offices for up-to-date advance booking information, or check announcements in the local press, including *The Donegal Democrat, The Leitrim Observer,* and *Sligo Champion.*

Theater In early June, during the **Ballyshannon Drama Festival,** the town hosts different drama companies for a program of mainly Irish plays. Sligo Town's **Hawk's Well Theatre** often features interesting programs. It brings in amateur and professional companies from all over Ireland (and occasionally from Britain) to stage a wide variety of shows. Most of the summer season is devoted to the works of popular Irish playwrights. *Temple St., Sligo, tel. 071/61526. Amateur shows: about £4; professional shows: about £5. Call for times. Box office open weekdays 10–6, Sat. 2–6.*

Music At the beginning of August, on the bank holiday weekend, the normally quiet town of Ballyshannon hosts one of Ireland's largest and best folk-music events, the **Ballyshannon Music Festival.** Visitors can hear both well-known and unknown folk and traditional musicians as they entertain in a riverside location. Impromptu performances occur at pubs. A party atmosphere prevails, attracting up to 12,000 visitors annually.

Hawk's Well Theatre in Sligo Town (*see* above) puts on concerts from time to time, including classical performances.

Nightlife

An evening out in the rural Northwest is generally an evening at a lively, popular pub with live music. Always ask locally or at your hotel if there is a nearby pub with "sessions," which are small-scale, informal performances of traditional folk music. For other entertainment, though, especially if you want something a little more sophisticated, you may have to look long and hard. Some hotels or large pubs, particularly at resort towns in season, put on a disco or dance on certain days of the week, or have performances by local groups with an emphasis on country-and-western music. These events generally don't deserve a special journey but can be entertaining if they are nearby.

For a small, old-fashioned village, Andara in County Donegal offers a surprising number of pubs, many of them offering evenings of traditional music. **Peter Oliver's** bar provides music almost every night. **Nancy's,** which is perhaps one of the smallest pubs in the whole of the Republic, finds space for a folk group several nights a week.

In Donegal Town, **The Abbey Hotel** (tel. 073/21014), on the Diamond, features dancing on the weekend and Irish folk music during the week. Letterkenny, also in County Donegal, offers folk music, jazz, or dancing on weekends at the **Mount Errigal Hotel** (tel. 074/22700). Sligo Town's **Southern Hotel** (tel. 071/62101) and **Sligo Park** (tel. 071/60291) have bands, country-and-western shows, and discos during the whole week.

10 Northern Ireland

Belfast, The Antrim Coast, Derry City, The Mountains of Mourne

By Andrew Sanger If Celtic legends are true, the giant Finn MacCool threw down the Giant's Causeway off the coast of Northern Ireland and marched across it in a few strides to reach the shores of Scotland, later returning to his homeland with equal ease. The story isn't entirely implausible. The channel between Scotland and Ireland, though turbulent, has never been much of a barrier to people moving in either direction, and the ancient Irish province of Ulster had close ties with its neighbor on the other side of the water.

Thanks largely to that strong Scottish influence, Ulster and its people have always been somehow separate from the rest of Ireland. Nearly 2,000 years ago the people of Ulster built the Black Pig Dyke—a great ditch and earth barrier—to mark the border between themselves and the other Irish regions to the south. To the southerners and to would-be conquerors, Ulster was known as a tough, indomitable land, home of a warlike people. The "Red Hand" at the center of its flag tells a typically ferocious tale: Two great Celtic warriors raced from Scotland to Ireland's northern coast to settle a dispute between them for possession of Ulster. The first to touch the foreign land could call it his own. In the last moments, one of the rivals cut off his own hand and threw it onto the shore and so, by blood and sacrifice, won Ulster.

Present-day Northern Ireland, a province under the rule of the United Kingdom, includes six of Ulster's nine counties (the others—Donegal, Cavan, and Monaghan—lie in the Irish Republic) and retains its sense of isolation. The hard-headed and industrious Scottish Presbyterians imported to make Ulster a bulwark against Ireland's Catholicism have had a profound and ineradicable effect on the place. Not least of the Scottish legacies are the North's distinctive accents. Northern Ireland has more factories, neater-looking farms, better roads, and more two-story redbrick houses (which are typical in Britain) than does the Republic. Of course, you'll also see, in Protestant districts, some of the odder manifestations of the pro-British Loyalists' zeal: curbstones and lamp posts painted in the British colors of red, white, and blue; entwined British and Ulster flags fluttering from tall poles raised in pocket-handkerchief front yards; and countless signs and crests declaring proud devotion to Ulster and the Queen.

For all that, the national frontier, which separates British Northern Ireland from the Irish Republic, is of little consequence to visitors, or even to residents, who may cross it freely at any time. The only inconvenience is that of waiting in line to be eyed warily by British soldiers, who are on the lookout for militant Republicans. No one should be deterred from traveling here on that account. The "Troubles"—almost always confined to a few city streets whose names come up again and again on news broadcasts—are not as bad in reality as they look on the screen. The truth is that Northern Ireland has a considerable number of attractions worth visiting and some of the very best of Irish scenery on its County Antrim coast and in the tranquil green lake country of County Fermanagh. It also maintains close links with the United States and Canada, to which many of its people have emigrated in the last century.

From the Norman period onward, the English made greater and greater inroads into Ireland, endeavoring to subdue what they believed (probably quite correctly) was a potential enemy and a collaborator with that great adversary of England's naval might, Catholic Spain. Ulster proved the hardest part to conquer, but in 1607 Ulster's Irish nobility were beaten and left their homeland in a great exodus known as the Flight of the Earls. Most went to Spain, abandoning their lands forever to confiscation by the English crown. The English distributed the territories among individuals called Planters—the name given to staunch Protestants from England and, even more often, from Scotland who came to Ireland to farm, work, and colonize. New Protestant towns were built, and Catholics became subjected to harshly repressive laws. Inevitably, tension between the two religious groups increased, often flaring into violence toward the end of the 19th century.

In the parliamentary elections of 1918, almost the whole of Ireland voted for Sinn Féin, the party that believed in independence for all of Ireland; in the six counties, however, the majority of votes went to the Nationalists (who were demanding Home Rule—local autonomy within the United Kingdom), and, especially in Counties Down and Antrim, to the Unionists (who wanted nothing less than to remain an integral part of the United Kingdom). In 1921, by a majority, leading Irish politicians in Dublin agreed to allow the North to remain in British hands, in exchange for complete independence for Ireland's remaining 26 counties. The North established its own parliament, housed in the imposing Stormont building just east of Belfast.

Although the "sectarian" conflict has clearly more to do with politics than religion, visitors may be surprised by the high degree of religious observance in the North. Protestants divide about equally into Anglicans and a variety of more or less austere nonconformists, especially Presbyterians. From the 1880s to the 1920s, the Nationalist movement included many Protestants. However, the passage of time caused positions to become more entrenched rather than less. The Unionists today are closely identified with the "planted" Protestant population, while the Nationalists or Republicans are inextricably associated with the native Irish community, which is almost entirely Catholic.

In the 1960s, after 40 years of living beneath the permanent Protestant majority, the Catholics launched a civil rights movement to demand equal rights in jobs, housing, and opportunities. The severity with which this was put down led to the return of direct rule from London and, at the same time, to a rebirth of the Irish Republican Army (IRA), which had lain dormant for decades. The war between the IRA and the British establishment has continued ever since. At the same time, Protestant paramilitary organizations wage their own war against the IRA. In an effort to undermine the extremism of both sides, in 1985 the London and Dublin governments signed the Anglo-Irish Agreement, which gives the Irish government a consultative voice in Northern Ireland's affairs.

The good news is that this tactic seems to be working, and in the last five years the political climate in Northern Ireland has become more relaxed. In 1990, a Fair Employment Commission was set up to integrate workplaces, and in the same year new legislation brought integration to schools, both of which institutions had traditionally segregated Protestants and Catholics. More and more people on both sides of the sectarian divide show a sincere willingness to make compromises and want only to live in peace with their neighbors. At the extremes, however, the violence between diehard Nationalists and fanatically pro-British Loyalists still continues.

For this reason, visitors to Northern Ireland still have to exercise a little care. Certain areas have seen frequent frightening incidents, particularly the poor working-class districts—both Protestant and Catholic—in west Belfast, and similar neighborhoods in Derry. Yet apart from these easily identified danger spots, Northern Ireland (including these two cities) is as tranquil, inviting, and friendly as the rest of the country.

Essential Information

Arriving and Departing by Plane

Airports and Airlines
Aldergrove Airport, or **Belfast International** (tel. 08494/22888), is Northern Ireland's principal air arrival point, situated 30½ km (19 mi) from Belfast. **Belfast City (Harbour) Airport** (tel. 0232/457745) is the second airport, 6½ km (4 mi) from Belfast. It receives flights from U.K. provincial airports and from Luton (near London). **Eglinton Airport** (tel. 0504/810784) is 8 km (5 mi) from Derry City.

Flights from Britain
British Airways (tel. 0232/240522) and **British Midland Airways** (tel. 0232/225151) operate most flights into Belfast. By far the cheapest flights are offered by **Capital Airlines** (tel. 0532/505550) and **Brittania** (tel. 0582/405737). Other main airlines include **Loganair** (tel. 041/889–3181) and **Air UK** (tel. 0345/666777).

Frequent services to Belfast are scheduled throughout the day from London Heathrow, London Gatwick, and 17 other U.K. airports. Flights take about 1¼ hours from London. British Airways' and British Midland Airways' shuttle services between London and Belfast are walk-on, no-reservation flights, and the airlines claim that no passenger will be turned away—another plane will be added if a scheduled flight is overbooked. Direct flights from Paris on Air France and from Amsterdam on Schiphol also arrive in Belfast. Scheduled flights to Belfast from the United States and Canada are routed via London, but sometimes charter services fly direct to Belfast from New York and Toronto. Eglinton, Derry City's airport, receives flights from Manchester, England, and Glasgow, Scotland, via Loganair.

Between the Airports and the Cities
Belfast: Ulsterbus (tel. 0232/320011) operates a shuttle bus every half-hour (cost: U.K.£3 one-way, U.K.£5 round-trip) between Aldergrove Airport and Belfast city center. From Belfast City Airport, you can travel into Belfast by train from Sydenham Halt to Central Station (East Bridge St.) or catch a taxi from the airport to your hotel.

Derry City: If you arrive at Eglinton Airport (8 km/5 mi from Derry City), you will need to call a taxi (tel. 0504/261911 or 0504/44100 or 0504/43813) to get to your destination.

Arriving and Departing by Car, Ferry, Train, and Bus

By Car While many roads from the Irish Republic into Northern Ireland have been closed, drivers can choose from a score of legitimate crossing points; "unapproved" routes across the border also exist but are not recommended. Visitors should expect an army checkpoint at all approved frontier posts, but few formalities are practiced. The fast N1/A1 road connects Belfast to Dublin (160 km/100 mi); sometimes you'll encounter delays at the border on this road (*see* Staying in Northern Ireland in Chapter 1).

By Ferry **Belfast Ferries** (tel. 051/922–6234; nine-hour crossing) offers car ferries to Belfast from the English port of Liverpool. **Sealink Ferries** (tel. 077/622620; 2½ hours) provides car ferries to Larne from Stranraer, Scotland, and **P&O European Ferries** (tel. 058/12276; 2½ hours) has car ferries to Larne from Cairnryan, Scotland. An interesting new option is to cross on the **SeaCat** (tel. 0304/240241, May–Sept. only)—the world's largest catamaran—which carries cars and passengers from Stranraer to Belfast in just 1½ hours.

By Train The Belfast–Dublin Express train travels nonstop between the two cities in two hours. Six trains run daily in both directions (three on Sundays).

By Bus Northern Ireland's bus company, **Ulsterbus** (tel. 0232/32011), crosses the border to connect with the Republic's **Bus Éireann** (tel. 01/746301 in Dublin) services. The ride from Dublin to Belfast takes four hours, with a change at Monaghan. Buses to Belfast also run from London and from Birmingham, making the Stranraer ferry (tel. 077/622620) crossing.

Getting Around

By Car
Driving In general, drivers will find that in Northern Ireland the roads are in much better shape, signposting is clearer, and gasoline is cheaper than in the Irish Republic. Northern Ireland visitors, however, must deal with army checkpoints; a soldier may ask you a few questions, or even wish to search your luggage; you'll pass through more quickly if you cooperate politely. Bad rush-hour delays can occur getting in and out of Belfast on highways A6 and A2. But on the whole, driving is quicker and easier in Northern Ireland than in areas south of the border.

Parking Always make sure you are not in a "control zone," where it is prohibited to leave a vehicle unattended. Most town centers are control zones, with free car parks situated within walking distance.

Car Rentals Visitors can choose among several local rental companies, but car rental isn't cheap. A compact car costs U.K. £130 to U.K. £160 per week (including taxes, insurance, and unlimited mileage). If you're planning to take a hired car across the border into the Republic, inform the company and check its insurance procedures. The following are some of the main rental offices. **Belfast: Avis** (Great Victoria St., tel. 0232/241414) and **Godfrey Davis** (58 Antrim Rd., 0232/757401). **Aldergrove Airport: Avis** (tel. 08494/22333), **Godfrey Davis** (tel. 08494/23444), and **Hertz** (tel. 08494/22533). **Belfast City Airport: Avis** (tel. 0232/240404). **Derry City: Hertz** (tel. 0504/360420).

By Train Northern Ireland Railways runs only three rail routes: Belfast–Derry via Coleraine, Belfast–Bangor along the shore of Belfast Lough, and Belfast–Dublin. Rail Runabout tickets allow seven days' unlimited travel (cost: U.K.£25): For information contact **Northern Ireland Railways** (17 Wellington Pl., Belfast, tel. 0232/230671), **Belfast Central Station** (East Bridge St., tel. 0232/230310), and local rail stations.

By Bus Visitors can take advantage of frequent and inexpensive Ulsterbus links between all Northern Ireland towns. The main bus stations in Belfast are located behind the Europa Hotel on Great Victoria Street and on Oxford Street near the Central Railway Station. A good bet for touring by bus is a Freedom of Northern Ireland Ticket, which allows unlimited travel (cost: U.K.£15 a day or U.K.£25 for a week; prices subject to change). For all specific fare and schedule details, call **Ulsterbus** (tel. 0232/320011). Within Belfast, visitors have access to good city bus service. All routes start from Donegall Square; you'll find a kiosk there where you can pick up a timetable. For **Citybus** inquiries, call 0232/246485.

Important Addresses and Numbers

Tourist Information The main information center for the whole of Northern Ireland is the **Tourist Information Office** (TIO) located in Belfast, which provides maps, advice, and information on every attraction in Belfast and the province, including upcoming events and festivals. *59 North St., tel. 0232/246609. Open weekdays 9–5:15; Easter–Sept., also open Sat. 9–2.*

Year-round local offices are located at **Armagh** (40 English St., tel. 0861/527808), **Carnlough** (Post Office, Harbour Rd., tel. 0574/85210), **Carrickfergus** (Town Hall, tel. 09603/51604), **Derry City** (Foyle St., tel. 0504/267284), **Downpatrick** (Down Leisure Centre, Market St., tel. 0396/613426), **Enniskillen** (Lakeland Visitor Centre, Shore Rd., tel. 0365/323110), **Giant's Causeway** (Visitor Centre, tel. 02657/31855), **Larne** (Larne Harbour, tel. 0574/70517), **Newcastle** (Central Promenade, tel. 03967/22222), **Newry** (Arts Centre, Bank Parade, tel. 0693/66232), and in more than a dozen other Northern Ireland towns. During June through August, many more towns and villages open tourist information offices.

Emergencies For **police, ambulance, fire,** or **coast guard,** dial 999 in all of Northern Ireland. The **main police station** (tel. 0232/650222) in downtown Belfast is located at 6–10 North Queen Street.

Hospitals In Belfast, the main hospitals with emergency rooms are **Belfast City Hospital** (Lisburn Rd., tel. 0232/329241) and **Royal Victoria Hospital** (Grosvenor Rd., tel. 0232/240503). In Derry City, **Altnagelvin Hospital** (Belfast Rd., tel. 0504/45171) has an emergency room.

Weather In Belfast, call Weathercall at 438544 (area code: 0232, if you're calling from outside Belfast).

Banks and Money Exchange

Northern Ireland uses British currency. Irish *punts,* or pounds, are not accepted. Rates change rapidly, but the British pound is worth a little more than the Irish (*see* Irish Currency in Chapter 1). You'll sometimes be given bank notes, drawn on Ulster banks, that are valid only in Northern Ireland; be sure not to get stuck with a lot of these when you leave, because they will be difficult to change at banks back home. As in the Irish Republic, credit cards are not widely accepted outside the main towns. Main banks are open weekdays 10–3:30. Changing money outside banking hours is possible at **Thomas Cook** branches at Belfast Airport (open weekdays 7 AM–8 PM, weekends 7 AM–10 PM) and 11 Donegall Place (open Mon.–Sat. 9–5:30).

Guided Tours

Orientation Tours   **Citybus** offers a Belfast city orientation tour that takes in the shipyards and heads out from the city center as far as Stormont (9½ km/6 mi east) and Belfast Castle on Cave Hill to the north. *Milewater Rd., tel. 0232/246485. Cost: U.K.£4 adults, U.K.£2.50 children, including afternoon tea. City tour leaves Castle Place June–Sept., Tues.–Thurs. at 2 PM.*

Ulsterbus (Milewater Rd., tel. 0232/331577) operates half-day or full-day trips during June to September from Belfast to the Glens of Antrim, the Giant's Causeway, the Fermanagh lakes, Lough Neagh, the Mourne Mountains, and the Ards Peninsula.

Special-Interest Tours   If you're seeing the province without a car, you could have diffi-
Tours   culty reaching the Giant's Causeway. Apart from a tour to that
Giant's Causeway/   destination from Belfast, Ulsterbus has also teamed up with
Bushmills   the Old Bushmills Distillery to run the **Bushmills Bus,** an open-top tour bus running from Coleraine to the Giant's Causeway via the coast resorts; you also visit Bushmills to observe whiskey-making. *Tel. 0265/43334. Cost: U.K.£2.50 adults, U.K.£1.85 children and senior citizens. Bus leaves Coleraine Mon.–Sat. 9:20, 11:30, 2:10, and 4; Sun. 2:10 and 4 only.*

Lower Lough Erne   **Kestrel** is a 63-seat water bus operated by **Erne Tours** (tel. 0365/22882); it sets off from Round O pier at Enniskillen during the summer for a two-hour trip on beautiful Lough Erne. On weekdays, the boat makes a half-hour stop at Devenish Island to allow visitors to see Ireland's best round tower. From May to June there are Sunday trips at 3 PM, and occasionally at other times of the year. *Cost: U.K.£3 adults, U.K.£1.50 children.*

Exploring Northern Ireland

Along the shores of Northern Ireland's coasts and lakes, green gentle slopes descend majestically into hazy, dark-blue water, against a background of more slopes, more water, and huge cloud-scattered skies. If time is short, you might decide to skip Belfast. (If you arrive by plane, you can easily bypass Northern Ireland's capital, because the Belfast Airport is several miles from the city.)

You certainly won't need to stick rigidly to the route in this guide. Belfast and Derry, however, do deserve a visit, if possible. Belfast is a naturally lively, friendly city with plenty of attractions; it is testimony to the spirit of the place that the long years of sectarian violence have not dimmed its vivacity. Derry still has a few problems but is facing them with great energy. Much of the bad housing has been swept away; new developments are being built both in the suburbs and in the small city center. British fortifications remain much in evidence, though, and soldiers patrol in force. Derry's center is still enclosed by its medieval walls, making it one of Europe's best-preserved examples of a fortified town.

If you want to see only one small area with plenty of variety, the best choice would be a stay in or near Enniskillen, in County Fermanagh. The town itself is bright and bustling; Lough Erne nearby has magnificent lake views, as well as one of Ireland's most impressive round towers, on Devenish Island. On the other side of Enniskillen stands Castle Coole, one of the most graceful mansions of the 18th-century Anglo-Irish nobility.

Highlights for First-time Visitors

The Giant's Causeway (*see* Tour 2)
The Glens of Antrim (*see* Tour 2)
Lower Lough Erne (*see* Tour 3)
Ulster Museum (*see* Tour 1)
Victorian (and older) pubs in Belfast (*see* Tour 1)

Tour 1: Belfast

Numbers in the margin correspond to points of interest on the Northern Ireland and the Belfast maps.

❶ **Belfast** is quite unlike any other city, Irish or British. Its unique charisma derives from a curious mixture of identities, its sense of separateness, and, of course, the notoriety it has received as a center of conflict. Belfast combines the hard-headed proletarian quality of a large industrial town with the dignified self-confidence of a respectable and well-to-do provincial capital. It was a great Victorian success story, a boom town whose prosperity was built on trade: Linen and shipbuilding brought in most of the wealth. Now Belfast struggles against decline; linen is no longer a major industry here, and shipbuilding has suffered severe setbacks. The quaysides along the River Lagan, however, are still impressively active, and the dry dock is one of the world's largest.

The city's central district, lying west of the docks, extends from the City Hall to St. Anne's Cathedral. The area is alive with commerce, shops, cafés, pubs, and historic (but now modernized) streets. Large redbrick or white Portland stone Victorian banks, as well as offices and department stores, occupy this old heart, symbols of Belfast's high standing before the creation of the Irish Free State. Now the whole of this district is pedestrianized for security reasons; the roads are closed to traffic by sturdy green railings with police checkpoints.

Perhaps the most astonishing thing about Belfast is its setting—high wild heath-green slopes rise abruptly at the end of the city-center streets. Until the Plantation period at the beginning of the 17th century, Belfast was an insignificant village called *Beal Feirste* (meaning "Sandbank Ford"). In the 1600s the district, formerly belonging to Ulster's ancient O'Neill clan, was granted to Sir Arthur Chichester, who was from Devon in southwest England. Chichester's son was made earl of Donegall, and he initiated the building of the town; he is remembered in many of the street names. A century later, French Huguenots (i.e., Protestants) fleeing persecution settled here, bringing their valuable skills in linen work. In the 18th century, Belfast saw a phenomenal expansion, with the population doubling in size every 10 years. The sectarian divide appeared during the 19th century when Presbyterian ministers began to preach bitterly against the town's Catholic residents. But the town's growth continued, factories were built, and industry expanded. In 1849, Queen Victoria paid a visit, and she is recalled in the names of buildings, streets, bars, monuments, and other places around the city. In the same year, the university opened and took the name Queen's College. Victoria granted Belfast full city status in 1888. Today its population is 400,000—one-third of all Northern Ireland's citizens.

When the working day is over, Belfast's central area closes down and the life of the town shifts south. Great Victoria Street down to Shaftesbury Square is known as the **Golden Mile,** though it is not at all as glittering as the name implies and is only about a third of a mile in length. Beyond it, down University Road to Stranmillis Road, is the **University Area.** Chances are that as well as drinking and eating in these two parts of the city, you'll also be staying nearby. The University Area is the safest part of town and features many good bed-and-breakfasts and guest houses.

② Belfast's best centrally located hotel, the **Europa** (tel. 0232/ 327000), at the northern end of Great Victoria Street, makes a good starting point for a walking tour of the city center. Many Belfast residents trace an improvement in the atmosphere of their city, and especially an upsurge in evening entertain- **③** ments, to the reopening in 1980 of the **Grand Opera House,** next door to the Europa. This typical Victorian theater, built in 1895, retains its original, richly decorated auditorium, where heavy gilt moldings, ornamental plasterwork, and frescoes depict Asian themes. Although the city already had a lively theater with its own company, the Lyric in south Belfast, the Opera House attracted bigger, more diverse audiences upon its reopening. Today it mounts touring performances of all kinds: musicals, operas, and children's plays, as well as conventional theater. The best way to see and enjoy this immaculate example of Victoriana is to attend a performance. *Great Victoria St., tel. 0232/241919. Seats range from U.K.£3 to U.K.£20.*

Turn right from the Opera House on to Howard Street to reach Belfast's central Donegall Square, dominated by its columned **④** and domed **City Hall** (built 1906). To appreciate the classical style and the setting of the building, first take a walk right around Donegall Square. In the gardens you'll see statues of Queen Victoria; a monument commemorating the unlucky ocean liner *Titanic,* which was built in Belfast; and a short column in honor of the U.S. Expeditionary Force, which landed in the city on January 26, 1942—the first contingent of the U.S. Army to land in Europe. Then step inside the City Hall; the public entrance is located at the rear of the building. If it happens to be a Wednesday morning, you can join the weekly guided tour and be shown the Council Chamber, the Great Hall, and the Reception Room. If not, you may at least walk into the Entrance Hall, to the foot of the Grand Staircase. Here you'll discover a riot of ornamental marble inlays and decorative plasterwork reaching up toward the dome. *Donegall Sq., tel. 0232/320202. Admission free. Guided tours: Wed. 10:30.*

Northern Ireland

Malin Head

Tory
Island

Fanad
Head

Malin
Culdaff

Horn
Head

Carndonagh

Inishowen
Head

Moville

Creeslough

Rathmullan

Carrowkeel

Lough
Foyle

Bla
Aghae

Milford

Muff

A2

Limavady

B66

Ramelton

Campsie

14

**Derry
City**

A6

Dungiven

B190

Letterkenny

R. Foyle

B48

Claudy

Lifford

B48

SPERRIN MOUNTAINS

DERRY

Stranorlar

Castlefin

Strabane

Glenties

Ballybofey

Sion Mills

A5

Newtownstewart

A505

Cookstow

BLUE STACK MOUNTAINS

Donegal Town

**Ulster-American
Folk Park**

15

Pomeroy

Omagh

B46

TYRONE

Dungannon

A4

Lower Lough
Erne

A7

Kesh

B4

A32

Dromore

Ballygawley

17

**White
Island**

■ **Castle Archdale**

Fintona

B122

Clogher

Augher

Aughnacloy

16

Belleek

A46

Lough
Melvin

FERMANAGH

B82

Fivemiletown

**Devenish
Island**

Ballinamallard

B80

18

Castle Coole

19

20

Lisbellaw

A4

Enniskillen

Florence
Court

A32

Lisnaskea

Rosslea

Upper
Lough
Erne

Newtown
Butler

R. Erne

Kintyre
(Scotland)

**The Giant's
Causeway** 13

Rathlin
Island

Carrick
-a-Rede

B15 Ballycastle

**Dunluce
Castle**

Portstewart

Bushmills

A29

Coleraine

Armoy

Cushendun

North Channel

Cushendall

Red Bay

Ballymoney

Glenariff

**Glens of
Antrim** 12

Carnlough Bay

Garvagh

R. Bann

Kilrea

ANTRIM

ANTRIM MOUNTAINS

Carnlough

A29

A43

A42

Maghera

Tobermore

Ballymena

A36

Ballygally

Magherafelt

A26

A8

Larne

Toome

Randalstown

Ballyclare

Antrim

Whitehead

Newtownabbey

Eden

Carrickfergus 11

Belfast Lough

Bangor

Crumlin

A52

25 **Ulster Folk
Museum**

*Lough
Neagh*

Ardboe

★

Belfast
1 — 10
**SEE DETAIL
MAP**

A20

Newtownards

Mt. Stewart

24

Greyabbey

Stewartstown

Comber

Lisburne

*Ards
Peninsula*

Craigavon

Lurgan

A26

A1

Hillsborough

A24

Saintfield

*Strangford
Lough*

A20

Portadown

A29

A3

Ballynahinch

Killyleagh

R. Bann

Strangford

Portaferry

Car Ferry

21

Armagh

Banbridge

DOWN

A25

23 **Downpatrick**

Markethill

ARMAGH

Castlewellan

Dundrum

Ardglass

Keady

A25

A2

Dundrum Bay

B133

Bessbrook

Newry

Newcastle

N

Camlough

A28

Warrenpoint

22 **Mountains
of Mourne**

*Slieve Donard
Mountain*

A2

Carlingford Lough

Kilkeel

0   10 miles

0   15 km

Albert Memorial
Clock Tower, **7**
Botanic Gardens, **9**
City Hall, **4**
Europa Hotel, **2**
Grand Opera House, **3**
Northern Ireland
Tourist Office, **6**
Queen's College, **8**
St. Anne's
Cathedral, **5**
Ulster Museum, **10**

Belfast

You'll notice many buses waiting on the western and eastern
sides of Donegall Square. This is the terminus for all city buses.
The gray building on Donegall Square's northwest corner (at
the junction with Wellington Place) is the **Linen Hall Library.**
This comfortable private library, founded in 1788, is not really
a tourist attraction, but you may want to stop here. Besides being a perfect hideaway for relaxing with a newspaper, the library has an unparalleled collection of local historical
documents. Paintings and prints that show Belfast views and
landmarks adorn the walls. The artworks are for sale and make
excellent and original souvenirs or gifts. Library members can
now peruse books while having a coffee and snack at the coffee
shop inside the reading room. *17 Donegall Sq. N, tel. 0232/
321707. Membership costs £28 per year. Open Mon.–Wed. and
Fri. 9:30–6, Thurs. 9:30–8:30, Sat. 9:30–4.*

Step round the corner of the library onto **Donegall Place,**
Belfast's main shopping street. You'll pass through the security gates into the pedestrians-only zone. Stroll up to Royal Avenue, a continuation of Donegall Place.

Time Out   Belfast offers dozens of intriguing pubs packed with relics of
the Victorian and Edwardian periods. At the start of Royal Avenue, turn left into Bank Street to find **Kelly's Cellars,** a typical
traditional bar with character. Specialties include Ulster fry
(fried bacon, sausages, egg, etc., with potato bread) and champ
'n' sausages (champ is creamy mashed potatoes with chopped
scallions), each for only about U.K.£2. Two centuries ago,
Kelly's Cellars was the regular meeting place of a militant Nationalist group, the Society of United Irishmen, whose leader,
Wolfe Tone, is remembered as the founder of Irish republican-
ism.

❺ To see **St. Anne's Cathedral,** continue to the end of Royal Avenue (crossing North Street), and then turn right onto Donegall
Street. St. Anne's, a large edifice built at the beginning of this
century, could almost be considered the spiritual headquarters
of the province's Anglican establishment. Frankly, though,
this is not an especially beautiful building. Its somber heavi-
ness and deep rounded arches are hallmarks of the Irish neo-
Romanesque style. Lord Carson, who was largely responsible
for keeping the six counties inside the United Kingdom, is buried here beneath a suitably austere plain gray slab. Almost opposite the cathedral in St. Anne's Court, off North Street, you
❻ will find the new premises of the main **Northern Ireland Tourist
Office.** Behind St. Anne's Cathedral, you'll find a run-down
area of narrow cobbled back streets and abandoned warehouses; this district is undergoing a major overhaul, with new
construction and businesses already promising to revive the
neighborhood.

Walk south down to Waring Street (it runs at the bottom of both
Hill Street and Donegall Street), turn left toward the River
Lagan, then right into busy Victoria Street. From here, as you
❼ walk toward the leaning **Albert Memorial Clock Tower,** you'll be
able to see parts of Belfast's famous shipyards and two of the
world's largest cranes, dubbed Samson (108 meters/350 feet
high) and Goliath (143 meters/462 feet). At the clock tower,
named for Queen Victoria's husband, Prince Albert (though he
never came to Northern Ireland), turn right onto High Street.

Off High Street, and especially down to the parallel Ann Street, run narrow lanes and alleyways called entries. Though mostly cleaned up and turned into chic shopping lanes, they manage to hang on to something of their former raffish character. Wandering along these lanes you'll discover some unique pubs with authentic Victorian interiors. For example, take a look inside **The Morning Star** (Pottinger's Entry, off High St.) with its large windows and fine curving bar. **White's Tavern** (Winecellar Entry, off High St.) is Belfast's oldest pub, founded in 1630. Although it has been considerably updated, it still has a warm and comfortable ambience, with plush seats and a big open fire.

Follow Ann Street back to Donegall Place, then retrace your steps through Donegall Square to Great Victoria Street.

Time Out   You might want a drink (and maybe a plate of oysters) in Belfast's best-preserved pub, the **Crown Liquor Saloon** (tel. 0232/325368), which is directly opposite the Europa Hotel on Great Victoria Street. The Crown, owned by the United Kingdom's official conservationist charity, The National Trust, dates back to the end of the 19th century and has been kept in immaculate condition, with opulent ornamentation, richly carved woodwork around cozy snugs (private rooms), leather seats, colored tiles, and abundant mirrors.

The Europa and the Crown bar mark the start of **The Golden Mile**, so called because most of Belfast's evening life takes place in bars and restaurants here. The Crown is far from being the only impressive old pub on this stretch. Indeed, if you would like to try another Victorian bar with more locals and fewer visitors, you only have to walk into **Robinson's,** next door to the Crown. **The Beaten Docket,** on the other side of the Crown, is snazzier and appeals to a younger crowd.

8 The **University Area** is centered on **Queen's College** (set well back from University Rd.), which was constructed in the 1840s. Queen's is modeled on the colleges at Oxford University in England, with their spires, turrets, and fine stonework. **University Square**, adjacent to Queen's, is another architectural treasure with its Georgian terraces.

9 Spreading out beside Queen's, the 19th-century **Botanic Gardens** provide a welcome haven of quiet and greenery. A pretty highlight of the gardens is the 150-year-old curved iron-and-glass Palm House, the oldest such structure in the world. *Stranmillis Rd., tel. 0232/324902. Admission free. Gardens open daily dawn–dusk. Palm House open weekdays 10–5, weekends 2–5.*

10 Within the gardens, to the left of the main entrance, the **Ulster Museum** offers three floors devoted to the history and prehistory of Ireland and, in particular, Northern Ireland, together with a considerable collection of 19th- and 20th-century fine art. In the natural history section, you'll see, among other things, a skeleton of the now-extinct Irish giant deer. The museum's centerpiece is the fabulous jewelry and gold ornaments (as well as cannon and other armaments) recovered from the Spanish vessel *Girona*, sunk off the Antrim coast in 1588. Perhaps the most imaginative, user-friendly sections are on the first floor—one colorfully traces the rise of Belfast's crafts, trade, and industry; the other tells the story of the Nationalist movement and explains the separation of Northern Ireland from the rest of the country. Visitors have access to a little café on level three. *Stranmillis Rd., tel. 0232/381251. Admission free. Open weekdays 10–5, Sat. 1–5, Sun. 2–5.*

The road south divides at the Botanic Gardens. Stranmillis Road leads into **Stranmillis,** a perfectly safe neighborhood with a cultured air and a choice of eateries. The community reaches over to the riverside towpath along the Lagan. **Malone Road** joins the river farther south, close to the out-of-town **Giant's Ring** (off Ballyleeson Road), a large, neolithic earthworks focused on an impressive *dolmen* (Celtic monument made of large stone slabs). To get this far, unless you're a keen walker (it's possible to come all the way on the Lagan towpath) you'll be happier driving in a car or taking a bus: bus No. 22 passes close to the site, and on the return journey it will take you back to Donegall Square.

Tour 2: Around Counties Antrim and Derry

Numbers in the margin correspond to points of interest on the Northern Ireland map.

This circular route starts and finishes in Belfast, passing through some fair-sized towns, but most of the way you're driving in open country. Scenery is the best thing about Northern Ireland, but the region has much more to offer. For example, you'll discover the roots of several Ulstermen who became distinguished Americans. To follow the whole tour as described here could take an unhurried three or four days.

Begin this tour by heading north out of Belfast along the industrialized west shore of Belfast Lough. Cave Hill (*see* Off the Beaten Track below), rising to the left, makes a popular day excursion for city dwellers.

⓫ Take the busy A2 toward **Carrickfergus.** This town on the shore of the lough grew up around **Carrickfergus Castle,** one of the first and one of the largest of Irish castles, which is still in good shape. Impressively located on a rock ledge, it was built in 1180 by John de Courcy, provincial Ulster's first Anglo-Norman invader. The castle stood as a bastion of British rule right up until 1928, at which time it was still an English garrison. In fact, when Carrickfergus was enclosed by ramparts at the start of the 17th century, it was the only English-speaking town in Northern Ireland. Not surprisingly, this was the loyal port where William of Orange chose to land on his way to fight the Catholic forces at the Battle of the Boyne in 1690. However, the English did have one or two small setbacks, including the improbable victory in 1778 of John Paul Jones, the American naval hero, over the British warship HMS *Drake.* That, by the way, was America's first naval victory during the Revolutionary War. After the sea battle, the inhabitants of Carrickfergus stood on the waterfront and cheered Jones because they supported the American Revolution.

Walk through the castle's 13th-century gatehouse into the Outer Ward; continue into the Inner Ward, the heart of the fortress. Here stands the five-story Keep, a massively sturdy building with walls almost 2½ meters (8 feet) thick. Inside the Keep, you'll find a Cavalry Regimental Museum with historic weapons and an impressive vaulted Great Hall. These days,

Carrickfergus Castle hosts entertaining medieval banquets (inquire at a local tourist office); if you're here at the beginning of August, you can enjoy the annual Lughnasa festival, a lively medieval costume entertainment. *Tel. 09603/51273. Admission: U.K.£1.50 adults, U.K.75p children under 16. Open Apr.–Sept., daily 10–6; Oct.–Mar., daily 10–4 (closed all year Sun. AM).*

Other structures that remain from Carrickfergus's past are St. Nicholas's Church, dating from the 13th and 14th centuries, and the handsomely restored North Gate in the town's medieval walls. **Dobbins Inn** (tel. 0574/51905) on High Street has been a popular hotel for more than three centuries. While in Carrickfergus, you might like to take a look at the **Andrew Jackson Centre,** in a thatched cottage a mile northeast of the town. This exhibit tells the tale of U.S. president Jackson, whose parents emigrated from Carrickfergus in 1765. This cottage was not their home, but it's thought to resemble it.

As you head away from the town on the A2, you'll pass through the village of **Eden,** where **Castle Dobbs** was the home of Arthur Dobbs, the 18th-century British governor of North Carolina. A mile and a half (2½ km) off the road, signposted on the left, **Dalway's Bawn,** built in 1609, is the best surviving example of an early *bawn,* or fortified farmhouse occupied by a Protestant Planter. Stay on the A2 to **Larne,** and pass through this workaday port town.

Soon after Larne, the coast of County Antrim becomes spectacular. Wave upon wave of high green hills curves down into the hazy sea, and the views are thrilling. The lower slopes are lush and intensively farmed, but rugged, too, while green moorland covers the rounded summits. Broad, rich glens, or valleys, cut through the hills toward the sea. In the 86 km (54 mi) between Larne and Ballycastle there are nine magnificent **Glens of Antrim.** The journey by these glens is mostly along a small, winding two-lane road close to the sea. **Carnlough** (24 km/15 mi out of Larne), a little resort made of white limestone, overlooks an endearing harbor within stone walls. There is a small tourist office inside the post office.

Time Out Carnlough's **Londonderry Arms** (20 Harbour Rd., tel. 0574/85255) is a fine old traditional inn by the harbor. It dates back to the 17th century and once belonged to Winston Churchill. Fresh seafood is, of course, the specialty—try the seafood gratiné or the lobster—and substantial homemade wheat bread is served as well.

Beyond Carnlough the scenery becomes even more attractive. **Glenariff,** opening onto Red Bay at the village of Glenariff (also known as Waterfoot), is considered the loveliest of the glens. At neighboring **Cushendall,** you'll see a curious fortified square tower of red stone—a 19th-century jailhouse—standing at a crossroads in the middle of the village. If you would like a break from the Antrim coast, stay on the A2 direct to Ballycastle. But if you would prefer to stay by the sea, turn left at the tower in the direction of **Cushendun,** a tiny jewel of a village. From this part of the coast you can see the Mull of Kintyre on the Scottish mainland. The coast road rejoins the A2 after a few miles and descends—passing the ruins of the Franciscans' 16th-century

Bonamargy Friary—into **Ballycastle,** the glens' main resort, at the northern end of the Glens of Antrim drive.

Every year since 1606, on the last Tuesday in August the town has hosted its **Oul' Lammas Fair,** a modern version of the ancient Celtic harvest festival Lughnasa. Ireland's oldest fair, this is a highly popular two-day event at which sheep and wool are still sold alongside more modern shopping stalls. If you're here at this time, treat yourself to the fair's traditional snacks, "dulse and yellow man" (edible seaweed and rock-hard yellow toffee). If you happen to be at Ballycastle in June, you might find yourself in the middle of the **Fleadh Amhran agus Rince,** a lively three-day music and dance folk festival.

From Ballycastle you have a view of *L*-shaped **Rathlin Island,** where in 1306 the Scottish king Robert the Bruce took shelter in a cave and was inspired to continue his armed struggle against the English by watching the patience of a spider spinning its web. It was on Rathlin in 1898 that Guglielmo Marconi set up the world's first radio link, from the island's lighthouse to Ballycastle. If the sea is not too rough (which it often is), a daily boat excursion journeys to the rocky windswept island; only 9½ km (6 mi) away from shore, Rathlin can take an hour to reach. Make sure that you'll be able to return the same day.

Follow the shore road (B15) to **Carrick-a-Rede,** famous for one simple thing: a rope bridge. The bridge, swinging 25 meters (80 feet) above the crashing sea, is the precarious link between the mainland and a salmon fishery on a tiny island 18½ meters (60 feet) offshore. The walk across the bridge is pretty scary, but perhaps that's why almost every man, woman, and child passing this way likes to try it. *Admission free. Bridge open daily May–Sept.*

Another 8 km (5 mi) along the coast brings you to Ireland's strangest and most impressive geological curiosity, **The Giant's Causeway.** This bizarre sight consists of huge masses of mostly hexagonal pillars of volcanic basalt, clustered like honeycomb; about 37,000 of these columns extend down the cliffs, far into the sea. They were apparently created from boiling lava crystallizing as it burst into the sea; the lava came from an underground fissure that stretched from Northern Ireland to the Scottish coast. According to legend, however, the columns were created when the giant Finn MacCool threw stepping-stones into the sea to make a causeway over to the Scottish island of Staffa.

Arriving by car, at first you'll reach a cliff-top parking lot beside the **Visitor Centre,** which provides displays about the area and an audiovisual exhibition explaining the formation of the causeway coast. Reaching the causeway itself requires a round-trip journey on foot of about 3 km (2 mi). If you can't face such a trek, a minibus from the Visitor Centre will take you to the site. You can walk or scramble over the rocks (beware—they can be slippery and dangerous), some of which have been given whimsical names such as the Organ and the Harp. Farther out, Port-na-Spania is the spot where the 16th-century Spanish Armada galleass *Girona* went down on the rocks. The ship was carrying an astonishing cargo of gold and jewelry, some of which was recovered in 1967 and is now on display in the Ulster Museum in Belfast (*see* Tour 1: Belfast, above). Beyond that, Chimney Point is the name given to one of the Causeway structures on which the Spanish fired, thinking that it was Dunluce Castle, which is 8 km (5 mi) west. *Giant's Causeway Visitor Centre, Causeway Head, near Bushmills, tel. 02657/31855. Car park: U.K.£1.50. Audiovisual exhibition: U.K.£1 adults, U.K.50p children. Static exhibition: U.K.50p adults, U.K.30p children and senior citizens. Open July–Aug., daily 10–7. Closes earlier according to demand, rest of year.*

Time Out The pleasant little tearoom in the Visitor Centre provides wholesome snacks at moderate prices. Enjoy panoramic sea views while you enjoy the cakes and scones.

Just inland from The Giant's Causeway about 3 km (2 mi) on the A2 is **Bushmills,** the village whose distillery produces the original, the best, and the most famous of Irish whiskeys. Enthusiasts of this elegant firewater who would like to see how it is made should call ahead at the Bushmills Distillery to join one of the guided tours. *Tel. 02657/31521. Admission free. Tours Mon.–Thurs. mornings and afternoons, Fri. mornings only.*

About 5 km (3 mi) west of Bushmills, still on the A2, the **Dunluce Castle** ruin lies dramatically on a cliff top. Originally a 13th-century Norman fortress, it was captured in the 16th century by the indomitable local MacDonnell clan chiefs, who enlarged it, making it an important base for controlling the area. Maybe they expanded the castle a little too much, for in 1639 the kitchens and the cooks plummeted into the sea. *Admission: U.K.£1 adults, U.K.50p children and senior citizens. Open Apr.–Sept., Mon.–Sat. 10–7, Sun. 2–7; Oct.–Mar., Mon.–Sat. 10–4, Sun. 2–4. Closed 1–1:30.*

To reach **Coleraine,** either take the A2 to the small resort of Portrush and turn inland on the A28 or turn back to Bushmills and take the B17 from there—either way, you'll drive about 13 km (8 mi) to Coleraine from Dunluce Castle. At Coleraine, cross the River Bann into County Londonderry (or Derry). The Bann, which cuts through Northern Ireland, marks the boundary between the fiercely Protestant Counties Antrim and Down and the other four counties.

Take the A37 west from Coleraine through **Limavady,** with its Georgian main street. At No. 51, in the year 1851, Jane Ross noted down the tune played by a traveling fiddler and called it "Londonderry Air," better known now as "Danny Boy." While staying at an inn on Ballyclose Street, William Thackeray (1811–1863) wrote his rather lustful poem "Peg of Limavaddy," about a barmaid. Among the many Americans descended from Ulster emigrants was President James Monroe, whose relatives came from the Limavady area.

⑭ As the road turns toward **Derry City,** the neat terraces rising gently from the Foyle Valley come into view. The town appears attractive and inviting, which is astonishing because of its reputation as one of Europe's most troubled cities. In reality, here as in Belfast, the publicity is out of proportion to the actual situation, though as always, it is prudent to avoid wandering about in certain sections of town, notably Bogside and Creggan. The name of the city, by the way, is now officially Derry, although staunch Loyalists (including many government departments) still like to call it by its old Plantation period name, Londonderry. The county, though, is still called Londonderry. The "London" part of the name was tacked on in

1613 after the Irish nobility were thoroughly trounced and the city and county were handed over to the Corporation of London, which represented London's merchants. They brought in a large population of Protestants, built new towns for them, and reconstructed Derry within the **City Walls,** which survive almost unchanged to this day.

These substantial ramparts of gray stone, pierced by eight gates (originally four), are about 8 meters (25 feet) high and as much as 9 meters (30 feet) thick. The walls are only 1.6 km (1 mi) all round, which indicates how small the walled area is. These days, Derry extends far beyond this fortified center; most of the life of the town actually takes place outside the walls. The best way to get the feel of Derry's history is to stroll along the parapet walkway atop the ramparts. The walkway has been closed for some time, but it is scheduled to be reopened for guided walks in 1993. If the ramparts walkway is still closed during your visit, a near-complete circuit can be made at ground level. The best starting point is Shipquay Gate on the north side, beside the ornate Victorian **Guildhall;** convenient parking is close by. The town's Tourist Information Office is located on Foyle Street, two minutes on foot from the Guildhall car park.

Over the centuries, the sturdy ramparts withstood many fierce attacks and were never breached, which explains Derry's coy sobriquet, "The Maiden City." The most celebrated siege occurred from 1688 to 1689, when James II (the Catholic king trying to regain the throne of England) reached the town with his army, expecting to be welcomed by Derry's governor, Colonel Lundy. But 13 Protestant apprentice boys had stolen the keys of the city gates; after throwing Lundy outside, these lads locked the gates to prevent James's entry. James, undeterred, blockaded the town with the intention of starving it into submission. Of the 30,000 people within the walls, a quarter of them died of hunger before reinforcements arrived from William of Orange (the Dutch Protestant claimant to the English throne). The blockade was broken, and James was forced to withdraw. The whole event is proudly recalled by Derry's Protestant community—now a minority of the population—who still hold colorful ceremonial marches in honor of the apprentice boys, reenacting the Protestants' triumph and annually burning an effigy of the hated Governor Lundy.

From Shipquay Gate, walk along Union Hall Street. You quickly reach **O'Doherty's Tower,** where a new and helpful interpretative center tells the story of the city from its beginnings as an oak grove right up to the present day; by summer 1993, an Armada Exhibition is planned with a permanent display of Spanish treasure found in the Foyle estuary. From here, turn up toward **Butcher Gate,** on the west side, which opens onto the Catholic Bogside district. The graffito "Doire Cholmcille" near this gateway is the old Irish name for Derry City—Columba's Oak. A five-minute walk downhill outside Butcher Gate into the Bogside will take you to **Free Derry Corner,** one of the city's compelling modern curiosities, a surviving gable wall, from a demolished terrace of houses, that is painted with the bold words YOU ARE NOW ENTERING FREE DERRY. From here you can see **Roaring Meg,** one of the original cannons from the 1688–89 siege, which still looks out from Double Bastion, a fortified corner on the ramparts. Go back inside Butcher Gate, and continue on Magazine Street to **Bishop Gate.** Here you'll discover one of the most extraordinary facts about the walls: The British army is still using them to defend the city. Bishop Gate, opening onto the Fountain Area, a Protestant quarter on the south side, is under exceptionally heavy guard.

Within the walls, Shipquay Street climbs steeply to the central square, the Diamond. On the way it passes an attractive new development lying to the right (look for a sign: THE VILLAGE). Beyond the Diamond, if you walk on Bishop Street Within, you'll pass **St. Columba's Cathedral.** Built in 1633 in simple Planter's Gothic style, the church is a treasure house of Derry Protestant emblems, memorials, and relics from the 1688–89 siege.

Time Out Among the several modest cafés suitable for a snack or lunch break in Derry City, one of the most agreeable is **The Boston Tea Party.** This small tea shop is situated in the new development called The Village, which is reached down an alley nearly opposite the Richmond Shopping Centre on Shipquay Street. Boston, by the way, has links with Derry dating back to the 17th and 18th centuries, when many Derry residents escaped their hardships at home by emigrating to that U.S. city and other parts of the New World.

Tour 3: Around Counties Tyrone, Fermanagh, Armagh, and Down

From Derry City, head across County Tyrone toward Enniskillen. Take the A5 south via Strabane to Omagh. **Strabane** does not offer much to hold your interest, apart from the well-preserved 18th-century **Gray's Print Shop** (49 Main St., tel. 0504/884094). John Dunlap (1746–1812), who apprenticed here as a printer before emigrating to Philadelphia, founded America's first daily newspaper, *The Philadelphia Packet,* in 1771, and was also the man who printed and distributed the American Declaration of Independence. James Wilson, grandfather of President Woodrow Wilson, also emigrated. The original **Wilson family home,** a simple thatched cottage, still with much of the original 18th-century furniture, survives at Dergalt, 3 km (2 mi) along the Plumbridge Road. It can be visited by knocking at the farmhouse next door, still owned and worked by the Wilson family. For a delightfully rustic alternative route, drive along the minor road B48, which skirts the foot of the **Sperrin Mountains** and reaches all the way to Omagh.

About 27 km (17 mi) south from Strabane on the A5, or 5 km (3 mi) north if you're coming from Omagh, you'll reach the ⑮ **Ulster-American Folk Park,** which has been designed to recreate a Tyrone village of two centuries ago, a log-built American settlement of the same period, and the docks and ships that the emigrants to America would have used. The centerpiece of the park is an old whitewashed cottage, now a museum, which is the ancestral home of Andrew Mellon (1855–1937), the U.S. millionaire banker. Another thatched cottage is a reconstruction of the boyhood home of Archbishop John Hughes, founder of New York's St. Patrick's Cathedral. Exhibitions trace the contribution of the Northern Irish people to American history. The park also features a crafts shop and café. *Camphill, Co. Tyrone, tel. 0662/243292. Admission: U.K.£2.60 adults, U.K.£1.30 children. Open Easter–Sept., Mon.–Sat. 11–6:30,*

Sun. and holidays 11:30–7; Oct.–Good Friday, weekdays
10:30–5. Last admission 1½ hrs before closing.

Drive south through **Omagh,** County Tyrone's capital, taking
the A32 in the direction of Enniskillen. After 9½ km (6 mi),
turn right onto the B4 to the village of **Kesh,** beside **Lower
Lough Erne.** The best of this highly scenic lake can be seen by
driving from Kesh to Enniskillen on the shore road (B82). Lovers of Belleek pottery should first skirt the northern edge of
🅰️ the lake to reach **Belleek,** where this distinctive fine porcelain is
made. You can tour the **Belleek Pottery Ltd.** factory, where
original methods of manufacture are still used; you can purchase some of the pottery, and enjoy a snack in the tea shop.
Tel. 0365/65501. Admission free. Tours Mon.–Thurs. 9:30–
4:15; Fri. 9:30–3:15.

Just a mile across the border, on the road to Ballyshannon in
County Donegal, you can visit **Celtic Weave China** (tel. 072/
51844), a small operation making handmade fine pottery similar to the items made in Belleek (*see* Shopping, below).

On the journey beside Lough Erne, apart from pausing to catch
your breath at the lovely views of green hills extending down to
the still lake water, you should also stop at **Castle Archdale
Country Park,** signposted down a narrow road about 6½ km (4
mi) from Kesh, where there's a lakeside marina, an open-air
country museum, and a World War II exhibition featuring the
Battle of the Atlantic. *Tel. 03656/21333. Admission free. No set
hours.*

From Castle Archdale a June–September ferry (tel. 0365/
22711; cost: U.K.£1; no boat Mon.) takes passengers to see the
🅱️ weird Celtic carved figures on **White Island.** After you drive 13
km (8 mi) farther from Castle Archdale Park, where the B82
joins the A32, a small sign shows the way to catch the little boat
from April–September (tel. 0365/22711; cost: U.K.£1; no boat
🆎 Mon.) over to **Devenish Island.** The extensive but ruined 12th-
century monastery on Devenish features Ireland's best example of a round tower and a richly carved high cross.

Another 5 km (3 mi) south along the A32 brings you to
🔟 **Enniskillen,** the pleasant capital of County Fermanagh, with
its town center strikingly situated on an island in the River
Erne between Upper and Lower Lough Erne. At the riverside,
the 16th-century **Water Gate** is handsomely turreted, and part
of the 15th-century **Castle Keep** contains the local history collection of the **Fermanagh County Museum** (tel. 0365/325050)
and the polished paraphernalia of the **Royal Inniskilling Fusiliers Regimental Museum** (tel. 0365/23142). Beyond the West
Bridge lies Portora Royal School, established in 1608 by King
James I. Its grounds contain the ruins of Portora Castle. Writers Oscar Wilde and Samuel Beckett were both educated at
Portora Royal School. The town's other sights are admittedly
modest. Yet the spires of its 19th-century churches and town
hall lend a certain charm to this friendly town. One satisfying
journey to make from Enniskillen is a complete tour of Lower
Lough Erne, allowing a full day to really enjoy it.

Time Out Among the several relaxed and welcoming old pubs in
Enniskillen's town center, the one with the most appeal is
Blakes of the Hollow on the main street, a place hardly altered
since it opened in 1887. Its name derives from the facts that the

heart of the town lies in a slight dip or hollow and the pub's landlord is named William Blake. Don't ask if he's related to the great poet of the same name—everybody does, and he isn't!

About 11 km (7 mi) south from Enniskillen on the A4 and the A32, **Florence Court** deserves a visit if you have the time. One of the most impressive of Northern Ireland's grand Anglo-Irish mansions, it was built in the 18th century for John Cole, father of the first earl of Enniskillen. The house features abundant Rococo plasterwork, 18th-century furnishings, and a fine porcelain collection. You can stroll around the estate grounds, and have a snack and coffee at the tea shop. *Tel. 0365/82249. Admission: U.K.£2.20 adults, U.K.£1.10 children. Open June–Aug., Wed.–Mon.; Apr.–May, Sept., weekends only. Grounds open 10–1 hr before sunset; house open 2–6.*

Next, drive east from Enniskillen on the A4, the main Belfast road (from Florence Court, backtrack on the A32 to Enniskillen), and 3 km (2 mi) from town, you'll see signs pointing to **⑳ Castle Coole** on the left. Another of the graceful mansions of the Anglo-Irish ruling class of the 18th and 19th centuries, this home is considered the finest of them all. The house stands in its own landscaped oak woods and parkland at the end of a long tree-lined driveway. In perfect Palladian symmetry, white colonnaded wings extend from either side of the white neoclassical mansion. In a recent restoration, anything not in keeping with the original design was removed. Inside, too, everything—from the lavish plasterwork to sumptuous period furniture—reflects the taste and wealth of its first owners, the earls of Belmore. Castle Coole is still the home of the present earl of Belmore. *Enniskillen, Co. Fermanagh, tel. 0365/322690. Admission: U.K.£2.20 adults, U.K.£1.10 children. Open Easter and June–Aug., Fri.–Wed. 2–6; May and Sept., weekends and holidays only; rest of year, grounds open, house closed.*

Continue in an easterly direction along the A4, through drumlin-dotted farmland (drumlins are tiny hillocks). At Augher village, pick up the A28 on the right.

㉑ After a 40-km (25-mi) drive, the road reaches the small but ancient ecclesiastical city of **Armagh.** Despite some pleasing Georgian streets (especially The Mall, east of the town center), the heart of Armagh can seem drab, and it suffers from having been a trouble spot in the religious conflict. Here St. Patrick founded a church, and the town has remained a religious center to the present day. In fact, *two* Armagh cathedrals are dedicated to Ireland's patron saint. Despite the 1921 partition of Ireland into two parts, the seat of the Catholic Archbishop of All Ireland remains in Armagh, as does the seat of the Archbishop of the Anglican Church of Ireland.

The pale limestone Victorian Gothic **Catholic Cathedral** with two pale spires, on a hill at the north end of town, is best seen from a distance. Nearer the town center, a squat battlemented tower identifies the **Protestant Cathedral,** in simpler early 19th-century Perpendicular Gothic style. It stands on the site of much older churches and contains several relics of Armagh's long history, including sculpted pre-Christian idols. This cathedral claims to be the burial place of Brian Boru, the great High King—that is, king of all Ireland—who drove the Vikings out of Ireland in the 11th century.

Walk down College Street, turning off English Street in the town center, to the broad Georgian esplanade called The Mall. At the north end of the green stands the 19th-century Courthouse, and at the other end, a dominating jailhouse. On the corner of The Mall East, the **Royal Irish Fusiliers Museum** (in Sovereign's House, tel. 0861/522911) features exhibits that illustrate part of the story of Britain's efforts to control this part of Ireland from the 1798 Rebellion onward.

On a completely different note, about 200 yards from the museum up College Hill—a continuation of College Street at the north end of the Mall—is Armagh's main attraction, the **Astronomy Centre and Planetarium**. It contains fascinating exhibits, including models of spacecraft, video shows of the sky, and hands-on computer displays. The observatory here has been in continuous use since 1791. *Tel. 0861/523689. Admission: U.K.£2 adults, U.K.£1.50 children under 18 and senior citizens. Open daily 1:30–4:45.*

Next, leave Armagh on the A28, driving toward Newry. Instead of going the whole way on the main road, after about 9½ km (6 mi), you'll have a more enjoyable drive if you take the B133, on the right. This will lead you through a rustic drumlin landscape of vivid green pastures. The appearance of villages changes as you return toward the River Bann; houses and farms begin to resemble homes and farms in Britain rather than those in the Republic. **Bessbrook** is a "model village" built in 1846 by Quaker linen manufacturer John Grubb Richardson. It has a naïve, dreamlike, toy-town quality, with its neat terraces and picture-book village stores. Richardson decreed that there would be no pubs at Bessbrook. Maybe that explains why there are no fewer than six in the neighboring village, Camlough. **Derrymore House,** a thatched cottage with a well-tended garden outside Bessbrook, is the place where in 1800 the fateful Act of Union was drafted.

From Bessbrook, the drive is only 3 km (2 mi) to the middle of **Newry,** a town with a history of vigorous Irish nationalism, despite having the first Protestant church in Ireland, St. Patrick's. Though still standing, the church has been altered a great deal since it was put up in 1578, having been frequently damaged and repaired. Some 18th-century buildings in Newry survive, especially on Upper Water Street and Trevor Hill, notably the White Linen Hall. On weekends and market days, Irish citizens fill the town, coming from across the Northern Ireland border, only 6½ km (4 mi) away, to take advantage of lower prices in the North.

Follow the east bank of industrialized Carlingford Lough via the A2 and then the wild Irish Sea to **Newcastle.** On the way you'll be circling the atmospheric and unspoiled **Mountains of Mourne,** which "sweep down to the sea" (in the words of a popular song) from 620-meter (2,000-foot) summits. This area was long considered ungovernable, its hardy inhabitants living from smuggling contraband into the numerous rocky coves on the seashore. Much of the Mourne range is still inaccessible except on foot. The countryside of high windswept pasture- and moorland, threaded with bright streams, is perfect for away-from-it-all walkers. Newcastle is the main center for visitors to the hills. Looming above the town is **Slieve Donard,** its panoramic 870-meter (2,805-foot) summit grandly claiming views into England, Wales, and Scotland—"when it's clear enough," or, in other words, rarely!

㉓ **Downpatrick,** 19 km (12 mi) away from Slieve Donard on the A2 and A25, used to be called plain and simple Down, but the town is proud of a suspected association with St. Patrick and changed its name in his honor. St. Patrick was a 5th-century Briton who, captured by the Irish, became a slave in the Down area; he escaped to France, where he learned about Christianity, and bravely returned to try to convert the local chiefs. Although it is not true that Patrick personally brought a new faith to Ireland (there was already a bishop of Ireland before Patrick got here), he must have been a better missionary than most because he did indeed win influential converts. The clan chief of the Down area gave him land at the village of Saul, near Downpatrick, to build a monastery.

Downpatrick's hilltop cathedral, built in 1790, preserves parts of some of the earlier churches and monasteries that have stood on the site since the 6th century. Even before that time, the cathedral site had long been an important fortified settlement (Down takes its name from the Celtic word "Dun," a fort). In the churchyard, a somber slab has been inscribed "Patric"— it's supposedly the saint's tomb, which is a bit of a fraud since no one knows where Patrick is buried. It might be here, at Saul, or, some scholars argue, more likely at Armagh. A lot of such mystery and legend surrounds Patrick. For some hard fact, visit the **St. Patrick Heritage Centre** next to the cathedral; it's housed, together with the **Down Museum,** inside a former 18th-century jail. *The Mall, tel. 0396/615218. Admission free. Open weekdays 11–5, weekends 2–5. Closed Sept.–June on Mon.*

From Downpatrick, head northeast on the A25 to **Strangford** (13 km/8 mi) and the **Ards Peninsula.** At Strangford, **Castle Ward** is an 18th-century mansion in a bizarre mixture of styles—classical on one side, Gothic on the other. The 700-acre estate has a "Victorian pastimes center" for children, a wildfowl collection, a restaurant, an information office, and the old tower house, which once guarded the shore. Holiday cottages are available for rentals as well. *Located .8 km (½ mi) west of Strangford on south shore of Strangford Lough, tel. 0396/ 86204. Admission: U.K.£2.30 adults, U.K.£1.15 children. House open May–Aug., Fri.–Wed. 1–6; closed Thurs. Estate open year-round, dawn–dusk.*

You'll have to cross Strangford Lough on the car ferry from Strangford to reach **Portaferry** (£2 per car, 60p per additional passenger, 25p for children and senior citizens), another quiet fishing village with old fortifications to guard this once-strategic channel, which joins the lough to the sea. The ferry crossing takes 10 minutes or less, and boats leave every half hour throughout the day all year long.

Time Out On the Portaferry waterside, **The Portaferry Arms** (tel. 02477/ 28230), an old, unpretentious bed-and-breakfast, has a full menu of inexpensive snacks and lunches. Take a window seat and watch the unhurried activity on the quay and the relaxed routine of the tiny ferry as it chugs to and fro across the lough.

Before moving on, you may want to take a look at Portaferry's unusual **Northern Ireland Aquarium,** which has models of the underwater environment in Strangford Lough and examples of 70 species that call the lough their home. Some of these creatures may not be what you expect—seals and some large, long-lived species of fish still live in the lake. *Northern Rope Walk, Portaferry, tel. 02477/28062. Admission: U.K.£1.50 adults, U.K. 85p children and senior citizens, children under 5 free; family ticket U.K.£3.85. Open Apr.–Aug., Mon.–Sat. 10–6; Sun., afternoons only. Sept.–Mar., Tues.–Sat. 10:30–5; Sun., afternoons only.*

The A20 makes its way north from Portaferry up the lakeshore. Strangford Lough is not really a lake; it is joined to the sea by the channel you crossed at Portaferry, and might be better described as a fjord. Although Strangford Lough is deep in the middle, it rises to shallow banks dotted with rounded islands (actually submerged drumlins). In fact, its original Norse name was *Strang Fjord* (Strong Fjord), referring to the powerful current that flows into and out of the water with every tide. Huge populations of wildfowl gather in and beside the water.

24 **Mount Stewart,** signposted on the right around 21 km (13 mi) from Portaferry, is the grand 18th-century family home of the marquesses of Londonderry. The marvelous landscaped gardens give the impression that the owners had more money than they knew what to do with; they created luxuriant flower beds, elaborate hedges, and planned views, and they populated the grounds with surprising stone carvings of rare and extinct creatures. The octagonal Temple of the Winds is a copy of a similar little structure in Athens. *Newtownards, tel. 024774/387. Admission: U.K.£3.30 adults, U.K.£1.65 children. Open June–Aug., Wed.–Mon. 1–6; May, Sept.–Oct., weekends and public holidays only.*

On the A20, from Newtownards west to Belfast direct is only 16 km (10 mi), but it's worth detouring via Bangor (6½ km/4 mi 25 from Newtownards on the A21) to visit the **Ulster Folk Museum,** which is also 11 km (7 mi) from Belfast on the A2. Devoted to the province's social history, the open-air museum is set in some 70 acres around Cultra Manor and encircled by a larger park and recreation area. It brings Northern Ireland's past vividly to life with a score of reconstructed buildings brought here from around the region; these structures represent different facets of Northern Ireland life—a traditional weaver's dwelling, terraces of Victorian town houses, an 18th-century country church, a village flax mill, a farmhouse, and a rural school. You start your visit with the Folk Gallery, which explains the background of each building. Across the main road (by footbridge) is the Transport Museum, with exhibits showing every kind of transport, including a miniature railway on Saturdays during the summer. *Cultra, near Holywood, tel. 0232/428428. Admission: U.K.£2.20 adults, U.K.£1.10 children and senior citizens. Open May–Sept., Mon.–Sat. 11–6, Sun., afternoons only; Oct.–Apr., Mon.–Sat. 11–5, Sun., afternoons only. May–June, till 9 PM Wed.*

Off the Beaten Track

Belfast's Churches   An amazing variety of religious denominations is represented in Belfast. The oldest house of worship is **Knockbreda Parish Church** (Church of Ireland), on Church Road, off the A24 on the south side of the city. This dark, sturdy, and atmospheric

structure was built in 1737, the work of architect Richard
Cassels, who designed many of Ireland's greatest mansions. It
quickly became *the* place to be buried—witness the vast 18th-
century tombs in the churchyard. The **First Presbyterian
Church** (Rosemary St.) dates from 1783 and has an interesting
elliptical interior. It hosts lunchtime concerts. **St. Malachy's**
(Roman Catholic; Alfred St.), built in 1844, features some fine
stonework, including an astonishing fan-vaulted ceiling. By the
riverfront is one of the most appealing churches, **Sinclair
Seamen's Church** (Presbyterian; Corporation Sq., off Donegall
Quay). It was designed by Charles Lanyon, the architect of
Queen's University, and has served the seafaring community
since 1857. A maritime theme pervades the building; even the
pulpit is shaped like a ship's prow.

Cave Hill On fine weekends, it seems that half of Belfast makes its way up
to this airy hill north of the city center, where you'll find walks
and fine views of the city spread out below. Up here visitors can
also visit the zoo, the grand 19th-century baronial mansion **Belfast Castle** (now a restaurant), and, at the summit, the ancient
earthworks of **MacArt's Fort**.

East Tyrone Tour 2 makes a quick dash across this large and most rural of
Northern Ireland counties, but you may want to explore the
area further. North of Omagh, the country is pretty and rustic,
with small farm villages within sight of the bare Sperrin Mountains. Heading east from the town on the A505, you'll discover a
pensive landscape of moist heath and bog. Left of the road,
Beaghmore is a strange Bronze Age ceremonial site preserved
for millennia beneath a blanket of peat: It has seven stone circles and 12 cairns. Farther along, the A505 reaches **Wellbrook Beetling Mill** (Corkhill, tel. 06487/51735; admission:
U.K.£1.20), where locally made linen was first "beetled," that
is, pounded with noisy water-driven hammers to give it a
smooth finish. The mill is kept in working order by the National
Trust. About 6½ km (4 mi) beyond Wellbrook is **Cookstown,** an
odd Plantation village with a single broad main street more
than 1½ km (1 mi) in length. From here, head down on the back
lanes to **Lough Neagh,** the largest lake in the British Isles (396
sq km/153 sq mi), noted for an abundance of eels. On its shore at
Ardboe stands a remarkable 10th-century high cross. It is
huge—more than 5½ meters (18 feet) tall—and richly carved
with biblical scenes.

Shopping

The best of Northern Ireland's traditional products, many
made according to time-honored methods, include the exquisite linen and superior handmade woolen garments that are
usually associated with the Republic of Ireland. Handmade
lacework also remains a handicraft from the countrywomen of
some Northern Ireland districts. Visitors should keep an eye
out for hand-cut crystal from County Tyrone. Highly regarded
as well is the mellow cream-colored parian china of Belleek,
which is not only beautiful, but also a good investment.

At the other end of the price scale, handcrafted miniatures of
the legendary leprechaun make an inexpensive and amusing (if
predictable) souvenir. Blackthorn walking sticks are another
popular memento from the province. Polished granite stones

from the Mountains of Mourne provide a pretty reminder of a haunting corner of the province.

Belfast

Belfast's main shopping streets include Donegall Place, High Street, Royal Avenue, and several of the smaller streets connecting with them. The whole area is traffic-free (except for buses), so visitors will find it pleasant to wander and window-shop. **Anderson McAuley** (Donegall Pl., tel. 0232/326681) stocks a good selection of linen, Tyrone crystal, Belleek china, and miniatures. **Smyth's Irish Linens** (14 Callender St., behind Marks & Spencer, no phone) carries a great selection of handkerchiefs, tablecloths, napkins, and other linen goods, which make excellent souvenirs or presents. If you've an interest in bric-a-brac, visit the **Variety Market,** a flea market you'll find on May Street every Tuesday and Friday morning.

Gifts

China   Anyone driving around Lower Lough Erne should pass through the village of Belleek, which sits right on the border with the Republic, beside the sparkling River Erne. On the riverbank stands the Visitor's Center of **Belleek Pottery Ltd.** (tel. 0365/65501), producers of world-famous Belleek chinaware and porcelain. Here a factory, a showroom, a permanent exhibition, a Belleek pottery museum, and a café are all under one roof. On weekdays, a tour of the factory starts every half hour. You'll find hardly any noise in the workshops, however—everything at Belleek is handmade, using the exact process that was invented in 1857. The showroom is filled with beautiful gifts, but prices are high: A cup and saucer costs about U.K.£25, and a bowl in a basket-weave style (very typical of Belleek) could cost you around U.K.£300. *Tel. 0365/65501. Admission free. Tours Mon.–Thurs. 9:30–4:15, Fri. 9:30–3:15.*

Celtic Weave China Ltd. (Cloghore, Ballyshannon, Co. Donegal, tel. 072/51844) is a family-run outfit just across the border from Belleek on the Ballyshannon road. You'll find it on the left side of the road as you approach the garda (police) checkpoint on the Irish Republic side. Celtic Weave specializes in the intricate basket-style design, decorated with sprays of colorful china flowers. The company's work has an excellent reputation, and many pieces are made on commission.

Glassware   Visitors can watch classic pieces of full lead crystal being mouth-blown and hand-cut at **Tyrone Crystal** (Killybrackey, Dungannon, Co. Tyrone, tel. 08687/25335). Tours are conducted on weekdays—phone ahead for tour times.

Sports

Northern Ireland is a favorite destination for connoisseurs of the great outdoors. Despite its popularity, the province offers open spaces, few crowds, and perfectly tranquil waterways and countryside. A free brochure, *Holiday Breakaways*, available from the Northern Ireland Tourist Board, details hotels and guest houses that especially suit sports and outdoor enthusiasts.

Participant Sports

Bicycling Roads are good and fairly traffic-free, so cycling is popular. There's no need to have a bike of your own—many towns have rental firms. Bicycle rentals cost around U.K.£3.50–U.K.£7 a day, U.K.£27 for a week. In Belfast, rent from **Ernie Coates** (108 Grand Parade, tel. 0232/471912) or **Bike It** (4 Belmont Rd., tel. 0232/471141). Local Tourist Information Offices can offer suggestions for good cycling routes.

Bird-watching The province has as wide a range of habitats for birds as could possibly be packed into such a tiny area, and the wealth of species satisfies all bird lovers. The best time to come is winter, but even in summer visitors can participate in first-class bird-watching, especially on the Antrim uplands, all down the Antrim coast, and on the offshore islands. For wildfowl and wading birds, the shores of Lough Neagh and Strangford Lough are exceptional. For information, ideas, and details of field-study groups, contact Northern Ireland Tourist Information Offices and the **Royal Society for the Protection of Birds** (Belvoir Park Forest, tel. 0232/692547).

Fishing With a 606-km (466-mi) coastline, part on the Atlantic and part on the Irish Sea, as well as major lakes and an abundance of unpolluted rivers, Northern Ireland is a great place for anglers. Set your rod for shark and conger off the Antrim coast, for big skate and tope in Strangford Lough, and for salmon and rainbow trout in the Glens of Antrim.

To catch fish, whether coarse or game, you'll need a license from either the **Fisheries Conservancy Board** (1 Mahon Rd., Portadown, tel. 0762/334666) or the **Foyle Fisheries Commission** (8 Victoria Rd., Derry, tel. 0504/42100), depending on where you're fishing, and you'll probably need a local permit as well. The license cost for 15 days is U.K.£9.70, for a whole season U.K.£14. In addition, you must get permission from the owner of the land where you plan to fish and you may have to pay a charge. If the landowner is the **Department of Agriculture** (Stormont, Belfast, tel. 0232/63939), you'll have to pay for an additional permit (cost: U.K.£15 for 15 days, or U.K.£6 a day). You don't have to approach these bodies individually: All licenses and Department of Agriculture permits are available from the Northern Ireland Tourist Board in Belfast (tel. 0232/231221) or the **Lakeland Visitor Centre** (Enniskillen, tel. 0365/323110), as well as from a number of tackle shops around the province.

Scores of tackle shops are situated around the province, and 10 of them are located in Belfast. Here are a few useful addresses in main angling areas: **J. A. Knaggs** (Main St., Ballinamallard, tel. 036581/321), **R. Bell** (38 Ann St., Ballycastle, tel. 02657/62520), **Carlton Park Fishing Centre** (Belleek, tel. 036565/8181), **Smyth's** (1 Park St., Coleraine, tel. 0265/43970), **Lakeland Tackle and Guns** (Sligo Rd., Enniskillen, tel. 0365/323774), **Four Seasons** (80 Main St., Newcastle, tel. 03967/25078), **Hook, Line & Sinker** (43 South St., Newtownards, tel. 0247/811671).

Golf Northern Ireland features more than 70 golf courses—many in spectacular coastal settings—that welcome visitors. Greens fees vary from about U.K.£7 to U.K.£20. A course is nearly always within reach of your hotel, with a dozen golf clubs within

8 km (5 mi) of Belfast. The **Royal County Down** (Newcastle, tel. 03967/23314) is considered by many golfers to be one of the finest courses in the world. Another championship course is at the **Royal Portrush Golf Club** (Portrush, Co. Antrim, tel. 0265/822311). All golf courses and clubs are listed in the Northern Ireland Tourist Board Information Bulletin No. 17, *Golf—Where to Play*, available from main tourist offices.

Hiking   Northern Ireland has plenty of magnificent walking country. The **Ulster Way,** in particular, is for the serious hiker, a 896-km (560-mi) trek right around the six counties. Apart from the ability to read a map, no special skills are needed, and the terrain never demands more than a pair of stout walking shoes. Of course, visitors do not have to walk the whole trail; some sections are easier than others, and some of the best stretches are clearly marked. The **Sports Council for Northern Ireland** (House of Sport, Upper Malone Rd., Belfast BT9 5LA, tel. 0232/381222) can give advice about the Ulster Way; it sells books covering each section of the route. Anyone who would like to try a hand at tougher walks in the hills should obtain the excellent and informative little handbook in the Irish Walks series, No. 4, *The North East,* by Richard Rogers (published by Gill & Macmillan, 15-17 Eden Quay, Dublin; the book should be available in local book and sporting goods stores in Northern Ireland). It gives precise details of 45 hill walks, complete with descriptions of the wildflowers you'll see along the way. For hikes in the Mountains of Mourne, you can obtain maps and details of suggested routes from **The Mourne Countryside Centre** (91 Central Promenade, Newcastle, Co. Down, tel. 03967/24059).

Horseback Riding/Pony Trekking   Sitting on the back of a horse or pony is a great way to travel into places that are out of bounds to motorists. Woodland, beaches, and rough country become accessible on guided rides, some suitable for complete beginners. Some 35 riding and trekking centers are located around the province, and several of them offer accommodations. Trekking rates are mostly U.K.£4–U.K.£5 an hour, with small reductions for children. The most convenient center in the Belfast area is **Lagan Valley Equestrian Centre** (172 Upper Malone Rd., Belfast, tel. 0232/614853). The center is open Monday through Saturday throughout the year, and it charges an hourly rate of U.K.£5 adults, U.K.£4 children (minimum age 7). The center runs pony treks through the Lagan Valley Regional Park, as well as residential summer camps. If you're over in the Enniskillen/Lough Erne area, **Drumhoney Stables** (Lisnarick, 5 km/3 mi west of Irvinestown, tel. 03656/21892) can teach you to ride, take you on a pony trek through Castle Archdale Country Park, or even rent you a pony and trap (suitable for two adults and up to four children). Hourly rates are U.K.£6 for adults, U.K.£4.50–U.K.£5 for children. The stables also have residential accommodations.

Lake and River Cruising   Inland cruising on the Erne waterway—777 sq km (300 sq mi) of lakes and rivers—is one of Northern Ireland's major treats. Upper and Lower Lough Erne are enclosed by some of Ireland's finest scenery and are studded with more than 100 little islands. Out on the lakes and the River Erne, which links them, you'll have all the solitude you want, but you'll find company at loughside hostelries. To hire a good standard-size boat, contact **Erne Charter Boat Association** (Lakeland Visitor Centre,

Enniskillen, Co. Fermanagh, tel. 0365/323110). Expect to pay at least U.K.£300 for a four-berth cruiser.

Spectator Sports

Ask any tourist office for the leaflet of the year's *Events*, which shows the dates and times of major sports occasions. Look out especially for the **hurling** and **Gaelic football** events. Dates of local matches are listed in local newspapers. During the summer, you'll come across **cricket** matches being played throughout the province. One oddity is the ancient precursor of bowls, called **bullets,** which is still played in County Armagh. It involves throwing bowls (originally they were cannonballs, hence the name) along a narrow winding country lane; the first to cover 3 km (2 mi) is the winner. The All-Ireland Championship for this sport is held in early August.

Dining and Lodging

Dining

Northern Ireland cuisine is similar to cooking in the Republic: Good-quality fresh local fish or meat is prepared in a simple style. Except in Belfast, acceptable Continental dishes are difficult to find. Vegetables receive an unimaginative treatment, and you'll find a heavy emphasis on potatoes, which are often served in two different ways on the same plate. Yet the hearty, unpretentious home cooking available is tasty, nourishing, and above all *filling*, because portions tend to be huge.

Visitors will not find much on the menu that is unfamiliar. Ulster fry, an inexpensive café and pub dish, is something like an Irish breakfast: a sizzling portion of bacon, sausages, tomatoes, and eggs, served with potato bread or soda bread. Champ is another potato dish, this time a creamy, buttery mash with scallions. Some other traditional favorites that remain popular include Guinness soup, oysters from Strangford Lough, Ardglass herring, and smoked salmon from Ballamena. Be sure to check out the variety of freshly baked breads, which you can sample at teatime. Tea, especially when described as high tea, is usually served around 6 PM; it's a full meal of breads and buns, accompanied with sandwiches or savory hot dishes, and followed by fruit cake. Among the delicious baked fare are scones (white or whole-meal), farls (triangular griddle cakes leavened with soda and buttermilk), potato bread (solid stuff, sometimes eaten fried), and wheaten bread (dark brown, very heavy). Most pubs will serve a pot of tea and a plate of scones.

Quite apart from cafés, pubs, and restaurants, Northern Ireland has discovered the convenience of fast food. Wine bars are another up-and-coming kind of eatery; in reality these are just inexpensive restaurants with good wine lists. Most diners, though, still prefer to take a pot of tea with their food.

Without being formal, the Northern Irish tend to dress soberly. Men often wear a jacket and tie when dining out; but if you prefer to dress more casually, that is quite acceptable at most establishments. By the standards of the Republic or the United States, or even the rest of the United Kingdom, restaurant prices are surprisingly moderate. Tax is usually included in the price of a meal. A service charge of 10% may be indicated on the bill; it is customary to pay this, unless the service was bad.

Category	Cost*
Very Expensive	over U.K.£20
Expensive	U.K.£15–U.K.£20
Moderate	U.K.£10–U.K.£15
Inexpensive	under U.K.£10

* *per person for a typical three-course meal, including tax and service but excluding drinks.*

Lodging

Northern Ireland has some good modern hotels but hardly any lodging in the more expensive categories. Travelers often find that the most enjoyable accommodations are low-cost guest houses (often family-run), offering bed and breakfast. Most B&Bs provide an evening meal as well, if needed. Visitors can choose from the humblest terraced town houses or farm cottages to the grandest country houses. Dining rooms of country-house lodgings frequently reach the standard of top-quality restaurants.

For details on Northern Ireland's six youth hostels, contact **Y.H.A.N.I.** (56 Bradbury Pl., Belfast BT7 1RU, tel. 0232/324733). All accommodations in the province are inspected and categorized by the Northern Ireland Tourist Board, which publishes all names, addresses, and ratings in the handbook *Where to Stay* (U.K.£2.95).

Category	Cost*
Very Expensive	over U.K.£110
Expensive	U.K.£70–U.K.£110
Moderate	U.K.£40–U.K.£70
Inexpensive	under U.K.£40

**All prices are for a standard double room, including breakfast and tax.*

Highly recommended restaurants and hotels are indicated by a star ★.

Belfast

Dining
★ **Roscoff.** This Golden Mile restaurant is now widely acclaimed as one of the best in the six counties. You're likely to hear the chat of barristers and government ministers at other tables. The curious decor is supposed to be reminiscent of the sea, with wave-shaped motifs, portholes, and a cloth-covered ceiling resembling billowing sails. The specialty is Breton fish and seafood (Roscoff is a port on the Brittany coast of France), though there are fine meat dishes as well. Portions are generous and accompanied by large quantities of vegetables. Among the imaginative starters is a gateau of baby leeks; as a main course you might try the "symphony of seafood," with wild rice and a

fennel sauce. From the delicious desserts, sample the roast pears with freshly made chestnut and honey ice cream. *Shaftesbury Sq. (at the end of Great Victoria St.), tel. 0232/ 331532. Reservations advised. Jacket and tie advised. AE, DC, MC, V. Closed Fri. evening and Sun. Very Expensive.*

★ **Restaurant 44.** This green-fronted establishment on a corner in the Golden Mile area is certainly one of the best and most agreeable eating places in Northern Ireland. Inside it has smart colonial decor, with green cane chairs, slatted shutters, a wooden ceiling fan, and a mural of elephants in India. The well-presented menu concentrates on imaginative French dishes. Start with Stilton mousse with poached pears in port sauce, try a main course of paupiettes of salmon filled with a prawn mousse and served with lobster sauce, and end with an unusual Floating Island with fresh caramel. There are excellent vegetarian dishes (clearly marked on the menu) for every course, such as baked papaya with a rich tomato sauce and crispy noodles. *44 Bedford St., tel. 0232/244844. Reservations required. Jacket and tie advised. AE, DC, MC, V. Closed Fri. evening and Sun. Expensive.*

Bananas. Adjoining Restaurant 44, with the same owners and kitchen, Bananas is as good as its neighbor. It features a similar but less opulent colonial style, with cane furniture, a plain wood floor, and ceiling fans. Palms grow in flowerpots that are made from old chimneys. The mixed international menu includes Continental and Asian cuisines, as well as many of the same dishes that are served next door. The choice ranges from Spanish tapas to Oriental stir-fry to pork escalope. There's a relaxed, brasserie-type atmosphere, and it's much brighter, noisier, and livelier than its neighbor. *44 Bedford St., tel. 0232/ 244844. Reservations required. Dress: informal. AE, DC, MC, V. Closed Fri. evening and Sun. Moderate.*

Belfast Castle. Ben Madigan's is the name of the more stylish upstairs restaurant inside this grand Belfast landmark in the pleasant park on top of Cave Hill. The table in the bay window has a panoramic view over the city and lake. The Castle is not ancient but is imposing, with big rooms, paneled ceilings, and a huge stairway. The misspelled menu offers elaborate, generous, and vaguely French dishes. The restaurant is recommended for its setting. In the basement there's an atmospheric, old-fashioned bar and a wine bar with cheaper meals. *Cave Hill, tel. 0232/370133. Reservations advised. Jacket and tie advised. AE, DC, MC, V. Moderate.*

La Belle Epoque. Relaxed and intimate, this well-established restaurant offers a French charm, with Art Nouveau decor reminiscent of Paris. The French menu features pigeon breast in raspberry sauce as an appetizer, and an excellent main course of pheasant in a cream and wine sauce. For dessert, you can't go wrong with the freshly made fruit sorbets. *103 Great Victoria St., tel. 0232/323244. Reservations advised (required on weekends). Dress: casual. DC, MC, V. Closed Sun. Moderate.*

The Strand. Situated in the popular University Area, this dark and intimate bistro with candlelighted tables attracts students and professors alike with its adventurous and unusual menu. Recommended dishes include chicken pancakes, peanut plaice, or cod in coconut and apple sauce. For dessert try the cream-laden gateaux. Several vegetarian entrées are available, such as broccoli and cashew-nut flan. *12 Stranmillis Rd., tel. 0232/*

682266. Reservations advised. Dress: casual. AE, DC, MC, V. Moderate.

Saints and Scholars. This University Area restaurant offers two distinct sections. The downstairs "library" has bookshelves on the walls, but the lively, noisy, and cheerful ambience could hardly be less studious. Upstairs, you'll find a calmer and more comfortable dining room. One of the special appetizers is deep-fried brie with gooseberry sauce. Main dishes include a hearty cassoulet (a rich, meaty stew with duck, sausages, and beans) and Seafood Harmony (a selection of baked or poached fish with thermidor sauce). Many vegetarian dishes are available, such as mushrooms stuffed with cream cheese and avocado. The rich dessert crepes, supposedly made according to a recipe from the Danish royal court, are truly fit for a king. *3 University St., tel. 0232/325137. Reservations required. Dress: casual. AE, DC, MC, V. Inexpensive.*

Lodging

★ **Culloden Hotel.** Located 8 km (5 mi) from the city center on the A2, this former 19th-century Scottish baronial mansion stands grandly amid 12 acres of woods and parkland. The public areas feature ornate woodwork, Louis XV chandeliers, decorative plasterwork, and stained glass. Bedrooms, both in the original section and in a newer wing, feature silk and velvet decor and fine views. The excellent dining areas include the large French Mitre Restaurant, with mahogany tables and a garden view, and a Grill Bar, which serves both snacks and meals. The hotel is situated in a peaceful part of town, close to the Ulster Folk Museum. *142 Bangor Rd., Holywood, Co. Down BT18 0EX, tel. 02317/5223. 93 rooms with bath. Facilities: restaurant, grill bar, tennis, squash, croquet, games room, snooker, laundry, 24-hr room service. AE, DC, MC, V. Very Expensive.*

★ **Europa Hotel.** This popular modern high-rise city-center hotel has long attracted visiting journalists and business travelers. What it lacks in period charm is compensated for by the polite and efficient staff and the comfortable ambience. Bedrooms are blandly decorated, but they are clean and functional and offer all the modern conveniences, including central heating and TV. The hotel, conveniently located near the Opera House, is only 1.6 km (1 mi) from the train station and 6.5 km (4 mi) from the airport. *Great Victoria St., Belfast BT2 7AP, tel. 0232/327000. 200 rooms with bath. Facilities: café, bar, restaurant, secretarial services, laundry, 24-hr security. AE, DC, MC, V. Very Expensive.*

Dukes Hotel. This delightful, modern hotel with a touch of style in the heart of the University area, though small, has a spacious lobby, good facilities, and an interesting restaurant (which leans toward healthy eating, with several vegetarian options). An unusual feature is the waterfall running down steps beside the stairs. Decor is smart gray, enlivened with plenty of greenery. The comfortable and well-laid-out rooms come with satellite TV, phones, and hairdryers, and many have good views of the hills beyond the city. *65–67 University St., tel. 0232/236666. 21 rooms with bath. Facilities: restaurant, bars, conference rooms, sauna, gym. AE, DC, MC, V. Expensive.*

Quality Plaza Hotel. This new, modern hotel, centrally located between Great Victoria and Bedford Streets, has a decor of muted grays and pretty floral fabrics. Bedrooms and bathrooms are rather small and cramped, but all rooms have cable TV, a phone, a hairdryer, and a trouser press. Room service can bring up a full three-course meal at any time of day or night. *15 Brunswick St., tel. 0232/333555. 83 rooms with bath. Facilities: restaurant, conference rooms. AE, DC, MC, V. Expensive.*

Templeton Hotel. Midway between the city and the airport, this new hotel has an interior with distinctive woodwork. Bedrooms feature pastel fabrics and polished pine and are equipped with hairdryers, trouser presses, cable TVs, and phones. There are three different places to dine; the main restaurant has good, hearty Irish cuisine and attractive blue and pink decor. *882 Antrim Rd., Templepatrick, Ballyclare (about 6 mi from Belfast), tel. 08494/32984. 20 rooms with bath. Facilities: restaurants, bar. AE, DC, MC, V. Expensive.*

Wellington Park Hotel. Formerly a private residence, this modernized establishment is among the best in the Queen's University area of town. Many evening visitors enjoy the relaxed bars, live music, and good food at this friendly family-run hotel. The quiet bedrooms are well-designed, with built-in wooden furniture; some of them feature loft sleeping areas. *21 Malone Rd., Belfast BT9 6RU, tel. 0232/381111. 50 rooms with bath or shower. Facilities: bar, restaurant, laundry. AE, DC, MC, V. Expensive.*

★ **Ash-Rowan Guest House.** Award-winning former restaurateurs Sam and Evelyn Hazlett own and run this outstanding B&B in a spacious Victorian home. Every bedroom has been decorated in a tasteful individual style, and each has a private bath and TV. Guests have access to a library. Breakfasts and dinners, prepared by the owners, are first-rate. This no-smoking house is located on a tranquil residential street near Queen's University and the Ulster Museum. *Mrs. E. Hazlett, 12 Windsor Ave., Belfast BT9 6EE, tel. 0232/661758. 4 rooms with bath. MC, V. Closed Dec. Moderate.*

Camera House. Mrs. Drumm runs this delightful B&B in a brick Victorian house with bay windows. Bedrooms are clean, cheerful, and simply furnished. You'll appreciate the friendly welcome and the generous breakfasts. *Mrs. A. Drumm, Camera House, 44 Wellington Park, Belfast BT9 6DP, tel. 0232/660026. 11 rooms, 7 with bath or shower. MC, V. Inexpensive.*

The Cottage. Aptly named, this lovely little B&B in Mrs. Muldoon's immaculate white home, located 8 km (5 mi) east of Belfast, has a charming flower-filled garden in the back. It's as rural a setting as you're likely to find so close to the city center. The traditional country-house decor combines beautiful antiques and modern comforts in the bedrooms. *Mrs. E. Muldoon, The Cottage, 377 Comber Rd., Dundonald, Belfast BT16 0XB, tel. 0247/878189. 3 rooms, 1 with bath. No credit cards. Inexpensive.*

Carrickfergus

Dining and Lodging **Dobbins Inn.** Still thriving after more than three centuries, this modest family-run hotel on High Street attracts locals to its convivial bar, especially during live music performances on Sunday, Monday, and Tuesday evenings. The adequate bedrooms offer private baths, TVs, and tea-making equipment. High tea is available, and the DeCourcy restaurant serves an acceptable dinner. *6–8 High St., Carrickfergus, Co. Antrim, BT38 9HE, tel. 09603/51905. 13 rooms with bath. Facilities: restaurant, baby-sitting service. MC, V. Moderate.*

Coleraine Area

Dining and Lodging ★ **Blackheath House.** Situated 13 km (8 mi) south of Coleraine, this fine country house, surrounded by magnificent countryside, was built as the home of the 18th-century bishop of Derry. The brown structure is within close driving distance of golf courses and the Causeway Coast beaches and cliff walks; the home retains a genteel character and stands amid 2 acres of landscaped gardens. Among its more modern comforts is an indoor swimming pool. The large bedrooms—including a four-poster room, a French Colonial room, and a pine room—have been individually decorated with a mixture of modern and antique furniture. The drawing room, with a fine marble fireplace, is filled with old pieces of furniture. Down in the cellars lies MacDuff's, a first-class expensive restaurant, open to nonresidents, where proprietors Joseph and Margaret Erwin provide excellent meals prepared with farm-fresh meats and local vegetables, game, and seafood. The menu offers steak in blue cheese sauce, sole in a sauce of tomato and herbs, and a good wine list. Breakfasts are filling, with a generous Ulster fry. *112 Killeague Rd., Blackhill, Coleraine, Co. Londonderry BT51 4HH, tel. 0265/868433. 6 rooms, 5 with bath. Facilities: pool, restaurant (closed Sun. and Mon.). No credit cards. Moderate.*

Greenhill House. This charming Georgian country house about 13 km (8 mi) south of Coleraine is run by Elizabeth and James Hegarty and provides a peaceful retreat. Guests enjoy the pleasantly decorated bedrooms, the substantial breakfasts, and the excellent dinners of locally caught fish, Ulster beef, and homemade bread and cakes. *24 Greenhill Rd., Aghadowey, Co. Londonderry BT51 4EU, tel. 0265/868241. 7 rooms, 6 with bath. No credit cards. Closed Nov.–Feb. Inexpensive.*

Lodging **Camus House.** Follow the road along the Bann valley south from Coleraine; 6½ km (4 mi) out of town, you'll arrive at this appealing Georgian farmhouse that dates back to 1685. Today it's a relaxed and gracious guest house, elegantly furnished, with a snug sitting room with a stone fireplace. Proprietor Josephine King provides a friendly atmosphere and a hearty breakfast. The pleasant bedrooms, decorated in pastel colors, have tasteful modern furnishings, reading lamps, and large closets. *27 Curragh Rd., Coleraine, Co. Londonderry BT51 3RY, tel. 0265/42982. 3 rooms without bath. No credit cards. Inexpensive.*

Derry City

Dining and Lodging **White Horse Hotel.** In the countryside overlooking Lough Foyle, yet only 8 km (5 mi) northeast of Derry City on the road to Limavady, this former inn has been enlarged into a comfortable modern hotel that caters to business and vacation visitors. Bedrooms are clean and unpretentiously furnished, with TVs and tea-making equipment. Locals and guests alike enjoy the good Irish meals served at the relaxed grill bar or more formal restaurant. *68 Clooney Rd., Campsie, Co. Londonderry BT47 3PA, tel. 0504/860606. 50 rooms with bath. Facilities: bar, restaurant, 24-hr valet service. MC, V. Moderate.*

Downpatrick/Ards Area

Dining and Lodging
Portaferry Inn. Standing on the quayside (or "strand") overlooking the narrow channel that connects Lough Strangford to the sea, this centuries-old whitewashed inn offers well-kept, simply furnished double rooms. The main action takes place in the popular bar and restaurant, where unadventurous but competent breakfasts, lunches, and dinners are briskly served. *10 The Strand, Portaferry, Co. Down, BT22 1PE, tel. 02472/ 28231. 14 double rooms with bath or shower. Facilities: restaurant, bar/lounge, boat mooring, laundry. AE, DC, MC, V. Moderate.*

Enniskillen and Environs

Dining and Lodging
★
Jamestown House. Tucked away in lush tranquil countryside near Lower Lough Erne and 11 km (7 mi) from Enniskillen, this dignified country house dates from 1760 and is run by Arthur and Helen Stuart. The large, attractive bedrooms feature modern furnishings, and elegant drawing and dining rooms contain older fine polished mahogany pieces. Staying here is just like visiting friends in the country. A river runs through the grounds—Mr. Stuart is keen on angling and advises visitors on the best spots to fish in the area. Breakfasts and the expensive set dinners are generous and satisfying. *Magheracross, Ballinamallard, Co. Fermanagh, tel. 036581/209. 3 rooms with bath or shower. No credit cards. Moderate.*

Glens of Antrim

Dining and Lodging
Ballygally Castle. At the Larne end of the North Antrim coast drive, 40 km (25 mi) from Belfast, you'll find an impressive little castle, complete with pointed turrets, facing the Ballygally Bay, which was built by a Scottish lord in 1625. After centuries of defending itself from invaders, the castle now cheerfully invites visitors to sample a good night's sleep and hearty breakfast within its substantial stone walls; modern plumbing and central heating have been skillfully integrated into the old Scottish-style design, but a recent extension, unfortunately, does not complement the castle architecture. Bedrooms, some of them located in the castle turrets, have been individually decorated with comfortable furnishings. In the dining room a decent table d'hôte evening meal is served (to music, on Saturdays), and a Sunday high tea is also available. *Ballygally Castle, 274 Coast Rd., Ballygally, Co. Antrim BT40 2RA, tel. 0574/83212. 30 rooms with bath. Facilities: bar, dining room, baby-sitting, fishing on grounds. MC, V. Moderate.*

Londonderry Arms. This ivy-covered traditional hotel by Carnlough Harbour, built as a coaching inn in 1848, features a lovely seaside garden, unique antique carved furnishings, regional paintings and maps, and Georgian period decor. The lodging once belonged to Sir Winston Churchill, and since 1947 it has been owned and run by the O'Neill family. A dozen of the bedrooms feature Georgian antiques, and the rest offer functional contemporary decor. Rooms 2, 8, and 9 are recommended for their spaciousness and good views. The hotel serves a substantial traditional Irish meal that relies on local seafood; bread and scones are homemade. Traditional Irish music is provided during the summer months. *Harbour Rd., Carnlough, Co. An-*

trim BT44 0EU, tel. 0574/885255. 21 rooms with bath. AE, DC, MC, V. Moderate.

Mountains of Mourne Area

Dining and Lodging **Slieve Donard Hotel.** A lavish redbrick monument to Victoriana, this turreted hotel stands like a palace on spacious green lawns at one end of Newcastle's 6½-km (4-mi) sandy beach. Guests will feel as if they are stepping back to the town's turn-of-the-century heyday as an elegant seaside resort, even though the rooms now have every modern comfort. Ask for a room overlooking the water. The relaxed gate-house pub/dining room serves adequate seafood dishes; folk music is presented every Saturday night. For daytime relaxation, walk the airy promenade or visit the Royal County Down Golf Club, right next door. *Downs Rd., Newcastle, Co. Down BT33 0AH, tel. 03967/23681. 120 rooms with bath. Facilities: pub/dining room, recreation center with 2 tennis courts and indoor pool. AE, DC, MC, V. Expensive.*

The Arts and Nightlife

The Arts

Just about all of Northern Ireland's arts and cultural activity is concentrated in Belfast. The *Belfast Telegraph* newspaper lists arts events. The high point of the province's cultural year is the **Belfast International Festival of Arts,** lasting a couple of weeks each November. It offers a full schedule of dramatic and musical events centered at Whitla Hall, at Queen's University. The **Belfast Folk Festival** in September is a weekend of traditional foot-tapping Irish music and dance at downtown locations.

Film **Cannon Cinema** (Great Victoria St., tel. 0232/322484), with four screens, and **Curzon Cinema** (Ormeau Rd., tel. 0232/641373), with three screens, are two of several city-center movie theaters showing new British and American releases and big box-office favorites.

Queen's Film Theatre is Belfast's art cinema, with two screens showing domestic and foreign movies. *University Sq. Mews, off Botanic Ave., tel. 0232/667687. Open during university semesters only.*

Music **The Ulster Hall** (Linenhall St., tel. 0232/241917) is the large city-center concert hall where classical orchestral pieces are performed; the center is the home base of the Ulster Orchestra. The hall has a splendid Victorian organ, so organ recitals are often held. Sometimes rock concerts are also scheduled here.

Whitla Hall (Queen's University, tel. 0232/245133) hosts classical concerts and recitals throughout the year.

Harberton Theatre (Harberton Park, Balmoral, tel. 0232/661302), in the southwest suburbs, is the home of the Ulster Operatic Society, which presents concerts and musicals.

Grosvenor Hall (Glengall St., tel. 0232/241917) is the place for some down-home music, including country-and-western, gospel, and folk concerts.

Theater and Opera The Arts Theatre (Botanic Ave., tel. 0232/324936), near the University Area, specializes in laugh-a-minute comedies and lightweight productions.

The Grand Opera House, a beautifully restored Victorian playhouse, has no company of its own but books shows from all over the British Isles and sometimes further afield. It puts on a constant stream of plays of widely differing kinds, plus occasional operas and ballets. *Great Victoria St., tel. 0232/241919. Tickets: U.K.£3–U.K.£20.*

The Group Theatre is a showcase for Belfast's local dramatic societies. *Bedford St., tel. 0232/329685. Tickets: Mon.–Thurs. U.K.£2.50, Fri. and Sat. U.K.£3.*

The Lyric Theatre, in the south of Belfast, stages thoughtful drama played by its resident company and draws most of its inspiration from traditional Irish culture. *Ridgeway St., tel. 0232/381081. Tickets: all seats U.K.£6 (except Mon., U.K.£5).*

Nightlife

A night out in Northern Ireland usually means an evening at a pub—that's where most entertainment takes place. The most popular pubs are those lively, convivial places where traditional Irish folk music is played frequently, and often quite spontaneously. They can be found in towns and villages all over the province, and the best way to locate them is to ask where to find a "singing pub." Pubs, by the way, close at around 11:30 PM.

Belfast
Golden Mile Area
Robinsons (next to the Crown Liquor Saloon, Great Victoria St., tel. 0232/329812) is a popular pub appealing to a young crowd. The Beaten Docket (also next to the Crown, tel. 0232/242926) is a noisier modern pub that attracts an even younger crowd than Robinsons; it features up-to-the-minute music. Limelight (Ormeau Ave., tel. 0232/325968) is a disco nightclub with cabaret on Tuesday, Friday, and Saturday, and music on other nights. The Linenhall (Clarence St., tel. 0232/248458) is a pub with a music lounge, where jazz is performed on Monday, Wednesday, and Saturday, and rock music on Thursday.

University Area
The Eglantine (tel. 0232/667994) and The Botanic (tel. 0232/660460), known as the Egg and the Bot to their student clientele, are two big, popular disco pubs facing each other across Malone Road.

City Center/Docks
Pat's Bar (Prince's Dock Rd., tel. 0232/744524) and Maddens (Smithfield, tel. 0232/244114) are popular pubs with first-rate sessions of traditional music. The Rotterdam (Pilot St., tel. 0232/746021) features folk, jazz, and blues performers. Kelly's Cellars (Bank St., tel. 0232/324835) offers blues on Saturday nights.

Index

Personal Itinerary

Departure *Date*

Time

Transportation

Arrival *Date*   *Time*

Departure *Date*   *Time*

Transportation

Accommodations

Arrival *Date*   *Time*

Departure *Date*   *Time*

Transportation

Accommodations

Arrival *Date*   *Time*

Departure *Date*   *Time*

Transportation

Accommodations

Personal Itinerary

Arrival *Date*   *Time*

Departure *Date*   *Time*

Transportation

Accommodations

Arrival *Date*   *Time*

Departure *Date*   *Time*

Transportation

Accommodations

Arrival *Date*   *Time*

Departure *Date*   *Time*

Transportation

Accommodations

Arrival *Date*   *Time*

Departure *Date*   *Time*

Transportation

Accommodations

Personal Itinerary

Arrival *Date*   *Time*

Departure *Date*   *Time*

Transportation

Accommodations

Arrival *Date*   *Time*

Departure *Date*   *Time*

Transportation

Accommodations

Arrival *Date*   *Time*

Departure *Date*   *Time*

Transportation

Accommodations

Arrival *Date*   *Time*

Departure *Date*   *Time*

Transportation

Accommodations

Personal Itinerary

Arrival *Date*   *Time*

Departure *Date*   *Time*

Transportation

Accommodations

Arrival *Date*   *Time*

Departure *Date*   *Time*

Transportation

Accommodations

Arrival *Date*   *Time*

Departure *Date*   *Time*

Transportation

Accommodations

Arrival *Date*   *Time*

Departure *Date*   *Time*

Transportation

Accommodations

Personal Itinerary

Arrival *Date*   *Time*

Departure *Date*   *Time*

Transportation

Accommodations

Arrival *Date*   *Time*

Departure *Date*   *Time*

Transportation

Accommodations

Arrival *Date*   *Time*

Departure *Date*   *Time*

Transportation

Accommodations

Arrival *Date*   *Time*

Departure *Date*   *Time*

Transportation

Accommodations

Addresses

Name	*Name*
Address	*Address*
Telephone	*Telephone*
Name	*Name*
Address	*Address*
Telephone	*Telephone*
Name	*Name*
Address	*Address*
Telephone	*Telephone*
Name	*Name*
Address	*Address*
Telephone	*Telephone*
Name	*Name*
Address	*Address*
Telephone	*Telephone*
Name	*Name*
Address	*Address*
Telephone	*Telephone*
Name	*Name*
Address	*Address*
Telephone	*Telephone*
Name	*Name*
Address	*Address*
Telephone	*Telephone*

Addresses

Name

Address

Telephone

Name

Address

Telephone

Name

Address

Telephone

Name

Address

Telephone

Name

Address

Telephone

Name

Address

Telephone

Name

Address

Telephone

Name

Address

Telephone

Name

Address

Telephone

Name

Address

Telephone

Name

Address

Telephone

Name

Address

Telephone

Name

Address

Telephone

Name

Address

Telephone

Name

Address

Telephone

Name

Address

Telephone

Notes